JUTLAND
1916

S0-AES-083

NIGEL STEEL & PETER HART

JUTLAND 1916

Death in the Grey Wastes

CASSELL

A CASSELL MILITARY PAPERBACK

First published by Cassell in 2003
This paperback edition published in 2004
by Cassell,
an imprint of Orion Books Ltd,
Orion House, 5 Upper Saint Martin's Lane,
London WC2H 9EA

An Hachette UK company

10

Copyright © Nigel Steel and Peter Hart 2003

The right of Nigel Steel and Peter Hart to be identified as the authors of
this work has been asserted by him in accordance with the
Copyright, Designs and Patents Act 1988.

All rights reserved. No part of this book may be
reproduced or transmitted in any form or by any means
electronic or mechanical including photocopying, recording
or any information storage and retrieval system
without permission in writing
from the publisher.

A CIP catalogue record for this book
is available from the British Library.

ISBN 978-0-3043-6648-4

**Printed and bound in Great Britain by
CPI Group (UK) Ltd, Croydon, CR0 4YY**

The Orion Publishing Group's policy is to use papers that
are natural, renewable and recyclable products and
made from wood grown in sustainable forests. The logging
and manufacturing processes are expected to conform to
the environmental regulations of the country of origin.

www.orionbooks.co.uk

CONTENTS

Preface   7

1. The Long Wait   11

2. First Contact   45

3. The Run to the South   78

4. The Run to the North   148

5. When Fleets Collide   166

6. Night Action   282

7. After the Battle   371

8. Who Won?   417

Appendices   436

Notes to the text   440

Index   465

This book is dedicated with love, gratitude but, most of all, with a deep sense of loss, to my parents:

Ruth Hart 1927–2000

Leslie Hart 1927–2002

PREFACE

JUTLAND WAS A truly terrible battle. The festering Anglo-German naval race that had ignited at the turn of the century had led to a burning desire in both countries for a naval Armageddon – '*Der Tag*' – that would settle the command of the seas once and for all. Never had a battle been so eagerly craved for so long in advance. Yet when battle commenced on 31 May 1916, two years into the Great War, death came quickly in the grey wastes of the North Sea for thousands of men who perished in their ships, blown to pieces in an instant. Others were less fortunate. Trapped behind locked doors and hatches in airtight, and shortly airless, chambers, they died slowly and alone in Stygian darkness, as their doomed ships slipped beneath the waves. Unluckiest of all were the mortally wounded, fated to die in miserable, hopeless agony hours, days, or even weeks later. Men had their heroic preconceptions ripped apart, just as surely as any shell fragment could flense their limbs. Many of those who survived the battle were left shocked and trembling by the sheer naked power of the destructive forces that had been unleashed around them. Yet, despite everything, men of both sides had stuck to their tasks, bolstered by their inculcated naval traditions of cheerful accept-ance of duty and sacrifice. The Somme and Passchendaele still weave their grim fascination, but, while the deaths of the men in the 'Pals Battalions' are morbidly 'celebrated', the sacrifice of the hapless crews of the *Indefatigable*, the *Queen Mary*, the *Invincible*, the *Defence*, the *Black Prince*, the *Shark*, the *Ardent* and the *Broke*, to name just a few, are commemorated mainly by a few dramatic photographs that linger round the edges of our folk memory.

This book aspires to return Jutland to the mainstream of public under-standing of the First World War. It examines the whole of the battle from the perspective of the participants of all ranks. It attempts to recreate the dramatic intensity of battle in all its awful grandeur: the silent moments of anticipation and fear before the guns opened up, the horrors, the excite-ments, the triumphs, the disasters, the all too sad aftermath as the ships and their crews slid to their last rest beneath the waves and the mind-numbing sense of loss for those left behind.

The Battle of Jutland has mesmerized generations of naval historians. There is just so much for us to argue about. Who, after all, had won? Who was to blame? Could better handling of the Grand Fleet have brought the British the crushing victory they craved? Why did British battlecruisers blow up while their German equivalents struggled back to port despite waves lapping over their decks? How could a defeat be a victory? Experts have pored over these unresolved issues for most of the past century. In the unresolved technical exchanges between specialists there has been too much attention paid to what *might have* happened and *did not* and not enough to examining what *did* happen. We wish to refocus this view of the battle, to move attention away from the now sterile controversy and to place it squarely onto the deeds of the men who fought and died at Jutland. Our sources are the voices, now stilled, of those who were actually there. Letters, diaries, books, reports, unpublished memoirs, tape-recorded interviews: these are the ocean into which it has been a pleasure to dip.

Our first port of call, as ever, was the Imperial War Museum. The superb Jutland collection administered by Rod Suddaby (one of the great unsung experts in twentieth-century naval history) and his sterling staff in the Department of Documents is second to none. Of his team we would particularly pick out Tony Richards, Amanda Mason and Daniel Scott-Davies, who have been helpful in the extreme, despite our numerous sins in following the correct archival procedure. It is a great pleasure to thank our colleagues past and present in the museum's Sound Archive: Margaret Brooks, Kate Johnson, David Lance, Laura Kamel, Jo Lancaster, Nigel de Lee, Richard McDonough, Harry Moses, Lyn Smith, John Stopford-Pickering; not forgetting the ageless, yet now officially aged, Rosemary Tudge and Conrad Wood. Together they have created an archive that will one day change perceptions of oral history and is there for anyone to use whatever their interests. We are indebted to Rose Gerrard of the Photograph Archive for her able assistance in locating photographs, and to the Keeper, our old *confrère* Brad King, for permission to reproduce the photographs. Neil Young and Terry Charman of the Research and Information Department have been fantastic in making available their photo-research. To them we cheerfully promise a slap-up fish supper and a crate of brown ale!

Among the historians who have donated their life's work to the IWM, we would particularly like to thank Robert Church, who created a magnificent Jutland archive in the early 1970s that is now freely available to other researchers through the museum's archive. An outstanding example of selfless generosity and dedication to the collective advancement of knowledge, his collection is absolutely invaluable to anyone wanting to understand 'what it was like'. We also salute the work of Henry Baynham, who conducted a series of interviews in his research for his book, *Men of the Dreadnoughts*. The irrepressible Max Arthur has also deposited his valuable collection of recordings with the Sound Archive.

One book, published in two separate editions, provided immeasurable assistance. This was compiled by H. W. Fawcett & G. W. W. Hooper, *The Fighting at Jutland: The Personal Experiences of Forty-Five Officers and Men of the British Fleet* (London: Macmillan, 1921). Other invaluable books were: Julian Corbett, *Naval Operations, Vol.III*; Arthur J. Marder, *From Dreadnought to Scapa Flow, Vol.III, Jutland and After* (London: OUP, 1966); Holloway H. Frost, *The Battle of Jutland* (Annapolis: US Naval Institute, 1936); John Campbell, *Jutland: An Analysis of the Fighting* (London: Conway Maritime Press, 1998); and last but by no means least, Andrew Gordon, *The Rules of the Game* (London: John Murray, 2000). We would urge everyone to buy these books if they want to breathe in themselves the authentic salty spray of Jutland.

The Library and Manuscript staff of the National Maritime Museum are truly remarkable and deserve our collective thanks for preserving in aspic the authentic flavour of the late nineteenth-century Royal Navy. We would also thank Richard Davies and the staff who administer the Liddle Collection, freely available as a public resource within Special Collections, Brotherton Library, Leeds University. Particular thanks are owed to the Library Assistant Sarah George, who was patience personified.

German time was two hours ahead and we have therefore taken the pragmatic step of converting *all* times to 'British' time. We should add that this is as much to avoid confusion in our own ragged minds as those of our readers! The timings throughout can only be held to be approximately accurate to within a minute or so and generally represent an average. As contemporary records are clearly not in chronological alignment it is not possible to produce precise timings. The maps also represent a diagrammatic representation of the squadron and ship movements. It is salutary to note that recent diving teams have reported the wreck of the *Indefatigable* to be some 5 miles to the west of where it should have been according to Admiralty calculations. Once again the multiple and often contradictory contemporary positional reports serve only to cloud, rather than clarify, the issue. In cases of doubt we have invariably made an assessment based on the balance of probability – which is really all anyone can now do.

In the writing and production of this book we would like to thank that promising novelist Keith Lowe and his team of designers at Cassell Military for their skill, patience and forbearance for deadlines missed. This book was originally commissioned by Angus McKinnon and we are grateful for his inspirational advice and encouragement. His successor, Ian Drury, has also been quietly supportive. As ever, with Cassell it has been a pleasure to deal with people who understand. Our good friends Bryn 'Tanky' Hammond and Polly Napper were kind enough to read and comment on the manuscript; their help was invaluable, especially as it was unpaid! Lily Hart was the soul of forbearance throughout the whole writing process.

Finally, we would like to dedicate this book to Wireman 2nd Class Francis Askins, just one of the 1,266 who lost their lives aboard the *Queen Mary* but who is, even now, generations later, occasionally in the thoughts of his now distant descendants. Let us follow their lead and remember the sacrifice of the men of Jutland, not in wholly inappropriate paroxysms of grief, but coolly, in recognition of lives cut sadly short before their time. He is formally commemorated on the Portsmouth Naval Memorial. On a personal note we would also dedicate it to the memory of Peter's mother and father, Ruth and Les Hart, who have both died in the last two years. Average life spans are created by the millions who die far too soon for those who loved them in times of both war and peace.

CHAPTER ONE

THE LONG WAIT

IN 1914 THE ROYAL NAVY had a lot to lose. Britain's fleet had attained its position of global pre-eminence during the succession of maritime wars that had rumbled on throughout the seventeenth and eighteenth centuries and culminated in the final defeat of a combined French and Spanish fleet at the battle of Trafalgar in 1805. While post-Napoleonic Europe slowly recovered from the ravages of war, Britain, free of Continental entanglements, exploited its undisputed control of the seas to ensure that the British Empire was in a pole position in the race to gain colonies and dominate large sections of the globe. The key was the sheer mobility and speed of naval intervention. The well-timed arrival of even just a single 'gunboat' could often settle a localized dispute before it got out of hand, long before other nations could begin to react. The Continental European powers found that, despite their large armies, their far-flung colonies only existed on sufferance and could not be seriously defended in a war with the British. Only the Royal Navy could move troops in almost total security around the globe. This naval ascendancy was maintained by having overwhelming numbers of all the types of ships that could possibly be required by a nation at war, ranging from the most modern battleships right through to the ubiquitous sloops and gunboats. The supremacy was so absolute that no one country could have a chance of naval victory against the Royal Navy.

By the end of the nineteenth century, naval experts had had time to consider how this maritime supremacy came into being. The first great sage was an officer of the United States Navy, Alfred T. Mahan, based at the US Naval War College. Mahan examined maritime policy and naval battles to seek the underlying reasons for the stunning success of the Royal Navy. He believed that to become a maritime power a country must steep itself in the sea in peacetime. Naval strength was rooted in and indivisible from a thriving maritime base of commerce and associated industries. There was, of course, no better way of achieving this than by the acquisition and commercial exploitation of colonies. To prepare for war, foresight was required to amass and maintain a navy of a size commensurate with the amount of merchant shipping and commercial interests that depended on the freedom of the seas. Furthermore, appropriate naval bases would be needed across the globe wherever the navy might be required to operate. The ultimate aim was to ensure that even amidst war, trade routes would be unaffected by enemy action. In essence this is what Great Britain had done and its traditional adversaries – Spain, Holland and France – had not. By failing to recognize the enduring importance of sea power, these nations allowed much of their empires to slip through their fingers.

Mahan was no mere materialist; he did not believe that simply having a certain number of ships and sailors would logically secure success. He maintained that the British had won many of their key battles because of the characteristics of dynamic leadership or the 'warrior spirit' inculcated in their admirals. Naval leadership had to be developed by the informed study of the lessons of past campaigns, within an overall culture that encouraged the rise of the courageous, self-confident and skilful commander, who would in turn be unafraid to share his 'secrets' with the next generation of officers. For Mahan, the ideal of leadership reached its apogee with the incomparable Horatio Nelson.

> Nelson, for the most part, shone upon the battlefield by his tactical combinations, by the rapidity and boldness with which he carried out plans previously laid, or, on occasion, by the astonishing *coup d'oeil* and daring with which, in unforeseen crises, he snatched and secured escaping victory.[1]
>
> Alfred Mahan

Mahan's doctrines were widely accepted and were seized upon both by various interested governments and by a generation of naval officers across the globe. In a sense, he supplied a template for any naval power that considered a challenge to the British hegemony. However, for the most part these acolytes ignored much of the more sophisticated thinking that informed his analysis and focused instead on the simple premise that it was the duty of a navy to seek out the opposing fleet, defeat them in a decisive battle and thereby secure 'command of the sea'.

The other great naval strategist who influenced naval thinking at the turn of the century was a British historian, Sir Julian Corbett, a lifelong civilian who nevertheless wielded great influence by means of his lectures to naval officers at the Royal Naval College, Greenwich. Inspired by his intensive study of the great military strategist Carl von Clausewitz, Corbett also studied the lessons of British naval supremacy. He adopted a more pragmatic approach than Mahan to the problems of conducting war at sea, which he eventually published in 1911 as *Some Principles of Maritime Strategy*. Corbett was less sanguine about the possibility of obtaining outright 'command of the sea', which he defined as the control of maritime communications, pointing out the impossibility of being everywhere at once across the limitless oceans. This uncertainty would be particularly acute if the weaker power chose not to engage in a decisive fleet action, but remained inviolate in harbour as a 'fleet in being', thus continuing to contest the 'command of the sea' from a position of safety. Many of Mahan's followers could not conceive of such a situation and the romantic cachet of the inevitable decisive battle seduced many otherwise sensible officers. But there were many attractions for the weaker naval power in not sacrificing its fleet in such an action. For a 'fleet in being' could render invasion almost impossible; by effective use of surprise a partial 'command of the sea' could be obtained temporarily in a specific location; it could demand the attention of the bulk of a stronger navy while sending out specially built commerce raiders to disrupt the sea lanes; while any attack on its harbour fastness would inevitably expose the superior naval power to such risks that its superiority would be forfeited. Corbett also clearly delimited the boundaries of maritime power. Although he believed it was of the utmost importance, in the end, to resolve a conflict, success on land was eventually required to secure any gains that might have been achieved by the wielding of naval power. True 'command of the seas' depended on decisive military victory on land.

Having highlighted some of the problems that existed in adopting a pure 'Mahanian' approach, Corbett proposed partial solutions based on the power of the blockade and indirect attacks. An effective blockade could produce 'command of the sea' by confining an enemy's naval fleet and commercial marine in harbour. It would not be uncontested. There might be breaches. But much of the military and commercial fruits of maritime supremacy could then be harvested as long as the blockade held. In the meantime, behind the line of the blockade, a vigorous policy of 'limited war' and 'indirect' attacks could harass the enemy coastline, threaten any overseas colonies and relieve pressure on the decisive theatre of land operations by distracting attention to secondary campaigns on the periphery of the enemy's sphere of control.

Corbett's theories, it can be seen with the passage of time, were built on the grounding principles already established by Mahan. Corbett did not contradict Mahan, but merely added a layer of reasoning to establish an alternative naval policy should the enemy fail to oblige in turning up for a decisive battle at the convenience of the stronger maritime nation. It is often forgotten that Mahan's hero, Nelson, spent two years aboard the *Victory* pursuing a blockade of the French and Spanish fleets before they were finally brought to account at Trafalgar. In the end both Mahan and Corbett were enormously influential, but influenced different schools of officers.

The balance of power was also changing across the world. By the end of the nineteenth century, Imperial Germany had emerged to pose a new threat to the British Empire. Following the military defeat of France in 1871, Germany was unquestionably the leading European Continental military power and already competing vigorously with Britain in the worlds of industry and commerce. Kaiser Wilhelm II, who had ascended to the throne in 1888, was a rabid convert to Mahan's view of the crucial importance of maritime power, and believed that Germany would never be able to reap the rewards of its military and industrial strength until it had commensurate naval power. After the appointment of the brilliant Admiral Alfred von Tirpitz as his Secretary of State for Naval Affairs in 1897, these ambitions were duly enshrined in the Navy Act passed by the Reichstag in 1898. This announced plans to create a new navy of some nineteen battleships together with a *mélange* of assorted coastal defence vessels and cruisers by 1904. But after the chastening demonstration of German powerlessness to intervene during the British colonial adventures in Southern Africa, which culminated in the outbreak of the Boer War in 1899, this estimate was revised to no fewer than thirty-eight battleships in a new Navy Act of 1900. This measure was clearly aimed at challenging the British hegemony of the seas.

To protect Germany's sea trade and colonies, in the existing
circumstances, there is only one means – Germany must have a battle
fleet so strong that, even for the adversary with the greatest sea power,
a war against it would involve such dangers as to imperil his position
in the world. For this purpose, it is not absolutely necessary that the
German battle fleet should be as strong as that of the greatest naval
power, because a great naval power will not, as a rule, be in a position to
concentrate all its striking forces against us. But even if it should succeed
in meeting us with considerable superiority of strength, the defeat of a
strong German fleet would so substantially weaken the enemy that, in
spite of a victory he might have obtained, his own position in the world
would no longer be secured by an adequate fleet.[2]

Memorandum, Naval Act, 1900

This theory developed by Tirpitz has become known as the 'Risk Fleet
Theory'. It was based on the expectation that Britain would not dare to
take on the German fleet for fear of exposing itself to its other enemies.
The old rule of thumb had been to ensure that the British possessed a
fleet large enough to face both France and Russia acting in harness – the
vaunted 'Two Power Standard'. The expansion of the German Navy
made this irrelevant and would eventually force Great Britain to seek
Continental alliances.

The Admiralty response to the increased pressure was amazingly bold.
For the long years of superiority wielded by the Royal Navy had not
brought it peace of mind. In between the death of Nelson and the
outbreak of the First World War, the Royal Navy managed to generate
a quite staggering amount of internecine conflict. Every development
in the design and nature of its ships was endlessly agonized over: the aban-
donment of sail for steam engines; the introduction of breech-loading
guns; the removal of extraneous masts; the introduction of turrets and
barbettes; the correct response to the threats to battleships posed by torpedoes, submarines, mines and destroyers. All were the focus of intense
controversy. The nature of tactics was the subject of endless debate, with
separate, but related, mayhem over the form and nature of the Signal
Book, by which means the ships of the line were guided in their manoeuvring. Nothing was simple; nothing could be taken for granted. Common

sense was just another weapon of debate to be twisted to the protagonist's own point of view. What had befallen Nelson's 'Band of Brothers'?

In essence, they had been traumatized by the incredible pace of scientific progress throughout the nineteenth century and the awful prospect that the Royal Navy could take a wrong technological turning. Many officers feared that some crucial new development could be missed and the fleet mortally embarrassed in facing an opposition armed with superior weapons. Others felt it would be equally disastrous to abandon the tried and tested for the possible culs de sac of the unproven. To confuse matters further, the progressives and traditionalists were fragmented and cross-cut depending on the matter at hand. In this febrile atmosphere, professional rivalries and imagined slights came to have a life of their own that transcended naval politics into the realm of lifelong personal feuds, with acolytes cheering on the main protagonists from the metaphorical sidelines. The tensions were so great that at some points it seemed almost impossible to guess what form a fighting ship of the future would take.

In these circumstances it might have been supposed that the Admiralty would be cautious in responding to the new German challenge. Yet, under the guiding hand of the First Sea Lord, Sir John Fisher, this very tension was used as the catalyst to achieve a root and branch revolution in the design of battleships. Recent advances in gunnery had greatly increased the effective range and accuracy of the guns, triggered in part by the necessity of getting out of torpedo range. As the ranges increased, the mixed armaments of 12-inch, 9.2-inch and 6-inch guns carried by the typical battleship at the turn of the century were increasingly called into question. The new techniques placed much importance on firing guns in salvo and straddling the target, but this process was hopelessly confused when a ship fired a mixture of gun calibres at the same time. What was required was an armament of eight or more guns of the same calibre. As heavier guns were relatively more accurate, and the shells naturally more devastating, the answer lay in an 'all-big-gun' ship: and so the *Dreadnought* was born with her ten 12-inch guns disposed to allow an eight-gun broadside. Such an armament would have rendered the *Dreadnought* so slow that she would have been unable to catch her more lightly armed contemporaries, had not the Admiralty commissioned another startling innovation in the method of propulsion. To get the speed that would allow the new ship to catch her victims, the new Parsons turbine engines were to be used, generating the then unprecedented speed for a British battle-ship of 21 knots. The defensive armour plating was less exceptional, although well up to prevailing standards, and strict regimes of watertight compartmentation were observed beneath the water-line. Once conceived, the *Dreadnought* was built in great secrecy in exactly a year and a day, instead of the usual three years, another phenomenal achievement. Suddenly, on 3 October 1906, when she sailed for her sea trials, all the navies of the other great powers, built at such enormous cost, were outdated. Magnificent ships that embodied the national pride of their countries overnight became belittled as mere 'pre-dreadnoughts'.

This sea change was not without risk for the British. Their huge numerical supremacy was rendered almost irrelevant at a stroke. Yet there were many advantages in deliberately instigating the revolution in naval design before a competing nation had a chance to seize the initiative. While the British assessed their prize and commissioned new dreadnoughts, foreign navies were forced to suspend their naval programmes and go back to the drawing board to design their own dreadnoughts from scratch. The Germans were faced with a choice of either abandoning their naval ambitions or embracing a stupendous new investment. They chose once again to challenge directly the Royal Navy. But it was not until July 1907 that the Germans could begin work on their first dreadnoughts. Even then they had to widen and deepen the Kiel Canal, which linked the Baltic and the North Sea, a task that would not be completed until the summer of 1914. When the mists cleared the British had once more secured their lead.

The *Dreadnought* was not the only innovative new ship launched on a startled naval world. Fisher, who strongly believed that speed was the most effective form of defence, had also instigated development of a new class of armoured cruiser that would in time become known as the battlecruiser. This new type would also have a uniform heavy armament, this time eight 12-inch guns, but instead of the thick armour plating of the *Dreadnought*, they were to be lightly protected, relying on their exceptional speed of 25 knots to whisk them away from danger. The battlecruisers were intended to sweep the seas clear of foreign cruisers, which would find themselves unable either to fight or to escape. The first battlecruiser was the *Invincible*, completed in 1908. The *Invincible* created much interest but the whole battlecruiser concept was deeply flawed from the start. The very strength of their massed 12-inch firepower created an irresistible temptation to use them as the fast wing of the battle fleet. Yet here they would inevitably encounter heavy shells from the enemy dreadnoughts that could easily penetrate their thin armour. And the question remained: what would happen when they met their inevitable direct equivalents that would be capable of the same speed? The Germans attempted to pre-empt the *Invincible* while she was on the stocks by building the *Blücher* armed with twelve 8.2-inch guns, in the apparent belief that the *Invincible* would only have eight 9.2-inch guns. Although the Germans got off on the wrong foot, they actually then came up with a better-balanced design for their subsequent battlecruisers. They were just as fast, but they incorporated a far superior overall level of armour protection. In the end they would test to destruction Fisher's dictum that speed is its own armour.

The naval race between Britain and Germany escalated remorselessly in the first decade of the twentieth century as each side sought to match and exceed the building programme of the other. The competition poisoned relationships between the two countries and forced Britain into ever closer informal links with its two former enemies, France and Russia. The Entente Cordiale was born and plans for military and naval co-operation in the event of war were hesitantly sketched out between the erstwhile rivals. Each successive class of dreadnoughts raised the stakes just as they increased in overall size, hitting power, armour and speed. Gunnery ranges expanded; new methods of fire control of ever-increasing sophistication were developed. Soon the *Dreadnought* herself was teetering on the brink of relative obsolescence.

In June 1914 the assassination of Archduke Franz Ferdinand of Austria lit the fuse that would explode Europe into the First World War. The escalating diplomatic crisis was rooted in the Balkans, but spread quickly across the whole of Europe. As nations teetered on the brink of war, the Admiralty had a slightly jaundiced view of the man *in situ* aboard his flagship the *Iron Duke* as Commander-in-Chief of the Home Fleet. Admiral Sir George Callaghan, a respected senior officer, had been in command since 1911 and had already had the normal two-year period of tenure extended until October 1914. However, it was precisely Callaghan's age that lay at the root of the problem. The Admiralty felt that at 62 he was simply too old to be entrusted with the onerous duty of wielding his country's main weapon in a war that would, one way or another, shape the twentieth century. It was these fears that caused Winston Churchill, the First Lord of the Admiralty, to appoint Sir John Jellicoe, then the Second Sea Lord, as second in command of the fleet. The stated intention was that Jellicoe would take over command of the fleet in the normal course of events when Callaghan had finished his term of office. But Jellicoe had long been marked for greater things.

John Jellicoe was born on 5 December 1859. His family had a variety of naval connections and he was duly sent as a cadet to the training ship *Britannia* at the tender age of 12. His tuition had its origins in the age of sail but Jellicoe thrived, passing out in 1874. His instruction had by no means finished but, by dutiful attention to his studies and duties, he invariably did well as he progressed through the ranks of junior officers. He eventually specialized in gunnery and soon caught the attention of Fisher, who was then commanding the *Excellent* gunnery school. Jellicoe spent the next few years divided between postings to experimental ships and ashore at the *Excellent* on Whale Island. In 1889 he acted as an assistant to Fisher on his appointment as Director of Naval Ordnance at the Admiralty. Jellicoe's mixture of intelligence and sheer hard work ensured that he reached the rank of commander in 1891. After his promotion he went back to sea as executive officer, first aboard the *Sans Pareil* and then on the *Victoria*, then the flagship of the Mediterranean Fleet. This plum posting could have been the end of him.

On 22 June 1893, as Jellicoe lay below decks in his bed struck down by a fever, Admiral Sir George Tryon committed a gross blunder in manoeuvring his fleet as he ordered the leading ships in each of the two columns to turn inwards, so that they were heading straight for each other. His subordinates failed for a variety of reasons to correct this elementary error, or indeed to take the necessary evasive action, and as a result the ram of the *Camperdown* crunched into the side of the *Victoria*, which duly heeled over and sank. Jellicoe, against the odds, was rescued from the water, although Tyron and many others perished. It was the low point of the Victorian navy and demonstrated the inherent inflexibility of mind of many, if not most, of its senior officers. They had been brought up and drilled to believe that their admiral was second only to God, with near papal infallibility. The inevitable consequences of such mental atrophy would bedevil the fleet for many long years.

Jellicoe's manifold qualities were recognized by the replacement Mediterranean Commander-in-Chief, Admiral Sir Michael Culme-Seymour, who selected him to serve as his commander aboard the new flagship, *Ramillies*. After a successful three-year commission, Jellicoe was made a captain and his gunnery specialization was reflected in his appointment to the joint service Ordnance Committee in 1897. At the end of the year he was made flag captain aboard the *Centurion* under Vice Admiral Sir Edward Seymour in command of the China Station. Here the naked colonialism of Britain, France, Germany and Russia, which were intent on cutting up Imperial China for their mutual profit, not unnaturally stirred up considerable antipathy among the Chinese, which culminated in the Boxer Rebellion instigated in mid-1900 by a mysterious, but influential, secret society violently opposed to Western penetration. The European embassy staffs were soon besieged in their Peking legations and Jellicoe was appointed Chief of Staff to a makeshift Anglo-German naval brigade sent by train to attempt their rescue in June 1900. As the Chinese Imperial troops began directly to assist the insurgent Boxers, the railway line was cut and the mission was perforce abandoned. The retreat was a confused nightmare that nearly cost Jellicoe his life. On 21 June he led an attack on a Chinese village which blocked their retreat alongside the banks of the Pei-Ho River.

> I was hit on the left side of the chest, the shock turning me half round.
> I thought my left arm had gone. Sat down on a stone, and Cross,
> Gunnery Instructor, came and cut away the sleeve of tunic and shirt
> and helped me behind a house where I lay down. After a bit Dr Sibbald
> came up and bandaged wound and told me that he thought I was
> finished. I made my will on a bit of paper and gave it to my coxswain. I
> was spitting up a lot of blood and thought the wound probably mortal.[3]
> Captain John Jellicoe, HMS *Centurion*, China Station

Jellicoe was successfully evacuated and the doctor's gloomy prognostications proved wrong as he made a good recovery, although he carried the bullet in his left lung for the rest of his life.

In 1901 he returned to England, where he was appointed as assistant to the Third Sea Lord and Controller, Sir William May. His role was to inspect the work of the various shipbuilders responsible for work on naval ships. His next sea command was as captain of the armoured cruiser *Drake* where, as might be expected, he showed great interest in absorbing the new techniques of gunnery with particular reference to the introduction of firing practice at much longer ranges than had been previously considered practical. In 1904 he was summoned back by Fisher to work on the committee charged with developing the plans for the *Dreadnought*. In 1905 Jellicoe was made Director of Naval Ordnance at the Admiralty with a special responsibility for overseeing the design and production of the heavy guns required for the dreadnoughts. Promoted to rear admiral in 1907, he went to sea aboard the *Albemarle* as second in command of the Atlantic Fleet, before returning to the Admiralty as Controller in 1908. Here he dealt with the many problems in trying to expand Britain's capacity to produce dreadnoughts during the height of the naval race with Germany.

Jellicoe was an admirer of German design and shipbuilding skills and warned repeatedly that German ships were utilizing their greater beam to carry more armour and secure superior underwater subdivision and compartmentation, making them far harder to sink than their British counterparts. He commissioned floating docks to repair damaged vessels, which would ease the possible pressure on the limited availability of suitable dock provision. He also raised pertinent questions about the quality of British shells. His capacity for sheer hard work was invaluable under a relentless pressure that might have broken a lesser man.

In 1910 he went back to sea, first in command of the Atlantic Fleet, and then in command of the 2nd Division of the Home Fleet under Sir George Callaghan. As he hoisted his flag in the *Hercules*, Jellicoe was, for the first time, serving aboard one of the dreadnoughts that would hold the fate of the country within their compass. During his command he was involved in the trials of the new 'director' firing systems for the main armament, which sought to direct and concentrate the fire of the multiple turrets on a dreadnought by the controlling hand of a single gunnery officer stationed high in the ship. Fisher and Churchill had by this stage clearly identified Jellicoe as the 'new Nelson' who would lead the Royal Navy to victory in the Armageddon that was envisaged in the near future.

Late in 1912 Jellicoe returned as Second Sea Lord to the Admiralty. Here he had to deal with the rumbustious character of Churchill, who was never one to let protocol dictate the limits of his powers or influence. The two were in conflict in many areas, but it is a testament to Jellicoe's tact and reasonableness that they never actually fell out. Indeed, when Jellicoe was given leave of absence to take command of the Red Fleet against the Blue Fleet commanded by Callaghan in the naval exercises of 1913, he did so well that once again the full sunlight of Churchill's approbation shone upon him. Jellicoe was the 'coming man', although he himself was not aware of how soon he would be thrust into the very front rank.

The gathering war clouds caused the Admiralty to cancel the scheduled dispersal of the fleet, which had by good fortune just undergone a rigorous test mobilization and was gathered together at full strength for a formal inspection by George V at Spithead on 17 July 1914. It would remain together and indeed began the move to its war stations at Scapa Flow. This disposition was another radical departure from tradition.

The Royal Navy had been weaned on a diet of close blockade. Its 'storm-tossed' ships had stood off French and Spanish ports throughout the endless wars that disfigured the elegant façade of the eighteenth century. Yet the emergence of the submarine as a credible weapon of war had left this policy in tatters; nothing, it seemed, could prevent the submarine from sneaking out of port to prey on the 'tethered goats' of any close blockading fleet. To this was added the ever-increasing threat posed by fast destroyers. Modern ships did not use the endlessly renewable wind power to fill their sails, but instead had to return to port regularly to take aboard coal or oil to power their vast engines. These problems were clearly discerned, but the ingrained traditional methods of warfare took some shifting and it was with considerable reluctance that the close blockade was abandoned in 1912. Wild schemes continued to emerge, such as an idea promulgated by Churchill to capture the offshore German island of Borkum as a forward base. Yet the eventually adopted policy of distant blockade was almost thrust upon it by circumstances of geography. The British Isles themselves effectively blockaded in the Germans, lying as they did four-square across the sea routes to Germany. Only two gaps remained. The English Channel to the south was narrow, only around 20 miles across at the Straits of Dover, and easily blocked by a combination of a strong minefield barrage patrolled by smaller ships and backed up by the nineteen second-line pre-dreadnoughts of the Channel Fleet. To the north, the 200 miles between Scotland and Norway would be patrolled by a force of cruisers. Meanwhile, the main battle fleet would be concentrated in the huge natural harbour of Scapa Flow, tucked away in the Orkneys. From here it could protect the cruiser line and sweep down as required into the North Sea if the German fleet should dare to emerge from harbour. Directly facing the German North Sea ports was the strong Harwich Force made up of fast light cruisers and destroyers charged with the task of patrolling the southern reaches of the North Sea and linking up with either the Channel Fleet or the battle fleet as required. This policy was almost pure Corbettism. It ceded absolute 'control' of the North Sea, which could not be achieved without insupportable risks, but it secured for Great Britain almost all the benefits of control of the wider oceans across the globe. The blockade was secure, the German fleet was effectively under house arrest and the impasse could not be broken unless it successfully assaulted its 'jailor' in a major fleet action.

Jellicoe was ordered north to join the fleet at Scapa. Churchill had already made him aware that he might well be appointed Commander-in-Chief should war break out. Jellicoe was appalled at the prospect. He had always liked and respected Sir George Callaghan, with whom he had served, and, although he had natural ambitions to command the fleet, he felt the timing could not have been worse. The anguish that would be caused to Callaghan by his removal, just at the moment when it seemed that his whole career would be fulfilled by wartime command, mortified the embarrassed Jellicoe. But it was not mere sentiment, or the feelings of an old friend and comrade, that made Jellicoe blanch. He was keenly aware that morale is a key element in warfare. If there was even a sneaking suspicion within the fleet that he had in any way connived to get the command, he could expect little loyalty from his aggrieved new subordinates. In battle this might be disastrous. The very concept of changing command at the point of war was inadvisable on principle. How could Jellicoe be expected to be as familiar with the intricate make-up of the fleet and its officers as its commander for the last three years? He could boast only a cursory knowledge of the detailed war plans and dispositions. Jellicoe sent multiple telegrams to the Admiralty attempting to persuade them of the irrationality of what they proposed, but they remained adamant. Finally, on 4 August as Britain entered the war, despite his vehement protests Jellicoe was ordered to open his secret orders and so take command of the battle fleet, henceforth to be renamed the Grand Fleet. He would be the man charged with the onerous responsibility of delivering the new Trafalgar that the British people expected and demanded. And so, as Jellicoe took over his staff, his flagship and his fleet, Callaghan left the pages of history.

The Grand Fleet that Jellicoe inherited was a formidable force, the concentrated essence of British naval power. It numbered 20 dreadnoughts, 8 pre-dreadnoughts of the King Edward class, 4 battlecruisers, 21 assorted cruisers and some 42 destroyers. In command of the 1st Battlecruiser Squadron was a man whose future was to become inextricably linked with Jellicoe: Vice Admiral Sir David Beatty.

David Beatty was born on 17 January 1871, the second son of an influential Irish family who had taken root in Cheshire. He passed through *Britannia* between 1884 and 1885, but achieved little of consequence other than a burgeoning reputation for carefree misbehaviour. Family influence brought him a sojourn as midshipman aboard the *Alexandria*, the then flagship of the Mediterranean Fleet, but poor examination results meant that his career was effectively stalled as a lieutenant on a variety of mundane postings that gave no indication of a glowing future. Then, in 1896, Beatty had a stroke of luck when he was appointed as second in command of river gunboats sent up the Nile to assist General Sir Herbert Kitchener in the campaign to avenge the death of General Charles Gordon and to recapture Khartoum. The first instalment of the protracted campaign was an exciting *Boy's Own Paper* affair and after his commanding officer was seriously wounded Beatty took over command. His leadership qualities were noticed and he was recalled at Kitchener's special request when the campaign was resumed in 1897. The river boats had a dramatic role scouting along the river ahead of the main army and providing support fire during the many skirmishes which culminated in the battle of Omdurman of 2 September 1898. Beatty's contribution was marked by early promotion to commander and the award of the DSO. His name was made.

Beatty's next commission was as executive officer aboard the *Barfleur* serving on the China Station. Like Jellicoe, Beatty was also drawn into the strange farrago of the Boxer Rebellion. Beatty was landed with a party of 150 naval personnel from the *Barfleur* to strengthen the impromptu naval brigade that was defending Tientsin from a mixed force of Chinese regular troops and the revolting Boxers. Once again he seems to have distinguished himself in the fighting until on 19 June 1900 he was wounded in his left arm. He soon discharged himself from the confines of hospital and joined an expedition to rescue the remnants of the naval column, which included the wounded Jellicoe. On his return to London the wounded hero courted social opprobrium but gained a fortune when he married the extremely wealthy American heiress and recent divorcee Ethel Tree. He did not return to sea until he was appointed as captain aboard a series of cruisers between 1902 and 1905. Beatty had advanced far beyond most of his contemporaries and the rapid expansion of the navy kept him ahead of the pack. An Admiralty appointment as the Naval Advisor to the Army Council then occupied him from 1905 to 1908. From late 1908 Beatty was in command of the pre-dreadnought *Queen* as part of the Atlantic Fleet, where he privately fulminated against the marked tactical rigidity employed in handling the fleet. Nevertheless, he impressed the powers that be and, on 1 January 1910, he was made an admiral at the age of 38, thus mirroring in this at least Nelson's achievement in 1797. Then in 1911 came a career-threatening spat as the financially secure Beatty refused to accept second fiddle as second in command of the Atlantic Fleet. Here he had overreached himself and might well have spent a considerable time ashore without a posting had he not been lucky in the timing of Churchill's appointment as First Lord of the Admiralty in October 1911. Beatty was just the kind of man to appeal to Churchill and in early 1912 he was soon appointed as his naval secretary. Beatty worked hard in his new role. He made considerable progress in understanding the new language of naval warfare and had the mental strength to stand up to Churchill where necessary without provoking a fatal falling out. Churchill was more than satisfied and exerted his influence once again to appoint his protégé above the heads of many other, more senior officers to the plum command of the Battlecruiser Fleet. So it was that on 1 March 1913 Beatty hoisted his flag in the ship that was to become synonymous with his name, the *Lion*.

In August 1914 the Grand Fleet was the sharp tip of the British naval iceberg. Elsewhere, scattered across the globe, were hundreds of miscellaneous ships busy on the manifold duties of king and empire. In particular, there were three more battlecruisers engaged in their original function of clearing the sea lanes by hunting down Germany's detached cruisers. The battlecruiser *Goeben* with the light cruiser *Breslau* were abroad in the Mediterranean, while the German East Asiatic Squadron posed a considerable threat further afield. The main German forces were concentrated into the High Seas Fleet, which it was presumed would choose the moment to deploy its full strength of 13 dreadnoughts, 16 pre-dreadnoughts, 5 battlecruisers, 17 cruisers and 88 destroyers. They were based largely at Wilhelmshaven, Germany's main port on its North Sea coast and linked by the recently completed Kiel Canal to the port of Kiel on the Baltic Sea.

After a decade of fevered speculation and anticipation, the general public, and no small proportion of the fleet, expected there to be a huge 'Mahanian' naval battle to resolve the command of the seas within days of the outbreak of war. It was widely predicted that the trigger for this naval Armageddon would be the despatch of the British Expeditionary Force across the English Channel, to take up its agreed place alongside the French Army in the war against Germany. The High Seas Fleet would surely emerge to contest the crossing. Unfortunately, as Corbett had predicted, the Germans declined to sacrifice their navy at the altar of popular British sentiment and remained safely in harbour as the BEF crossed the Channel. German strategy was based firmly on securing an early land victory. In order to defeat both France in the west and Russia in the east, they aimed to move decisively against the former while the latter was still mobilizing its unwieldy forces. For over a decade the Germans had nurtured a plan first proposed by their Chief of Staff, von Schlieffen, to wheel through Belgium, evading the French armies massed on the Franco-German border. The intention was to capture Paris in a matter of weeks. With France eliminated they could turn their combined forces onto the hapless Russians. The German General Staff was confident that the BEF would have a negligible impact on the outcome of the overall campaign in the west. The BEF was a minnow alongside the leviathan conscript armies of Germany and France. There was no need to risk the fleet, which had a key role to play in defending the open German flanks from the possibility of coastal assault in the Baltic or North Sea, in order to destroy a contemptible little army that was doomed in any event.

The Commander-in-Chief of the High Seas Fleet, Admiral Friedrich von Ingenohl, was ordered not to risk his ships and he duly complied. The Germans believed that the British were still committed to the idea of a close blockade of German ports. The Grand Fleet was expected to appear off the German coast as soon as war was declared. The chances of successfully launching submarine and destroyer attacks against the anticipated British blockade in the Heligoland Bight whetted the German appetite. A drip, drip string of losses to torpedoes and mines would soon render the Grand Fleet vulnerable to a decisive attack at the moment of Ingenohl's choosing. Even when it became apparent that the Royal Navy was not going to provide an easy target off the coast of Germany, the original tactic of trying to erode the majesty of the Grand Fleet through the use of mines and torpedoes remained in force, although with far less chance of real success. Meanwhile the High Seas Fleet stayed in harbour.

In contrast, the Grand Fleet did not. Day after day was spent at sea, sweeping down into the North Sea hoping to intercept any German effort to interfere with the passage and supply of the BEF. On 28 August a major raid was carried out by elements of the Harwich Force, supported by the 1st Battlecruiser Squadron, into the Heligoland Bight. A confused action between the light cruisers of both sides was effectively resolved in the British favour by the thunderous intervention of Beatty's battlecruisers. Shortly afterwards the Germans ceased their tempting advanced patrols and replaced them with massed and impenetrable minefields that almost filled the Heligoland Bight.

If the opening exchanges of the first month of the war had been unexpectedly restrained, as early as September 1914 it became clear that German submarines were considerably more advanced and deadly than had been realized. One signifying moment was the success of the *U9* on 22 September in sinking three British cruisers, the *Aboukir*, *Cressy* and *Hogue*, that were patrolling, with the utter serenity and over-confidence that only comes with ignorance, off the Dutch coast. The ships were not a significant loss in material terms, but their crews were. The death toll

was unpalatable in the extreme. The incident showed that no dreadnoughts or battlecruisers could proceed in safety without a proper
destroyer screen to keep down and harass any lurking submarines. The
destroyers, significantly formerly known as torpedo-boat destroyers, were
armed with their own torpedoes which could cause havoc in an enemy
fleet. The extension of their defensive role to provide a constant cover
against submarines led to an immediate shortage of destroyers, exacerbated by their limited sea endurance of just three days, in sharp contrast
to the nine or ten days the ships they guarded could stay at sea. Jellicoe
was convinced that the Germans had a clear superiority in the numbers
of *available* destroyers. He was deeply concerned about this imbalance and
was convinced that in a fleet action that could be initiated by the Germans
at their selected moment, the destroyers of the Harwich Force, nominally
part of the Grand Fleet, were unlikely to be present.

An even greater cause of concern was the apparent vulnerability to
submarines of the Grand Fleet's anchorage at Scapa Flow. As it had only
recently been designated as a main base, no proper defences had yet been
built and German U-boats were soon sighted exploring the entrances to
the harbour. Submarine alarms were frequent and although they were
almost invariably unfounded, no chances could be taken. While the proper
defences were being put in place to secure Scapa, the Grand Fleet made
itself scarce, taking temporary shelter on the west coast of Scotland and
even as far away as Northern Ireland. It was undignified, but the dreadnoughts were beyond all price. They could not be placed at risk to the
depredations of submarine intruders, whose capacity for destruction was
limited only by the number of torpedoes they could carry.

Submarines were not Jellicoe's only worry. Although on paper the
Grand Fleet was apparently superior in numbers of dreadnoughts and
battlecruisers, in practice this advantage was whittled away in the most
unnerving manner. Just as Tirpitz had predicted in the 1900 Navy Act,
the Royal Navy, despite all its strength, had many responsibilities to fulfil
and it could not concentrate all its striking forces in the North Sea at a
given moment. Engine problems, the necessity for refits and the sinking
of the new dreadnought *Audacious* by a mine on 27 October left Jellicoe
with a superiority of just seventeen to fifteen dreadnoughts and a parity
of five battlecruisers. As Jellicoe was convinced that German dread-

noughts possessed both better armour protection and superior underwater compartmentation, this smallest of advantages was in fact all but nullified. In November 1914 the humiliating British defeat by the German East Asiatic Squadron at the battle of Coronel prompted the post-haste detachment of three of the battlecruisers to extract vengeance. The temporary loss of these ships severely tested Jellicoe's nerve. The return of the battlecruisers in triumph after defeating the German squadron at the battle of the Falklands came not a moment too soon. From that time, early in 1915, the strength of the Grand Fleet climbed inexorably relative to the High Seas Fleet as new dreadnoughts rolled off the stocks. Ironically, the Germans' reluctance to expose their precious dreadnoughts in the opening months of the war robbed them of their only realistic chance for a true naval victory.

It was against this strategic and tactical background that Jellicoe began to draft and issue formal Grand Fleet Battle Orders to guide and co-ordinate his subordinates in action. It was in this exercise that his preoccupations and generally cautious demeanour found their natural expression. His predecessor, Callaghan, had issued little more than a review of the functions of the different classes of ships coupled with an injunction for his squadron commanders to use their initiative. Jellicoe's approach was markedly different, motivated as he was by an earnest desire to bring as high a degree of order as possible to the mad confusions of battle.

> The tactics to be pursued by the different units of the Fleet in action under all conceivable conditions were provided for as far as possible.[4]
>
> Admiral Sir John Jellicoe, HMS *Iron Duke*, Grand Fleet

Through the Grand Fleet Battle Orders his subordinates would be given their 'orders' in advance; orders which sought to predict almost any eventuality of war and to provide ready-made answers. The overall tone was centralist and in this Jellicoe reflected the preoccupations of the Royal Navy. For an organization that worshipped leadership and assigned autocratic powers to the admiral in charge, the Royal Navy was remarkably keen on stamping on all signs of individuality in junior officers. From the moment they joined the navy, they were expected to fall in line, to excel by devotion to duty and a rigid adherence to orders. Then, on finally becoming an admiral they were miraculously to blossom forth with the instincts, insight, daring and command abilities of a new Nelson. In theory Jellicoe recognized that no commander could exercise complete command and control in battle.

> He cannot be certain, *after* deployment, of being able to control the movements of three Battle Squadrons when steaming fast and making much funnel smoke; with the noise and smoke of battle added, the practicality of exercising general control would be still further reduced. It therefore becomes necessary to decentralise command to the fullest extent possible, and the Vice Admirals commanding squadrons have discretionary power to manoeuvre their squadrons independently whilst conforming generally to the movements of the Commander-in-Chief and complying with his known intentions.[5]
>
> Admiral Sir John Jellicoe, HMS *Iron Duke*, Grand Fleet

Although the intellectual acceptance of the need for decentralization was therefore clearly made, unfortunately it did not reflect the reality of Jellicoe's approach in practice. Elsewhere in the Grand Fleet Battle Orders the freedom to launch such independent action was limited by a series of caveats and a list of special circumstances, all of which further reinforced the habits of implicit obedience inculcated in his senior officers. This was exacerbated by Jellicoe's failure in all the hundreds of exercises undertaken by the Grand Fleet over the next few years ever to rehearse the circumstances whereby independent action or manoeuvring might be required by a subordinate officer. The exercises bore more in common with the parade ground drill of a regimental sergeant major than the manoeuvring together of a 'Band of Brothers' guided by a common set of principles to a common end.

The need for control originated from Jellicoe's desire to enter combat in a single line of battle. Any encounter would, as far as possible, be fought at long range to nullify the threat of torpedo attack and to rely on the massed heavy-calibre guns of the dreadnoughts to pulverize the Germans before closing in for the *coup de grâce*. Line ahead was the traditional fighting formation of the Royal Navy and it could not be surpassed in providing an unfettered concentration of broadsides onto the opposing line. It did however presuppose a certain amount of co-operation from the opposing fleet. The vagaries of the winds had once limited the manoeuvring possibilities that lay before an admiral, but the onset of steam gave them an almost unlimited freedom to pursue any course of action. In particular, it allowed the prospect of a sudden retreat artfully covered by artificially generated smoke-screens.

Jellicoe was aware that, when battle came, it might be difficult to bring it to a decisive conclusion. Yet he was determined not to take unnecessary risks in trying to secure such a victory. At the root of all his tactical thinking was the overall strategic position and his full acceptance of his personal responsibility to his country. 'Our fleet was the one and only factor that was vital to the existence of the Empire.'[6] The British Empire could not withstand a serious defeat at sea, nor, indeed, could the Allies. Allied strategy was underpinned by the command of the oceans guaranteed by the Grand Fleet. Above all, Jellicoe was preoccupied with avoiding serious losses to the Grand Fleet which might occur if he ran into some kind of underwater trap. The twin perils of mines and torpedoes filled his waking thoughts. These anxieties were clearly defined in a forceful letter sent to the Admiralty as early as 30 October 1914.

> The experience gained of German methods since the commencement of the war makes it possible and very desirable to consider the manner in which these methods are likely to be made use of tactically in a fleet action. The Germans have shown that they rely to a very great extent on submarines, mines, and torpedoes, and there can be no doubt whatever that they will endeavour to make the fullest use of these weapons in a fleet action, especially since they possess an actual superiority over us in these particular directions. It, therefore, becomes necessary to consider our own tactical methods in relation to these forms of attack. In the first place, it is evident that the Germans cannot rely with certainty upon having their full complement of submarines and minelayers present in a fleet action, unless the battle is fought in waters selected by them and in the southern area of the North Sea. Aircraft, also, could only be brought into action in this locality. My object will therefore be to fight the fleet action in the northern portion of the North Sea, which position is incidentally nearer our own bases, giving our wounded ships a chance of reaching them, whilst it ensures the final destruction or capture of enemy wounded vessels, and greatly handicaps

a night destroyer attack before or after a fleet action. The northern area is also favourable to a concentration of our cruisers and torpedo craft with the battle fleet; such concentration on the part of the enemy being always possible, since he will choose a time for coming out when all his ships are coaled and ready in all respects to fight. Owing to the necessity that exists for keeping our cruisers at sea, it is probable that many will be short of coal when the opportunity for a fleet action arises, and they might be unable to move far to the southward for this reason. The presence of a large force of cruisers is most necessary, for observation and for screening the battle fleet, so that the latter may be manoeuvred into any desired position behind the cruiser screen. This is a strong additional reason for fighting in the northern area.[7]

Admiral Sir John Jellicoe, HMS *Iron Duke*, Grand Fleet

He then turned to the actual tactics to be pursued in a battle, deliberately exposing the cautious nature of his plans and virtually inviting the Admiralty either to endorse them or sack him.

If, for instance, the enemy battle fleet were to turn away from an advancing fleet, I should assume that the intention was to lead us over mines and submarines, and should decline to be so drawn. I desire particularly to draw the attention of Their Lordships to this point, since it may be deemed a refusal of battle, and, indeed, might possibly result in failure to bring the enemy to action as soon as is expected and hoped. Such a result would be absolutely repugnant to the feelings of all British Naval Officers and men, but with new and untried methods of warfare new tactics must be devised to meet them. I feel that such tactics, if not understood, may bring odium upon me, but so long as I have the confidence of Their Lordships I intend to pursue what is, in my considered opinion, the proper course to defeat and annihilate the enemy's battle fleet, without regard to uninstructed opinion or criticism. The situation is a difficult one. It is quite within the bounds of possibility that half our battle fleet might be disabled by under-water attack before the guns opened fire at all, if a false move is made, and I feel that I must constantly bear in mind the great probability of such attack and be prepared tactically to prevent its success.[8]

Admiral Sir John Jellicoe, HMS *Iron Duke*, Grand Fleet

In this letter Jellicoe may only have mentioned submarines and the threat of mines laid by minelayers or destroyers, but he was also fully aware of the risk of an effective ambush in circumstances of low visibility, or from behind smoke-screens, by massed German destroyers. This was especially the case if his detached destroyers in the Harwich Force had been unable to rendezvous with the Grand Fleet before the action ensued. On 7 November 1914 the Admiralty replied, fully endorsing Jellicoe's intended actions.

> I have laid before My Lords Commissioners of the Admiralty your
> letter of the 30th ultimo., and I am commanded by them to inform
> you that they approve your views, as stated therein, and desire to assure
> you of their full confidence in your contemplated conduct of the Fleet
> in action.[9]
> Admiralty

Jellicoe's letter clearly outlined the tactical framework within which any battle would eventually be fought. In understanding what happened when the two fleets ultimately met on 31 May 1916, it is essential to keep these principles in mind as they informed and underlay all his actions that day.

Having defined the parameters within which he would act, Jellicoe began an intensive programme of exercises designed to bring the Grand Fleet to a peak of efficiency. If manoeuvring, station-keeping, signalling, gunnery and damage control were the language of naval warfare, then Jellicoe was determined that his men would be fluent in all of them. If the Grand Fleet ever had any doubts about their new leader, they were soon washed away by a combination of his transparent decency, manifest competence and evident capacity for hard work. One of the staff he inherited from his predecessor was more than impressed.

> Jellicoe worked with an amazing rapidity. When in harbour it was not his
> habit to sit at his ordinary large writing table, but at a tiny little affair in
> the middle of his cabin. To see him there reading despatches and
> memorandum, making pencil annotations and corrections, interrupted
> from time to time by the mass of matters and signals requiring immediate
> action, was to see a man who through years of training and control had
> brought the power of concentration to a fine art. Physical fitness was

combined with this power of concentration. In the evenings in harbour he could be seen hard at the ball game, going at it with the terrific energy he put into everything he undertook. The exercise that he got out of a game of golf on the Flotta Links is well known ... This physical fitness combined with the mental and moral attributes he so abundantly possessed enabled him serenely to sustain his vast responsibilities – responsibilities always great, but greater perhaps in the early stages of the war when so much was in the making. Never did the writer see him out of temper or anything but cheerful, and infusing everyone with the joy of carrying out the work in hand. His calm outlook never deserted him. Care and responsibilities were when possible thrown off the last thing at night by the reading of thrillers of a particularly lurid description.[10]

Lieutenant Commander Roger Bellairs, HMS *Iron Duke*, Grand Fleet

This eulogy, which might appear sycophantic, is made real by this last intriguing detail. It does more than anything else to bring Jellicoe to life.

Jellicoe had made it explicitly clear to the Admiralty that it could not command the southern area of the North Sea. That domination had been sacrificed at the moment it was decided to enforce a distant rather than close blockade of the German ports. The only dilution of the Grand Fleet was the move of Beatty and the 1st Battlecruiser Squadron to the Cromarty Firth in October. This was thrown into high profile by the German decision to launch battlecruiser hit-and-run raids on the British east coast. After the aperitif of a quick raid on Yarmouth on 3 November 1914, Ingenohl decided to chance his arm further by bombarding Scarborough and Hartlepool on 16 December. The idea was to draw out the Grand Fleet right across a newly laid minefield – just as Jellicoe had predicted. But at this point the Admiralty deployed one of the most powerful weapons at its disposal.

Accurate intelligence of an enemy's movements is invaluable in war. In a supreme act of Allied co-operation the Russians had passed to the Admiralty copies of German cipher books and the squared charts of the North Sea used by the High Seas Fleet for all positional reports, which they had obtained from the German light cruiser the *Magdeburg*, run aground on the island of Odensholm in the Baltic off the coast of Estonia. A special group of decoding experts was established under the collective title of Room 40 which soon mastered the German signal code and began to forward to the Admiralty Operations Division a constant stream of decoded signal traffic. The Germans changed their code frequently, but a lack of wireless discipline, coupled with already identified routine patterns of signals, allowed the decoders to track their every twist and turn right through the war. This intelligence coup was further backed up by the establishment of a series of directional-finding wireless stations along Britain's east coast, which could accurately pinpoint the position of German ships every time they used their wireless. This information was also channelled through Room 40 to the Operations staff. The challenge lay in using these intelligence sources effectively without jeopardizing their continued provision. If the Admiralty did not preserve absolute secrecy relating to the activities of Room 40, then the Germans would inevitably change their wireless protocol and codes so radically that all the advantage would be lost.

It is perhaps ironic that the first major operational use of this gold-mine of information nearly led a part of the Grand Fleet to disaster. On 14 December the Admiralty was made aware that the 1st Scouting Force commanded by Admiral Franz von Hipper would set off on 15 December 1914 to carry out a further raid on the vulnerable east coast of England. It therefore ordered Jellicoe to intercept the German ships by sending Beatty's battlecruisers accompanied by the detached Second Battle Squadron of six dreadnoughts – a more than adequate force to deal with five German battlecruisers. Jellicoe wanted to send the whole Grand Fleet, but the Admiralty prevailed and so the trap was set to catch the German battlecruisers off the east coast at dawn on 16 December. Unfortunately, it was the British who almost trapped themselves. Room 40 did not in fact know the whole story. They did not realize that Ingenohl intended to bring out the whole High Seas Fleet in support of the battlecruiser raid. It was only through a combination of Ingenohl's pusillanimity and sheer luck in the murk and mists of the foul winter weather that the British did not lose the differential between the two fleets in one fell swoop. As it was, Ingenohl fled for home and Hipper was in turn lucky to escape from a vengeful Beatty after a bombardment of Scarborough, Hartlepool and Whitby.

The outcry that resulted among the general public was whipped up and orchestrated by the more unscrupulous elements of the press in England. The question was simple. With the most powerful and expensive navy in the world, how was it possible for an enemy to bombard their homeland unscathed? To its credit, the Admiralty rode out the storm, recognizing the sheer stupidity of trying to guarantee the security of the whole east coast. However, it did move Beatty and the battlecruisers from Cromarty to a new base a little further south at Rosyth in the Firth of Forth. This would enable them to respond more quickly should the alarm be sounded again. For the Germans the raid was a heady mixture of defiant gesture, near disaster and golden opportunity. It boosted morale throughout their fleet and counterbalanced the growing feeling that they were not justifying their place in the overall scheme of things. They could not resist trying again.

On 23 January 1915 Ingenohl sent out the I Scouting Force under Hipper in an attempt to entrap any British light forces found sweeping through the Dogger Bank area. Once again, Room 40 warned the Admiralty that the game was afoot. Yet the curse of over-confidence meant that Beatty was sent out to intercept Hipper without the full and close support of the Grand Fleet. Beatty had with him his flagship the *Lion*, the battlecruisers *Tiger*, *Princess Royal*, *New Zealand*, *Indomitable*, and the 1st Cruiser Squadron. He was to rendezvous with the Harwich Force close to Dogger Bank. A dawn clash between the light scouting forces of both fleets on 24 January alerted Hipper to the likelihood of a British trap and without hesitating he immediately turned for home. At 07.50 Beatty finally sighted the German battlecruisers *Seydlitz*, *Moltke*, *Derfflinger* and *Blücher*, at a distance of some 35,000 yards. A determined stern chase began. Straining their engines to the utmost, the *Lion*, *Tiger* and *Princess Royal* surged ahead, leaving behind the slower *New Zealand* and *Indomitable*. Gradually they began to overhaul Hipper and, as they came into range at about 20,000 yards, they began to concentrate on the *Blücher*, the rear ship of his line. The *Blücher* was not really a battlecruiser at all, but a strange hybrid built in the period immediately before the nature of the battlecruiser concept was realized on the launch of the *Invincible*. As each of Beatty's ships came into range, they assailed the hapless *Blücher* before moving on to the next in line. Before long battle was properly joined.

The events of the battle of Dogger Bank need not be covered in detail, but there were several points of interest which had a great bearing on the battle of Jutland over a year later. First, Beatty had quite correctly reasoned that, if there was to be any chance of action, he could not keep his force together, but must allow the faster ships their head if they were to have any chance of catching the fleeing Germans. Second, overall the British battlecruisers' fire was very largely inaccurate and they failed to distribute it evenly, which not only added to the overall confusion, but allowed a dangerous German concentration of fire to be developed on the *Lion*, leading the British line. The *Lion* was badly damaged, her port engines failed and she slowly dropped back down the line of battle. Third, an imaginary submarine was sighted and, without hesitating, in accordance with the prevailing doctrine, Beatty turned his precious ships sharply away, fearing a massed submarine 'trap'. Finally, as the *Lion* lost touch and dropped out of line, Beatty's efforts to direct his remaining ships resulted in an embarrassing blunder. His signals lacked clarity and inadvertently prompted his four undamaged battlecruisers to abandon the chase and gather like a pack of dogs to finish off the badly damaged *Blücher*. A relieved Hipper took his chance, left the *Blücher* to her inevitable fate and made straight for the safety of harbour.

It was a British victory, but the farcical circumstances by which the Germans had been allowed to escape meant it was hardly an occasion for self-congratulation. Unfortunately, it was enough of a success to shroud the real cause for concern; for it was not properly recognized within the Battlecruiser Force that their overall standard of gunnery was inadequate. Many of their crews were convinced during the battle that they were raining shells down on their enemies, mistaking the German gun flashes for the detonation of their shells, which were in fact whistling harmlessly well over their intended targets. With the exception of the short-range demolition of the *Blücher*, which suffered some seventy hits, in total the British ships had scored only three hits. In return the German I Scouting Force had thudded home some twenty-two heavy calibre shells onto the *Lion* and *Tiger*.

Yet the *Seydlitz* suffered dreadfully from one of the two British shells that hit her. It crashed through the quarterdeck and penetrated the barbette armour of the aft turret. Here it ignited the charges held in the working chamber. The flash spread in an instant into the magazine handling room. Desperate men, trying to escape the searing flames, futilely opened the door that led to the superimposed turret and thus exported the disaster and condemned their neighbours. Flames roared right through the two turrets, killing some 159 men, and the outright disaster of a magazine explosion was only avoided by the rapid flooding of the after-magazine. The Germans launched an investigation into the disaster that revealed the necessity for increased anti-flash precautions to prevent a flash travelling between a turret gunhouse, handling chamber and the magazine. They had been lucky, and they took advantage of their good fortune to try to minimize the future risk on all their dreadnoughts and battlecruisers. While the Admiralty congratulated itself that all was well, and indeed renamed Beatty's force the Battlecruiser Fleet, indicating an independence from the Grand Fleet which it did not really possess, the Germans were alleviating one of the potentially cataclysmic flaws at the heart of their battlecruisers.

The Battlecruiser Fleet gunnery problems were recognized by some officers in the Grand Fleet, but there was little that could be done immediately to resolve the problem. The relatively narrow confines of the Firth of Forth where the battlecruisers were stationed simply did not have the space for gunnery ranges that could be defended against any possible incursions by German submarines. The main body of the Grand Fleet had the wide-open spaces of the Scapa Flow anchorage and took full advantage with regular practice firing. As a solution to their lack of range firing, the battlecruisers attempted to compensate by increasing their rate of fire on the faulty principle that pumping out more shells would inevitably lead to more hits, while the sheer flurry of shells landing around their intended victims would blind them with water spouts. This was dangerous nonsense. The margin of error was not just a matter of a few hundred feet. At Dogger Bank the battlecruisers were often guilty of firing thousands of yards over the target. This did not inconvenience anybody, except perhaps the accompanying German destroyer screen. Furthermore, in their efforts to increase their rate of fire, corners were cut in gun drill, particularly in the magazines and working chambers. The lids of ammunition cases containing the volatile cordite bags were often removed in advance to save vital seconds, magazine doors were left ajar in order not to have to open and shut the doors and, perhaps worst of all, charges were piled up outside the doors ready to be thrust in the hoists that took them up to the gunhouse. As the German ships improved their anti-flash precautions, what anti-flash screening that existed aboard the British battlecruisers was carefully circumnavigated in the quest for ever greater firing speed.

Although they only lost one ship, the fact that they were forced to flee rankled deeply with the Germans, despite the awe-inspiring gallantry of the *Blücher*'s last fight. On 2 February Admiral von Ingenohl was summarily dismissed and replaced by Admiral Hugo von Pohl. This change in command did not precipitate any real change in policy with regard to the deployment, or rather non-deployment, of the High Seas Fleet. Instead the German Navy turned its attention to the thorny problem of submarine commerce raiding. The internationally accepted 'rules of war' severely restricted the effectiveness of their submarine operations. Allied merchant ships could not be sunk without warning and proper provision for the safety of the crews. Neutral ships were sacrosanct: they could be stopped and searched, but even if the cargo carried was contraband, they could not be sunk. Such rules rendered useless the invisibility with which submarines could strike, for they were forced to surface, where they were excessively vulnerable. Up until February 1915 the Germans had played by these rules, but they could not carry on allowing one of their most powerful weapons of war to be casually rendered impotent. They announced that from 18 February any merchant ship found in the 'war zone' surrounding the British Isles would be sunk without the usual warnings, while neutrals were warned of the severe risks inherent in passing through the zone. The unleashed U-boats were sent out, easily breaking the blockade to reach the Atlantic and Irish Sea, where they preyed on shipping in the Western Approaches to British ports.

Strangely, for a country fixated on its own glorious naval history, the Admiralty had completely forgotten the painful lessons of earlier wars that commerce raiding is best countered by a system of convoys that gathers together potential victims and provides them with a strong escort force through any area of danger. Convoys could force the submarines to expose themselves to the accompanying escorts if they wanted to attack the vulnerable merchant ships. Instead of convoys, every ship that could mount a gun was pressed into service to try to criss-cross the seas to hunt down the elusive U-boats. But the oceans are inexhaustibly large and the hunt was for the most part futile. The need for destroyers was so pressing that even those of the Grand Fleet were pressed into service to hunt submarines, which left the dreadnoughts vulnerable and forced the cancellation of the periodic sweeps into the North Sea. As the shipping losses mounted, the British seemed to have no answer to this increasingly serious problem. But German successes were undermined by the risk of international outrage inherent in attacking ships without due warning. The sinking of the liners *Lusitania* and *Arabic,* with a consequent loss of life among American civilian passengers, brought a strong protest from the United States government. Faced with a possible new enemy, Germany backed down and the U-boats were withdrawn from the Western Approaches in September 1915. During the unrestricted submarine campaign the High Seas Fleet made only token excursions that barely cleared Heligoland before returning to port. In these circumstances, it was the prospect of recommencing unrestricted warfare that continued to exercise many minds in Germany. Indeed, for the rest of 1915 the sea war seemed stalled. The impetus for change was the departure of Admiral von Pohl, his health utterly broken, and his replacement on 24 January 1916 by Admiral Reinhard Scheer.

The new Commander-in-Chief had joined the German Navy as a cadet on 22 April 1879. His early career was not outstanding but he was steadily promoted until he attracted attention in command of a torpedo-boat flotilla in 1900. His progress then accelerated as he gained promotion to Kapitän zur See on 21 March 1905 and rose to be Chief of Staff of the High Seas Fleet. At the outbreak of war he was the admiral in command of the pre-dreadnoughts of the II Battle Squadron and subsequently commanded the dreadnoughts of III Battle Squadron. Scheer brought a fresh mind, and a good deal more vigour, to the problem of finding a real role for the High Seas Fleet.

> England's purpose of strangling Germany economically without
> seriously exposing her own fleet to the German guns had to be defeated.

This offensive effort on our part was intensified by the fact that the prohibition of the U-boat trade-war made it impossible for us to aim a direct blow at England's vital nerve. We were therefore bound to try and prove by all possible means that Germany's High Seas Fleet was able and willing to wage war with England at sea.[11]

Admiral Reinhard Scheer, SMS *Friedrich der Grosse*, III Battle Squadron,
High Seas Fleet

He recognized that a straight battle with the Grand Fleet was to be avoided at all costs. Instead he sought to attain his ends by trying to provoke the Admiralty and Jellicoe into rash action by applying a policy of systematic and constant pressure across the whole gamut of naval warfare. Submarines and mines would play their part, but he also aimed to use the High Seas Fleet on active sorties. He meant to seize upon the confusion of action to attain a temporary local superiority that if vigorously exploited could erode the ever-increasing British superiority in bald numbers. Slowly he began to raise the lazy tempo of the naval war. In February a destroyer sweep was launched across the Dogger Bank; in March a bolder sweep south with the High Seas Fleet in an attempt to entrap British light forces in the area off Lowestoft. Later the same month, when the British launched a seaplane carrier attack supported by the Harwich Force with Beatty in close support, Scheer once more emerged to try to catch Beatty, although the rough weather caused him to abort the operation.

Scheer next tried a return to the hit-and-run tactics employed by Ingenohl in 1914. The High Seas Fleet left port on 24 April. Once more the activities of Room 40 gave advance warning to Jellicoe. But, in the event, severe weather hampered the Grand Fleet and it was left to the Harwich Force alone to harass the German battlecruisers as they bombarded first Lowestoft and then, briefly, Yarmouth on 25 April. The raid was to have notable consequences. The British public renewed their outcry: 'Where was the navy?' Jellicoe came under increasing pressure to adopt a more active offensive policy with the Grand Fleet to try to force the Germans to come out and fight. But Jellicoe was not the kind of man to abandon a strategically successful policy out of a vague sense of boredom and desire for change. The Germans would not win the war by landing a few shells on British east coast towns. But the Royal Navy could lose it if it lost control of the world's oceans. His policy therefore remained rooted in caution.

> It is not, in my opinion, wise to risk unduly the heavy ships of the Grand Fleet in an attempt to hasten the end of the High Seas Fleet, particularly if the risks come, not from the High Seas Fleet itself, but from such attributes as mines and submarines. There is no doubt that, provided there is a chance of destroying some of the enemy's heavy ships, it is right and proper to run risks with our own heavy ships, but unless the chances are reasonably great, I do not think that such risks should be run, seeing that any real disaster to our heavy ships lays the country open to invasion.[12]
>
> Admiral Sir John Jellicoe, HMS *Iron Duke*, Grand Fleet

Jellicoe was also required to explain once again why he preferred to stay at Scapa Flow, too far north to intercept hit-and-run raids on the east coast. Could he not move the Grand Fleet further south, down to the Firth of Forth or even into the Humber? Jellicoe refused to budge from his northern fastness. He accepted that strategically Rosyth had advantages over Scapa Flow, but pointed out that lack of secure anchorage space, the prevailing foggy weather, vulnerability of the exits to German submarine mining operations and the crucial general absence of adequate submarine defences made the move to Rosyth an impractical and dangerous suggestion. Only when the area to the east of the Forth Bridge had been made secure from submarines could the Grand Fleet consider moving there. As a sop, he agreed to relocate the obsolete pre-dreadnoughts of the Third Battle Squadron to Sheerness, to act as an added deterrent and general support to the Harwich Force, with the overall objective of forcing Scheer to bring his heavy ships on any raid. They were no longer needed in the Grand Fleet as he had received substantial reinforcements in the shape of the Fifth Battle Squadron made up of the much vaunted *Queen Elizabeth* class.

The *Queen Elizabeth* class were the first super-dreadnoughts, the next stage in the battleship revolution. Armed with eight mighty 15-inch guns that could project a huge 1,920-pound shell up to 25,000 yards, protected with armour up to 13 inches thick over their vitals, powered by huge oil-fired turbine engines that could drive them along at some 24 knots, they were truly a new breed of ship that marked the demise of the battlecruiser concept. They had it all; there was no longer any need to compromise protection in the search for speed. Beatty soon coveted these magnificent ships as an addition to the Battlecruiser Fleet. He was initially thwarted by Jellicoe, who pointed out that although the super-dreadnoughts were fast, they were still not as fast as the battle-cruisers. Their active service speed wavered between 23 and 24 knots, which would have been a small but significant drag on battlecruisers in offensive actions, and an endangerment if withdrawing towards the support of the Grand Fleet in the event of meeting the High Seas Fleet. Jellicoe also cherished the notion of employing the squadron as the fast wing of his battle line, to bring a crushing concentration of fire on the van or rear of the High Seas Fleet as required. Beatty was undeterred and continued to press his case.

> They would in all cases be able to keep with us until the moment when we sighted the enemy. If we are then east of the enemy, the Fifth Battle Squadron would be invaluable. Taking the worst case, we may be west of them and may have a long chase at full speed. After chasing for three hours, i.e. a distance of at least 75 miles, the Fifth Battle Squadron with their 23½ knots would then be at most 4½ miles astern of the 3rd Battlecruiser Squadron. I can imagine no better or more valuable support.[13]
>
> Vice Admiral Sir David Beatty, HMS *Lion*, 1st Battlecruiser Squadron

Jellicoe was worried that Beatty might overreach himself by taking on the High Seas Fleet alone, if he had such a strong supporting squadron.

> I am sure it would be wrong to send them to him. It would for one thing lead to his getting far afield from me, which is wrong, and in thick weather might be almost disastrous.[14]
>
> Admiral Sir John Jellicoe, HMS *Iron Duke*, Grand Fleet

Jellicoe knew that there could be no tastier morsel for Scheer to entrap and swallow than the Fifth Battle Squadron. Yet the twin pressure of the Admiralty's expressed desire for a stronger force to cover the southern waters of the North Sea and the evident need for real gunnery practice by the Battlecruiser Fleet eventually tipped the scales against him. It was decided that Beatty's 3rd Battlecruiser Squadron would have to join the Grand Fleet temporarily for intensive gunnery practice. In its absence the Battlecruiser Fleet had to be strengthened, and the Fifth Battle Squadron was the only real option. Doubtless gritting his teeth, Jellicoe sent the vessels down to join Beatty at Rosyth on 22 May. The *Queen Elizabeth* was booked for a refit at the Rosyth dockyard, but her sister ships *Barham*, *Malaya*, *Valiant* and *Warspite* were at Beatty's disposal until the 3rd Battlecruiser Squadron returned.

As the British adjusted their dispositions, to the Germans the successful raid on Lowestoft on 25 April was seen as a triumph. The latest campaign of unrestricted submarine warfare, which had been relaunched in March 1916, had already started to falter after the sinking of the *Sussex* on 24 March. Once again, American casualties provoked strong protests from the US ambassador. The German high command decided to suspend the controversial campaign, return operational control of the submarines to the High Seas Fleet and thus give Scheer the chance finally to harness all the elements of the German Navy in an effort to ensnare a portion of the Grand Fleet.

In mid 1916, as the climax of the naval war approached, Jellicoe and the Grand Fleet had achieved all but one of their war aims. The BEF and endless reinforcements had been safely deposited on the Western Front. There was no chance of the Germans launching a successful invasion of Britain. They had *de facto* control of the vast oceans that lay beyond the narrow confines of the North Sea, and German commercial links to the rest of the world had been neatly severed. All that now remained was the task of achieving victory over the High Seas Fleet. The time for this remained uncertain. The Germans were determined to pick their moment of greatest advantage, the British were in no hurry to be drawn into battle except on their own terms. Of one thing the men of both fleets were sure: sooner or later '*Der Tag*' would come – and every week that passed brought that day closer. The scene remained set for a North Sea confrontation between the two fleets.

CHAPTER TWO

FIRST CONTACT

IN MAY 1916 the war in the North Sea entered a dramatic new phase. Both Admiral Sir John Jellicoe and Admiral Reinhard Scheer were planning significant operations for the end of May and early June. Jellicoe intended on 2 June to try to tempt Scheer and the High Seas Fleet out into the open North Sea by dangling a couple of light cruiser squadrons in front of him, sweeping through the Kattegat channel between Denmark and Sweden. Behind them in the Skagerrak would be a battle squadron, which in turn would be supported by the Battlecruiser Fleet and rest of the Grand Fleet. The seaplanes from the carrier *Engadine* would be responsible for fending off inquisitive Zeppelins. Jellicoe was not overly optimistic of the chances of bringing Scheer far enough north to get to grips with the High Seas Fleet properly and so in addition he planned a trap made up of lines of newly laid mines and lurking submarines across the northern exit channel from the Heligoland Bight minefields to the south of Horns Reef. This plan was to be rendered stillborn as Scheer struck first.

Scheer determined to make the fullest possible use of the submarines released by the suspension of the short-lived second unrestricted submarine campaign. Hipper's battlecruisers would be sent to bombard Sunderland in the certain knowledge that Beatty and Jellicoe would rush down to intercept them. The German submarines, some of them minelayers, would be lying in ambush across the exits from Rosyth and Scapa Flow ready to do their worst when the fleets emerged. In the resulting confusion, Hipper would then engage Beatty and draw him inexorably to his doom at the hands of Scheer and the High Seas Fleet lurking in the Dogger Bank area. Zeppelins would ensure that the Germans were not themselves ambushed by superior forces. The operation was intended for 17 May, but the repairs to the *Seydlitz*, which had been mined in the hit-and-run raid on Folkestone, took longer than expected and it was rescheduled for 29 May. The weather then intervened, ruling out the long-range Zeppelin reconnaissance that underpinned the whole operation. Unwilling to proceed blindfolded, Scheer switched his plans to a less ambitious sweep by Hipper up into the Skagerrak with the intention of preying on any British light forces in the area. After flaunting themselves off Norway in the hope of attracting the attention of Beatty, the German battlecruisers would fall back on Scheer following up in support with the High Seas Fleet. In the continued absence of Zeppelins, the whole operation would be covered by his light forces scouting to the west of their path of progress.

Scheer's plans were however fatally flawed. The Germans had still not realized that their signals were being swiftly decoded by Room 40. The departure of numerous U-boats had been noted and they had been traced to the northern North Sea, which indicated that some major German operation was brewing. As every signal was decoded a new piece of the jigsaw fell into place. At 12.00 on 30 May, they were able to warn Jellicoe that the High Seas Fleet would be putting to sea next day. At 17.40 the Admiralty could hesitate no longer and ordered Jellicoe and Beatty to sea.

At Rosyth the Battlecruiser Fleet and attached Fifth Battle Squadron lay tranquilly at anchor.

> Things seemed as peaceful as could be on the afternoon of Tuesday, May 30th, when Maurice Bethell and I went ashore for a round of golf at Bruntsfield near Edinburgh. After a thoroughly enjoyable game over this course, whose delightful inland surroundings reflected all the charm of early summer, we adjourned for tea to 'Rospletha', the little house I had rented on the side of the links, and then found our way down to Queensbury Pier at the regulation hour of 6pm, in order to catch the routine boat. While we stood waiting on the pier amid a throng of fellow officers, all eyes were suddenly drawn in the direction of the *Lion*, from whose masthead there floated a string of flags with this message to all ships. "Raise steam for 22 knots and bank fires at half an hour's notice."[1]
>
> Commander Barry Bingham, HMS *Nestor*, 13th Flotilla

Gradually word of what was happening spread among all those who had gone ashore as the laggards congregated at piers to catch the boats back to their ships.

Went ashore in the afternoon for a walk with the Fleet Paymaster, returning to Hawes Pier at 7.30. Our boat was one of the last to shove off and whilst waiting we noticed a light cruiser, the leader of a flotilla of destroyers anchored off South Queensferry, hoist a long string of flags, which appeared to be a steaming signal. We were not certain about this however, but on our way off we noticed unmistakeable preparations for going to sea being made by the battlecruisers and on our arrival on board found that we also had been ordered to raise steam as quickly as possible, for full speed. Further signals came through indicating the urgency of the need for despatch and we eventually got under way at about 8 o'clock British Summer Time.[2]

Surgeon Gordon Ellis, HMS *Warspite*, Fifth Battle Squadron

The nurses and doctors of the hospital ship *Plassy* watched them go.

Today the whole fleet of battlecruiser and cruisers have gone out; we watched them steaming up. I wonder if there is really anything doing this time, there have been so many false alarms.[3]

Naval Nursing Sister Mary Clarke, Hospital Ship *Plassy*

The image of silent power was impressive as the fleets moved through the Forth, passing Edinburgh and Leith on their starboard beam.

Imagine darling if you can, a fine though starless night and 12 great ships steaming out of the Forth, no lights visible and not a sound to be heard but the swish of the waves.[4]

Seaman Torpedoman Harry Hayler, HMS *Warspite*, Fifth Battle Squadron

The huge ships raised anchor, manoeuvred round and then moved under the Forth Bridge. The mighty super-dreadnoughts, the epitome of modern naval engineering, passed one by one beneath the proud symbol of the Victorian railway age.

At high water we actually cleared the bridge by some 12 feet, but on approaching the bridge it always appeared, right up to the last moment almost, that we must inevitably hit it. Hardened seafarers on the upper deck have been seen starting to turn up their collar or even disappear under cover in order to dodge the falling topmast! Then at the last moment the topmast seemed to oblige by dipping clear. Looking astern, it then just as suddenly reappeared as high as before. This phenomenon never ceased to fascinate me.[5]

Midshipman Richard Fairthorne, HMS *Warspite*, Fifth Battle Squadron

The Battlecruiser Fleet was a formidable naval force. The fleet flagship was the *Lion*, accompanied by the 1st Battlecruiser Squadron of the *Princess Royal*, *Queen Mary* and *Tiger;* the 2nd Battlecruiser Squadron of the *New Zealand* and *Indefatigable*; the Fifth Battle Squadron consisted of the mighty *Barham*, *Valiant*, *Warspite* and *Malaya*. All around them were their screening light forces: the 1st, 2nd and 3rd Light Cruiser Squadrons, the 1st and 13th Destroyer Flotillas, parts of the 9th and 10th Flotillas and finally the seaplane carrier *Engadine*. The battlecruiser *Australia* and the *Queen Elizabeth* were left behind undergoing repairs in dry dock.

At Scapa Flow the Grand Fleet, Britain's final bulwark against the world, simultaneously prepared to leave harbour for the umpteenth time. There was nothing to indicate to the ships' crews that this was anything other than a normal sweep, but the atmosphere was pregnant with possibilities sharpened to a point only perhaps in retrospect.

On a calm summer's evening of 30th May, just about cocktail time, the C-in-C, Admiral Jellicoe in the *Iron Duke*, hoisted the momentous signal, 'Q.P.' or in plain language, 'Raise steam for Fleet Speed and report when ready to proceed!' Though we had received the same order many times before, it never failed to raise a thrill of wild excitement in the expectation that this time perhaps, 'Der Tag' as we also called it had dawned at last. That evening the thrill was immensely multiplied for everybody seemed to have a premonition that the day had really arrived. There was an almost electric atmosphere of expectation and suppressed excitement as officers and men went about the work of preparing for sea.[6]

Midshipman John Croome, HMS *Indomitable*, 3rd Battlecruiser Squadron

Every ship primed itself for sea. For the crews of these most complex of war machines there were myriad tasks to undertake.

Usual activity on deck, securing against rough weather, getting boats inboard, closing watertight compartments etc. I proceed to my usual routine, first to inform the engine room staff that air compressors are needed. Then to forward submerged torpedo flat. Fleet orders are that

all torpedoes are to be topped up from normal air pressure of 2,200 PSI
to 2,500 PSI to give a longer range. The torpedo crew are assisting the
Petty Officer Instructor to withdraw torpedoes from the tubes to fit
warheads with firing pistols, also spare primers and pistols are being
brought to the 'ready' for immediate use. I check firing gear and
instruments from conning tower firing position. Topping up completed,
I then proceed to various compartments around the ship to close stop
valves on the air ring main so that in the event of damage, each gun
turret is independently supplied. This high pressure and water is
automatically blown through the gun as the breach opens to douse any
burning debris left and to cool the gun barrel.[7]

Electrical Artificer Nelson White, HMS *Colossus*, Fifth Division, First Battle Squadron

It was a stirring sight to watch the men scurrying across the decks as the
leviathans stirred themselves into action.

To see thirty or so of the biggest and most powerful vessels afloat
spread over the calm wide anchorage of Scapa Flow, together with their
masses of attendant light cruisers and destroyers, and to watch them as
the sun set. Simultaneously every one of them began to send up clouds
of heavy smoke into the still air as the stokers got busy at the boilers,
forced draught fans began to hum the familiar tune and on deck, men
like busy ants, formed in orderly groups as the bugle calls floated across
the immense harbour and set about hoisting boats and gangways;
uncovering guns and searchlights and making the many preparations
for taking the gigantic floating forts to sea for battle.[8]

Midshipman John Croome, HMS *Indomitable*, 3rd Battlecruiser Squadron

The hours, days, months and years of intensive training were clearly
visible as they formed up for sea.

The grey monsters wheeled in succession round us and followed out to
sea with that uncanny precision and silent majesty which marks the
departure to sea of a perfectly trained fleet. Finally as the last of the
long line passed us, we in turn began to swing, weighed the last few links
of cable and stole stealthily away in the wake of the Grand Fleet. A
more powerful exhibition of majestic strength and efficiency devised
solely for the utter destruction of the enemy it would be hard to imagine

and the impression upon my youthful mind can never be erased.
Moreover, I was proudly conscious that I was a part of this huge
machine and firmly convinced that the machine was invincible,
if not even invulnerable.[9]

Midshipman John Croome, HMS *Indomitable*, 3rd Battlecruiser Squadron

Calmly, carefully, almost unobserved in its remote Scottish fastness, the
great fleet left harbour, ever hopeful that this might be the sweep that
brought battle.

It was a magnificent sight as we steamed out of Scapa. Ahead of us the
minesweepers clearing a safe passage and as we passed from the safety
of Scapa the crews on the boom defence ships that controlled the net
defence gave us a loud cheer. Out into the damp cold mist we steamed
a mighty Armada of ironclads.[10]

Able Seaman Torpedoman Joseph Moss, HMS *Ajax*, 1st Division, Second Battle
Squadron

As Commander-in-Chief, Jellicoe flew his flag in the *Iron Duke*
and the names of his ships reflected and perpetuated the vibrant spirit
of hundreds of years of British military and naval history. The Fourth
Battle Squadron included the *Iron Duke* herself, the *Royal Oak*, *Superb*,
Canada, *Benbow*, *Bellerophon*, *Temeraire* and *Vanguard*. The First Battle
Squadron was the *Marlborough*, *Revenge*, *Hercules*, *Agincourt*, *Colossus*,
Collingwood, *Neptune* and *St Vincent*. Temporarily attached were the 3rd
Battlecruiser Squadron of the *Invincible*, *Inflexible* and *Indomitable*. From
the secondary base at Cromarty emerged the Second Battle Squadron
composed of the *King George V*, *Ajax*, *Centurion*, *Erin*, *Orion*, *Monarch*,
Conqueror and *Thunderer*. Forming the protective screens around the
powerful yet vulnerable dreadnoughts were the 1st and 2nd Cruiser
Squadrons, the 4th Light Cruiser Squadron, the 4th, 11th and 12th
Destroyer Flotillas. Together they slipped through the submarine
defences and out into the open seas.

The ship is now under way and passing through Hoxa Gate boom
defence, this is three lines of trawlers joined together with anti-
Submarine steel nets. We are now in the Pentland Firth and increasing
speed, there are signs of urgency, more so than usual for the many times

that we had left Scapa Flow for exercises and sweeps in the North Sea.[11]

Electrical Artificer Nelson White, HMS *Colossus*, Fifth Division, First Battle Squadron

There was just one exception to the fleet's smooth departure. The seaplane carrier *Campania* was stationed some 5 miles from the main fleet anchorage and, although she had acknowledged the signals ordering her to prepare to leave harbour, she somehow failed to receive the general signal giving the actual intended time of sailing. Almost unbelievably, the crew did not observe the disappearance of the largest fleet in the world from under their noses. Doubtless there was considerable consternation aboard the *Campania* when the absence of the Grand Fleet was finally noticed at 23.45.

The North Sea

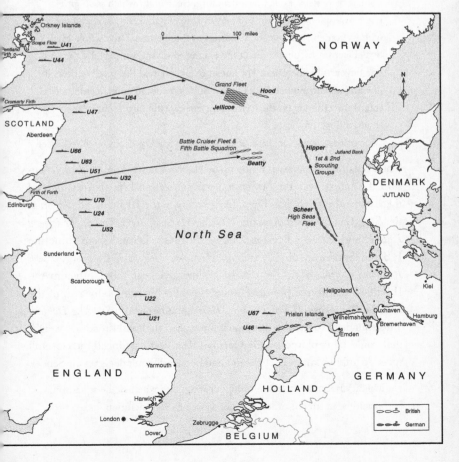

Much chastened, they set sail at once, only to be ordered home by Jellicoe, who feared that the unescorted carrier would fall prey to the submarines which he knew were swarming in the area. This calamity deprived him at a stroke of his sole source of aerial reconnaissance for the main body of the Grand Fleet. Beatty of course still had the seaplanes of the *Engadine*.

The success of British naval intelligence in correctly divining the German plans can be judged by the fact that both Jellicoe and Beatty were at sea before 23.00 on 30 May. Scheer himself did not even leave harbour until 02.30 on the following morning.

> We had spent the night at anchor in the Schillig Roads, off the entrance to the Jadebusen. Ahead of us stretched the small cruisers and some flotillas of destroyers. It was a beautiful, clear night which soon gave place to a splendid morning. The sun rose magnificently, covered the sea with its golden rays and soon showed us the picture of the whole High Seas Fleet proceeding to meet the enemy, always a wonderful sight and one never to be forgotten. Far ahead of us steamed the small cruisers in line ahead, surrounded by a cordon of destroyers steaming ceaselessly round the cruisers, on the lookout for enemy submarines, like dogs round a flock of sheep.[12]

Commander Georg von Hase, SMS *Derfflinger*, I Scouting Group, High Seas Fleet

The I Scouting Group was made up of Hipper's newly commissioned flagship, the *Lützow*, with the *Derfflinger, Seydlitz, Moltke* and *Von der Tann*. Behind them came the High Seas Fleet. In the van was the III Battle Squadron of the *König, Grosser Kurfürst, Kronprinz Wilhelm, Markgraf, Kaiser, Kaiserin, Prinzregent Luitpold* and Scheer's flagship *Friedrich der Grosse*. Behind them came the I Battle Squadron of *Ostfriesland, Thüringen, Helgoland, Oldenburg, Posen, Rheinland, Nassau* and *Westfalen*. In addition, Scheer took with him the II Battle Squadron of pre-dreadnoughts, which brought up the rear of the line: the *Deutschland, Hessen, Pommern, Hannover, Schlesien* and *Schleswig-Holstein*. This squadron may have marginally increased the total broadside weight that could be deployed by the German fleet, but it reduced their overall speed to only 18 knots. Its inclusion had been a difficult decision for Scheer.

> Military reasons entered into the question as to whether the squadron should be taken out or left behind, as well as consideration for the

honour and feeling of the crews, who would not hear of being reduced, themselves and their ships, to the second class. For battleships to have their activity limited absolutely to guarding the German Bight without any prospect of getting into touch with the enemy – to which they had been looking forward for a year and a half – would have caused bitter disappointment; on the other hand, however, was the responsibility of sending the ships into an unequal fight where the enemy would make use of his very best material. I cannot deny that in addition to the eloquent intercession of Rear Admiral Mauve, the Squadron Commander, my own former connection with Squadron II also induced me not to disappoint it by leaving it behind.[13]

Admiral Reinhard Scheer, SMS *Friedrich der Grosse*, III Battle Squadron, High Seas Fleet

The Germans, too, shrouded their fleet with a protective screen of the light cruisers of the II and IV Scouting Group and seven flotillas of destroyers. The total surface forces at Scheer's disposal were 16 dreadnoughts, 6 pre-dreadnoughts, 5 battlecruisers, 11 light cruisers and 61 destroyers. Against him Jellicoe deployed 28 dreadnoughts, 9 battlecruisers, 8 cruisers, 26 light cruisers and 78 destroyers.

The Grand Fleet clearly outnumbered the High Seas Fleet in every department that mattered. Yet although Jellicoe's long-expressed fears of being outnumbered in the destroyer department had proved groundless, he was proved right in his outright scepticism that the Harwich Force would ever be able to join him in battle. The Harwich Force was under the command of the able Commodore Reginald Tyrwhitt and it had been ordered by the Admiralty to remain in harbour until the Admiralty was certain that Scheer, still a relatively unknown force, was not launching some kind of desperate thrust south towards the Channel ports and the Dover Straits. Tyrwhitt was thus left champing at the bit in enforced inactivity with his five light cruisers and eighteen destroyers.

As the fleets deployed into the North Sea, the intentions of the two commanders can be simply stated. Jellicoe aimed to defeat the High Seas Fleet if he could bring it to battle without exposing his fleet to the risk of serious losses from mines and torpedoes. He preferred the maintenance of the strategic status quo to fighting in anything but favourable circumstances. Scheer intended to draw detached elements of the Grand Fleet, most probably the Battlecruiser Fleet, into a trap, whereby he could achieve and exploit a local superiority. Only when the two fleets had been 'equalized' would he risk an out-and-out fleet action. His ambition as he left harbour was to take the first steps towards overturning the British naval hegemony slowly suffocating his country.

Scheer suffered an early disappointment when the submarine ambush that he had set around the British bases proved a damp squib. The eighteen German submarines were meant to begin that process of attrition that would eventually bring the Grand Fleet down to size. But his hopes were dashed. The new minefields laid by submarine minelayers were ineffective and indeed one of them suffered the indignity of being caught and destroyed by an armed trawler. Once the Battlecruiser Fleet and Grand Fleet had left harbour they simply disappeared into the vastness of the seas. Only the *U32* managed to fire torpedoes at the *Galatea* of the 1st Light Cruiser Squadron when she was about 70 miles out of Rosyth. They missed. The wireless intelligence reports they sent to Scheer were positively misleading.

> At 5.30, U32 reported at about 70 miles east of the Firth of Forth, two battleships, two cruisers, and several torpedo-boats taking a south-easterly course. At 6.30 a second wireless was received stating that she had intercepted English wireless messages to the effect that two large battleships and groups of destroyers had run out from Scapa Flow. At 6.48am a third message came through from U66 that about 60 nautical miles east of Kinnairel, eight enemy battleships, light cruisers, and torpedo-boats had been sighted on a north-easterly course. These reports gave no enlightenment as to the enemy's purpose. But the varied forces of the separate divisions of the fleet, and their diverging courses did not seem to suggest either combined action or an advance on the German Bight or any connection with our enterprise, but showed a possibility that our hope of meeting with separate enemy divisions was likely to be fulfilled. We were, therefore, all the more determined to keep to our plan.[14]
>
> Admiral Reinhard Scheer, SMS *Friedrich der Grosse*, III Battle Squadron, High Seas Fleet

Jellicoe had arranged to rendezvous with Beatty about 90 miles off the entrance of the Skagerrak. The intention was for their two fleets to reach their designated points some 69 miles apart at 14.00 on 31 May. If there were no signs of life from the German High Seas Fleet, then Beatty would join forces with Jellicoe for a final sweep towards the Horns Reef sector north of the Heligoland Bight.

> I felt no anxiety in regard to the advanced position of the force under Sir David Beatty, supported as it was by four ships of the Fifth Battle Squadron, as this force was far superior in gun power to the I Scouting Group, and the speed of the slowest ship was such as to enable it to keep out of range of superior enemy forces.[15]
>
> Admiral John Jellicoe, HMS *Iron Duke*, 3rd Division, Fourth Battle Squadron

As the great fleet pounded across the North Sea, the routine drudgery of shipboard life at sea commenced.

> The day started off as usual, dull grey and very cold. We boys, our trousers turned up to our knees and bare from the waist, having lashed up and stowed our hammocks at 6 o'clock, make our way to the upper deck. There, placed ready overnight, large water butts in which we give ourselves a good scrub, being observed the while by the Petty Officer instructor and being passed by him as OK. Down to the messdeck where there is a kettle of thick hot cocoa and a couple of biscuits to be had. 6.15am. We scrub decks, water rushing over the deck, the boys lined across with long handled scrubbers. "Scrub forward, scrub aft!" until 10 to 7. Squeeze down, dry up deck. Down to the messdeck breakfast, hungry as a horse. Maybe porridge, maybe a kipper. Bread and margarine, tea, never enough sugar. Change into rig of the day, as usual duck suits. We curse the one who invented it. 8am. Fall in on deck detailed for cleaning ship, two from each mess to scrub out and prepare dinner for 14 others. 9am. Divisions on the upper deck, inspected for cleanliness in dress and person. Marine band on top of midship turret strikes up. Everyone under 35 starts to gallup all round the ship leaping hatches on the way, sliding down ladders. Band plays faster and faster as we fly round in time with it. 9.15. Fall in. Detailed for instruction, take up messenger and call boy duties, rifle

drill, seamanship, signals, splicing rope work etc – and on through the rest of the day. Boy, are we hungry? Not so you'd notice! What's for dinner – stewed corned beef with a coating of cinders from the funnels – glad to eat it.[16]

Boy 1st Class A. E. Cooper, HMS *Conqueror*, 2nd Division, Second Battle Squadron

The specialist personnel had their intricate duties to perform, combined with endless checks to make to ensure that everything was in working order. Petty Officer Gunner's Mate Ernest Francis was ordered to check 'X' Turret aboard his ship, the *Queen Mary*.

I knew before I went round that I should find everything quite all right. Because Lieutenant Ewart was wrapped right up in his turret and many an hour have I spent with him explaining the working of the different machinery. His one aim was efficiency; if at any time a new man came into the turret he would worry about him till I reported to him that the new man knew his job and could be trusted to fill up any other number if we had casualties in action. I went over 'X' Turret from top to bottom and I really felt quite pleased with everything. It was complete, right down to spare lengths of flexible piping, urinal buckets, biscuits and corned beef, drinking tank and plenty of first aid dressings. I went back to Commander (Gunnery) and made my report.[17]

Petty Officer Ernest Francis, HMS *Queen Mary*, 1st Battlecruiser Squadron

As far as the men of the lower deck were concerned this was just one more sweep into the North Sea, another part of the endless routine. There was nothing to indicate otherwise.

The morning breaks fine and clear and the two fleets commenced exercising. How little did any of them think that this mimicry would soon become grim reality, they had been out so often and nothing had happened, so they went on in blissful ignorance of the fact that the German Fleet was even then on its way to give battle. All this time the sun has been shining and the sea is as calm as a millpond, everything seems so peaceful.[18]

Seaman Torpedoman Harry Hayler, HMS *Warspite*, Fifth Battle Squadron

It was indeed a pleasant day for a cruise.

There was nothing much going on. So the hands were given a 'make and mend'. That means that apart from those employed in keeping the ship steaming, we could have a 'doss' down, have a lie up. And that afternoon in the sun – it was nice and warm – I had a nice little sleep on the quarterdeck. We didn't know anything was around. No excitement at all.[19]

Midshipman John Ouvry, HMS *Tiger*, 1st Battlecruiser Squadron

The morale in both the Grand Fleet and the Battlecruiser Fleet was high: they had trained hard, they had learned much and they accepted the weight of public expectation that lay upon them. Aboard Beatty's battle-cruisers they were buoyed even further by their taste of German blood at the battles of Heligoland Bight and Dogger Bank. Confidence reigned supreme and they fully believed that the Royal Navy had a natural right to untrammelled victory.

We were ready for battle, hopeful and confident, under a leader in whom every officer, petty officer and man had complete confidence. We considered the Battlecruisers the spear point of the Grand Fleet, like the cavalry of a great army, and behind us we had that vast, powerful fleet of battleships which, if they could get into action, would have little difficulty in annihilating the enemy.[20]

Flag Captain Alfred Chatfield, HMS *Lion*, 1st Battlecruiser Squadron

At 11.30 the Second Battle Squadron, which had been stationed at Cromarty, linked up with the Grand Fleet, enabling it to shake down into its final cruising order of six tight columns of four dreadnoughts, screened on all sides from attack. It was shortly after this that things started to go wrong. In London, the experts of Room 40 received a visit from the Director of Naval Operations, Captain Thomas Jackson, who had little sympathy for his civilian 'boffins' and no respect for their acquired expertise. He made the classic mistake of asking a specific question which would not in fact elicit the information he required. Jackson asked where the wireless directional stations had placed Scheer's wireless call sign 'DK'. He received the answer, 'Wilhelmshaven', asked no further questions, turned on his heel and left. This was extremely unfortunate to say the very least. It was Scheer's practice when at sea to transfer his normal 'DK' call sign to a shore establishment and adopt another call sign while he was at sea. This simple ruse was designed to put directional stations off the scent. The Room 40 staff had already worked this out after their experiences during previous German excursions into the North Sea. But Jackson did not know this vital information and Room 40 did not, or more likely did not have the opportunity to, enlighten him. Thus Jackson reported that Scheer was still in harbour. Rear Admiral Henry Oliver, the Chief of War Staff at the Admiralty, had no reason to doubt this information and therefore sent an entirely misleading signal to Jellicoe and Beatty at 12.30 on 31 May.

> No definite news enemy. They made preparations for sailing early this morning Wednesday. It was thought fleet had sailed but direction signal placed flagship Jade at 11.10 GMT. Apparently they have been unable to carry out air reconnaissance which has delayed them.[21]
>
> Rear Admiral Henry Oliver, Admiralty

This signal clearly told Jellicoe that the High Seas Fleet was in harbour and that whatever Scheer had been planning had been delayed or even cancelled. The consequence was that although he continued to head towards the rendezvous point, from that moment, for him, the whole character of the mission had changed from an interception to just another sweep. The Grand Fleet continued at a mean speed of 15 knots but carried out several inspections of passing neutral ships which might have been forgone in circumstances of greater urgency. Beatty carried on at 19 knots.

In direct contradiction of the misleading Admiralty signal, the High Seas Fleet *was* at sea. In front was the light cruiser screen of the II Scouting Group, behind them came the battlecruisers of Hipper's I Scouting Group. Fifty miles behind Hipper was the High Seas Fleet covered by the IV Scouting Group. Aboard the *Derfflinger*, second in line in the I Scouting Group, the gunnery commander took a well-earned rest and pondered his future.

> I went to my cabin, lay down for a siesta, watched the blue rings from my cigar, and dreamed of battle and victory. If only it came to gunnery action this time! My whole career seemed so incomplete, so much of a failure if I did not have at least one opportunity of feeling in battle on

the high seas what fighting was really like. Blow for blow, shot for shot, that was what I wanted.[22]

Commander Georg von Hase, SMS *Derfflinger*, I Scouting Group, High Seas Fleet

As he lay there, day-dreaming, his thoughts drifted along familiar lines.

I was possessed by a burning desire to engage our proud *Derfflinger* in action with an English battlecruiser worthy of her. Day and night this thought never left me. I pictured to myself how, on outpost duty or one of our reconnaissances, we came across an English battlecruiser, how the *Derfflinger* joined action and thus a gigantic gun duel developed while we both tore along at delirious speed. I could see how every salvo from the enemy was replied to by one from us, how the fight became ever faster and more furious, and how we struggled together like two mighty warriors who both know well enough that 'only one of us will survive'. In my dreams I saw the English gunnery officer get his periscope on to my ship; I heard his English orders and my own. This thought of such a contest between giant ships intoxicated me, and my imagination painted pictures of monstrous happenings.[23]

Commander Georg von Hase, SMS *Derfflinger*, I Scouting Group, High Seas Fleet

The Germans had every intention of provoking a clash with a portion at least of the Grand Fleet, but they had no idea that Room 40 had first revealed and then, through no fault of their own, obfuscated their plans to Jellicoe.

That the entire English fleet was already at sea and bearing on the same point as ourselves, not a man in the German fleet suspected, not even the Commander in Chief. And in the same way, according to all published reports, no-one in the English fleet knew that the German fleet had put to sea. There is no reason to believe that this was not the case, and yet in the inland parts of the country the question is always being asked, "How did the English get to know that we were off the Skagerrak?"[24]

Commander Georg von Hase, SMS *Derfflinger*, I Scouting Group, High Seas Fleet

Unaware that they were heading directly towards each other, the scene was set for battle when the fleets collided in the North Sea.

By 13.30 Beatty had disposed his force so that the 2nd Battlecruiser Squadron lay some 2 miles to the north-east of the *Lion* and the 1st Battlecruiser Squadron, a distance of little tactical significance. However, the mighty Fifth Battle Squadron was stationed some 5 miles north-north-west of the *Lion*. This failure to concentrate his forces made a hollow mockery of his earlier claim to Jellicoe that

> Taking the worst case, we may be west of them and may have a long chase at full speed. After chasing for three hours, i.e. a distance of at least 75 miles, the Fifth Battle Squadron with their 23½ knots would be at most 4½ miles astern.[25]

Even at their cruising stations the gap was already greater than the 'worst case' scenario. It is possible that Beatty intended to close up his forces as they approached the area where they were considered likely to contact the German fleet, but the misleading telegram from the Admiralty had turned his mind more towards the mundane practicalities of the junction with the Grand Fleet and the imminent exchange of the Fifth Battle Squadron for the 3rd Battlecruiser Squadron. Whatever the reason, it was to prove a grave error and have a significant impact on the course of the looming battle. Ahead of Beatty, to the east, was the screen provided by the 1st Light Cruiser Squadron, while the 2nd and 3rd Light Cruiser Squadrons covered the approaches from the south and south-east. The whole force was zigzagging as an additional precaution against submarine attack. At 13.58, as they neared the designated rendezvous point, Beatty signalled his ships to be ready to make the turn at 14.15 to the north-east to move towards a junction with the Grand Fleet. Hipper was at this time pursuing a northerly course some 50 miles to the east of Beatty and, as their light cruiser screens were still some 16 miles apart, both admirals were in total ignorance of each other's presence at sea.

At this moment in the epic drama that was about to unfold, an archetypal strolling player crossed the world stage. A Danish tramp steamer, the *N. J. Fjord*, chose this moment to pass midway between the outlying scouts of both sides. Just before 14.00 she was sighted by the German light cruiser *Elbing* of the II Scouting Group and as a matter of course two destroyers were sent to investigate. Lieutenant Heinrich Bassenge was on the bridge of the *Elbing*.

Madlung had just sent *B110* to investigate. Through our binoculars we
watched, with excitement, our torpedo boats circling around the
steamer, going alongside it and examining their papers.[26]

Lieutenant Heinrich Bassenge, SMS *Elbing*, II Scouting Group, High Seas Fleet

At 14.10 the *Galatea*, the flagship of Commodore Edwyn Alexander-Sinclair
of the 1st Light Cruiser Squadron and the most easterly ship of Beatty's
screen, also sighted the *N. J. Fjord*. They too moved in to investigate, accompanied by the *Phaeton*. As the outer margins of both screens converged on
the hapless *N. J. Fjord*, the *Galatea* was startled to sight the two German
destroyers alongside with their boats lowered and their boarding parties
already setting out to check the *N. J. Fjord*'s cargo documentation.

We sighted two German ships on the horizon. Full speed was at once
put on and everything possible was done by the staff below to make
sure they did not get away this time. When we got near enough, we
discovered them to be two destroyers with a big merchant packet. Our
Commodore at once challenged them with a signal. They attempted a
reply, but gave wrong one. He tested them with another and again they
could not answer correctly.[27]

Engine Room Rating T. Farquhar, HMS *Galatea*, 1st Light Cruiser Squadron

Realization soon dawned on both sides.

After a short time a signal came from *B110*, we thought they must have
found something important. I read the message myself, but all it said
was, "Smoke clouds from the west, it looks like an enemy battleship".
This message was unexpected.[28]

Lieutenant Heinrich Bassenge, SMS *Elbing*, II Scouting Group, High Seas Fleet

'*Der Tag*' had finally dawned with a rosy glow of understatement.
Immediately, the *Galatea* started to pursue the destroyers. Commodore
Alexander-Sinclair, who had initially mistaken them for light cruisers,
hoisted the signal flag, 'Enemy in sight' at 14.18 and submitted a wireless
sighting report.

Urgent. Two cruisers probably hostile in sight bearing east south east
course unknown.[29]

At 14.28 the *Galatea* opened fire. Finally, after years of anticipation, battle had commenced.

> They were Huns all right and bang went our 6″ guns. They soon left the merchant packet and fled eastwards with the *Galatea* and the *Phaeton* after them, at the same time pouring as much lyddite as possible into them.[30]
>
> Engine Room Rating T. Farquhar, HMS *Galatea*, 1st Light Cruiser Squadron

As the German destroyers fell back on the II Scouting Group, the *Elbing* returned fire at a range of about 14,000 yards and made her own contact report: 'Enemy armoured cruiser in sight bearing west by north.'[31] The Germans had been deceived by the sheer volume of smoke made by the British light cruisers.

> At 14.32, the first shells were fired at the enemy, and the big battle had started. The distance was 13–14 kilometres despite the high speed. We managed to direct the first hit of the battle at the *Galatea*. The shell hit the bridge through two or three decks. Both English cruisers returned fire but did not hit us.[32]
>
> Lieutenant Heinrich Bassenge, SMS *Elbing*, II Scouting Group, High Seas Fleet

This shell caused a considerable amount of superficial damage aboard the *Galatea*.

> They put a shell through our ship's side, through our dispensary, through another bulkhead and finally made a dimple in the other side of the ship, but luckily for us it did not explode, as it was right over the 4″ magazine chamber and I don't think it necessary to state here what would have happened.[33]
>
> Engine Room Rating T. Farquhar, HMS *Galatea*, 1st Light Cruiser Squadron

The *Galatea* wireless reports were picked up aboard the *Iron Duke*. Jellicoe, although he still believed that the High Seas Fleet was safely tucked in harbour thanks to the earlier Admiralty signal, nevertheless realized that something was afoot, and immediately ordered the Grand Fleet to raise steam ready to proceed at full speed. Beatty was steering on a north-easterly course when he received the message from the *Galatea* at about 14.20. At 14.25 he hoisted a preparatory signal to his destroyers ordering them to take up position to form a submarine screen, so that he could turn his battlecruisers onto a new course of south-south-east. At 14.30 a second wireless message from the *Galatea* reported the presence of a German light cruiser. At 14.32 Beatty ordered the flag signal to be hoisted for the general change of course to south-south-east. In doing so he spawned one of the most bitter, never-ending disputes in the whole history of the Royal Navy. The moment the signal was hoisted, the *Lion* turned to the new course accompanied by the 1st Battlecruiser Squadron and the 2nd Battlecruiser Squadron. At the same time, Beatty increased speed to 22 knots. Unfortunately, the Fifth Battle Squadron failed to accompany the battlecruisers. What had gone wrong?

In essence, the *Barham*, the flagship of the Fifth Battle Squadron, was too far away to read the flag signal made by the *Lion*. The super-dreadnoughts had been zigzagging, controlled from the *Lion* by signal flags which had been repeated for them by flashing searchlight from the *Tiger*. The flags may have been large, but they could not easily be read at a distance of five miles. It is also vital to understand that they would have been only briefly displayed before being hauled down, which was the sign to execute the order. The dense smoke that poured from the battlecruisers, as they simultaneously raised steam to accommodate the increase in speed, exacerbated the difficulty of reading the signals at long range. Unfortunately, the *Tiger* confounded these problems by failing to repeat the signal by searchlight. In these circumstances, naturally expecting the fresh signal to be a continuation of the pattern of course changes in the zigzag pattern they had been following, the *Barham* ordered the squadron to turn from their north-easterly course to the north-west at 14.32. The two elements of Beatty's force thus began to head in opposite directions.

> The visibility as it was, together with the intense smoke made by the battlecruisers bringing fires forward, it was impossible to see what *Lion* was doing until most of the Squadron had turned. *Barham* was zig-zagging at the time, which caused delay, but as *Lion* had been signalling to *Barham* with a searchlight previously to the turn, and had made all alterations of course by that method, there was no reason why a signal should not have been made for *Barham* to turn with *Lion*, by searchlight, if not by wireless, had he wished her to do so.[34]
>
> Rear Admiral Sir Hugh Evan-Thomas, HMS *Barham*, Fifth Battle Squadron

As the battlecruisers raced off, each precious minute added immensely to the distance between themselves and the super-dreadnoughts that were supposed to ensure their superiority over Hipper's battlecruisers. This has rightly been seen as a serious failure in command and control by Beatty:

> After all isn't it one of the fundamental principles of naval tactics that an Admiral makes sure that his orders are understood by distant parts of his fleet before rushing into space, covered by a smoke screen.[35]
>
> Rear Admiral Sir Hugh Evan-Thomas, HMS *Barham*, Fifth Battle Squadron

Rear Admiral Hugh Evan-Thomas, as a new arrival, was unaware of the intricacies of the standing Battlecruiser Fleet Orders, which warned that Beatty would not wait for acknowledgements from his subordinate admirals. Yet Evan-Thomas himself was not entirely free from blame in this calamity. As the battlecruisers disappeared into the middle and then far distance, he was lamentably slow in taking any action himself – in fact about seven minutes passed before they swung onto the south-south-east course – and even then it was only because the order was belatedly repeated to him by searchlight from the *Lion*. As such he was culpable for standing on precious little else but his dignity and due ceremony for far too long. It was surely obvious that the 1st and 2nd Battlecruiser Squadrons were no longer zigzagging in concert with his ships and, by failing to take the independent corrective action that was clearly within his power, Evan-Thomas was also guilty of an egregious blunder.

The consequences of this seemingly minor signal mix-up were to be serious. The original gap of 5 miles which already separated Beatty from Evan-Thomas was overly large for proper close support. That gap had now opened up to around 10 miles. At 14.35 the *Galatea* made another report: 'Urgent. Have sighted large amount of smoke as though from a fleet bearing east-north-east.'[36] Whoever was over the horizon, the battlecruisers would now have to meet them on their own.

On the German side, Hipper's opening manoeuvres were less fraught with controversy. As the first signal from the *Elbing* was received at 14.27, he turned to a west-south-west course. A subsequent garbled message from the *Elbing* seemed for a moment to indicate they were approaching twenty-four to twenty-six battleships, which caused him to form line ahead steering south-south-west as it seemed that battle was imminent. When subsequent signals made it apparent that they were at that stage facing just four British light cruisers, Hipper swung in stages round, until at 15.10 he was steering a north-westerly course in hot pursuit of his imagined prey.

As the British battlecruisers hared off, eventually to be followed by the Fifth Battle Squadron desperately engaged in cutting corners to try to diminish the gap, there was a lengthy period of calm before the storm that would engulf them. Sighting reports from the two light cruiser screens meant that the British and Germans were aware of the possible presence of the other's battlecruisers. But distances at sea are vast and there was a good deal of hard steaming to endure before they could actually see their opposite numbers. As they searched the empty grey horizons that bound them, excitement mingled with occasional tremors of entirely natural trepidation and a grim sense of purpose as they eagerly antici-pated the cathartic moment of release when they would actually see their enemies.

> A message from the captain reached me in the fore control, "Enemy
> battlecruisers have been reported." I passed this message on to the gun
> crews. It was now clear that within a short time a life and death struggle
> would develop. For a moment there was a marked hush in the fore
> control. But this only lasted a minute or so, then humour broke out again,
> and everything went on in perfect order and calm. I had the guns trained
> on what would be approximately the enemy's position. I adjusted my
> periscope to its extreme power. But still there was no sign of the enemy.[37]
>
> Commander Georg von Hase, SMS Derfflinger, I Scouting Group, High Seas Fleet

At about 14.45 Beatty ordered his seaplane carrier, the *Engadine*, stationed in the cruiser screen, to launch an aircraft to investigate the smoke reported by the *Galatea*. The *Engadine* carried two Short seaplanes and two 'Baby' Sopwith seaplanes.

> Word came through, "Investigate with aircraft!" There was some activity
> just on the horizon in the direction of Schleswig Holstein. I was on the
> aft deck with my old Short Seaplane 8359 on the aft deck all ready to go
> – clad in flying gear sitting in the cockpit waiting for instructions, engine
> warming up, chain hooked on ready to hoist – I'd have been in the
> water and away in about a minute and a half. Unfortunately just as I got

my engine nicely warmed up, our senior flying officer, Flight Lieutenant Rutland, appeared, waved me down with my observer and told me that he'd got the Captain's sanction – he was to go! So my Short Seaplane 8359 went – but without me![38]

Flight Lieutenant Graham Donald, Royal Naval Air Service, HMS *Engadine*, Battlecruiser Fleet

Before the seaplane could be launched, the *Engadine* had to pull round into the wind and it was not until 15.08 that the usurper Rutland took off with his observer, Assistant Paymaster George Trewin. It was a historic moment, the first aerial reconnaissance to be carried out at sea during a battle. The cloud conditions were such that Rutland was forced to come down low in order to carry out any effective observation.

After about ten minutes sighted the enemy. Clouds were at 1,000 to 1,200 feet, with patches at 900 feet. This necessitated flying very low. On sighting the enemy it was very hard to tell what they were, and so I had to close to within a mile and a half at a height of 1,000 feet. They then opened fire on me with anti-aircraft and other guns, my height enabling them to use their anti-torpedo armament. When sighted they were steering a northerly course. I flew through several of the columns of smoke caused through bursting shrapnel.[39]

Flight Lieutenant Frederick Rutland, Royal Naval Air Service, HMS *Engadine*, Battlecruiser Fleet

Lieutenant Bassenge sighted Rutland's aircraft from the *Elbing*.

Just before the order was given, to sail to the south, a little enemy seaplane came up from the south-west. We were very much taken aback it was not known that there were any enemy planes at this time, it must have been kept aboard an enemy ship. We had never thought of this idea. The whole manoeuvre took about two minutes. The aircraft inspected us from front to back (600–700 metres) in length and then disappeared into the mist.[40]

Lieutenant Heinrich Bassenge, SMS *Elbing*, II Scouting Group, High Seas Fleet

The change of course by the German light forces was spotted by Rutland while Trewin was in the process of making his wireless report.

When the observer had counted and got the disposition of the enemy and was making his W/T report, I steered to about three miles, keeping the enemy well in sight. While the observer was sending one message, the enemy turned 16 points. I drew his attention to this and he forthwith transmitted it. The enemy then ceased firing at me. I kept on a bearing on the bows, about three miles distant of the enemy, and as the weather cleared a little I observed the disposition of our fleet, and judged by the course of our battlecruisers that our W/T had got through.[41]

Flight Lieutenant Frederick Rutland, Royal Naval Air Service, HMS *Engadine*, Battlecruiser Fleet

The immediate value of aerial reconnaissance seemed to have been proven at the first attempt. However, Rutland's confidence was misplaced as their efforts were in vain. Signalling difficulties meant that their reports do not appear to have been received aboard the *Lion*.

Three W/T signals were received from it, reporting three large enemy cruisers and ten destroyers, and that they were turning to the Southward. By this time the *Lion*, leading the battlecruisers, was passing us on our starboard side steaming into action. We tried to pass the seaplane's report in code by searchlight, but could get no reply. Probably, as the Yeoman suggested, the report had been received by W/T direct from the seaplane, and in any case the battlecruisers would soon be in visual contact with the enemy. The haze had closed down again to a certain extent and the great ships were quickly outside visual signalling distance. Following the battlecruisers came the four battleships of the Fifth Battle Squadron and we made another attempt to pass the signal to the *Barham*. She answered our call sign, but would not take the signal as she also was preparing to go into action.[42]

Signaller H. Y. Ganderton, HMS *Engadine*, Battlecruiser Fleet

The first aerial reconnaissance had achieved little but to act as a signpost to the inevitable future of naval warfare.

◆ ◆ ◆

As the fleets closed on each other, the visibility was favourable to Hipper, for it was considerably clearer looking west than east. As a result, at 15.20

Hipper, from his flagship the *Lützow*, caught his first glimpse of the smoke of the approaching British battlecruisers several minutes before he was sighted by his opposite number on the bridge of the *Lion*. At first Hipper was unsure as to their course and formation and for a few minutes he continued to the north as he allowed the situation to clarify, although as a precaution he slowed down to 23 knots. At around 15.25 the first British sighting reports were made from the *New Zealand* and *Princess Royal*. Beatty finally sighted the German battlecruisers from the *Lion* at about 15.30 and immediately ordered his ships back onto an easterly course to close rapidly with the Germans while at the same time placing himself squarely between Hipper and his base.

> It was a lovely day and a flat calm. Many of the sailors were sun-bathing on deck. To the eastward the visibility was about 20,000 yards but more to the westward. I checked our position and had a general look round. The other destroyers of the 13th Flotilla were scattered around as a submarine screen with the *Champion* dead ahead of the *Lion*. I had a good look round and then saw flying at the *Lion*'s yardarm a flag which I knew well meant, "Enemy in sight!" I rang the alarm and called the Captain.[43]
>
> Sub-Lieutenant Hilary Owen, HMS *Moorsom*, 9/10th Flotilla

By this time Hipper had a clearer view of the six dark grey British battlecruisers and he realized that not only were the British present in greater strength, but he was in imminent danger of being cut off. He had already recalled the light cruisers pursuing the *Galatea* and at 15.33 he turned 16 points to starboard, in effect reversing his course right round to the south-east. This would take him straight back towards the High Seas Fleet and, if Beatty followed, it would draw him straight into Scheer's welcoming steel embrace.

> The British light cruisers came in view, and behind them dense clouds of smoke. Then tripod masts and huge hulls loomed over the horizon. There they were again, our friends from the Dogger Bank.[44]
>
> Kapitän zur See Moritz von Egidy, SMS *Seydlitz*, I Scouting Group, High Seas Fleet

Aboard the *Derfflinger*, von Hase watched the approach of the British battlecruisers. The fantasy appeared to be unfolding before his eyes.

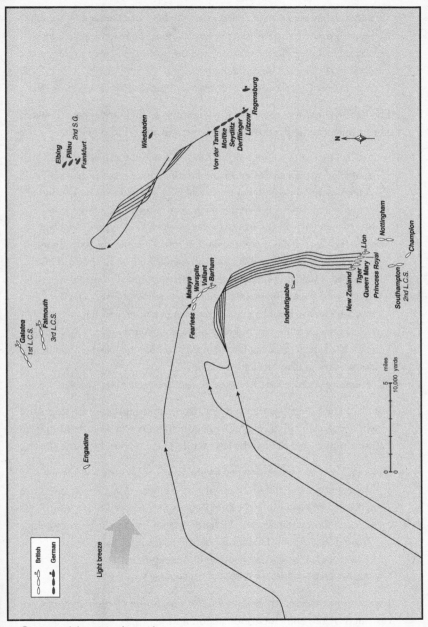

Galatea
1st L.C.S.
Falmouth
3rd L.C.S.

Engadine

Elbing
Pillau 2nd S.G.
Frankfurt

Wiesbaden

Von der Tann
Moltke
Seydlitz
Derfflinger
Lützow
Regensburg

N

Malaya
Warspite
Valiant
Barham

Fearless

Indefatigable

New Zealand
Tiger
Lion
Queen Mary
Princess Royal
Southampton
2nd L.C.S.

Nottingham

Champion

5 miles
10,000 yards

British
German

Light breeze

Contact and the run to the south

Suddenly my periscope revealed some big ships. Black monsters; six tall, broad-beamed giants steaming in two columns. They were still a long way off, but they showed up clearly on the horizon and even at this great distance they looked powerful, massive.[45]

Commander Georg von Hase, SMS *Derfflinger*, I Scouting Group, High Seas Fleet

The British ships, too, soon had firm sightings of their arch-rivals. As word passed through the fleet, the crews were galvanized into action.

At 3.30pm, just as we were sitting down to tea in the gunroom, the 'snottie' of the watch dashed in and informed us that the *Galatea* had sighted enemy ships and that we should be going to action stations in ten minutes time. Knowing that this might lead to anything, we made the best of that ten minutes, stowing away as much food as possible. They say a 'Britisher' fights best on a full stomach. Then, for the second time in my life, I heard the real 'Action' call sounded off on the bugle. This same call is used for practice, but preceded and ended by a long 'G'. Today's call meant the real thing and I'm sure it sent a joyful thrill through everybody and scattered us to our action stations full of eagerness with a spice of Nelson's 'peerage or Westminster Abbey' spirit. I just had time to grab my Gieve's waistcoat from my sea-chest and dash down below to the transmitting station.[46]

Midshipman Gordon Eady, HMS *New Zealand*, 2nd Battlecruiser Squadron

Not all of the hungry young 'snotties', as the midshipmen were popularly known, were as lucky as Eady. As action stations was sounded bang on tea-time, many were denied the last chance to eat before the battle started.

At half past three tea was piped for the hands. That means the Bosun's Mate went around and just shouted out, "Hands to tea!" I woke up and slouched off towards the Gun Room where I hoped to get a cup of tea. Almost immediately – I'd hardly got up – when the bugles went, "Immediate Action!" That meant instead of having a fatheaded tea I had to run off as fast as I could to my action station.[47]

Midshipman John Ouvry, HMS *Tiger*, 1st Battlecruiser Squadron

It was not just the midshipmen who lost out. Some of their seniors were frustrated by the coincidence of action and tea-time.

I had had the morning watch and had seized the opportunity of two hours sleep after lunch in the gunroom armchair, before going on again for the first 'dog'. I was woken by some excited conversation on the part of the midshipmen, one of them had just come down from the bridge and said there was a 'buzz' that a German destroyer had been sighted by 'someone', 'somewhere' – it didn't sound very promising. The steward was laying the table for tea but, we never sat down to it, as just at 3.30 the bugles sounded for 'Action' and we all ran to our stations.[48]

Sub-Lieutenant Clifford Caslon, HMS *Malaya*, Fifth Battle Squadron

Many officers were mildly irritated by the timing and at first did not believe that this was any more than an exercise.

I woke up and was going to the Wardroom for a cup of tea before going on watch. Just as I got to the Wardroom door 'action stations' was sounded off. I was slightly indignant having to go to action stations at that time of day, thinking that it could only be an exercise action and not the real thing – our usual time for exercising action being the forenoon. I thought I had misheard the call of the bugle, but I soon found out I was wrong. The enemy were really out and on the warpath.[49]

Lieutenant Henry Hill, HMS *Tiger*, 1st Battlecruiser Squadron

This was the real thing; fierce excitement and frenetic activity filled the air.

Everything was orderly disorder. Sailors running to their guns, down to the shell rooms etc, up to the controls etc etc; stokers rigging hoses, and shutting hatchways.[50]

Able Seaman Edward Sharpe, HMS *Valiant*, Fifth Battle Squadron

As the bugles sounded action stations, Petty Officer Francis ran to his post in 'X' Turret aboard the *Queen Mary*.

I took the first hatchway up, as doors were closing and came up to the foremost 4″ Battery, starboard side and raced for 'X' Turret. When I got inside everyone was there. I yelled out, "Turret's crew, number!" They were correct from top to bottom and I reported to Lieutenant Ewart. He said, "Test loading gear, but for goodness sake don't let them go too rash I wouldn't miss one round in this smash for worlds." The loading gear and machinery was tested and immediately afterwards came the order to load all cages. As soon as they were loaded it was reported to the transmitting station and then came the order to load.[51]

Petty Officer Ernest Francis, HMS *Queen Mary*, 1st Battlecruiser Squadron

Aboard the *Malaya*, Frederick Arnold reported to the main wireless office on the Royal Marines' mess deck where he waited to be assigned to duties.

We could feel the ship hastily increasing speed, the racing up of the engines from the boiler and engine rooms below our feet, the whining of the electric fans, the shivering of the ship at intervals – all tending to create a tense situation – everybody below decks wondering what is going on outside. Down below decks we, like the vast majority of ships companies of the modern warships, never see any of the actual enemy of the fighting. We, like the stokers, engine room personnel and many, many others, we were all 'wheels' within one big machine, with our parts to play, we just had to carry on with our vital duties, as part of the fighting machine, just guessing, wondering, hazarding what was actually occurring up on deck.[52]

Wireless Telegraphist Frederick Arnold, HMS *Malaya*, Fifth Battle Squadron

Commander Humphrey Walwyn was the executive commander aboard the *Warspite* and his responsibilities as the bugles sounded were legion. The hour had arrived when all the apparently endless training routines would be put to good use.

There was not much time and I was thankful we had always done everything so thoroughly. Passed the word round to everybody that we were in for the real thing and went all round mess decks, wetted decks, put all tables and stools on the deck and lit all 'action candles' etc. etc. Saw all doors and everything closed and went up on deck; they were just finishing washing down the weather decks, and I sent all hands away to their stations and went up and reported everything was ready. On my way down from the bridge, went into my sea cabin and put on my Gieve waistcoat and 'action' things, then went on to 'B' Turret.[53]

Commander Humphrey Walwyn, HMS *Warspite*, Fifth Battle Squadron

It is perhaps unsurprising that, to others, Walwyn appeared a little brusque as he rushed around his ship.

I went up onto the forecastle deck and just as I arrived there met the Commander coming aft again. He was hurrying and, as he passed, told me to get along forward at once and get everything shifted out of the Sick Bay into the Distributing Station as quickly as I could. He did not say why, but it was evidently urgent.[54]

Surgeon Gordon Ellis, HMS *Warspite*, Fifth Battle Squadron

The *raison d'être* of the battlecruisers and super-dreadnoughts was their main armament gun turrets. The 12-inch gun turrets carried by the *Indefatigable* and *New Zealand*, the 13.5-inch gun turrets of the *Lion*, *Princess Royal*, *Queen Mary* and *Tiger*, and the 15-inch gun turrets of the *Barham*, *Valiant*, *Warspite* and *Malaya* were very similar in the way in which they operated. They were guided by a director system, an elevated position that transmitted gun elevation and training angles to the turrets. In the gunnery control tops high above the ship were installed Dumaresq trigonometrical calculating machines which worked out the deflection required by the guns when set with the German range, bearing, course and speed as determined by the various appropriate instruments. The first effective fire-control system had been invented in 1901 by Arthur Pollen, though it was not officially accepted. Ultimately the Admiralty preferred the system developed from Pollen's original by Lieutenant Frederic Dreyer, who was, by 1916, Jellicoe's flag captain aboard the *Iron Duke*. Both systems were designed to reduce the problems experienced in long-range fire in tracking the relative movements of the firing ship and its target during the period the shell was actually in flight.

Most of the ships in the Grand Fleet were now fitted with 'directors' which meant that the actual firing was done by the gunnery officer from a position high up just above the bridge. Gunlayers and trainers in the turrets followed a system of electrically controlled pointers on dials so that when each gun was ready to fire, left and right alternately, a switch was made and the gunnery officer pressed the trigger when his Director sights were 'on'. Rangefinders provided the range and deflection was estimated by special instruments, this information being passed to the turrets through the transmitting station, somewhere low down in the ship.[55]

Midshipman Roger Frampton, HMS *Barham*, Fifth Battle Squadron

The range-finders and director system provided the initial information, after which 'spotting' the fall of shot was used to correct the range up or down as required. If the gunnery officer could be regarded as the eyes of the ship, then the transmitting station was its brain. It contained the fire-control table that continuously recorded the data for the range and bearing of the target ship as it received them from the Dumaresqs aloft. This was then fine-tuned by a continuous process of comparing the results with the actual ranges as estimated by the range-finders and spotting gunnery officers in the gunnery control top. As befits such a precious organ it was tucked away deep in the bowels of the ship.

> My action station was down below in the transmitting station – a kind
> of telephone exchange. The lower conning tower opened out of the
> transmitting station and we were able to get a rough idea as to the ship's
> movements by noting the alterations of course on the gyro compass
> receiver. The upper conning tower was connected with lower by a tall
> armoured tube containing an iron ladder. This tube was very narrow
> which prevented anyone from climbing up at any but the slowest pace.
> As two armoured hatches were slammed down on top of us, this tube
> was our only means of escape in an emergency and it would have taken
> some time for the thirty-odd people down there to get out. However as
> there was a 12″ magazine on each side of us, a 4″ one below and the
> foremost boiler equally close, we should probably have all been blown to
> glory together.[56]
>
> Midshipman Gordon Eady, HMS *New Zealand*, 2nd Battlecruiser Squadron

It was a strange, claustrophobic environment in which to fight a battle. Yet on their ability could depend the whole fighting efficiency of the ship.

> Imagine then dearest, a room 18 feet square, in the centre of which
> is a table, on one side of it is a roll of paper, this is stretched across
> the table to another roller which is being revolved by a motor and so
> keeps the paper constantly on the move, on this is plotted out all the
> information which the men at the guns want to know. All around the
> walls of the transmitting station are the different electrical instruments
> for sending the information up to the guns, besides voice pipes and
> telephones, in all there are about 20 men in this room and each one has

so many of these instruments to attend. The first order which comes
from the control officer is to inform all guns to load with lyddite shell
and the battle commences.[57]

Able Seaman Harry Hayler, HMS *Warspite*, Fifth Battle Squadron

As the battlecruisers sighted their enemies, the range-finders and directors began their vital work. The first readings began to be charted in the
transmitting stations.

Ranges now began to come through to us from the rangefinders in the
turrets and foretop. The action, in so far as I and my assistant 'snotty'
were concerned, had begun. Facing us were six range transmitters
worked by the men at each rangefinder. As these flicked round altering
the ranges it was our job to mark them down on a large moving roll of
paper spread out on a table in front of us. This was called the plotting
table and each range transmitter was shown by a different coloured
pencil. Two 'snotties' and two able seamen as voicepipe men completed
the plotting table crew. Making marks in coloured pencils on a piece of
paper seemed a funny way of fighting a naval action, but by plotting the
ranges we were able to determine at what rate the enemy were opening
or closing on us. The rates so obtained were passed up to the gunnery
lieutenant in the foretop.[58]

Midshipman Gordon Eady, HMS *New Zealand*, 2nd Battlecruiser Squadron

Thus, the precise directions for laying the big guns were transmitted to
each of the main turrets. To load the guns, the shells and cordite charges
that propelled them with such devastating power out of the guns had to
be brought up from the shell room and magazine directly underneath
the turret gunhouse.

The guns crews were closed up and eventually the order to load was
passed. That meant that the shells and the cartridges had to come
up from the bottom of the ship where there were shell rooms and
magazines. It was all mechanical, being hydraulic. They were brought
up, the shell first, then the rammer operator pushed the shell into the
gun, followed by four quarter charges of cordite. We stayed in this
position until the order to bring the guns to the ready was passed. In a
turret you are simply in a steel box. The box completely surrounds you

with thick armoured plating all round. Three ways of getting out were possible. One out through a manhole at the top of the turret, one through a manhole at the bottom of the turret and it is possible to leave the turret by going down through the trunking into the magazines and shell rooms. One feels, while you are in a turret, that you are naturally cut off from anything going on outside – except the telephone communication with the bridge and the control towers. It is a feeling of being fastened in a big box. The atmosphere is good, the crew, numbering about 16, have all got their individual jobs which they attend to and work as one. The turret trainers were moving the turret. The guns being loaded the next order was passed, "Bring the guns to the ready!" When the guns are brought to the ready you simply wait for the open fire, we were looking forward to a chance to have a crack at the enemy. We were keen – this was the day we were waiting for.[59]

J. J. Hazelwood, HMS *Warspite*, Fifth Battle Squadron

Morale was indeed high. Although many of the battlecruiser crews had been in action before at Dogger Bank, the vast majority of the crews had in no sense been fully exposed to the horrors that lurked behind the glories of naval warfare. To them it was the supreme moment of realization.

Our excitement and surprise may be imagined. Faces at once brightened and glasses scanned the horizon for a sight of the enemy. The pessimists still held out that, in all probability, it was some wretched enemy light cruisers that would easily escape us.[60]

Lieutenant Patrick Brind, HMS *Malaya*, Fifth Battle Squadron

At all levels of command, officers and men made their final preparations.

I had a hurried look round to see that all was well and told the men what I could, viz, "That we might expect to meet anything from an enemy light cruiser to the High Seas Fleet and that 'B' Turret had to get off the maximum number of rounds allowed by the control. We had, up to date, been favoured by luck, but we must be ready for anything and not miss a salvo." The men were greatly cheered by the news, assured me that not a chance would be missed to ease off a round at the Huns and at once began to make little extra preparations, taking off superfluous clothing etc. They made all sorts of weird and wonderful jokes as to what would happen to any German ship that should be so unfortunate as to come within range of us.[61]

Lieutenant Patrick Brind, HMS *Malaya*, Fifth Battle Squadron

Aboard the German ships, the same type of 'Action Stations' routine, and possibly variations of the same jokes, were being made as the Germans too prepared for battle.

> As always at the beginning of an operation, all watertight doors were thoroughly examined, every piece of apparatus tested and spare parts broken out to be handy in emergencies. The watch kept a sharp look out for submarines, while the men off watch dozed. When the message "Enemy in sight" came in, bugles and drums sounded the 'General March' to call all hands to battle-stations. Within minutes, every station reported to the bridge that it was ready for action.[62]

Kapitän zur See Moritz von Egidy, SMS *Seydlitz*, I Scouting Group, High Seas Fleet

Like the British they had been waiting for so long for '*Der Tag*'. Their admirals and high command may have been wary of exposing the German fleet in battle but the vast majority of their crews were in a veritable fervour of anticipation and excitement. They too had absolute confidence in themselves and their mighty warships.

> The distant thunder of the salvoes announced the coming storm. "Clear for action!" Who has once heard this resounding command can never forget the inspiring magic of the moment. In a few seconds the final preparations had been made and after a short bustle all were at their stations. It seemed to us as if, in the moment of calm before the storm broke, the spirits of the mighty dead, whose names shone out on the steel sides of the ships, were gathered together in the heavens above our heads watching to see if the coming battle should be worthy of them.[64]

Commander Albert Scheibe, I Scouting Group, High Seas Fleet

Neither side had the monopoly of purple prose or vastly inflated expectations. Both fleets believed that victory would be theirs. Neither conceived of the possibility of defeat. As the great turret guns on both sides swung round to track the movements of their opposite numbers all was ready for a naval Armageddon.

CHAPTER THREE

THE RUN
TO THE SOUTH

As HIS BATTLECRUISERS closed with the I Scouting Group, Vice Admiral Sir David Beatty made some final adjustments to his dispositions. Somewhat belatedly, he ordered Rear Admiral William Pakenham, aboard the *New Zealand* leading the 2nd Battlecruiser Squadron, to take up their battle stations in line behind the 1st Battlecruiser Squadron, led by the *Lion*. At the same time Beatty signalled Vice Admiral Sir Hugh Evan-Thomas to turn east and to increase speed to 25 knots. This was easier said than done, for the super-dreadnoughts' designed maximum speed was only 24½ knots. Furthermore, by specifying the course and speed in the finest parade ground manner, Beatty also precluded the use of any initiative that Evan-Thomas might have wished to display to close the still yawning gap between his battleships and the battle-cruisers. The 9th Flotilla was ordered to take station ahead of the *Lion*, with the 13th Flotilla further round on her starboard bow. Beatty also sent a contact report by wireless to Admiral Sir John Jellicoe. At 15.45 Beatty ordered a complicated manoeuvre whereby his ships would all turn together to form a compass line of bearing north-west while pursuing an east-south-east course. His intention was to clear the smoke that was obstructing their view and bring as many guns as possible to bear on the German line.

From the foretop of the *Derfflinger*, Commander Georg von Hase tracked his 12-inch turrets onto his putative opponents, ready to fire the moment the order was given.

> Ship turning to starboard! Normal direction for starboard fire! 17,000!
> 16,500! Heavy guns armour piercing shell! Direction on second
> battlecruiser from the right, 102 degrees! Ship making 26 knots, course
> east-south-east! 17,000! Our target has two masts and two funnels, as

well as a narrow funnel close to the foremast! Deflection 19 left! Rate 100 minus! 16,400! Still no permission to open fire from the flagship![1]

Commander Georg von Hase, SMS *Derfflinger*, I Scouting Group, High Seas Fleet

The ship he was aiming at was the *Princess Royal*. The Germans were both surprised and relieved that the British had not yet opened fire, for they were only too aware that the 13.5-inch guns of the 1st Battlecruiser Squadron had a far superior range to the German 11- and 12-inch guns. The 13.5-inch guns could propel a shell up to about 24,000 yards while the German guns could only manage between 19,000 and 21,000 yards at maximum. This difference in ranges marked a zone in which the British could hit the Germans without any prospect of return fire. This was a missed opportunity.

Midshipman Hill was at his action station on high angle guns on the compass platform of the *Lion*.

I could not bring myself to realise that we were in the presence of the enemy. What struck me as being rather strange was that while the range of the enemy on sighting them was only about 23,000 yards, we did not open fire till the range was 18,500 yards on the gun sights.[2]

Midshipman Rupert Hill, HMS *Lion*, 1st Battlecruiser Squadron

There were a number of factors that prevented the British ships from opening fire earlier. Foremost among these was that their range-finders were considerably overestimating the range. The weakness of their range-finders was the Achilles heel within the British director system. Their importance was obvious, but their accuracy was directly linked to the base-length of the instrument. The British Barr & Stroud range-finders were largely limited to a 9-foot base-length, except in the latest battleships, which had a 15-foot base-length. The operators had to line up two images until they exactly coincided, a system that could be badly affected by the vibrations inevitable when a ship worked up to full speed or was firing guns. The German system relied on the operators making a difficult value judgement on a stereoscopic rangefinder, adjusting an 'x' shaped 'wandermark' until it appeared to be the same distance away as the target. The process could be adversely affected by mental stress or plain nerves! Overall it seems that the German range-finders were quicker to get the range correct. As the battlecruisers closed in on each other a further delay in the British opening fire can be attributed to the fact that Beatty was not at his usual station, being, not unnaturally, preoccupied with his duties as an admiral.

We were now steaming at 19 knots on a south-south-easterly course. The enemy battlecruisers were rapidly closing us steering south-westerly. The range receiver on the bridge showed 20,000 yards. I was on the compass platform with my navigator, Commander the Hon. Arthur Strutt, and my small staff. Beatty remained for a time on his own bridge, below me, with Commander Bentinck, Seymour, Commander Bailey and Spickernell, his Secretary. I wanted him to come on the compass platform and sent a message to Seymour, telling him to advise Beatty that the range was closing rapidly and that we ought almost at once to be opening fire. This was a duty that I had actually handed over to the Chief of Staff. But I could get no reply, the Vice Admiral was engaged in an important message to the Commander in Chief. 18,000 yards. I told Longhurst to be ready to open fire immediately. The turrets were already loaded and trained on the leading enemy ship, the *Lützow*.[3]

Flag Captain Alfred Chatfield, HMS *Lion*, 1st Battlecruiser Squadron

The British had lost part of the advantage given to them by their heavier main armament.

Finally, the Germans found themselves within range and took the liberty of opening fire first at 15.48.

Our rangefinders gave us good ranges commencing at 240hm and it seemed an eternity, actually it was 20 minutes, before we had reached our range of 190hm. Even then we had to wait for the *Seydlitz* till the range was further reduced. Five points – 57 degrees is the enemy's bearing. Estimated speed 26 knots, course 110 degrees. This made the rate of closing 4hm a minute. At a range of 167hm by our calculations the first turret salvo from 'A' and 'B' Turrets was fired at 4.48. Time of flight 22 seconds.[4]

Commander Günther Paschen, SMS *Lützow*, I Scouting Group, High Seas Fleet

Hipper ordered his battlecruisers to distribute their fire from left to right as they steamed to the south. Thus the *Lützow* fired at *Lion*, *Derfflinger* at

Princess Royal, *Seydlitz* at *Queen Mary*, *Moltke* at *Tiger* and the *Von der Tann* left the *New Zealand* in peace and fired at the *Indefatigable*. Facing them, Beatty ordered his first two ships to fire at the leading German ship, so that *Lion* and *Princess Royal* fired at the *Lützow*, *Queen Mary* at *Derfflinger*, *Tiger* at *Seydlitz*, *New Zealand* at *Moltke* and *Indefatigable* at *Von der Tann*. In accordance with Hipper's instructions, Commander von Hase had the guns of the *Derfflinger* trained on the *Princess Royal*.

All was ready to open fire, the tension increased every second, but I could not yet give the first order to fire. I had to wait for the signal from the flagship. "15,000!" As my last order rang out there was a dull roar. I looked ahead. The *Lützow* is firing her first salvo and immediately the signal, "Open fire!!" is hoisted. In the same second I shout, "Salvoes fire!" and like thunder our first salvo crashes out. The ships astern follow suit at once and we see all round the enemy jets of fire and rolling clouds of smoke.[5]

Commander Georg von Hase, SMS *Derfflinger*, I Scouting Group, High Seas Fleet

The British could no longer stand on ceremony, and in the continued absence of Beatty his flag captain took action on his own initiative.

The range was 16,000 yards. I could wait no longer and told Longhurst to open fire. At the same moment the enemy did so. Seymour hoisted the '5' flag (engage the enemy) and off went the double salvoes.[6]

Flag Captain Alfred Chatfield, HMS *Lion*, I st Battlecruiser Squadron

Midshipman Anthony Combe was at his post in the foretop of the *Lion* above the bridge when he heard the momentous order to open fire.

Almost immediately after the enemy had opened fire the Captain said, "Open Fire!" to the foretop and the Gunnery Lieutenant Commander opened fire with four 13.5″ guns all at once. You could hear the firing bell in the transmitting station ring and the direction layer pressed the trigger, at which the guns went off with a tremendous great crash. Then I sat myself down at my voice-pipes trusting to luck that the foretop would be spared![7]

Midshipman A. B. Combe, HMS *Lion*, I st Battlecruiser Squadron

All along the British line the guns finally blazed out.

A blinding flash through our gun port and the rattle of a hail of shell splinters on our ship's side told us that Jerry was already straddling us with a near miss. Our guns thundered out, the great 13.5″ heavies speaking for the first time. The Armageddon of war seemed to me like a mighty Ajax trying to crack the universe with a terrible, prolonged roaring of the fearful guns.[8]

Able Seaman Victor Hayward, HMS *Tiger*, 1st Battlecruiser Squadron

The fears and individual inner tensions that lurked behind the widespread wild enthusiasm for action were often dissipated by sheer physical exertion once the fighting started.

All hell was let loose. It was very frightening at first but you soon forgot once it got into full swing and you had something to do.[9]

Boy 1st Class, Richard Hogg, HMS *New Zealand*, 2nd Battlecruiser Squadron

In 'X' Turret aboard the *Queen Mary*, as the salvoes rang out Petty Officer Ernest Francis was watching his men like a hawk to make sure that they did not miss a beat in the tattoo of gunfire.

We had started on the great game. I had no means of telling what the time was and if I had I probably should not have looked, because getting a turret started is an anxious rushing time for a Captain of a Turret – once started it is easy to keep going. The gun's crew were absolutely perfect, inclined to be a little swift in loading, but I gave them a yell and pointed out to them that I wanted a steady stride, and after that everything went like clockwork. Lieutenant Ewart came out of the cabinet twice and yelled something to encourage the guns' crews and yelled out to me, "All right, Francis?"[10]

Petty Officer Ernest Francis, HMS *Queen Mary*, 1st Battlecruiser Squadron

The loading was a complicated process and any problems had to be dealt with immediately to minimize the disruption to the firing. Any fault had to be correctly diagnosed, a feasible solution devised and remedial action taken – all without causing additional knock-on effects which could further delay firing.

Suddenly both rammers gave out, my gun going first. This was caused through No 3 opening the breech before the gun had run out after firing;

the carrier arm must have hit the rammer head and slightly metal bound it. I dropped the elevating wheel, got hold of a steel pinch bar, forced the end in behind the rammer head, at the same time putting the rammer lever over to 'run out'; out went the rammer, I rushed it back again and then out again and it all went gay once more. Then the lever was passed over to the right gun and both rammers were once more in working order. I was pleased to get them going again as it would have been such a damper on the crew if we had had to go into hand loading.[11]

Petty Officer Ernest Francis, HMS *Queen Mary*, 1st Battlecruiser Squadron

The guns operated with an awe-inspiring power and each detonation had an inevitable effect on the slim battlecruisers as the recoil mechanism strained to control the explosive forces that had been unleashed.

It seemed as if we were never going to open fire and when our first salvo at last did go off it was speeded on its way with a huge sigh of relief. Whatever that salvo may have done to the enemy I do not know, but it certainly played havoc with us in the transmitting station. The concussion of the discharge brought large quantities of dust and cordite smoke down the voicepipe and set us all choking and spluttering. Orders still had to be passed and to see a fat marine bandsman bawling a message up a voicepipe and suddenly receive a torrent of dust in his mouth as another salvo went off, was as good as a pantomime.[12]

Midshipman Gordon Eady, HMS *New Zealand*, 2nd Battlecruiser Squadron

But such discomforts were overshadowed by the knowledge that at last they were in action.

The place was filled with dust and smoke and as hot as an oven, owing to all the hatches being shut. It was a real genuine 'Tag' at last and everybody revelled in it. It all seemed too good to be true, to think that at last we were really doing something and hammering the Hun after close on two years of weary waiting and watching.[13]

Midshipman Gordon Eady, HMS *New Zealand*, 2nd Battlecruiser Squadron

The first German salvoes screamed towards their targets. Although they too had overestimated the range, for the most part they corrected the error and soon began straddling their targets. But aboard the *Derfflinger*,

Commander von Hase was almost beside himself with impotent fury as he rang through the changes to his guns, yet still found his shells sailing far beyond the *Princess Royal*.

> The second salvo crashed out. Again it was over. 'Down 400' I ordered. The third and fourth salvoes were also over in spite of the fact that that after the third I had given the order, "Down 800!" "Good God, Stachow, there's something wrong." I cursed. "Down 800!" It appeared later from the gunnery log that the midshipman had probably not understood the first "down 800", or at any rate it had not been acted upon. This time, however the "Down 800" was effective. The sixth salvo, fired at 3.52 straddled, three splashes over the target, one short! We had meanwhile reached a range of 11,900, as the elevation clock had shown a rate of 200 closing and then 300 closing per minute. We had already been in action four minutes and only now had we straddled our target. That wasn't a very cheering result. Our first rounds had been well over.[14]
>
> Commander Georg von Hase, SMS *Derfflinger*, I Scouting Group, High Seas Fleet

The German range-finders depended a great deal on the unflustered skills of the range men operating the stereoscopic sights. But human beings cannot be isolated from outside influences.

> The range-takers were completely overwhelmed by the first view of the enemy monsters. Each one saw the enemy ship magnified 23 times in his instrument! Their minds were at first concentrated on the appearance of the enemy. They tried to ascertain who their enemy was. And so when the order suddenly came to open fire they had not accurately fixed the estimated range. It cannot be put down to incapacity, for throughout the remainder of the action the range-takers did their work excellently. Nor can it be put down to the inefficiency of our instruments; on the contrary our Zeiss stereoscopic finders worked admirably throughout.[15]
>
> Commander Georg von Hase, SMS *Derfflinger*, I Scouting Group, High Seas Fleet

The German mistakes, however, paled into insignificance compared to the massive uncorrected overestimate of the range by the British range-finders. Given the difficult visibility conditions that faced the British gunners, any extra smoke drifting across between the fleets was a desperate nuisance that made a bad situation far worse.

Spotting was very difficult due to interference near own ship of torpedo boat destroyers' smoke and enemy shorts, which frequently obscured you just as salvo was going to pitch. The smoke and mist round the enemy was so thick at times that it was difficult to pick up the correct target but bearing reports to and from director and assistant spotter glasses on bearing plate helped in this. Time of flight gear was absolutely essential to identification of shot. Few 'overs' were seen. The system of large down corrections and smaller up was used together with maximum rate of fire whenever enemy range appeared to be found. But it was frequently necessary to re-start the bracket, when the fall of two or three salvoes had been missed. Owing to possible large errors in initial range and rate, big spotting corrections had to be used.[16]

Lieutenant Commander Walter Lapage, HMS *Tiger*, 1st Battlecruiser Squadron

The problem with smoke from the British destroyers was caused as they passed up the engaged side of the British battlecruisers in an attempt to regain their correct station in the screen.

The sudden switch to the south-south-east threw the destroyers out of station. We had been assembled ahead of *Lion* but the rapid 70 degree turn to starboard left us trailing and there was a mad scramble to regain our battle station in the van. Most of our flotilla mates steamed up the disengaged side of our battlecruisers, but *Obdurate* and *Morris* found themselves on the engaged side and as we crept up between the battle lines we were much inhibited by the necessity to moderate our speed so that excessive funnel smoke would not obscure the big ships' view of the enemy.[17]

Sub-Lieutenant Harry Oram, HMS *Obdurate*, 13th Flotilla

The accurate ranging and spotting of their shells was not the only problem that afflicted the British battlecruisers during the opening minutes of the encounter. As at the battle of Dogger Bank, they had managed to blunder in their distribution of fire. The orders had been made by signal flags and, once again, not all of the intended recipients had received their orders. Thus, while *Lion* and *Princess Royal* were concentrating on the *Lützow* as ordered, the *Queen Mary*, instead of taking on the second ship in the German line – the *Derfflinger* – was firing at the third in line, *Seydlitz*.

This left the *Derfflinger* totally undisturbed and it was not long before von Hase realized that he was being given a free ride.

> What astonished me was that so far we had apparently not been hit once. Only quite rarely did a shot stray near us. I observed the gun turrets of our target more closely and established that this ship was not firing at us. She too was firing at our flagship. I observed the third enemy ship for a moment; by some mistake we were being left out. I laughed grimly and now I began to engage our enemy with complete calm, as at gun practice and with continually increasing accuracy.[18]
>
> Commander Georg von Hase, SMS *Derfflinger*, I Scouting Group, High Seas Fleet

Behind the *Queen Mary*, the *Tiger* also missed the gunnery distribution signal and, instead of aiming at the *Seydlitz*, was aiming at her opposite number in the German line, the *Moltke*. To compound matters, the *New Zealand* was firing as intended by Beatty at the fourth in line, so she too was firing at *Moltke*. Meanwhile the *Indefatigable* and *Von der Tann* exchanged fire to the satisfaction of both admirals.

As the huge shells flew over his head, Oram found himself effectively naked before his enemies as his frail destroyer moved between the lines.

> Throughout this opening stage of fierce action we were in the front row of the stalls, one might almost say in the orchestra pit, and the clamour was awe-inspiring. I had by now taken up my station at the foc'sle gun and as we were not then in action there was time to watch developments. Standing with my gun's crew on the open foc'sle, I felt peculiarly exposed and curbed an urge to seek spurious shelter on the disengaged side of the gun mounting. Instincts of self preservation were, however, quickly submerged by waves of intense excitement set up by the sheer magnitude of passing events.[19]
>
> Sub-Lieutenant Harry Oram, HMS *Obdurate*, 13th Flotilla

To ensure that all his guns could bear, Beatty ordered a series of small incremental turns to the south to bring their targets squarely to beam. Nevertheless, the range was still dropping sharply and the German gunnery was proving effective. It is ironic that although the *Moltke* was receiving the undivided attention of both the *Tiger* and *New Zealand*, she was the first ship of either side to hit home really hard. At around 15.54

a series of her shells crashed down on the *Tiger*, putting both 'Q' and 'X' Turrets temporarily out of action and causing considerable damage elsewhere. The medical teams rushed into action, assisted in their grim duties by the ship's padres. One of the badly wounded in 'Q' Turret was a young midshipman.

> Three or four of us went including a doctor. He was got safely down
> the turret and along the messdeck to the distributing station. The poor
> fellow was wounded in several places. I took off his sea boots and found
> a piece of shell had gone through into his foot. He was also wounded in
> the arm and side. His left eye was lying on top of a mass of bruised flesh
> that filled up the cavity of the eye. He was later taken to the Padre's
> cabin where he died during the night.[20]
>
> Reverend Thomas Bradley, HMS *Tiger*, 1st Battlecruiser Squadron

The destructive force of the 11-inch shells was huge and capable of causing the most dreadful wounds. Men were smashed by the explosive blast, maimed by the flying steel shards, burnt by the searing flames, or gassed by the noxious poisonous fumes.

> We had not been in action a few minutes before the wounded began to
> arrive in the distributing station. The stretcher parties worked splendidly.
> The cries of the wounded and burnt men were very terrible to listen to.
> They were brought in sometimes with feet or hands hanging off. Very
> soon the deck of the distributing station was packed with wounded
> and dying men, and when fresh cases were brought in one had some
> difficulty in avoiding stepping on the others. Very little operating, save of
> an urgent kind was done during the action, though we had an operating
> table ready. The doctors occupied themselves chiefly in first aid work.
> Morphia was given to a lot of the wounded. After a time they all settled
> down and we were able to sort them out putting the slightly wounded
> in one place and the more serious in the other. A certain number of
> men were gassed and it was a sad sight to see them die. They began by
> coughing insistently and then gradually went off in a stupor. The greater
> number of injuries were caused by burns – some men had all their head,
> hands and arms burned, but there were not many burned about the
> body. Those that died were taken out and put in the messdeck port side

abreast of the distributing station. When there was no longer room for the wounded in the distributing station they were placed in the corresponding messdeck, starboard side.[21]

Reverend Thomas Bradley, HMS *Tiger*, 1st Battlecruiser Squadron

The fight grew in severity as the battlecruisers continued to converge on each other and both sides risked severe punishment as the range closed rapidly to about 13,000 yards. In recognition of this, at 15.55 Hipper ordered his ships to turn away to the south-east. A couple of minutes later, Beatty also ordered his ships to turn away from their south-south-east course round by 2 points to the south. This meant that both sides in effect turned away from their enemies and the range began to open out.

In these opening minutes the British rate of fire was increasing, but only the *Queen Mary*, widely considered the crack gunnery ship of the Battlecruiser Fleet, managed to score any hits, as she landed two shells in succession at 15.55 and 15.57 to leave her mark on the *Seydlitz*.

We had not gone unscathed. The first hit we received was a shell that struck the Number Six 6″ casemate on the starboard side, killing everybody except the Padre who, on the way to his battle-station down below, had wanted to take a look at the men and at the British, too. By an odd coincidence we had, at our first battle practice in 1913, assumed the same kind of hit and by the same adversary, the *Queen Mary*. Splinters perforated air leads in the bunker below and smoke and gas consequently entered the starboard main turbine compartment.[22]

Kapitan zur See Moritz von Egidy, SMS *Seydlitz*, I Scouting Group, High Seas Fleet

The second 13.5-inch shell from the *Queen Mary* knocked out the 'C' Turret aboard the *Seydlitz*. This proved a critical test of the new German flash control modifications introduced in response to the harsh lessons meted out at the battle of Dogger Bank aboard the same ship.

The gunnery central station deep down reported: "No answer from 'C' turret. Smoke and gas pouring out of the voice pipes from 'C' turret." That sounded like the time on the Dogger Bank. Then it had been 'C' and 'D' turrets. A shell had burst outside, making only a small hole, but a red-hot piece of steel had ignited a cartridge, the flash setting fire to 13,000 pounds of cordite. 190 men had been killed, and two turrets had been put out of action. Afterwards, a thorough examination showed that everything had been done in accordance with regulations. I told the gunnery officer: "If we lose 190 men and almost the whole ship in accordance with regulations then they are somehow wrong." Therefore we made technical improvements and changed our methods of training as well as the regulations. This time only one cartridge caught fire, the flash did not reach the magazines, and so we lost only 20 dead or severely burned, and only one turret was put out of action.[23]

Kapitän zur See Moritz von Egidy, SMS *Seydlitz*, I Scouting Group, High Seas Fleet

Meanwhile the *Princess Royal* was also beginning to suffer. Just before 16.00 she was hit by a series of shells from the *Derfflinger*. Able Seaman James Herford and several other gunners had been ordered to retire from their action stations on the 4-inch guns to take shelter in the lower deck flats.

There were quite a few sailors there, all dancing to mouth organ music. I said to the Officer in charge, "The shells are dropping all round us, Sir!" "All right", he replied, "Get your respirator, there may be gas shells." Then, all of a sudden, we got an armour piercing liquid fire shell in the flat. Everything went red hot. I fell to the deck. After a while I heard people moaning. Everything was in darkness. No lights. I came to and put my hands to my head and I thought, "I'm not dead, my head's still on!" Then I was picked up by the First Aid men. I could walk after a moment or two and they took me to the sick bay. When I got to the sick bay there seemed to be about 150 dead and wounded, worse than me, I thought, so I walked away and went to the mess deck. An hour later, I blacked out.[24]

Able Seaman James Herford, HMS *Princess Royal*, 1st Battlecruiser Squadron

The *Derfflinger*'s undisturbed target practice was ended after about ten minutes as the *Princess Royal* at last began to return her fire. Now it was von Hase's turn to be transfixed as he watched shells flying towards him.

I again fixed the enemy gun turrets with my periscope and watched them carefully. I now saw that they were directly trained at us. I made a further discovery which astonished me. With each salvo fired by the enemy I was able to see distinctly four or five shells coming through the air. They looked like elongated black spots. Gradually they grew bigger, and then – CRASH! – they were here. They exploded on striking the water or the ship with a terrific roar. After a bit I could tell from watching the shells fairly accurately whether they would fall short or over, or whether they would do us the honour of a visit.[25]

Commander Georg von Hase, SMS *Derfflinger*, I Scouting Group, High Seas Fleet

Aboard the *Lion* they gradually became aware of the accuracy of fire from the *Lützow*.

On the bridge we were blissfully ignorant of the fact that two large shells had exploded in the ship; the rush of wind and other noises caused by the high speed at which we were travelling, together with the roar of our own guns as they fired, four at a time, completely drowned the noise of bursting shell. There was no doubt, however, that we were under heavy fire, because all round us huge columns of water, higher than the funnels, were being thrown up as the enemy shells plunged into the sea. Some of these gigantic splashes curled over and deluged us with water. Occasionally, above the noise of battle, we heard the ominous hum of a shell fragment and caught a glimpse of polished steel as it flashed past the bridge. One of these went clean through the plotting room and dislodged the clock. It was a service clock, however, and seeming to realise the importance of its duty, continued to tick merrily as if nothing unusual had happened![26]

Lieutenant William Chalmers, HMS *Lion*, 1st Battlecruiser Squadron

It was a wild, exhilarating scene with danger scything towards them from seemingly every angle.

Shells were all over the place and splinters by thousands were flying all over the whole ship and the air was full of them. It was a wonder the officers and men on the bridge weren't hit, as it was, the ladder from the bridge to the director tower was shot way at the bottom and consequently had to be made fast to one of the stanchions on the fore-bridge.[27]

Midshipman Anthony Combe, HMS *Lion*, 1st Battlecruiser Squadron

The rate of fire was increasing and at last the *Lion* began to get the range right.

As to the enemy, it appeared as though he had commenced at 167hm, been well over and had spent an endless time in getting on. *Lion*'s first straddling salvo after nine minutes was therefore quite a surprise.[28]

Commander Günther Paschen, SMS *Lützow*, I Scouting Group, High Seas Fleet

At 16.00 the *Lützow* struck what could have been a decisive blow, as a 12-inch shell burst on the top of the left gun of 'Q' Turret. The blast peeled back the roof and front of the turret as if it were cardboard and killed or wounded most of the crew.

The enemy's shooting at the *Lion* became extremely accurate and she sheered a little to starboard, the effect as to fall of shot being very noticeable. Just as she came back again she was very heavily hit and I saw a large plate, which I judged to be the top of a turret, blown into the air. It appeared to rise very slowly, turning round and round, and looking very much like an aeroplane. I should say it rose some 400 or 500 feet and looking at it though glasses I could distinctly see the holes in it for the bolts. My attention was drawn from this by a sheet of flame by her second funnel, which shot up about 60 feet and soon died down, but did not immediately disappear. It seemed to have no effect on the ship, except that her midship turret seemed out of action. One gun was about horizontal and the other one at a considerable elevation.[29]

Commander Alan Mackenzie-Grieve, HMS *Birmingham*, 2nd Light Cruiser Squadron

The roof of the turret crashed back onto the deck of the injured *Lion*. The now open-topped turret caught fire and there was an obvious danger to the whole ship if the fire spread to the magazine.

A heavier explosion than usual occurred and dense smoke came down the trunk, stopping progress until we had shipped our respirators. Two men were then brought up from the shell room, both had been working in the gunhouse, and were badly wounded, they were passed along the messdeck to the medical station. Standing by the magazine door I heard the Officer of Turret give the order, "Close magazine doors – 'Q' Turret out of action!" The Corporal and I closed the port magazine door and clipped it up.[30]

Private H. Willons, Royal Marine Light Infantry, HMS *Lion*, I st Battlecruiser Squadron

The 'Q' Turret was manned by the Royal Marines under Major Francis Harvey. He was mortally wounded and had lost both of his legs. But in the last moments of his consciousness he retained the presence of mind to issue crucial orders to flood the magazine and for his sergeant major to report the situation to the bridge.

> I heard a resounding "Clank!" behind me. Turning round from the compass which I was watching carefully to ensure that the Chief Quartermaster below in the conning tower was steering that steady course which is so important for gunnery, I saw a large flame spring up from 'Q' Turret. Those on the bridge who had been looking aft told me the armoured roof of 'Q' Turret had gone up in the air and fallen on the upper deck. Realising that the magazine might be in danger, I told the conning tower to order 'Q' magazine to be flooded immediately. My order, however, had been forestalled by Major Harvey, RMLI, the turret commander. It was lucky he had done so, for every second counts in such an emergency and, as is well known he gave the order with his last words. A little later my attention was drawn to a figure which had just come up the bridge ladder. His face was black from fire, his hair singed, his clothes burnt. Saluting in strict formality, he reported, "'Q' Turret knocked out, Sir!"[31]
>
> Flag Captain Alfred Chatfield, HMS *Lion*, 1st Battlecruiser Squadron

Although there is some confusion as to whether Major Harvey's orders were actually carried out prior to the intervention of Captain Chatfield, he has been generally given the credit for the prompt flooding of the 'Q' magazine, which was to have great significance before the battle was through. In recognition of his gallant actions, Harvey was awarded a posthumous Victoria Cross. Nevertheless, the *Lion* was badly damaged and for a moment she staggered out of the line to starboard, a move possibly exacerbated by a mistake in the handling of the ship. From the German perspective, the *Princess Royal* seemed to have taken over the leadership of the British line.

> Seventeen minutes after fire was opened *Lion* turned sharply away, until we could see her from aft and *Princess Royal* pushed in front. I counted six hits in 31 salvoes. We have been hit three times; one of these exploded between 'A' and 'B' Turrets and cleared out the forward action

dressing station. All are dead there. Hit No. 3 seems to have hit the belt somewhere, a heavy shock but nothing put out of action.[32]

Commander Günther Paschen, SMS *Lützow*, I Scouting Group, High Seas Fleet

As the battle raged, some miles behind the Fifth Battle Squadron were desperately trying to catch up although they were still steering east rather than heading south. The super-dreadnoughts were too far away to engage the German battlecruisers but as they raced along at around 24 knots they seized the chance at about 16.00 to engage the German light cruisers of the II Scouting Group. Commander Humphrey Walwyn was at his duty station in 'B' Turret of the *Warspite*.

Got orders to "Load and train Red 20". Could not see anything at all; hazy and a lot of smoke about. We were now steaming very hard. Wondered if our steering jackstaff would be shot away, as we had just fitted a new one. Everybody in the turret in very good spirits, and I asked Grenfell if he had any cotton wool. He said he hadn't and passed me a lump of cotton waste, enough to stop the ears of a donkey, which I chucked back at him.[33]

Commander Humphrey Walwyn, HMS *Warspite*, 5th Battle Squadron

Although visibility was not good, the *Warspite* opened fire at long range on the German light cruisers. The complexity of the battle was deepening. It was no longer just another battlecruiser encounter.

I made out five columns of smoke in the mist and that was all I could see, no masts or anything else. Opened fire on light cruisers, range about 21,000 yards. Could see the fall of shot well, but could not see at all what we were firing at. Fired a few rounds by director and saw *Barham* and *Valiant* were firing too; light cruisers were getting clearer now. Suddenly saw on No. 2 a column of smoke break out into a bright flame; this dropped astern and at first I thought she was hit, but later I thought it was a smoke box, as it looked like an enormous calcium life buoy, bright flame and huge white smoke cloud drifting astern.[34]

Commander Humphrey Walwyn, HMS *Warspite*, 5th Battle Squadron

As Walwyn speculated, a buoy had indeed been dropped from the *Frankfurt* in an effort to distract the British fire. For in sharp contrast to the performance of the British battlecruisers, the super-dreadnoughts immediately demonstrated a much greater accuracy of fire. With only their third salvoes they straddled the German line and it was noticeable that the shells were all tightly grouped together.

> Out of the blue came a heavy barrage of fire from the south west. We were suddenly surrounded by high fountains of water. Out of the distance four big ships appeared which Bödicker thought to be of the 2nd British Battle Squadron but very soon we could see a second mast and it was clear that it belonged to the very modern battleships of the 5th Battle Squadron of the *Queen Elizabeth* class. The distance was 17km. We could just see the enemy on the horizon. With our 15cm guns we could only manage about 13–14km and under these circumstances we could hardly fight back. We were not equipped for anything like this. We turned quickly, glad to get out of it.[35]
>
> Lieutenant Heinrich Bassenge, SMS *Elbing*, II Scouting Group, High Seas Fleet

The German light cruisers and the accompanying destroyer made smoke to conceal their rapid retreat. At 16.06 the Fifth Battle Squadron turned from their easterly course in stages round to the south-east. Evan-Thomas was following the battlecruisers and cutting corners wherever he could to try to close the distance between them.

The pace of the main engagement between the battlecruisers remained frenetic. At the rear of the line the *Indefatigable* was engaged in a rancorous single-ship duel with her opposite number, the *Von der Tann*. A few minutes before 16.00 one of the signallers was ordered aloft to clear their signal flags which had become entangled round the mast as the ship manoeuvred in battle.

> The message came up for someone to go aloft to clear the flags. I went up, took my sea boots off first, climbed out the foretop, went up the 'Jacob's Ladder' right to the very top. I unfurled the flag and I sat on the wireless yard looking around, naturally watching the firing.[36]
>
> Signaller C. Falmer, HMS *Indefatigable*, 2nd Battlecruiser Squadron

From the still distant *Malaya* of the Fifth Battle Squadron, Sub-Lieutenant Caslon watched this Wagnerian duel through a 5-inch slit in the armour.

I could not see the enemy, who were on the far side of the battlecruisers, but I could see the splashes of their shells falling round our ships. Both Tillstone and I were watching absolutely fascinated, and suddenly he said, "Look at that!" I thought for an instant that the last ship in the line had fired all her guns at once, as there was a much bigger flame, but the flame grew and grew till it was about 300 feet high, and the whole ship was hidden in a dense cloud of yellow brown smoke. This cloud hung in the air for some minutes and when it finally dispersed there was no sign of the ship. Although I did not know the order of the battlecruiser line, I had a feeling it was the *Indefatigable* in which I had a very great friend.[37]

Sub-Lieutenant Clifford Caslon, HMS *Malaya*, Fifth Battle Squadron

It was indeed the hapless *Indefatigable*. In a highly visible disaster, which occurred right in front of the aghast Battlecruiser Fleet, a salvo from the *Von der Tann* had crashed down onto the ship at 16.02. By accident or design the *Indefatigable* sheered out of line to starboard and a few seconds later was hit by a second salvo, which provoked the huge explosion. Accounts as to exactly what happened are slightly contradictory and until her sunken wreck can be examined in detail by marine archaeologists it will not be possible to say with any certainty what the sequence of events was. But it seems likely that the cordite charges in the 'X' Turret were ignited and a flash passed down to the magazines aft. However, it is entirely possible that a shell penetrated right through the armour and set off the magazine directly.

There was a colossal double explosion in our line, which we could see was the *Indefatigable*. It was an awful sight, even at the distance we were off; I could clearly see huge funnels, turrets etc flying through the air, while the column of flame and smoke must have been at least 1,500 feet high.[38]

Sub-Lieutenant Edward Cordeaux, HMS *Lapwing*, 1st Flotilla

The fortunate Falmer was still aloft in the foretop when the 11-inch shells struck. From within the eye of the storm he witnessed a moment of stupefying destruction.

There was a terrific explosion aboard the ship – the magazines went. I saw the guns go up in the air just like matchsticks – 12″ guns they were – bodies and everything. She was beginning to settle down. Within half a minute the ship turned right over and she was gone. I was 180 foot up and I was thrown well clear of the ship, otherwise I would have been sucked under. I was practically unconscious, turning over really. At last I came on top of the water. When I came up there was another fellow named Jimmy Green and we got a piece of wood. He was on one end and I was on the other end. A couple of minutes afterwards some shells came over and Jim was minus his head – so I was left on my lonesome.[39]

Signaller C. Falmer, HMS *Indefatigable*, 2nd Battlecruiser Squadron

The battle moved on and he was left isolated in the North Sea surrounded by nothing but debris from the ship that had been his home.

There was nothing to be seen, only the Fifth Battle Squadron coming along. They started to open fire and the German shells were dropping short. I could feel them myself in the water – my feet, my legs. They went and about half an hour later four German cruisers came along so I ducked my head down, because, probably, if they had seen me they would have put in a shot at me – they would have done, to put you out of your misery you see. Then they cleared off and it turned dark. There wasn't a sound, nobody near me. It was pitch dark, I'd given up all hope practically – I let go once but I struggled back again quick. Between half past two and three all of a sudden I could hear something coming towards me. I gazed up and it was a destroyer. They stopped, two German sailors got down on the fender, grabbed me by the shoulders and pulled me aboard. I didn't remember nothing till next morning. When I came to I was in the engine room, they were mopping me down with waste – I was smothered in oil fuel.[40]

Signaller C. Falmer, HMS *Indefatigable*, 2nd Battlecruiser Squadron

There was just one other survivor, Able Seaman Elliott, who had also been in the top. The other 1,017 men serving aboard were all killed. A whole ship's company not wounded, crippled or mentally scarred – just dead. From the alternative German perspective it was a moment of triumph and the first inkling that the British battlecruisers that had harried them across the North Sea for the past two years were by no means invulnerable.

Suddenly we saw in the distance a big pillar of fire which grew bigger and bigger. It was too misty to see exactly what was going on, but it was clear that they were Beatty's battlecruisers and one of them must have been hit. Everybody was overjoyed. Now we became very hopeful after a deep depression.[41]

Lieutenant Heinrich Bassenge, SMS *Elbing*, II Scouting Group, High Seas Fleet

Perhaps the most cold-blooded reaction of all came from the bridge of the *Lion*. Captain Chatfield, for one, clearly took such matters in his stride.

The *Lion* was hit early several times, but we seemed also to be hitting the *Lützow* and were going along joyfully, when, at 4.00pm, the Yeoman of Signals saw (and reported) the rear ship, the *Indefatigable* blow up. A vast column of smoke rose to the sky. This seemed at the moment just a disappointment. The *Indefatigable* was a smaller and more weakly protected ship than those of the first division and was not a really serious tactical loss.[42]

Flag Captain Alfred Chatfield, HMS *Lion*, 1st Battlecruiser Squadron

Following the loss of the *Indefatigable* the two battlecruiser fleets were now equally matched in number, and both sides, as a matter of course, tried to take on their opposite numbers in the line. This was often easier said than done in the assorted confusions of a smoke-wreathed battle. The initial problems encountered by the British in sorting out their fire distribution had been an irritant and more symptomatic of a lack of professionalism within the Battlecruiser Fleet than a significant disturbance to the course of events. What had proved more serious was the absence during the early stages of the action of the Fifth Battle Squadron, left trailing behind and still heading east. Their fire at the German light cruisers was irrelevant to any rational assessment of the outcome of the main battle and occurred while the *Indefatigable* was losing her single-ship duel with the *Moltke*. If the Fifth Battle Squadron had been in close support alongside Beatty as Jellicoe had intended, then, although the *Indefatigable* might still have been lost, it is reasonably certain that Hipper's battlecruisers would have suffered a much more severe pounding as the price for their success.

It was only at 16.05 that the 'forgotten squadron' finally sighted the German battlecruisers, and they opened fire at extreme range a minute or so later. After the initial rounds the *Barham* and *Valiant* fired at the *Moltke* while the *Warspite* and *Malaya* aimed at the *Von der Tann*. Sub-Lieutenant Eric Brand was at his station as rate officer operating the Dumaresq instrument in the 15-inch gun control tower aboard the *Valiant*.

> When rather idly searching the horizon with my glasses out of the port slit of the tower, I saw a German ship and exclaimed, "My God, it's the *Von der Tann*!" and getting busy estimating her 'inclination' and speed. As soon as we could we opened fire at a range of 22,000 yards or at any rate the time of flight was around 45 seconds. In those days we only fired one four-gun salvo and waited to see the splash before making any correction to the range and firing the next salvo. Nobody had thought of double salvoes separated by a definite amount of range in those days. That was one of the lessons we learnt that day.[43]
>
> Sub-Lieutenant Eric Brand, HMS *Valiant*, Fifth Battle Squadron

The belated arrival of the British super-dreadnoughts was a serious matter for the *Von der Tann* and *Moltke*, for as battlecruisers they had not been designed to cope with the crushing impact of the huge 1,920-pound shells that almost immediately began falling around them.

> Our navigation officer came back and said we had the British Fifth Battle Squadron in front of us now. He said they were all dangerous fellows, they only fire 38cm shells. We continuously heard the noise, through the battle, of the shells passing over our heads, but in spite of it they missed. Suddenly we received a hit. It was most peculiar, it entered the stern of the ship without damaging any screws or rudder. *Von der Tann* continued unperturbed but the hit in the stern had a funny effect. The vibration travelled from the stern to the front and back to the stern. Altogether we received four heavy hits from 38cm shells and quite a bit of water entered the ship. My navigation officer sent me to his room to fetch something and I had a little time to look round. There was lots of damage and a few dead. Lots of blood everywhere. A young sailor was crouched on the floor looking very bad, losing a lot of blood, he had been hit in the arm. He was trying to bandage his own arm. I tried to help him but he said, "No!" in a very weak voice. "Go upstairs and fight!"[44]
>
> Seaman Carl Melms, SMS *Von der Tann*, I Scouting Group, High Seas Fleet

As the action widened, the seriously outnumbered German battlecruisers inevitably suffered some painful blows.

> We also sustained some injury and the steel hulls trembled under the weight of the impact. Led by the first lieutenants, there commenced in the interior of each ship a hard fight against the destruction wrought by the great shells, and against all that they brought in their wake, fire and water, which, fighting blindly against friend and foe alike, developed their powers of evil.[45]
>
> Commander Albert Scheibe, I Scouting Group, High Seas Fleet

The German attempts at damage control were hampered by the shells that continued to crash round them.

> All around heavy shells are falling, raising waterspouts as high as the tops, often so close to the vessels that the masses of water they raise fall on the decks. Splinters of shell are hurled screaming across the deck and through the superstructure. Huge flames blaze up roaring from the bursting of giant shells, melting and charring everything that they touch.[46]
>
> Commander Albert Scheibe, I Scouting Group, High Seas Fleet

At 16.18 the *Von der Tann* had no option but to switch her fire onto the *Barham*. Unsubdued by the unequal match, her general accuracy was still impressive.

> Blast from 'A' Turret was awfully bad and blew salt water and dust into my eyes, which watered like blazes. I saw several of their salvoes splash short of us; they fell into an extraordinary small spread and made the devil of a noise. Caught sight of *Valiant* and *Barham* through the corner of my eye, and saw *Barham* 'straddled' once or twice. I realised we were steering south and it crossed my mind whether we should meet the High Seas Fleet.[47]
>
> Commander Humphrey Walwyn, HMS *Warspite*, Fifth Battle Squadron

Aboard the *Barham*, Midshipman Roger Frampton was at his post in 'X' Turret.

> It soon became very stuffy in our turret and an occasional fault in the air blasts (blowers which blew the smoke out of the guns after firing) caused

smoke to lie about in the gunhouse with an unpleasant smell so that we had to keep open the breech-blocks for a time to let it out. Enemy shells hitting the water close to the ship made a noise like a gun going off and heard through the open guns, had a very disagreeable metallic ring which jarred one's eardrums.[48]

Midshipman Roger Frampton, HMS *Barham*, Fifth Battle Squadron

But the fight was always going to be an unequal one. The heavy British shells took a visible toll on the rear of the German line.

They 'straddled' us once or twice, but we had not been hit at all so far. I think they were zig-zagging very much, as their deflection was very hard to pick up. I distinctly saw one salvo hit No. 5, and she turned away about 6 points to port and went away in a cloud of black and white smoke. We turned our attention to No. 4, as No. 5 was by this time out of range and the guns on the stops at 23,000 yards. It was a wonderful and rather horrible sight to see the constant orange flicker of flame along the line when they fired. After the flame there was a white cloud, like steam, which was very deceptive and looked like hits.[49]

Commander Humphrey Walwyn, HMS *Warspite*, Fifth Battle Squadron

As the Fifth Battle Squadron came up into the fray, Beatty returned to the attack. At 16.09 he ordered Captain James Farie, commanding the 13th Flotilla, to launch his destroyers into an attack on the German line. Three minutes later he turned his battlecruisers back to the east, giving him a course of south-south-east – closing with the Germans. At the same time Hipper turned to the west and, at 16.17, once more the great ships were on a rapidly converging course and the battle ratcheted up to a new and awful intensity.

In peacetime gunnery exercises, the firing of a salvo of heavy guns, when you are as close to them as we were on the compass platform, is disturbing; you seem momentarily to be slightly lifted from the deck, perhaps you put your fingers in your ears, as it had not become the fashion in those days to use cotton wool, or ear plugs to save your delicate ear-drums. But in action all this feeling vanishes. So often and so rapidly do the salvoes follow each other that you do not hear many of them at all; your mind becomes attuned to the four, or eight, 13.5″ guns

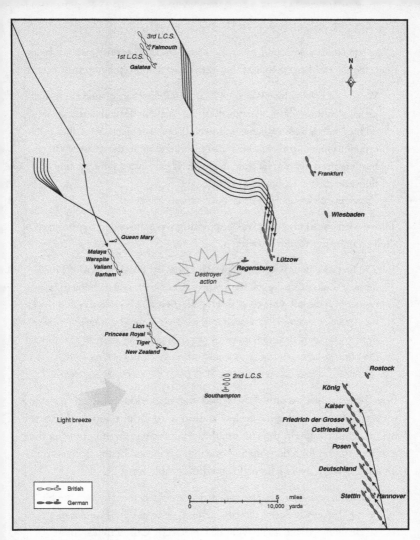

The end of the run to the south

with their quite severe blast – which had actually blown my cap off my head and overboard already. Rather is your feeling, "Why do they not fire quicker?" At one moment in this action I turned to Seymour, the Flag Lieutenant, and said, "Why are they not firing?" He told me a salvo had been fired five seconds before I spoke. I had not heard it![50]

Flag Captain Alfred Chatfield, HMS *Lion*, 1st Battlecruiser Squadron

As the shells continued to crunch into the *Lion* even those far below decks could not but be aware that they were taking heavy punishment.

> We were receiving hits. We could hear a rumbling sort of noise as a shell penetrated through the armour deck and then the deafening roar as it erupted into a mass of flame and steel. If one was near one of these eruptions there seemed to be a big quivering flash in the midst of the hurtling mass like a great shining mirror. It only lasted for a fraction of time and then it was gone.[51]
>
> Stoker D. Maclachlan, HMS *Lion*, 1st Battlecruiser Squadron

Those who could see what was happening were absorbed by the sight of shells screaming towards them.

> The first half hour was very unpleasant from my point of view as I had nothing to do except watch the enemy salvoes, each one seeming to be nearer than the last. One could feel the ship being hit occasionally and twice the conning tower was illuminated by the flash of a shell bursting somewhere near. Fortunately the noise made by our own guns was so great that one did not take so much notice as would otherwise have been the case.[52]
>
> Midshipman Nevill Garnons-Williams, HMS *Lion*, 1st Battlecruiser Squadron

Boy Telegraphist Arthur Lewis had the hazardous duty of carrying messages from the main wireless station across the open decks to the bridge. Unfortunately, the vulnerable aerials were soon put out of action, a serious matter for a flagship and one that prevented Beatty from communicating directly with Jellicoe for a considerable time.

> The main aerials of the *Lion* got carried away, whether through the hit on 'Q' Turret which was directly under it, or by gunfire I cannot now say. I volunteered to go up with the Chief Petty Officer Telegraphist to repair and rig up the battle (jury) aerial and secure it to the main mast. It was a particularly bad time, shrapnel bursting all around, shells whistling overhead, our speed, approximately 26 knots, did not make the task any easier. My hat whisked away and landed in one of the picket boats; it was then I felt really scared and prayed I might be spared to be able to get down into the comparative safety of 'below decks'.[53]
>
> Boy Telegraphist Arthur Lewis, HMS *Lion*, 1st Battlecruiser Squadron

It took around twenty minutes to complete the work of erecting the jury aerial, but to young Lewis it felt like a lifetime.

Behind them, the *Queen Mary* was still engaged in an evenly balanced contest with the *Seydlitz* until an unfortunate set of circumstances severely disadvantaged the *Queen Mary*. When the damaged *Lion* weaved to starboard and temporarily dropped out of the British line, von Hase, aboard the *Derfflinger*, could not see what was happening. In consequence, when he attempted to engage the second battlecruiser he could see in the British line, he actually inadvertently switched his fire from the *Princess Royal* to the *Queen Mary* at 16.17. Hampered by smoke, for a while von Hase handed over direct control to his spotting officer in the foretop. Now his pre-battle fantasies were becoming a reality, as the leviathans exchanged mighty blows – although it was hardly a fair fight at two to one. With both the *Seydlitz* and *Derfflinger* firing hard at the *Queen Mary*, the barrage of accurate shells soon began to tell.

> There was a heavy blow, struck, I should imagine in the after 4″ Battery and a lot of dust and pieces flying around on top of 'X' Turret. My attention was called by the turret trainer, A. B. Long, who reported the front glass of his periscope blocked up. This was not very important because we were in director training, but someone in the rear heard him report his glass foul and without orders dashed on top and cleared it. He must have been smashed as he did it, for he fell in front of the periscope, groaning and then apparently fell off the turret. I wish I knew his name, poor chap, but it's no use guessing.[54]
>
> Petty Officer Ernest Francis, HMS *Queen Mary*, 1st Battlecruiser Squadron

Another crunching blow landed on the midship turret of the *Queen Mary*.

> Everything went beautifully until, 4.21, when 'Q' Turret was hit by a heavy shell and the right gun put out of action. We continued firing with the left gun for two or three minutes and then a most awful explosion took place which broke the ship in half by the foremast. Our left gun broke off outside the turret and the rear end fell into the working chamber; the right gun also slid down. The turret was filled

with flying metal and several men were killed. A lot of cordite caught
fire below me and blazed up and several people were gassed.[55]

Midshipman Jocelyn Storey, HMS *Queen Mary*, 1st Battlecruiser Squadron

As the next German salvoes crashed home the situation span out of
control. One shell detonated a forward magazine of either 'A' or 'B'
Turret.

Then came the big explosion, which shook us a bit, and on looking at the
pressure gauge I saw the pressure had failed. Immediately after that came
what I term the 'big smash' and I was dangling in the air on a bowline,
which saved me from being thrown down on to the floor of the turret.
These bowlines were an idea I brought into my turret and each man in
the gunhouse was supplied with one. As far as I noticed the men who
had them on were not injured in the 'big smash'. No 2 and 3 gun crew of
the left gun slipped down under the gun and the gun appeared to me to
have fallen through its trunnions and smashed up these two numbers.[56]

Petty Officer Ernest Francis, HMS *Queen Mary*, 1st Battlecruiser Squadron

For a moment there was an illusion of silence, probably caused by a
mixture of temporary deafness and mind-numbing shock.

Everything in the ship went as quiet as a church, the floor of the turret
was bulged up and the guns were absolutely useless. I must mention here
that there was not a sign of excitement. One man turned to me and
said, "What do you think has happened?" I said, "Steady everyone,
I will speak to Mr Ewart." I went back to the cabinet and said,
"What do you think has happened, Sir?" He said, "God only knows!"
"Well, Sir", I said, "it's no use keeping them all down here, why not send
them up round the 4″ guns and give them a chance to fight it out."[57]

Petty Officer Ernest Francis, HMS *Queen Mary*, 1st Battlecruiser Squadron

Francis was ordered to check on the state of the 4-inch battery but he
did not get far before he realized that the game was up.

I put my head up through the hole in the roof of the turret and I nearly
fell through again. The after 4″ Battery was smashed right out of all
recognition and then I noticed that the ship had an awful list to port.
I dropped back inside the turret and told Lieutenant Ewart the state of

affairs. He said, "Francis, we can do no more than give them a chance, clear the turret." "Clear the turret!" I called out, and out they went.[58]

Petty Officer Ernest Francis, HMS *Queen Mary*, 1st Battlecruiser Squadron

Throughout the ship it was apparent that something was seriously wrong. The damage was such that the ship could never survive.

There was a terrific explosion forward and I was sent out on the top of our after turret to see what was happening. I had to put on lung respirators owing to clouds of smoke and fire. I could see nothing for about a minute and then all cleared away as the foremost part of the ship went under water. I then told the officer of the turret that the ship was sinking rapidly and so as many as possible were got up out of the turret.[59]

Midshipman Peregrine Dearden, HMS *Queen Mary*, 1st Battlecruiser Squadron

Midshipman John Lloyd Owen was still inside 'X' Turret.

There was a terrific explosion in the fore part of the vessel. I asked the working chamber if they had anything to report. They answered all pressure had failed, both guns being out of action. I reported this to the officer of the turret, Lieutenant Ewart. He told me that the ship was going down and would probably sink in a few minutes. I asked him for orders and he told me to send up the gunhouse crew on deck which I did.[60]

Midshipman John Lloyd Owen, HMS *Queen Mary*, 1st Battlecruiser Squadron

The scramble to escape from deep inside the turrets was desperate, but some men had personal courage that led them far beyond the normal call of duty. They could not bring themselves to escape until all their men were accounted for.

Petty Officer Stares was the last I saw coming up from the working chamber and he told me it was no use as the water was right up the trunk leading from the shell room, so the bottom of the ship must have been out of her. Then I said, "Why didn't you come up?" He simply said, "There was no order to leave the turret." I went through the cabinet and out through the top and Lieutenant Ewart was following me; suddenly he stopped and went back into the turret. I believe he went back because he thought there was someone left inside.[61]

Petty Officer Ernest Francis, HMS *Queen Mary*, 1st Battlecruiser Squadron

By this time the ship was in its death throes. The deck heeled over to port at an angle of more than 45 degrees.

> The ship had an awful list to port by this time, so much so that men getting off the ladder went sliding down to port. I got on to the bottom rung of the ladder and could not by my own efforts reach the stanchions lying on the deck from the ships side, starboard side. I knew if I let go that I should go sliding down to port like some of the others must have done – and probably got smashed up sliding down. Two of my turret's crew, seeing my difficulty, came to my assistance; they were A. B. Long, turret trainer and A. B. Lane, left gun No. 4. Lane held Long at full stretch from the ship's side and I dropped from the ladder, caught Long's legs and so gained the starboard side. These two men had no thought for their own safety. They saw I wanted assistance and that was good enough for them, they were both worth a VC twice over.[62]
> Petty Officer Ernest Francis, HMS *Queen Mary*, 1st Battlecruiser Squadron

Behind them aboard the *Tiger*, Able Seaman Victor Hayward watched as Francis and the rest of the 'X' Turret men struggled onto the deck.

> One by one, men could be seen coming out of the after turret and climbing down on to the exposed bilge keel and jumping into the water. Also, rolls and rolls of white paper came streaming out of her after hatch situated on her quarterdeck. These must have been spare rolls of Dreyer's chart paper, because her gunnery office was situated close to the after hatch. It went trailing away over the boiling sea like a shaking toilet roll. When quite a few men were already in the water, the second explosion occurred.[63]
> Able Seaman Victor Hayward, HMS *Tiger*, 1st Battlecruiser Squadron

Inevitably, some men hesitated before entering the water. Although they were all supposed to be able to swim, it is a fool who entrusts his life to the waves of the North Sea unnecessarily. As ever, some were convinced that their ship would yet survive despite the overwhelming evidence to the contrary.

> When I got to the ship's side there seemed to be a fair crowd and they did not appear to be very anxious to take to the water. I called out to

them, "Come on, you chaps, who's coming for a swim?" Someone answered, "She will float for a long time yet!" But something, I don't pretend to understand what it was, seemed to be urging me to get away, so I clambered up over the slimy bilge keel and fell off into the water, followed, I should think, by about five more men.[64]

Petty Officer Ernest Francis, HMS *Queen Mary*, 1st Battlecruiser Squadron

After emerging from the turret Lloyd Owen faced a damnable scene. Repeated explosions were tearing the *Queen Mary* to pieces about him.

After all the men had gone out of the turret I went up myself and found the ship lying on her side. She was broken amidships, her bows were sticking up in the air and the stern was also sticking out at an angle of about 45 degrees from the water. I was standing on the back of the turret which was practically level, the turret still being trained to port fore most bearing, the vessel lying on her port side. I looked towards the stern and saw that it was red hot and that all the plates had been blown away, nothing but the framework remained. All around us men were falling off into the water. A few moments afterwards a tremendous explosion occurred in the fore part of the vessel, which must have blown the bows to atoms. The stern part gave a tremendous lurch, throwing me off into the water. Just before entering the water another explosion occurred, apparently just above my head. I sank a considerable distance and on reaching the surface could see nothing of the ship only a great deal of wreckage and oil fuel floating on the surface.[65]

Midshipman John Lloyd Owen, HMS *Queen Mary*, 1st Battlecruiser Squadron

Amidships, Midshipman Storey and remnants of the 'Q' Turret crew were emerging into a scene of devastation.

The men left and myself got to the ladder leading out of the turret and climbed quickly out. There was no panic or shouting at all, the men were splendid heroes. Just as I got out of the turret and climbed over the funnels and masts which were lying beside the turret, and had got off my coat and one shoe, another awful explosion occurred blowing me into the water. The remaining part of the ship, the after part, blew up, the 'X' Turret magazine going off.[66]

Midshipman Jocelyn Storey, HMS *Queen Mary*, 1st Battlecruiser Squadron

Preferring the cold of the water to the weight of wet clothing, Midshipman Dearden had removed his heavy uniform, leaving nothing but his shirt and vest, before entering the water.

> As soon as I was in the water I swam clear and astern of the ship about 30 yards when she suddenly blew up completely. I was luckily sucked under water and so all the wreckage chucked about did not come with its full weight on my head. I held my breath for a long time and at last came to the surface. I started looking round for something to support me as much as possible.[67]
>
> Midshipman Peregrine Dearden, HMS *Queen Mary*, 1st Battlecruiser Squadron

Their last glimpses of the stricken giant that had been their home were through masses of billowing black smoke and falling debris. The final convulsions of the *Queen Mary* were visible right across the fleet as she disappeared in a final paroxysm.

> The *Queen Mary* was obliterated by an 800-feet-high mushroom of fiery smoke, in this case I remember seeing bits of her flying up. As I watched this fiery gravestone, it seemed to waver slightly at the base and I caught a momentary but clear glimpse of the hull of the *Queen Mary* sticking out of the water from the stern to the after funnel.[68]
>
> Lieutenant Stephen King-Hall, HMS *Southampton*, 2nd Light Cruiser Squadron

The final explosions which tore the ship apart were cataclysmic and probably killed most of the men in the water near the ship as the crushing shock waves passed through the water followed by a storm of debris falling from the sky. Of her company of 1,286 men there were just twenty survivors.

> I struck away from the ship as hard as I could and must have covered nearly 50 yards when there was a big smash. Stopping and looking round the air seemed to be full of fragments and flying pieces, a large piece seemed to be right above my head and acting on an impulse I dipped under to avoid being struck and stayed under as long as I could and then came to the top again. Coming behind me I heard a rush of water, which looked very much like a surf breaking on a beach and I realised it was the suction or backwash from the ship which had just

gone. I hardly had time to fill my lungs with air when it was on me.
I felt it was no use struggling against it, so I let myself go for a moment
or two, then I struck out, but I felt it was a losing game and remarked to
myself mentally, "What's the use of you struggling – you're done!" and
actually eased my efforts to reach the top, when a small voice seemed to
say, "Dig out!" I started afresh and something bumped against me.
I grasped it and afterwards found it was a large hammock; it undoubtedly
pulled me to the top, more dead than alive. I rested on it, but I felt I was
getting very weak and roused myself sufficiently to look around for
something more substantial to support me. Floating right in front of me
was what I believed to be the centre bulk of our pattern four target.
I managed to push myself on the hammock close to the timber and
grasped a piece of rope hanging over the side. My next difficulty was to
get on top and I was beginning to give up hope when the swell lifted me
nearly on top and with a small amount of exertion I kept on. I managed
to reeve my arms through a strop and I must have become
unconscious.[69]

Petty Officer Ernest Francis, HMS *Queen Mary*, 1st Battlecruiser Squadron

Midshipman Storey, too, was almost drawn down for ever by the incredible suction generated as the huge bulk of the *Queen Mary* slid down
beneath the waves.

I was sucked down and down in the water, swallowed pints and a lot
of oil and gave up hope, but eventually got to the surface and got hold
of a floating lifebelt. There was nothing left of the ship except some
wreckage and a few heads bobbing in the water. After about five minutes
the Fifth Battle Squadron passed me firing grandly and all the German
shells were falling short and near us in the water. The swell they made in
passing washed me under again, and then I got hold of a plank. About
ten minutes later, a Division of our destroyers passed and appeared not
to see us, in reality they did and signalled for help, being unable to stop
themselves. This was the worst part and a lot of people gave up hope
and sank. I was again washed clear of my wood by the swell of these
destroyers and went down a bit, but eventually got two bits of wood
under my arms and was kept up.[70]

Midshipman Jocelyn Storey, HMS *Queen Mary*, 1st Battlecruiser Squadron

Men clung on to whatever floating wreckage they could find. It may have been summer but the North Sea was bitterly cold.

> The surface of the water was simply covered with oil fuel which tasted and smelt horrible. I smothered myself all over with it, which I think really saved my life as the water was really frightfully cold. I should say that about 50 hands went over the side, but about half of these were killed during the second explosion. Most of the remainder of us held out on two or three spars and other wreckage on the surface. Shortly afterwards several of our destroyers came up but only one stopped.[71]
>
> Midshipman Peregrine Dearden, HMS *Queen Mary*, 1st Battlecruiser Squadron

The destroyer was the *Laurel*, which had been stationed on the starboard – disengaged – beam of the *Queen Mary*. Able Seaman Albert Hickson was at his action stations as the sight setter on her forward 4-inch gun.

> We turned to port and under very heavy fire started to pick up survivors. This was made extremely difficult, because in addition to the very heavy shelling the sea was a mass of wreckage and all sorts of ship's parts, wood and masses of bits of boats and decking. We had lowered our whaler but the wreckage was so thick we could not force the boat through it. We abandoned the boat and somehow we were hauled aboard. Then nearly all our guns crew and the upper deck hands were hanging over the side on fenders, lines and nets trying to get the survivors aboard. This was made so very difficult because they were all soaked in oil and we could not hold on to them for very long, especially as we were steaming ahead so as not to present a sitting target to the enemy. We picked up 11 survivors, all except one were in a very bad state. As we steamed away we noticed about half a dozen survivors on a raft. They cheered us and I believe they hoped we would pick them up. The only uninjured *Queen Mary* survivor we picked up was the left gunlayer of 'X' Turret. He was a Petty Officer and though shocked, he stood with some of us at the break of the foc'sle, drinking a basin of soup.[72]
>
> Able Seaman Albert Hickson, HMS *Laurel*, 9/10th Flotilla

As Hickson observed, many of the men in the water were wounded and many were in a pretty bad way. Midshipman Storey was one of the lucky few picked up by the *Laurel*, as was Midshipman Lloyd Owen, who had been knocked unconscious by the incredible concussive effect of a German shell bursting close to him in the water. He awoke to find himself safe on the forecastle with no idea of how he had got there.

Of necessity, the *Laurel*'s search for survivors, however pitiful their state, was by no means exhaustive. A mass of flotsam and jetsam covered the sea and shells were still falling in the vicinity. Destroyers could not afford to lose their station as part of the screen covering the battlecruisers against the threat of submarines. Inevitably, some survivors suffered the mortifying fate of being abandoned to their fate as the *Laurel* steamed off.

> It nearly drove one frantic when she steamed off when I was only about 25 or 30 yards away from her. She would not even leave her whaler behind to pick up the remaining 15 or 20 of us in the water, although I shouted to them to do so. Afterwards it was terrible seeing everyone else collapse and drown and I had not the strength to help any of them.[73]
>
> Midshipman Peregrine Dearden, HMS *Queen Mary*, 1st Battlecruiser Squadron

From the *Derfflinger*, the destruction of the *Queen Mary* seemed literally a dream come true for Commander von Hase.

> Since 4.24pm, every one of our salvoes had straddled the enemy. When the salvo fired at 4.26 and 10 seconds fell, heavy explosions had already begun in the *Queen Mary*. First of all a vivid red flame shot up from her forepart. Then came an explosion forward which was followed by a much heavier explosion amidships, black debris of the ship flew into the air, and immediately afterwards the whole ship blew up with a terrific explosion. A gigantic cloud of smoke rose, the masts collapsed inwards, the smoke cloud hid everything and rose higher and higher. Finally nothing but a thick, black cloud of smoke remained where the ship had been. At its base the smoke column only covered a small area, but it widened towards the summit and looked like a monstrous black pine.[74]
>
> Commander Georg von Hase, SMS *Derfflinger*, I Scouting Group, High Seas Fleet

But the German gunnery officers took their triumph with another display of the cool professionalism that had marked their performance throughout the battle.

The spectacle was overwhelming, there was a moment of complete
silence, then the calm voice of a gunnery observer announced
"*Queen Mary* blowing up", at once followed by the order "Shift target
to the right" given by the gunnery officer in the same matter-of-fact
tone as at normal gunnery practice.[75]

Kapitän zur See Moritz von Egidy, SMS *Seydlitz*, I Scouting Group, High Seas Fleet

During the last moments of the stricken *Queen Mary*, the *Tiger* and *New
Zealand* had to take emergency action to avoid running into her. The *Tiger*
passed by on her engaged port side, the *New Zealand* to the starboard. Both
ran through the enormous black funeral pyre of smoke, the famous picture
of which has come to sum up much of the tragedy of the battle of Jutland.

I observed a salvo pitch abreast 'Q' Turret of *Queen Mary* (this was the
first time I had seen *Queen Mary* hit) and almost instantaneously there was
a terrific upheaval and a dense cloud of smoke. This could not altogether
be avoided as *Tiger* was close up (about 2 cable) from *Queen Mary*. As *Tiger*
passed through the cloud there was a heavy fall of material on her decks,
but no sign whatever could be seen of the *Queen Mary*.[76]

Captain Henry Pelly, HMS *Tiger*, 1st Battlecruiser Squadron

The filthy smoke was sucked into the air inlets of the *Tiger* and naturally
caused concern among those imprisoned within her steel walls who had
no opportunity to see what was going on.

Suddenly we passed though some dense black smoke. I thought it was a
gas shell that had exploded somewhere. I shouted out, "On gas masks!"
and put my own on, which incidentally was only a piece of sponge on a
tape, wetted a bit – it wasn't very efficient. But it wasn't a gas shell at all
it was the smoke from the *Queen Mary* blowing up.[77]

Midshipman John Ouvry, HMS *Tiger*, 1st Battlecruiser Squadron

The explosion that finally sank the *Queen Mary* was of such force that the
impact was transmitted through the water until it could be felt deep in
the bowels of the following ships.

We again felt a tremendous concussion in the transmitting station as if
from an underwater explosion, but all parts of the ship reported, "All
well!" in answer to our telephone inquiries as to whether they had been

hit. It was not until the action was over that we learnt that this had been caused by the *Queen Mary* blowing up.[78]

Midshipman Gordon Eady, HMS *New Zealand*, 2nd Battlecruiser Squadron

For the British the overall situation was now grim.

The scene was now a terrible one, the *Lion* was afire somewhere amidships, and of the *Indefatigable* and *Queen Mary*, nothing remained but two great columns of smoke.[79]

Sub-Lieutenant Colin Buist, HMS *Southampton*, 2nd Light Cruiser Squadron

This latest loss was a truly stunning blow for Beatty. He had entered into combat filled with confidence with a numerical superiority of six battle-cruisers to the German five. Now within forty-five minutes he had lost two and his own flagship had been severely pounded. Perhaps the *Indefatigable* was old before her time; not a 'serious tactical loss', as Chatfield had claimed. But the *Queen Mary* was the pride of the whole Battlecruiser Fleet. Completed in 1913, she was one of the most modern type of battlecruiser and as such meant to be superior to any German equivalent. As Beatty and Chatfield stood on the bridge of the *Lion*, Beatty summed it all up in one pithy phrase that has since secured his place in popular history.

I was standing beside Sir David Beatty and we both turned round in time to see the unpleasant spectacle. The thought of my friends in her flashed through my mind; I thought also how lucky we had evidently been in the *Lion*. Beatty turned to me and said, "There seems to be something wrong with our bloody ships today!" A remark which needed neither comment nor answer. There *was* something wrong.[80]

Flag Captain Alfred Chatfield, HMS *Lion*, 1st Battlecruiser Squadron

This remark, so simple, was later the subject of a protracted historical argument, but it is of little significance. One of the signal ratings present later claimed to have heard a slightly different phrasing.

On reaching the bridge on one occasion, I was almost pushed over the side by the Admiral Sir David Beatty, as he stormed up and down and actually heard him angrily exclaim, "What's the matter with our bloody ships today?"[81]

Boy Telegraphist Arthur Lewis, HMS *Lion*, 1st Battlecruiser Squadron

Another remembered it in almost exactly the same way.

> I was standing alongside Admiral Beatty and the Captain A. E.
> Chatfield, when *Queen Mary* blew up. It was on that occasion that the
> Admiral made his famous remark, "What is the matter with our bloody
> ships today, Chatfield?"[82]
>
> Leading Signalman Alec Tempest, HMS *Lion*, 1st Battlecruiser Squadron

Sir David Beatty was without doubt a brave man and an inspirational
leader. He had led his ships into a serious action at the battle of Dogger
Bank against the same opponents and, while there had been frustrating
command and control problems, and the *Lion* had been severely damaged,
there had been nothing that prepared them for this scale of disaster. Yet
in a way he was lucky, although it was the sort of luck that distinguishes
a disaster from an outright calamity. For, at approximately 16.28, the wreck
of 'Q' Turret, smouldering quiescently since the hit at 16.00, suddenly
blazed up with a renewed and deadly vigour. Private H. Willons, who
had helped close the magazine door, was fortunate to escape once again.

> The handling crew had gone up the iron ladder to the switchboard
> flat which is immediately above, and being rather a small place, was
> rather crowded; from this flat is another iron ladder which leads to the
> messdeck. About then the Chief Gunner came along to see everything
> was in order, finding the turret was out of action he ordered several of
> us to put out fires on the messdeck. Just as he and I got clear the ignition
> of the cordite occurred and the blast pushed us along. The space of
> about ten minutes elapsed between the projectile exploding and the
> ignition of the cordite, which happened to be in the cages, hoppers and
> possibly a charge in the handling room – broken quarter charges that
> got damaged while handling. Doubtless some burning clothing fell from
> one of the ramming numbers into the open cage and caught the cordite
> afire. Owing to the fact that the top of the turret was partially blown off,
> there was no explosion, but the flames travelled right through the turret
> and the adjacent compartments.[83]
>
> Private H. Willons, Royal Marine Light Infantry, HMS *Lion*, 1st Battlecruiser Squadron

As the charges in the hoist exploded, the flames swept through 'Q' Turret
charring battered steel and consuming human flesh in the inferno. The

magazine bulkheads bent inwards under the pressure of the detonation, but they held and the ship survived although the flames vented out as high as the masthead. Some took confidence from their survival against the odds.

I gradually overcame this feeling of fear. I think it was seeing so many dead and horribly wounded and so much destruction. It gave me a conviction nothing could happen to harm me; or indeed the ship. Surely were she destined to go she would have gone when hit between the twin guns of 'Q' Turret. So I had this feeling of relief, felt happier. There was a feeling of pride; I thought, this is going to end as the greatest naval battle in history and I have taken part in it – and it's going to be a big victory for us.[84]

Boy Telegraphist Arthur Lewis, HMS *Lion*, 1st Battlecruiser Squadron

Only a matter of moments had stopped the *Lion* sharing the same grim fate as the *Indefatigable* and *Queen Mary*. And it could have been worse. At 16.26 the *New Zealand* had been hit by an 11-inch shell.

We felt the impact down in the transmitting station and knew that a shell had found a billet somewhere on board. We phoned through to all the action stations in different parts of the ship, "Report if you have been hit!" Presently 'X' Turret replied, "Yes, no casualties." The shell exploded against the glacis port side for'ard, filling the turret with thick yellow fumes. Respirators were used, but the fumes were found to have no ill effects. Considerable blast was felt in the gunhouse and working chamber, but luckily no-one was hurt. Two more rounds were fired before the turret jammed and there was a delay of some 20 minutes while splinters of shell and armour were removed from the roller path.[85]

Midshipman Gordon Eady, HMS *New Zealand*, 2nd Battlecruiser Squadron

The *New Zealand* had built up a reputation as a lucky ship. As the shells rained down on the British battlecruisers she seemed almost inviolate. The crew later put it down to the ceremonial wearing by the ship's captain of Maori good luck symbols.

The only casualty suffered by the *New Zealand* was that of a Maltese messman's canary, killed by our own blast. The matelots put our luck down to the various Maori mascots and charms associated with the ship. There was a special steering wheel which had to be shipped in action –

this was made from different New Zealand woods and was inscribed with a Maori war cry, "Ake, Ake, Ake, Kia, Kaha" that is "Fight on, Fight on, Fight on, for ever." The Captain had a greenstone tiki and a Maori mat to be worn in action; the former round his neck and the latter round his middle. He wore the tiki, but, being a rather portly person, had the mat handy in the Conning Tower ready to put on should things become too hot for us.[86]

Midshipman Gordon Eady, HMS *New Zealand*, 2nd Battlecruiser Squadron

A reliance on superstition is an unreliable method of conducting war. But it was perhaps better than nothing in circumstances where it was becoming apparent that any hit on a British battlecruiser turret was serious and could easily be the catalyst to disaster.

There were a number of factors that made the British battlecruisers so vulnerable to flash fires and magazine explosions whenever a turret was penetrated. The first lay in the different nature of the British and German cordite charges.

Our powder was contained in brass cases. Thus a 30.5 centimetre cartridge looked exactly like a giant sporting cartridge except that the whole case was made of brass. Large cases such as these were very difficult to manufacture; they were also expensive and extremely heavy. Notwithstanding these drawbacks we used these brass cases in the German Navy even for the heaviest calibres ... Of course we could not keep all the powder required for a shot from a large calibre in a brass case and so, in addition to the so-called main cartridge, we had a secondary cartridge the powder of which was contained in a doubled silk pouch only. These naturally caught fire much more easily than the others. But our enemy kept *all his* powder in silk pouches! Further, we kept all the cartridges which were not by the gun or on the ammunition hoists in tin canisters so that they could not easily catch fire, while the packing of the English ammunition must have been very defective.[87]

Commander Georg von Hase, SMS *Derfflinger*, I Scouting Group, High Seas Fleet

The British cordite charges were far more unstable than those used by the Germans, which tended to burn rather than explode with such devastating consequences.

Second, the British had not introduced effective anti-flash precautions; they had not had the 'benefit' of the timely warning given to the Germans by the near demise of the *Seydlitz* at the battle of Dogger Bank. The Germans had adopted precautions that restricted the potential for disaster, although it should be emphasized that they were not actually flash-tight. Ignorant as they were of the high degree of risk they were taking, the British had not grasped just how easily a flash could be communicated from the turret, down via the handling and working chambers to the magazines. The relentlessly competitive culture of the Royal Navy undoubtedly played its part in promoting these disasters. In peacetime an officer's entire career could be determined by his ability to perform certain tasks faster and smarter than his contemporaries. The level of gunnery competition was intense and, as one might expect, cheating or cutting corners to gain a second or two's advantage was endemic. Peacetime habits died hard and it was common for ammunition cases to be left open or stacked up ready for instant use, while access ladders were left open between the gunhouse and the working chamber. Many gunnery officers were obsessed with increasing the rate of fire and hitting the enemy rather than any worries as to the possible consequences in the event of being hit themselves. The crews of the *Indefatigable* and the *Queen Mary* paid the inevitable price.

German shells continued to rain down on the attenuated British line after the demise of the *Queen Mary*. Von Hase switched the fire of the *Derfflinger* to the second ship in the line: the *Princess Royal*. Within one minute five seconds his first salvo landed home. It was truly remarkable shooting. At the front of the British line there was continued chaos on the *Lion*, as various small fires blazed amidships.

The last salvo of the first run hit the second cutter which blazed up and the foremost 4″ crews were ordered to close up and put out the fire. I went down and found the second cutter in a blaze and the whole of the lower part of the port side of the second funnel blown in. The crews were already at the fire, but none of the hoses that were rigged were long enough to reach the biggest part of the fire, which was right inside the blast screen. However we managed to get one of the hoses lengthened and soon got the fires under, but not before everything inside

the blast screen had been burnt away. There was a German 12″
projectile lying perfectly whole just abaft the cutter. It must have been a
ricochet as the shell was absolutely whole. It had a round nose and no
cap, and was base fused.[88]

Midshipman Nevill Garnons-Williams, HMS *Lion*, 1st Battlecruiser Squadron

In circumstances like these there were many deeds of heroism.

I got hold of a large wooden stave and rolled the shell to the ship's side
and, after a struggle, managed to roll the shell over the side. The Flag
Lieutenant, Lieutenant Kemble had been watching and later
recommended me for the DCM.[89]

Leading Signalman Alec Tempest, HMS *Lion*, 1st Battlecruiser Squadron

Still more German shells rained down on the sadly reduced British line
and the *Tiger* was again hard hit, causing some flooding and a slight
list to port. Many aboard the battered British ships were beginning to
realize that perhaps war really wasn't a one-sided, risk-free entertain-
ment after all.

After the *Indefatigable* and the *Queen Mary* had gone there was the fear
that we might suffer the same fate and that one of their shells might
get at one of our magazines, we would all be entombed in the ship.
The hatchways leading from the engine rooms on to the gangways and
those leading from the messdecks above are all, or almost all battened
down. Only one other way up is left free so that we had the somewhat
unpleasant knowledge that if the ship went suddenly we would be
drowned like rats in a cage – or perhaps a worse fate awaited in the
submerged flats which are watertight. We had a very unpleasant list due
to the flooded magazines. We did not know the cause and every time the
ship turned to port the list increased and as we did not know what was
happening, there was the dread fear the ship was turning over.[90]

Reverend Thomas Bradley, HMS *Tiger*, 1st Battlecruiser Squadron

While the battlecruiser battle had reached its peak, the destroyers had
been fighting a brisk, but savage, war of their own between the lines of
behemoths. As may be recalled, Beatty had issued orders at 16.09 for the

13th Flotilla to attack the German battlecruisers. At 16.15 Captain James Farie, the flotilla leader aboard the light cruiser *Champion*, issued his orders and, in response, Commander Barry Bingham aboard the *Nestor* moved across the *Lion*'s bows and led the destroyers off towards the German line. The deployment was disturbed as the *Nottingham* of the 2nd Light Cruiser Squadron cut through the line of destroyers, compelling the *Petard* to take fairly rapid avoiding action. As a result, *Nestor* was followed closely only by the *Nomad* and *Nicator*; some distance behind came the *Petard*, *Obdurate* and *Nerissa*, which acted independently in the ensuing action. Sadly, the *Pelican* and *Narborough* were left completely behind in the somewhat confused circumstances.

> I immediately hoisted the signal for full speed and ordered the destroyers
> to form a single line stern of me. Then, shaping course a point and a
> half in towards the enemy, we ran full speed at 35 knots for half an
> hour, in order to reach an advantageous position on the enemy's bows,
> such as would enable me to launch the torpedo attack with the greatest
> possible prospect of success. On drawing out to this position, we
> observed the enemy's 15 destroyers coming out with the object of
> making a similar torpedo attack on our battlecruisers.[91]
>
> Commander Barry Bingham, HMS *Nestor*, 13th Flotilla

The German riposte was all but inevitable. Eleven destroyers of the IX Flotilla, followed subsequently by four of the II Flotilla and their flotilla leader, the light cruiser *Regensburg*, moved out to meet the British thrust, aiming to launch their own torpedo attack on the British battlecruisers.

As the two destroyer forces charged out to meet each other in true 'light cavalry' fashion, the British destroyers lost all concept of lines or tight formation. Instead they charged recklessly into the attack at speeds of over 30 knots. Haphazardly joining the fray came the *Turbulent*, *Termagent*, *Moorsom* and *Morris* of the 10th Flotilla. Sub-Lieutenant Hilary Owen was in charge of the after deck 4-inch gun aboard the *Moorsom*.

> We were not connected to any division but Hodgson tagged on to
> *Nestor*'s (Commander Bingham) Division, with *Nomad* and *Nicator*.
> We followed to get a position ahead of their battlecruisers to fire our
> torpedoes. But then we saw a Flotilla of about 15 German destroyers

coming out to attack our battlecruisers and *Nestor* altered course down towards them.[92]

Sub-Lieutenant Hilary Owen, HMS *Moorsom*, 9/10th Flotilla

The German destroyers raced towards them and the range closed at a fantastic speed. Unlike the distant combat of the battlecruisers, fought through range-finders and binoculars, this action would be a close- quarter fight conducted at breath-taking speed.

By sheer coincidence the hounds on both sides had been unleashed simultaneously to steam at full speed into a fierce mêlée between the lines. The opposing forces were evenly matched and their combat was spectacular, highly exciting and chaotic – 30 ships at 30 knots weaving about in a restricted area striving to find a way through to a torpedo firing position and hotly engaged in frustrating enemy craft. The approaching German torpedo-boats with gushing funnels, high bow waves and sterns tucked down in foaming wakes looked sinister and menacing. I remember feeling that they were a pack of wolves that must, at all costs, be killed.[93]

Sub-Lieutenant Harry Oram, HMS *Obdurate*, 13th Flotilla

Once the destroyer action began, it swirled round like a mad dogfight, too fast for any single man to take in and control. Individual captains reacted with spur-of-the-moment decisions and their crews responded instinctively to the demands of the moment as best they could.

At the foc'sle gun we waited expectantly for the Captain's order and, with a sense of relief opened rapid fire at the leading ship in the advancing pack. In a matter of minutes we were caught up in a maelstrom of whirling ships as we swerved and jockeyed for a break-through position. We were under helm most of the time, the ship heeling as she spun. Events moved far too quickly for stereotyped gun control procedure and we let fly at anything hostile that came within our arc of fire. It became a personal affair and I have a vivid recollection of the sweating Trainer cursing as he strove to change his point of aim from ship to ship as I tried to seize fleeting opportunities. Quite apart from the difficulty in making split second decisions on friend or foe our legitimate enemies swept past at aggregate speeds of up to 60 knots and there was scant time to make a wild guess at range and deflection and get the gun pointed and fired before the chance passed and we were frantically trying to focus on a new target. It was quite impossible to pick out one's own fall of shot in a sea pocked with shell splashes, nor was there time to correct the range had we been able to do so. We fired many rounds at more or less point blank range but had no idea if any found their mark though several bright flashes gave hope that we had inflicted punishment. In the heat of swift action senses become keyed up by the high tempo and feeling for time is lost. I would have been at a loss to say if we had been engaged for minutes or hours. Crowding incidents made it seem an eternity and yet the period of action passed in a flash.[94]

Sub-Lieutenant Harry Oram, HMS *Obdurate*, 13th Flotilla

As the destroyers cut and weaved, their tracks resembled nothing more than a ball of string tangled by a particularly irresponsible kitten. The gun crews, frantic with excitement and nerves, put into action the gun drills they had rehearsed so many times. As ever, the stresses of action caused problems unforeseen or unnoticed in innumerable practice shoots.

Under bridge control we engaged the German boats, but after three or four rounds, all went dead and we found that the voice pipe and electric lead from the bridge had been cut and so we went on to local control, which was much pleasanter. The gun crews were very steady except for an Ordinary Seaman, who was the projectile loading number, getting a bit excited because he could not get the pins out of the lyddite shells. The Chief Stoker, who was finding things a bit dull in the storeroom and had more or less adopted our gun, produced a pair of pliers.[95]

Sub-Lieutenant Hilary Owen, HMS *Moorsom*, 9/10th Flotilla

The British had one great advantage in such an engagement. Their destroyers were rated as torpedo-boat destroyers, while the German destroyers were simply torpedo-boats. This reflected the fundamental differences in their core function. The German destroyers were intended to launch torpedo attacks and so reduce the margin of superiority of the British dreadnoughts. The British destroyers, although armed with torpedoes, had as their first duty the protection of the Grand Fleet. This fact was clearly distinguishable in the relative armaments that they had at their disposal.

Then I saw a mini-splash just abreast of where I was standing and
I realised I was at last under fire. The German destroyers only had
12 pounders and we had 4" (30 pounders) semi-automatic and almost
felt sorry for the poor German destroyers. Just then I heard a frightful
howl overhead and a tight salvo of 5.9" or 4.7" shells landed 200 yards
over. This was from the secondary armament of the German
battlecruisers and was followed by many others.[96]

Sub-Lieutenant Hilary Owen, HMS *Moorsom*, 9/10th Flotilla

This fire of the German battlecruisers' secondary armament went a good
way to redressing the British destroyers' superior firepower. Having
entered the skirmish in a state of disorganization, once they came under
heavy fire there was no chance of the British destroyers subsequently
forming any sort of cohesive line to concentrate their firepower.

It was a very confused affair with everybody getting in each other's way
at great speed and no chance of following a straddle on one of the
enemy but a boat of one's own side would come surging past, or else
Hodgson would have to put his helm hard over and we had to hold on
to anything to avoid going overboard, because the guard rails were
down. But we got off about 30 rounds in local control, but due to
interference, I cannot honestly say I got any hits. One felt that, if we
could have got into line ahead we should, with our superior fire power
at 2,000 yards have knocked seven bells out of the enemy flotilla.[97]

Sub-Lieutenant Hilary Owen, HMS *Moorsom*, 9/10th Flotilla

However, such a concentration into line ahead would have provoked an
equally concentrated response to which they would have been more
vulnerable.

Into the middle of this confusion dropped salvoes of 5.9" and 4.7" shells
from the German battlecruisers and the light cruiser, but I think our
confusion also confused their gunnery control officers and they were
just firing into the brown as one does at a covey of partridges – with the
same negative results. All this lasted I suppose about a quarter of an
hour and all the excitement and activity warmed my feet which had got
rather cold when the first salvoes came howling over or, what was worse,
falling short without a howl, but all the time I was looking over my

shoulder feeling that we ought to be supported in part against the enemy light cruiser who was not engaged at all.[98]

Sub-Lieutenant Hilary Owen, HMS *Moorsom*, 9/10th Flotilla

Early on in the fray, the *Nomad* was quickly disabled and wallowed to a stop.

Our misfortune lay in getting a shell from one of their light cruisers clean through a main steam pipe, killing instantly the Engineer Officer and, I think, a Leading Stoker. At the same time from two boilers came the report that they could not get water. We then shut off burners from the upper deck engaging the enemy meanwhile. The ship finally stopped, though steam continued to pour from the engine room.[99]

Lieutenant Commander Paul Whitfield, HMS *Nomad*, 13th Flotilla

In the mêlée it was difficult for the destroyers to see beyond their immediate foes to target the more distant battlecruisers. But the *Petard* found success in using her torpedoes on nearby German destroyers.

We opened fire on what seemed to be our opposite number at about 6,000 yards range and rapidly closed to about 3,000 yards. I cannot say I remember much about our shooting or about the German shooting, as I was fully occupied with handling the ship, but I remember our steaming light falling down with a crash from aloft when the halliards had been cut through by a shell. At this time Mr Epworth, my torpedo gunner, fired a torpedo, which was set to run at 6 feet deep, high speed setting, at a bunch of four German destroyers which were close together and the tubes' crews state they shortly afterwards noticed a very large explosion in the after part of them, which I hope was caused by this torpedo.[100]

Lieutenant Commander E. C. O. Thomson, HMS *Petard*, 13th Flotilla

A torpedo hit amidships on the *V29* was attributed to this speculative effort from the *Petard*. As the *Petard* passed her crippled foe she poured in a series of salvoes from her 4-inch guns.

The German destroyers were unable to press home their attack on the British battlecruisers or super-dreadnoughts to an effective torpedo range and although some were fired they had no effect other than to cause Evan-Thomas to turn his Fifth Battle Squadron some 2 points away as a precautionary measure. At around this point in time, the German destroyers of the IX Flotilla retired back to their line, having rescued the crews of the sinking *V27* and *V29*. This retirement gave some of the British destroyers the chance they had been waiting for; the rest seemed in the confusion of the moment to have melted away. With the *Nomad* stopped in her tracks by a direct hit in the engine-room, the *Nestor* and *Nicator* turned to carry out a torpedo attack on the German battlecruisers. It was at this point that the four more powerful 'G' class German destroyers of the II Flotilla made their presence felt, with powerful back-up from the *Regensburg*. The *Nestor* missed her battlecruiser targets with her first two torpedoes as Hipper turned away, but Bingham was a determined man.

> Thus I found myself with the solitary *Nicator* hot in the track of the fleeing destroyers and now rapidly approaching the head of the German battlecruiser line, who were not slow in giving us an extremely warm welcome from their secondary armament. At a distance of 3,000–4,000 yards the *Nestor* fired her third torpedo and immediately afterwards turned away eight points to starboard, in order to get clear of the danger zone and to regain the line of the British battlecruisers. Suddenly from behind the head of the enemy's line there came a German light cruiser, who opened hot fire and straddled us.[101]
>
> Commander Barry Bingham, HMS *Nestor*, 13th Flotilla

The light cruiser *Regensburg* certainly made her presence felt among the other British destroyers and even aroused a grudging admiration from her opponents.

> He had done his homework in the tactical school at Wilhelmshaven had that Captain and he could not support his destroyers with their miserable popguns better. He had a regrettable skill in concentrating his tight salvoes on the turning point when our leader altered course. Twice when *Nestor*, who was still leading us on an opposite course to the German destroyers, altered course, this light cruiser sent salvo after salvo into the turning point. Twice Hodgson altered course, well inside, and each time a salvo landed where we would have been if we had not altered our course.[102]
>
> Sub-Lieutenant Hilary Owen, HMS *Moorsom*, 9/10th Flotilla

Despite the disparity in firepower, Owen decided to take the light cruiser on himself with the 4-inch gun of the *Moorsom*.

I observed our enemy light cruiser seemed to have ceased fire and yet was within range. I decided on a private war with her, "7,000 yards, fire!" A splash right in line with her mainmast – perfect! "Up 400, 7,400, fire!" No sign, evidently over. We had got a straddle. "Down 200, 7,200, three rounds rapid!" I was just about to say, "Fire!" when the voice of L. H. K. Hamilton behind me, "Cease Fire! She is out of range!" "No she is not, I have got a straddle!" "Well, don't waste ammunition, we may want it later on!" I have regretted many things in my long life and foremost among them is the memory of the three rounds rapid which we never fired![103]

Sub-Lieutenant Hilary Owen, HMS *Moorsom*, 9/10th Flotilla

The *Nestor* got her torpedo off, but was hit almost in the same instant.

As we turned one of their light cruisers got a 6″ right into our forward boiler room. This shell came right through, hit the whaler, through the steel deck, into the boiler room to the bottom of the ship and exploded. I was up to my neck in salt water, boiling water – all the lot! We couldn't do much about that. Norman Roberts, the Engineer Officer, he went down the engine room and found out then that they'd got a packet in the engine room – all put out – all the lot. Tanks and everything, hence the water coming through to us. I decided to shut that one off. So there we were stuck. The after boiler room with one little single boiler – he struggled on as much as he could with that but eventually Jerry stopped us altogether and we were a sitting target.[104]

Petty Officer George Betsworth, HMS *Nestor*, 13th Flotilla

Bingham realized that the game was up.

Two boilers were put out of action by direct hits. From the bridge I saw at once that something of the kind had happened. A huge cloud of steam was rising from the boiler room, completely enshrouding the whole ship and it was painfully apparent that our speed was dropping every second.[105]

Commander Barry Bingham, HMS *Nestor*, 13th Flotilla

The *Nestor* was still far from helpless.

Although crippled, we had guns that were still intact, and a hostile destroyer, swooping down on what she thought an easy prey, was greeted with volleys of salvoes from our invaluable semi-automatic guns. After such a warm reception, the German destroyer sheered off post-haste.[106]

Commander Barry Bingham, HMS *Nestor*, 13th Flotilla

The damaged *Nomad* was also not to be underestimated despite the serious damage she had suffered in the flurry of action.

With the ship stopped bad luck had it that the only gun that would bear was the after one, and that couldn't be fought owing to the steam from the engine room obliterating everything. Several of our destroyers passed close, but I did not signal to them for assistance as I saw they were all busy. I then noticed that we had started to list to port considerably, and so thought that rather than let the torpedoes go down with the ship, and before the list became too bad, I would give them a run for their money, and fired all four at the enemy's battleships who were on the starboard beam.[107]

Lieutenant Commander Paul Whitfield, HMS *Nomad*, 13th Flotilla

The next two British destroyers to seize the moment and attack the German line were the *Petard* and *Turbulent*.

We fired another torpedo at about 9,000 yards range at the German battlecruiser line and then turned to starboard to a slightly converging but nearly parallel, course, to the German battlecruisers. We steamed ahead a little and when about four points on their bow fired the remaining two torpedoes. By this time the German destroyers seemed to have disappeared.[108]

Lieutenant Commander Evelyn Thomson, HMS *Petard*, 13th Flotilla

With the rendezvous with the main body of the High Seas Fleet now becoming imminent, there was no longer any need for Hipper to risk the combined danger of the increasingly concentrated fire from the Fifth Battle Squadron coupled with the deadly torpedoes launched from the destroyers. He therefore turned away three times after 16.30, until he was steering due east and had effectively broken off his duel with Beatty. The torpedoes from the gallant *Nestor*, *Nicator* and *Turbulent* missed their targets.

But the *Petard* was credited with a success, as it is believed that it was her torpedo that ran a considerable distance eventually to strike home on the *Seydlitz* at 16.57.

Our foretop reported first one, then more torpedo tracks. We tried to avoid them by sharp turns, but finally one got us a bit forward of the bridge. The blow was much softer than gunnery hits or near misses, no loud report, but only a rattling noise in the rigging. It was almost the same spot near the forward torpedo flat where we had struck a mine five weeks before. For the damage control party it was a repeat performance, and although they grinned it was otherwise not much of a joke. The torpedo bulkhead held, but it was seriously strained, as were parts of the armoured deck. Where the rivets had gone completely, the holes could be stopped with wooden pegs. Where they only leaked, which they did in great numbers they became a distinct menace because there was no way to plug them effectively. Both forward generators were casualties; one stopped entirely, while the other ran but failed to generate any current. Soon all this part of Compartment XIII was flooded, and with one third of our electric supply gone, all circuits had to be switched to the generators aft. There the air leads had been damaged by splinters, and in the dynamo room the temperature rose to 72°C (164°F). The men had to put on gas masks but some fainted and had to be carried out. Eventually, the room had to be evacuated, although a stoker returned from time to time to lubricate the bearings. The lights failed, but the petty officer at the electrical switchboard succeeded in re-switching all the circuits from memory. In view of the intricate battle arrangements this was quite a feat. He could do it only because he simply lived for his work and among his work. Besides this, the turbo-fans, the strong lungs of the ship, repeatedly failed because their leads were damaged, casings bent and vents perforated. However, the repair parties took special note of them and got them working again every time. In the conning tower we were kept busy, too. "Steering failure" reported the helmsman and automatically shouted down from the armoured shaft to the control room, "Steer from control room." At once the answer came, "Steering failure in control room." The order, "Steer from tiller flat" was the last resort. We felt considerable relief when the red helm indicator followed orders. The ship handling officer drew a deep breath, "Exactly as at the Admiral's inspection." "No," I said, "then we used to get steering failure at the end, whereas now the fun has only just started." Fortunately, we soon found that some springs holding down levers in the steering leads had not been strong enough for the concussions caused by the hits. Quite simple, but try finding that under heavy fire.[109]

Kapitan zur See Moritz von Egidy, SMS *Seydlitz*, I Scouting Group, High Seas Fleet

As the *Petard* turned back from her torpedo run she passed the damaged *Nestor*. But the attention of the two crews was soon diverted in another direction.

She was steaming in the same direction but at a reduced speed. I eased down near her and steamed alongside her for a few moments; she had obviously been hit, but there did not seem to be anything I could do for her then. About this time I caught my first sight of the German Battle Fleet coming up, bearing about south-east from us and I can remember a long line of grey ships.[110]

Lieutenant Commander Evelyn Thomson, HMS *Petard*, 13th Flotilla

The supposed heartfelt wish of every man in the Royal Navy was about to be granted as Scheer and the High Seas Fleet entered the battle, but not perhaps in the circumstances that they would have wished. Out-fought in the battlecruiser duel, the four remaining British battlecruisers and still trailing four super-dreadnoughts found themselves facing the combined might of the whole German High Seas Fleet. The First Act was drawing to a close and the main drama was about to begin.

Hipper had performed his reconnaissance and entrapment role to perfection. Throughout the early exchanges he had kept Scheer admirably well informed as to events and had succeeded in enticing a significant section of the Grand Fleet into the maw of the entire High Seas Fleet. Scheer's plans were about to reach fruition.

The message received at 3.45 pm, from the Chief of Reconnaissance that he was engaged with six enemy battlecruisers on a south easterly course showed that he had succeeded in meeting the enemy, and as he fought was drawing him closer to our main fleet. The duty of the main fleet was now to hasten as quickly as possible to support the battlecruisers, which were inferior as to material, and to endeavour to hinder the premature retreat of the enemy. At 4.05, therefore, I took a north-westerly course at a speed of 15 knots, and a quarter of an hour later altered it to a westerly course in order to place the enemy between two fires, as he, on his southerly course, would have to push through between our line and that of the battlecruisers. While the main fleet was still altering course, a message came from Scouting Division II that an English unit of warships, five ships (not four!) had joined in the fight. The situation thus was becoming critical for the Scouting Division I, confronted as they were by six battlecruisers and five battleships. Naturally, therefore, everything possible had to be done to get into touch with them, and a change was made back to a northerly course. The weather was extremely clear, the sky cloudless, a light breeze from the north west, and a calm sea. At 4.30 pm the fighting lines were sighted. At 4.45 pm, the Squadrons I and III opened fire, while the Chief of Reconnaissance, with the forces allotted to him, placed himself at the head of the main fleet.[111]

Admiral Reinhard Scheer, SMS *Friedrich der Grosse*, III Battle Squadron, High Seas Fleet

As the British and German fleets converged, the first British ships to sight elements of the High Seas Fleet were the 2nd Light Cruiser Squadron dutifully performing their scouting role some 3 miles ahead of Beatty. Their initial wireless sighting report of a German cruiser heading towards them from the south-east was made at 16.30. All such signals were made through Morse code and spark transmission.

When the fleet put to sea wireless silence was of paramount importance as direction finding stations could easily plot a ship's position during a transmission. Once action was joined, wireless silence was no longer essential. This caused a unique situation as the two fleets were now free to use wireless transmission. As the fleets, both British and German, were in very close proximity, the noise in the headphones was absolutely deafening. So much so that we had to keep relieving the operators after a stint of about ten minutes duration. Many ships were transmitting at full power at one and the same time, so it became almost impossible to either send or receive a complete message. Vital signals were sent, but whether they were ever received, either in full or in part, I very much doubt.[112]

Telegraphist G. F. Spargo, HMS *Dublin*, 2nd Light Cruiser Squadron

It was soon apparent from the bridge of the flagship, *Southampton*, that this was not just a stray German cruiser that they had encountered but something of far greater import.

We saw ahead of us, first smoke, then masts, then ships. "Look, Sir," said Arthur Peters, "this is the day of a light cruiser's lifetime. The whole of the High Seas Fleet is before you!" It was: 16 battleships with destroyers disposed around them on each bow. That was reported.[113]

Commodore William Goodenough, HMS *Southampton*, 2nd Light Cruiser Squadron

At 16.33 they sent the momentous signal by searchlight, 'Battleships south-east'. This was a tremendously exciting report, even on the bridge of the *Lion* which was fast becoming acclimatized to surprises.

We had no information that the German Battle Fleet was at sea. Rather had the Admiralty told us that they were still in the Jade River. It was therefore a surprise, yet not a great one, as it was a possibility Beatty always had in mind.[114]

Flag Captain Alfred Chatfield, HMS *Lion*, 1st Battlecruiser Squadron

Beatty, to his credit, acted immediately. Leaving the Fifth Battle Squadron, which was still firing at Hipper's battlecruisers, to hold their course, Beatty turned his battlecruisers to port and headed directly towards the reported sighting. Although he had confidence in the reported sighting of the German dreadnoughts it was imperative that he confirm this by seeing them for himself as soon as possible. As he did so another signal came in from Goodenough at 16.38.

Have sighted enemy battle fleet bearing approximately south-east. Course of enemy, north.[115]

Beatty did not have to pursue his south-easterly course for long. After just a couple of minutes, at 16.40, he sighted the advance ships of the

High Seas Fleet and instantly his position was transmogrified. No longer the gallant admiral accepting casualties in the pursuit of his weaker prey, now he was the prey. The situation had changed completely. His sole duty was to lead the High Seas Fleet under the guns of the Grand Fleet while simultaneously ensuring that he passed as much intelligence as possible to his Commander-in-Chief, who would assume the sole responsibility for achieving the destruction of the German fleet. With a commendable lack of hesitation, Beatty issued a general signal by flags ordering his force to 'Alter course in succession 16 points to starboard', which, two minutes later, he changed from a north-west course to north to allow them to pass on the engaged port side of the Fifth Battle Squadron, which was still steaming south. He timed it almost perfectly, for, as the battlecruisers turned, the first shells from the still distant German dreadnoughts splashed around them. But at 20,000 yards the range was too long, and the opportunity too fleeting, for any but the most fortuitous of hits. Beatty's luck held as his ships escaped unscathed and turned their turrets round to starboard ready to re-engage the German battlecruisers.

Meanwhile Goodenough's light cruisers, right under the noses of the High Seas Fleet, were even more dangerously exposed. Yet Goodenough knew that any extra detail he could secure as to the composition and formation of the High Seas Fleet would be invaluable to his ultimate master Jellicoe, still some 50 miles away to the north. He thus decided to ignore Beatty's signal temporarily and to hold on to the south as long as possible. They were perhaps fortunate that their continued approach under the guns of their enemies initially led to some confusion among the German ranks.

Why they did not blow us out of the water is a mystery to me, unless the German Admiral mistook us for some of his own light cruisers. Anyhow not a shot was fired until we turned and then they gave it to us hot and strong. It seems a miracle how we escaped; I could never imagine how so many heavy projectiles could fall around four ships and not hit. All four of us were straddled repeatedly and one could easily see the shells as they ricocheted screaming over the ship. Sometimes too you could distinguish a salvo approaching if you watched the flashes of their guns and counted the seconds of flight sufficiently accurately.[116]

Sub-Lieutenant Colin Buist, HMS *Southampton*, 2nd Light Cruiser Squadron

At 16.45, when they were only some 14,000 yards from the leading ships of the High Seas Fleet, Goodenough had seen enough and at last ordered his ships to turn onto a northerly course.

> We hung on for a few minutes to make sure before confirming the message. My Commander, efficient and cool, said, "If you're going to make that signal, you'd better make it now, Sir. You may never make another." Other remarks, some acid, some ribald, passed.[117]
>
> Commodore William Goodenough, HMS *Southampton*, 2nd Light Cruiser Squadron

At 16.48 he sent the signal for which he had risked the lives of his men.

> Urgent. Priority. Course of enemy's battlefleet North Single Line ahead. Composition of van Kaiser class. Bearing of centre east. Destroyers on both wings and ahead. Enemy's battlecruisers joining battle fleet from northwards.[118]

For the *Birmingham*, steaming behind the *Southampton*, it was a tight situation.

> By this time we had approached pretty close to the battle fleet and I began to wonder what was going to happen to us when the *Southampton* turned to starboard, and think just then the enemy battleships opened fire. We turned in succession and in consequence I think we in the *Birmingham* got closer to them than anyone. We were very heavily shelled and the enemy's shooting was very good. We did not reply, though the other ships did with, I think, no possible effect. Heavy shells were falling all around the four ships, and to me it seemed unlikely that we should get away at all. One salvo fell all around us about abreast the after-funnel, three to starboard and two to port, and so close that the ship shook as if we had rammed something. I do not think the three starboard ones fell 20 feet away at the outside. I had the time of flight taken as near as possible and it was 40 seconds towards the end of the shelling. Splinters were plainly audible and often visible, and the noise of the bursting of shells was very impressive. Once what appeared to be half a shell passed us ricocheting, seemingly quite slowly, but making a noise like an express train and falling in the water some hundreds of yards ahead.[119]
>
> Commander Alan Mackenzie-Grieve, HMS *Birmingham*, 2nd Light Cruiser Squadron

From the perspective of the German dreadnoughts that were harrying them, the evasive antics of the 2nd Light Cruiser Squadron looked almost comical.

> The light enemy forces veered at once to the west, and as soon as they were out of firing range turned northwards. Whether the fire from our warships had damaged them during the short bombardment was doubtful, but their vague and purposeless hurrying to and fro led one to think that our fire had reached them and that the action of our warships had so surprised them that they did not know which way to turn next.[120]
>
> Admiral Scheer, SMS *Friedrich der Grosse*, III Battle Squadron, High Seas Fleet

During their flight to the north, Goodenough continued to send out regular reports to Jellicoe. Unfortunately, the constant manoeuvring of course necessary to evade the German shells rendered their navigational dead reckoning erroneous. As a result, the reports made by Goodenough were marred by seriously inaccurate estimates of the position by latitude and longitude of the High Seas Fleet.

Yet the 2nd Light Cruiser Squadron was not the only squadron that had held on to the south. For the Fifth Battle Squadron was also still steaming south, engaging the German battlecruisers and keeping a precautionary watchful eye on the activities of the German destroyers involved in the mêlée between the lines. It has been persuasively argued[121] that the general signal to turn did not at this stage apply to Evan-Thomas, as Beatty intended to concentrate his forces for the run to the north by waiting until the super-dreadnoughts grew level with the battlecruisers before ordering them to turn and fall in behind the battlecruisers. If this was not the case, then once again Beatty's signals team had an extremely optimistic view of the distance at which signals flags could be read, for around 8 miles separated the two flagships. In addition, the signal was not repeated by searchlight, which might raise an eyebrow given the failure to communicate with Evan-Thomas at only 5 miles earlier in the day. Unfortunately, the smooth operation of whatever Beatty had in his mind all depended on the correct timing of the orders by Beatty and their immediate execution by Evan-Thomas. Where almost everyone is in agreement is that something went seriously wrong in the timing of the turn of the Fifth Battle Squadron to a northerly course. As no two accounts of this phase of the battle seem to agree on anything else, this turn has become another huge bone of contention between those who blame Beatty for unnecessarily imperilling his super-dreadnoughts, and others who censure Evan-Thomas for once again standing on signalling protocol and failing to carry out an obvious order. The issue cannot now be resolved without causing an unseemly plethora of angels to tumble from the points of their needle. Let us let them rest in peace.

For the few aboard the super-dreadnoughts who had a view of what was happening, it was somewhat of a surprise when they realized that the battlecruisers were now running back to the north, passing between them and the German battlecruisers.

> I suddenly saw our battlecruisers coming close by about 4 cables in the opposite direction and I realised they had turned back. I saw *Queen Mary* and *Indefatigable* were adrift, but never for a moment realised they had gone. Before this we had passed through a mass of black water with an 'M' Class picking up people, I heard afterwards this was the *Queen Mary*. 'X' Turret of *Lion* was trained towards us, guns at full elevation, several hits showing on her port side, great black splashes.[122]
>
> Commander Humphrey Walwyn, HMS *Warspite*, Fifth Battle Squadron

The four super-dreadnoughts were still hard at it, hammering away at Hipper's battlecruisers.

> When the *Seydlitz* was hit she turned about 5 points away, but shortly afterwards resumed her course. Very soon after, I remember thinking they must be zig-zagging as we were several times wrong for deflection. During this time the enemy were firing quickly but wildly. We fired quickly for the first few salvoes, but as the light grew worse, our firing became more deliberate and the range closed. I did not have much time to note how the firing of the other ships fared. All I remember is that the enemy ships all seemed to be having a bad time and that they appeared to be obliterated by splashes of our shell. I distinctly remember noting that the *Seydlitz* appeared badly on fire shortly after being hit by our shells, and that the third ship also appeared to be on fire. The battle continued in this manner till 4.50pm.[123]
>
> Lieutenant Patrick Brind, HMS *Malaya*, Fifth Battle Squadron

At 16.48, as they came up to the point where they would pass the battle-cruisers, Beatty hoisted a flag order that was unambiguously directed at Evan-Thomas: 'Alter course in succession 16 points to starboard.' The specification of the manner of the turn 'in succession' as opposed to a 'turn together' would not have been overly important if there had not then been a serious breakdown in signals procedure. A flag signal became 'executive', in the sense that it should be carried out instantly, only after it had been acknowledged by the relevant subordinate admiral and *at the*

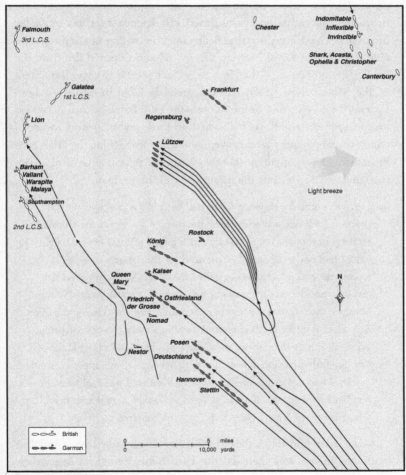

The turn and run to the north

moment at which it was hauled down aboard the flagship. Beatty's signals officer aboard the *Lion* was Lieutenant Ralph Seymour, who was under severe pressure at this point to keep up with the signals being received and sent as the repercussions of the sighting of the High Seas Fleet made themselves felt. It was under this pressure that the system failed. The signal was not made executive at the ideal moment that would allow the Fifth Battle Squadron to swing round and into line close behind the battle-cruisers. Evan-Thomas, for a second time that day, chose to rely on correct naval signal procedure, rather than use his common sense to turn before the formal 'executive' order was issued. His defence is terribly weak, for he could not have imagined that Beatty intended to expose the most valu-able ships in the Royal Navy to the risk of concentrated fire from the leading dreadnoughts of the High Seas Fleet, merely to cover the retreat of the battlecruisers which had the speed in hand to escape anyhow. Instead, for another four or five minutes the Fifth Battle Squadron carried on racing to the south. As it dawned on those few who were aware of what was happening, that they were now fast approaching the High Seas Fleet alone, it was apparent that they had good reason to be afraid, even though they were aboard the most powerful ships afloat.

> Up to this time the shooting for us had been like a 'peace' battle
> practice. I felt that according to all the rules of the game, the German
> battlecruisers ought not to remain much longer afloat if only the light
> held. I had not up to date thought much of the dangers of being hit by
> a projectile except perhaps just before the action, when my mind did
> certainly wander on the gruesome prospects of a naval action. Now,
> however, matters took a different complexion. We were closing the High
> Seas Fleet at a rate of 40 knots and there was every prospect of being
> engaged with them in a very short space of time. My feelings at that
> time are rather hard to analyse, for as things were then happening quite
> quickly, I had not much time for thinking whether I was frightened or
> not, but I dare say that if I had stopped to think, I should have been.[124]
> Lieutenant Patrick Brind, HMS *Malaya*, Fifth Battle Squadron

At last, at around 16.54, the offending signal was hauled down and thus made executive. Only then did the Fifth Battle Squadron begin their delayed turn. At this point the order to turn in succession, which had earlier seemed merely overly fussy, was supremely dangerous. The German III Battle Squadron could concentrate their fire on the point at which the super-dreadnoughts would all pass in their turn. True, their spotting would be rendered difficult by the forest of splashes in such a small area, but, on the other hand, their target was a static point in the ocean.

> I must confess to a feeling of relief when I realised we were to turn round, though not at it being done in succession. When it was the turn of the *Malaya* to turn, the turning point was a very hot corner, as of course the enemy had concentrated on that point. The shells were pouring at a very rapid rate and it is doubtful if we, the last ship in the line, could get through without at least a very severe hammering. However, the Captain decided that point, by turning the ship early. When we had turned, or rather as I was turning my turret to the starboard side, I saw our battlecruisers who were proceeding northerly at full speed, were already quite 8,000 yards ahead of us, engaging the German battlecruisers. I then realised that the four of us alone – *Barham*, *Warspite*, *Valiant* and *Malaya* – would have to entertain the High Seas Fleet.[125]
>
> Lieutenant Patrick Brind, HMS *Malaya*, Fifth Battle Squadron

Thanks to the decisive action precipitated by Captain Algernon Boyle, the *Malaya* had got through her moment of extreme peril. But she was not entirely without a scratch.

> We were hit twice, both times on the armour, with no damage. This was my first experience of being hit. The whole ship seemed to jar, but I didn't notice the noise of the explosion to any particular extent. One might compare the sensation to the feeling in one's arms if one takes a sledge hammer and brings it down as hard as possible on an anvil, keeping one's arms rigid.[126]
>
> Sub-Lieutenant Clifford Caslon, HMS *Malaya*, Fifth Battle Squadron

Although it had been a close-run thing, the Fifth Battle Squadron had, for the moment, got away with their over-close exposure to the full force of their many enemies.

Meanwhile, at 16.43, Beatty had also ordered the recall of his destroyers from between the lines. But, perhaps not unnaturally, their main attention was fixed on their German targets, rather than in looking back to the *Lion*. Lieutenant Commander John Hodgson of the *Moorsom* found himself, almost by chance, in a good position to launch an attack against the oncoming juggernauts.

Then Hodgson altered course 16 points to the south and I saw the south horizon filled with ships. These were 20 battleships of the High Seas Fleet in sub-divisions in line ahead disposed quarterly to port. The sun was shining on them and they looked almost white. At the moment they were not engaged and the secondary armament of the enemy battlecruisers was firing chiefly at *Nestor*, *Nomad* and *Nicator*. For the moment we were having a quiet time. The Chief (Engineer Lieutenant Commander Wheeler) was giving her all he could get and I realised we were making a torpedo attack on the High Seas Fleet. I think they were so surprised that they thought there was a catch in it, but we were approaching at a relative speed of 53 knots, nearly a mile a minute. About this time I remember seeing *Nicator* also making an attack, but no sign of *Nestor* or *Nomad*. Then the High Seas Fleet opened fire and our gunner (Mr Condon) related how he saw a salvo of 11" 'like a flight of wild duck'; which fell only 100 yards short and the large shell splinters found lying about the deck bore him out. We were approaching so fast that most of the salvoes were over. Then at a range of about 6,000 yards we turned to port and fired two torpedoes, one from each tube, and then we legged it for the safety of our own line.[127]

Sub-Lieutenant Hilary Owen, HMS *Moorsom*, 9/10th Flotilla

It was a bold and plucky move, but inevitably they did not get away with it entirely.

Our relative speed of escape was only 13 knots, and we came under very heavy fire. If I had my life again I would have opened fire while we were still within range in order to give the gun's crew something to do. As it was we just stayed there waiting for the inevitable to happen, and happen it did. We were just beginning to feel that we were soon to be out of range when there was a frightful explosion and we were totally enveloped in black smoke. I felt that the ship must be going down and I nearly felt the water in my boots – but when the smoke cleared I found we were still afloat and still making our 33 knots. Except for the projectile number, who had a bit of a cut on one hand, we were quite unscathed but there was a 6″ hole in our torpedo winch. The after shelter round the cabin had disappeared, the mainmast was towing along on the starboard quarter, there was a large hole in the deck above my cabin and the cabin flat, the after torpedo tube was riddled with splinters and so was the searchlight and the after funnel. As the smoke cleared I observed to my horror the torso of Stoker Armstrong, the Chief's servant, clinging to the edge of the hole in the deck. I assumed that this was all that was left of him and approached gingerly, but the Chief got there before me and seizing his servant by the shoulders, pulled him out and he lay moaning on the deck but outwardly unimpaired. I asked him, "Are you hurt Armstrong?" and he said, "No, Sir, only shell-shocked!" and I was not surprised because he was very close to the explosion which pierced the deck of the cabin flat in many places and cut the fire main which proceeded to flood the area. I then discovered that the Leading Torpedo Operator of the after torpedo tube was lying between his tubes with multiple splinter injuries, but not really serious. Our Surgeon Probationer soon had him bandaged up and quite comfortable. I was worried about the mainmast towing alongside in case it fouled our propeller, but I could not slip the shrouds. Once again the Chief Stoker came to the fore with a fireman's axe and we cut them away.[128]

Sub-Lieutenant Hilary Owen, HMS *Moorsom*, 9/10th Flotilla

Shortly after she was hit the *Moorsom* began to lose speed. It was discovered that the water from the broken fire main had got through the splinter holes into the main oil tanks.

All seemed set for our departure from the danger zone and we were beginning to draw out of range when, to my surprise and horror, Hodgson turned 16 points and steered once more towards the High Seas Fleet. I am afraid to admit that, if I had been in his shoes I would not have continued with it. The reason for his decision was that, now the after oil tanks were full of water, we only had enough oil left to return to Rosyth and Hodgson was determined to fire our two remaining torpedoes before we quit the battle. So once more we were approaching the High Seas Fleet at an approach speed of 53 knots and once more most of their salvoes were over. We were soon at about 6,000 yards and turned to port and fired our two remaining torpedoes, one of which having several splinter holes in it, sank immediately. Then away with us once more to regain the safety of our line. This was the worst we went through with splashes all round and we just stood there feeling naked and would have been glad of anything, even a canvas screen, against the enemy fire. We passed half a mile from *Nomad* who was stopped with splashes all around her, a sitting target. Hodgson and Hamilton considered taking her in tow but decided we could not do it with the High Seas Fleet hot on our heels. I cannot remember Hodgson using a smoke screen or dodging like a snipe. Then I was surprised to see that our battlecruisers had disappeared and in their place were the four '*Queen Elizabeth*' class battleships. They maintained their rate of fire and appeared indestructible, although receiving many hits.[129]

Sub-Lieutenant Hilary Owen, HMS *Moorsom*, 9/10th Flotilla

As the full might of the High Seas Fleet bore down on them the crews of the *Nestor* and *Nomad*, disabled and left stranded earlier in the fight, had the macabre experience of watching death steaming towards them in slow motion. There was nothing they could do.

This was more than I had ever bargained for, and, using my own glasses, I was dumbfounded to see that it was in truth the main body of the German High Seas Fleet, steaming at top speed in a north westerly direction. Their course necessarily led them first past the *Nomad* and in another ten minutes the slaughter began. They literally smothered the destroyer with salvoes. Of my divisional mate nothing could be seen: great columns of spray and smoke alone gave an indication of her whereabouts.[130]

Commander Barry Bingham, HMS *Nestor*, 13th Flotilla

The Germans opened fire on the helpless *Nomad* at a range of about five miles.

The High Seas Fleet spotted us, and started battle practice at us with 6" or bigger guns. Salvo after salvo shook us and wounded a few. The ship sinking fast, I gave the order to abandon her and pull clear. About three minutes after, she went down vertically by the stern. It was grand practice for them, but murder for us, and so exasperating that we could not hit back. The officers and crew behaved splendidly, and while waiting for 'the end', or my order to abandon ship, they might have been having their usual forenoon stand easy, to look at them. I nearly cried as she went down. With my usual luck, I met three different salvoes and am wounded as follows: upper and lower lips torn to pieces (since sewn together); three teeth removed; shrapnel hole through the throat – each hole about the size of a four shilling piece; splinter hole in the right forearm and right ear cut; shot or splinter hole in right chest; left hand burned.[131]

Lieutenant Commander Paul Whitfield, HMS *Nomad*, 13th Flotilla

The stunned onlookers aboard the *Nestor* knew beyond doubt that in a matter of minutes they would receive the same treatment. There was nothing they could do to avert their fate so they set about their duties as required by King's Regulations, supplemented with a little rearranging of metaphorical deckchairs to help maintain their collective morale in the desperate circumstances they found themselves in.

Of what there was in store for us there was now not the vestige of doubt and the problem was how to keep all hands occupied for the few minutes that remained before the crash must come. While the Sub-Lieutenant and myself were 'ditching' all charts, confidential books and documents, the First Lieutenant and the men were executing my orders in providing biscuit and water for the boats; lowering these to the water's edge; hoisting out Carley floats; and generally preparing for the moment when we should be obliged to leave the ship. These orders were rapidly executed and there was still time on our hands; for nothing had as yet happened. By a brilliant inspiration, Bethell then suggested to me that the cables might be ranged on deck – ostensibly for use in case of a friendly tow, but in reality to keep the men busy to the last.[132]

Commander Barry Bingham, HMS *Nestor*, 13th Flotilla

Then the slaughter began again.

Very soon we were enveloped in a deluge of shell fire. Any reply from our own guns was absolutely out of the question at a range beyond the possibilities of our light shells; to have answered any one of our numerous assailants would have been as effective as the use of a peashooter against a wall of steel. Just about this time we fired our last

torpedo at the High Seas Fleet and it was seen to run well. It was a
matter of two or three minutes only before the *Nestor*, enwrapped in a
cloud of smoke and spray, the centre of a whirlwind of shrieking shells,
received not a few heavy and vital hits and the ship began slowly to
settle by the stern and then to take up a heavy list to starboard.[133]

Commander Barry Bingham, HMS *Nestor*, 13th Flotilla

The end had come. In the final moments the usual heart-rending dramas
that mark the last moments of a sinking ship were played out.

The Sub-Lieutenant left the bridge. He went aft and ditched some
books, he knew it was going down. When he got down there they got a
couple right on the aft part and blew her stern right off. She began to
sink. "Abandon ship!" I went over and saw some of the lads come up
out of the engine room, most of them got away in a whaler and a few
Carley floats. This kid, he'd only just joined the ship before we left the
Forth, he was smothered in blood and silicate cotton from the lagging of
the steam pipes. It was awful to see this kid – he hadn't left home for five
minutes you might say – quick bit of training and sent to us, like many
others. I got hold of him in all the hurry and scramble, and this kid died
in my arms. I couldn't do anything else with him.[134]

Petty Officer George Betsworth, HMS *Nestor*, 13th Flotilla

The orders to abandon ship had been given by Bingham. He too made
his way to the side of the ship.

The motorboat and Carley floats were quickly filled and as the dinghy
was badly broken up by shell fire, there seemed to remain for me only the
possibility of a place in the whaler. Bethell was standing beside me and I
turned to him with the question, "Now, where shall we go?" His answer
was only characteristic of that gallant spirit, "To Heaven, I trust, Sir!"[135]

Commander Barry Bingham, HMS *Nestor*, 13th Flotilla

It was a prophetic remark. The next moment, as Bethell stooped to assist
a wounded signaller, he disappeared in the detonation of a bursting shell.
The ship's doctor made a last round to check for any remaining wounded.

I was no sooner in and we were about to shove off when someone
shouted, "What about Freeman?" This man had been left on the bridge

with his leg half shot away, so I rushed up on top only to find poor Freeman dead. In about 30 seconds more I was in the boat again. There was a frightful shriek and the whole bridge crashed over the side. If Freeman had been alive and it had been necessary for me to carry him down, I would have assuredly have gone that time, for he was a heavy man and the going was none too easy.[136]

Surgeon Probationer A. Joe, HMS *Nestor*, 13th Flotilla

At last the time had come for Bingham himself to abandon his beloved *Nestor*.

I clambered into the whaler, where I found about eight others waiting and we remained alongside until the last possible moment, hailing the partially submerged ship vigorously, in the unlikely event of any survivors being still on board. Finally we pushed off clear. The whaler, however, had also been hit, probably at the same time as the dinghy, and before we had gone half a dozen strokes she filled and sank. We then struck out, I luckily having my 'Miranda' life saving waistcoat on, for the well loaded motorboat, lying some 50 yards ahead of the *Nestor*, where some of us were pulled in, the rest supporting themselves by holding on to the gunwhale. Looking now towards the *Nestor*, we saw the water lapping over the decks, and the forecastle high in the air, still the target of the German gunlayers, some of whose projectiles fell uncomfortably near us.[137]

Commander Barry Bingham, HMS *Nestor*, 13th Flotilla

Not all of the crew had been able to find a berth in any kind of a boat. Many went straight into the sea.

Everybody else had more or less left the ship. I thought, "Well there's only one thing for it now – over the side!" I dived over and swam away from the ship or what was left of it as she was gradually sinking. I swam out to a bit of sunken wreckage I spotted – it must have been the bow of a boat or something. I got hold of this and stopped on that.[138]

Petty Officer George Betsworth, HMS *Nestor*, 13th Flotilla

The *Nestor* did not last long without them. At about 17.30 she finally sank.

The destroyer suddenly raised herself into an absolutely perpendicular position and thus slid down, stern first, to the bottom of the North Sea, leaving a quantity of oil and wreckage to mark the spot where she had last rested. As she sank, her sharp stem and stockless anchors alone visible, we gave our gallant, but cruelly short-lived *Nestor* three rousing cheers and sang, 'God save the King'. A reverential pause followed, broken almost immediately by the voice of a typical Able Seaman, "Are we down-'earted? No!" Then, "Wot abart 'Tipperary'?" His words and spirit were infectious and all joined lustily in the chorus of that hackneyed but inspiring modern war song. The song was thus in no small degree responsible for a frame of mind in which it was possible calmly to face a situation of finding oneself afloat, 60-odd miles from the nearest shore, in an over-laden, leaking, and broken down motorboat, with nothing in sight except the enemy's High Seas Fleet vanishing in the distance.[139]

Commander Barry Bingham, HMS *Nestor*, 13th Flotilla

Their ordeal was by no means over, but after some hours in the water, many of the *Nestor* survivors were picked up by German destroyers after dark.

The German destroyers were rushing around and one of them flashed a searchlight – they must have spotted me and a signalman hanging on to something else. She gradually came towards where I was and the searchlight was still blinding me, sidling alongside and then I saw an iron ladder come over the focsle and two matelots. One at the top and one got half way down. He reached over and he got hold of me and hauled me up onto the foc'sle deck. Six hours in the water – that was long enough. There was me and the signalman, both of us, I never saw anybody else then. They picked us up, took us aboard. They took everything away from us, we didn't have much on, an overall suit, only an old thing. There was a German sentry on the hatchway, at the bottom of the ladder. When we recovered our composure a bit, I asked him for a drink of water and he said, "We go into action tonight against the British fleet!" Speaking a bit of pigeon English. I said, "You do, do you! You do that and they'll put you right down there and I'll come with you!" He went for me like blazes.[140]

Petty Officer George Betsworth, HMS *Nestor*, 13th Flotilla

Commander Bingham was also picked up by the Germans and survived both the battle and the war to receive the Victoria Cross, awarded for his powers of leadership and his personal courage in the face of over-whelming odds.

◆ ◆ ◆

As the Battlecruiser Fleet wheeled round to the north, the few remaining survivors of the *Queen Mary* were oblivious to any nuances of the tactical situation as they fought their last battle against the most implacable of enemies: the sea. One by one they began to expire as the last residues of their physical and mental strength drained away. The combined effects of their wounds, shock and the insidious cold racked their bodies until the waves seemed to offer nothing but peace and an end to suffering.

> I only saw two officers in the water: an assistant paymaster McGilp and Sub Lieutenant Percy. As you know I never had a Gieve waistcoat and am now glad I had not. The people with Gieve waistcoats on were the first I noticed to drown, as they were held a little too high out of the water and when they became weak their heads fell forward in the water. After a while I thought everyone else had given up as I could see no one else apparently swimming. In the end I was picked up more or less unconscious with an Able Seaman from my turret also in the same state. The others were not to be seen except for one dead in a waistcoat. I was put to bed and had a good 10 hours sleep after which I got up and had breakfast feeling somewhat revived.[141]
>
> Midshipman Peregrine Dearden, HMS *Queen Mary*, 1st Battlecruiser Squadron

Dearden estimated he had been in the water for about seventy to seventy-five minutes. Many men were left totally isolated, seemingly without hope. But some indefinable quality deep inside made the stronger ones fight on regardless.

> When I came to my senses again I was half way off the spar, but managed to get back again. I was very sick and seemed to be full up with oil fuel. My eyes were blocked up completely with it and I could not see. I suppose the oil had got a bit dry and crusted. I managed, by turning back the sleeve of my jersey which was thick with oil, to expose

a part of the sleeve of my flannel, and thus managed to get the thick oil off my face and eyes, which were aching awfully. Then I looked round and I believed that I was the only one left out of that fine ship's company.[142]

Petty Officer Ernest Francis, HMS *Queen Mary*, 1st Battlecruiser Squadron

Francis had not been seen by the *Laurel*. But he hung on for some time until he was encouraged by the appearance of more destroyers.

How long I was in the water I do not know. I was miserably cold, but not without hope of being picked up, as it seemed to me that I had only got to keep quiet and a ship would come for me. After what seemed ages to me, some destroyers came racing along, and I got up on the spar, steadied myself for a second and waved my arms.[143]

Petty Officer Ernest Francis, HMS *Queen Mary*, 1st Battlecruiser Squadron

It was the *Petard*, returning from her gallant torpedo run against the German battlecruisers. On her way back to the British lines she spotted a large patch of oil.

We stopped on the edge of the patch and picked up one man who was swimming about; when we got him on board we learnt that he was the captain of the after turret of the *Queen Mary*. We then noticed in the middle of this patch of oil that there was just showing a portion of the bilge of a ship, which was floating about a foot out of the water.[144]

Lieutenant Commander Evelyn Thomson, HMS *Petard*, 13th Flotilla

Francis had been extremely fortunate. Like a needle in a haystack he had been found clinging to life and his pathetic spar.

The *Petard*, one of our big destroyers, saw me and came over, but when I got up on the spar to wave to them the swell rolled the spar over and I fell off. I was nearly exhausted again getting back. The destroyer came up and a line was thrown on me, which needless to say, I grabbed hold of for all I was worth and was quickly hauled up on to the decks of the destroyer. The first words I heard spoken were English, not German, and I must have managed to convince them that I was English.
I remembered no more until I came to and found I was lying on what seemed to be a leather settee. Someone was telling me I was all right

and not to struggle. I could not see the faces around me so concluded
I was blind, but did not feel then that it mattered much – my thoughts
flew to the fine crowd that had gone under.[145]

Petty Officer Ernest Francis, HMS *Queen Mary*, 1st Battlecruiser Squadron

The opening phase of the Battle of Jutland – which has ever since been
known as the 'Run to the South' – had been an unmitigated disaster for
the British Battlecruiser Fleet. Although immeasurably stronger than the
German I Scouting Group, they had failed to concentrate their forces at
any time during the engagement. Had Beatty's ships been more effectively
deployed, they would have levelled a vastly increased concentration of fire
on each of Hipper's battlecruisers and this would have undoubtedly
affected the accuracy of fire directed against them. There is no doubt
that, given their vulnerability to plunging fire, a single well-placed salvo,
or series of salvoes might still have destroyed the *Indefatigable* or *Queen Mary*,
but it would have been a little less likely. In addition, it can be said with
certainty that the I Scouting Group would have suffered much greater
damage if they had been forced to contend with the Fifth Battle Squadron
right from the start. As it was, Beatty had started with a numerical
superiority of six to the German five battlecruisers. Yet Hipper had
triumphed and the British finished the run with just four battlecruisers
facing the original German five. Beatty's failure to concentrate his forces
was the root cause of the British defeat in the Run to the South and the
responsibility therefore clearly lies at his door.

CHAPTER FOUR

THE RUN
TO THE NORTH

S UCCESSIVE COMMANDERS-IN-CHIEF of the High Seas Fleet had long
schemed to isolate and destroy a significant section of the Grand
Fleet. As the surviving battlecruisers and the super-dreadnoughts of Vice
Admiral Sir David Beatty's Battlecruiser Fleet began their run to the
north they represented the most glittering of prizes. Although Admiral
Reinhard Scheer must have been aware that it was possible that the
Grand Fleet was out, he was prepared to take the risk of an encounter
to secure the prize that lay tantalizingly within range of his guns. If any
of Beatty's ships were incapacitated, then the High Seas Fleet would
inevitably overhaul them and their destruction would surely be assured.
At a stroke the Germans would seriously erode the measure of superiority possessed by the Grand Fleet, remove for ever the myth of British
invincibility and perhaps then acheive a decisive confrontation on an
equal footing. For the Germans the overall result of the battle would
surely be decided in this phase. If they could destroy Beatty's force
without suffering serious losses themselves, then they would have achieved
their objectives and won the battle before Admiral Sir John Jellicoe could
get the mighty Grand Fleet into action. The sinking of the *Indefatigable*
and the *Queen Mary* during the Run to the South represented a good start,
but it was not nearly enough to tip the naval balance of power towards
the Germans. For Beatty this phase of the battle was merely concerned
with survival while he lured the High Seas Fleet into Jellicoe's grasp. And
so, with the Germans apparently in control, an intriguing passage of the
battle began.

After their turn the Fifth Battle Squadron steamed north, following
Beatty's battlecruisers. Behind them in hot pursuit came the III Battle
Squadron of the High Seas Fleet. The *Barham*, *Valiant*, *Warspite* and *Malaya*
were thus exposed to an alarming concentration of fire from the guns of

the leading German dreadnoughts with many miles to cover before there was any chance of meeting the Grand Fleet.

> Very soon after the turn, I suddenly saw on the starboard quarter the whole of the High Seas Fleet; at least I saw masts, funnels and an endless ripple of orange flashes all down the line, how many I didn't try and count, as we were getting well strafed at this time. [1]
>
> Commander Humphrey Walwyn, HMS *Warspite*, Fifth Battle Squadron

Under this concentration of fire the *Barham* was beginning to take a fair amount of punishment, with three hits being recorded within the six minutes between 16.56 and 17.02.

> I saw all four rounds of the salvo which hit *Barham* in mid air as they came. One hit penetrated the deck six feet from where I stood. It went on to explode below without doing much harm. Another hit below the water line and blew a hole in the opposite side of the ship, causing jagged edges which may have slowed us up. It wiped out a torpedo detachment. [2]
>
> Lieutenant Commander Stephen Tillard, HMS *Barham*, Fifth Battle Squadron

Not every sailor at Jutland had complete control of their nerves. Harold Dawson was acting as a range setter in the 6-inch gun control tower and it was all a bit too much for a young lad not yet 18 years old.

> I was no hero and I'm afraid that applied to my confreres in the control tower during the action. The crew consisted of three ratings, two boys and an officer, in this instance a two-ringed RNVR lieutenant. As you will perceive the aperture in the tower was equipped with a sliding shutter that lifted up and down. We had been busy firing our six 6″ guns, in control firing, when all of a sudden the 15″ guns got busy. This dislodged the shutter and brought it down with a bang. The officer was looking through his sights, when what with all his concentration and the fact that he could not see he jumped up in an understandable panic, shouting out, "What's happened, Dawson?" Seeing that I was just as petrified and doing a bit in my trousers, I was speechless. We soon recovered, ascertained the trouble and took up our positions again, but I feel I must say from then on my concentration on my job was negligible.

I could not stop looking out of the aperture, watching the gun flashes of
the Germans and then the splashes of their shells as they dropped
within yards of us, absolutely unforgettable.[3]

Boy 1st Class Harold Dawson, HMS *Valiant*, Fifth Battle Squadron

The German dreadnoughts unable to claw themselves within range of
the real targets amused themselves by tormenting the fleeing minnows of
Goodenough's 2nd Light Cruiser Squadron.

I can truthfully say that I thought each succeeding minute would be our
last. For a solid weary hour we were under persistent 11″ shell fire from
the rear of the German Battle Fleet, that is to say from all the German
battleships who could not quite get the Fifth Battle Squadron and
therefore thought they might as well while away the time by knocking us
out. Needless to say, we could not fire a shot in return, as the range was
about 16,000 yards. I crouched down behind the ¹/₁₀″ plate of the After-
Control with Hayward-Booth (the Sub) and the Clerk and we gnawed a
bit of bully beef. However my throat was so dry that I could not get
much down and we could not get any water. About once a minute, or
perhaps thrice in two minutes, a series of ear-splitting reports would
indicate that another salvo had burst around the ship. Against my will,
I could never resist hanging over the edge and then I saw half a dozen
or four muddy foamy looking circles in the water, over which black
smoke hung. Sometimes these pools were on one side, sometimes the
other. Some were literally absolutely alongside the ship and those threw
masses of water on board drenching us to the skin. I should say (and this
is a carefully reasoned and considered estimate) that 40 large shells fell
within 75 yards of us within the hour; and many others varying
distances out. We seemed to bear a charmed life, but it was obvious that
such a position could not last forever.[4]

Lieutenant Stephen King-Hall, HMS *Southampton*, 2nd Light Cruiser Squadron

At 16.52 Admiral Franz von Hipper had executed his own 16 point
turn in succession and began to steer north some 7 miles ahead of Scheer.
Following this, the I Scouting Group resumed fire at the four British battlecruisers, with each ship aiming at its opposite number in the line, while
the already severely battered *Von der Tann*, still bringing up the rear, aimed

her sole remaining operational 11-inch turret at the *Malaya* of the Fifth Battle Squadron. The German battlecruisers were indeed beginning to fray at the edges under the accumulated weight of hits they had suffered. But they still had teeth and the *Tiger* received a further hit, while two more shells crashed down on the already wounded *Lion*. If anything, visibility was even worse for the British battlecruisers than in the preceding Run to the South and their return fire remained generally ineffective.

At 17.01 Beatty reacted to this renewed pressure on his battlecruisers. Conscious that his first duty was to draw the Germans towards Jellicoe, rather than engage in an irrelevant fire-fight at a disadvantage, he decided to minimize the risk during the run north. He ordered a turn away onto a north-westerly course, which naturally had the effect of opening out the range, and from 17.08 the firing between the rival battlecruisers gradually died down. At the same time he ordered Vice Admiral Hugh Evan-Thomas to 'prolong the line by taking station astern'. At this stage there was about 4,000 yards between the leading *Barham* and the *New Zealand* bringing up the rear of the battlecruisers. As the battlecruisers were making some 25 knots in contrast to the 23½ that could be achieved by the super-dreadnoughts, this gap was opening all the time. They could only 'take station astern' if Beatty cut his speed below 24 knots to allow them to do so. This he did not do and thus, in effect, the Fifth Battle Squadron were left to act as a powerful rearguard for the battlecruisers. As they swung round their turrets and generally sorted themselves out after the disruption of fire caused by their turn, they were only able to resume fire at 17.05. The *Barham* and *Valiant* targeted the German battlecruisers; behind them the *Warspite* and *Malaya* aimed at the leading German battleships. At first, Evan-Thomas seems to have continued to pursue a northerly course, in effect interposing himself between the High Seas Fleet and the British battlecruisers, before conforming to Beatty's north-westerly course at 17.14.

Meanwhile, at 17.05, Scheer had ordered a turn to give the High Seas Fleet a course of north-north-west, and at the same time called for maximum speed, which naturally caused the German battle line to begin to spread out as the faster, more modern dreadnoughts of the III Squadron gradually eased ahead of their slower consorts.

It was around this time that the destroyers *Moresby* and *Onslow* launched an opportunistic attack on the German battlecruisers. Originally left behind to stand by the seaplane carrier *Engadine,* they had eventually been released from this mundane duty, and surged after the main body. By sheer luck, as the Run to the North began they found themselves situated between the battle lines in a good position to launch their torpedoes, 2 points before the beam of the *Lützow,* leading the German battlecruisers.

We were about abreast of the middle of their line and were therefore closing in to a good position on the bow of their rearward half. When they opened fire with their secondary armament I suppose the range was about 11,000 yards. Their salvoes were extraordinarily neat with a spread of about 50 yards. I think now that only one ship could have been firing at us. This neatness of spread was our salvation, as both ships snaked the line all the way in, altering towards the direction of the last splash. When the first lot came over everyone on the bridge ducked. At any rate I know I did, and the coxswain and telegraphman. It's shameful to think of – but also rather humorous. We did nothing with our guns at the time as there was nothing for them to do. I was the Gun Control Officer, with a voicepipe on the bridge. I remember being free to watch their salvoes arrive and also thinking that I wouldn't have dared say a word to old 'R.V.' *(Lieutenant Commander Roger V. Alison)* with his old chin sticking out over the bridge screen. But I didn't really appreciate then what a grand act he was putting up. We turned to fire at, I believe, 7,000 yards. In those days it wasn't the fashion to let off all one's fish at once, so we only fired two and then streaked for home.[5]

Sub-Lieutenant Anthony de Salis, HMS *Moresby*, 13th Flotilla

Shortly after they turned, the *Moresby* parted company with the *Onslow* and ran into a different kind of trouble in a case of mistaken identity that could easily have proved fatal.

Moresby wasn't a fast steamer at any time and always made clouds of smoke when hard put to it to keep up with the rest of the flotilla. On this occasion we were probably excelling ourselves. We must have been steaming nearly bows on to the *Tiger* who, taking us for a German destroyer attack under the famous smoke screen, opened a brisk fire on us with her 6" guns. This was a totally different thing to the German fire, as it had a spread of around about 400 yards and there wasn't any possibility of dodging it. It straddled us pretty soon. R. V. saw what was happening and at once put his helm over to give them a broadside view of the ship. This sounds an obvious thing to do. But actually it wasn't a bit and if he hadn't been extremely quick to grasp the situation and to see the best action to take in it, we should have suffered heavily. As it was we were only hit once before they realised their mistake. A piece of shell was picked up on the upper deck afterwards – unmistakeable service yellow-brown and subsequently produced to taunt the control officer of the *Tiger*'s starboard battery.[6]

Sub-Lieutenant Anthony de Salis, HMS *Moresby*, 13th Flotilla

Their bold efforts were all in vain, as the torpedoes they launched missed.

The problems of the Fifth Battle Squadron were increased when at 17.13 Hipper turned to adopt a north-north-west course and reduced speed, opting to linger with his new-found enemies rather than pursue at full tilt the battlecruisers. Despite their fraught situation and the increasing pressure that engulfed them, the super-dreadnoughts demonstrated the sting that they carried in their collective tail. Several hits were scored on the now struggling *Seydlitz*; one shell hit the *Lützow*. Other shells crashed into the leading German dreadnoughts, the *Grosser Kurfürst* and *Markgraf*. Both sides were now exchanging hammer blows.

The noise of their shells over and short was deafening, that frightful crack, crack, crack, going on the whole time. Felt one or two very heavy shakes, but didn't think very much of it at the time and it never occurred to me that we were being hit. We were firing pretty fast about Green 120. I distinctly saw two of our salvoes hit the leading German battleship. Sheets of yellow flame went right over her mastheads and she looked red fore and aft like a burning haystack; I know we hit her hard. Told everybody in the turret that we were doing all right and to keep her going. Machinery working like a clockwork mouse and no hang-up of any sort whatever.[7]

Commander Humphrey Walwyn, HMS *Warspite*, Fifth Battle Squadron

Lieutenant Desmond Duthy, at his station on the starboard 6-inch gun control tower, could now actually see the Germans – and found it an intimidating sight.

> The first thing I saw as we steamed on our new course was what I thought were about six German battleships. They were blazing away like 'HELL!' and got our range fairly soon. We swung into a course nearly parallel with them and got going with plenty of noise, incidentally banging my face against my spotting glasses and giving me two slight black eyes. Their shot fell all around us and how we were not hit dozens of times is beyond me. We had great difficulty in seeing them, but they could easily see us against the setting sun. It was not unadulterated bliss seeing the flash of their guns and wondering whether the shell would touch you or not, but I can't say that I was thinking of much else than what an infernal nuisance it was we could not fire oftener. They were just out of range of my 6″ guns. [8]
>
> Lieutenant Desmond Duthy, HMS *Valiant*, Fifth Battle Squadron

At 17.14 the *Warspite* was hit by a shell that crashed into the base of the after funnel.

> We got our first hit. It seemed to be on the armour abreast of our station, on the water line, from the closeness of the sound, but actually it was some way further aft I believe. One could hear the distinct sound of metal striking against metal and it was quite different to any of the subsequent hits we received, as if it had struck broadways on without exploding. [9]
>
> Surgeon Gordon Ellis, HMS *Warspite*, Fifth Battle Squadron

A minute later, at 17.15, Scheer ordered another turn to port to a course of north-west. Whatever the imagined maximum speed of the Fifth Battle Squadron it was clear that they could not shake off the German *König* class dreadnoughts that made up the III Battle Squadron. As the German battleships slowly clawed themselves into range, the concentration of fire they achieved against the rear ships increased exponentially.

> Their salvoes began to arrive thick and fast. From my position in the turret I could see them fall just short, could hear them going just over

and several times saw a great column of black water fall on the top of the turret roof. I expected at any moment we should get a nasty knock and I realised that if any one of those many shells falling round us should hit us in the right place, our speed would be sadly reduced and that we should not then stand a very good chance. The salvoes at this time were coming at a rate of six to nine a minute.[10]

Lieutenant Patrick Brind, HMS *Malaya*, Fifth Battle Squadron

At 17.19, enthused by the possibilities inherent in the situation, Scheer issued the order that threw caution to the winds: 'Pursue the enemy!' The *Malaya*, as the hindmost ship, was in severe danger and to some extent her continued survival depended purely on luck. If any hit slowed her speed by an appreciable amount she would face obliteration. Her armour would not be able to protect her against the kind of close-range battering she would inevitably receive if the entire High Seas Fleet overhauled her.

Malaya was at first very lucky and although shells were falling all round and the ship deluged in spray, she wasn't hit much. During this time the range was still too great (about 18,000 yards) for my 6″ guns to be in action, and I remained a spectator. It was extraordinarily fascinating – the visibility was bad and it was difficult to see the German battleships distinctly, but one could see the flashes of their guns with great distinctness, and then after an interval of 30 seconds the salvoes would fall round the ship. During this time we never had less than three ships firing at us and sometimes more.[11]

Sub-Lieutenant Clifford Caslon, HMS *Malaya*, Fifth Battle Squadron

Her luck could not, and did not, last. At 17.20 the *Malaya* received a serious hit abreast of her 'B' Turret where Lieutenant Patrick Brind was stationed.

I saw a large column of water rise up between my guns and felt the turret shake heavily. We had been hit abreast the turret, below the water line and so heavy was the shock that I feared that our fighting efficiency must have been gravely impaired, not so much that the shell had pierced any part of the turret, but that the shock of the impact had seriously impaired our loading arrangements. I went into the gunhouse to enquire whether all was well below and received the report that they had been somewhat shaken by the blow, but that everything seemed all right. This proved too optimistic an estimate, for when the main cage arrived in the working chamber it was found that the shell could not be withdrawn and there was a proper jam up. I dashed down and we had to work hard to clear it. After what seemed an age, but could not really have been long we succeeded and by extemporary means managed to get the cage into working order again. During this time the secondary method of loading was in use for the right gun and although five rounds had to be loaded in this manner the turret never missed a chance to fire. This was very pleasing as the secondary method of loading is considered very slow.[12]

Lieutenant Patrick Brind, HMS *Malaya*, Fifth Battle Squadron

At 17.27 they received a further heavy hit, this time further aft on 'X' Turret. To try to baffle the German range-finders, Captain Algernon Boyle ordered his starboard secondary battery of 6-inch guns to fire deliberately well short into the sea in order to throw up a wall of waterspouts. Royal Marine Private John Harris was detailed to man the ammunition hoist of the starboard battery.

I was put on ammunition hoist by Sergeant Wood, affectionately known as 'Timber', who gave me the orders, "Pass up common shell, lyddite, shrapnel ..." Orders given through the voice pipe to the shell room below. We had now gone into independent firing, when the First Gunnery Lieutenant came up and I asked, "How are we doing, Sir?" "Not too bad!" he replied, you have one to your credit, another on fire astern. Going to the voice pipe he said, "You all right below?" A voice came up, "All right down here, Jack!" thinking it was me! It was misty, bad visibility, hit and run.[13]

Private John Harris, Royal Marine Light Infantry, HMS *Malaya*, Fifth Battle Squadron

Although imaginative, the water-screen idea was to be stillborn, for at 17.30 the *Malaya* received a severe direct hit into the starboard 6-inch battery. The consequences were dreadful.

A German battleship took up position on our right and let us have it broadside on with everything she had. Shells ripped through the armour plating like a knife through cheese. One shell dropped amidships, came down through the deck head and exploded. It ignited our ammunition

charges throwing every man off his feet. We lay half stunned until the
dreaded cry, "FIRE!!" It was soon roaring like a furnace and we were
trapped by watertight doors.[14]

Private John Harris, Royal Marine Light Infantry, HMS *Malaya*, Fifth Battle Squadron

The shell burst on the No. 3 gun, killing all the crew and igniting the
cordite that had been placed on trolleys to the rear of the guns by the
ammunition party. Even from his position high aloft in the foretop
Paymaster Keith Lawder could see the seriousness of the fire.

I looked over the top and the flames from the burning cordite were coming
out through the gun ports pretty well as far as the muzzles of the 6″ guns.[15]

Assisstant Paymaster Keith Lawder, HMS *Malaya*, Fifth Battle Squadron

The flash fire swept from end to end of the starboard battery, causing
severe casualties.

My Gun Control Tower was filled with fumes and blue smoke, and we
were knocked backwards, but it cleared immediately and there was no
damage. Souther again called down from the foretop to know if I was
all right, and I told him, "Yes". I put my face to the battery voicepipe to
enquire for them, but there was no need to ask, I could hear the most
terrible pandemonium, and the groans and cries of wounded men. I
heard one man call out, "Water, we're burning."[16]

Sub-Lieutenant Clifford Caslon, HMS *Malaya*, Fifth Battle Squadron

In these desperate circumstances, Caslon was given permission to go down
and see what he could do to help. But reaching the scene of the fire proved
easier said than done.

The only way down was by a ladder which led into the port battery, and
on arrival there I found all the lights out, and a crowd of men who were
having difficulty in joining up a hose to the fire main. This was soon put
right and then a Petty Officer said that the door at the forward end
dividing the port battery from the starboard was jammed. In the
meantime the Lieutenant and Midshipman of the port battery went to
the dividing door at the after end of the battery with a party, to try and
get a hose in that way.[17]

Sub-Lieutenant Clifford Caslon, HMS *Malaya*, Fifth Battle Squadron

They had no time to lose and Caslon decided to back a hunch.

I felt sure that the forward door was not jammed, as it was much too
heavy, and so went forward to see, and, as I expected, found that they
had missed one of the clips in the darkness. While I was knocking this
back the men with the hose just behind me were playing it all over me,
and I remember very distinctly using bad language at them about it.
I only mention this because, when the door swung open, a big sheet of
flame came through, and the fact of my being wet probably saved me
from being nastily burnt. Immediately afterwards five blackened figures
rushed out – they were the survivors from No 1 gun.[18]

Sub-Lieutenant Clifford Caslon, HMS *Malaya*, Fifth Battle Squadron

The mental anguish and corresponding relief of those men seemingly
doomed to the most horrible of deaths, only to be reprieved at the very
last moment, can barely be imagined.

I ran to the nearest door, pulled down the levers but could not open it –
jammed. I got back jumped at it three times and knocked it open.
The guns crew on the port side scattered like sheep as fire came over my
head. A naval officer came up and said, "What happened?" I replied,
"Get the men out quickly or they will soon be dead!" As I spoke he
pulled a mask over his head down to his waist and went through – it was
not to save the men but to turn on the water which flooded the gun deck
and so saved the ship. He should have been awarded the VC.[19]

Private John Harris, Royal Marine Light Infantry, HMS *Malaya*, Fifth Battle Squadron

Caslon and others went through to rescue any survivors and to try to
put out the flames.

The first person I saw in the battery was the gunroom steward, who
had been laying the table for tea – these ratings usually form part of the
ammunition supply party, or stretcher bearers, or something like that –
he was half burnt from head to foot. The right half of his hair, face,
shirt and right trouser all gone and seemed dazed, but walking and
otherwise all right. He asked me where to go and I gave him to a
leading seaman to be taken to the dressing station.[20]

Sub-Lieutenant Clifford Caslon, HMS *Malaya*, Fifth Battle Squadron

Speed was of the essence if the burnt men were to be saved, the fire put out and an assessment made of how many of the 6-inch guns were still serviceable if crews could be found.

We got the fire under to a certain degree and were able to pull a number of the wounded out. I left the men from the port battery doing this and returned to the port battery myself, where I found McCulloch, who had got in by the door at the after end, but considered we would get at the fire best by getting through the ship's galley which was directly abreast it. We had some trouble with this door, which was a light one and was badly jammed by the explosion, but eventually broke it down and got the hose through.[21]

Sub-Lieutenant Clifford Caslon, HMS *Malaya*, Fifth Battle Squadron

The cordite fire was blazing fiercely and was not easy to suppress.

The poor devils of the supply party were like moths in a candle. I went forward and found Lieutenant McCulloch, Sub Lieutenant Caslon, and Engineer Sub and some men handling the high pressure hoses. We were faced by a wall of flame, I believe it reached mast high. After what seemed like half an hour – I believe it was only five minutes – we got it out and what a sight. Blackened bodies everywhere and feet of water swishing about.[22]

Midshipman Gerald Norman, HMS *Malaya*, Fifth Battle Squadron

The aftermath of the fire as the casualties and corpses were brought out was stomach-churning.

We in the main wireless office could see the first aid parties passing our door, going to the aft deck carrying bodies and wounded. Laying them out and treating, where possible, the badly burned and shock cases. Some of the dead were so burned and mutilated as to be unidentifiable. The living badly burned cases were almost encased in wrappings of cotton wool and bandages with just slits for their eyes to see through, in fact, the few 'walking cases' who could wander about the after deck presented a grim, weird and ghoulish sight.[23]

Wireless Telegraphist Frederick Arnold, HMS *Malaya*, Fifth Battle Squadron

In a narrow passage below decks, Surgeon Lieutenant Duncan Lorimer manned the aft distribution station with his medical party. Many of the burn casualties were brought to him, but there was little he could do in the worst cases but look on as they suffered.

Shortly after our guns got going, we felt a different concussion and soon the ship took a severe list to starboard. I could not help wondering how much damage was done, as, I have no doubt, all the rest of the party wondered. However, we soon were far too busy to think of anything but our job and a good thing too. The wounded began to come down in great numbers, mostly burns, and very bad burns they were, entailing very extensive dressings and of course morphia. I don't quite understand the immediate cause of death. We talk vaguely of shock, but I don't know that this explains it. A man will walk into the dressing station, or possibly be carried in, with face and hands badly scorched, not deeply burned, nor disfigured. One would call it a burn of the first degree. Very rapidly, almost as one looks, the face swells up, the looser parts of the skin become enormously swollen, the eyes are invisible through the great swelling of the lids, the lips enormous jelly like masses, in the centre of which, a button-like mouth appears. I have an idea that it must be due to the very high temperature of the burning cordite applied for a very short time. It is quite unlike any burns I have ever seen in civil life and would be very easily avoided by wearing asbestos gloves and masks, or similar anti-fire substance. The great cry is water, not much pain, and that is easily subdued by morphia. There is then great and increasing restlessness, breathing rapid and shallow, and final collapse. The bodies stiffen in their twisted attitudes very rapidly. The scorched areas are confined to the exposed parts: face, head, and hands, hair, beard and eyebrows burnt off. The skin of the hands, the whole epidermis including the nails, peels off like a glove. In many cases one has to look twice to be certain that one is cutting off only skin, and not the whole finger. In very few cases does the burning appear to go any deeper than this. And yet they die and die very rapidly. Cases looking quite slight at first become rapidly worse and die in an appallingly short time. It is possible in such circumstances to try many remedies. Stimulants such as spirits and strychnine were useless. We had no time to transfuse. Whether it would have done any good I don't know. I doubt it, the end came so rapidly in many cases. Brandy, hot bottles and drinks, with, of course, the dressing of the cases and some operations were the utmost we could do.[24]

Surgeon Lieutenant Duncan Lorimer, HMS *Malaya*, Fifth Battle Squadron

The gunroom steward rescued by Lieutenant Caslon was one of the walking wounded who succumbed in this fashion from his burns a few days later. Of the 121 men in the starboard battery, no fewer than 104 were killed or wounded.

At 17.35, just as this drama was starting to unfold, two more shells holed the *Malaya* below the water-line, with consequences that could well have made all heroics in the starboard battery irrelevant. The sea rushed in and flooded the neighbouring compartments, which caused a serious list of some 4 degrees which resulted in a slight, but significant, reduction in the ship's speed. As fast as possible the oil fuel was switched between fuel tanks to counterbalance the weight of the water and as far as possible correct the list. The *Malaya* needed every knot if she was to draw clear of the pursuing German dreadnoughts. In addition an oil fuel tank had also been penetrated, which corrupted the fuel supply to 'A' Boiler. The water put out the burners and again speed was lost. The engine-room staff acted with considerable presence of mind as they diagnosed the fault and switched over to another fuel tank. Although the *Malaya* dropped a little further astern she regained her speed and kept her place in the line.

Just ahead of the *Malaya*, the *Warspite* had also been hit by a salvo of shells that crashed down onto the quarterdeck and her 'X' Turret at around 17.30.

The *Warspite* received one hit from an 11″ shell which hit right aft. Even in 'A' Turret at the other end of the ship, we felt the hit, which made the ship give a sort of wriggle, very like the feel of a trout on the end of a line.[25]

Assistant Clerk Gilbert Bickmore, HMS *Warspite*, Fifth Battle Squadron

Commander Walwyn was ordered by the captain to go aft and see what was happening.

I thought for a few seconds, "Should I go over the top of the turret or down through the shell room", but realised I ought to get there quickly and decided to go over the top. I didn't waste much time on the roof as the noise was awful and they were coming over pretty thick. As I got

down the starboard ladder of 'B' turret both 'A' and 'B' fired and made
me skip a bit quicker. Ran down ladder and tried to get into the port
superstructure – all clips were on, so I climbed over second cutter. Just as
I got up, one came through the after funnel with an awful screech and
spattered about everywhere. I put up my coat collar and ran like a stag,
feeling in a hell of a funk.[26]

Commander Humphrey Walwyn, HMS *Warspite*, Fifth Battle Squadron

At first he could find nothing wrong, despite searching through the mess
decks. Then he actually saw a shell hit.

Went through to foc'sle mess deck and was just going forward when a
12″ came through the side armour on the boys' mess deck. Terrific sheet
of golden flame, stink, impenetrable dust and everything seemed to fall
everywhere with an appalling noise.[27]

Commander Humphrey Walwyn, HMS *Warspite*, Fifth Battle Squadron

One of the ship's doctors was close to the seat of the explosion.

We were again struck. This time the shell came in through the armour
into the boys' mess deck, on the starboard side, just overhead and a
little forward of where we were. There was a loud crash as it exploded
and mess tables and forms seemed to be being thrown about all over
the place judging from the noise and clatter. Some of the fumes came
down into the distributing station and made the atmosphere rather
unpleasant for breathing for a short while, but they were soon
exhausted by the fans.[28]

Surgeon Gordon Ellis, HMS *Warspite*, Fifth Battle Squadron

At least one casualty was carried to their dressing station.

This shell resulted in our first casualty forward. Portions of it struck a
Stoker (Frederick Plater by name) in the left side of the neck, causing a
small perforating wound through into the pharynx, from which there was
at first considerable frothy haemorrhage. He was very collapsed from
shock also when brought down, but the bleeding was stopped by packing
the wound with thin strips of gauze and he subsequently did well. We put
him in one of the canvas bunks suspended between decks by wire stays.[29]

Surgeon Gordon Ellis, HMS *Warspite*, Fifth Battle Squadron

Walwyn swung into action organizing the various damage control parties. Speed was essential.

> Called for No. 2 Fire Brigade, and they ran up from the flat below
> and we got hoses on and put out a lot of burning refuse; directly water
> went through this 'glow' it vanished and I can't say what was burning.
> Personally, I think it was water gas or something like it. Several of the
> fire brigade were sick due to the sweet, sickly stench, but there was no
> sign of poison gas. The shell hole was clean and about the size of a
> scuttle; big flakes of armour had been flung right across the mess deck
> wrecking everything. Many armour bolts came away. The flooding
> cabinet was completely wrecked and all voice pipes and electric leads
> overhead were cut to pieces. Smoke was pouring up through holes in
> the deck, and it occurred to me that the high angle magazine was very
> near. Told Pring to disconnect all flooding gear from main deck and
> stand by to flood from middle deck position. Water from the cut fire
> mains was pouring below and smoke soon stopped. Plugged fire mains
> as far as we could. Everybody busy 'souvenir' hunting and had to put
> hose over them to make them take cover below again.[30]
>
> Commander Humphrey Walwyn, HMS *Warspite*, Fifth Battle Squadron

The severed fire mains allowed thousands of gallons of water to flood the decks below 'X' Turret with awful consequences for one trapped sailor.

> The working chamber was flooded, a shell had severed the 4″ fire main
> and water was pouring into the handling room. I reported this to the
> gunhouse, they soon had this under control, but the sentry who was in
> charge of the escape hatch was drowned.[31]
>
> Able Seaman Gunner Percival Cox, HMS *Warspite*, Fifth Battle Squadron

When he got aft, Walwyn found that there was considerable damage and even as he investigated its scope another shell arrived which wrecked his cabin.

> Lot of burning debris in my cabin which we put out. In the middle of
> this heap was Eileen's miniature without its case, but otherwise perfect.
> Sleeping cabin was not so bad and only spattered with splinters. There
> were about four bursts in the lobby, trunk to steering compartment was

wrecked, stanchions cut through, captain's pantry in heaps and
everything in a filthy state of indescribable wreckage. Realised things
were pretty warm aft and nothing could be done so went forward before
any more shells arrived.[32]

Commander Humphrey Walwyn, HMS *Warspite*, Fifth Battle Squadron

Unsurprisingly, Walwyn at last was forced to pause to catch his breath.

Had a cigarette on the port side of the cooks lobby, or rather started
one to steady my feelings. Had a yarn with the Paymaster who was
wandering about in a 'kapok' waistcoat using appalling language as to
when the Grand Fleet were going to turn up. Had a laugh together,
anyway. Whilst there a 12″ came into warrant officers' galley and blew
through deck. A stoker alongside me looked up and said, "There goes
my _ _ _ dinner!"[33]

Commander Humphrey Walwyn, HMS *Warspite*, Fifth Battle Squadron

Despite all the alarums and hits, the second distinct phase of the battle
of Jutland, subsequently known as the Run to the North, was characterized
by the almost miraculous survival of the Fifth Battle Squadron. Yet British
super-dreadnoughts were by no means quiescent victims. Through all their
trials and tribulations, the *Barham*, *Valiant*, *Warspite* and *Malaya* distinguished
themselves through the prowess of their magnificent gunnery as they
continued to score repeated hits on the German ships that threatened them.

The *Seydlitz* was systematically battered, as were the *Lützow* and the
Derfflinger. All of these battlecruisers felt the crushing weight of the huge
British 15-inch shells. Given the high expectations that they held after
their successes in the Run to the South, it was a deeply disappointing phase
of the battle for Hipper's men.

This part of the action, fought against a numerically inferior but more
powerfully armed enemy, who kept us under fire at ranges at which we
were helpless, was highly depressing, nerve-wracking, and exasperating.
Our only means of defence was to leave the line for a short time, when
we saw that the enemy had our range. As this manoeuvre was
imperceptible to the enemy, we extricated ourselves at regular intervals
from the hail of fire.[34]

Commander Georg von Hase, SMS *Derfflinger*, I Scouting Group, High Seas Fleet

The long ranges, coupled with passages of uncertain visibility and drifting smoke, reduced the efficiency of the German battlecruisers.

> I only fired to make quite sure that the enemy were still out of range, and then, to save ammunition, I contented myself with isolated shots from one turret. The guns were again trained on the upper edge of the funnels or the mastheads. At these long ranges the enemy's shooting was not good either, though their salvoes, it is true, fell well together and always over an area of not more than 300 to 400 metres diameter. The control, however, was not very efficient, perhaps owing to the poor visibility. At any rate, the salvoes fell at very irregular distances from our ship. Nevertheless, we suffered bad hits, two or three heavy shells striking us during this phase. When a heavy shell hit the armour of our ship, the terrific crash of the explosion was followed by a vibration of the whole ship, affecting even the conning-tower. The shells which exploded in the interior of the ship caused rather a dull roar, which was transmitted all over by the countless voice-pipes and telephones.[35]
>
> Commander Georg von Hase, SMS *Derfflinger*, I Scouting Group, High Seas Fleet

A faint odour of sour grapes may be discerned in von Hase's comments on the accuracy of the Fifth Battle Squadron gunnery. In the event, neither side suffered the kind of disaster that might have been expected. The heavy armour of the super-dreadnoughts proved able to prevent the kind of damage that might have reduced their speed or combat efficiency; the armour of the German battlecruisers could not prevent severe damage from the 15-inch shells that severely eroded their fighting powers, but it proved sound enough to protect their vitals. Scheer did not succeed in significantly reducing the strength of the Grand Fleet. The purpose of his sortie into the North Sea – the opportunity to entrap and destroy a significant portion of the British fleet – that he had sought and worked hard to realize had been presented to him, but, through the resilience of the British super-dreadnoughts, it had slipped through his fingers. Scheer's period of ascendancy had passed. There was no clear victor in the Run to the North, except perhaps for the man who lurked over the horizon. Jellicoe's long-awaited moment was approaching.

CHAPTER FIVE

WHEN FLEETS COLLIDE

A S THE BATTLE RAGED in the south, Admiral Sir John Jellicoe's Grand Fleet was thundering down across the North Sea, desperate to reach the scene of the action. His twenty-four dreadnought battleships were drawn up in six line abreast columns of four ships. Surrounding the main body of the fleet, to foil any attempted submarine attacks, were the 4th Light Cruiser Squadron and the screening destroyers of the 4th, 11th and 12th Flotillas. Ahead of them were the widely spread armoured cruisers of the 1st and 2nd Cruiser Squadrons, which acted as a further screen to prevent surprise and to reconnoitre the way forward. Finally, some 25 miles ahead, acting as an advance guard to the whole fleet, there was the 3rd Battlecruiser Squadron. The Grand Fleet was the mightiest fleet that had ever existed and represented the vast bulk of Great Britain's naval strength.

> A ripping day, fairly clear – light breeze – and a fearfully imposing sight the whole lot piffing along at 17 knots plus screening destroyers all round led by Flotilla Leaders and four funnel cruisers (mine bumpers) ahead of all. Yet it seemed impossible that these few ships represented the whole of England's might bar battlecruisers – 24 battleships in all.[1]
>
> Midshipman Arthur James, HMS *Royal Oak*, 3rd Division, Fourth Battle Squadron

In Nelson's day there had been many more ships of the line and teeming hundreds of minor vessels. If the battle of Trafalgar had ended in defeat, then the Royal Navy could have fallen back on its other fleets and fought on if not regardless then at least with some hope of success. But twentieth-century technology had demanded that all Britain's eggs were placed in just a few baskets. An awareness of this vulnerability was at the heart of Jellicoe's assessment of the naval war in 1916.

It is interesting to compare this situation with that existing a century earlier. In September, 1805, the month before Trafalgar ... in addition to Nelson's force of 26 capital ships and 19 frigates, the Navy had, therefore, in commission in home waters and the Mediterranean a yet more numerous force of 47 capital ships and 50 frigates. The main portion of this force was with Cornwallis off Ushant, and was watching Brest. Between the Shetlands and Beachy Head we had 155 sloops and small vessels. In 1916, in addition to the Grand Fleet of 39 capital ships (including battlecruisers) and 32 cruisers and light cruisers, we had in commission in home waters and the Mediterranean only 13 capital ships (all of pre-Dreadnought types and, therefore, obsolescent) and 5 light cruisers. Between the Shetlands and Beachy Head we had, exclusive of the Grand Fleet and Harwich force, about 60 destroyers (mostly of old types), 6 P boats, and 33 old torpedo boats. In September, 1805, we had building 32 ships of the line in England, besides 10 under construction in Russia, and 36 frigates. In May, 1916, we had building five capital ships and about nine light cruisers. A consideration of these figures will show that the situation at these two periods was very different, in that, in 1805, the force engaged at Trafalgar was only a relatively small portion of the available British Fleet; yet Mahan has declared that, "Nelson's far distant, storm-beaten ships on which the Grand Army never looked, stood between it and the dominion of the world." In 1916 the Grand Fleet included the large majority of the vessels upon which the country had to rely for safety.[2]

Admiral Sir John Jellicoe, HMS *Iron Duke*, 3rd Division, Fourth Battle Squadron

If the Germans were successful in isolating and destroying any significant number of his dreadnoughts without suffering comparable losses themselves, then Britain would be vulnerable to complete and utter naval defeat with no meaningful recourse. This was the burden that Jellicoe carried on his shoulders.

The initial wireless report of the first contact with the Germans, made at 14.18, from the *Galatea*, had been intercepted aboard the *Iron Duke*. Jellicoe immediately ordered the fleet to raise steam to allow full speed.

The Fleet Wireless Officer ordered me to the Admiral's charthouse, a small steel shelter high up on the bridge superstructure, a splendid viewing point if one had the time to look out through its portholes. Whilst climbing the several ladders to the bridge, I noticed that the battle fleet had stopped zig-zagging, hurrying forward at a speed in excess of normal cruising. The majestic and menacing looking battleships, surrounded by destroyer flotillas and with cruisers fanned out ahead, gave me a stirring and reassuring feeling, yet the urgency of the occasion did not affect me in the least; so many times before we had gone to action stations which had led to nothing.[3]

Petty Officer Telegraphist Arthur Brister, HMS *Iron Duke*, 3rd Division, Fourth Battle Squadron

Gradually, further reports came in, culminating in Vice Admiral Sir David Beatty's report at 15.40 that he had sighted Admiral Franz von Hipper's five battlecruisers. As the various elements of the Battlecruiser Fleet and Grand Fleet were out of any visual contact there was a complete reliance on wireless messages. Petty Officer Arthur Brister thus had an important role in the communications chain that was so vital to the effective control of the various elements under Jellicoe's command.

In the charthouse my duty was the manning of the W/T remote control position, a panel of instruments and switches for:

a) The reception of operation priority signals from the Main and Auxiliary W/T Stations by buzzer in Morse code exactly as received by the operators in the cabinets below. These signals were of the highest priority and generally were enemy sighting reports or other information vital to the C-in-C. It had been amply proved during exercises that the transit of these O-P signals in Morse from the W/T offices to the bridge was the most expedient method provided the operators worked at high speed, making no mistakes nor needing repetitions. From the charthouse the signals were sent to the Cypher Room just beneath.

b) Taking over control of the two transmitters for the purpose of sending manoeuvring signals direct to the battle fleet at the same time as the flag signals were made. Simultaneous signalling by flag and W/T was necessary when the battle fleet was spread out or in bad visibility. Ships other than the battle fleet, i.e. battlecruisers, cruisers and light cruisers could also hear these manoeuvring signals being made by W/T and thus be kept informed of the battle fleet's movements, it being most essential they knew when and how the battle fleet was deploying.

c) Switching into the receiver in the Main W/T Office when it was necessary to receive direct from the ships.

From the charthouse, Commander Phipps, the Assistant Fleet Signal Officer, controlled the distribution of all signals by the use of telephone, voice-tube and pneumatic tube, the most used of these being connected to the Upper Compass Platform immediately above, the Cypher Room, War Room and Signal Platform underneath the charthouse. The only piece of furniture in the charthouse apart from the C-in-C's chart table was a wooden settee in one corner; therefore the Commander and myself had to stand, using the chart table as a desk for writing down signals.[4]

Petty Officer Telegraphist Arthur Brister, HMS *Iron Duke*, 3rd Division, Fourth Battle Squadron

Jellicoe adjusted the fleet's course to close directly on the Battlecruiser Fleet, ordered his ships to prepare for action at 15.00 and increased speed as fast as possible until by 16.00 they had reached a fleet speed of 20 knots. Meanwhile the 3rd Battlecruiser Squadron, commanded by Rear Admiral Sir Horace Hood aboard the *Invincible* and accompanied by the *Inflexible* and *Indomitable*, was sent forward to reinforce Beatty as quickly as possible. Hood increased speed to 25 knots and moved rapidly ahead.

We could feel the vibration as speed was increased and the grim calm of suppressed excitement settled on everybody. At this moment the grizzled old Sergeant Major came up to me to report everything in the turret correct and I noted the curious fact that for the first time since I had been in the turret he saluted me with the perfect precision that he reserved for Marine Officers and added a rolling, "Sirrr!" at the end of his report – an honour not previously accorded to me as a sailor of tender years. I thought that perhaps there was at least one old-timer who felt as excited as I did myself.[5]

Midshipman John Croome, HMS *Indomitable*, 3rd Battlecruiser Squadron

Although Jellicoe was confident in the superiority of his four super-dreadnoughts and six battlecruisers over the German five battlecruisers, he was left in considerable suspense by an absence of reports from any of his subordinates in the Battlecruiser Fleet. Deeply concerned, he

signalled to Vice Admiral Hugh Evan-Thomas to check that the Fifth
Battle Squadron were in action alongside Beatty and received the distinctly
terse confirmation: 'Yes, I am engaging enemy.'[6]

Jellicoe's orders to prepare for action naturally caused an outburst of
frenetic activity in the Grand Fleet.

> We were told by signal to "Assume complete readiness for action in every
> respect". This consisted of clearing away guard rails, frapping, rigging
> and placing shot mantlets where not already done, rigging hoses which
> were left running on the upper deck to keep it wet for a fire precaution.
> Other fire precautions comprised the striking down of hammocks,
> officers' bedding, mess stools and tables, and other inflammable objects
> from the cabins and messdecks on the main deck. Ready use ammunition
> was got up for the 6″ and 3″ guns from the magazines and shell rooms, a
> limited amount only; again as a fire precaution. Three or four extra white
> ensigns were hoisted at the mast and yards.[7]
>
> Lieutenant Angus Cunninghame Graham, HMS *Agincourt*, 6th Division, First Battle
> Squadron

In all the ships, whatever their size, there was an almost endless list of
preparations to complete, designed to increase battle efficiency, reduce
the risk of fire and generally facilitate damage control. Some were routine.

> A few hours before we were expected to be in action our Gunnery
> Officer Lieutenant Commander Erol Manners mustered men off watch
> and instructed us to make preparations i.e. get a good meal, draw the
> galley fires, use the heads, sling hammocks to check flying metal, sling
> gangways, fit hoists over magazines, check guns and torpedoes, close
> all bulkheads and watertight doors etc. During the afternoon watch we
> were 'stood to' at action stations and were steaming at about 25 knots.[8]
>
> Boy 1st Class Seaman William Bennett, HMS *Comus*, 4th Light Cruiser Squadron

Others were more intensely personal but no less vital for the individuals
concerned.

> We boys had been previously warned to put on clean underwear in case
> of wounds and this I had done.[9]
>
> Boy 1st Class David Frost, HMS *Conqueror*, 2nd Division, Second Battle Squadron

Although nobody really knew what was happening to the south, it did not prevent rumours circulating round the ships that Beatty and the Battlecruiser Fleet were in action. Men had to come to terms with the idea that '*Der Tag*' – the day they had dreamed of for so long while swinging at anchor in Scapa Flow or carrying out seemingly fruitless sweeps through the grey wastes of the North Sea – was finally at hand.

> Now we really did sit up and take notice, believing that at long last the
> day for which we had been patiently working and waiting had arrived.
> My cursed imagination started playing me tricks and it was only by a big
> effort that I was able to stifle it and persuade myself that I really was
> itching for a scrap.[10]
>
> Midshipman John Brass, HMS *Orion*, 2nd Division, Second Battle Squadron

Overall it seems that most of the men responded to the bugles' clarion call to action with a complex mixture of entwined trepidation and anticipation. '*Der Tag*' was nigh, but they could not but be aware of their own personal mortality and a fear that they might not survive the battle ahead.

> We all flew to our action stations, each man doing his best to look
> comfortable and happy. Judging by my own feelings, I arrived at the
> conclusion that what had really sounded on the bugle must have been
> 'Trembling Stations'. It was hard to realise the fact that after all those weary
> non-leave-giving months we were at last to meet the Huns, and it was with
> mixed feelings that we eagerly scanned the horizon and strained our ears.[11]
>
> Ordinary Seaman William Robinson, HMS *Royalist*, 4th Light Cruiser Squadron

In the hustle and bustle, as they rushed to their myriad stations, friends took the chance where possible to acknowledge each other for what could be the last time.

> When action stations was sounded I proceeded from the bridge to 'Y'
> Turret on the quarterdeck, which was the Marines' turret. On the way
> I remember passing my best pal on the ship, named Len Riddles, who
> was going in the opposite direction to his station in the port torpedo
> room. We had just time for a quick handshake and a "Good luck!" as
> we passed each other.[12]
>
> Signalman Victor Jensen, HMS *Collingwood*, 5th Division, First Battle Squadron

For one Royal Marine, John Beardsley, there was a very real problem in taking up his designated position. It took all his strength of mind just to enter his turret.

> Taking up my station in the turret was a real test of my morale, I suffered from claustrophobia since as a boy spending four years down a coal mine. I dreaded action stations at each rehearsal prior to the battle. But the firm orders issued by our commanding officer, Captain Colley and his reassuring smile to all his crew, drove the nightmare of the steel coffin away.[13]
>
> Private John Beardsley, Royal Marine Light Infantry, HMS *Hercules*, 6th Division, First Battle Squadron

Claustrophobia was not the only reason for nerves. Anxiety as to how they would perform under the stress of battle loomed large in some minds.

> My post was in the gunhouse of my turret and my business was to keep an eye on the loading arrangements. Inside the turret, there is no means of seeing out except for a periscope but as there was a special man detailed for this position, the rest of us were kept in an unpleasant state of suspense and complete ignorance of any developments that might be taking place or expected. It must have been like waiting to go over the top and wondering if there was to be a bullet labelled, "Me!?" I noticed that some of the younger members of the gun crew looked as though they were feeling very much like myself, in a state of nervous tension. The older sailors and petty officers cracked jokes and spun yarns, partly to allay their own excitement and partly to calm the nerves of the younger men, and I found that taking part in this badinage helped me a lot. I am quite certain however, that there *was* a fear at the back of each of the older men's heads, not of the enemy, but of the possibility of the youngsters in their excitement making a slip in the drill which might cause a jam in the complicated loading mechanism and put that gun out of action and thus getting off fewer rounds than the other guns in the ship. A petty officer gunlayer would find it difficult to 'live down' a misfire in action due to faulty drill![14]
>
> Midshipman John Brass, HMS *Orion*, 2nd Division, Second Battle Squadron

The gun turrets were fearsomely complicated monsters, pushing their crews and the modern technology they sought to harness to the limits. It was no simple affair firing huge shells from moving platforms, across some 15 miles of waves to hit a weaving target measuring only around 90 feet wide. The turret crews needed to work closely as a team to ensure that nothing disturbed the regular pattern that each gun needed to fire its round at the split second required.

A full charge for a turret gun consists of a projectile weighing the best part of a ton and four quarter charges each weighing about 55lbs. This explosive little load is brought up from the working chamber immediately below, to the breech of the gun, by a lift called a cage. This cage consists of a trough in which the projectile lies and a steel box made in two compartments one above the other in each of which are laid two quarter charges. As soon as the cage reaches the mouth of the gun a folding telescopic rammer shoots out, butts the tail of the projectile and propels it at great speed into the yawning breech. The rammer then flicks back and as soon as it is back clear of the tray, the flap door of the cage springs open and the lower two quarter charges drop down onto the tray. These are rammed in a little way and as soon as the rammer is back the door of the cage is again opened and the last two quarter charges drop out and are rammed into the gun – the rammer is withdrawn, the cage drops, the breech is closed and locked and all is ready.[15]

Midshipman John Croome, HMS *Indomitable*, 3rd Battlecruiser Squadron

Deep in the bowels lurked the engineers, charged with keeping the great engines beating to supply power to the muscles and sinews of the ships. Below the water-line and often in ignorance of what was happening above them, some men were understandably prone to morbid fears.

My responsibility was the maintenance of the four hydraulic engines supplying pressure at 1,100 lbs per square inch to the five 13.5″ gun turrets and the boat hoist and four air compressors supplying air at 2,500 lbs per square inch for charging and firing torpedoes. The engineer officer of the watch was an engineer lieutenant fairly new to the ship, who was a survivor from a previous action when the three fairly old cruisers, HMS *Aboukir*, *Hogue* and *Cressy* were torpedoed and sunk in that order. He had been in HMS *Hogue* and when she was hit and foundered, he swam to HMS *Cressy* only in time to be torpedoed again. His nerves were still in a very bad state. News began to come through to the engine room. This news had a marked effect on the engineer officer of the watch. He became very agitated, could not remain still and repeatedly left the engine room to try and get further news. He was not of course leaving his post of duty; we were not at action stations so it was within the scope of his duty to visit other parts of the department such as the boiler rooms.[16]

Engine Room Artificer 4th Class Harold Wright, HMS *King George V*, 1st Division, Second Battle Squadron

As the ships raced on and the tension inside them mounted, the men stuck far below decks would not have been human had they not considered exactly how they might fare if the worst came to the worst in the coming battle.

My station was down in the torpedo flat well below the water line, which I shared with the torpedo tubes crews and the atmosphere was pretty tense. One cannot get out of these places too easily. I think that most of us were concerned with the sliding watertight door – would the 'up top' people close it or not? Lying in a steel box was not ideal. Awaiting to hear that frightful thud against the side, wondering how I was going to get out, those were my thoughts and feelings.[17]

Electrical Artificer Frank Hall, HMS *George V*, 1st Division, Second Battle Squadron

Whatever their inner feelings, most of the men behaved just as they were expected to do, in the finest traditions of the Royal Navy. It may on occasions have been a façade, but it was a good one.

It was a most inspiring fact for me (as their Captain) to notice the smiles on everyone's face; to see the cheerfulness and enthusiasm throughout the ship at the idea of at last having a 'go' at the Germans. Though the prevalent thought throughout the Fleet was not so much the actual killing of Germans and sinking their ships, as the thought that at last the navy was to have the chance of proving their worth and showing our folks at home that their continued trust in us was not misplaced. And further a feeling that at last we could show our professional skills against a strong adversary rather than any particular bitterness against them as individuals.[18]

Lieutenant Commander Arthur Marsden, HMS *Ardent*, 4th Flotilla

When, at 16.38, news was received from Goodenough aboard the *Southampton* that the High Seas Fleet had been sighted, Jellicoe was not at all perturbed. Thanks to the incompetent handling of their intelligence sources by the Admiralty, he was not expecting to meet the High Seas Fleet, which he had imagined still secure in Wilhelmshaven harbour. He remained content that the reasoning behind his original dispositions remained sound.

> At this time I was confident that, under the determined leadership of Sir David Beatty, with a force of four of our best and fastest battleships and six battle cruisers, very serious injury would be inflicted on the five battle cruisers of the enemy if they could be kept within range. The report of the presence of the German Battle Fleet, which was communicated to our Battle Fleet, did not cause me any uneasiness in respect of the safety of our own vessels, since our ships of the Fifth Battle Squadron were credited with a speed of 25 knots. I did not, however, expect that they would be able to exceed a speed of 24 knots; the information furnished to me at this time gave the designed speed of the fastest German battleships as 20.5 knots only. Even after making full allowance for the fact that our ships were probably carrying more fuel and stores proportionately than the Germans, and giving the Germans credit for some excess over the designed speed, no doubt existed in my mind that both our battleships and our battle cruisers with Sir David Beatty could keep well out of range of the enemy's Battle Fleet, if necessary, until I was able to reinforce them.[19]
>
> Admiral Sir John Jellicoe, HMS *Iron Duke*, 3rd Division, Fourth Battle Squadron

Jellicoe might have expected that this definite sighting of the Grand Fleet would allow the Admiralty to release the Harwich Force from their enforced inactivity. Commodore Reginald Tyrwhitt obviously thought so, as at 17.15 he set sail on his own authority. Unfortunately, the caution of the Admiralty knew no bounds and, at 17.35, it bluntly ordered him to, 'Return at once and await orders.' Presumably it feared that some elements of the High Seas Fleet might give Beatty and Jellicoe the slip to launch a marauding raid into the English Channel. Tyrwhitt was incandescent with barely suppressed fury. Whatever happened, it was apparent that the Grand Fleet, as Jellicoe had always suspected, would not be getting any destroyer reinforcements from Harwich.

Goodenough's signal meant there was no doubt now that Admiral Reinhard Scheer and the High Seas Fleet were not only out, but sailing directly towards the Grand Fleet. And so at 16.51 Jellicoe made the long-awaited signal: 'Fleet action is imminent.'[20] This confirmation of what many had suspected and hoped was the case acted as the trigger for a cathartic release of emotion aboard many ships.

In my turret the men spontaneously forgot discipline and let forth a hearty cheer which also came echoing up the shafts from the shell room and magazine down below, and reverberated in the confined space. Of course we couldn't hear others cheering elsewhere in the ship, but the ship almost literally seemed to shake with the cheering in some places as large numbers of voice pipes connect the various compartments and stations, and down these the cheers came booming from the boiler rooms, torpedo flats, turrets, gun positions and everywhere in the ship as the infection spread. The Captain's delight in the conning tower where the majority of voice pipes and telephones are collected must have been intense, but his sole remark was, "I had better put on my red waistcoat!" A startling scarlet garment which he was alleged to have worn in every action in which he had served.[21]

Midshipman John Croome, HMS *Indomitable*, 3rd Battlecruiser Squadron

As the fleets raced towards each other it was essential that Jellicoe should be given all possible intelligence of the exact location and course of the High Seas Fleet if he was to make an informed decision as to the method and direction of deployment of the battle fleet from the existing six columns into a single line.

The 'plot' made on the reports received between 5pm and 6pm from Commodore Goodenough, of the 2nd Light Cruiser Squadron, and the report at 4.45pm from Sir David Beatty in the *Lion* giving the position of the enemy's Battle Fleet, showed that we, of the Battle Fleet, might meet the High Seas Fleet approximately ahead and that the cruiser line ahead of the Battle Fleet would sight the enemy nearly ahead of the centre.

Obviously, however, great reliance could not be placed on the positions given by the ships of the Battle Cruiser Fleet, which had been in action for two hours and frequently altering course. I realised this, but when contact actually took place it was found that the positions given were at least twelve miles in error when compared with the *Iron Duke*'s reckoning. The result was that the enemy's Battle Fleet appeared on the starboard bow instead of ahead, as I had expected, and contact also took place earlier than was anticipated. There can be no doubt as to the accuracy of the reckoning on board the *Iron Duke*, as the movements of that ship could be "plotted" with accuracy after leaving Scapa Flow, there being no disturbing elements to deal with.[22]

Admiral Sir John Jellicoe, HMS *Iron Duke*, 3rd Division, Fourth Battle Squadron

In fact, confident as he was, Jellicoe was wrong in this assumption. It now appears that, although Beatty's positions were indeed out by some 7 miles west, the *Iron Duke* also had an error of some 4 miles east – a collective error totalling nearly 11 miles. At 17.33 the first contact between the respective screens of the Battlecruiser Fleet and the Grand Fleet occurred as the *Falmouth*, one of Beatty's screening light cruisers some 4 miles to the north of the *Lion*, sighted the *Black Prince*, the extreme starboard wing ship of Jellicoe's cruiser screen. Beatty was obviously miles to starboard of where Jellicoe expected him to appear from.

As Beatty approached the Grand Fleet, he adjusted his course to north-north-east, bending across the area from which he presumed Jellicoe would emerge, thus screening Jellicoe from view and at the same time closing in once again on Hipper and his indomitable battle-cruisers. At 17.40 firing once again broke out at a range of about 14,000 yards. During this period the combination of Beatty's battle-cruisers and the leading two ships of the Fifth Battle Squadron managed a formidable concentration of fire onto Hipper's battle-cruisers, which delivered a considerable number of hits, particularly on his flagship the *Lützow*.

At 5.41, we are heavily fired at by him and are hit four times. Two of these pierce the large 6″ casemate from above, destroy both W/T sets and cause severe casualties. Another bursts amidships without seriously injuring the main armour deck; but the fastenings in the gunnery

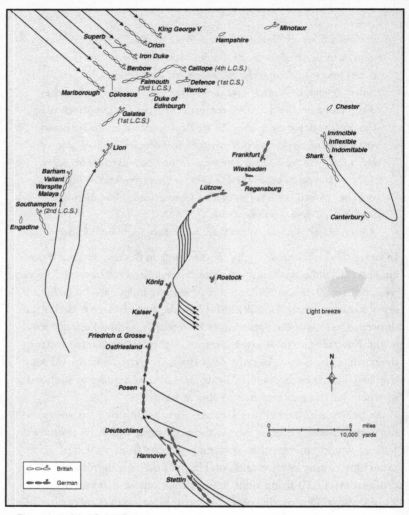

The arrival of the Grand Fleet

transmitting station, which were underneath, came adrift and smoke penetrated everywhere. The fire control was interrupted momentarily but was restarted shortly afterwards. Our own smoke becomes a nuisance; for a short time I had to let the after position carry on fire control. The enemy has for the moment the upper hand and I cannot get rid of the idea that trouble is brewing.[23]

Commander Günther Paschen, SMS *Lützow*, I Scouting Group, High Seas Fleet

Meanwhile, the *Indomitable* and the rest of the 3rd Battlecruiser Squadron had pressed on their south-south-east course to such an extent that they had passed beyond the line at which they should have seamlessly joined their comrades in the Battlecruiser Fleet. As a result, the *Lion* was actually to the south-west, as opposed to straight ahead, of the *Invincible*. Around Hood's battlecruisers were the usual screen of light cruisers and destroyers. The *Canterbury* was 5 miles ahead, the *Chester* was 5 miles to the west and the destroyers *Shark*, *Acasta*, *Ophelia* and *Christopher* were immediately ahead. The whole force was still proceeding. At 17.27 Captain Robert Lawson commanding the *Chester* heard the muffled roar of heavy guns to the south-west and was ordered to investigate by Hood. As they moved towards the gunfire the men aboard the *Chester* soon sighted flashes through the general mist and murk.

> Visibility was down to about 2,000 yards. We sighted enemy ships, four cruisers, to port and opened fire. The enemy soon got our range and were registering hits. One shell passed under the upper bridge going through the captain's sea cabin and hit a sounding machine on the starboard side before exploding, killing and wounding 12 signal staff on the flag deck leaving just two special lookouts on the upper bridge. Two signal boys were slightly wounded but they did not tell us until next morning. Exposed cordite was exploded and flames shot up about 200 feet. Guns' crews were walking over the side blinded and hurt. During the action I saw a man's hair stand on end – a thing I never thought possible. Captain Lawson was cut around the throat by a loose stay and he was the only one injured on the upper bridge. We showed the enemy a clean pair of heels.[24]
>
> Ordinary Signalman Charles Rudall, HMS *Chester*, Attached 3rd Battlecruiser Squadron

The *Chester* had run straight into the *Frankfurt*, *Wiesbaden*, *Pillau* and *Elbing* of the German II Scouting Group. The *Chester* was a new ship, commissioned less than a month earlier on 2 May. Her crew was barely trained, with a mass of new recruits only slightly leavened by a few old salts. As Lawson sighted the light cruisers, he swung round to starboard in an attempt to bring his main armament of ten 5.5-inch guns to bear, but he soon realized the perilous nature of his position and ran for it to the north, heading towards Hood and the battlecruisers.

My attention was given to dodging enemy's salvoes by steering towards the last fall of shot; thus maintaining the mean to the north-eastward and keeping the enemy's salvoes falling alternately on either side, on account of the constantly changing deflections. This was apparently successful as regards saving the ship from a large amount of further damage. In the last few minutes I believe she was seldom hit, but the changes in course rendered it impossible for the after guns to make effective shooting, even if the gun crews had been in a fit state and sufficient numbers to do so. But it was obvious to me that *Chester* was smothered with enemy's fire and I considered only the best way of getting out of action, without any heavy loss, by zig-zagging and taking shelter to the north-eastward of the Battlecruisers.[25]

Captain Robert Lawson, HMS *Chester*, Attached 3rd Battlecruiser Squadron

Lawson was livid that his inexperienced crew had been thrust without warning into such a maelstrom.

I may say that no case of actual flinching or deserting a post has come to my notice, although 47 out of 100 men at the guns crews were killed or wounded. But confusion undoubtedly occurred among gun crews – utterly inexperienced in all that appertains to sea life – when they found themselves on an open deck, with mutilated men all around, officer of the battery either killed or wounded and apparently no enemy to shoot at. Nothing to do in fact. The natural and sensible instinct in such cases is to take cover. The only apparent cover was the light bulkheads of superstructures, which appear to offer protection, but are in point of fact most efficient shell bursters. And disengaged crews endeavoured to take such shelter. The only real shelter is the off side of the gun shield. And had a larger proportion of experienced seamen been among the crews, it is not improbable that valuable lives would have been saved. Moreover it would not have been necessary to have an officer at each gun to direct the fire of those that would bear independently. A ship with open batteries, carrying this proportion of raw human material, with no gun director and the control voice-pipes unprotected, would be heavily handicapped against even one enemy cruiser of about the same type, fitted with an excellent gun director and manned by a properly trained crew. If a larger proportion of trained ratings cannot be found for the fleet, then a larger proportion of untrained ratings should go to armoured ships, where such a mass of casualties can hardly occur in such a short space of time and in full view of many other men.[26]

Captain Robert Lawson, HMS *Chester*, Attached 3rd Battlecruiser Squadron

Given the fate of the *Indefatigable* and *Queen Mary*, Lawson may have been over-sanguine, but his argument, and his palpable concern for his crew, nevertheless remain powerful.

As the shells splintered across and scored through the *Chester*'s upper works, Sub-Lieutenant Windham Hornby, who was relatively safe below decks in the gunnery transmitting station, became aware that all was not well.

Occasional bangs which I heard, I attributed to our guns being fired under 'local control' by the battery officers or even individual gunlayers. What I suppose I had been hearing was the bursting of German shell. As a matter of routine I 'challenged' the after fire control position, but all I got in reply was a loud bang which may have been the bursting of the shell which exploded and wrecked the position. There was also a loud bang and shock when a shell burst against the side armour abreast of, but a few feet above the level of the transmitting station. That shell did not penetrate, but the burst of it drove pieces of the side armour inboard which destroyed (though at the time we did not realise it) most of the transmitting station communications (voice-pipes) with the rest of the ship.[27]

Sub-Lieutenant Windham Hornby, HMS *Chester*, Attached 3rd Battlecruiser Squadron

Below decks the first-aid parties were battened down in the store-room to keep them safe. But they remained ready to carry out their task of ministering to the many wounded when called upon to do so.

There was about six of us including a young surgeon named Lieutenant Bloomfield, a brilliant Doctor. The first shot put all our lights out and we were in total darkness. After a lull in the fighting we were let out to the upper deck and what a sight – which will remain in my memory forever. An officer was lying dead with both legs severed in sea boots. I stepped over a body that had been disembowelled. I had to hold a seaman's foot while the Doctor cut it off as it was just hanging. We laid the bodies side by side and were told to turn them over on their stomachs.[28]

Officers Steward 1st Class Reginald Gulliver, HMS *Chester*, Attached 3rd Battlecruiser Squadron

Casualties and battle damage littered the upper decks. Sub-Lieutenant Hornby had a similar shock when he emerged from the transmitting station.

When I got up to the stokers' messdeck above the fore ammunition lobby I saw that already a slightly wounded man had come down and was being attended to by a first aid party. Another more serious casualty was being carried down on a stretcher. I found my way to the forecastle deck via what was known as the torpedo hatch and there I saw lying the first dead man I had ever seen – I was only 20 at the time. As signal officer of the ship I made my way to the bridge and discovered a sad state of affairs. A shell that had burst on the starboard sounding machine had wrecked the starboard side of the bridge and the port side had also suffered damage. Roy, the Chief Yeoman of Signals, had been killed as he was taking a signal up to the upper bridge for the Captain to see. He was lying on his back, the signal pad still clutched in his dead hand.[29]

Sub-Lieutenant Windham Hornby, HMS *Chester*, Attached 3rd Battlecruiser Squadron

Jinking from side to side, narrowly evading the shells that crashed into the sea all around her, the *Chester* fled for her life. But rescue was close at hand.

We sighted ships on the starboard beam and I was told to hoist the challenge. Going down the ladder to the flag deck I fell on the body of the Yeoman of Signals; a step had been shot away from the ladder. I hoisted the challenge and using the telescope I noticed three large ships, one veered slightly and I saw that it was the 3rd Battlecruiser Squadron. I called out, "*Invincible* crowd, Sir!" It was a great relief. They steered past us and gave us a great cheer. My leading hand asked for me; he was lying on the flag deck port side. He was quite natural and asked for a cigarette. He took a couple of pulls then was sick. He said he was dying, I said, "No!" and tried to cheer him up. He was leading Signaller

George Dinn, about 30. I know he was getting married next leave, but it wasn't to be as he died two days later.[30]

Ordinary Signalman Charles Rudall, HMS *Chester*, Attached 3rd Battlecruiser Squadron

From the many casualties among the *Chester*'s gun crews, one was picked out for special attention following the battle. The boy sight setter on the forecastle 5.5-inch gun crew remained at his post awaiting orders, despite the severe wounds he received in a shell burst, which had killed the rest of the crew. Jack Cornwell, aged just 16, emerged from subsequent newspaper accounts of the battle as the epitome of youthful British valour and selfless dedication to the higher cause. By that time he had already succumbed to his mortal wounds but his story encapsulated many of the virtues held dear by a nation at war. Jack Cornwell became a hero. He was awarded a posthumous Victoria Cross, becoming the youngest recipient of that award in the twentieth century. The exact circumstances of his courageous deed are now blurred. There were few direct witnesses and what factual evidence did exist was quickly overshadowed by the propaganda value of his example to British youth in a time of conflict. But there can be no doubt that Jack Cornwell stands as a fair and deserving representative of all the inexperienced members of the *Chester*'s gun crews who died during their violent baptism of fire. Cornwell's VC can be seen today in the Imperial War Museum in London, together with the 5.5-inch gun alongside which he stood firm, enduring symbols of all those ordinary young men who fought and died at Jutland.

At 16.37 Hood, aboard the *Invincible*, had heard the firing and at once turned to support the *Chester*, arriving in the nick of time. Once in position the battlecruisers' guns roared out. Here they were truly in their element. They had caught a group of German light cruisers cold and had little to fear from their relatively diminutive opponents. Croome was in the port midship turret of the *Indomitable*, second in the line.

The elevation and direction pointers began to get really agitated and ranges started coming through thick and fast. A minute later the gunlayers simultaneously cried, "There she is!", and the "Commence Fire!" sounded off. Even then it was fully another minute before the first salvo went off, quickly followed by the left gun salvo. I remember feeling inside the identical feelings that I was accustomed to experiencing when bending over the table for 'six of the best'. Outwardly I felt unnaturally calm and so self possessed as to remember to check the time it took to reload with my fire control stop watches. It was not particularly good but we had an unusually long interval to wait before the next two salvoes went off. This time both guns reloaded in 11½ seconds, equalling the record, and I felt pretty good about things in general.[31]

Midshipman John Croome, HMS *Indomitable*, 3rd Battlecruiser Squadron

The recent intensive gunnery practice at Scapa Flow paid off as they hit home almost immediately. There is no doubt that the II Scouting Group was in extreme danger.

A few minutes later a signal came through from Admiral Hood commanding our Squadron, saying simply, "Good shooting *Indomitable!*" and the message was passed to the guns and cheered us considerably. We now really felt that we were '*Indomitable*' and our Admiral was '*Invincible*' and fell to congratulating ourselves.[32]

Midshipman John Croome, HMS *Indomitable*, 3rd Battlecruiser Squadron

The *Wiesbaden* was worst hit as the 12-inch shells crashed down and disabled both of her engines, leaving her stationary. The *Pillau* also received engine damage, but retained a speed of 24 knots, which enabled her to keep her place in the line as they escaped, fleeing to the south in considerable confusion. Given the poor visibility and briefness of the contact, it is not surprising that Konteradmiral Friedrich Bödicker and his subordinate captains in the II Scouting Group should misidentify their opponents. They sent reports to Scheer that they were under fire from a group of dreadnoughts. It is one of the great ironies of the battle that while Jellicoe was desperately waiting for news giving the position and course of the High Seas Fleet, Scheer received a plethora of reports claiming to have sighted the dreadnoughts of the Grand Fleet, all of which were essentially wrong.

In the confused situation, Kapitänleutnant Lahs commanding the XII Half Flotilla, who had also misidentified Hood's battlecruisers as dreadnoughts, moved in to the attack. The German destroyers *V46*, *V69* and *S50*, despite heavy fire from the battlecruisers, managed to approach within 6,500 yards of their target before launching four torpedoes. The *V45* and *G37* got even closer, but only fired two torpedoes as they became embroiled in a spirited action with the four British destroyers of the 4th Flotilla led by Commander Loftus Jones aboard the *Shark*. The British destroyers sought to distract the superior forces from their target by the sheer vigour and *élan* of their attack.

> The destroyers were supported by cruisers and things very quickly became unpleasantly warm. The German shooting was undoubtedly good, their salvoes falling close together – perhaps too close together, really – but at first we were little hit, although a piece of shell scalped a signalman on our bridge, and a lot of shell splinters were flying about. We afterwards picked out 30 to 40 pieces of shell from the mattresses slung round the bridge. Also, on the bridge we were all soaked through by the spray thrown up by shell, causing the sub-lieutenant to remark that, "An umbrella would be handy!"[33]
>
> Lieutenant Commander John Barron, HMS *Acasta*, 4th Flotilla

The following waves of German destroyers, made up of the IX and II Flotillas, were severely hampered by their predecessors retiring through their line of fire, the limited visibility and the spirited spoiling tactics of the four British destroyers. Only the *V28*, *S52*, *S35* and *G104* managed to fire a torpedo each. The torpedoes were subsequently sighted by the *Invincible*, *Inflexible* and *Indomitable*, which were able to evade them. Not enough torpedoes had been fired to make hits impossible to avoid. The four destroyers of the 4th Flotilla had performed their defensive function well in emphatically distracting the Germans from their larger prey. Unfortunately, the *Shark* was severely hit and slowed almost to a stop, unable to steer.

> It was then that our steering was hit. I reported, "Steering gear gone, Sir!" on which the Captain gave orders to me to man the after wheel. It was then that I got wounded in the head and over the right eye. We then went to starboard making use of our guns on the port side. This was when the forecastle gun's crew were completely blown away gun and all. About this time the *Acasta* arrived and the Captain of the *Acasta* asked if he could assist us and the Captain replied, "Don't get sunk over us!"[34]
>
> Torpedo Coxswain William Griffin, HMS *Shark*, 4th Flotilla

Recognizing that it would surely doom the *Acasta* as well, Loftus Jones refused the offer of a tow and prepared for his last fight. However, iron-ically, the position had now changed as German battlecruisers began to emerge from the mists to the south. The surviving 4th Flotilla destroyers now appeared well placed to threaten a torpedo attack and Able Seaman Clement Ford was acting as quartermaster on the bridge of the *Ophelia* when Commander Lewis Crabbe ordered his ship into action.

> As we turned to fire we saw the *Shark* put out of action and she was sinking fast. The next destroyer, *Acasta*, went to her assistance but was ordered away by Loftus-Jones as the *Shark* was sinking and the *Acasta* was heavily damaged. We passed both with *Christopher* following us. We already had our forecastle gun put out of action and the gun crew lying dead around it except for one of the loading numbers who was standing up with his arm jammed in the breech of the semi-automatic gun. I was at the wheel steering at the time. Shrapnel was bursting overhead, which caught this poor fellow and opened up his skull. It was a sickening sight to look down on this from our small bridge. The Captain said to me, "Ford, go down and tell the Doctor to come up and drop him by taking off his arm." When I got down the steps, which were only three in number, the Doctor was standing under the canopy with all his instruments and shouting out, "Where are the Germans?" I tried to calm him but to no avail and just as I was about to return to the bridge to explain to the Captain, we were caught in a shower of shells from all quarters, some hitting us, some missing. So the Captain decided to fire our last torpedo and then to extract ourselves if possible – as there was only us and the *Christopher* left.[35]

Able Seaman W. J. Clement-Ford, HMS *Ophelia*, 4th Flotilla

The threat to Hipper's battlecruisers was not terribly serious given the isolation of the British destroyers, but, taken in conjunction with the renewed vigour of the fire from Beatty's battlecruisers and the Fifth Battle Squadron, it seems to have been the final straw. At 17.59 Hipper ordered a reversal in course to south-west, to reduce the immediate pressure and seek sanctuary closer to the High Seas Fleet. His retreat lasted for just a matter of minutes, before he effected a junction with Scheer and the High Seas Fleet. At 18.14 Hipper was therefore once more able to revert to his original course and lead the whole battle line back towards the north-east and the crippled *Wiesbaden*.

As he made this manoeuvre Hipper again found himself plagued by British destroyers on both sides of his line. The *Acasta* was just moving away from the *Shark* when she spotted the German battlecruisers emerging from the mist at about 4,500 yards on her port quarter. Without hesitating she fired a single torpedo and claimed a hit, although this cannot be verified. From the other side of the German battlecruisers and dreadnoughts another lone destroyer entered the fray. The *Onslow* had already made one brave but fruitless attack on the High Seas Fleet. But Lieutenant Commander John Tovey was a resourceful officer and, as he still had torpedoes remaining, he remained on the engaged starboard bows of Beatty's battlecruisers, awaiting another opportunity. As soon as he sighted the stationary light cruiser *Wiesbaden*, Tovey made straight for her at speed, closing to a range of 2,000 yards. His main concern was that although the *Wiesbaden* may have been immobile, she still represented a serious threat. Engine damage would certainly not prevent her from firing her torpedoes at Beatty's battlecruisers as they passed close by. The *Onslow* opened fire with her 4-inch guns.

> At one time we came so close that, with a range of only 1,000 yards on the gun sights, our shots were still not falling short. The enemy cruiser replied vigorously, but with little success. Her firing was very much easier to endure than the firing which we had suffered an hour previously, when we had simply to sit still under a heavy 'bombardment' unable to make any reply. I should not say perhaps that this cruiser's fire exercised no strain on us, for one man of my gun's crew, for example, was found sheltering behind a flimsy bit of canvas, apparently acting on an extension of the ostrich principle that, if he was out of sight of the enemy, their shell could not hit him![36]
>
> Lieutenant John Knox, HMS *Onslow*, 13th Flotilla

Uninhibited by the fire directed against them, Tovey moved into position to finish the *Wiesbaden*. Suddenly they sighted Hipper's battlecruisers advancing as the vanguard to the whole German fleet. Opportunity and death beckoned in equal measure for Tovey and his men.

We were now brought 45 degrees on their port bow at only about 11,000 yards from them – an ideal position for a torpedo attack – so the Captain closed the enemy, and when 8,000 yards from the leading enemy battlecruiser gave the signal to the torpedo tubes to fire, and turned the ship to port to bring the sights on.[37]

Lieutenant John Knox, HMS *Onslow*, 13th Flotilla

In this moment of near fulfilment, their dreams of glory were shattered as the *Onslow* was hit by a shell from the almost forgotten *Wiesbaden*.

We were ordered to make a torpedo attack, increasing speed a lot to do this. I went down to the after-mast to hoist a black flag to denote this, when I noticed an enemy light cruiser off our starboard bow, listing a bit and stopped but at her after gun two or three men were still firing. A shell struck our engine room killing one and injuring one or two more.[38]

Signalman A. W. Gutteridge, HMS *Onslow*, 13th Flotilla

The shell could not have struck at a more inconvenient time and the ship was enveloped in clouds of steam escaping from the damaged engine-room.

Immediately there was a big escape of steam completely enveloping both torpedo tubes. On enquiring I received a report that all torpedoes had been fired and consequently turned away at greatly reduced speed, passing about 3,500 yards from the enemy's light cruiser previously mentioned. I sent Sub-Lieutenant Moore to find out the damage done; while doing this he discovered that only one torpedo had been fired and observing the enemy's light cruiser beam on and apparently temporarily stopped, fired a torpedo at her. Sub-Lieutenant Moore, Leading Signalman Cassin, also several other ratings and myself saw the torpedo hit the light cruiser below the conning tower and explode.[39]

Lieutenant Commander Jack Tovey, HMS *Onslow*, 13th Flotilla

In an action conducted at this frenetic pace, minutes seem like hours.

My action station at the break of the foc'sle with my rangefinder was both uncomfortable and terrifying. I kept shouting ranges up to the bridge and once, when I glanced up I saw Jack Tovey alone and manning the helm himself. When a shell exploded in the engine room,

I got permission to go down to see if I could help in any way, but found all the occupants dead and we were still being shelled. Tovey ordered me out, and, whilst I was some time groping about in the gloom, he shouted that if I was not out in five minutes he would secure the hatch. I came up pretty quickly after this and the heel of my sea boot was cleanly removed by a shell splinter as I arrived on deck.[40]

Probationary Surgeon Lieutenant Thomas D'Arcy, HMS *Onslow*, 13th Flotilla

After receiving fresh reports from Sub-Lieutenant Moore that there were still two torpedoes left and that the ship could still make 10 knots, Tovey decided that he must use them against the High Seas Fleet just 8,000 yards away.

He pointed out that his policy was sound, as we were in a position of torpedo advantage, and if we cleared out without firing our last two torpedoes they would be wasted, for we were far too damaged to take any part in the action later on. The probability was that the ship would be lost, as our reduced speed made us an easy target, but what was one destroyer more or less compared to a torpedo hit on one of the enemy battle line?[41]

Lieutenant John Knox, HMS *Onslow*, 13th Flotilla

In they went again. Both torpedoes were fired and Tovey was confident that they had crossed the line of the German battlecruisers, though neither found its mark. The net results of his lone attack were limited, but fortune partially favoured the brave for, against all the odds, the *Onslow* escaped and started her long journey back to Blighty. She suffered just five casualties, which was remarkable under the circumstances. Tovey would have to wait another twenty-five years before he got his next chance to sink a German battleship: the *Bismarck*.

Throughout this time the main bodies of both fleets continued to close on each other though neither commander had any clear idea of where his opponent was situated. Jellicoe knew that somewhere, just over the horizon, was the High Seas Fleet and a collision point was inevitable in the very near future. His need for accurate intelligence was becoming ever more desperate as the Grand Fleet was still deployed in its cruising formation of six columns abreast. The deployment into a single battle line had to be achieved before the High Seas Fleet hove into view and wreaked havoc on the densely packed columns of the Grand Fleet. All the much vaunted superiority in numbers would count for nothing if they failed to deploy, or deployed over-hastily into a tactically inferior position. As he waited, Jellicoe made all the professional preparations that were in his power to inform his eventual decision.

> At about 5.40pm Jellicoe ordered me to have ranges taken on various bearings and report to him what would be the most favourable directions in which we could engage the enemy fleet, then coming north in pursuit of Beatty. As a result I reported to him that the most favourable direction was to the southward, and would draw westwards as the sun sank … It was typical of Jellicoe's clear mind that he should deal fully with the enormously important question of the light-gage-for-gunnery advantage just prior to the main battle.[42]
>
> Captain Frederic Dreyer, HMS *Iron Duke*, 3rd Division, Fourth Battle Squadron

But, in the absence of accurate contact reports, Jellicoe was effectively operating in the dark. With every passing second his quandary grew worse. At 17.56 there came the first visual contact between the main units, when the *Lion* sighted the leading battleships of the Grand Fleet some 7,000 yards to the north of him as he continued to bend to the east across the front of Jellicoe's approach area, thus forcing back Hipper's force under the weight of their fire. Admiral Burney aboard the *Marlborough* leading the starboard column also sighted Beatty's battlecruisers. The collective error in the reckoning of navigational position between the Grand Fleet and the Battlecruiser Fleet meant that the Grand Fleet had got far closer to the danger zone before deploying than Jellicoe would have wanted. Unfortunately, both Beatty and Burney failed to realize that in the poor visibility Jellicoe could not see what they could see and their reports to him were either unhelpful or shamefully opaque. In desperation, at 18.01 Jellicoe signalled, 'Where is the enemy's battle fleet?'[43]

> Then at somewhere around 6pm we spotted just above the horizon a light calling pendants 22 by Morse code of course. That was *Lion*'s visual

call sign. We discovered it was the Commander in Chief in the *Iron Duke* with his battle fleet. When we answered we got a message asking in what direction and where was the enemy? I am not quoting what Beatty said on being given the message. We replied by giving the direction and distance the enemy were from us.[44]

Petty Officer Edwin Downing, HMS *Lion*, 1st Battlecruiser Squadron

The signal Beatty actually sent in response to Jellicoe's plea was: 'Enemy's battlecruisers bearing south east.'[45] This rather missed the point of where the enemy *battle fleet* was and in addition criminally failed to give Hipper's course. Jellicoe was faced with making the most important decision of his life based on a series of incompatible reports.

It became apparent by the sound of the heavy firing that enemy's heavy ships must be in close proximity, and the *Lion*, which was sighted at this moment, signalled at 6.6pm that the enemy's battle cruisers bore south-east. Meanwhile, at about 5.50pm, I had received a wireless report from Commodore Goodenough, commanding the 2nd Light Cruiser Squadron, to the effect that the enemy's battle cruisers bore south-west from their Battle Fleet; in other words, that his Battle Fleet bore north-east from his battle cruisers. In view of the report from Sir Cecil Burney that our battle cruisers were steering east, and observing that Sir David Beatty reported at 6.6pm that the enemy's battle cruisers bore south-east, it appeared from Commodore Goodenough's signal that the enemy's Battle Fleet must be ahead of his battle cruisers. On the other hand, it seemed to me almost incredible that the Battle Fleet could have passed the battle cruisers. The conflicting reports added greatly to the perplexity of the situation, and I determined to hold on until matters became clearer.[46]

Admiral Sir John Jellicoe, HMS *Iron Duke*, 3rd Division, Fourth Battle Squadron

What was rapidly becoming apparent was that the Grand Fleet would meet the High Seas Fleet some ten to twelve minutes earlier than expected, and that the Germans would be rather more to the starboard than straight ahead, as had originally been expected. But not one of his advanced British ships reported to him exactly where Scheer and the High Seas Fleet actually *were* in relation to the Grand Fleet. Jellicoe was a man of considerable intelligence and showed an admirable forbearance in subsequently reviewing the performance of his subordinate officers in the Battlecruiser Fleet.

These officers had been in sight of the German Fleet, or a large part of it, for some two hours before the battle fleets met and, of course, were fully aware of all the information which I lacked. They too, from their position well ahead of the British Battle Fleet after deployment, did not have their view of the enemy fleet obstructed, as did those in the British Battle Fleet by the smoke of the battlecruisers, light cruisers and destroyers ahead of the Battle Fleet. Their range of vision was limited only by the misty weather, and the conditions were nothing like so difficult in the way of visibility as were those confronting me as Commander in Chief in the centre of the Battle Fleet. The result may well be that these officers could not get out of their minds their own experience during the battle, and, when replying to my observations, they still looked at the conditions as they saw them, and failed to grasp the great difference in those conditions which made the situation so difficult for me.[47]

Admiral Sir John Jellicoe, HMS *Iron Duke*, 3rd Division, Fourth Battle Squadron

As he stood aboard the *Iron Duke*, with every passing moment propelling him inexorably towards the battle that would decide the future of the British Empire, Jellicoe was faced with an intractable problem.

Before it is possible for anyone to realise the difficulties which confronted me as Commander in Chief of the Grand Fleet at the Battle of Jutland it is essential for a clear idea to be formed and continually kept in view of the two main factors to which those difficulties were entirely due. These two factors were: 1. The absence of even approximately correct information from the Battlecruiser Fleet and its attendant light cruisers regarding the position, formation and strength of the High Seas Fleet. 2. The lack of visibility when the Battle Fleet came in sight of a portion of the High Seas Fleet, due largely to mist, and partly to smoke from our own battlecruisers and other vessels.[48]

Admiral Sir John Jellicoe, HMS *Iron Duke*, 3rd Division, Fourth Battle Squadron

The tactics that the Grand Fleet were to follow in action had long been enshrined in Jellicoe's Grand Fleet Battle Orders. It was no secret that he was a cautious admiral and that, though his battle line would ironically be composed of 'dreadnoughts', he made it abundantly clear right from the start of the tenure of his command that in almost no circumstances would they be exposed to ambush by German submarines, destroyers or mines. He was a member of the Sir Julian Corbett school who believed that the Royal Navy had harvested most of the fruits of maritime supremacy across the globe without needing to risk it all to secure complete control in the North Sea. The destruction of the High Seas Fleet was desirable, but not essential, to the British Empire. They already had the fruits of victory and had everything to lose. Jellicoe would take no risks with the dreadnoughts that underpinned Britain's maritime supremacy.

By now the *Lion* and her battered survivors of the Battlecruiser Fleet were drawing across the front of the Grand Fleet. As they did so, the *Marlborough*, *Colossus* and *Benbow*, leading the three starboard divisions of the Grand Fleet, had splendid views of one of the most dramatic vistas of the Great War.

> I must confess it was a magnificent sight seeing the *Lion*, slightly on
> fire forward, leading the other ships and firing salvo after salvo, with
> the enemy's flashes visible in the haze, but not the ships themselves,
> tremendous volumes of water being thrown up by the enemy's shots,
> none of which hit the cruisers when in my vision.[49]
> Lieutenant Thomas Norman, HMS *Benbow*, 4th Division, Fourth Battle Squadron

The sight was utterly absorbing. Aware that they would soon be in action themselves, the men could not tear their eyes away.

> The sight was very interesting and I found it extremely hard to pay any
> attention to keeping station at all, and in fact was once politely reminded
> by the Captain that it was my job. The Battlecruiser Squadron and the
> *Queen Elizabeths* were about two points on our starboard bow, about
> 6,000 to 10,000 yards, firing heavily and steaming about 80 degrees to
> our course. The *Lion*, leading the line, was on fire forward and a thin
> stream of smoke, looking as if it came out of a scuttle, was coming from
> just below the upper deck, just before 'A' Turret. The enemy could not
> be seen without glasses against the misty background, but a few columns

of smoke could be seen. The flashes of both sides showed very clearly, a sort of deep orange and also the splashes of the enemy's shots and a few of our own.[50]

Lieutenant Patrick Lawder, HMS *Benbow*, 4th Division, Fourth Battle Squadron

From their perspective, the leading players in the drama were equally delighted to see the Grand Fleet. The sight of their old comrades from Scapa Flow was a welcome boost to the hard-pressed Fifth Battle Squadron.

At 6.10 the report was passed round the ship that the Grand Fleet was in sight and would shortly deploy into action. This was extremely welcome news for matters were not looking too cheery for our squadron. It could hardly be hoped that we four ships could continues to engage the whole German Battle Fleet for much longer without sustaining very serious damage, to say the least of it.[51]

Lieutenant Patrick Brind, HMS *Malaya*, Fifth Battle Squadron

At last, at 18.14, clear information finally reached Jellicoe aboard the *Iron Duke* confirming the exact location of the High Seas Fleet. 'Have sighted the enemy's Battle Fleet bearing south-south-east.'[52] It arrived in the nick of time. Jellicoe could have waited no longer. Now was the moment of decision; the moment that would define him as an admiral and decide his place in history. As might be expected, given the nature of the man, his post-war account of this cliff-hanging moment was characteristically dry, understated and largely technical.

The first definite information received on board the fleet-flagship of the position of the enemy's Battle Fleet did not, therefore, come in until 6.14pm, and the position given placed it thirty degrees before the starboard beam of the *Iron Duke*, or fifty-nine degrees before the starboard beam of the *Marlborough*, and apparently in close proximity. There was no time to lose, as there was evident danger of the starboard wing column of the Battle Fleet being engaged by the whole German Battle Fleet before deployment could be effected. So at 6.16pm a signal was made to the Battle Fleet to form line of battle on the port wing column, on a course south-east by east, it being assumed that the course of the enemy was approximately the same as that of our battle cruisers. Speed was at the same time reduced to 14 knots to admit of our battle

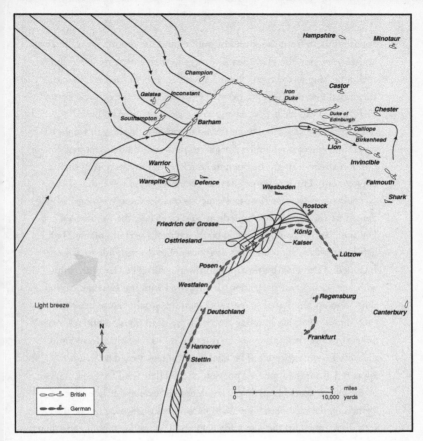

Jellicoe deploys

cruisers passing ahead of the Battle Fleet, as there was danger of the fire
of the Battle Fleet being blanketed by them. During the short interval,
crowded with events, that had elapsed since the first flashes and sound
of gunfire had been noted on board the *Iron Duke*, the question of most
urgent importance before me had been the direction and manner of
deployment. As the evidence accumulated that the enemy's Battle Fleet
was on our starboard side, but on a bearing well before the beam of the
Iron Duke, the point for decision was whether to form line of battle on
the starboard or on the port wing column. My first and natural impulse
was to form on the starboard wing column in order to bring the Fleet
into action at the earliest possible moment, but it became increasingly

apparent, both from the sound of gunfire and the reports from the *Lion* and *Barham*, that the High Sea Fleet was in such close proximity and on such a bearing as to create obvious disadvantages in such a movement. I assumed that the German destroyers would be ahead of their Battle Fleet, and it was clear that, owing to the mist, the operations of destroyers attacking from a commanding position in the van would be much facilitated; it would be suicidal to place the Battle Fleet in a position where it might be open to attack by destroyers during such a deployment. The further points that occurred to me were, that if the German ships were as close as seemed probable, there was considerable danger of the First Battle Squadron, and especially the *Marlborough*'s Division, being severely handled by the concentrated fire of the High Sea Fleet before the remaining divisions could get into line to assist. Included in the First Battle Squadron were several of our older ships, with only indifferent protection as compared with the German capital ships, and an interval of at least four minutes would elapse between each division coming into line astern of the sixth division and a further interval before the guns could be directed on to the ship selected and their fire become effective. The final disadvantage would be that it appeared, from the supposed position of the High Sea Fleet, that the van of the enemy would have a very considerable "overlap" if line were formed on the starboard wing division, whereas this would not be the case with deployment on the port wing column. The overlap would necessitate a large turn of the starboard wing division to port to prevent the "T" being crossed, and each successive division coming into line would have to make this turn, in addition to the 8-point turn required to form the line. I therefore decided to deploy on the first, the port wing, division.[53]

Admiral Sir John Jellicoe, HMS *Iron Duke*, 3rd Division, Fourth Battle Squadron

Jellicoe's cool account gives us no real sense of the huge burden of responsibility that he bore. But Captain Frederic Dreyer, who commanded the *Iron Duke*, captured the moment when a slight, self-effacing man made the decision that could have changed the course of history. Dreyer was standing by the standard compass on the manoeuvring platform, watching the steering of the ship which acted as the guide of the whole fleet, when Jellicoe appeared beside him.

I then heard at once the sharp, distinctive step of the Commander-in-Chief approaching – he had steel strips on his heels. He stepped quickly onto the platform round the compasses and looked in silence at the magnetic compass card for about 20 seconds. I watched his keen, brown, weather-beaten face with tremendous interest, wondering what he would do. With iron nerve he had pressed on through the mist with his 24 huge ships, each weighing some 25,000 tons or more, until the last possible moment, so as to get into effective range and make the best tactical manoeuvre after obtaining news of the position of the enemy Battle Fleet, which was his objective. I realised as I watched him that he was as cool and unmoved as ever. Then he looked up and broke the silence with the order in his crisp, clear-cut voice to Commander A. R. W. Woods, the Fleet Signal Officer, who was standing a little abaft me, "Hoist equal-speed pendant south-east." Woods said, "Would you make it a point to port, Sir, so that they will know it is on the port-wing column?" This was a small matter and not actually necessary in view of Jellicoe's habit of commencing the deployment in the *Iron Duke* while the signal was being answered. Jellicoe replied at once, "Very well. Hoist equal-speed pendant south-east by east."[54]

Captain Frederic Dreyer, HMS *Iron Duke*, 3rd Division, Fourth Battle Squadron

And so the signal was sent. Petty Officer Arthur Brister was at his station at the W/T remote control position in the charthouse alongside the 2nd Signals Officer, Commander Phipps.

Gunfire was heard in due course, becoming louder. Excitement rising within me, I was sorely tempted to peep through the portholes, but I had to keep my head down and concentrate on the important signals buzzing in; however, when handing signals to the Commander I managed a glance. A mile or two ahead, amidst a cauldron of gunfire, smoke and columns of water, a line of our cruisers were in the thick of it and living dangerously. Just then the Signal Commander gave me the first manoeuvring signal, ordering, "At once!" Having transmitted the signal to "JJJ" (battle fleet) I was waiting for acknowledgements when the Commander shouted, "Executive now!"[55]

Petty Officer Telegraphist Arthur Brister, HMS *Iron Duke*, 3rd Division, Fourth Battle Squadron

Subsequent controversy over the deployment centred on whether Jellicoe should have deployed onto the starboard or central column and engaged the High Seas Fleet earlier on and at correspondingly closer range. In the face of Jellicoe's reasoned exposition of why he deployed on the port column no one has ever been able to substantiate such criticisms other than by recourse to vague generalizations born of foolishness and wish-fulfilment.

As the deployment of the Grand Fleet commenced, the 1st Cruiser Squadron, under the command of Rear Admiral Sir Robert Arbuthnot aboard the *Defence*, found itself in an extremely awkward and dangerous situation. The obsolescent armoured cruisers had been acting as a dispersed screen and now found themselves in the dangerous waters between the Grand Fleet and the High Seas Fleet. Arbuthnot pulled the *Defence* and *Warrior* together, with the *Duke of Edinburgh* trailing slightly behind, and seems to have set off towards the sound of the guns, heading direct for the *Wiesbaden*. This put them on a collision course with the *Lion* and the Battlecruiser Fleet. One young boy aboard the *Duke of Edinburgh* got a profound shock as he looked at the battered survivors of Beatty's fleet.

> To tell the truth I had been brought up to believe that the British Navy was untouchable in warfare, I was expecting the German ships to go down one after another. So that when our Squadron, with the Grand Fleet, arrived at the scene of action, I was surprised to see some of our ships – they were Beatty's battlecruisers – burning and out of control, sinking and helpless. I was not frightened, but *surprised* to discover that the Germans had men and ships that were as good, maybe better, than ours. Our Squadron steamed on. Three heavy cruisers, the *Black Prince* had fallen out, we were firing our 9.2"s to starboard where the enemy were. Then our Admiral, Robert Arbuthnot, made the signal for the Squadron to turn into the enemy.[56]
>
> Boy 1st Class John Davies, HMS *Duke of Edinburgh*, 1st Cruiser Squadron

As a result of Arbuthnot's orders, the armoured cruisers cut right across the battlecruisers just as the Grand Fleet began to deploy into its battle line. This manoeuvre could have caused an absolutely disastrous collision.

At that exciting moment I saw the 1st Cruiser Squadron leading from
port to starboard across my bows. It was clear that unless I altered
course drastically I should collide with one of his ships, so I jammed the
Lion's helm over and swung her under the stern of their second cruiser,
which only cleared us by a cable's length. By forcing the Battlecruiser
Squadron off its course in the low visibility, which was then only five
miles, Arbuthnot caused us to lose sight of the enemy fleet and he
himself took the place of the battlecruisers as their targets.[57]

Flag Captain Alfred Chatfield, HMS *Lion*, 1st Battlecruiser Squadron

No one really knows what was going through Artbuthnot's mind, but his
actions came as little surprise to Lieutenant Leslie Hollis, who was serving
as a Royal Marine aboard the *Duke of Edinburgh*.

Admiral Arbuthnot had made it abundantly clear in a series of
addresses to the ships' companies of the vessels under his command,
that when he encountered the enemy he would close to the rather
meagre range of our guns and engage remorselessly. In the action he
put his precepts into practice, but the old ships of the 1st Cruiser
Squadron were no match for the German battlecruisers.[58]

Lieutenant Leslie Hollis, HMS *Duke of Edinburgh*, 1st Cruiser Squadron

The *Defence* and *Warrior* cut across the battlecruisers and began to pour
their 9.2-inch shells into the *Wiesbaden,* which had survived the malevo-
lent attentions a few minutes earlier of the *Onslow.* It may be that, like
Tovey, he was worried the still lurking *Wiesbaden* might use her torpedoes
against the deploying Grand Fleet. Arbuthnot had a high contemporary
reputation as a Christian gentleman, obsessed with physical fitness and
the highest authoritarian standards of discipline mercilessly enforced.
Such qualities have not been as highly prized by modern commentators;
indeed, one has described him as: 'in a colloquial if not a clinical sense,
insane'.[59] It may be that he was merely intending to regain his correct
station at the rear of the deployed battle line. But, on balance, it seems
probable that, having engaged the stationary *Wiesbaden*, like a bulldog with
its teeth firmly into its prey, he was not about to let go, and failed to appreciate the consequences of his actions to all those around him. Whatever
the reason, he led his squadron on, getting ever closer to the *Wiesbaden*

and blasting away at his stationary prey, as if only he and they existed on the high seas. No thought of his smoke obfuscating the view of the all-important battlecruisers and dreadnoughts. No thought of what might lie ahead cloaked in the poor visibility. No thought, really, at all, at least as far as can now be judged.

Unfortunately for the men under his command, he was not alone. Whether or not Arbuthnot could see the German battlecruisers from the bridge of the *Defence*, they could certainly see him through the variegated mist and smoke.

> From left to right there appears in the field of the periscope, a ship, improbably large and close. At the first glance I recognise an old English armoured cruiser and give the necessary orders. My arm is clutched, "Don't fire, that is the *Rostock*!" But I can see the turrets fore and aft. "Action! Armoured Cruiser. Four funnels. Bow left. Left 30. Range 76hm. Salvo!" Fire salvoes rapidly follow, of which three straddled; then there was repeated the now familiar sight of a ship blowing up.[60]
>
> Commander Günther Paschen, SMS *Lützow*, I Scouting Group, High Seas Fleet

Behind the *Lützow*, the *Derfflinger* did not even have time to turn her guns onto the *Defence* before it was all over. In just an instant, at 18.20, Arbuthnot and his men met their doom.

> In the misty grey light the colours of the German and English ships were difficult to distinguish. The cruiser was not very far away from us. She had four funnels and two masts, like our *Rostock*. "She is certainly English," Lieutenant Commander Hauser shouted, "may I fire?" "Yes, fire away!" I was now certain she was a big English ship. The secondary armament was trained on the new target. Hauser gave the order, "6,000!" Then, just as he was about to give the order, "Fire!" something terrific happened. The English ship, which I had meanwhile identified as an old English armoured cruiser, broke in half with a tremendous explosion. Black smoke and debris shot into the air, a flame enveloped the whole ship, and then she sank before our eyes. There was nothing but a gigantic smoke cloud to mark the place where just before a proud ship had been fighting.[61]
>
> Commander Georg von Hase, SMS *Derfflinger*, I Scouting Group, High Seas Fleet

It was another raw human tragedy, played out in seconds on the most dramatic and public of stages. As the ship exploded the scene was visible to friend and foe alike.

> Poor fellows, I had only had such a cheery lunch with them all a few days ago. She had never a chance. As the fleets closed so rapidly that she couldn't get out of the way, though trying to do so. She went up in a huge sheet of flames 1,000 feet high, and not a vestige remained five minutes after, but falling bits of iron which fell all around us. No-one could have known, they died instantaneously.[62]
>
> Commander John Champion, HMS *Maenad*, 12th Flotilla

Contemporary descriptions of the demise of the *Defence* have been slightly undermined by divers and marine archaeologists, who recently discovered the wreck to be in remarkably good condition for a ship reported blasted to smithereens. Yet despite this new evidence there seems little doubt that it was an impressive explosion. It was clearly witnessed from the ships of the Fifth Battle Squadron as they manoeuvred to fall in behind the emerging battle line of the Grand Fleet.

> When I first saw them, I felt they were doomed. They were steaming at their utmost speed between the lines, endeavouring to get clear round us, ie round the end of the Grand Fleet, smoking very heavily, being continually straddled and frequently hit. They were soon on fire in several places, especially the *Defence*, but still they continued to fire to the very last. The *Defence* suddenly disappeared in an immense column of smoke and flame, hundreds of feet high. It appeared to be an absolutely instantaneous destruction, the ship seeming to be dismembered at once. Wreckage continued to fall into the water for quite a considerable time after the explosion, but when the smoke cleared, there was absolutely nothing to be seen, where only a minute before, had been the *Defence*.[63]
>
> Lieutenant Patrick Brind, HMS *Malaya*, Fifth Battle Squadron

Once again the German gunnery had been excellent; the range may have been short, but the execution had been fearsomely quick. There were no survivors from the crew of 903. Admiral Arbuthnot had taken his shipmates to their deaths. But the casualties did not stop there. Behind the

Defence came the *Warrior*, and the Germans shells now started to crash down all around her, scoring fifteen or more direct hits.

I stopped to have another look and saw one of our four funnelled cruisers being heavily shelled. Splashes were all round her and one salvo straddled her quarterdeck, with one or two shots this side. At the same time, as the splashes rose a tall column of smoke, 200–300 feet high, rose from her quarterdeck, the smoke being lit up by the flame inside it in a very pretty way. She went on, however, and immediately afterwards was again straddled, but I didn't notice any hits. There was a good deal of smoke about and I didn't see what damage had been done by the explosion.[64]

Lieutenant Patrick Lawder, HMS *Benbow*, 4th Division, Fourth Battle Squadron

Among the plethora of hits one shell pitched into the aft engine-rooms. The Engineer Commander was confronted by a scene of mounting chaos as he attempted to inspect the damage.

I heard a tremendous explosion at the after end, a heavy jar went through the whole fabric, and most of the lights went out. Immediately afterwards there was a heavy roar of water and steam, and my impression was that we had been torpedoed. Several men came running forward from that end, one of them with blood streaming down his face. In that moment I realised fully what cold drawn funk is like. But I had to make a decision, and advancing towards the after end, I tried to gauge the extent of the damage. The engines still went on running, which seemed to show that the cylinders had not been hit, but in the dim uncertain light I perceived what appeared to be Niagara at the after end of the engine room, though whether the sheet of water was rising up from below or pouring down from above I couldn't be sure at the time. Anyhow, a blast of steam on my face warned me that I hadn't long to think about it, and I soon made up my mind that no pumps could deal with the quantity of water that was coming in, and that the only thing to do was to get the men out as quickly as possible.[65]

Engineer Commander Henry Kitching, HMS *Warrior*, 1st Cruiser Squadron

Their attempts to escape from the complex warren of machinery and gangways were tortuous. As they stumbled through the Stygian darkness, pursued by water and threatened by flame, it became a terrifying nightmare.

> At first the men didn't know what to do, as the ladders at the after end were inaccessible, but I shouted to them to go up the midship ladder and hustled all towards it in front of me. As soon as it appeared that they had all gone up, I followed them myself, but by that time all the lights had gone out and it was pitch dark. When I got to the top, knowing it was hopeless to go aft, I turned forward and felt my way by the handrails along the platform at the tops of the cylinders towards the door at the fore end, which communicated with the port engine room and with the mess deck. When I got there, however, a stoker told me that we could not get through there, as the mess deck was on fire, and when I tried to do so I was met by a rush of thick smoke and blinding fumes that drove me back. At this moment with this in front and the roar of steam behind me I felt like a trapped rat, for there seemed no possibility of lifting the heavy armour hatches overhead, and a spasm of sheer terror came over me; but just then I realised that the man was calling my attention to a glimmer of light above, and the next minute I found myself climbing out through a torn rent in the deck.[66]
>
> Engineer Commander Henry Kitching, HMS *Warrior*, 1st Cruiser Squadron

The maelstrom of shell continued unabated as the German battlecruisers poured shell into the near helpless *Warrior* and the end seemed inevitable.

> From my sheltered action stations, I was ordered to go up aloft to clear some halyards which were fouled. Just as I was about to climb the rigging a shell whistled overhead, shattering some superstructure. My mission was abandoned. I was near a hatchway to the boiler room; a burst main steam pipe caused some injured stokers to come from below scalded by steam. With the noise of guns, explosions and the knowledge that the ship was crippled and likely to sink, I prayed.[67]
>
> Signalman Reuben Poole, HMS *Warrior*, 1st Cruiser Squadron

The damage control parties were clearly fighting a losing battle. Nothing human could hope to staunch the ship's wounds as the shells crashed home time and time again. Stoker David Williams was one of the repair parties on the mess deck.

A shell came through the upper deck and killed three of my mates
working with me – another mate had his leg blown off. After that the
firing was so heavy that we could not move around like we should have
done. I got hit myself. The sick berth steward tried to bandage me and
as he did another shell came and blew off his two middle fingers – they
fell on my leg so I picked them up and gave them back to him as he did
not feel what had happened. The only thing he could do now was to tie
my trousers over my thigh with my cap ribbon.[68]

Stoker 1st Class David Williams, HMS *Warrior*, 1st Cruiser Squadron

Surgeon Charles Leake was at his action station in the ammunition
passages, standing ready to assist the forward and aft sick bays or to move
onto the bridge and upper deck as required by events.

News was brought to me by a messenger of a fearful explosion aft: the
aft dressing station had been wiped out and no-one knew if there were
any survivors. Hearing this, and as wounded were being reported,
I resolved to try to do my best to get there. It was impossible to get aft
owing to gas fumes, except by way of the upper deck, so I took a risk
which a Medical Officer is not supposed to take, as circumstances were
exceptional. On arriving aft and whilst attending to the wounded, much
to my surprise, the Surgeon Macdonald appears, somewhat shaken, but
none the worse for his experience. His sick bay steward had had his left
hand shattered as the result of the explosion and many people were
killed near that spot – about 40 or more by one shell alone. We set to
work and rendered first aid and gave morphia to the wounded as fast as
we could. Meanwhile the forward dressing station was becoming
untenable owing to gas fumes and fumes from burning paintwork so it
was deemed advisable to evacuate the position.[69]

Surgeon Lieutenant Charles Leake, HMS *Warrior*, 1st Cruiser Squadron

The *Warrior*'s engineer commander found all his attempts to reach the
port engine-room were thwarted by a combination of smoke and flames.
It was not only the sick bay attendants who had difficulty in carrying out
their duties in such dreadful circumstances.

I then endeavoured to collect my scattered wits with a view to putting
out the fire, but I found that I had the greatest difficulty in getting my

brain to work at all. I have heard other fellows say that they have been seized with this temporary mental paralysis, which seems to last for ages, but really lasts for moments only. On such occasions when it is difficult to originate anything, evolutions rehearsed at drill work automatically, and at this moment I found my subordinates readier than myself in carrying out measures that I had myself devised.[70]

Engineer Commander Henry Kitching, HMS *Warrior*, 1st Cruiser Squadron

Once again it was apparent that there was much truth in the old principle that a bad character can be a wonderful man in a crisis. At least one man aboard the *Warrior* seized the chance of redemption.

One of our crew members was under punishment and was in the cells when we went into action. He was immediately released as the first salvoes hit us driving great holes in *Warrior*. If you had seen this man go into action pulling hosepipes along the decks to tackle the fire with great speed, pushing anyone in his way aside – it was very humorous and brave.[71]

Signalman William Robertson, HMS *Warrior*, 1st Cruiser Squadron

Quite a considerable distance behind the *Warrior* came the *Duke of Edinburgh*; making smoke like a factory chimney, she bore a charmed life. Able Seaman Ewart Eades was serving as the spare sight setter on 'Y' Turret.

Our Gunlayer, Petty Officer Gunners Mate Rawles, said that the lens of the gunlayer telescope was getting fogged up with the spray and cordite smoke. I was sent out with some cloth to see if I could wipe the telescope lens from the top of the turret. Now I had a desire to see what was happening being young and without nerves or fear. However I looked and found that it seemed to me that we were between the Grand Fleet and German Fleet. Shells were going over us both ways. I saw that the *Defence* went up in flames and then the *Warrior* took a broadside and dropped out of line. I never did make the top of the turret for it seemed that the helm was put hard over. I was nearly decanted into the sea.[72]

Able Seaman Ewart Eades, HMS *Duke of Edinburgh*, 1st Cruiser Squadron

The *Duke of Edinburgh* managed to extricate herself successfully from the situation with very little damage, although she caused significant problems for the deploying battle line of the Grand Fleet by steaming up the engaged side while pumping out an excessive amount of black smoke from her funnels, adding to the all-pervading murky conditions. The crippled *Warrior* limped back with much reduced engine power towards the British lines under continued heavy fire, augmented with a will by the leading dreadnoughts of the High Seas Fleet. She was saved by an amazing conjunction of events.

As the Fifth Battle Squadron approached the area of the Grand Fleet deployment, Evan-Thomas had very little idea of what was going on. Sighting the starboard division led by the *Marlborough*, he made the not unreasonable assumption that she was leading the whole battle line; in other words, that the fleet had already deployed to starboard. His first move was therefore to attempt to take his rightful pre-designated station at the head of the line in front of the *Marlborough*. This led the Fifth Battle Squadron eastwards, back into the cauldron of fire from the leading ships of the High Seas Fleet. Then, having gained a clearer view of the Grand Fleet deployment, Evan-Thomas realized his error and turned sharply back to the north-east, in order to tag on to the end of the battle line as the deployment was completed. Suddenly, as this second manoeuvre was taking place, without warning the *Warspite* seemed to veer out of line and head directly for the Germans. She began executing a huge circle that took her dangerously near the German line, but to the intense relief of the beleaguered crew of the *Warrior,* she acted as a magnet, naturally attracting German shellfire from a disabled old cruiser to the much more lustrous target of a super-dreadnought offered on a plate at close range. The *Kaiserin*, *Friedrich der Grosse*, *König*, *Helgoland*, *Ostfriesland*, *Thüringen*, *Nassau* and *Oldenburg* all blasted away at the *Warspite* at various times with both main and secondary armaments at varying ranges from 9,500 to 15,500 yards.

At first no one aboard the *Warspite* really knew what had happened, although most guessed that it was some kind of steering breakdown that had caused the strange circling, rather than mental confusion on the part of their captain.

The steering gear episode was rather extraordinary. The hit by the port wing engine room had buckled the after bulkhead of the centre engine room on which the steering engine is secured. This gave it a hot bearing

and it was labouring heavily. When turning to port to deploy astern of
the Grand Fleet we were very close to and inside the *Valiant*. The
Captain did not think we could turn safely and gave the order, "Port 20"
to swing under the *Valiant*'s stern. The Quartermaster got a bit 'rattled'
and forced the wheel too quick which overrode the telemotor gear due
to the engine lagging with a hot bearing. Having got a swing out, the
order was given "Starboard 20 degrees" and they could not get more
than 5 degrees starboard on, the ship had therefore 10 degrees port
helm on and completed the circle twice, turning through 32 points
towards the enemy's fleet.[73]

Commander Humphrey Walwyn, HMS *Warspite*, Fifth Battle Squadron

This misfortune could not have been worse timed, but it did give a
demonstration that the huge investment locked up in the super-
dreadnought had been worth while. The great ship seemed to shrug off
the German shells.

Warspite was being continually straddled and I remember seeing the
greater part of a salvo land on her. She appeared to do something that
can best be described as 'bounce' under it. The whole ship seemed to
move or 'give' to port under it momentarily; and she rolled a little;
but seemed to recover and went on firing immediately afterwards.
I remember thinking what magnificent ships they were. The impression
made on me of the essential value of heavy armour for any ship in the
battle line has remained as a conviction with me to this day.[74]

Sub-Lieutenant Anthony de Salis, HMS *Moresby*, 13th Flotilla

The men aboard her were totally reliant for their survival on the strength
and resilience of her armour protection. This was no battlecruiser with
a mere 6 to 9 inches of armour; the *Warspite* had 13 inches of protection
over her turrets, magazines and main belt. It was intended to keep shells
out of the vitals and for the most part that was exactly what it did despite
the severity of the situation.

For about 20 minutes we received the fire of about 20 German ships,
using guns of all calibres at what was virtually point blank range. Only
the fact that the ship was continuing to turn circles like a kitten chasing
its own tail saved us from being sunk. The noise of shells hitting or

bursting close alongside sounded like rapid independent fire from a battery of 6″ guns. The ship was heavily hit.[75]

Assistant Clerk Gilbert Bickmore, HMS *Warspite*, Fifth Battle Squadron

There was nothing Evan-Thomas could realistically do for his wounded charge, for the fleet action was imminent, and so he carried on and took up his station at the rear of the battle line.

The men aboard the *Warspite* were left in a world of their own, surrealistically circling and still smothered by waterspouts thrown up by shells spattering all around them, as the German gunners sought to pin down their elusive target. If Commander Walwyn had thought himself busy directing the damage control parties during the Run to the North, he was thrown into a whole new chaotic dimension, as shell after shell crashed home on his precious ship. One of the most threatening hits came when a shell penetrated the starboard 6-inch gun battery casemate and caused a severe cordite fire. Fortunately, the fire was restricted to just one gun and did not spread along the whole battery as had earlier occurred on the *Malaya*. Midshipmen quickly rigged up fire hoses to damp down the seat of the fire before they moved in to rescue the survivors.

There was a great noise going on in No 6 casemate. We knew that the gun crew must be burnt pretty badly and this did not altogether make it a pleasant job spraying cold salt water into the casemate. But still it had to be done because if the rest of the cordite had caught fire there is no knowing what might have happened. We played the hose on the fire until no actual flames could be seen. I then went to the breakwater of the casemate. The after end of the battery was in absolute darkness except for one solitary electric light which looked a dull red. The air was thick with smoke so I donned my trusty respirator and went to see if I could rescue any of the gun's crew. I saw one dilapidated looking figure stagger forward and lean against the breakwater. I found it was the gun layer Petty Officer Yeo. He was quite calm and told me he was burnt all over and could not touch anything with his hands, so I helped him over the breakwater, which was almost too hot to touch, and supported him into the other battery. I found he could walk all right so long as I held him up. I got him into a cabin at the after end of the battery. Betson

and myself then laid him on some blankets on the deck. I then went
along to No 4 Gun Port and got a medical bag from there. On the way
back I found another man, lying on the deck. He must have been burnt
in the starboard battery and run across to the port side before collapsing
on the deck. I picked him up and he told me he had been burnt about
the hands and face but I found him unable to stand and so got Batson to
help me. Between us we carried him into the cabin and placed him on
the bed. There were two or three other men belonging to No 6 Gun's
crew starboard in the cabin as well and the chaplain and a sick berth
steward were doing what they could for them.[76]

Midshipman John Bostock, HMS *Warspite*, Fifth Battle Squadron

Another shell smashed home. Walwyn rushed to the scene.

I went below again and found a second shell had come through into the
boys' mess deck, through the embrasure overhead. Smoke was pouring
out of the wet provision room and seeing Pring leaning up against
bulkhead told him to flood it. He seemed dazed and silly and I 'bit' him
for not getting on quicker. I didn't know at the time that he was very
badly hit, anyway he did the job before he was too far gone. Looked
through the hole in the armour on the boys' mess deck, it looked red,
lurid and beastly, heavy firing all around and splashes everywhere,
thought we were steaming slow.[77]

Commander Humphrey Walwyn, HMS *Warspite*, Fifth Battle Squadron

Two decks below them in the transmitting station one of the young
midshipmen manning the plotting table was terrified by the after-effects
of the shell, which were exaggerated out of all proportion by their over-
wrought imaginations.

Then came an appalling crash. We were all knocked off our stools
and probably slightly dazed. My first recollection was that I was sitting
in a pool of water in almost complete darkness. All noise had ceased.
I remember being speechless and very, very scared. But stood up and
saw streaks of water shooting into the transmitting station through the
voice-pipes, that ALL instruments had ceased to function and that
engines were stopped. I could only think of the three armoured hatches
that were shut above us. Emergency lamps were coming on, the smoke

clearing, the influx of water rapidly stopping – but above all I could hear and feel the engines again.[78]

Midshipman William Fell, HMS *Warspite*, Fifth Battle Squadron

The *Warspite* had by this time taken on a strange and awful appearance. She had been physically disfigured by the multiple hits that had smashed and distorted much of her unarmoured superstructure.

Decks were all warped and resin under corticene crackling like burning holly. The upper deck and superstructure looked perfectly awful, holed everywhere. I think at this time the firing had slackened, but the noise was deafening, shells bursting short threw tons of water over the ship. The superstructure itself was in an awful state of chaos. Port shelter completely gone and starboard side had several big holes in it, everything wrecked and it looked like a burnt out factory, all blackened and beams twisted everywhere.[79]

Commander Humphrey Walwyn, HMS *Warspite*, Fifth Battle Squadron

Eventually, Captain Edward Phillpotts managed to regain control of his ship and their nerve-racking ordeal came to an end.

She was checked at the end of the second circle by going astern port, and brought out by the screws. The whole leading division concentrated on us and we got very heavily hit and everybody thought we had gone. The Huns thought so too and ceased firing, luckily for us, but they no doubt could not see us for splashes, spray and smoke.[80]

Commander Humphrey Walwyn, HMS *Warspite*, Fifth Battle Squadron

The *Warspite* had survived against seemingly overwhelming odds and had protected her crew as well as could possibly be expected in such a hail of fire from heavy-calibre shells.

Our casualties were comparatively slight. The worst cases we had sent down to us forward were of burns, due to a cordite fire breaking out in the starboard battery. Eleven cases, including Father Pollen, the Roman Catholic Chaplain, were brought down suffering from very severe and extensive burns of the face, body and limbs. They were so badly burnt that one could do very little to relieve them of the pain and shock, injections of morphia seeming to have very little, if any, effect on them.

As regards dressings, the specially prepared picric acid lint was at first applied, but they could not be kept on owing to the pain causing the patients to tear their bandages off, and they were accordingly dressed afterwards with either boracic ointment or oil. This proved more successful, but the restlessness of the patients all the time they were on board made it a very difficult matter to keep them protected by dressings. One couldn't keep them still even with repeated hypodermic injections of morphia. Sepsis can't be helped, because the burns are bound to get septic in any case, and one's chief treatment is directed towards alleviating the pain and severity of the shock to the patient as much as possible. Father Pollen sustained his burns (face, hands and legs) through helping to rescue the men of the guns' crews who were on fire from the cordite. He is 56 years old, but stood the shock well and at no time whilst he remained a patient on board uttered any complaint that he was suffering. Griffiths was also burnt about the face, arms and neck in assisting to extinguish the fire.[81]

Surgeon Gordon Ellis, HMS *Warspite*, Fifth Battle Squadron

As the *Warspite* emerged from an ordeal that would have tested the mettle of any ship, her captain only had one thing on his mind.

I got a message from the Captain that he wanted me at once. I was by this time as black as a sweep and wet through, but quite untouched. The Captain asked me how things were and I started to tell him. He said, "I don't care a damn about the damage, can we join the line?" I hadn't the faintest idea what the situation was or what had happened and must have seemed a bit queer, anyway I said, "If she gets another heavy hit on the port side I don't think she will stand it."[82]

Commander Humphrey Walwyn, HMS *Warspite*, Fifth Battle Squadron

The whole incident had lasted about ten minutes. As they emerged, they found that they could only safely make about 16 knots and that they had become considerably separated from the rest of the Grand Fleet, which by then had completed their deployment and moved on. When Captain Phillpotts gamely wirelessed to find the position of the fleet, he was peremptorily ordered back to Rosyth.

◆ ◆ ◆

Meanwhile, the 3rd Battlecruiser Squadron, having to some extent 'over-shot' the battle, headed on a westerly course straight towards the orchestrated tangle of ships that marked the deployment of the Grand Fleet, later known as 'Windy Corner'.

Two columns of smoke appeared – the Grand Fleet. To me at my action stations, armed with one set of semaphore flags and Morse flags and with not even a canvas screen between me and the enemy, it was a welcome sight. When they opened fire it looked as if the whole of the horizon was ablaze. To a lad of 17 things were rather puzzling, especially as he was frozen stiff and everyone forgot about me up the tripod mast.[83]

Ordinary Signaller Harold Webber, HMS *Indomitable*, 3rd Battlecruiser Squadron

Rear Admiral Horace Hood, aboard his flagship the *Invincible*, quickly assessed the situation. At 18.17 he swung his squadron round in succession, to place himself neatly in front of the emerging battle line, some 2 miles ahead of the oncoming *Lion*.

At that time I happened to lift the 'deadlight' to have a look out. *Invincible* was steaming away from us (we were just ready to follow) and she was a glorious sight which I will never forget. A huge bow wave and white wake, her smoke streaming back and her battle flag flying.[84]

Stoker Sidney Blackman, HMS *Inflexible*, 3rd Battlecruiser Squadron

As the 3rd Battlecrusier Squadron settled onto its new course, the German battlecruisers suddenly emerged from the mists on their starboard beam. To Signaller Harold Webber, aloft in his perch in the tripod mast of the *Indomitable*, it was a terrifying sight.

On the starboard bow we had the German Fleet throwing everything they had, including their toothbrushes at us and the Battlecruiser Force returning the compliment. As one can imagine there was a lot of smoke and flame around.[85]

Ordinary Signaller Harold Webber, HMS *Indomitable*, 3rd Battlecruiser Squadron

Far below him in the transmitting station they were hard put to keep up with the changes in course and the appearance of new enemies.

Arranged before us were pieces of graph paper around rollers which
moved slowly at calculated speeds. Ranges would be flashed down on
a receiving instrument from each of the turrets preceded by a warning
buzz. From other points these ranges would be transmitted by voice
pipe. We had a different coloured pencil for each transmitting agent
and the graph resulting from blobs of the same colour indicated the
range of closing or opening on the enemy. I recollect that our first
range was about 18,000 yards and this rapidly fell till it reached
6,000-odd yards. This caused us to look at each other in horror
since this could be called point-blank range. Actually however it later
transpired we had been firing our secondary armament at enemy
small craft including the luckless *Wiesbaden* which we disabled and then
passed at close range leaving her to become a target for all following
ships. Every time we fired a salvo of our main armament the whole
ship lurched and shivered to a disturbing degree – we were very heavily
armed for our tonnage.[86]

Assistant Clerk Hubert Fischer, HMS *Indomitable*, 3rd Battlecruiser Squadron

In such a confined space, as the cordite fumes drifted in, the atmosphere
became increasingly fetid. Nevertheless, the sounds of battle probably
came as a light relief to the young officers round the plotting table, who
had created their own form of auditory torture.

In order to help in keeping up our morale, we had brought down with
us no less than three gramophones (the ship abounded in these) and
someone would snatch a moment every few minutes to change the
records. I can remember 'Chalk Farm to Camberwell Green' especially
as one of the tunes and one or two others I can no longer name.
When we had all three gramophones going during a temporary lull
the cacophony in that confined space can be imagined. One wit
amongst us described it as the worst horror of the battle![87]

Assistant Clerk Hubert Fischer, HMS *Indomitable*, 3rd Battlecruiser Squadron

The 3rd Battlecruiser Squadron made excellent shooting at the German
battlecruisers, which found themselves almost helpless in front of their
enemies. As had been predicted by Jellicoe, the poor visibility towards the
north rendered them unable to make any effective response.

Even though the ranges were short, from 6,000 to 7,000 metres,
the ships often became invisible in the slowly advancing mists, mixed
with the smoke from the guns and funnels. It was almost impossible to
observe the splashes. All splashes that fell over could not be seen at all,
and only those that fell very short could be distinguished clearly, which
was not much help, for as soon as we got nearer the target again it
became impossible to see where the shots fell.[88]

Commander Georg von Hase, SMS *Derfflinger*, I Scouting Group, High Seas Fleet

The capricious mists did not allow for a parity of vision between the
combatants, and for the Germans it was a severely lopsided contest.

Meanwhile we were being subjected to a heavy, accurate and rapid fire
from several ships at the same time. It was clear that the enemy could
now see us much better than we could see them. This will be difficult to
understand for anyone who does not know the sea, but it is a fact that in
this sort of weather the differences in visibility are very great in different
directions. A ship clear of the mist is much more clearly visible from a
ship actually in the mist than vice versa.[89]

Commander Georg von Hase, SMS *Derfflinger*, I Scouting Group, High Seas Fleet

It may have been their recent gunnery practice at Scapa Flow that made
a real difference to their gunnery; or possibly it was just the closeness of
the range and favourable gunnery conditions. Whatever the reason, the
Invincible, *Inflexible* and *Indomitable* left their indelible mark on Hipper's ships,
which were also coming under fire from Beatty's battlecruisers and
increasingly beginning to attract the attention of elements of the
deploying Grand Fleet as, minute by minute, more of them swung round
into the unified battle line.

There began a phase compared with which all that had hitherto
happened was play. While our own smoke completely hid the target
from me so that I had to hand over to the after control, a hail of hits
descended on us from port aft and port ahead. There nothing can be
seen but red flashes, not the shadow of a ship. Our turrets are trained
right aft and are firing as well as they can at our old friends, Beatty's
battlecruisers. From this direction a shell pierces the upper deck abaft the
fore funnel, penetrates the casemate and bursts behind the under part of

'B' Turret, causes a serious fire and throws outwards both the armoured doors which lead from the casemate to the deck. The explosion occurred directly under the control position but did no damage to this and the two fore 6″ single casemates which were quite close. A hit from forward hits the right gun of 'A' Turret, on the right hand side just in front of the turret, tears a big bit out and goes slantwise upwards against the right side of 'B' Turret. The shell breaks up but the 10″ plate is pierced and the piece broken out is hurled into the turret. There it destroys the breech gear of the right gun, kills the men standing there and sets alight the front and rear portions of a cartridge which were ready in the upper lift. The officer of the turret is dead, the gunner unconscious, lights out, all the fuses of the power and light current fused, the pumps empty, the turret full of smoke and swimming with glycerine, but the left gun and its crew behind the splinter bulkhead are unharmed.[90]

Commander Günther Paschen, SMS *Lützow*, I Scouting Group, High Seas Fleet

Amidst the mass of hits was one which, although relatively unnoticed at the time, eventually was to doom the *Lützow*.

Every ship has weak spots; our Achilles heel was the broadside torpedo flat, situated forward of 'A' Turret. Here, unfortunately, for reasons of space, the torpedo bulkhead, that incomparable protection against hits below the water line, which was such a marked advantage in German ships as compared with foreign ones, had been left out. So two heavy enemy shells succeeded in penetrating under the belt and burst so effectively that the whole of the ship forward of 'A' Turret filled practically at once.[91]

Commander Günther Paschen SMS *Lützow*, I Scouting Group, High Seas Fleet

Under heavy pressure, Hipper's line bent back to the east and began to lose coherence. Individual ships took avoiding action to try to mitigate the effects of the salvoes crashing around them.

A severe, unequal struggle developed. Several heavy shells pierced our ship with terrific force and exploded with a tremendous roar, which shook every seam and rivet. The Captain had again frequently to steer the ship out of the line in order to get out of the hail of fire.[92]

Commander Georg von Hase, SMS *Derfflinger*, I Scouting Group, High Seas Fleet

As reports began to filter through to Scheer, it became apparent that this was more than the Battlecruiser Fleet he was facing.

Admiral Scheer had stood freely on the open upper bridge. Now, however, the enemy's heavy shells began to land around *Friedrich der Grosse* and a saltwater torrent rained over the ship reminding us to seek the shelter of the conning tower. We arrived in the conning tower. It was a narrow intimate space measuring only a few metres in space, with the front protected by armour almost a half metre thick. It was only possible to see or use the observation glasses through the vision slits, which went through the armour. One could feel the strain on the nerves that affect men serving in this intimate space, and a sense of power. Not one unnecessary word was spoken, only brief reports and orders. Here is the brain of the ship, and the brain of the entire fleet.[93]

Chief of Staff Adolf von Trotha, SMS *Friedrich der Grosse*, III Battle Squadron, High Seas Fleet

The question was, just how much of the Grand Fleet had he stumbled into? Had he finally achieved his dream of entrapping an isolated portion of the fleet that he could destroy and thereby equalize the balance of dreadnoughts? Or had he inadvertently walked into the nightmare of Jellicoe's crushing embrace? Scheer still had scant available evidence on which to judge his next and most crucial course of action.

We, on our flagship, were occupied debating how much longer to continue the pursuit in view of the advanced time. There was no longer any question of a cruiser campaign against merchantmen in the Skagerrak, as the meeting with the English fighting forces which was to result from such action had already taken place. But we were bound to take into consideration that the English fleet, if at sea, which was obvious from the ships we had encountered, would offer battle the next day. Some steps would also have to be taken to shake off the English light forces before darkness fell in order to avoid any loss to our main fleet from nocturnal torpedo-boat attacks.[94]

Admiral Reinhard Scheer, SMS *Friedrich der Grosse*, III Battle Squadron, High Seas Fleet

Finally Scheer could see the scale of the problem that faced him. He had run into the full power of the Grand Fleet. This was no isolated detachment ripe for plucking; the tables had been turned and it was Scheer who faced defeat.

It was now quite obvious that we were confronted by a large portion of the English Fleet and a few minutes later their presence was notified on the horizon directly ahead of us by rounds of firing from guns of heavy calibre. The entire arc stretching from north to east was a sea of fire. The flash from the muzzles of the guns was distinctly seen through the mist and smoke on the horizon, though the ships themselves were not distinguishable. This was the beginning of the main phase of the battle. There was never any question of our line veering round to avoid an encounter. The resolve to do battle with the enemy stood firm from the first.[95]

Admiral Reinhard Scheer, SMS *Friedrich der Grosse*, III Battle Squadron, High Seas Fleet

As the twenty-four dreadnoughts of the Grand Fleet completed their fraught deployment from columns into battle line, one by one the mighty dreadnoughts, their very names reflecting two centuries of British naval hegemony around the globe, opened a thunderous fire.

Our long line of battleships stretching away literally for miles to the north east and generally curving round the Germans presented an inspiring and heartening spectacle, as they proceeded majestically along. Salvo after salvo belched out from the long line of those great ships, now confronted for the first time in their career with the enemy they had waited to see for so many weary months.[96]

Lieutenant Stephen King-Hall, HMS *Southampton*, 2nd Light Cruiser Squadron

The Battlecruiser Fleet had suffered grievous losses but it had accomplished its primary mission. It had delivered the High Seas Fleet right under the guns of the Grand Fleet.

That I suggest to you was a tremendous moment in anybody's life. At last the two main fleets were in action. I remember thinking to myself, "Well, we've lost a lot and we're going to lose more. But we don't mind losing this and that as long as the two fleets meet." This moment had arrived and there was a feeling of extraordinary relief – rather patriotic relief perhaps. It was absolutely wonderful to see the battleships opening fire. I thought, "Well, this is the end!"[97]

Midshipman John Ouvry, HMS *Tiger*, 1st Battlecruiser Squadron

In an echo of days gone by the dreadnoughts were bedecked in their fighting colours. Midshipman Hugh Tate, now serving aboard the *Royal Oak*, was already a veteran of the Gallipoli landings more than a year earlier.

Through my periscope in 'A' Turret I could just make out the enemy on the horizon like little black splodges. We were now in battle line, every ship flying as many ensigns as she could. We flew one at the ensign staff, one at the port main yard, a jack the other side, an ensign forward, and a huge silk ensign at the peak. *Iron Duke* ahead of us had three ensign staffs aft.[98]

Midshipman Hugh Tate, HMS *Royal Oak*, 3rd Division, Fourth Battle Squadron

The dreadnoughts moved into their battle stations and the tension mounted as they waited for the chance to let fly their first salvo and finally to join in the action.

The worst part of the whole thing was waiting for that first round to go off. The guns were at the 'Ready' for about half an hour. The gun crews were simply standing there and sweating from the tension of it. However as soon as the first round went off they were all as happy as sand boys.[99]

Midshipman John Farquhar, HMS *Benbow*, 4th Division, Fourth Battle Squadron

The stress in those final moments before the guns finally roared out was almost indescribable.

Picture to yourself the sound of guns heard off the bow, getting louder and louder; then the flashes clearly seen; then ships heavily engaged (our cruisers); then the long looked-for signal is seen and the ships turn – and, after all these many months of waiting, the Grand Fleet is at last in action.[100]

Chief of Staff Captain Percy Grant, HMS *Marlborough*, 6th Division, First Battle Squadron

Without any doubt this was '*Der Tag*'. But the hour was late; there was only a limited amount of daylight left on 31 May. Hope rose supreme; surely the Germans were now trapped. Without doubt they would fight it out, as nature and the British Empire ordained, with the two fleets slugging it out in two parallel lines until the inevitable end.

> It was 'some' sight – too wonderful and literally awe inspiring to describe. After 22 months of war they were the first German ships I had seen – and it was jolly nice to feel one was firing at them; though honestly at first it was very hard to realise that those were the Huns opposite us and that it was not simply an extra special target practice. Similarly it was very difficult to realise the ship might get hit, although one did occasionally see shells making a splash in the water. They might hit *other* ships, but I could not conceive of them hitting *us*.[101]
> Sub-Lieutenant Reginald Elgwood, HMS *Vanguard*, 4th Division, Fourth Battle Squadron

The *King George V* had the honour of leading the whole British line and, deep in her bowels, Harold Wright was at his action stations on the engine-room platform.

> Everyone I suppose had their own thoughts at this moment in time. For myself, I just felt tensed and eager to get started, a certain amount of pride in being the leading ship mixed with some apprehension at being in what seemed a fairly vulnerable position.[102]
> Engine Room Artificer 4th Class Harold Wright, HMS *King George V*, 1st Division, Second Battle Squadron

There were many isolated action stations below decks where men could have little idea of what was going on far above them. In claustrophobic, confined spaces men found themselves alone with their thoughts.

> Just before the firing started an order came through that the stern torpedo was to be made ready. This would only be used when retreating. This meant that I would have to go aft with a gyroscope and fit it into the torpedo. I now had to go the whole length of the mess decks, opening and closing seven watertight bulkhead doors. As I entered the wardroom flat I was confronted by the the figure of the Commander.

He did not question me, as he probably understood my presence by the fact that I was carrying the box with the gyroscope. He was the only person that I had seen and it struck me how lonely he looked and that also, he had his revolver strapped around his waist. I did not see another soul until I reached the aft flat; it seemed like an empty tomb. We were enclosed in a steel box and all we could do was just obey orders.[103]

Electrical Artificer Nelson White, HMS *Colossus*, 5th Division, First Battle Squadron

As they went into battle, some thought of honour and glory, some of their wives, their families and some of themselves. Yet even the prospect of an apocalyptic battle could not wrench some from the more mundane concerns of their routine duties.

At the time I had 360 lbs of dough proving in the tins, and as my bakehouse is situated on the upper deck it is very exposed. My orders were to leave it and get under cover below as soon as the position became critical. I went to the Commander and obtained permission to remain in the bakehouse until the latest moment, which was the firing of the first gun. This order gave me the opportunity of witnessing the opening of the battle fleet action. While my dough was proving in the tins, I went out on the quarterdeck and witnessed a magnificent spectacle, one never to be forgotten. The whole visible horizon which was not more than four miles was one long blaze of flame. I was so intensely interested that I could not realise the risk until observing a cruiser close handy on fire. I went back to the bakehouse and endeavoured to save my batch of bread. My staff which consists of three men had gone down under cover. The fire party by this time had orders to extinguish my fire. The dough required at least 20 minutes more proof. But being very loathe to waste the material and labour, I put it in and trusted to luck if it would be possible to save it later. Then my superior officer gave me orders to leave everything. Having done this I hastened down below, by the time I got to my station we were in the thick of it.[104]

Warrant Officer Walter Greenway, HMS *Vanguard*, 4th Division, Fourth Battle Squadron

The guns were the *raison d'être* of the Grand Fleet. The massed 15-inch, 13.5-inch and 12-inch guns were designed and built for one reason only: to engage and eliminate the enemies of the British Empire. The dénouement of the drama was approaching as this vast array of almost unimaginable artillery strength and power was turned at last on the High Seas Fleet. After all the drills and exercises, the guns roared out in fulfilment of their primary function: to smash, to destroy, to rend and, above all, to kill Germans.

> At last after what seemed to me to be an eternity, we got the order, "Load! Load! Load!" This really meant business and the crash of the mechanism and hiss of the hydraulic pressure made me feel better. Another long pause – and I found my mind concentrating on the breeches of our own guns containing the huge 1,350 lb shells and accompanying cordite. I have never really got used to the shock of the first gun to be fired in any action, either practice or realistic and I suffered the same apprehension at Jutland. It quite took my mind off the possibility of the enemy hitting us and a good thing too. "Bring all guns to the ready!" A moment of deathly silence and then, "CRASH!" The first salvo was off. Immediately, the tension snapped and the whole turret, men and machinery, sprang into life whilst one broadside after another was pumped into the enemy.[105]
>
> Midshipman John Brass, HMS *Orion*, 2nd Division, Second Battle Squadron

The noise was terrible. The percussive shock ripped into their ears, assaulting their sensory perception anew with each salvo. Although no louder than in the endless training shoots, it was devastating just the same.

> They made a real ringing boom when they fired. All we had was a little cotton wool in our ears as protection against the noise. The lads setting the ranges had earpieces, but at times blood oozed out of their ears.[106]
>
> Signalman Victor Jensen, HMS *Collingwood*, 5th Division, First Battle Squadron

As the power of each cordite charge was detonated, the guns violently recoiled and even the mighty dreadnoughts trembled with an after-shock that no hydraulic buffers could entirely smother.

The concussion of five 12″ guns going off absolutely together is, as you may imagine, pretty considerable. Even on the bridge it is difficult to keep one's cap on and after each discharge the ship is enveloped for a moment in a dense brown fog.[107]

Assistant Paymaster Harold Foot, HMS *Colossus*, 5th Division, First Battle Squadron

Fragile fixtures and fittings paid the price as the shock waves surged around the superstructure.

During the firing there was a steady fall of broken glass onto the conning tower, as all the glass round the bridge was broken by the concussion, as also was the glass in the searchlights. [108]

Midshipman Michael Hoyle, HMS *Monarch*, 2nd Division, Second Battle Squadron

In the turrets, the epicentres of the man-made thunderbolts, the results of ceaseless drills and training were sharply in evidence as the gun crews sprang to reloading, maintaining the essential rhythm of fire.

Crouched over the fire-control instruments, behind those twin giant guns, it was also my duty to 'keep an eye' on the crew loading the huge projectiles and charges into the gaping breeches. Rattle, rattle, rattle, went the automatic rammer – then a thud as the rifling bit deep into the copper driving band. Rattle, rattle – in goes the cordite – the red ends of the heavy charges seemed to convey a mute warning as the slam of the breech hid them for ever from view. "Right Gun – Ready!" "Left Gun – Ready!" The steady voices of each gunlayer reporting, "On, on!" to indicate that they are 'on' the target. Then that portentous silence unbroken except for the hiss of the hydraulic machinery as the director layer high up the mast waits for a favourable roll. "Ting! Ting!" from the fire gongs and CRONCH! The heavy recoil of those tons of steel to within an inch of my busy head. I can always remember the placid face of the big Marine who worked the breech mechanism. He chewed tobacco and radiated quiet efficiency and I used to hope that my own youthful face registered a similar professional indifference to these tremendous proceedings. [109]

Midshipman Robert Goldreich, HMS *Thunderer*, 2nd Division, Second Battle Squadron

As the guns roared, an infectious excitement mingled with the cordite fumes in the air. As the adrenalin surged through them not all the younger officers were able to control themselves.

> Lieutenant Bishop arrived at the foot of a vertical steel ladder leading up to the only exit on to the upper deck. The ladder had no guard rails, it was near to where I sat with my instrument, close to the pedestal and seat of the rangefinder. With a grin the Lieutenant said, "What's going on up there?" Climbing the ladder he opened the 'manhole' cover, popping his head out to look round. A shell came very near to the turret – at that moment Captain Colley appeared and roared, "What the hell are you doing up there, Bishop? Come down you bloody fool!" Lieutenant Bishop staggered down minus his moustache, eyebrows and lashes, he just looked as if he had been to the barbers for a singe. I felt like a good laugh, but dare not. He appeared none the worse for his foolish adventure, except that the affected parts were very sore.[110]
>
> Private John Beardsley, Royal Marine Light Infantry, HMS *Hercules*, 6th Division, First Battle Squadron

The gunhouse of the turret was just the tip of the iceberg. Below them were the working chamber and the magazine – the source of the ship's destructive power and containing the seeds of their own destruction if it were breached by a cordite flash.

> The only thing below us is the shell room, where they are busy loading shells to send up to the guns followed by cordite charges from our magazine. We don't want to hold them up so dozens of cases are opened ready to pass up. The guns fire, the ship heels over, there's a thud. We don't know if we are hit or if it's our own guns. There are kettles of water and tins of corned beef in corners in case we are down here very long. As charges and shells are sent up, comments come down to us by voice tube.[111]
>
> Boy 1st Class A. E. Cooper, HMS *Conqueror*, 2nd Division, Second Battle Squadron

The desire for speed at all costs, typified by the dozens of open cordite cases, would have doomed them were the turret to be penetrated by a German shell. The atmosphere quickly became fetid.

I was working down in the magazine. We were taking off the lids of these quarter cordite charges. They were sealed with a sort of putty type thing called lutin. This kept them watertight and airtight. Directly we took the lids off all the fumes of the cordite came out. We were in a confined place, couldn't have fans and we all began to get headaches. The officer in charge passed up a message through the voice-pipe, he asked for permission for us to go on deck. We were nearly all sick, cordite fumes and no fresh air.[112]

Boy Seaman Charles Blunt, HMS *King George V*, 1st Division, Second Battle Squadron

At the bottom of the chain was the shell room.

My station was the shell room with my mates, sending shells up to the turret by hydraulic power. I had to help clamp the shell from the bins and guide them to the tray for sending up to the gun. My mates were chalking the shells as they were sent up. 'Hit old Kaiser Bill', 'Hit the Bastards' etc. The morale was good. I cannot explain to you our feelings in battle. The guns were firing away, shaking the ship. I must say I felt very scared. I could not see anything that was happening on deck. We were shut down in the shell room, watertight doors.[113]

Ordinary Seaman William Macey, HMS *Collingwood*, 5th Division, First Battle Squadron

Before the deployment of the Grand Fleet had even been completed, many of the dreadnoughts had sighted targets and opened fire. At first the hapless *Wiesbaden* was the main victim, trapped as she was like a rabbit in the headlights of the approaching juggernaut.

We could see a small three funnelled cruiser and hear heavy explosions from the direction of the battlecruisers. All guns were loaded with Capped Armour Piercing Lyddite and at last we had orders to train on the above cruiser. At 6.29 we opened fire, range 10,500 yards (about 5¼ miles) and straddled her with our first salvo, and continued to do so till she heeled over and went down with flames pouring out of her side. We fired 36 15″ at her and though she was in a pretty bad way already, we undoubtedly finished her.[114]

Midshipman Hugh Tate, HMS *Royal Oak*, 3rd Division, Fourth Battle Squadron

In such accounts, the *Wiesbaden* was reported sunk many times. But she clung to life with a tenacity that was an awesome testimony to the skills of German shipbuilders. As Beatty's battlecruisers ran ahead and cleared sight lines, more and more of the Grand Fleet dreadnoughts sighted their real enemies, the High Seas Fleet. In the prevailing conditions of uncertain visibility there was no chance of systematic target assignment; each ship picked the target her crew could see best in the murk.

> We fired on a big black German battleship with a funnel close against each mast. We had the satisfaction of landing two hits on this '*Kaiser* class' ship. The hits showed very red against the hull and she only fired from the foremost guns after, so I take it we strafed the two turrets on her quarterdeck.[115]
>
> Midshipman Robert Goldreich, HMS *Thunderer*, 2nd Division, Second Battle Squadron

In the gloom it was difficult to identify specific ships. It was also hard to determine which ship had fired which shells with so many firing at once at the same targets. Nevertheless, there were clear signs that numerous hits were being scored.

> What we were firing at I couldn't at first see owing to the infernal mist, but at last I could make her out. I thought it was one of their *Kaiser* class at first, but afterwards found it was the *Derfflinger*, a battlecruiser. I couldn't see where our shells were dropping. The whole horizon was lit up by flashes, but no shell came near us at first. I think they were firing at the end of our line. After about four shells we got a hit. She had been hit before and I could see the flames running along her quarterdeck. That lyddite must be awful. She was fairly flaming and also amidships but I didn't see it. I don't believe she even fired at us as she was engaging the battlecruisers. She was the only ship I saw clearly, but the fleet must have been firing at us. *We* were not hit at all.[116]
>
> Midshipman Geoff Congreve, HMS *Benbow*, 4th Division, Fourth Battle Squadron

The Germans were hamstrung by the one-way visibility. Blinded not by light but by mist, they could not respond properly to their tormentors. Many British observers mistook their ineffectiveness for a sign that they had lost their nerve under pressure.

The German gunnery when they were knocking out the armoured cruisers was absolutely drill perfect, salvoes falling beautifully. As soon as we got on the scene though they must have lost their heads completely and just pumped the stuff overboard. It was a quaint sensation being under fire. The *Benbow* was being fired at by some ship, but we couldn't make out by which. Most of the stuff fell about 800 short or else about 1,000 over. Only one salvo came really near to us; it seemed to pass right underneath the top and made a horrid noise – a sort of cross between a wail and a whistle. Our men were perfect; as happy and as cheery as if at a picnic. The stokers came up on deck, parties of 20 at a time, to have a look at the fight. The Commander was the worst offender of the lot.[117]

Assistant Paymaster Noel Wright, HMS *Benbow*, 4th Division, Fourth Battle Squadron

Without warning, at about 18.30, just for a fateful moment, the visibility situation changed. The mists seemed to open up, and the Germans finally saw the 3rd Battlecruiser Squadron right in front of them. Demonstrating that they had not lost any of their nerve, once handed back a fair chance, the German gunners did not take long to react.

Meanwhile we had turned to the south and suddenly there appeared, plainly and comparatively near, an English battlecruiser of the *Invincible* class, four points aft. I cannot express the delight I felt at having one of these tormentors clearly in sight, and like lightning the orders are given.[118]

Commander Günther Paschen, SMS *Lützow*, I Scouting Group, High Seas Fleet

As the Germans sprang into action, their shells soon began to fall around the *Invincible*, *Inflexible* and *Indomitable*. Aboard the *Indomitable*, as they were steering to the east with the Germans to the south, the port midship turret was naturally unable to bear to starboard. Unable to restrain his curiosity as to what was happening, Midshipman J. C. Croome climbed out onto the roof of the turret to see what was happening. He used the telescope of the 4-inch gun mounted on the turret roof to get a good view while taking advantage of the limited protection provided by the gun shield against shell splinters.

I could now see very clearly our shot and those of the rest of the squadrons falling all around the enemy, but I didn't see much sign of

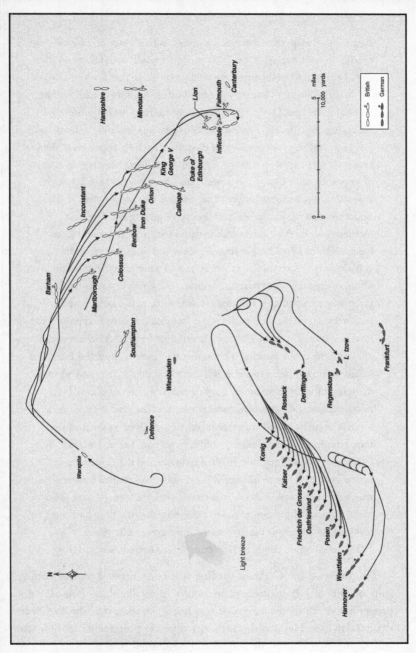

Scheer's battle turn away

hitting. About this time there was a hiss of falling water and I looked up quickly to see what might easily have been a waterspout falling on the ship. I realised from the immense volume of water that it was a salvo of 11″ or 12″ which had landed just ahead of us. A moment after another colossal water spout went up immediately astern of us completely obscuring the *Inflexible*. The column of water was probably at least 100 feet high and from the smoke and disturbance which appeared at the bottom it was apparent that the German shells were bursting on contact or very soon after hitting the water. This wasn't so good but I thought I would wait a moment longer to see the *Inflexible* and the rest of the Squadron emerge just to see how they were getting on. The next moment four or five express trains roared past my left ear and I was lying as flat as I could make myself on the top of the turret and gabbling my prayers as fast as might be and wondering whether the rush of air as the salvo went past had knocked me down or my knees had given way, or whether it was just instinct, while at the same time I tried to convince myself that it really was a fact that the salvo had passed at least one fifth of a second before I heard it or I wouldn't have heard it at all. From my prone position with some other part of my mind I saw the splash set up by the salvo some 100 yards beyond the ship and noticed the series of splashes made by a solitary shell which continued ricocheting into the distance, turning over and over like a big stone as it went. The arrival of the next salvo some 50 yards or so short of the ship, but plumb in line with our midships section, instantaneously followed by the whining hiss of shell splinters and the simultaneous appearance of a few small jagged holes in the two funnels between which my turret was situated, made me wonder where the next salvo might land and I jumped to my feet deciding that the time had come to seek such sanctuary as the armour of the turret might afford.[119]

Midshipman John Croome, HMS *Indomitable*, 3rd Battlecruiser Squadron

The worst of the German shelling was concentrated on the leading ship of the 3rd Battlecruiser Squadron, their flagship, *Invincible*, the progenitor of all battlecruisers. It was not a situation that she had been designed to face. Her speed was meant to be her protection, but here she was facing two heavily armed, better armoured and all round more modern German battlecruisers, at a range where it was only a question of where shells would hit that would determine her fate. The light armour protection of the *Invincible* could not hope to withstand this kind of punishment. Only luck could be her salvation in these circumstances.

> Her guns were trained on us and immediately another salvo crashed out, straddling us completely. "Range 9,000!" roared Leading Seaman Hanel. "9,000 – salvoes fire!" I ordered, and with feverish anxiety I waited for our splashes. "Over. Two hits!" called out Lieutenant Commander von Stosch. I gave the order, "100 down. Good, Rapid!" And 30 seconds after the first salvo the second left the guns. I observed two short splashes and two hits. Von Stosch called, "Hits!" Every 20 seconds came the roar of another salvo. At 6.31pm the *Derfflinger* fired her last salvo at this ship. [120]

Commander Georg von Hase, SMS *Derfflinger*, I Scouting Group, High Seas Fleet

On board the *Invincible*, Gunnery Commander Hubert Dannreuther, the equivalent of both Commander von Hase and Commander Paschen, was stationed in the foretop.

> *Invincible* then turned and came into action at about 6.15pm with the leading enemy battlecruiser which was thought to be the *Derfflinger*. Fire was opened at the enemy at about 8,000 yards and several hits were observed. Admiral Hood hailed the Control Officer in the Control Top from the forebridge, "Your firing is very good, keep it as quickly as you can, every shot is telling." This was the last order heard from the Admiral or Captain who were both on the bridge at the end. [121]

Commander Hubert Dannreuther, HMS *Invincible*, 3rd Battlecruiser Squadron

Paschen's view from the *Lützow* was obscured by her own drifting smoke and he was forced to pass over control of the guns to the gunnery officer manning the after control. Both the *Lützow* and the *Derfflinger* were now concentrating on the *Invincible*.

> Lieutenant Commander Bode quickly and clearly takes over and to the unspeakable delight of the whole ship, 15 seconds later our turrets, except 'B' speak again. I hear through the telephone everything said by Bode at the gunnery centres and look again at the enemy. Over! "4

Down." "Salvo." A straddle! "Salvo." As the sound of the fall of shot indicator squeaks, the red flame flashes up nicely and unmistakeably from the water columns round the enemy. Signs of a hit like these make a very definite impression if one has seen them twice. And sure enough, only a few seconds pass before the red glow breaks out everywhere and this ship too blows up. It was the *Invincible* – the unconquerable conquered. *Derfflinger*, as well as ourselves, had fired at her. For myself, I would not claim the credit from my highly esteemed brother-in-arms, but to be just to Lieutenant Commander Bode, I must say that I have no doubts as to our being responsible. The squeaking sound, the straddling salvoes and the red flames, all were unmistakeable.[122]

Commander Günther Paschen, SMS *Lützow*, I Scouting Group, High Seas Fleet

The *Invincible* blew up at 18.34. Yet again, the thin armour of a British battlecruiser had been found wanting under the random probing of heavy-calibre shells.

The moment a German shell penetrated the midships turret of the *Invincible* she was doomed as the flash raced down through the working chamber into the magazines below. Like a box of fireworks when a match is thrown in, she went up for all to see.

Suddenly a dark smudge seemed to pass along the leading ship's side, the *Invincible*. Then she disappeared into a huge cloud of smoke and flame. The upper bridge awning was blown high above the smoke and looked like a huge parachute with the iron stanchions that supported it dangling below it. As soon as the force of the explosion was over the whole thing plunged into the sea. It was awful, that a ship could go in seconds like that, not so much the ship but those living souls with her.[123]

Leading Seaman Reginald Bowden, HMS *Yarmouth*, 3rd Light Cruiser Squadron

Marine Bryan Gasson was at his post as a range-finder, actually inside the ill-fated 'Q' starboard midship turret of the *Invincible*, when the world exploded around him.

Suddenly our starboard midship turret manned by the Royal Marines was struck between the two 12″ guns and appeared to me to lift off the top of the turret and another of the same salvo followed. The flashes passed down to both midship magazines containing 50 tons of cordite.

The explosion broke the ship in half. I owe my survival, I think, to the fact that I was in a separate compartment at the back of the turret with my head through a hole cut in the top. Some of the initial flash must have got through to my compartment as I was burnt on the hand, arms and head – luckily my eyes escaped, I must have instinctively covered them with my hands. The rangefinder and myself had only a light armour covering. I think this came off and, as the ship sunk, I floated to the surface.[124]

Royal Marine Bryan Gasson, HMS *Invincible*, 3rd Battlecruiser Squadron

Despite his best intentions, Midshipman Croome had not had time to get back to the shelter of his turret aboard the *Indomitable* and thus he had a grandstand view of the dreadful explosion which he captured for posterity in a photograph.

There was a terrific flash from the *Invincible*, then in sight as we turned towards the enemy a point or so, and she went up in a column of smoke several hundred feet high decorated at the edges by bits and pieces of what a second before had been a battlecruiser and the flagship of our squadron. Of this astonishing spectacle I took a photograph, which I expect was probably unique. I must have got the explosion almost at its height since the column of smoke and debris took certainly three or four seconds to get to its full height. So utterly unexpected and sudden was this calamity that I don't think it made much impression on me until quite a time afterwards. I remember some small bits of falling debris bouncing on top of the turret drove me back to the shelter of my 4" gun shield. One of these pieces, which happened to stay on top of the turret, I picked up as a souvenir two or three minutes later. I burned my hand quite nicely doing so to my surprise and disgust as it looked cold enough.[125]

Midshipman John Croome, HMS *Indomitable*, 3rd Battlecruiser Squadron

Elsewhere in the *Indomitable*, men helplessly watched the death throes of their comrades in arms. For all of them it was a profound and ominous moment.

We observed two dull glows amidships. The appearance was that the armour was withstanding the impact of the shells. But a few moments later a great mushroom of smoke rose to the clouds. When it cleared our flagship was in two halves sticking out of the water in opposite directions and slowly sinking into it. We young *Indomitable* officers had particularly poignant feelings since the day before we sailed, the junior officers of *Invincible* had come aboard us and a merry and riotous evening was had by all. Now every one of those was 'asleep in the deep'.[126]

Assisstant Clerk Hubert Fischer, HMS *Indomitable*, 3rd Battlecruiser Squadron

For some onlookers, caught up in the middle of the battle, personal grief and shock were hidden behind a façade of professional sang-froid. Their real emotions would surface later.

I saw an enormous sheet of flame shoot up in the air, it was really a most appalling sight, the flames dissolved into a cloud of black smoke, when it cleared the *Invincible* had practically entirely disappeared, just a bit of her bow and a bit of her stern entirely separate were sticking up out of the water. Nobody took the slightest notice of it, that struck me as being rather extraordinary, but everything went on exactly as before. I had dined in that ship only three nights before. The whole thing is too awful for words.[127]

Sub-Lieutenant Reginald Servaes, HMS *Comus*, 4th Light Cruiser Squadron

For others, the almost instantaneous destruction of a proud warship in the throes of her duty had a salutary effect. It struck home in brutal fashion that neither they, nor their ship, were either invulnerable or immortal, as the triumphal ethos of the Royal Navy had encouraged them to believe.

We heard a very loud explosion, we had another look out and *Invincible* seemed covered in a cloud of smoke. Then she passed out of my range of vision and I never saw her break up and sink. At this point one of my mates having, like me, stood stupefied at the sight, said, "Shut that bloody dead light or we shall get one!" And we hastily closed it, which of course was a futile gesture. I was entirely unafraid until I saw *Invincible* in trouble. That was not because I was brave, but I was so inexperienced and naïve that it never struck me that we could be sunk.[128]

Stoker Sidney Blackman, HMS *Inflexible*, 3rd Battlecruiser Squadron

For those battened down far below the water-line, the grim reality of their position began to prey on their nerves. In the plotting room of the *Indomitable*, Fischer considered his minimal options if the worst should happen.

> There were seven of us cramped into a space about 10 feet by 8 feet. The only exit was through a manhole in the deck above and as soon as action was joined this was battened down from above. In the event of the ship sinking we could only hope for someone to come round to open up. I still shiver when I think of those poor souls in a similar position in our ill-fated flagship. I can only hope they were killed or knocked out immediately by the force of the explosion and had not just to wait for the water to rise to the deck above via the voice pipes and other points of entry.[129]
>
> Assistant Clerk Hubert Fischer, HMS *Indomitable*, 3rd Battlecruiser Squadron

It was another well-deserved triumph for the battered but still game ships of Hipper's I Scouting Group They had seized their brief opportunity delivered by the breaking mists and struck another mighty blow for their country.

> I shouted into the telephone, "Our enemy has blown up!" And above the din of the battle a great cheer thundered through the ship and was transmitted to the fore-control by all the gunnery telephones and flashed from one gun position to another. I sent up a short, fervent prayer of thanks to the Almighty, shouted, "Bravo Hanel, jolly well measured!" And then my order rang out, "Change target to the left!"[130]
>
> Commander Georg von Hase, SMS *Derfflinger*, I Scouting Group, High Seas Fleet

Of the crew of 1,032 men, just six survived, including Commander Dannreuther, who later estimated that the *Invincible* sank in about 15 seconds.

> She went down with a crash and I was pushed out of her. When I came up to the surface again, I was a bit out of breath and I saw a target floating by, so I went and got on it, found two other fellows there. The bow and the stern were right up, leaning on the bottom.[131]
>
> Commander Hubert Dannreuther, HMS *Invincible*, 3rd Battlecruiser Squadron

The force of the detonation in her midships turret rent the *Invincible* in two. As the middle section disappeared in the titanic explosion the wreck took up a bizarre configuration with both bow and stern standing erect out of the water.

The two halves were drifting past us, we would be doing about 26 knots. There were about 12–14 survivors clinging to the bow and stern, there may have been more. The thing which struck me was the terrific spirit shown by these men, to the best of their knowledge, there was only the most remote chance of them being picked up – yet they hung on with one hand and waved and cheered us on – many being swept off by our wash. A terrific spirit.[132]

Leading Signalman Alec Tempest, HMS *Lion*, 1st Battlecruiser Squadron

As the Grand Fleet steamed past, men died in the water in front of the horrified observers.

Right aft she was crowded with men but owing to the slippery state of the deck and ship's side many of these poor fellows fell into the water and soon the sea around was alive with bobbing heads of swimming men and, although a destroyer was there picking up survivors, many were drowned before our eyes.[133]

Able Seaman John Myers, HMS *Monarch*, 2nd Division, Second Battle Squadron

The destroyer *Badger* was detailed by Beatty to pick up survivors. The ship had not witnessed the explosion and at first, as the crew presumed it was a German wreck, they detailed an armed guard to take care of the antic-ipated prisoners.

As we neared the wreck we could see the water all around thick with flotsam and jetsam, mainly composed of floating seaman's kitbags, with a few hammocks scattered amongst them. We also spotted a raft, on which there were four men, and on the bridge they spotted two other survivors in the water. By orders from the Captain I lowered and sent away the whaler, with our gunner in charge armed with a service revolver. The Captain brought the ship alongside the raft, and I waited with the doctor and the armed guard ready to receive German survivors. Judge of my surprise, when the raft was almost alongside, to see a Commander R.N., a Lieutenant R.N., and two seamen ratings on it. In my surprise I forgot to dismiss the armed guard, who, no doubt

234

considering that it was that for which they were there, wanted to seize
on the unfortunate survivors as we hauled them on board. However,
I quickly sent the guard away and apologised to the Commander, who
only treated it as a good joke. The Commander was really marvellously
self-possessed. I can hardly understand to this day how a man, after
going through what he had, could come on board us from the raft as
cheerily as if he was simply joining a new ship in the ordinary course of
events. He laughed at the armed guard and assured us that he hadn't a
scratch on his whole body, and that he had merely – as he put it –
stepped into the water when the foretop came down.[134]

Anon Lieutenant, HMS *Badger*, 1st Flotilla

The Commander was Dannreuther, and in both escape and rescue he
displayed a level of sang-froid that has rarely been bettered. The *Badger*
also picked up the two men struggling in the water. One of them was
Gasson, who was in great pain from the burns he had suffered during the
explosion.

After about half an hour the destroyer HMS *Badger* approached,
lowered boats and picked the survivors up. Luckily for me the destroyer
carried a doctor and my burns were carefully treated.[135]

Gunner Bryan Gasson, HMS *Invincible*, 3rd Battlecruiser Squadron

Dannreuther lived until 1977, Gasson until 1980 – two very lucky men
from an unlucky ship.

The horned remnants of the *Invincible* stood as macabre monuments
to the failure of British battlecruiser design. As the ships of the Grand
Fleet passed by during the succeeding minutes, many, like the crew of the
Badger, had no idea what it was they were looking at.

I felt quite sure it was a German ship. So I passed to my 6″ gun crews,
"The wreck of a German ship is now in view on the starboard side!"
and the 6″ crews gave a great cheer. Two minutes afterwards the Signal
Bosun on our bridge rang me up. He said, "Did you see that ship on the
starboard side?" I said, "Yes I did!" He said, "Did you read the name of
the ship on the stern?" I said, "No!" He said, "It was the *Invincible*!"
I was terribly depressed.[136]

Midshipman John Ouvry, HMS *Tiger*, 1st Battlecruiser Squadron

The wreck was truly a strange sight. The erect bow and stern remained standing for some time and few observers could conceive that these were the remains of a proud British warship.

> I had been keeping my eye open for Zeppelins, as I felt sure they must be about and although I couldn't see one in the air, great was my joy when I thought I saw one wounded, lying in the water some distance on the bow. As we got closer I found it wasn't a 'Zepp' but a ship, and felt rather elated at seeing the fruits of our labours. Alas, on getting closer, I found it was the *Invincible* with her bow and stern above water, sticking up in the air at an angle of about 45 degrees, her back broken and resting on the bottom. A destroyer was standing by her with some survivors on board, a quantity of wreckage of course about, but no one in the water that I could see.[137]
>
> Lieutenant Thomas Norman, HMS *Benbow*, 4th Division, Fourth Battle Squadron

Ahead of the Grand Fleet, the *Inflexible* and *Indomitable* passed their former flagship and continued the fight undaunted.

> We now led the line for some time and were under heavy fire from the big German ships opposite us, but we were fortunate enough not to be hit at all the whole time. How we escaped I don't know, as shells were falling about us and ships astern of us thought we were having a very bad time. We were also lucky in avoiding torpedoes which were seen coming and very skilfully dodged by our Captain, who all through the action was in the open, on the bridge, not in the conning tower behind armour. In my turret I could not see much except the ship we were firing at and I was glad to see that we got some hits on her – that was probably why we weren't getting hit.[138]
>
> Captain Robert Sinclair, Royal Marine Light Infantry, HMS *Inflexible*, 3rd Battlecruiser Squadron

As the mists closed in again and their visibility deteriorated, the Germans had renewed difficulty in ranging on their opposite numbers. Methodically the *Inflexible* and *Indomitable* took their revenge on Hipper's flagship the *Lützow*.

I very soon forgot the disaster to the *Invincible* in the excitement of seeing a steady series of red splashes of flame and much fewer and more irregular flashes of yellow along the enemy's long line which indicated that we were hitting with some regularity and effect while the enemy was no longer hitting back with his previous vigour and rapidity. Also every now and then a single shot would spring into view ridiculously far down the range showing that somebody's shooting, presumably the enemy, was going most erratically. The enemy was just beginning to turn away and for the moment was showing up more clearly than at any time before. The leading ship *Lützow*, on which we had been firing in concentration with *Inflexible* since *Invincible* went up, was out of line and obviously badly hit. Shells were falling all round her while red splashes in almost every salvo and clouds of smoke made it quite clear that she was being hit repeatedly. The three battlecruisers which had been following her were also having a hot time of it.[139]

Midshipman John Croome, HMS *Indomitable*, 3rd Battlecruiser Squadron

The sinking of the *Invincible* was a triumph, but it did not change the tactical morass into which the High Seas Fleet was now sinking. As the Grand Fleet columns evolved into a fully fledged battle line, their shells began to crash down on the German battlecruisers and leading dread-noughts of the III Battle Squadron. The *König*, in particular, was hard hit by the *Iron Duke* and the *Monarch*.

At this time, owing to smoke and mist, it was most difficult to distinguish friend from foe, and quite impossible to form an opinion on board the *Iron Duke*, in her position towards the centre of the line, as to the formation of the enemy's Fleet. The identity of ships in sight on the starboard beam was not even sufficiently clear for me to permit of fire being opened; but at 6.30 p.m. it became certain that our own battle cruisers had drawn ahead of the Battle Fleet and that the vessels then before the beam were battleships of the "*König*" class. The order was, therefore, given to open fire, and the *Iron Duke* engaged what appeared to be the leading battleship at a range of 12,000 yards on a bearing 20 degrees before the starboard beam; other ships of the 3rd and 4th Divisions (the Fourth Battle Squadron) opened fire at about the same time, and the van divisions (Second Battle Squadron) very shortly afterwards; these latter ships reported engaging enemy battle cruisers as well as battleships. The fire of the *Iron Duke*, which came more directly under my observation, was seen to be immediately effective, the third and fourth salvoes fired registering several palpable hits. It appeared as if all the enemy ships at that time in sight from the *Iron Duke* (not more than three or four, owing to smoke and mist) were receiving heavy punishment.[140]

Admiral Sir John Jellicoe, HMS *Iron Duke*, 3rd Division, Fourth Battle Squadron

The *Iron Duke* claimed some six or seven hits with her 13.5-inch guns, causing serious damage to the *König*. Shells crashed down on her forecastle deck, denting the 'A' Turret armour and causing fires to blaze up which undoubtedly looked worse than they were. Damage was also caused by two hits on the forward section of the port 5.9-inch battery. In addition, one shell holed the lower armour belt beneath the water-line and caused extensive flooding to adjacent compartments and bunkers, which led the *König* to settle slightly in the water and take on a 3 degree list to port. Finally, a glancing blow to the conning tower generated splinters which slightly wounded Rear Admiral Paul Behncke in his exposed station on the upper bridge. Behind the *König*, the *Markgraf* was hit by a shell on a port 5.9-inch casemate, and damaged more seriously by another that actually missed but detonated so close to the port propeller shaft that it was bent. As a result, the bearings started to overheat and the *Markgraf*'s port engine had to be closed down, resulting in a significant loss of speed.

The slowly failing light, coupled with the prevalent mists and rolling smoke clouds, rendered visibility difficult for both sides. For the German gunners clear opportunities to hit back began to diminish. Aboard the *Friedrich der Grosse*, Scheer could see little of the British other than the encircling flashes of their guns. Now it was his turn to make the decision that would decide the future of his command. How could he withdraw the High Seas Fleet from the fatal position into which it had been drawn?

I could see nothing of our cruisers, which were still farther forward.
Owing to the turning aside that was inevitable in drawing nearer,
they found themselves between the fire of both lines. For this reason
I decided to turn our line and bring it on to an opposite course.
Otherwise an awkward situation would have arisen round the pivot

which the enemy line by degrees was passing, as long-distance shots from the enemy would certainly have hit our rear ships. As regards the effectiveness of the artillery, the enemy was more favourably situated, as our ships stood out against the clear western horizon, whereas his own ships were hidden by the smoke and mist of the battle. A running artillery fight on a southerly course would therefore not have been advantageous to us.[141]

Admiral Reinhard Scheer, SMS *Friedrich der Grosse*, III Battle Squadron, High Seas Fleet

The manoeuvre selected and ordered by Scheer was the splendidly named '*Gefechtwendung nach Steuerbord*' or battle turn to starboard. It had been designed to extricate the High Seas Fleet rapidly from just such a disadvantageous situation by the naval equivalent of a handbrake turn. Each ship in the German line would turn individually in a fast, decisive manoeuvre demanding a high degree of seamanship. The ship at the rear of the line would put her helm over first; each successive ship would then follow in sequence, rippling along the line towards the van. Despite Scheer's later dissembling, his sole idea was to use this reversal of course to escape from the trap that had been brilliantly sprung upon him by Jellicoe.

The swing round was carried out in excellent style. At our peace manoeuvres great importance was always attached to their being carried out on a curved line and every means employed to ensure the working of the signals. The trouble spent was now well repaid; the cruisers were liberated from their cramped position and enabled to steam away south and appeared, as soon as the two lines were separated, in view of the flagship. The torpedo boats, too, on the leeside of the fire had room to move to the attack and advanced.[142]

Admiral Reinhard Scheer, SMS *Friedrich der Grosse*, III Battle Squadron, High Seas Fleet

The *Gefechtwendung* did not in fact go entirely smoothly in the pressured combat situation. The pre-dreadnoughts of the II Battle Squadron bringing up the rear of the line were left out and it was the *Westfalen*, the rear dreadnought, that began the movement at 18.37. At the front of the dreadnoughts, the hard-hit *König* missed Scheer's wireless signal, but the plunging shells from the Grand Fleet, coupled with a realization of what was happening behind them, caused them to turn until they too had reversed their course.

After their protracted pummelling, the German battlecruisers were in such a state that all semblance of order had disappeared as they sought to evade the torrents of shells that plagued them. The *Lützow* was so badly battered, well down at the bow, that to steam at any more than 15 knots would be to invite disaster through the collapse of her straining internal bulkheads. At this speed she could no longer lead the line and she therefore pulled out of line altogether to the south-west, trying to evade her enemies as best she could.

> *Lützow* sheers out of the line to slacken speed; the water is pouring in too fast at our bows. Four of our destroyers put up an enormous black veil of smoke between us and the enemy and at once we are out of the heavy fire. A rest from action![143]
> Commander Günter Paschen, SMS *Lützow*, I Scouting Group, High Seas Fleet

It was obvious that the *Lützow* could no longer perform the functions of flagship to the battlecruisers. Hipper therefore reluctantly decided to shift his flag and boarded the destroyer *G39,* temporarily handing over effective command of his precious battlecruisers to Captain Paul Hartog of the *Derfflinger*. But the *Derfflinger* herself was in a dire state.

> The masts and rigging had been badly damaged by countless shells, and the wireless aerials hung down in an inextricable tangle so that we could only use our wireless for receiving; we could not transmit messages. A heavy shell had torn away two armour plates in the bows, leaving a huge gap quite six by five metres, just above the water line. With the pitching of the ship water streamed continually through this hole.[144]
> Commander Georg von Hase, SMS *Derfflinger*, I Scouting Group, High Seas Fleet

From the British perspective the High Seas Fleet simply disappeared in the confusion of the misty conditions. No one realized for a while what had happened. At best, most British ships had only been able to see a few of the German ships and at first it was presumed that they had merely been swallowed up by the mists and would shortly reappear.

Above: Jellicoe aboard his flagship the
Iron Duke (IWM Q 55499)

Right: Beatty in his pomp
(IWM SP 3129)

Reinhard Scheer (AKG)

Franz Hipper (AKG)

Above: The *Lützow* (IWM HU90054)

Opposite: High Seas Fleet on a
North Sea sweep, 1916
(IWM HU 58253)

Above: Lion followed by the *Princess Royal* and *Queen Mary* on the morning of 31 May (IWM HU 69073)

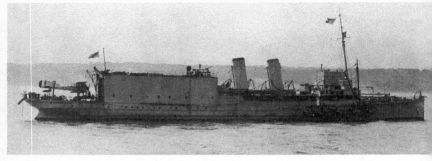

Above: Seaplane Carrier *Engadine* (IWM SP 413)

Above: The *Warspite* (IWM SP 836)

Below: The *Queen Mary* (IWM RP 2222)

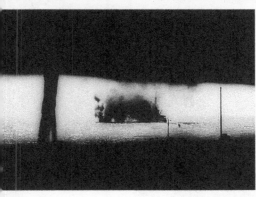

Left: A German battlecruiser firing the first salvo, 31 May 1916
(IWM HU 58254)

Below: Seydlitz firing a salvo, 1916
(IWM HU90055)

Above: Last moments of the *Indefatigable* (IWM Q64302)

Left: Final explosion of
the *Queen Mary*
(IWM SP 1708)

Below: German shell
spouts around
the *Birmingham*
(IWM SP 474)

Below: Iron Duke opens fire (IWM Q 20439)

Above: Forecastle of the *Iron Duke* (IWM Q 55500)

Jack Cornwell VC
(IWM Q 20883)

Forecastle gun of the *Chester* at which Jack Cornwell won his Victoria Cross (IWM SP 191)

Above: The *Warrior* (IWM SP 3102)

Below: The *Tipperary* (IWM SP 45)

Opposite: Men on the deck of the damaged *Chester* (IWM SP 1592)

Above: Explosion of the *Invincible* taken from the *Indomitable* (IWM SP 2469)

Explosion of the *Invincible* (IWM SP 2468)

Wreck of the *Invincible* (IWM SP 2470)

Below: Seydlitz down by the bows as she limped back to port (IWM SP 2157)

Below: Stern view of the battered *Seydlitz* (IWM SP 2158)

Below: Shell damage aboard *Seydlitz* (IWM HU 90056)

Above: Badly burned wounded sailors aboard *Plassy* (IWM Q 83512)

Right: Hole made by German shell in Q Turret of the *Tiger* (IWM HU 69071)

Below: The *Lion* after the battle (IWM Q 70605)

After what seemed a very short time there was a violent ringing of the 'cease fire' gongs bringing everything to a standstill. We in the gunhouse wondered what it could be – had we sunk our opposite number in the enemy line or what? The lieutenant in charge of the turret put us out of suspense by reporting, "Enemy obscured by mist". Another low down trick on the part of the weather.[145]

Midshipman John Brass, HMS *Orion*, 2nd Division, Second Battle Squadron

Fulfilling one of Jellicoe's greatest fears, at the same moment as they executed their battle turn away, the Germans launched a covering destroyer attack. But, in the confusion of the moment, it was recalled and only a few torpedoes were fired towards the British line, to no real effect. They had missed an excellent opportunity of causing real damage. However, the German destroyers did succeed in laying a smoke-screen that masked the retirement of the High Seas Fleet. As they in turn fell back, the destroyers encountered the previously crippled *Shark* and without mercy closed in for the kill. The gallant Commander Loftus Jones manned the last remaining 4-inch gun with a scratch crew of officers and men.

The Captain came off the bridge and spotted for the midship gun; during that time he gave me orders for the boats and rafts to be lowered and got out, but the boats were useless. He also gave orders for the collision mat to be got out which was done. All this time the enemy's cruisers and destroyers were constantly shelling us; several of the enemy destroyers came very close to us in line formation, the range being only 600 yards. We were still firing our only gun. By this time the gun's crew consisted of three men, the Midshipman T. Smith R.N.R, J. Howell, A.B., Gunlayer II and C. Hope, A.B. The Captain was wounded slightly in the leg, but he managed to control the gun.[146]

Torpedo Coxswain William Griffin, HMS *Shark*, 4th Flotilla

Although immobile, they still had a sting in their tail and at least one of their shells scored a vital hit on the *V48*, bringing her to a stop. Under a hail of German shells they stuck it out to the end. Eventually, Loftus Jones had his leg smashed off below the knee by a shell which failed to explode. But he continued to encourage his crew in their hopeless defiance. Able Seaman Charles Hope attempted to help his wounded skipper.

The gaff on which the ensign was flying was shot away, and
Commander Jones, seeing the ensign was hanging down the mast, asked
what was wrong with the flag, and appeared greatly upset as he lay on
the deck wounded. Twice he spoke of it. Then I climbed and unbent
the ensign from the gaff. I passed it down to Midshipman Smith, R.N.R.
who then hoisted it on the yardarm. Commander Jones seemed then to
be less worried when he saw the flag hoisted again.[147]

Able Seaman Charles Hope, HMS *Shark*, 4th Flotilla

As the battle swept past them, the White Ensign, the traditional symbol
of defiance in adversity, continued to fly, and was flying still when the
battered husk that had been the *Shark* finally slipped beneath the waves
at around 19.00. Some thirty of her crew, including the mortally wounded
Loftus Jones, managed to take to the rafts. They were only a mile or so
from the course of the battle line, but they were not picked up. Many
months after the action, Able Seaman Joseph Howell, one of the survivors,
wrote in plaintive tones to the captain of one of the many ships that
passed, asking why they had not made any effort to rescue them despite
all desperate attempts to hail them.

I have often wondered if my simple little signal was ever read, as we
were in the water on a raft on the glorious Jutland day. I am one of the
survivors of the gallant little *Shark* who died so game that day. Of course
I can see now that you had more important work that evening than
saving life, but it was a dying man's appeal. When you passed us, Sir,
I made with my arms, the best I could, the simple message, "We are
British". I remember reading *G22* on your bow, if I am not mistaken
and I have been told that that was the *Onslaught*. Dear Sir, if you have
not heard of this, would you kindly ask your Yeoman of Signals if he
read it. I have always been wanting to know. Perhaps some of the other
boats read it. We had quite a lot alive in the raft at that time but they
were fast dying off from exposure. I was badly wounded in the knee and
I will have a stiff knee for life, but I am far from better yet. The poor
Shark fought about five light cruisers and about ten destroyers that
evening. Our plucky Captain made a gallant attempt to get his
torpedoes home but the enemy were too great in numbers and I'm
afraid we failed. Me (gunlayer) and my Number 2 was left at the gun

fighting them all. But at last we sank, having no upperworks left at all. After doing six hours in the water we were picked up by a Danish ship. So, dear Sir, if I am not asking too much would you kindly answer this note, if you were informed of my little signal, "We are British"?[148]

Able Seaman Joseph Howell, HMS *Shark*, 4th Flotilla

Just six of her crew survived and Commander Loftus Jones was subsequently awarded a posthumous VC. The *V48*, which the *Shark* had disabled in her death throes, remained marooned under the guns of the Grand Fleet. She too fought with great courage as the shells crashed all around her. Like the *Shark*, though helpless and doomed, she still carried the torpedoes that could pose a potent threat to the mightiest dreadnought.

Aboard the *Iron Duke*, Jellicoe was once more faced with a considerable quandary. The guns were falling silent as their targets 'disappeared' and it became apparent that the Germans were not going to engage on a parallel course if they could possibly avoid it. He needed to take precipitate action if he was to regain contact.

The course of the Fleet on deployment had been south-east by east, as already stated, but the van had hauled in to south-east without signal shortly after deployment in order to close the enemy, and at 6.50pm, as the range was apparently opening, the course was altered by signal to south 'by divisions' in order to close the enemy. The *King George V*, leading the van of the Battle Fleet, had just anticipated this signal by turning to south. The alteration was made 'by divisions' instead of 'in succession' in order that the enemy should be closed more rapidly by the whole Battle Fleet.[149]

Admiral Sir John Jellicoe, HMS *Iron Duke*, 3rd Division, Fourth Battle Squadron

Jellicoe has since been criticized for not turning more sharply to the southwestwards to pursue Scheer. However, this criticism is unfounded and overlooks a number of critical factors. Jellicoe had made it clear as early as 1914 that he would not follow a retreating force for fear of their use of mines, submarines and co-ordinated destroyer attacks. Given the largely unplanned way in which the battle had come about at a place that no one could have predicted, it would have taken an act of supreme serendipity to put German submarines in the right place to 'ambush' the

Grand Fleet. Yet throughout the battle there were numerous reports of submarines that must have seemed all too real and threatening at the time. They are all now known to have been false and generated by a variety of flotsam and jetsam in the waves, which to the anxious look-out appeared exactly to duplicate the sinister appearance of a periscope. Such submarine reports do not appear to have overly affected Jellicoe's decision-making process. Yet they were clearly in his mind and placed yet another pressure on him. In addition, Jellicoe believed that most, if not all, of the German destroyers had the capacity to carry mines. While again this was not so, their ability to launch a massed torpedo attack from behind a smoke-screen was real enough. Although it failed, Scheer's attempt to utilize his destroyers to cover his disengagement fully justifies Jellicoe's actions. Through his skilful deployment Jellicoe had managed to 'cross the T' of the High Seas Fleet, putting his ships in the dominating position sought by any naval commander and simultaneously securing the best possible light for his gunners. By turning south after the German fleet turned away, he had then placed himself across the line of their homewards retreat and once again maximized the best available light for his fleet as the sun set in the west. These were considerable achievements within the 'no risk' framework that governed him.

As the Grand Fleet turned south, an incident occurred that was to provide yet another bone of bitter contention during the post-war analysis of the battle. After passing the wreck of the *Invincible*, the *Inflexible* and *Indomitable* had successfully manoeuvred to fall into line behind Beatty so that the *Lion* was once again leading all the battlecruisers. But almost as soon as this had been achieved, at around 18.54, Beatty began a turn of 180 degrees to starboard with the apparent intention of closing the distance that separated the *Lion* from the Grand Fleet. The gap was about 8,000 yards, which probably was too much in the murky conditions. Owing to a failure of her gyroscopic compass, the *Lion*, followed by the whole Battlecruiser Fleet, continued this turn right through 360 degrees, in other words a complete circle. Little sense has ever been made of this. Beatty stoutly denied it ever happened, but the evidence has been preserved by many of the navigation tracks of his subordinates. Beatty adamantly claimed that in fact the 180 degree turn to starboard was followed by a 180 degree turn to port. As the manoeuvre had no conse-

244

quence it remains relatively unimportant within the overall history of the battle. After their eccentric manoeuvre the battlecruisers did end up closer to the Grand Fleet by around 19.05.

While Beatty was chasing his own tail, a more significant incident occurred in the line of the Grand Fleet. A single torpedo, probably fired by the stranded *V48*, struck the *Marlborough* a grievous blow at 18.54. It was the first blow struck against the main body of the British dreadnoughts.

> After we had been firing for 10 or 12 minutes there was a sudden tremendous shock. I was almost thrown off my feet and the shells, which were halfway into the loading cages were up-ended and jammed against the tops of the cages. For a second there was a tense silence, then the voice of Jimmy Green, "There goes my flippin' eggs!" With a shout of laughter we set about righting the shells to keep the guns in action.[150]
> Midshipman Angus Nicholl, HMS *Marlborough*, 6th Division, First Battle Squadron

The impact of the detonating torpedo was far greater than that of any single shell and the concussion reverberated throughout the ship.

> There was a terrific explosion, it simply lifted the ship like a ball and bounced her up and down just like a rubber ball would be in the water. My action station there was first aid station down in one of the flats. We felt the ship gradually going further over and over and over. Of course everybody's faces turned pale, we wondered how far the ship was going over, whether she was going over altogether and we were going to be drowned in this little compartment. It wasn't a very pleasant position to be in knowing that the ship was probably turning turtle, because we didn't know what had hit her, whether it was gunfire or what it was. We had a Surgeon Lieutenant Commander there who was in charge, he said, "Look, there'll be no VCs won on this station. You all remain where you are!" And I think he calmed everybody down. As a matter of fact he sat on the companionway, the ladder that led out and refused to let anyone out – not that anybody did attempt to go out – I think she fetched up about ten degrees.[151]
> George Fox, HMS *Marlborough*, 6th Division, First Battle Squadron

The ships behind could see at once that she had been hit and was in considerable trouble.

The *Marlborough* was hit by a torpedo. Although almost right ahead of us I could just see her – she heeled right over to starboard and I thought she was going, but in spite of this tremendous list she kept her place in the line.[152]

Sub-Lieutenant Clifford Caslon, HMS *Malaya*, Fifth Battle Squadron

With the ship listing it was important to avoid panic. But no one knew whether or not she would eventually sink. To date, British ships had shown little resistance to torpedo hits. The crew faced the prospect of capsizing with varying degrees of uncertainty.

Someone suggests it would be advisable, as the ship is listing, to open the conning tower door. The reply comes back, "The door is jammed!" However, everyone takes it quite calmly and, with a little persuasion, the door is opened; but no-one seems to bother much about it. Judging by the absolute discipline and quiet that prevail it might be a general-quarter day in harbour.[153]

Captain Percy Grant, HMS *Marlborough*, 6th Division, First Battle Squadron

Not everyone in the conning tower was so icy calm. Bugler Thomas Clark had a much more anxious few moments before the door was forced open.

With a foot of armour all around me I felt very secure, when all of a sudden the ship was struck by a torpedo right under the bridge on the starboard side, which of course gave the ship a considerable list. By this time there were orders to open the door of the conning tower, but concern grew when the door would not move and I began to wonder if ever I would get out alive from the armoured room as one might call it. At last they got the door open and the first one out was your humble servant. I certainly took a deep breath, glad to be outside. The whole personnel could have been drowned like rats in a trap if the ship had sunk right away.[154]

Bugler Thomas Clark, Royal Marine Light Infantry, HMS *Marlborough*, 6th Division, First Battle Squadron

As the Grand Fleet settled on a southerly course, Scheer, still deeply aware of his predicament and conscious that night was drawing in, took a decision that has variously been regarded as bold, reckless or downright stupid depending on the perspective of the commentator. At 18.55 he ordered a second *Gefechtwendung* or battle turn to bring his ships onto an easterly course – heading directly towards the centre of Jellicoe's line. This was an amazing decision but Scheer had his reasons.

> It was still too early for a nocturnal move. If the enemy followed us our
> action in retaining the direction taken after turning the line would partake
> of the nature of a retreat, and in the event of any damage to our ships in
> the rear, the Fleet would be compelled to sacrifice them or else to decide
> on a line of action enforced by enemy pressure, and not adopted
> voluntarily, and would therefore be detrimental to us from the very outset.
> Still less was it feasible to strive at detaching oneself from the enemy,
> leaving it to him to decide when he would elect to meet us the next
> morning. There was but one way of averting this – to force the enemy

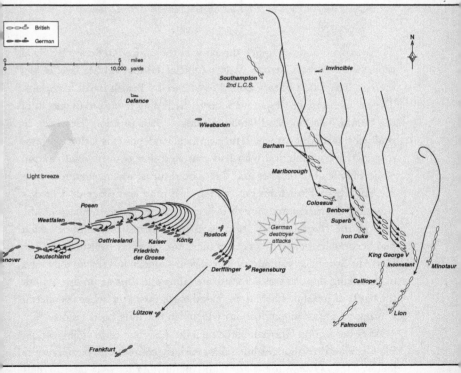

Scheer's second battle turn away

into a second battle by another determined advance, and forcibly compel his torpedo-boats to attack. The success of the turning of the line while fighting encouraged me to make the attempt, and decided me to make still further use of the facility of movement. The manoeuvre would be bound to surprise the enemy, to upset his plans for the rest of the day, and if the blow fell heavily it would facilitate the breaking loose at night. The fight of the *Wiesbaden* helped also to strengthen my resolve to make an effort to render assistance to her and at least save the crew. Accordingly, after we had been on the new course about a quarter of an hour, the line was again swung round to starboard on an easterly course at 6.55pm. The battle-cruisers were ordered to operate with full strength on the enemy's leading point, all the torpedo-boat flotillas had orders to attack, and the First Leader of the torpedo-boats, Commodore Michelsen, was instructed to send his boats to rescue the *Wiesbaden*'s crew.[155]

Admiral Reinhard Scheer, SMS *Friedrich der Grosse*, III Battle Squadron, High Seas Fleet

These explanations are much the same as those given in Scheer's official report and in the German Navy's Official History. Other, less noble, motives have often been ascribed to Scheer by British naval historians. They contend that a desperate Scheer was aiming to pass to the north of the Grand Fleet and had fatally misjudged their position. However, in positing this theory, for which no empirical evidence exists, they perhaps misjudge a bold admiral who had reasoned that conventional caution could only lead to disaster and that a bold thrust was needed to rescue the High Seas Fleet from destruction at a time and place of Jellicoe's choosing. Furthermore, though Scheer's anxiety for the welfare of the crew of the *Wiesbaden* may seem excessive to British sensibilities, which had become hardened by frequent maritime sacrifices over the ages, the German Navy always made every effort to support and rescue the crews of its sinking ships, as was demonstrated time and time again throughout the battle of Jutland. There is no reason to suppose that Scheer's concern was not an important contributory factor in reaching his decision.

After the second German battle turn the *König* was once again leading the German dreadnought line on an easterly course. The battlecruisers followed the *Derfflinger* to the north and then swung across to take up their position in the van. Almost immediately the German dreadnoughts sighted Commodore William Goodenough and his 2nd Light Cruiser Squadron, who had initially taken up station at the rear of the British line, but were now cutting inside further to the south to seek out the High Seas Fleet and possibly to have one final crack at trying to sink the seemingly indestructible *Wiesbaden*. Once again the *Southampton* and her cohorts were surrounded by shell spouts as fire opened from the German line. Goodenough quickly appraised the situation and managed to turn back unscathed to escape on a northerly course. As he withdrew he signalled a sighting report, which was received by Jellicoe at 19.00: 'Enemy battle fleet steering east-south-east. Enemy bears south-south-west, number unknown.'[156]

Although some imprecision remained over the location of the High Seas Fleet, as Jellicoe was not in sight of the *Southampton* the signal from Goodenough was coupled in his mind with a simultaneous sighting report from Beatty ahead of the battle line: 'Enemy are to westward.' Combined, these reports made it pretty clear that Scheer was once again steering directly into the Grand Fleet's lethal embrace. Jellicoe's battle line was in a state of considerable disorder, as the turn by divisions had almost undone the initial deployment, while the various adjustments ordered to the speed had caused further confusion all along the line. Yet these were inconveniences rather than serious problems. For, at around 19.10, they were suddenly granted a second bite at the cherry as the German destroyers, battlecruisers and leading dreadnoughts emerged from the mottled mixture of mist, smoke and sunset haze.

> The whole picture was soon apparent. We were steaming on a southerly course with the whole Battle Fleet stringing out behind us. The German fleet was to westward, apparently in single line, silhouetted against the setting sun – a perfect target, each ship standing out black and clear. The wind was also from the west, hence the reason why the smoke from *our* ships' guns was curling upwards and obscuring the gunnery control positions. One was soon able to distinguish the difference between the flash from the German guns and the resulting explosion when one of the German ships was hit. I am sure we served out a lot of punishment at this particular time and it soon became like a football match. Every

time there was a hit, a roar would go up from the lads; with a few appropriate adjectives for emphasis and everyone was very excited. It must have been nearly half an hour before German shells began to fall near and I believe one of our screening destroyers was hit. Immediately the Captain shouted down from the bridge that everyone was to return to Action Stations. Myself, as a Chief Petty Officer, and I expect everyone else with a rating on their arm, were quick to obey, but some were so excited, or possibly did not hear the order, that Admiral Jerram himself shouted down before the deck was cleared.[157]

Engine Room Artificer 4th Class Harold Wright, HMS *King George V*, 1st Division, Second Battle Squadron

Unfortunately, not every ship could take due advantage of the opportunity. Strung out in divisions as they were, some ships were badly masked and could not fire.

I was in 'Y' Turret, the after turret in the working chamber which is in the barbette just below the gun house. I was in charge of the training of the turret which was by director. I stood beside the trainer who trained by means of a wheel, watching a dial and keeping two pointers in a line. I regret to say that my ship was unable to fire as, during the short time the enemy was in sight, the *Orion*, who was next to us in the line, had failed to take station astern of us and was lying between us and the enemy. Subsequently at Scapa Flow, when our Captain, The Hon. Victor Stanley, repaired on board the Flagship, Jellicoe asked him why he had not fired, to which he answered, "There stands the reason!" indicating the Rear Admiral who flew his flag on *Orion*.[158]

Midshipman Robert McLean, HMS *Erin*, 1st Division, Second Battle Squadron

Although the visibility was much better for the British than for the Germans, it was variable and there were still several ships dogged by drifting smoke or the frustrations engendered by localized sea mists.

The Commander was in the gun control tower and very quiet and good; 'Guns' being a bit excited; Morris very forgetful and slow; and self a bit bewildered but not the faintest trace of funk. The whole thing struck me as fearfully disorganised and happy-go-lucky – we appeared to be circling to surround the enemy. The mist was fearfully handicapping and I had to be continually wiping my glasses to keep the spray off. Added to this the continual listing due to turning and firing made it impossible to press the bearing plot button half the time, as I had to manoeuvre the glasses with one hand and the handle with the other.[159]

Midshipman Arthur James, HMS *Royal Oak*, 3rd Division, Fourth Battle Squadron

In these conditions there could be no systematic distribution of fire. Each ship selected the target that suited it best without recourse to central direction. The benighted *Wiesbaden* and *V48*, limply lolling in the centre of the confrontation, still offered tempting targets.

During lulls in the battle, I had the opportunity of looking at the outside world through the lens of the rangefinder. I saw the German light cruiser *Wiesbaden*, wallowing in its gallant death throes. That scene lived long in my memory – on fire, half submerged, defiant – I've asked myself – could it have been hatred? I would rather like to think it was devotion to duty.[160]

Royal Marine Private John Beardsley, Royal Marine Light Infantry, HMS *Hercules*, 6th Division, First Battle Squadron

If part of Scheer's reason for turning directly to the east was to facilitate the rescue of the surviving crew of the *Wiesbaden*, then it became almost immediately apparent that the destroyers of the III Flotilla assigned to the mission were not going to get anywhere near her without being sunk themselves. They were sighted by many of the dreadnoughts towards the rear of the British line, which not unnaturally assumed that they were launching a serious torpedo attack and opened up a vigorous barrage with their secondary batteries.

We were now treated to a destroyer attack from the mists ahead. There were apparently several destroyers engaged on this expedition, but only one came really clearly into view. There was no time to waste if we were to stop her firing her torpedo which she would probably do at about 3,000 yards. Several ships concentrated on her quickly however and there was no more destroyer. The *Colossus* claims to have fired the final salvo that finished her.[161]

Assistant Paymaster Harold Foot, HMS *Colossus*, 5th Division, First Battle Squadron

The *Colossus* was over-optimistic in her claims, but she may have scored hits on the *V48*, which seems to have regained some engine power and to have been slowly moving southwards at this time. Lieutenant Commander Gautier aboard the *V71*, accompanied by the *V73* and the *G88*, pressed on as far as was possible, but eventually they were recalled by their flotilla commander, Korvettenkapitän Hollman, who reluctantly decided he had no option but to abandon the *Wiesbaden*'s crew to their fate. As the destroyers turned back they launched several torpedoes at the British line at a range of around 6,600 yards that just missed the *Neptune*, which was forced to take emergency avoiding action.

As the High Seas Fleet hove into view the British fire doubled and redoubled. From his position in the middle of the line aboard the *Friedrich der Grosse*, Scheer remained largely unaware of what was actually happening directly ahead of him and generally the Germans could see next to nothing except the wall of gun flashes.

> Suddenly we were practically surrounded. We were being fired at from every side. The entire British fleet had suddenly appeared. We were in a tight corner and I said to myself, "You will be a lucky fellow if you get out of this!"[162]
>
> Obermatrose (Leading Seaman) Albert Blessman, SMS *Posen*, I Battle Squadron

Scheer realized that, whatever his intentions may have been, he had made a disastrous mistake. A man of quick decisions, at 19.13 he issued an amazing order, by signal flag: '*Schlachtkreuzer! Ran an den Feind. Voll einsetzen.*'[163] This is perhaps best translated as 'Battlecruisers at the enemy, attack, give it everything!' A similar signal with different wording was sent by wireless: 'Battlecruisers turn towards the enemy and engage him closely! At him!'[164] Just a minute later Scheer added the rider that the battlecruisers were to operate against the British van. None the less, they were still to attack regardless of consequences. The possibility of a 'death ride' by a major unit in a fleet action had been expressly presaged in orders only recently issued to the pre-dreadnoughts of the II Battle Squadron of the High Seas Fleet on 10 May 1916.

> If the battle develops into a *circular action*, the enemy van is to be concentrated on as much as possible. Should the Commander-in-Chief

expect the II Battle Squadron to *push home an attack regardless of consequences*, he will indicate the same by the signal: "The II Battle Squadron is to operate on the enemy's van.[165]

Admiral Reinhard Scheer, SMS *Friedrich der Grosse*, III Battle Squadron, High Seas Fleet

Scheer intended to use this desperate measure to buy him time to cover another *Gefechtwendung* of the main dreadnought fleet to escape onto a westerly course. The standard tactic of a torpedo attack launched by the destroyers would in these circumstances not be enough. A charge of the battlecruisers was the only feasible option remaining to him as they would dilute the British fire and allow his destroyers to get into decisive torpedo range. He ordered the battle turn to starboard at around 19.18 as soon as his battlecruisers and destroyers had commenced their attack. This time things did not go as smoothly because conditions were extremely unfavourable for any complicated manoeuvre. The III Battle Squadron at the head of the line had already begun to deploy to starboard and was hence in a state of considerable confusion. Its ships were too close together and the orders forced them to manoeuvre in an extremely congested area under heavy fire.

Scheer's subordinate admirals and captains showed immense skill and gratifying powers of independent thought. They evaded many collisions by a hair's breadth as the huge ships whirled round at high speed. But they did not get through unscathed. The *Grosser Kurfürst* was hit by a veritable deluge of shells, many of them 15-inch monsters from the *Barham* and *Valiant*, as she was forced to move out of line in company with the struggling *Markgraf*, which was still hampered by the damage to her port engine.

We had to take over as leading ship as one of our ships had lost speed due to damage caused by a loosened screw. The English fleet knew this and concentrated heavily on us. After a few minutes we were hit eight times by their 38cm shells. We had 19 dead, among which were two officers. Water was flooding the ship due to a hit near the waterline. Due to so many misses a wall of water had built up restricting their view, which was an advantage for us which nobody had reckoned upon.[166]

Lieutenant Beissel von Gymnich, SMS *Grosser Kurfürst*, III Battle Squadron, High Seas Fleet

The cumulative effect of these body blows to the *Grosser Kurfürst* was a series of leaks and a list of 4 degrees, which was only reduced after carefully controlled counter-flooding on the opposite side of the ship.

While his friends retreated, Captain Paul Hartog, still in temporary command of the I Scouting Group, did not shirk in the blood sacrifice that Scheer demanded. He wheeled his badly damaged ships round to starboard to take up a southerly course, for what he must surely have envisaged would be their last great service for the Fatherland. They were to act as a giant magnet for British fire, drawing it away from the battle line as it turned behind them. This plan certainly worked. It has been estimated that eighteen British dreadnoughts fired at the four German battlecruisers, while just seven fired at the German dreadnoughts. The *Derfflinger*, leading the line, suffered worst.

> Salvo after salvo fell round us, hit after hit struck our ship. They were stirring minutes. My communication with Lieutenant-Commander von Stosch was now cut off, the telephones and speaking-tubes running to the fore-top having been shot away. I was now left to rely entirely on my own observation of the splashes to control the gun-fire. Hitherto I had continued to fire with all four heavy turrets, but at 7.13pm a serious catastrophe occurred. A 38cm shell pierced the armour of the 'Caesar' turret and exploded inside. The brave turret commander, Lieutenant-Commander von Boltenstern had both his legs torn off and with him nearly the whole gun crew was killed. The shell set on fire two shell-cases in the turret. The flames from the burning cases spread to the transfer chamber, where it set fire to four more cases, and from there to the case-chamber, where four more were ignited. The burning cartridge-cases emitted great tongues of flame which shot up out of the turrets as high as a house; but they only blazed, they did not explode as had been the case with the enemy. This saved the ship, but the result of the fire was catastrophic. The huge tapering flames killed everyone within their reach. Of the seventy-eight men inside the turret only five managed to save themselves through the hole provided for throwing out empty shell-cases, and of these several were severely injured. The other seventy-three men died together like heroes in the fierce fever of battle, loyally obeying the orders of their turret officer. A few moments later this

catastrophe was followed by a second. A 38cm shell pierced the roof of the 'Dora' turret, and here too, exploded inside the turret. The same horrors ensued. With the exception of one single man, who was thrown by the concussion through the turret entrance, the whole turret crew of eighty men, including all the magazine men, were killed instantly. The crew of the 'Dora' turret, under the leadership of their brave turret officer, Stuckmeister Arndt, had fought heroically up to the last second. Here, too, the flames spread to the cartridge chamber and set fire to all the cases which had been removed from their protective packing. From both after-turrets great flames were now spurting, mingled with clouds of yellow smoke, two ghastly pyres.[167]

Commander Georg von Hase, SMS *Derfflinger*, I Scouting Group, High Seas Fleet

Shell after shell, some fourteen in all, plunged down onto the smoking remnants of von Hase's once proud warship. The damage was just incredible and her continued survival provided convincing testimony to the skill with which she had been designed and built. No British battlecruiser could have survived the punishment that was meted out to her in just a few minutes, which must have seemed like hours to her beleaguered crew. There was nothing wrong with Hipper's bloody ships that day.

Now hit after hit shook the ship. The enemy had got our range excellently. I felt a clutch at my heart when I thought of what the conditions must be in the interior of the ship. So far we in the armoured tower had come off very well . . . my train of thought was sharply interrupted. Suddenly, we seemed to hear the crack of doom. A terrific roar, a tremendous explosion and then darkness, in which we felt a colossal blow. The whole conning tower seemed to be hurled into the air as though by the hands of some portentous giant, and then to flutter trembling into its former position. A heavy shell had struck the fore-control about 50cm in front of me. The shell exploded, but failed to pierce the thick armour, which it had struck at an unfavourable angle, though huge pieces had been torn out. Poisonous greenish-yellow gases poured through the apertures into our control. I called out: 'Down gas-masks!' and immediately every man pulled down his gas-mask over his face. I went on controlling the fire with my gas-mask on, which made it very difficult to make myself understood. But the gases soon dissipated, and we cautiously took off the masks. We assured ourselves that the gunnery apparatus was still in order. Nothing had been disturbed. Even the delicate mechanism of the sighting apparatus was, strange to say, still in order. Some splinters had been flung through the aperture on to the bridge, where they had wounded several men, including the navigating officer. The terrific blow had burst open the heavy armoured door of the tower, which now stood wide open. Two men strove in vain to force it back, but it was jammed too tight. Then came unexpected assistance. Once more we heard a colossal roar and crash and with a noise of a bursting thunderbolt a 38cm shell exploded under the bridge. Whole sheets of the deck were hurled through the air, a tremendous concussion threw overboard everything that could be moved. Amongst other things, the charthouse, with all the charts and other gear, and – 'last but not least' – my good overcoat, which I had left hanging in the charthouse, vanished from the scene for ever. And one extraordinary thing happened: the terrific concussion of the bursting 38cm shell shut the armoured door of the fore-control. A polite race, the English! They had opened the door for us and it was they who shut it again. I wonder if they meant to? In any case it amused us a good deal. I looked towards the enemy through my periscope. Their salvoes were still bursting round us, but we could scarcely see anything of the enemy, who were disposed in a great semicircle round us. All we could see was the great reddish-gold flames spurting from the guns. The ships' hulls we saw but rarely. I had the range of the flames measured. That was the only possible means of establishing the enemy's range. Without much hope of hurting the enemy I ordered the two forward turrets to fire salvo after salvo. I could feel that our fire soothed the nerves of the ship's company. If we had ceased fire at this time the whole ship's company would have been overwhelmed by despair, for everyone would have thought, "A few minutes more and it will be all up!" But so long as we were still firing, things could not be so bad.[168]

Commander Georg von Hase, SMS *Derfflinger*, I Scouting Group, High Seas Fleet

In such manner the Germans returned the fire as best they could, but, looking to the east, they were severely hampered by dreadful visibility.

Despite this handicap, they did manage to deliver a fair concentration of fire at the First Battle Squadron towards the rear of the convoluted British battle line.

> Meanwhile events were developing on our beam, for when we looked round there were at least three of the enemy capital ships comparatively close on our starboard beam (about five and a half miles off), having apparently suddenly come out of a bank of mist. The leading ship was a battlecruiser and we both concentrated on each other as speedily as possible. Things became very lively now, so much so that it was impossible to take in all that was actually happening. One of her 12" made a fine mess of our superstructure just abaft the foremost funnel and a huge blaze ensued.[169]
>
> Assistant Paymaster Harold Foot, HMS *Colossus*, 5th Division, First Battle Squadron

Flag Lieutenant David Joel was a man who coupled a wry sense of humour with a keen sense of self-preservation. Both were truly invaluable qualities in what looked to be the commencement of the naval Armageddon.

> When it was obvious to HMS *Colossus* that the situation was, 'Let Battle commence' I at once hustled the 'old Navy' Admiral to whom I was Flag Lieutenant Signal Officer into the 12" thick armoured conning tower – for his own protection! Here I was much unnerved by the noise of the full calibre firings of the two twin 13.5" turrets just forward of us. Suddenly we were struck by a large shell, fired by the cruel Germans, which burst amongst the 4" Battery just abaft the conning tower. All their ready use ammunition blew up all around us. My urgent desire was to escape and jump into the sea! But unfortunately my Admiral of small stature was standing on our boxes containing gas masks with his head out of the small hole in the roof, which was the only way in and out. He always made me carry, wherever we went the King's Regulations and Admiralty Instructions. This I quickly consulted and learned that to drag him down by his feet so that I could escape would be an 'act to the prejudice of good order and naval discipline'. So with the utmost courage I remained in the shelter of the conning tower. For this I was

'mentioned in despatches'. My natural modesty prevents me from allowing any mention of my bravery in that action to be made publicly.[170]

Flag Lieutenant David Joel, HMS *Colossus*, 5th Division, First Battle Squadron

The *Seydlitz* was credited with two hits from this salvo that bespattered the *Colossus*. At the same time a near miss caused more damage and a couple of casualties.

Almost at the same moment the forepart of the ship was plastered with splinters of a 12″ shell that burst about 30 yards short of the ship. The range taker who was standing just beside me in the bridge had his right arm completely shattered and another man in the foretop was severely wounded. After settling the poor wounded fellow on the deck, I jumped down below for a stretcher party, but finding the fire more urgent duty, sent a messenger instead and bore a hand in putting out the remains of the fire which was quickly under control.[171]

Assistant Paymaster Harold Foot, HMS *Colossus*, 5th Division, First Battle Squadron

These relatively minor hits on the *Colossus* were the only successes scored by the Germans during this phase of the battle. This was a clear measure of the superior position that a combination of Jellicoe's caution and Scheer's reckless thrust had given the Grand Fleet. The ship credited with hitting the *Colossus* was paid back for her efforts with a good deal of interest.

Visibility decreased and there seemed to be an endless line of ships ahead. But we saw only incessant flashes, mostly four discharges in the peculiar British 'rippling' salvoes. Our ship received hit after hit, but our guns remained silent because we could not make out any targets. This put us under a heavy strain which was relieved, to some extent, by ship handling, changes of formation and zigzagging towards and away from previous salvoes. The port casemates suffered heavy damage, and chains had to be formed to get ammunition from the lee battery. In 'B' turret, there was a tremendous crash, smoke, dust, and general confusion. At the order, "Clear the Turret" the turret crew rushed out, using even the traps for the empty cartridges. Then they fell in behind the turret. Then compressed air from Number 3 boiler room cleared away the smoke and gas, and the turret commander went in again, followed by his men. A shell had hit the front plate and a splinter of armour had killed the right gunlayer. The turret missed no more than two or three salvoes.[172]

Kapitän zur See Moritz von Egidy, SMS *Seydlitz*, I Scouting Group, High Seas Fleet

As the tables were turned on the gallant German battlecruisers, below decks men endured appalling conditions to perform their duties, usually so mundane but now pregnant with risk.

In the port low-pressure turbine, steam leaked out and the men had to put on gas masks. The leak was repaired by a man creeping on his belly in the bilge directly under the turbine casing. Electric light and boiler room telegraphs also ceased to operate under the frequent concussions. Fortunately we had practised working in the dark. Our men called these exercises "blind-man's-bluff" because they were blindfolded to learn handling valves etc by touch. The stokers and coal trimmers deserved the highest praise, for they had to wield their shovels mostly in the dark, often up to their knees in water without knowing where it came from and how much it would rise. Unfortunately, we had very bad coal, which formed so much slag that fires had to be cleaned after half the usual time, and grates burnt through and fell into the ash-pits. The spare ones had to be altered in the thick of the battle because even the beams supporting the grates were bent by the heat.[173]

Kapitän zur See Moritz von Egidy, SMS *Seydlitz*, I Scouting Group, High Seas Fleet

The *Von der Tann* had been reduced to the status of a decoy within a decoy squadron, as every one of her guns was by then out of action. Her sole remaining role was to act as a target, sucking in shells that might otherwise be directed at her sisters, who still retained the use of their main armament. But she stuck it out, and escaped reasonably lightly in the circumstances. Only one more shell scored a hit and smashed into her conning tower, although the splinters killed or wounded all the occupants.

Our ship was in great danger during the evening. It was so bad that I thought our time had come and we would sink. We received a direct hit in the foundations immediately behind the Commander. I heard afterwards that nearly everybody there had been killed. The ship moved from side to side so badly that I had to hold on tight in order to remain standing.[174]

Seaman Carl Melms, SMS *Von der Tann*, I Scouting Group, High Seas Fleet

Having already dropped out of the German battlecruiser line, the *Lützow* was not directly involved as such in the death ride, although as she limped away to the south-west she soon found she was not yet out of the metaphorical woods. To the despondency of her crew, she was sighted by the *Monarch*, *Orion* and *Centurion* of the Second Battle Squadron.

> Then the dance starts again. Red flashes to port out of the mist. "To the guns!" In a moment I am in the control. Rangefinder 100hm. "At the muzzle flashes!". "Salvo." Not a shot! It is impossible for the gunlayers to get on. If only we had 'the director'. Two or three hits shake the ship further aft. One of these bursts in the lower deck, between 'C' and 'D' Turrets, causing serious casualties in the after action dressing station, among the wounded, surgeons and sick bay attendants. At the same time it destroys part of the electric power leads to 'D' Turret, which here, for a short distance, contrary to the usual practice, lie above the main armoured deck. Enemy shells find places like this with deadly accuracy; as a result 'D' Turret is reduced to training by hand which, in the case of a 12″ turret, means practically complete inaction.[175]
>
> Commander Günther Paschen, SMS *Lützow*, I Scouting Group, High Seas Fleet

The battlecruisers were not the only German ships risking their survival for the greater good of the precious dreadnoughts. At 19.15 their destroyers were ordered to launch a desperate charge of their own. Destroyers had already been detached to nursemaid the ailing *Lützow* as well as to attempt to bring succour to the mortally wounded *Wiesbaden*. In the event, the II, V and VII Flotillas were out of position for an immediate attack and only thirteen destroyers of the VI and IX Flotillas were able to make the initial attacks. Later they were augmented by the remaining five destroyers from the III Flotilla. Several of the destroyers had already expended some of their torpedoes, which naturally further diluted the essence of their threat. The massed attack of Scheer's dreams and Jellicoe's nightmares therefore never materialized. The first to pass through the smoke-screen drifting across the sea were the four destroyers of the IV Flotilla led by Korvetten Kapitän Max Schultz aboard *G41*. They were probably the first to get a full view of the Grand Fleet laid out in all its glory before them. But by emerging into the limelight, they drew the unwelcome attention of a large number of British secondary, and even main, armaments that immediately blazed out and soon scored hits on three of their diminutive foes.

> Because of the smoke and haze I could not discern the enemy ships now away to the westward, with the exception of the German torpedo boats who stood out clearly between the two fleets. In line abreast, cream waves curving away from their sharp bows, the black painted narrow-waisted boats raced in towards us to deliver an attack. Shell splashes rose up around them to increase as our secondary armament commenced firing.[176]
>
> Petty Officer Telegraphist Arthur Brister, HMS *Iron Duke*, 3rd Division, Fourth Battle Squadron

Despite the heavy concentration of fire, the German destroyers succeeded in launching some eleven torpedoes at a range of between 7,500 and 9,000 yards. Although their speed was reduced by the shell damage they suffered, the IV Flotilla skilfully used the smoke-screens that they themselves had laid as they approached to cut and run when the moment came. Next to emerge from the drifting smoke, slightly further to the north in a 'V' formation, were the IX Flotilla, led by Korvetten Kapitän Goehle. They too were met with a storm of shell.

> After we had fired about four salvoes, ten or so destroyers then came right across between the line, going very fast, pouring out clouds of black smoke and hiding the whole horizon. They were being fired at by the secondary armament of nearly the whole fleet and several must have been hit, but they did their job and we had to check fire. They must have fired torpedoes too and I think we were hit by one that failed to explode.[177]
>
> Midshipman Geoff Congreve, HMS *Benbow*, 4th Division, Fourth Battle Squadron

Even the devastated starboard battery of the *Malaya* was called into urgent action to beat off the destroyers. They were all too aware of the threat they posed for even the super-dreadnoughts.

> I must get as many guns going as possible, as the Germans were sending a destroyer attack down on us. So I returned to the battery and took a volunteer gun's crew from the port battery to No 1 Starboard – No 6

Starboard had escaped from the explosion and were able to man their own gun. I then returned to the gunnery control tower and arranged a curious system of control for the two guns – as all electrical circuits and most voice-pipes were destroyed. I called No 1 gun direct and gave orders; they had a messenger who ran across to a man in the port battery, passed the orders to him, he ran aft along the port battery, through the aft door and gave the orders to No 6 gun. When I returned to the gunnery control tower I found that the German destroyer attack had developed and could see the boats coming towards us. I think that there were about nine of them. The attack was met by our gunfire and also by the gunfire of some of our destroyers, who moved out from the rear of our line.[178]

Sub-Lieutenant Clifford Caslon, HMS *Malaya*, Fifth Battle Squadron

These makeshift arrangements were pressed into service to allow the starboard battery to fire.

Caslon had returned to the starboard 6″ control tower and I remember an ERA at No 1 shouting his orders down the wrecked starboard battery to me, who shouted them to No 6. We fired about five or six rounds and then, "Attack beaten off!" Of course Able Seaman Bright the gunlayer at No 1 said he had sunk his destroyer! Very likely he did![179]

Midshipman Gerald Norman, HMS *Malaya*, Fifth Battle Squadron

Certainly someone was successful in hitting one of the German destroyers as they closed in on the super-dreadnoughts.

Only one destroyer got within close range, although I think they all fired torpedoes. The one destroyer which came close got to within about 6,000 yards and was received with an overwhelming fire, in which was included the two guns of my battery. Splashes were falling all around her like rain falling in a puddle of water. After about five minutes she was hit by several shells at once and sank.[180]

Sub-Lieutenant Clifford Caslon, HMS *Malaya*, Fifth Battle Squadron

The destroyer *S35* was literally split asunder by a heavy shell and sank with the loss of all her crew plus the survivors she had picked up earlier from the doomed *V29*.

As they approached to within torpedo range they appeared to be bent on suicide, but I only had time to see one of them pull up suddenly and then to drift away helplessly, when I had to make another manoeuvring signal, the turn-away which received much criticism from the clever 'after the event' boys, although it undoubtedly saved several battleships and probably the *Iron Duke* from being torpedoed. I remember that German torpedo attack as the most exciting and bravest incident I saw at Jutland, bearing in mind that my observation throughout was strictly limited. It was the kind of dashing naval action prominent in boyish dreams.[181]

Petty Officer Telegraphist Arthur Brister, HMS *Iron Duke*, 3rd Division, Fourth Battle Squadron

There was a magnificence about the Germans' raw courage that touched even the men charged with extinguishing them. They also created enough havoc to allow the German battlecruisers to be released from their 'death ride'. At 19.20 they turned away from the Grand Fleet first to west-south-west and finally swung round to follow the retreat of the High Seas Fleet to the west.

The German destroyer attack triggered the standard naval response from Jellicoe. At 19.22 he ordered the 4th Light Cruiser Squadron into the attack to counter the German thrust and at the same time issued orders for his dreadnoughts to turn away in two separate turns by divisions. In this way he greatly reduced the chance of torpedoes hitting his precious but strangely vulnerable giants. This left the British dreadnoughts following a south-south-east course, with the obvious consequence that they were sailing almost directly away from the High Seas Fleet.

At a sufficient interval before it was considered that the torpedoes fired by the destroyers would cross our line, a signal was made to the Battle Fleet to turn two points to port by subdivisions. Some minutes later a report was made to me by Commander Bellairs (the officer on my Staff especially detailed for this duty, and provided with an instrument for giving the necessary information) that this turn was insufficient to clear the torpedoes, as I had held on until the last moment; a further turn of two points was then made for a short time. As a result of this attack and another that followed immediately, some twenty or more torpedoes were observed to cross the track of the Battle Fleet, in spite of our turn, the large majority of them passing the ships of the 1st and Fifth Battle Squadrons at the rear of the line.[182]

Admiral Sir John Jellicoe, HMS *Iron Duke*, 3rd Division, Fourth Battle Squadron

Jellicoe was not prepared to risk it. As far as he was concerned, torpedo attacks on a large scale meant a mathematical certainty that ships in close order line ahead would be hit if the appropriate measures were not taken.

Frequent exercises carried out at Scapa Flow showed conclusively that the percentage of torpedoes that would hit ships in a line when fired from destroyers at ranges up to 8,000 yards was comparatively high, even if the tracks were seen and the ships were manoeuvred to avoid them. One very good reason is that torpedoes are always a considerable but varying distance ahead of the line of bubbles marking their track, making it difficult to judge the position of the torpedo from its track.[183]

Admiral Sir John Jellicoe, HMS *Iron Duke*, 3rd Division, Fourth Battle Squadron

Jellicoe was aware that he could have turned towards, rather than away from, the torpedoes, but having analysed the risks as he saw it, he once again played safe with the fleet that guaranteed the naval supremacy of the British Empire. In making this decision he was not helped by some faulty intelligence work on the powers of German torpedoes.

The alternatives to a turn away were a turn towards, or holding the course and dodging the torpedoes. A turn towards would have led to great danger if the first attack had been followed up by a second and third, and no one could say that this would not be the case. To hold on and dodge might meet with success if the tracks could be seen. Information had reached me that the Germans had succeeded in making the tracks of their torpedoes more or less invisible. Therefore there was danger in this alternative.[184]

Admiral Sir John Jellicoe, HMS *Iron Duke*, 3rd Division, Fourth Battle Squadron

His source was the Directorate of Naval Intelligence, which believed that the Germans had been successful in devising a torpedo that did not leave an obvious trail on the surface. This was of great significance. If approaching torpedoes could be seen, then they could be evaded far more easily. As it turned out, the German torpedoes seem to have been slightly more visible than the British torpedoes. Furthermore, the threat of hundreds of torpedoes did not materialize. Just thirty-one torpedoes were fired at the British dreadnoughts, of which only twenty-one seem to have actually passed through the line. Most at risk were the ships of the First Battle Squadron at the rear of the line. Individual ship's captains took emergency avoiding action as they saw fit. There were some close shaves which indicates that Jellicoe was probably right to assume there would have been losses if they had not turned away from the threat. Even though the British dreadnoughts turned away and reduced the profile of the target being offered, there were moments of high drama as the torpedoes inexorably approached the British dreadnoughts.

> We saw a torpedo coming straight for us but order hard to starboard
> and it went by our stern. A little later another torpedo came straight at
> us but, lucky for us, it surfaced about 200 yards from us having spent its
> run.[185]
>
> Gunner Horace Phipp, Royal Marine Light Infantry, HMS *Agincourt*, 6th Division,
> First Battle Squadron

The *Marlborough*, the *Revenge*, the *Hercules*, the *Agincourt*, the *Iron Duke*, the *Thunderer* and the *Colossus* all sighted torpedoes that they managed to evade with manoeuvres of varying degrees of desperation.

The Grand Fleet turn away has been roundly criticized by many commentators. They contend that the main threat posed by the German destroyers, given the position and direction of their attack, was to the rear of the British battle line. It has been suggested that only the rear should therefore have turned away. Others believe that Jellicoe missed his tryst with destiny by not turning towards the torpedoes, thus precipitating a close action that would surely have doomed the German battlecruisers at the very least. These points are well made and there is no doubt that the combination of the successful German battle turn away and the Grand Fleet turn away conclusively prevented any chance of a decisive action before night fell. Yet how could Jellicoe have known that this was not just the first wave of a much larger attack employing the whole destroyer strength of the High Seas Fleet? Many of his subordinate admirals later objected in retrospect to the turn away, but Jellicoe had always made it clear what he would do in these circumstances. Their objections were based largely on hindsight and ignored the fact that his intentions had been long enshrined in the Grand Fleet Battle Orders. Furthermore, even as it was, with the torpedoes slowing down at the extremity of their range and travelling in the same direction as the ships, there were several close shaves. A turn towards would have meant those torpedoes that did come close would have been encountered earlier on in their run travelling faster, with a much higher relative speed as the ships ran towards them. With the dreadnoughts in close order just 500 yards apart, it is quite possible that a disaster might have resulted. Speculation cuts both ways.

During all the excitement, as the fates of nations hung in the balance, Warrant Officer Greenway, truly a man with a mission, seized upon the chance to check his precious bread. The ovens had been hot enough to do their work even after being doused.

> I discovered that my batch of bread had actually baked without any fire, and turned out fairly creditable. As I did not know how long the bakehouse would remain intact, I was anxious to save it, knowing full well we may be glad of it if anything happened. I went to my action station. Firing had commenced, so I requested the Fleet Surgeon to allow me to go and draw my oven. He was very reluctant to let me do this but eventually consented at my own risk. I asked for two volunteers from my staff and without any hesitation two came forward. Of course their risk was no greater than many others, but I tell you this to show the spirit that prevailed. No-one seemed excited.[186]
>
> Warrant Officer Walter Greenway, HMS *Vanguard*, 4th Division, Fourth Battle Squadron

And so the *Vanguard*'s bread was saved and Greenway lived to bake another day!

Others had more pertinent considerations. In accordance with Jellicoe's orders, the 4th Light Cruiser Squadron moved out from ahead of the Grand Fleet to counter the German destroyers, although its ships were severely restricted by his warning that they were not to mask the firing of Beatty's battlecruisers. So far, these light cruisers had had a privileged view of the battle from their position in the van.

Our guns were of no avail against the big ships of the enemy,
which were only within range of the big guns of the battleships and
battlecruisers. 'Carry on Smoking' was piped, and we were in the
position of being spectators of the fight now raging with intensity
around us. Some difficulty had been experienced in keeping our men,
who were engaged in ammunition supply and other multifarious duties
below, at their stations. They had now been some hours standing by
doing nothing and naturally wanted to see the 'scrap'. When the word
was passed to 'Carry on Smoking,' they scrambled up on deck keeping
handy to hatchways, and ready to jump down to their stations should
the necessity arise. It was a glorious sight to see our big ships firing their
broadsides. On two occasions, when their shells had found their billets
on an enemy ship, which would be observed by the shells bursting
against their sides, our men, who also clapped as if witnessing a football
match, gave loud cheers! The men were quite unconcerned about the
big shells that only too frequently passed over our heads or dropped in
the water near the ship.[187]

Carpenter Frederick Fielder, HMS *Caroline*, 4th Light Cruiser Squadron

It was a grand, yet awful sight, one that inspired conflicting emotions in
the watching men.

Guns were hurling 15″ shells into the opposing fleets with roars and
flashes, as if scores of thunderstorms had met and got angry. The sea,
which before had been calm, became churned into waves and foam, this
being caused by the speed and movements of scores of ships of all sizes.
The falling of enemy shells around us caused huge columns of water,
rising many feet high. The sky became thick and overcast by vast clouds
of dense black smoke, belched out by scores of funnels.[188]

Officers' Steward 2nd Class Albion Smith, HMS *Caroline*, 4th Light Cruiser
Squadron

There were many such ships that found themselves on the periphery of
the action. As their crews watched the unfolding drama, they realized that
at any moment the holocaust could reach out and engulf them. The
Caroline certainly had an extremely narrow escape when several torpedoes passed through the line of light cruisers.

The firing was now going on with increased intensity, and this ship in particular was extremely fortunate in avoiding not only shells but torpedoes, two of which were observed to be coming towards the ship, but by splendid handling of the helm, one passed on either side of the ship. On another occasion, a torpedo was seen making for us, but fortunately, it was nearing the end of its run and was travelling at only about six knots. As it neared our ship, the wash of our propellers turned it away just sufficient to clear the stern by inches.[189]

Carpenter Frederick Fielder, HMS *Caroline*, 4th Light Cruiser Squadron

Shortly after the first two waves of the German destroyer attack, the III Flotilla launched its own assault. It emerged from the smoke to run into and engage several destroyers of the British 12th Flotilla. A brief and inconclusive action took place, which served to distract the Germans from their main mission, although they did fire some torpedoes towards the British line, which again failed to strike their target. The attacks meant to be launched by the II, V and VII Flotillas were either cancelled or never really got started. Meanwhile the 12th Flotilla came across the *V48*. Like a pack of dogs overhauling their prey they casually tore her to pieces.

We came across a German destroyer leader. She'd been damaged but she was still operative and firing the guns. So we engaged her and there was a couple of German seaman there, despite the fact the ship was badly damaged, they were still firing their gun and I said to a pal of mine, "God I hope them blokes don't get killed! I feel really sorry for them!" Anyway she was sunk, we had to, she was still flying the German ensign and whether they were saved I don't know.[190]

Able Seaman George Wainford, HMS *Onslaught*, 12th Flotilla

They probably were not, as only three survivors from *V48* were picked up by a Swedish ship later that night.

Amidst all the grand tragedy, sometimes it was the small details that left an indelible impression.

I'll always remember the amount of dead fish there were floating about. I think they'd been killed by concussion when ships blew up. There was fish everywhere floating about on the surface.[191]

Able Seaman George Wainford, HMS *Onslaught*, 12th Flotilla

Meanwhile Jellicoe, relieved to have survived the destroyer attack unscathed, returned his attention to the question of closing with the High Seas Fleet, which he discovered had by then long disappeared off to the west. Once again he had been let down by elements of the fleet who had seen what was happening, but wrongly assumed that anything they could see was visible to all. Thus, although many of his subordinate commanders actually saw the German battle turn, none reported it to the only man who mattered: Jellicoe. His subsequent frustration at their failure to keep him informed may be glimpsed in the long list he included in his post-war account of the battle of sightings of the turn away that were not reported to him.

Although this retirement was not visible from the *Iron Duke* owing to the smoke and mist, and was, therefore, not known to me until after the action, it was clearly seen from the rear of our line, as is indicated by the following citations: The Captain of the *Valiant* stated in his report, "At 7.23pm enemy's Battle Fleet now altered course together away from us and broke off the action, sending out a low cloud of smoke which effectually covered their retreat and obscured them from further view." The Captain of the *Malaya* reported, referring to this period, "This was the last of the enemy seen in daylight, owing to their Battle Fleet having turned away." Sir Cecil Burney stated in regard to this period, "As the destroyer attack developed, the enemy's Battle Fleet in sight were observed to turn at least eight points until their sterns were towards our line. They ceased fire, declined further action, and disappeared into the mist." The Captain of the *St. Vincent* said, "The target was held closely until 7.26pm (32 minutes in all), when the enemy had turned eight or ten points away, disappearing into the mist and with a smoke screen made by destroyers to cover them as well." Rear-Admiral Evan-Thomas remarked, "After joining the Battle Fleet the Fifth Battle Squadron conformed to the movements of the Commander-in-Chief, engaging the rear ships of the enemy's battle line, until they turned away and went out of sight, all ships apparently covering themselves with artificial smoke." The Captain of the *Revenge* recorded, "A flotilla of destroyers passed through the line and made a most efficient smoke screen. At this period the enemy's fleet turned eight points to starboard and rapidly drew out of sight."[192]

Admiral Sir John Jellicoe, HMS *Iron Duke*, 3rd Division, Fourth Battle Squadron

At 19.35 Jellicoe turned his divisions back towards where the High Seas Fleet had been and began manoeuvring to form a single line. He received signals from Beatty and Goodenough that indicated the Germans were to the west, although both were flawed in their details. But, taken together, they confirmed the general position of the High Seas Fleet and at 19.40 Jellicoe ordered the Grand Fleet onto a south-westerly course.

For the moment at least, the High Seas Fleet had escaped. Yet this time the price of its withdrawal had been high. The battlecruisers in particular had suffered heavily. Worst of all was Hipper's former flagship, the *Lützow*, which was in a truly dreadful state, with water lapping over her lower decks in an ominous fashion.

> I could not believe my eyes! About 100 metres away I could see the *Lützow* with only the upper deck showing. I could not understand that the ship was still able to float. She must have been badly damaged but she still sailed very slowly. I thought, "Poor Hare, you will never reach home again!"[193]
>
> Lieutenant Heinrich Bassenge, SMS *Elbing*, II Scouting Group, High Seas Fleet

The damage was not confined to the German battlecruisers. The horrors of war were becoming excruciatingly apparent even aboard the German dreadnoughts.

> It was my job to help a dying signalman from our crows nest and I told him that we all might have to face it one day, as we were all in great danger. During an interval in the battle I had to take a message to the lower deck, which meant I had to pass the kitchen. There I saw a dead cook with his head and both arms in the coffee kettle. Several seamen were so thirsty that they were pouring coffee from the same kettle into their cups. Who worries about dead men in cases like these? Some of the incidents which took place below deck are not repeatable.[194]
>
> Signalman Franz Motzler, SMS *König*, III Battle Squadron, High Seas Fleet

Respite for the High Seas Fleet was only temporary. The German ships may have eluded Jellicoe for the moment, but the danger of their situation had not fundamentally diminished. Although they had struck several painful blows to the British, they knew that they remained seriously outnumbered and still at severe risk if a general fleet action was renewed. The whole of the Grand Fleet stood squarely between themselves and their home port. By hook or by crook they had to get past them. But the question was how and when. At 19.45 Scheer, rather than sail even further west and hence further than ever from sanctuary, changed course to south. This placed the British and German fleets on slowly converging courses.

As Scheer changed course the British battlecruisers were some 6 miles in front of the leading division of the Grand Fleet. Two minutes later, at 19.47, Beatty sent a remarkable signal to Jellicoe: 'Submit that the van of the battleships follow me: we can then cut off the whole of the enemy's fleet.'[195] It is regrettable that Beatty's phrasing was so unclear. Despite his dramatic implications it seems that at this point he had neither the German battlecruisers nor the High Seas Fleet in sight although he thought he knew where they were. The intention was for the battlecruisers to lead the search to the west for the High Seas Fleet, but, sensibly in the light of his earlier experiences that day, he wanted the heavy-duty support that could only be offered by the leading divisions of dreadnoughts. Beatty was rightly concerned that, in the declining visibility, he might run into a little more than he could cope with. Yet the wording of the signal was undoubtedly unfortunate. Interpretations vary from depictions of a heroic call to arms or a desperate attempt to chivvy a reluctant superior into action. It has also been characterized as oozing bluster and displaying naked ambition with an obvious eye to posterity. Whatever the true intent, it is generally accepted that by the time Jellicoe received the message on the *Iron Duke* he had already decided to order the Grand Fleet to turn by divisions to a westerly course. Thus he duly informed Beatty of the new course and in turn ordered Vice Admiral Sir Martyn Jerram of the Second Battle Squadron to follow Beatty – essentially as requested. Unfortunately, as Jerram was not in sight at the time either of Beatty or the High Seas Fleet, he to some extent ignored the wishes of both Beatty and Jellicoe and continued on much the same westerly course as the rest of the fleet.

Once again the two fleets were on a collision course. The British dreadnoughts, once again in six columns not a single line, were heading directly west. Beatty, some 6 miles ahead of them, was steering to the south-west. The High Seas Fleet was set on a southerly course.

Nearest to the Grand Fleet were the four battlecruisers, then the dreadnoughts, with the I Squadron leading the III Squadron, with a considerable gap between the squadrons. The pre-dreadnoughts of the II Squadron were further to the west, but slightly more to the south. The crippled *Lützow* and her escort of destroyers were heading west with the sole intention of survival. Scheer was not aware that the British were following him and was still intent on organizing renewed destroyer attacks once his somewhat scattered flotillas had re-formed to the west of the main force.

Amongst the first ships to make contact were the 4th Light Cruiser Squadron and the 11th Flotilla, which were feeling their way forward in front of the Second Battle Squadron, acting in their role as scouts and seeking to protect the dreadnoughts against any threat that might be posed by German destroyers. At 20.11 the commodore of the 11th Flotilla, Commander Commodore James Hawksley aboard the *Castor*, sighted German destroyers to the north-west which appear to have been the V Flotilla, returning from their abortive attempt to attack the Grand Fleet. He turned to the attack and Commodore Charles Le Mesurier commanding the 4th Light Cruiser Squadron aboard the *Calliope* moved to support him accompanied by the *Constance* and *Comus*. Sub-Lieutenant Servaés was the officer on watch on the bridge of the *Comus*.

> We, half the Squadron, and half a flotilla were sent off again to beat off another destroyer attack. Personally I was too busy keeping station and never saw any destroyers. Our leading ship opened fire about three minutes later, almost as soon as she had opened fire, I saw three Hun battleships who promptly opened fire on our leading ship. Our destroyers had already turned back as the Hun destroyer attack had failed to develop. The Commodore however held on so as to fire a torpedo. His ship started getting straddled and as she turned she was hit once or twice, and we were straddled. One salvo burst close astern of us and I heard the splinters going pit-a-pat against the funnels and casings.[196]

Lieutenant Reginald Servaes, HMS *Comus*, 4th Light Cruiser Squadron

Thus, at around 20.26, the British screen had encountered the main German battle line moving south. Le Mesurier ordered the other two light

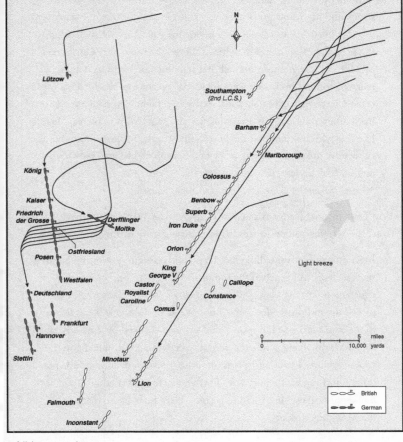

Night approaches

cruisers away to starboard to clear his run. It does, with hindsight, seem strange that all three light cruisers did not seize the chance to launch a proper co-ordinated attack. Although only a few of the German dreadnoughts were in sight, the range was short, initially around 8,000 yards. Most of the German fire was concentrated on the *Calliope* as she made a solo torpedo run. The *Prinz Regent Luitpold*, *Kaiser* and *Markgraf* opened up with a combination of heavy and secondary batteries. Under this heavy concentration of fire, the *Calliope* was hit several times as she ran back towards the Grand Fleet.

Shrapnel was falling all about us, the gun just below the bridge was struck and the whole gun's crew was killed except for one, the gunlayer, who lay unconscious on the deck beside his gun. Another shell caught the port after 4″ gun and that crew suffered the same fate. Our Sergeant of Marines was gunlayer and all that remained of him was a hand, a piece of leg and his brains were splattered on the gun shield. This was caused through a fall of shrapnel exploding the lyddite shell already in the loading tray, and the breech of the gun was blown to pieces. Directly in a line with this gun and the line of fire was the ice house and that was riddled. A stoker standing near by had the top of his head blown off and both of his legs, the sight was awful.[197]

Albert Nickless, HMS *Calliope*, 4th Light Cruiser Squadron

Boy Telegraphist James Algar was employed as a runner to provide a link from the wireless office to the bridge, carrying incoming messages.

I ran up a ladder using little hand hold and a 6″ gun just overhead fired unexpectedly as I reached the top of the hatchway. Surprise and concussion sent me back to the deck below – on my backside. I was picked up and proceeded some, but not much, the worse. I ran forward to the starboard side but soon found my way checked by the body of a Royal Marine lying across the gangway between a gun shield and the superstructure. I felt that to step on or jump over a dead man was not done – so I ran to the port side. There a worse sight met me – parts of a body or bodies – but I had to go on – there must be no delay in delivering my message.[198]

Boy Telegraphist James Algar, HMS *Calliope*, 4th Light Cruiser Squadron

Splintered metal screamed through the air and splattered across the decks of the *Calliope*. But despite the damage and casualties that were sustained, the torpedo attack was continued.

The ship at this point caught fire but this was quickly extinguished thanks to the promptitude of a few stokers. A shell of large calibre hit us amidships but the shell had only penetrated some superstructure casing and the upper deck and caused comparatively little damage and few casualties. The ship at this juncture turned 16 points and while slewing fired a torpedo at an enemy dreadnought of the *Kaiser* class. A violent explosion was seen to take place, proclaiming a hit for us. During this period (which lasted only seven minutes) ours was the only ship of the squadron actually under fire. Several more hits were scored by the enemy, before we managed to get clear.[199]

Boy Telegraphist James Algar, HMS *Calliope*, 4th Light Cruiser Squadron

Despite Algar's optimism, no claim for a torpedo hit was subsequently confirmed. As soon as the torpedo was launched the *Calliope* turned and tried to make her escape.

Our speed and the Commodore's seamanship were saving us, we were also getting out of range of their guns, but at what price – 9 killed and 29 seriously wounded, several others with smaller injuries – but I thank God that we had escaped and trust that we shall never be in such a tight corner again. When we came to reckon up, our little action only lasted seven minutes, but what a seven minutes it was. An eternity – never in all my life shall I forget the sight: the whizzing of shells; the falling of stays and halliards; the sight of the dead; and the flesh and blood scattered round about the guns.[200]

Albert Nickless, HMS *Calliope*, 4th Light Cruiser Squadron

There was to be an amusing postscript to the *Calliope*'s encounter.

There was a popular belief in *Calliope* that the ship was the fastest man of war in the Royal Navy, if not in the World. A day or two after our return to base the C-in-C visited *Calliope*. After he had had an informal look around at the damage sustained, Sir John Jellicoe addressed the ship's company assembled on the quarterdeck. Among the things he said I remember particularly his remark that at one time he had seen *Calliope* straddled with shot and he thought any moment would be our last. He thought that for our escape we should be thankful for the consummate skill of our Commodore in his handling of the ship and the ship's wonderful speed. He added, "I hope that the next time you beat your speed record it will be towards the enemy and not away from him!"[201]

Boy Telegraphist James Algar, HMS *Calliope*, 4th Light Cruiser Squadron

Further south, the 3rd Light Cruiser Squadron commanded by Rear Admiral Trevylyan Napier had been ordered by Beatty to scout to the

west in an effort to locate the main body of the German fleet. At 20.09
they sighted ships to the north-west. These were the IV Scouting Group
screening and reconnoitring ahead of the High Seas Fleet as it progressed
on its southerly course. In the skirmish that followed there was a vigorous
but fairly ineffective exchange of fire for about fifteen minutes. Two hits
were scored on the *München* but the Germans could not effectively respond
as they were rendered almost blind by the failing light conditions and eventually turned away to the west. This engagement attracted Beatty's attention. He had turned to a westerly course paralleling the Grand Fleet at
20.15, but now changed to west-south-west in an attempt to close on this
new manifestation of battle. Almost immediately the British battlecruisers
sighted the German battlecruisers and the head of the I Battle Squadron.
As the sun was setting, once again the old enemies opened up on each
other, at around 20.19. By a strange coincidence the twists and turns of
the battle had brought the duelling forces almost back to where they had
started many hours before.

> As twilight fell I found myself gazing almost with rapture at the twinklings
> of the enemy salvoes away on the horizon. One never knew what their
> target was until they made a hit, or nigh to, over or under. I suppose
> others felt as I did, but though one was part of the possible object, I never
> felt more than an exaggerated interest as to whether or not the projectiles
> would arrive. The actual fear, or funk, that one in days of anticipation
> thought would be the dominant feeling, did not seem to mature.[202]
>
> Paymaster Henry Horniman, HMS *Inflexible*, 3rd Battlecruiser Squadron

The German battlecruisers were not really in a fit state to resume the
battle. They had suffered too much in the last three hours, many of their
guns were out of action, fires still blazed below decks and they were listing
drunkenly from the effect of hits below the water-line. In contrast, although
the *Lion*, *Princess Royal* and *Tiger* had suffered damage, their fighting potential was only partially restricted, while the *New Zealand*, *Indomitable* and
Inflexible were almost untouched. When the British guns opened up, hits
were scored once again on the wretched *Seydlitz* and *Derfflinger*.

> "Clear for action!" sounded once more through the ship and a few
> seconds later I had trained the 'Anna' turret on the target and fired. In

the thick mist the 'Bertha' turret could not find the target, so I had to fire as well as I could with the 'Anna' turret alone. Then this, too, was interrupted. A heavy shell struck the 'Anna' turret and bent one of the rails on which the turret revolves, so that it stuck. Our last weapon was snatched out of our hands![203]

Commander Georg von Hase, SMS *Derfflinger*, I Scouting Group, High Seas Fleet

Quick repairs got the turret working again, but even so they could only fire intermittently. Range finding and shell spotting were almost impossible for the Germans, as the British battlecruisers were wrapped in the general murkiness of the looming night sky. In contrast, the British gunners could still see well enough with the sun setting behind the Germans. Then rescue came from the most unlikely of quarters. The pre-dreadnoughts of the German II Battle Squadron appeared from the gloom.

Suddenly the enemy saw seven big ships heading for them at top speed. At the same time the unwearying destroyers again pressed home the attack. That was too much for them; the enemy turned about and disappeared in the twilight. We did not want to see any more of them … I wonder if they would have turned about had they known what kind of ships these were! They were the famous German 'five minute ships', to settle which the Englishman could not spare more than five minutes, but bravely withdrew![204]

Commander Georg von Hase, SMS *Derfflinger*, I Scouting Group, High Seas Fleet

Von Hase's account is mischievously misleading and questions the courage of Beatty's ships quite unfairly. Actually, the German battlecruisers themselves turned sharply to the west to evade the fire of the British ships. In doing so, they fouled the course of the I and III Battle Squadrons, which were close behind them and had little choice but also to turn to starboard. Ships of the II Battle Squadron, which held on to the southerly course, thereby interposed themselves between the withdrawing battlecruisers and Beatty. This was not to say that the sudden appearance of the pre-dreadnoughts did not rattle some of the men aboard the battlecruisers.

When we were engaged on the starboard side some German battleships closed us in failing light and opened fire on us. I remember seeing the flashes of the German guns firing and wondering whether the shell was on its way to blow me up; whether I'd actually seen the gun fire which was going to cause me to pack up. That was just a little thought.[205]

Midshipman John Ouvry, HMS *Tiger*, 1st Battlecruiser Squadron

The combined strength of Beatty's battlecruisers opened fire on these new targets, scoring hits on the *Schleswig-Holstein*, the *Pommern* and the *Schlesien*. Admiral Mauve recognized the physical limits of his ships and, after just a few minutes, it was he who turned away to the west at 20.35. At considerable risk the pre-dreadnoughts had covered the withdrawal of their comrades in the battlecruisers. Although Beatty did not follow, unsure what was happening as the light faded and not willing to venture too far out on a limb, he had been successful in beating back the bulk of the High Seas Fleet to the west once more. Overall the situation remained the same, with the Grand Fleet standing squarely across the German route home.

Throughout the simultaneous engagements fought by Beatty, Napier and Le Mesurier, between 20.15 and 20.40, Jellicoe was once again left in the literal and metaphorical darkness. Those reports that did come in were confusing and often lacked the necessary details of bearings and positions. Many of his subordinates were understandably confused as the darkness closed in and they realized that their situational awareness was weak or non-existent.

I, with sandwich and dividers in hand, pored over the chart in a vain endeavour to work out our position. It was a case of making bricks without straw because the Captain had been far too pre-occupied to jot down our many changes of course and speed. The pages of the navigator's notebook, which I had hopefully left on the chart table, were virginally blank. However, navigation was not in the forefront of our problems at the moment and drawing an optimistic circle on the chart and marking it "20.30 (approx)".[206]

Sub-Lieutenant Harry Oram, HMS *Obdurate*, 13th Flotilla

Many of Jellicoe's officers no longer understood what was going on and simply eschewed responsibility for making a decision. They did not want to make a mistake and therefore preferred to do nothing rather than risk their reputations through error. At 20.28 Jellicoe altered course by divisions from west to south-west, thus in effect forming a single line once again, determined to stay across the German line of retreat. Nothing could have demonstrated more clearly the creeping paralysis of initiative endemic among many of his officers than the next clash as night fell.

The German's deflection to the west did not last long before they reverted once again to a southerly course and at the same time inadvertently resumed their collision course with the Grand Fleet. At 20.45 the *Caroline* and *Royalist* of the 4th Light Cruiser Squadron were positioned about 2 miles ahead and to the starboard of the Second Battle Squadron, followed by the *Castor* and eight destroyers of the 11th Flotilla, when they sighted German dreadnoughts approaching from the north-west.

> One half of the officers and men went below to get a meal as we had been some hours without an opportunity of getting one. A short time afterwards our alarm rattlers sounded off, and on rushing to our stations, found that we were steaming on an almost parallel course to a line of German battleships or battlecruisers. I had just come up on deck to observe them, and noticed that they were German ships, which could easily be identified by their distinctive funnels.[207]
>
> Carpenter Frederick Fielder, HMS *Caroline*, 4th Light Cruiser Squadron

Captain Ralph Crooke of the *Caroline* had no doubt what he could see and ordered a joint torpedo attack. Behind the cruisers, Admiral Jerram, aboard the *King George V*, could also see the ships, but convinced himself that they were Beatty's battlecruisers and duly signalled: 'Negative the attack. Those are our battlecruisers.'[208] Crooke knew what he could see and he signalled again confirming his identification. Jerram merely replied, 'If you are quite sure, attack.'[209] But he remained unconvinced and at the same time signalled to Jellicoe: 'Our battlecruisers in sight bearing 280 degrees, steering 210 degrees.'[210] Crooke was having none of it and he went into the attack regardless.

> Our starboard torpedo tubes were trained on them, and as we fired two torpedoes, so the nearest ship to us opened fire with a broadside of eleven inch guns, but we were lucky enough not to be struck, although it was a straddle, some shots falling short, others going over. By all the rules of gunnery, the next broadside should have finished our career,

especially as we were at such close range. The enemy set up a large star shell to light us up, but our 'Guardian Angel' was still protecting us, for the next broadside missed us, going over. The shells screamed over our heads, some dropping between us and our own ships on the other side. By this time, we had set up a smoke screen and escaped from an extremely perilous position, for the small ship would have been literally blown off the water had any of the broadsides fired at us got home. However, we did escape, due no doubt to the erratic German shooting, their men probably being in a state of panic or blue funk as they must have received fearful punishment from our hands.[211]

Carpenter Frederick Fielder, HMS *Caroline*, 4th Light Cruiser Squadron

In a poor repayment for Crooke's skill and courage the torpedoes missed, and as a direct result of Jerram's grave error of judgement, the Second Battle Squadron and the attendant 11th Flotilla carefully maintained their station and did not get involved.

I turned the flotilla away from the battlecruisers and expected the fleet to open fire on them. The leading battlecruiser then fired a star shell, which appeared to justify the opinion that they were enemy ships; but as the fleet still held their fire, it was not dark enough to make an attack unsupported by fire from the fleet. The battlecruisers turned off to starboard and were lost sight of.[212]

Commander James Hawksley, HMS *Castor*, 11th Flotilla

For the British a splendid opportunity had been missed but, as darkness fell for the short summer night, Jellicoe still had the whip hand.

The main fleet action was over. The British had suffered serious casualties, mainly through the traumatic loss of the *Invincible* and *Defence* during the frenetic minutes as the fleets collided and Jellicoe strove to deploy his battle fleet. Yet the Germans had entirely failed to isolate and destroy a significant portion of the Grand Fleet as they had intended. Throughout the whole phase, Jellicoe had controlled the course of the battle. His brilliant deployment and subsequent cool manoeuvring had crossed the German 'T' on two separate occasions. Although he had lost some of the initiative by turning away in the face of the German destroyer attack, he had continued to direct the overall shape of the battle, despite all the problems of command and control endemic in the handling of a large fleet in poor visibility. During the brief battle fleet engagements his ships had battered with near impunity the battlecruisers and leading dreadnoughts of the High Seas Fleet. As a result, several of Scheer's ships were severely damaged and in considerable danger of sinking; indeed, he could not afford to delay long his return to harbour.

Yet for the British the battle remained unresolved. Could Jellicoe convert the undoubted positional advantage he had secured blocking the German route home into convincing victory on a new 'Glorious First of June'? He had suffered the loss of the three battlecruisers, but they did not materially affect the overall superiority of his fleet, especially as the German battlecruisers had been reduced to a shadow of their former fighting strength. The vast majority of ships in Jellicoe's Grand Fleet were unscathed and ready for action. His men were still eager and more than ready to play their part.

It was getting very dark and rumour had it that the enemy had received such a hammering that he had bolted. This cheered us very much, although I rather wondered at the time why we hadn't gone after him! Perhaps it was the result of not being hit, but my fear had completely vanished and I really was at this time as keen as mustard to have another go at the enemy.[213]

Midshipman John Brass, HMS *Orion*, 1st Division, Second Battle Squadron

NIGHT ACTION

B Y 21.00, WITH the light rapidly fading away, the battle of Jutland still rested in the balance. The High Seas Fleet could be devastated by losses during the night or, come the dawn, find itself still trapped far from home with the Grand Fleet firmly astride its chosen escape route. In contrast, the Grand Fleet might be hard hit during the night by German destroyer attacks or lose more ships in the frenetic uncertainties of night action. Alternatively, the High Seas Fleet could evade retribution, slip past the vigilant foe and escape back to port. Nothing was certain. Everything was still to play for. Two men bore the responsibility of making the command decisions which would decide the outcome.

Admiral Sir John Jellicoe knew the High Seas Fleet was effectively trapped to the west of the Grand Fleet and he had to decide whether to seek, accept or try to avoid a night action. Given his personality and determination to avoid unnecessary risk to Britain's naval superiority, this was not in truth a difficult decision. He had already shown, earlier in the evening, his instinctive wariness with regard to destroyers. He would prefer not to fight a night action.

> In the first place, such a course must have inevitably led to our
> Battle Fleet being the object of attack by a very large destroyer force
> throughout the night. No senior officer would willingly court such an
> attack, even if our battleships were equipped with the best searchlights,
> and the best arrangements for the control of the searchlights and the
> gunfire at night. It was, however, known to me that neither our
> searchlights nor their control arrangements were at this time of the best
> type. The fitting of director firing gear for the guns of the secondary
> armament of our battleships (a very important factor for firing at night)
> had also only just been begun, although repeatedly applied for. The
> delay was due to manufacturing and labour difficulties. Without these

adjuncts I knew well that the maximum effect of our fire at night could not be obtained, and that we could place no dependence on beating off destroyer attacks by gunfire. Therefore, if destroyers got into touch with the heavy ships, we were bound to suffer serious losses with no corresponding advantage. Our own destroyers were no effective antidote at night, since, if they were disposed with this sole object in view, they would certainly be taken for enemy destroyers and be fired on by our own ships.[1]

Admiral Sir John Jellicoe, HMS *Iron Duke*, 3rd Division, 4th Battle Squadron

Concern over attack by massed destroyers was not Jellicoe's only reason for caution. To a man who laid great store by the exercise of hard-earned professional skills, there seemed too great a risk involved when those skills were smothered by darkness.

The result of night actions between heavy ships must always be very largely a matter of *chance*, as there is little opportunity for skill on either side. Such an action must be fought at very close range, the decision depending on the course of events in the first few minutes. It is, therefore, an undesirable procedure on these general grounds. The greater efficiency of German searchlights at the time of the Jutland action, and the greater number of torpedo tubes fitted in enemy ships, combined with his superiority in destroyers, would, I knew, give the Germans the opportunity of scoring heavily at the commencement of such an action.[2]

Admiral Sir John Jellicoe, HMS *Iron Duke*, 3rd Division, Fourth Battle Squadron

So Jellicoe determined to avoid a night action if possible, and as this represented the prevailing orthodoxy, it was a decision that was heartily endorsed by his subordinate admirals. Jellicoe has since been criticized for his 'timidity'. Some consider that he should have risked a night action and his refusal showed that 'His continual thought was of what the Germans could do to him rather than what he could do to the Germans.'[3] But this was precisely the rationale behind his tactics, rooted as they were in a naval strategy inspired by the teachings of the naval historian Sir Julian Corbett. Jellicoe had no need to offer hostages to fortune. In the end, he merely had to maintain the status quo for his fleet to prevail.

Anything else was a windfall dividend; more than welcome but not essential to the continued well-being of his country.

After he had decided to avoid a night action, the next point of decision for Jellicoe was which course to steer. He might not want to seek out and confront the High Seas Fleet until dawn, but he did want to prevent them slipping past him to the east in the direction of their home ports.

> The first desideratum was to keep the British Fleet between the enemy and his bases, so as to be in a position to renew the action at dawn. Daylight was rapidly disappearing; it was necessary to form the Fleet for the night as quickly as possible to avoid visual signalling after dark; and it was also necessary to place our destroyers in a position where the chances of their coming in contact with our own ships was reduced to a minimum, and yet giving them an opportunity of attacking the enemy's capital ships during the night. The Grand Fleet was formed at the time in practically a straight line, steering approximately west-south-west. I considered that a southerly course would meet the situation.[4]
>
> Admiral Sir John Jellicoe, HMS *Iron Duke*, 3rd Division, Fourth Battle Squadron

The Germans had a number of options for escape. The first was to sail back to the north-east, pass through the Skagerrak, round Denmark and back to reach the Baltic and safety. Jellicoe decided to ignore this possibility as the length of the journey would mean the sacrifice of any ships with severe hull damage. It would also be impossible to cover this route effectively without abandoning other, more likely options. The second route was via Horns Reef, to the north of the huge minefields that almost filled the Heligoland Bight. This offered Admiral Reinhard Scheer the quickest, most direct route to safety – around 100 miles – but it was also a regular haunt of patrolling British submarines. The third route was a passage through the minefields that the Germans were known to have used on the way out. It was considered unlikely that they would try to locate the mouth of the passage after the navigational stresses and imprecision of a fleet action. The fourth route lay via the north Frisian coast past the mouth of the River Ems, which lay about 180 miles away. It was this option that Jellicoe considered the most likely based on Scheer's last reported position and course of west-south-west. He believed that his dreadnoughts had the speed to prevent Scheer passing in front of him heading to Ems and therefore in accordance with these deliberations he set a fleet course of south at a speed of 17 knots. Mindful of the other options open to Scheer, he decided to station his destroyer flotillas 5 miles behind the fleet to prevent the High Seas Fleet sneaking astern of the British fleet heading for the sanctuary of the Horns Reef channel or the alternative gap through the Heligoland Bight minefield.

> If I put the destroyers astern, they would fulfil three conditions: first, they would be in an excellent position for attacking the enemy's fleet should it also turn to the southward with a view to regaining its bases during the night (which seemed a very probable movement on the part of the enemy); secondly, they would also be in position to attack enemy destroyers should the latter search for our fleet with a view to a night attack on the heavy ships; finally, they would be clear of our own ships, and the danger of their attacking our battleships in error or of our battleships firing on them would be reduced to a minimum.[5]
>
> Admiral Sir John Jellicoe, HMS *Iron Duke*, 3rd Division, Fourt Battle Squadron

Jellicoe considered that massed torpedo attacks by his destroyer flotillas would soon drive the Germans back off to the west. Great import has subsequently been attached to the fact that he failed to issue any specific instruction to attack any German ships they encountered and nor were they informed of the last known location of the High Seas Fleet. Jellicoe however subsequently contended that the duty to attack the enemy when sighted was axiomatic and that the destroyers knew the High Seas Fleet was to the west – which was all that he as their Commander-in-Chief knew. To bolster further the barrier to the Horns Reef channel, at 21.32 he ordered the fast minelayer *Abdiel* to proceed to lay a further minefield in that area.

His deliberations complete, at 21.01 Jellicoe ordered the battle line to turn by divisions onto a southerly course. Then, at 21.17, he ordered his ships to get into their close order formation for night cruising. Each of the three dreadnought squadrons was to form a column, separated from each other by a single mile, with the sensible intention of staying well within sight of each other to prevent any tragic cases of mistaken identity. At 21.16 Vice Admiral Sir David Beatty received a signal from Jellicoe informing him that the fleet would be adopting a southerly course. Beatty, who was by then some 13 miles to the west-south-west of the main fleet body, decided against closing on the main body for fear once again of some disastrous night mix-up.

> I did not consider it desirable or proper to close the enemy battle fleet during the dark hours. I therefore concluded that I should be carrying out the Commander-in-Chief's wishes by turning to the course of the fleet, reporting to the Commander-in-Chief that I had done so. My duty in this situation was to ensure that the enemy fleet could not regain its base by passing round the southern flank of our forces. I therefore turned to south at 9.24pm at 17 knots.[6]
>
> Vice Admiral Sir David Beatty, HMS *Lion*, 1st Battlecruiser Squadron

Beatty's new course in effect placed the British battlecruisers in the slightly surreal position of leading the German battle line, although neither side was aware of this. The advance units of the High Seas Fleet would effectively be boxed in if they were to continue to sail south. However, even before Jellicoe had ordered his dispositions, Scheer had also reached a momentous decision and decided on his escape route.

There is no doubt that Scheer's situation was desperate. At some point he had to get to the east of the Grand Fleet. Although his subsequent published accounts are full of understandable posturing that he wanted to retain the option to resume the battle next day, there is little doubt that a renewal of the battle was not uppermost in his mind.

> It might safely be expected that in the twilight the enemy would endeavour by attacking with strong forces, and during the night with destroyers, to force us over to the west in order to open battle with us when it was light. He was strong enough to do it. If we could succeed in warding off the enemy's encircling movement, and could be the first to reach Horns Reef, then the liberty of decision for the next morning was assured to us. In order to make this possible all flotillas were ordered to be ready to attack at night, even though there was a danger when day broke of their not being able to take part in the new battle that was expected. The main fleet in close formation was to make for Horns Reef by the shortest route, and, defying all enemy attacks, keep on that course.[7]
>
> Admiral Reinhard Scheer, SMS *Friedrich der Grosse*, III Battle Squadron, High Seas Fleet

At 21.10 Scheer had made his decision and ordered a course of south-south-east-¼-east at a speed of 16 knots. Given the perilous condition of several of his most valuable ships, he was going to take the shortest route straight for Horns Reef. There was to be no diversion; the only real chance of survival was to press on regardless. Speed was of the essence both to capitalize on the natural surprise of night encounters, and to prevent the British having any time to react effectively to what was going on around them. It was a bold decision. He was risking everything, but at least the goal was clear – despite his subsequent blustering – escape was the only priority. This was clearly demonstrated at 21.46, when he tweaked the course to south-south-east-¾-east as he considered that this would enable him to pass around the stern of the Grand Fleet. As his battle line reorganized for the perilous night odyssey, the *Westfalen* leading the I Battle

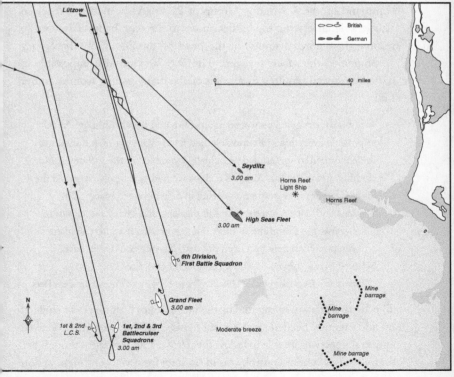

Scheer escapes

Squadron was in the van, followed by the III Battle Squadron with the more vulnerable pre-dreadnoughts of the II Battle Squadron behind them. The II Scouting Group would act as a cruiser screen ahead with the IV Scouting Group on the starboard wing. The German flotillas had already been ordered to prepare for action and had commenced manoeuvring to optimize their starting positions. Unfortunately, they were not sure exactly where the main body of the Grand Fleet was located, especially after it had contracted into the much more compact night cruising station. The German destroyers were therefore split up and assigned to search for their prospective prey across the various segments of the battlefield.

Scheer ordered the battered battlecruisers to take up station at the rear of the line. Some confusion was caused by the belated arrival of Vice Admiral Franz von Hipper aboard the *Moltke*, ready to resume his command of the I Scouting Group at 21.15. As he had not received Scheer's signal placing the battlecruisers to the rear, he initially tried to resume their normal station at the head of the line. Only the *Seydlitz* accompanied the *Moltke* forward. The *Derfflinger* found it impossible to match the speed required as a result of the many gaping wounds in her hull:

> A stubborn struggle was waged against fire and water. Although as far as possible everything inflammable had been taken out of the ship, the fire continued to spread, fed principally by linoleum, the wooden decks, clothing and oil paints. About 8 o'clock we had practically mastered the flames, the fire now only smouldering in a few isolated places. The 'Caesar' and 'Dora' turrets were still smoking and giving out clouds of thick yellow gas from time to time, but this gradually ceased after the ammunition chambers had been flooded. No-one could ever have believed that a ship could endure so much heavy fire.[8]
>
> Commander Georg von Hase, SMS *Derfflinger*, I Scouting Group, High Seas Fleet

The *Von der Tann* was hampered by the fact that her furnaces were clogged up and urgently needed cleaning out. This could not be further delayed and so she too was unable to follow the *Moltke*. The *Derfflinger*, though her fires were now under control, was in no state for a vigorous night action with destroyers or indeed anything else.

Only the *Derfflinger* and the *Von der Tann* took station in the rear of the line. We certainly did not feel very well suited to this station. Our starboard was our best side, for it still had all six 15 centimetre guns intact. But one single searchlight was hardly enough. On the port side only two 15 cm guns were still in action. We should therefore have to urge the English destroyers to confine their attacks as far as possible to the starboard side. There we were still capable of administering a cold douche![9]

Commander Georg von Hase, SMS *Derfflinger*, I Scouting Group, High Seas Fleet

The battlecruisers' confusing situation was, however, soon resolved. As Hipper moved forward up the German line, he drew level with Scheer aboard the *Friedrich der Grosse*, who repeated his orders. Once he had received them, Hipper began to drop back to his unaccustomed role bringing up the rear. As its formation settled down, the High Seas Fleet began its fateful voyage.

Ahead of the bridge of SMS *Friedrich der Grosse* the next ahead was visible only as a black silhouette, accompanied by the weak shimmering light of his stern lantern playing on the foam of the propeller wash, and a point of light on the forecastle which gave the helmsman the correct line for our own ship, but otherwise there was overall darkness. Half of the crew already lay with the guns, and all important posts were occupied. The speaking tubes and telephones were manned, the searchlights were clear for immediate illumination and the torpedo arm was ready to fire. Also the engine department, who had to give the highest performance in their difficult work, were careful not to produce any sparks from the funnels which would betray our position. Not a word sounded, only whispers, no light was shown. Silent darkness! Tense attentiveness! Each sector of the dark horizon was searched with night glasses under the direction of an officer. Hundreds of eyes spied into the night, hundreds of senses tensed themselves in the highest expectation and readiness. From time to time Admiral Reinhard Scheer appeared on the bridge and received the reports; he also looked out into the dark wall of the night.[10]

Chief of Staff Adolf von Trotha, SMS *Friedrich der Grosse*, III Battle Squadron, High Seas Fleet

The course set by Scheer of steering south-south-east-¾-east meant that the High Seas Fleet was on a collision course with the Grand Fleet steering south with some 100 miles of perilous waters before it reached the Horns Reef channel through the Heligoland Bight minefields. The only question was, when would they cross the track of the Grand Fleet and who would be there waiting for them? For both fleets the die was cast.

As the German fleet swung round to its new course, the natural result was that it started gradually to part company with Beatty and his battlecruisers, who were directly ahead of it but still persisting on a southerly course. For the battlecruisers '*Der Tag*' had ended, although of course they were not yet aware of this. As they gradually realized that, at least for the time being, the fighting had stopped, men emerged from their action stations and peered into the darkness.

> About 9pm we were allowed to go to the Gun Room for food and I can well remember that the gramophone was on the deck playing, "I want to settle down in some old one horse town away from all the care and strife!" which was a popular tune at the time.[11]
>
> Midshipman John Boldero, HMS *Inflexible*, 3rd Battlecruiser Squadron

After being locked for seemingly endless hours in their stations, the prime imperative for many was to get some food and drink. It was only when they began to forage through their ships that the enormity of the widespread destruction sustained during the battle started to dawn on them.

> We had been hotly engaged for the best part of five hours, but had lost all sense of time and only now began to realise that we were very hungry. A couple of hands from each turret or action station were allowed to go and get food for the remainder. I was the lucky one to be despatched from the transmitting station. We had no idea when we might open fire again so I had to forage around as fast as possible. This was not easy, as on emerging from the hatch to the transmitting station I found the messdeck in total darkness and everything in utter confusion. With the help of my electric torch I picked my way aft to the gunroom flat. Here the wreckage was even worse and I began to think we must

have been badly knocked about. A fire main had burst outside and the
gunroom was swishing about a good six inches deep in water, the long
table had collapsed, chairs were smashed to pieces, lockers had crashed
to the deck from overhead, while gramophone records, sextants,
telescopes, books and newspapers floated about in the water which
was diluted with red ink, beer, champagne and the rest of the contents
of the wine cupboard. All the lamps had been smashed and were
temporarily replaced by hand lanterns such as were used in Nelson's
day. The place was an absolute shambles and with each roll there issued
dismal crashes from the pantry as the broken crockery careered from
side to side. What food there had been was now keeping the china
company in the water on deck. Naturally we were very thirsty and made
for the wine cupboard, but the stokers' fire brigade, whose action station
was in our flat, had been there before us, carrying off all they could lay
hands on besides boxes of cigars and cigarettes. The place was filled
with cordite smoke and in the gloom I managed to have a few words
with 'snotties' who had come in from the turrets and elsewhere.
It was now that I first received the news of the loss of the *Queen Mary*,
Indefatigable, *Invincible* and *Defence*. It seemed scarcely credible at first –
the very idea that any of our ships could be sunk by the Germans
seemed preposterous. We were so proud of the superlativeness of our
squadron that we had come to believe it was invulnerable. My chest was
floating about outside the gunroom and I was able to find some apples
and a box of chocolates and peppermints. This was all I had in the
transmitting station until next afternoon, to share with my assistant
'snotty' at the plotting table.[12]

Midshipman Gordon Eady, HMS *New Zealand*, 2nd Battlecruiser Squadron

During his brief foray, Eady came across Rear Admiral William
Pakenham, the commanding officer of the 2nd Battlecruiser Squadron.

Admiral Pakenham came down from the bridge for a few moments
when I happened to be on deck. It was the one and only time that I had
not seen him in his usual spotless clean array. His uniform was begrimed
and dirty, and his face and beard were blackened with cordite smoke.
He had remained in an exposed position on the bridge throughout the
action and refused to take refuge in the conning tower. He kept his flag

lieutenant on the run the whole time maintaining a supply of cigarettes for him. His stock of cigars he sent below to the stokers.[13]

Midshipman Gordon Eady, HMS *New Zealand*, 2nd Battlecruiser Squadron

As the night wore on, for most of the men a combination of physical discomfort and nervous tension made sleep impossible. The search for food and drink offered limited relief, as well as a distraction from the lingering signs of death and destruction.

The night was not a restful one. Anything like turning in was out of the question. We all felt horribly tired. The men lay down in any dry place they could find and the doctors, after they had finished the operations, lay down in the distributing station. I had nothing to eat since lunch and so at about 10.00 I made my way to the wardroom. The teacups were still on the table, but there was nothing to eat except the remains of a loaf. We managed to get hold of some ginger beer and later coerced the messmen's assistant to give us bully beef and some biscuits. We also got some soda water and half a bottle of whisky. But these did not go far amongst a lot of hungry officers. I was very wet and tired and hungry and bully beef, and ginger beer and biscuits were very welcome, only one was impeded by the dirt and blood on one's hands from touching anything directly.[14]

Reverend Thomas Bradley, HMS *Tiger*, 1st Battlecruiser Squadron

One gallant midshipman earned himself what could have been a career-threatening notoriety in his quest for sustenance.

Lieutenant Commander Longhurst told us in the foretop to get as much sleep as possible as we may be having another action during the night and next day. Before we went to sleep we ate some ham, which I had procured! Another ham had also been brought up for Admiral Beatty but in the heat of the action had been temporarily set aside for consumption later on! It was at this moment that he happened to glance up at the foretop and observed to his intense amazement the picture of me climbing to the foretop with a ham sticking out of my monkey jacket! I was thereafter known throughout the Fleet as the 'Snotty' who had pinched the Admiral's ham![15]

Midshipman Anthony Combe, HMS *Lion*, 1st Battlecruiser Squadron

After the intense fighting, which had lasted longest of all for the battle-cruisers, the grisly task of collecting the wounded could finally proceed unhindered. As they wandered through the damaged ships, men encountered some bizarre sights in which horror mingled strangely with humour.

> Passing along the stokers' mess deck, first aid parties were bringing wounded stokers up from the engine room. One of them had his leg blown off at the knee. He was yelling his head off, "Where's my bloody leg? Where's my bloody leg?" Repeatedly. The leg was eventually recovered and it was found to have the stoker's roll of bank notes tucked into his sock. The money was obviously of more importance than the loss of his leg.[16]
>
> Leading Signalman Alec Tempest, HMS *Lion*, 1st Battlecruiser Squadron

The wounded were being brought to the medical distributing stations, where the hard-pressed medical staff struggled to keep pace with the demand. For them there was no rest from the call of duty. Even more gruesome was the awful task of retrieving the corpses littered about the ships. Private Willons, who had been so lucky to escape the inferno that devastated the *Lion*'s 'Q' Turret, found himself recalled to the scene.

> There was about four inches of water on all the messdecks from the fire hoses, and washing about in it were odds and ends of clothing, boots and burnt articles; the electric light gave out and we had to stumble through the water in the dark, striking matches or by the dim light of a candle. The Chief Gunner and I went down to the shell room at about six o'clock to find out if it was possible to salve any of the ammunition. The handling room, switchboard, flat and shell room were completely burned out, the crew were lying in all directions, some still hanging on the ladder in a last attempt to get out. On finding that it was impossible to salve any of the projectiles for use in the other turrets the shell room was flooded. The Captain of Marines sent for me then to go to the gunhouse to find the Major and remove some of the casualties. I got into the gunhouse through the manhole on top and assisted by another Marine got out seven people from the right cabinet. The Chaplain was one of these. The Major was in the rangefinder position close by the voice-pipe. There was a great deal of smoke coming from behind the

293

ready use shell bin and we gave the alarm that four common shell were being roasted and were likely to cause another explosion. With the assistance of several more Marines the fire was put out and the remainder of the casualties were removed. They were then taken aft, identified if possible and sewn into hammocks. This carried on most of the night of 31st May.[17]

Private H. Willons, Royal Marine Light Infantry, HMS *Lion*, 1st Battlecruiser Squadron

The ships of the Grand Fleet had some problems in taking up their designated night cruising stations. Mostly these were caused by the damage inflicted on the *Marlborough* by the successful torpedo strike against her, which reduced her speed to around 16 knots. As the rest of the 6th Division, First Battle Squadron continued to keep station with her; this caused the four dreadnoughts in the division gradually to fall back until they were eventually 4 miles behind the main body of the fleet. The Fifth Battle Squadron took up station in the gap between the main formation and the 6th Division. The 4th Light Cruiser Squadron screened ahead of the Grand Fleet; the 2nd Light Cruiser Squadron was to the west. At 21.27 the destroyer flotillas began their move to their allotted stations at the rear of the Grand Fleet. They turned about and passed back down between the columns of darkened battleships before reversing back onto a southerly course. The 11th Flotilla sat off the western flank of the fleet, then came the 4th Flotilla, 13th Flotilla, a small combined force of the 9th and 10th Flotillas and finally the 12th Flotilla on the eastern flank. Many of these flotillas had not yet been in action during the day and were thus as ready as they would ever be to face the challenges of the night ahead. Unfortunately, the British destroyers had not been trained in the different skills and procedures essential for effective night fighting.

It was the policy of the Royal Navy, whenever possible, to avoid the risks and imponderables of night action and consequently it had adopted a 'head in the sand' approach to it. Jellicoe, the great trainer, had an unfortunate blind spot when it came to night fighting and had lamentably failed to make any proper preparations throughout the Grand Fleet. Unstable, low-level, shutterless searchlights, an absence of star shells, rudimentary night identification signals and a pervasive confusion over the importance of the dual defensive and attacking roles of the destroyers formed an excellent recipe for disaster. In contrast the Germans were far better equipped for a serious night battle. They too were wary of the problems posed by a fleet night action, but, in their situation as the weaker naval power, it had been recognized as imperative to make the most of any opportunities that might occur under cover of darkness. Their first advantage lay in the development of proper searchlight controls, stationed above the swirling smoke likely to mask any low-level positions. They had proper iris shutters, which meant that the searchlight could warm up to full power behind shutters before being opened up at full blaze onto their targets. They could also be switched off and covered in a moment should the situation require it.

> When we switched off our searchlights we had to find tarpaulins to throw over them to hide the glowing carbons that stood out like full moons and gave the enemy the chance to have a bang at us. When the German searchlights were switched off there was damn all to see – we learned later his lights had iris shutters fitted.[18]
> Boy 1st Class Seaman William Bennett, HMS *Comus*, 4th Light Cruiser Squadron

The Germans had also successfully introduced star shells, which had the great advantage of simultaneously illuminating and dazzling their target at a distance without revealing their source to the enemy. Although neither side had director control of their secondary batteries, the German dreadnoughts had, through night practice, achieved a far higher ability to concentrate their fire effectively onto any target that suddenly revealed itself before them. The Germans also seem to have known at least part of the British night recognition signal. This has often been attributed to a startling lack of common sense displayed by the signal team aboard the *Lion*. At 21.32 they signalled to the *Princess Royal* by flashing lamp asking for a reminder of the night recognition signal: 'Please give me challenge and reply now in force as they have been lost.'[19] Unbeknown to them the German light cruisers were close enough to intercept at least part of the signals flashed back in response. As it was a simple signal which could have been easily discerned the first time the British used it as a challenge to a German ship, this is perhaps more interesting as an instance of a breakdown in security than something that can be held to have had a substantial effect on the course of the night fighting. Overall, the German system of recognition signals was far superior as it involved a more complicated sequence of coloured lights that could not easily be replicated.

For the British the hope was that, by not actively seeking a night confrontation for which they were so poorly prepared, they could avoid it, while retaining their tactical position for the next daylight round of the battle. However, Scheer had no intention of leaving the Grand Fleet in peace. It was perhaps fortunate for Jellicoe that, in the event, Scheer's destroyers proved almost totally ineffective in their task of hunting down and destroying the Grand Fleet. Otto Frost, as the engineer on watch on the German destroyer *V1*, was in charge of two engines and three boiler-rooms. The separate boiler-rooms could only be entered from the deck. As a result, he constantly moved around the ship.

> The twilight made visibility bad. The fleets parted. The state of the enemy was uncertain. Motionless and alone, lay the German battlecruiser *Lützow* and a terrific pall of smoke was rising out of the after smoke stack. Toward 9pm, my Flotilla was ordered to make a torpedo attack on the British Fleet. We sailed close to the aft of the *Lützow*. We searched for the British Fleet in a 21 sea miles sweep. But in that direction there was no British Fleet to be found.[20]
>
> Wachmachinist Otto Frost, *V1*, V Torpedo Boat Flotilla

In the inky darkness of night, with no precise bearings or sightings on which to base any search, the German destroyers had great difficulty finding their quarry. On the occasions where they did manage to get near the British capital units, they suffered from a series of technical problems that wholly negated their efforts. They struggled to overcome reduced speed resulting from dirty, choked boilers that severely hampered them in their efforts to get forward and attain a position in the van ahead of the British line from which they would be able to launch an effective attack. They were further dogged by signalling difficulties and by the necessity for extreme caution in approaching and passing through their own battle line. They searched far and wide across the sea, but failed to look in the direction in which the Grand Fleet lay. Overall, the German destroyers did not cover themselves in glory that evening.

The dark night was by no means silent. No one knew what was happening with any degree of certainty and all were aware that once a shell or torpedo had been despatched at a target it could not be recalled if the target proved friendly. At the short ranges of night action the risks of opening fire in haste and repenting at leisure were evenly balanced against the rewards for getting one's retaliation in first. A couple of well-directed salvoes or a torpedo could effectively end a potentially hazardous night action before it had begun. But it was so easy to make a mistake.

> At approximately 9.45 we suddenly saw a flotilla of destroyers rushing
> at us. Just as we were about to open fire, we saw that they were our own.
> As they dashed past our line (how we cursed their haphazard behaviour)
> one of them fired a 4″ at us, but didn't hit anyone – I imagine a
> gunlayer lost his head.[21]

Lieutenant Stephen King-Hall, HMS *Southampton*, 2nd Light Cruiser Squadron

Smothered by a blanket of uncertainty and fear, both fleets edged awkwardly into the night. Moving like wraiths through the dark, the British destroyer flotillas took up their positions 5 miles behind the main body of the Grand Fleet. As they did so, the High Seas Fleet was moving inexorably towards them on their course of south-south-east-¾-east. Even before the destroyers had completed their reverse turn back onto their southerly course behind the Grand Fleet there were small-scale clashes, as elements of the respective probing destroyer and light cruiser shields bumped into each other. At first the British barely noticed they were under threat. At 09.50 the 4th Flotilla was in the act of reversing course back to the southward. As it swung round, the *Garland*, lying fourth in the line, sighted four German destroyers. The German destroyers were cautious, as they thought the murky shapes could be their own II Flotilla. They hoisted their designated recognition signals, but as they got no response, without further hesitation fired a torpedo each and turned away. The *Garland* was the only British ship seemingly aware of the threat and she briefly opened fire to little effect while turning away. The German torpedoes were sighted but successfully evaded by both the *Garland* and the *Fortune*.

A similar clash occurred at 21.58: as the 11th Flotilla was moving into its night station at the rear of the Grand Fleet, it was sighted by the

Frankfurt and *Pillau* of the II Scouting Group at a range of only about 1,000 yards. The two German light cruisers may have mistaken the British destroyers for light cruisers but in any event they silently fired a torpedo each and turned back into the dark night without being sighted by the British. The British were lucky, for the torpedoes missed as they turned back onto the southerly course to follow the fleet. A few minutes later there came another augury of a busy night. At 22.05 they bumped into more of the II Scouting Group. Once again the British ships may well have been distracted by the complications of their manoeuvres onto a new course in difficult circumstances.

In the dark we saw, in an easterly direction, the shadows of English ships, the *Castor* with their XI Flotilla. We showed them English recognition signals which they acknowledged. As we were sure that it was the enemy we opened up heavy fire from about 1,000 metres distance. *Castor* returned fire straight away and turned back.[22]

Lieutenant Heinrich Bassenge, SMS *Elbing*, II Scouting Group, High Seas Fleet

It appears that the Germans had correctly shown the first two letters of the British recognition signal, although they got the rest wrong.

They fired only at us, being apparently unable to see our destroyers, which were painted black. We were hit direct four times: one shell hit the forecastle just under the bridge and, bursting inside, made a hole about five feet in diameter, and the splinters from it wounded a large number of men in the fore ammunition lobby; one shell went right through the fore messdeck and burst outside the disengaged side of the ship; one hit the motor-barge, bursting in her and setting her on fire; another shell hit the disengaged side of the forebridge and wiped out everybody in the way of signalmen, messengers, etc., who had gathered there, with the exception of one man. This man had a miraculous escape, the 4″ shell bursting practically between his legs, but all the force of the explosion must have gone on in the direction in which the shell was travelling, for it blew a large hole in the deck of the bridge, and through this the man fell. He landed on another man who had been killed by that same shell, but he himself was practically unhurt. Besides these direct hits, the ship was covered with splinter dents from shells

298

which burst on hitting the water short and several men at the midship guns were laid out by them. We fired a torpedo at the leading Hun and the two after 6″ guns, which were not being directly fired at, were making very good practice at the enemy.[23]

Anon officer, HMS *Castor*, 11th Flotilla

Behind the *Castor*, all aggressive instincts among the 11th Flotilla were strangled by doubt, even when the *Elbing* and *Hamburg* switched on their searchlights and opened fire. Although the *Marne* and *Magic* both managed to fire a single torpedo, the rest of the destroyers were totally bemused. The stabbing, blinding lights, the indistinct shapes all conspired to paralyse them. Although the enemy ships they had prayed for so long to meet were just 1,000 or so yards away, with their searchlights providing an ideal target for torpedoes, they embraced any excuse to avoid action. Dazzled and blinded, they were afraid that the *Castor* had made a dreadful error of judgement and was pouring shells into friendly ships. And so they did nothing. As both sides turned away, Hawksley on the *Castor* seems to have considered the whole incident closed. His failure to keep in touch with his assailants, or to attempt to find out what was going on behind the screen of light cruisers, has been harshly criticized in some quarters. He may, quite understandably, have been distracted by the aftermath of the shells that had burst all around his bridge. In all, the *Castor* suffered some twelve killed and twenty-three wounded. But, unfortunately, he might also have been too preoccupied with keeping station behind the Grand Fleet, regardless of anything else detrimental to the completion of that duty.

The Flotilla then proceeded south after the battle fleet, my object being to be within reach of the fleet at daybreak should the fleet have found the enemy and a fleet action take place.[24]

Commodore James Hawksley, HMS *Castor*, 11th Flotilla

Whatever the reason, a fine opportunity was missed. Hawksley could not communicate with his destroyer captains to tell them what was happening, as the first German salvoes had disabled his wireless and signalling lamps. Only a vague report was ever sent in to Jellicoe, which omitted any details of the position, course or identification of the German ships encountered.

Just a few minutes later, at 22.20, the 2nd Light Cruiser Squadron under Commodore William Goodenough was pursuing a southerly course a little to the east of the 11th Flotilla. Having seen the recent 11th Flotilla skirmish, Goodenough was aware that German ships were in the vicinity. But of course so too were a large number of British ships. Lieutenant Harold Burrough was stationed in the after gun control of the *Southampton* when he first saw a line of 'mystery' ships sailing towards them on a slightly converging course.

> We three light cruisers were steaming along guarding our Battle Fleet
> from destroyer attack when we fell in with five German cruisers. It was a
> very tense moment while we were trying to make out in the dark
> whether they were friends or foes.[25]
>
> Lieutenant Harold Burrough, HMS *Southampton*, 2nd Light Cruiser Squadron

The 'mystery' ships were the light cruisers *Stettin*, *München*, *Frauenlob*, *Stuttgart* and *Hamburg* of the German IV Scouting Group, which were closely followed by the *Elbing* and the *Rostock*. In the dark the German screen had been unable to take up their correct positions and both the II Scouting Group and IV Scouting Group had drifted in error to the port wing of the High Seas Fleet. All too aware of the peril of the situation, Goodenough brought his ships to the highest state of readiness, guns loaded and trained on their putative targets, torpedo tubes at the ready. On the bridge of the *Southampton*, he bore the ultimate responsibility for making a decision. Unfortunately, he had only minimal information and no really compelling evidence either way. Of course, in this game of nerve, the first to break and formally challenge the other would cede the advantage.

> The Commodore looked at them through night glasses, and I heard a
> whispered discussion going on as to whether they were the enemy or
> the 3rd Light Cruiser Squadron. From their faint silhouettes it was
> impossible to discover more than the fact that they were light cruisers. I
> decided to go aft as quickly as possible. On the way aft I looked in at the
> after control, where H.B. said to me, "There are five Huns on the beam.
> What on earth is going on?" They were evidently in as much doubt as

us, for, as I got down into the waist by the mainmast, a very great many things happened in a very short time.[26]

Lieutenant Stephen King-Hall, HMS *Southampton*, 2nd Light Cruiser Squadron

As the ships gradually converged in rising tension, it seems that both sides lost their nerve almost simultaneously in an exchange of challenges at about 22.35. It was like a sharp pin bursting a balloon.

We began to challenge; the Germans switched on coloured lights at their fore yardarms. A second later a solitary gun crashed forth from the *Dublin*, who was next astern of us. Simultaneously I saw the shell hit a ship just above the water line and about 800 yards away. As I caught a nightmare-like glimpse of her interior, which has remained photographed on my mind to this day, I said to myself, "My God, they are alongside us!" At that moment the Germans switched on their searchlights, and we switched on ours. Before I was blinded by the lights in my eyes, I caught sight of a line of light grey ships. Then the gun behind which I was standing answered my shout of, "FIRE!"[27]

Lieutenant Stephen King-Hall, HMS *Southampton*, 2nd Light Cruiser Squadron

The gun teams on both sides sprang into action. As the ships were in such close proximity, in an instant the shells did terrible execution.

Apparently they made up their minds at the same time as ourselves, for at the same moment that the Commodore ordered us to open fire, they switched on their searchlights and opened fire on us. The ships astern were unmolested and all the five enemy ships concentrated on us. We received a most intense fire which killed or wounded practically all my gun crews so that we were practically helpless to reply to their fire.[28]

Lieutenant Harold Burrough, HMS *Southampton*, 2nd Light Cruiser Squadron

Such an exchange of fire was probably unprecedented in modern naval warfare and the German concentration of fire on the *Southampton* and to a lesser extent on the *Dublin* behind her made matters even worse.

The range was amazingly close – no two groups of such ships have ever fought so close in the history of this war. There could be no missing. A gun was fired and a hit obtained – the gun was loaded, it flamed, it roared, it leapt to the rear, it slid to the front – there was another hit.

But to load guns there must be men, flesh and blood must lift the shells and cordite, and open and close the hungry breeches. But flesh and blood cannot stand high explosives and there was a great deal of high explosive bursting all along HMS *Southampton*'s upper deck from her after screen to the fore-bridge. The range was so close, the Germans shots went high, just high enough to burst on the upper deck and around the after superstructure and bridge. And in a light cruiser *that's* where all the flesh and blood has to stand. So in a very few seconds my guns stopped firing, all through lack of flesh and blood – it was a great pity. In fact, the Sergeant Major, with a burnt face, and myself seemed to be the only bits of flesh and blood left standing.[29]

Lieutenant Stephen King-Hall, HMS *Southampton*, 2nd Light Cruiser Squadron

The process was by no means one-sided. As she was returning fire, the *Southampton* even managed to launch a torpedo.

On the bridge the full glare of the searchlights of the leading enemy ship was on us and we could see nothing, but I had already received enough impression of the general direction of advance of the enemy for the purpose of torpedo fire, so I passed down an order to the torpedo flat and waited impatiently for a reply. When it came through – the report, "Ready!" – I fired at a group of hostile searchlights, which were the only things visible.[30]

Anon Lieutenant, HMS *Southampton*, 2nd Light Cruiser Squadron

The torpedo ran true and struck a mortal blow. Midshipman Stolzmann was at his station on the upper bridge of the *Frauenlob*.

I at once switched both available searchlights on to the cruiser opposite us. The guns immediately opened fire. This was followed by such a furious rain of shell, which nearly all hit the after part of the ship, that it looked as if several enemy ships were concentrating their fire on us. A very few seconds later I heard a shout, "Fire in the after part of the ship!" and then, only a few seconds later, a terrific crash there, with the characteristic tremor of a ship which has been hit by a torpedo. We had been torpedoed.[31]

Midshipman Stolzmann, SMS *Frauenlob*, IV Scouting Group, High Seas Fleet

Down below in the engine-rooms the water rushed in, overwhelming the damage control efforts of the crew.

> At the same moment, both engines stopped, probably owing to damage
> in the propellor shafts, the light went out and there was a roar of water
> pouring in. As I followed the sound, to find out where the hole was, the
> water was already rushing over the floor plates, so that it was no longer
> possible to locate the hole. I went on deck and enquired through the
> speaking tube to the starboard engine room, whether the engine room
> was still intact. The chief engineer replied, "We will try to get rid of the
> water from the port engine room." This took some time, and meanwhile
> the action was proceeding on the port side with unabated fury. The ship
> had a heavy list to port. At the same time the water was rushing over the
> deck and flooding the port side.[32]
>
> Machinist Max Müller, SMS *Frauenlob*, IV Scouting Group, High Seas Fleet

As Stolzmann left the upper bridge and moved aft, he was aware that the ship had already begun to list to port.

> For the first minute the ship merely seemed to sink slightly, but after that it
> went down rapidly. On reaching the after bridge, I barely had time to
> fasten on a lifebelt, and glance hastily at the havoc in the after part of the
> ship – a shapeless mass of wreckage cowls and corpses – before the water
> reached the deck of the after bridge, and I threw myself onto a raft which
> was floating in the angle between the fore and aft bridge and the after
> bridge. I found two men who with great difficulty helped me to clear the
> raft from the fore and aft bridge, so as not to be caught in the latter. A few
> seconds later we saw the ship sink without any internal explosion. Some of
> our guns continued firing when the gunlayers were already standing in the
> water and the ship was sinking. As the last tremor ran through the vessel,
> three cheers for His Majesty the Kaiser rang out.[33]
>
> Midshipman Stolzmann, SMS *Frauenlob*, IV Scouting Group, High Seas Fleet

The *Frauenlob* took with her to the bottom all but five of her crew of over 320.

Despite her well-timed show of defiance, the *Southampton* had been thoroughly peppered from end to end, suffering under the heavy concentration of German fire and receiving no fewer than eighteen direct hits.

On top of this the ship was heavily on fire forward, amidships and aft. In the darkness it was rather an appalling sight and I think we all made up our minds it was the end. Luckily we got off a torpedo at their leading ship (which I am certain was *Frauenlob*) which sank her. This I believe is the reason they retired after 3½ minutes. I am personally very thankful that they did for we could not have stood much more.[34]

Lieutenant Harold Burrough, HMS *Southampton*, 2nd Light Cruiser Squadron

Below decks the effect was incredible as the shells crashed home time and time again. At this range very few missed.

The shellfire was very heavy, some of the shells hitting one side of our ship going right through and out the other side. The sick bay was badly damaged. I was standing by a fire main in between decks near the big racks. I thought it was a stupid place to stand so I got at the back of the racks. And just then a shell came through the ship's side. My six mates were killed and a piece of shrapnel hit me on the forehead.[35]

Stoker Andrew Stewart, HMS *Southampton*, 2nd Light Cruiser Squadron

Boy Telegraphist Arthur Gash was standing by the main wireless office when the battle began.

It seemed as if all hell was let loose: shells bursting and projectiles thumping into the ship's side and the coal bunkers. This lasted for about five minutes and stopped as suddenly as it had begun. Then the wounded casualties began to be brought down. One, a leading stoker, was helped into the W/T office. He had his right leg shot off just below the knee and was bleeding badly. I tried to help to stop the bleeding by pressing my weight in a vital spot. Then a sick bay attendant brought a tourniquet and he was removed to the wardroom which was being used as a casualty ward. Then my job was to clear up the blood and mess in the office – not a nice job at all.[36]

Boy Telegraphist Arthur Gash, HMS *Southampton*, 2nd Light Cruiser Squadron

Next in line behind the *Southampton*, the crew of the *Dublin* watched aghast as their flagship endured the firestorm. They also were under fire, but the assault against them paled into insignificance compared to the plight of the *Southampton*.

Fire was opened up immediately by both sides and a running fight
continued. *Southampton* and *Dublin* were both heavily engaged, the
other two ships, *Nottingham* and *Birmingham* veered away to port and
disappeared into the darkness. *Southampton* was hit and her upper deck
was ablaze and she looked to be in dire trouble.[37]

Telegraphist G. F. Spargo, HMS *Dublin*, 2nd Light Cruiser Squadron

They could see the shells driving home into the target, almost as they fired.
Yet the opposing ships were still unidentified.

Our firing was excellent and I saw a great many of our shells get well
home, but I don't know whom it was I was engaging which in itself is
very unsatisfactory.[38]

Captain Albert Scott, HMS *Dublin*, 2nd Light Cruiser Squadron

The *Dublin* did not go unscathed. Telegraphist G. F. Spargo had a close
escape from one of the many shells sweeping across her decks:

An urgent cipher message was decoded and had to be taken and handed
personally to the Captain, who was directing operations from the
'Monkey's Island', the upper bridge. As I was going up the ladder
from the upper deck to the bridge the foremost 6″ gun fired and
simultaneously a shell passed right through the charthouse. The blast
threw me down the ladder and I picked myself up again on the upper
deck, dazed, but otherwise unhurt. Unfortunately, the navigating officer,
who was in the charthouse was hit and killed – a small piece of shrapnel
had severed his jugular vein – how unlucky can one be! During the
action the ship was hit repeatedly, shells were passing right through the
starboard side and out through the port side. In one instance a shell had
penetrated about midships on the starboard side and its passage could
be traced right through two or three bulkheads and then out through the
bows on the port side. On my way back to the wireless office I decided
to go down along the main deck, instead of using the upper deck to
reach the office which was in the after part of the ship. Down the ladder
to the main deck I went, there to find the ship's commander dashing
about, revolver in hand, directing operations. This rather startled me but
I went on my way with very mixed feelings. A shell had pierced the
main deck quite near to the magazine hoist and had made a hole about

12 feet square and started a fire. This was quickly got under control and an order to flood the magazine was rescinded by the Commander just in time. On reaching the wireless office I found that the deck insulator which carried our main wireless aerial had been shot away, the aerial itself was also down and part of our receiving and transmitting gear had been put out of action. Temporary repairs were made and we retuned the various circuits and were able to receive signals again.[39]

Telegraphist G. F. Spargo, HMS *Dublin*, 2nd Light Cruiser Squadron

The repeated successes that the Germans had attained in hitting the bridge area suggests that they may have been trained to aim for this point. If so, it was certainly a policy that paid dividends by swiftly eradicating the senior officers directing the ship.

I was dreadfully sad at losing my Navigating Officer who was killed when standing close beside me. He was a splendid fellow and I miss him very much. He was married and they were a most devoted couple. Beside poor Stickland, we lost two signalmen killed and 22 ratings wounded.[40]

Captain Albert Scott, HMS *Dublin*, 2nd Light Cruiser Squadron

Shaken by the sudden loss of the *Frauenlob*, the Germans withdrew into the protective cover of the night. As the action ended, the *Southampton* metaphorically licked her wounds.

Darkness succeeded light and groping my way forward, I passed a number of dead men, and came across a boy (Mellish), a splendid little chap, one arm and a leg was off. He was bleeding to death, quite conscious and most plucky. I had him taken below as well as many others. Mellish died one hour afterwards. On reaching the bridge I met the Commodore who sent me to report on the casualties. I went down aft, stopping to see some dead put over the side, and then went down the Hatch 'F', to the central passage way, which was in places running with blood. The Doctors were operating in the Stokers' bathroom, they were doing an amputation when I arrived.[41]

Lieutenant Stephen King-Hall, HMS *Southampton*, 2nd Light Cruiser Squadron

There was a brutal logic to the choice of location by the ship's medical team for their makeshift operating theatre.

The size of this room was about 8 feet high, 12 feet broad and 12 feet long. The centre of the room was occupied by a light portable operating table. A row of wash basins ran down one side and the steel walls streamed with sweat. Four bright electric lights were fixed to the roof, but with its faults the stokers' bathroom had some advantages. It had a tiled floor and a drain in the corner.[42]

Lieutenant Stephen King-Hall, HMS *Southampton*, 2nd Light Cruiser Squadron

By the time the lightly wounded Stoker Andrew Stewart reached the scene, his cut forehead was small beer compared to the horrifying sights in front of him.

The doctors were in the stokers' bathroom operating on the badly injured, some having limbs amputated. My injury seemed very trivial when I saw the other poor fellows and as the doctors were so busy I just got a bit of sticking plaster and stuck it on the wound and carried on with my watch in the stokehole. I felt safer down there anyway.[43]

Stoker Andrew Stewart, HMS *Southampton*, 2nd Light Cruiser Squadron

From the stokers' bathroom Lieutenant King-Hall moved on. In the wardroom he found more wounded men waiting patiently for relief with an air of resigned stoicism.

I then went to the wardroom where we had about 20 serious cases. Not a murmur rose, not a sound, not a groan came from those wrecks of humanity lying on the deck, the tables and the sideboard. A whispered request for a cigarette was all I heard.[44]

Lieutenant Stephen King-Hall, HMS *Southampton*, 2nd Light Cruiser Squadron

Sub-Lieutenant Charles Marsden, the acting Navigating Officer, was one of the wounded facing the efficient but not particularly tender ministrations of hard-pressed doctors.

I was being attended to in the action sick bay, having a nasty wound in my left leg about the size of a cricket ball. I always remember our Surgeon Commander, Commander Schofield, saying to the Surgeon Lieutenant – Lieutenant Carey, "Sit on his head!" He then proceeded to pour most of a bottle of iodine inside the wound – very lucky my head was held well down![45]

Sub-Lieutenant Charles Marsden, HMS *Southampton*, 2nd Light Cruiser Squadron

In just a few short minutes the *Southampton* had suffered some eighty-nine casualties, of whom twenty-nine were killed and the vast majority of the rest seriously wounded.

> As one young boy lay dead, Commander Rushton looked at him and said to Goodenough, "He has died a glorious death." Admiral Goodenough said, "So long as England lives." When I heard that remark it made me think what it was all about.[46]
>
> Stoker Andrew Stewart, HMS *Southampton*, 2nd Light Cruiser Squadron

At least one German was profoundly surprised in this vicious skirmish. Lieutenant Heinrich Bassenge had seized the chance of some sleep in his wireless-room aboard the *Elbing*, when his slumbers were disturbed by the unheralded arrival of a 4-inch shell through the wall.

> I was awakened by a strong jet of flame, burning my face and hands and I felt a terrific blast. I was thrown through the wall taking it with me onto the middle deck. I thought my last hour had arrived. There was no time to think of being frightened or shocked. I thought, "Now, I know what it is like when one dies!" I neither fainted nor died but looked round and saw flames all around me. I quickly crawled out on my hands and knees. As I could not use my burned hands I used my elbows. A 15 centimetre shell was standing in front of the wireless station. The ship was rolling and this pulled the shell out. As it rolled it landed on my hand and crushed the tips of several of my fingers. I hardly noticed as I tried desperately to get out of the flames. I managed to escape to safety and I was still able to get up and walk the few steps to the ship's sick-bay. When I arrived I had to lie down and was unable to carry on. What had happened?[47]
>
> Lieutenant Heinrich Bassenge, SMS *Elbing*, II Scouting Group, High Seas Fleet

Bassenge had suffered multiple minor splinter wounds. But searing flames from the shell burst caused the real damage. A quick count revealed that the *Elbing* had suffered four dead and fourteen wounded.

> The Doctor was busy with my heavily bleeding comrades. When he had time for me he gave me a morphia injection because my heart was not too good and my burns very painful. They took me to the officers' mess,

cleaned me up and reassured me that I still had my nose and ears – I was not quite sure of this – but I moved my eyes and found I could still see.[48]

Lieutenant Heinrich Bassenge, SMS *Elbing*, II Scouting Group, High Seas Fleet

◆ ◆ ◆

The next possible barrier to the progress of the High Seas Fleet across the rear of the Grand Fleet was the 4th Flotilla, under the command of Captain Charles Wintour aboard the *Tipperary*. Behind him steamed the *Spitfire*, *Sparrowhawk*, *Garland*, *Contest*, *Broke*, *Achates*, *Ambuscade*, *Ardent*, *Fortune*, *Porpoise* and *Unity*. Tired after their difficult day, men settled for as comfortable a night as was possible in the circumstances.

I was not inclined to go below, so I made myself comfortable on a camp-stool abaft the after funnel alongside the engine room hatch. My pitch was warm, I could see what little there was to see, I was out of the way and I had a convenient funk-hole handy. I remember a pipe added materially to my comfort.[49]

Surgeon Lieutenant Henry Breese, HMS *Ambuscade*, 4th Flotilla

Any thoughts of a quiet reverie were soon to be violently disturbed. As they settled down to sit out the tense night hours, the main German battle fleet, led by the *Westfalen* and the accompanying screen of light cruisers, was fast approaching them. At around 23.15 Leading Torpedoman Cox was at his action station on the foremost torpedo-tube aboard the *Garland*, which was fourth in the long line.

Having excellent eyesight in those days, I sighted the blur of three ships on our starboard quarter, their bow waves showing faintly. They were apparently converging on our line of destroyers and were becoming more distinct. I reported these facts to the bridge. With night-glasses, ships were seen by the bridge and so reported to the *Tipperary*. It appeared that the *Tipperary* rather ignored the fact that ships were in the vicinity, although at the time we had wonderful targets.[50]

Leading Torpedoman Maurice Cox , HMS *Garland*, 4th Flotilla

Aboard the *Tipperary*, Captain Wintour was in every sence in the dark. He had no idea where the Germans were. But, of equal concern, he also was in woeful ignorance of the state of the British dispositions, other than a vague awareness that the 11th Flotilla was somewhere to the west, effectively off the *Tipperary*'s starboard bow. It was a recipe for disaster. For the ships that had been sighted on the starboard quarter were the *Stuttgart, Hamburg, Rostock* and *Elbing*. Lurking close behind this light cruiser screen was the *Westfalen,* followed by the whole long line of the High Seas Fleet still steadily pursuing their course chopping right through the British destroyer flotillas stationed at the rear of the Grand Fleet.

> It can only be imagined *Tipperary* had no knowledge of the disposition of British units. If she had a challenge should not have been made, but an order for a torpedo attack to all the flotilla. We were at a very close range to the enemy without them knowing of our presence. A full discharge of torpedoes would undoubtedly have turned the course of the battle.[51]
>
> Leading Torpedoman Maurice Cox, HMS *Garland*, 4th Flotilla

At around 23.30, riddled with uncertainty, Wintour felt he had to challenge the approaching ships as the range inexorably closed below 1,000 yards. It was to be his first and last mistake. The moment the British recognition signals were hoisted, the blinding German searchlights flicked on and the deadly shadows opened up with a searing barrage of fire from a point-blank range of about 600 yards. The fire of the light cruisers was supplemented to deadly effect by the secondary 5.9-inch batteries of the *Westfalen* and *Nassau* in the van of the long column of German battleships. Sub-Lieutenant Newton William-Powlett was at his station aboard the *Tipperary* on the small after control platform for the three aft 4-inch guns.

> They were so close that I remember the guns seemed to be firing from some appreciable height above us. At almost the same instant the *Tipperary* shook violently from the impact of being hit by shells. I was told afterwards that the first salvo hit the bridge and it must have killed the Captain and nearly everyone there. I opened fire with the after guns as soon as the enemy opened on us. Proper spotting was out of the question, but crouching behind the canvas screen of my control position – I felt much safer with this thin weather screen between me and the enemy guns, though it wouldn't have kept out a spent rifle bullet – I yelled at the guns to fire. I don't think they heard me, but they opened fire all right. During this time both our starboard torpedo tubes were

fired, but the enemy was so close that I think that the initial dive which torpedoes usually take as they enter the water made them go under the enemy ships. The enemy's second salvo hit and burst one of our main steam pipes, and the after part of the ship was enveloped in a cloud of steam through which I could see nothing.[52]

Sub-Lieutenant Newton William-Powlett, HMS *Tipperary*, 4th Flotilla

Most of the German searchlights and guns were trained on the hapless *Tipperary*. Behind them, despite the surprise and the shock of the encounter, the *Spitfire, Sparrowhawk, Garland, Contest* and *Broke* leapt into action, fired their torpedoes and sheered away to port.

We immediately opened fire and at the same time the Captain turned the ship away to bring the after torpedo tube to bear. We fired a torpedo, then waited until, much to our joy and relief, it was seen to get the second enemy's ship between the after funnel and the mainmast and she seemed to stop firing, heel over and all her lights went out. But instead of the violent explosion we expected to see there appeared a kind of dull red glow and then fire seemed to spread forward and aft from where she was hit.[53]

Lieutenant Athelstan Bush, HMS *Spitfire*, 4th Flotilla

The path of each torpedo was a matter for speculation. Hits depended on a complicated formula of luck, mathematical probability and the degree of skill demonstrated on both sides in the opposed disciplines of torpedo aiming and evasion.

We fired our torpedoes and turned away to reload – in those days they were single tube ships with spare torpedoes on either side deck. Our helm was put hard over and in the spot we had just vacated half a cable astern at least half a dozen salvoes landed which drenched our ship from bow to stern – an extraordinary experience[54]

Leading Torpedoman Maurice Cox, HMS *Garland*, 4th Flotilla

They were fortunate not to have more ships crippled in the initial burst of fire from the much larger German ships.

We found ourselves close astern of the *Tipperary* and the latter was suddenly attacked from starboard by two Hun light cruisers. They put their lights on and fairly peppered the '*Tipp*' – we saw her fall out and burst into flame, how we avoided their lights I can't imagine – however we did and hauled out to port, firing a 'mouldy' at the after of the two cruisers as the bearing came on. We claim a hit and much hope we are allowed it, although there is some doubt I'm afraid.[55]

Lieutenant Irvine Glennie, HMS *Broke*, 4th Flotilla

Each destroyer captain went through the same torment. The quiet of their evening had been rudely shattered but no one knew exactly what was happening. Once again the crippling doubt and uncertainty of night fighting undermined their resolve and thereby their combat effectiveness. It was almost impossible to shrug off the fear that, after all, perhaps a terrible mistake had been made. Aboard the half flotilla leader *Broke*, the situation was typical.

I still felt certain that these ships were our own cruisers and so did the Captain, for without any hesitation he ordered me not to turn away and fire torpedoes until we could definitely establish the fact that they were Germans. Fortunately, at this moment, one stray searchlight beam from the leading ship swept aft and rested on the rear ship of her squadron. Although it was only for an instant, it was time enough for us to recognise the ship as an enemy. The Captain at once gave the order, "Carry on!" and we turned away and fired the starboard after torpedo tube, increasing to full speed immediately afterwards.[56]

Anon Navigating Officer, HMS *Broke*, 4th Flotilla

Each skipper made his own lightning assessment, and it is no surprise that some of the rearmost ships failed to fire their torpedoes as they remained utterly confused. A further problem was caused by the prevailing doctrine among many torpedo specialists that all the 'eggs' should not be put into one basket. Only one, or at most two, torpedoes were fired by each destroyer. The remainder were retained for later use. Success depended on the number of torpedoes thrown across the enemy line. In concert, sheer numbers of torpedoes could make it almost impossible to evade a strike and hence would generate a substantial number of hits. As not many torpedoes were fired it is not surprising that the results were meagre. Of the torpedoes fired during the course of this frenetic action, it seems that only one had any success, when the *Elbing* appears to have been struck. Various claims for this success were put forward by the *Spitfire*, *Garland*, *Broke* and *Sparrowhawk*. Only one could be true, but circumstances meant that no one could tell who had done the deed. The combination of sheer pandemonium, the impossibility of following the torpedo tracks at night, the frequency of impressive explosions and a natural unquenchable optimism inevitably led to a multiplicity of claims.

As the German light cruisers moved away to starboard to avoid the British torpedoes, they had to pass through the oncoming line of the German I Battle Squadron, which had also bent away from the torpedo threat, until they were steering well away from the course required to make Horns Reef. Chaos duly ensued and the *Elbing*, perhaps hampered by torpedo damage, did not quite make it as she tried to slip in front of the mighty *Posen*.

> Then our aft searchlight revealed a great warship. We expected a hail of shells, but it was a German ship. It rammed us during an avoiding manoeuvre in the darkness of the night. Next, the *Elbing* developed a heavy list to starboard and then painfully and slowly, returned to normal.[57]
>
> Max Meier, SMS *Elbing*, II Scouting Group, High Seas Fleet

The *Posen* had crashed into the weakened *Elbing*, causing yet more damage and untold anxiety to her crew. Below decks in the sick bay, the badly wounded Lieutenant Bassenge followed this further trial with considerable concern.

> I had noticed the heavy knock and was worried. I was too weak to go and see what was happening. Soon everything around us was quiet, all engines stopped, the battle noise ceased. Doctors and attendants went to the upper deck to see to the badly injured. The lights went out, an uncanny silence after 10 hours of battle made us feel very uneasy. I was worried that our dear *Elbing* was sinking and looked continuously at the floor and walls to see whether water was coming through. But I also thought that my comrades would come to fetch me if there was any danger because they would never have left the injured behind.[58]
>
> Lieutenant Heinrich Bassenge, SMS *Elbing*, II Scouting Group, High Seas Fleet

For a few minutes, the 4th Flotilla succeeded in deflecting the High Seas Fleet from the very precise course of its escape route. Unfortunately, when Scheer reached the 'bend' in the line caused by the leading ships bending away, he instantly realized what was happening and issued an immediate course correction that swung the line back on target for the Horns Reef sanctuary. Meanwhile, the *Spitfire*, which had already been hit by several German shells and was thus unable to fire her remaining torpedoes, turned back to go to the assistance of the burning *Tipperary*.

> We closed the *Tipperary*, now a mass of burning wreckage and looking a very sad sight indeed. At a distance her bridge, wheelhouse and charthouse appeared to be one sheet of flame, giving one the impression of a burning house and so bright was the light from this part that it seemed to obliterate one's vision of the remainder of the ship and of the sea round about, except that part close to her which was all lit up, reflecting the flames.[59]
>
> Lieutenant Athelstan Bush, HMS *Spitfire*, 4th Flotilla

They saw a German ship looming out of the dark, coming towards them across their port bow. Lieutenant Commander Clarence Trelawny of the *Spitfire* acted immediately. He ordered the helm to be put hard over at full speed, to avoid being hit amidships and cut in two. By swinging the destroyer round so that it would face the impact head-on, he would at least give them some kind of a chance of survival. Having issued the orders he leaned over the bridge and shouted to his men to clear the foc'sle, for a collision was clearly inevitable. The limited nature of their night vision meant that he and his crew were convinced they were facing a German light cruiser. In fact it was the 20,000-ton battleship *Nassau* that the 935-ton destroyer was preparing out of necessity to ram.

> The two ships met end on, port bow to port bow, we steaming at almost 27 knots, she steaming at not less than ten knots (perhaps 20 or more). You can imagine how the eighth inch plates of a destroyer would feel such a blow. I can recollect a fearful crash, then being hurled across the deck, and feeling the *Spitfire* rolling over to starboard as no sea ever made her roll. As we bumped, the enemy opened fire with their foc'sle guns, though luckily they could not depress them to hit us, but the blast

of the guns literally cleared everything before it. Our foremast came tumbling down, our for'ard searchlight found its way from its platform above the fore-bridge down to the deck, and the foremost funnel was blown back until it rested neatly between the two foremost ventilation cowls, like the hinging funnel of a penny river steamboat.[60]

Lieutenant Athelstan Bush, HMS *Spitfire*, 4th Flotilla

Just before the impact, two shells had crashed through the screen of the bridge killing almost everyone there. Captain Trelawny miraculously escaped with only a scalp wound, though he was blown right off the bridge onto the main deck. The coxswain and one other able seaman were later found trapped in the wreckage. To be released the unfortunate seaman subsequently had to have his leg amputated without any anaesthetic, while lying among the tangled ruins of the bridge. The *Spitfire* was in a dreadful state.

Fires started breaking out forward and to make matters worse all the lights were short circuited, so that anyone going up to the bridge received strong electric shocks. Moreover, all the electric bells in the ship were ringing, which made things feel rather creepy. It was extraordinary the way fire spread, burning strongly in places where one thought there was hardly anything inflammable, such as on the fore-bridge and the decks, but flags, signal halliards and the coconut matting on the deck all caught fire, and sparks from the latter were flying about everywhere. We thought the light would be sure to draw some enemy's fire on us, but fortunately it didn't. There was a large hole in the base of the second funnel through which flames were pouring out, and every single hosepipe in the ship seemed to be cut by splinters and useless.[61]

Lieutenant Athelstan Bush, HMS *Spitfire*, 4th Flotilla

The enormous impact of the head-on collision at a combined speed of around 40 knots had been such that not even the mighty *Nassau* escaped unscathed in this brief 'David and Goliath' encounter. Heinz Bonatz was on duty in the 5.9-inch port battery.

We sustained a direct hit on the forward group of lights and, soon after, rammed HMS *Spitfire* which had not seen us. The destroyer brushed against the 15cm gun in my casemate and ripped it and its carriage from the deck. Just a few seconds before the collision, I had been looking through the telescopic sight on the right side of the gun but was then called away to my proper battle station of the starboard side, because destroyers were reported there. Thus I stood right in the doorway of the middle casemate which lay between the two 15cm gun casemates. With the tilt of the ship, the armour plated door struck me on the right foot and the back. We believed the British ship to be destroyed at the time, especially as a great number of pieces of wreckage, both great and small, were floating round us.[62]

Cadet Heinz Bonatz, SMS *Nassau*, I Battle Squadron, High Seas Fleet

Despite the horrendous damage she suffered, the *Spitfire* did not sink but limped off to lick her wounds. Some 20 feet of the *Nassau*'s armour plating had been wrenched off her port side and came to rest on the forecastle of the *Spitfire*. It was the ultimate souvenir of their encounter.

Meanwhile, some of the survivors of the 4th Flotilla formed up behind the *Broke*, commanded by the half flotilla leader, Commander Walter Allen. Their new leader led them back into the attack, but it should not for a moment be imagined that anyone had any clear idea of what was happening. At about 23.40 they sighted once again indistinct shadows in the gloom on the starboard bow.

I was in the main office decoding all the wireless signals, which were coming through at a decent rate. About 11.45, I looked out the door of the office and saw the outline of a big ship, then she played her searchlight on a destroyer a little way from us, evidently not seeing us at first. But the searchlight, whilst taking a sweep, just caught sight of our ensign which was flying at the foreyard arm. From there it was played right on us. The ship was a big battlecruiser and German as she proved by challenging us with four green lights across the yardarm.[63]

Telegraphist J. J. R. Croad, HMS *Broke*, 4th Flotilla

In fact the ship was the *Westfalen*. Once again, before anyone on the destroyer could react, their huge adversary opened up with a torrent of well-directed shell fire.

I gave the order to challenge, but immediately the stranger challenged by a green light system, followed by switching on searchlights and opening fire. The order was given to fire the remaining starboard tube, full speed ahead both and fire was opened by *Broke* and after a slight pause for the firing of the torpedo I gave the order "Hard a starboard!"[64]

Commander Walter Allen, HMS *Broke*, 4th Flotilla

Just a few seconds of concentrated fire was all it took for the *Westfalen* to nullify any threat that the *Broke* might have posed. Her crew were effectively helpless in the face of their enemies.

We ran foul of a Hun battleship – she was to starboard and converging. She put on her challenge and the Skipper said, "Look out, a Hun!" We were just putting the helm over to fire the other 'mouldy' and I had just given the order to train on the light (to the guns) when her challenge went out and her searchlights came on bang on the bridge. She flicked aft to see who we were, I suppose, and came back to the bridge (we were on the upper bridge) opening rapid fire at once. It was perfectly damnable having their light right in our faces (about four or five cables off) and being properly biffed.[65]

Lieutenant Irvine Glennie, HMS *Broke*, 4th Flotilla

The range would have been familiar to seamen of Nelson's day. But it was high-explosive shells, not cannon-balls, that smashed into the *Broke*.

She then switched off her lights and began pouring salvoes into us at the range not being more than 150 yards, naturally not a shot missed. The first shot swept our gun crews clean off the deck, the next cleared the forebridge. The helmsman was shot dead at the wheel. The lad that was actually on watch in the wireless office was killed, I don't know to this day how I got saved. I was at that moment outside of the silent cabinet door inside which he was killed. The watch of stokers that were off watch were sleeping on the mess deck and nearly all of them were killed by shrapnel bullets or by the steam escaping from the broken steam pipes which were cut asunder by the shells.[66]

Telegraphist J. J. R. Croad, HMS *Broke*, 4th Flotilla

Once more, despite having made the challenge, the Germans got in the vital first broadside at a range where every shot counted and markedly reduced the chance of any effective reply.

We got off two or three rounds and never fired the 'mouldy' as the captain of the tube considered that he had not got a good target. I say two or three rounds because all hands were laid out before any more could be got off. We were hit many times, mostly by 6″ – or I suppose 5.9″ really. They did a lot of damage – killing or wounding all the guns' crews, the Quartermaster and all the fore supply and fire parties – 50 killed and 30 wounded all told – not bad work for one or two minutes. I was hit in the face by a few very small splinters and had rather a shock from one 6″ which burst quite close – in fact how we all escaped I don't know. Our helm and telegraphs were out of action and the steam from the foremost boiler was roaring off drowning all orders.[67]

Lieutenant Irvine Glennie, HMS *Broke*, 4th Flotilla

To compound the damage there came a crushing blow.

When the helmsmen fell dead, as he dropped he took the wheel with him, the ship answering to the helm thus given her, we turned away to port and having no time to warn HMS *Sparrowhawk* we crashed right into her.[68]

Telegraphist J. J. R. Croad, HMS *Broke*, 4th Flotilla

At the time the *Sparrowhawk* was under heavy fire and could do nothing to avoid the collision. As men in battle often observe, things seem to happen slowly and with an irresistible fascination.

So in addition to the enemy's gunfire which was straddling us with every salvo, we saw *Broke* coming straight for our bridge, absolutely end on, at 28 knots. I remember shouting a warning to everybody in hearing to hold on, and cried out to the foc'sle gun's crew to clear off the foc'sle. Then I leant over the bridge and watched *Broke*'s bow coming absolutely dead straight for us. I really don't know why, but it was a fascinating sight; I clean forgot all about the Germans and their gunfire. Just as she hit us I remember shouting out, "Now!" and then nothing more till I found myself lying on the foc'sle, not of our ship, but of the *Broke*.[69]

Sub-Lieutenant Percy Wood, HMS *Sparrowhawk*, 4th Flotilla

The impact was terrible. Most of the shocked crews from the two ships were thrown bodily off their feet.

We hit very hard, doing much damage and it took some seconds, as you may imagine, to collect oneself and try and grasp what had happened. I am afraid that I was more rattled than I should have been. But my eyes were full of blood and I thought I was much worse than I really was.[70]

Lieutenant Irvine Glennie, HMS *Broke*, 4th Flotilla

The collision had caused considerable damage to both ships and at first no one knew what was going on in a situation made more bizarre by the fact that several of the *Sparrowhawk*'s crew had been thrown overboard to land on the deck of the *Broke*.

On picking myself up I at once saw that we had one of our own destroyers bumping alongside and an ugly looking rent in her side abreast of the bridge showed where we had hit her. Steam was roaring out of our foremost boiler rooms and it was extremely difficult to see or hear anything. Our ship appeared to be settling by the bow and at intervals gave unpleasant lurches from side to side, which for the moment made me feel that she might be sinking. I went down on the forecastle to try and find out the extent of our damage, and to see what had happened, and to my surprise found a strange officer standing there, who turned out to be the sub-lieutenant of the *Sparrowhawk*, the destroyer which we had rammed. He informed me he had been pitched on board by the force of the collision, and I afterwards found out that three of her men had had the same experience.[71]

Anon Navigating Officer, HMS *Broke*, 4th Flotilla

Clasped together, the two ships drifted out of the centre of the battle. The stray sub-lieutenant reported to Captain Allen of the *Broke*, who in turn ordered him to report back to his captain aboard the *Sparrowhawk*, Lieutenant Commander Sydney Hopkins. In sending him back to his own captain, Allen directed him to take a message explaining that he wanted arrangements made for *Sparrowhawk* to take aboard the crew of the *Broke* as he believed she was in a sinking condition. By this time the German fire had died down and they had switched off their searchlights. But the drama continued, with tragedy descending unerringly into the realms of farce.

I found my Captain and gave him the message from the Captain of the *Broke*. His remarks were, "But that's a pity Sub, because I've sent across precisely the same message to him. This ship is also sinking fast!" The orders for the men to cross had actually been given and about 20 of our ship's company went into the *Broke* and about 15 men from the *Broke* came across into us.[72]

Sub-Lieutenant Percy Wood, HMS *Sparrowhawk*, 4th Flotilla

With the situation spiralling out of control, to make matters worse, in the interval another ship crashed into the two entangled destroyers. In the dark, it was almost impossible for the ships astern to see what was happening and a further collision was no surprise.

While we stood jammed into each other, another of our destroyers, HMS *Contest* ran into the *Sparrowhawk*, missing us by a hair's breadth, which was a marvellous piece of seamanship on the part of the man at the wheel. After about 30 minutes we managed to get clear from the *Sparrowhawk*, whom we left, having about 30 of their crew on board our ship.[73]

Telegraphist J. J. R. Croad, HMS *Broke*, 4th Flotilla

The *Contest* neatly sliced some 6 feet from the *Sparrowhawk*'s stern, but other than some collateral bow damage that marginally cut her speed, she was relatively uninjured and managed to carry on into the night regardless.

The *Broke* and the *Sparrowhawk* were left behind in the fast-moving action. Locked together, it took some thirty minutes before the *Broke* was able to back away from the jealous embrace of the *Sparrowhawk*. After their torrid but mutually unsatisfying encounter, the two crippled ships eventually parted like strangers in the night.

We soon got clear and commissioned the after bridge, hauled away to the north and tried to repair the damage and shore up bulkheads – the bows having vanished in the collision.[74]

Lieutenant Irvine Glennie, HMS *Broke*, 4th Flotilla

Strangely enough, the *Broke* was still seaworthy, despite the missing bows, though not by any means fit for action. As long as her forward bulkheads held, she could slowly make her way home. Yet as she slowly struggled away from the scene of her downfall, the Germans reappeared to try to finish their work of destruction.

We had got things well underway when we were again attacked at 1.30am by Hun destroyers. They came up from the port quarter, put their lights on and opened fire. I must confess that I felt that that was the end. But not so! We fired one round and then for some unknown reason they pushed off after hitting us several times.[75]

Lieutenant Irvine Glennie, HMS *Broke*, 4th Flotilla

Men who had celebrated their miraculous escape from the earlier rain of shells found that once again they had to face up to the threat of death.

A German destroyer came up and fired about six rounds of 3pdr shell killing a few men. I had managed to get to the after part of the ship and I lay flat on the deck and only got a small splinter in the arm, which I looked at as nothing compared with some of my poor messmates. One shell killed Able Seaman Palmer, who during the first attack had a leg shattered. He had been put in a life raft amidships, where he was killed.[76]

Telegraphist J. J. R. Croad, HMS *Broke*, 4th Flotilla

Once again the injured *Broke* was alone in the night.

As a result of this series of mishaps, the prospect of any cohesive attack by the remnants of the 4th Flotilla had inevitably broken down as each destroyer took emergency evasive action to avoid adding to the pile-up in front of them. At the same time, many of the destroyer captains were still labouring under the delusion that either some terrible accident had occurred or British ships were now located in between them and the German ships. Only the *Contest* and the *Ambuscade* seem to have fired their torpedoes at this stage.

Then we did a quick turn to avoid a steady searchlight beam which was upon the *Broke* and several others of our flotilla – I could see the shots falling thick and fast amongst them. For a few moments the excitement abated and amidst 'Alarums and excursions' our torpedo party worked with feverish activity to load our spare torpedo. The manoeuvre was executed in record time and I am glad to remember that when the tube was loaded I helped to train it.[77]

Surgeon Lieutenant Henry Breese, HMS *Ambuscade*, 4th Flotilla

The other captains hesitated and so missed one of the finest torpedo opportunities that anyone could wish for as the High Seas Fleet steamed past at close range. Even so, one of the three or four torpedoes that were fired seems to have struck lucky and hit the light cruiser *Rostock*, causing severe damage which eventually caused her crew to abandon ship about four hours later. The luck in question was, in this case, only relative. While the *Rostock* was a worthwhile mark, she seems to have been struck while darting between the far more rewarding targets of dreadnoughts *Westfalen* and *Rheinland*. To have disabled or sunk one of these would have been a triumph indeed. For both sides the difference between success and absolute triumph was truly separated only by the narrowest of margins. A salvo of sixteen torpedoes and a *soupçon* more luck might have changed the course of the battle considerably.

Despite these vicissitudes, a significant part of the 4th Flotilla managed to collect together for another strike. This time the cursed baton of leadership was passed to Commander Reginald Hutchinson of the *Achates* and behind him were the *Ambuscade, Ardent, Fortune, Porpoise* and *Garland*. They had lost contact with the German ships, but as soon as they had formed up in line, Hutchinson turned back to a southerly course. For a while all was quiet. Yet it could not last. On this course they were once more closing in on the long line of German dreadnoughts crossing the wake of the Grand Fleet.

> I clearly perceived four big ships on a parallel and slightly converging course to us on our starboard quarter. They challenged several times and their challenge was not an English one. They then switched on their searchlights, picked up the *Fortune* and opened fire on her.[78]
>
> Lieutenant Commander Arthur Marsden, HMS *Ardent*, 4th Flotilla

As had happened several times already during the night, the British destroyers should really have firmly identified the ships as German, well before they were 'surprised' by the deluge of fire. Hampered by their complete lack of training in night tactics, their commanding officers waited far too long 'to be sure' and thus surrendered the vital initiative of being first to open fire.

I was sitting on the tube, it was pitch dark and quiet when a dark shape appeared in front of me about 200 yards away – apparently the *Derfflinger*. I knew it was the enemy, but must wait for orders to fire. Then she made her recognition lights and when I got no order to fire, I looked to the bridge and it was blown away … So I got the tube to bear and fired my torpedo. Waiting for the splash as she hit, I was blown off the tube by gunfire. We were that close I could see searchlight crew on the big ship. I got up and helped to get any survivors into the Carley float. All boats were blown away. At last only Sub-Lieutenant Patterson and I were left on the quarterdeck. He was thinking of 33 golden sovereigns he had down in his cabin, when another forward bulkhead collapsed and the stern rose to a sharper angle, so I suggested we dive over the side. If you know what it is like to jump into the black unknown then diving in is worse![79]

Leading Seaman Thomas Clifford, HMS *Fortune*, 4th Flotilla

It was actually the dreadnought *Oldenberg* that the *Fortune* had attacked. High above them the German searchlight officer was impressed by the last fight of the little destroyer.

It was the most gallant fight I have ever seen. She was literally riddled with shell; but clear in the glare of our searchlights, I could see a petty officer and two seamen loading and firing her after gun until she disappeared. We would have liked to have saved her brave survivors, but you can well understand we could not stop in the middle of a night battle.[80]

Searchlight Control Officer Fritz Otto Busch, SMS *Oldenburg*, I Battle Squadron, High Seas Fleet

Of course, Clifford was one of those men struggling for their lives below him.

At about 00.10 I entered the water and for five hours I was on my own. I was sitting on a lifebelt. Knowing I had miles to swim either way, I reserved energy and stopped where I was. At daylight I saw a Carley Float, I swam over, but it was too full so I swam around until only six were in the raft – many having passed out due to exposure, a wonderful death many smiling at the last. I nearly went twice myself and it feels like turning into warm blankets and going to sleep. Well, at about

6.30am a cruiser dashed by and threw a line. They missed us and as
they were not allowed to stop to pick up survivors they disappeared –
but they signalled a destroyer, HMS *Moresby*, to rescue us. They lowered
their boat and got us on board.[81]

Leading Seaman Thomas Clifford, HMS *Fortune*, 4th Flotilla

Ahead of the doomed *Fortune* was the *Ardent*, commanded by Lieutenant
Commander Arthur Marsden. They too managed to despatch a
torpedo.

The leader of my line appeared to increase speed and turn away to
port. I could see the *Fortune* was hard hit, so altered round to starboard
and fired a torpedo at the leading enemy ships. We could all see it hit
most clearly and there was an enormous upheaval of water right
forward. Her foremost lights went out and she turned away. By this time
other searchlights were on us from the second ship, and fire was opened
on us, but we got through and away with very little damage. We caught
a last glimpse of the *Fortune*, on fire, in a sinking condition, but fighting
still and firing her guns in a most inspiring manner.[82]

Lieutenant Commander Arthur Marsden, HMS *Ardent*, 4th Flotilla

The *Ambuscade* also fired a torpedo in the general direction of the German
ships.

We encountered enemy's battle fleet steering south-east. Third torpedo
was fired at ships concentrating on *Ardent*. A red flash was observed at
water level between searchlights and they momentarily went out, giving
the possibility of another hit, observing that *Ardent* may have fired. *Ardent*
and *Fortune* were not seen after this. Having discharged all torpedoes, by
smoke screen and continual alterations of helm, I got away to the
eastwards.[83]

Lieutenant Commander Gordon Coles, HMS *Ambuscade*, 4th Flotilla

Once again several ships failed to fire their torpedoes for the usual *mélange*
of reasons. Perversely, those that did were ill rewarded for their efforts.
Although some torpedoes were sighted passing through the German battle
line, there were simply not enough of them to render hits a certainty, and
a little subtle manoeuvring took the dreadnoughts past unscathed. The

claims of both the *Ambuscade* and *Ardent* to have scored hits seem to be unjustified, although several 4-inch shells certainly did cause damage and casualties to the bridge of the *Oldenburg*. This may have been what the harassed officers saw in the split seconds of action under the dazzling strobe effects of a night battle. Following their encounter the *Ardent* lost touch with the remnants of 4th Flotilla.

> I found myself alone, and so resumed the course of the fleet and increased speed, hoping to pick up the rest of my division. Smoke was reported right ahead, which I thought would be theirs but as I got nearer realised that it was a big ship on exactly the opposite course. I attacked at once and from very close range our remaining torpedoes were fired, but before I could judge the effect the enemy switched on searchlights and found us at once. I then became aware that *Ardent* was tackling a division of German battleships. However, we opened fire and ran on at full speed. The next moments were perhaps the most thrilling that anyone could experience. Our guns were useless against such big adversaries; our torpedoes were fired; we could do no more but just wait in the full glare of the blinding searchlights for the shells that could not fail to hit us at such close range. There was perfect silence on the bridge and not a word was spoken. It must have been only seconds but it seemed like hours. At last it came, and as the first salvo hit I heard a seaman ejaculate almost under his breath. "Oh-ooh!" as one does to a bursting rocket. Shell after shell hit us and our speed diminished and then stopped; then the dynamo stopped and all lights went out. Our three guns that had been barking away like good'uns ceased firing one by one. I looked on the forecastle and saw and heard the captain of the forecastle exhorting the only remaining man of his gun's crew to, "Give them one more!" but that one more was never fired and I saw later both those brave souls stretched out dead. I myself was wounded by almost the first salvo but felt no great pain or discomfort. The actual feeling when I was struck was as if I had been hit on the thigh with an iron bar, though eventually a piece of shell about as big as my little finger was taken out of me. The enemy ships suddenly switched off lights and ceased fire.[84]

Lieutenant Commander Arthur Marsden, HMS *Ardent*, 4th Flotilla

It was clear to Marsden that his ship would soon sink. Calmly he began to make the preparations for the end; hampered by the fact that he had been wounded in the leg, he made his way aft from the bridge. The morale of his men remained high, but it soon became evident that it would be difficult to get them away safely.

> The ship was nearly gone so it only remained for us to try and save as many as we could. A terrible scene of destruction and desolation was revealed to me as I walked aft, with some difficulty. All boats were in pieces. The funnels looked more like nutmeg graters. The rafts were blown to pieces, and in the ship's sides and deck there were holes innumerable. In the very still atmosphere the smoke and steam poured out from the holes in the deck perfectly straight up into the air. Several of my best men came up and tried to console me, and were all delighted that we had at length been in action and done our share. But many were already killed and lay around their guns and places of duty. Most of the engine room and stokehold brigade must have been killed outright.
> I walked right aft and sat down on the wardroom hatch. I could do no more as my leg was stiff and bleeding a lot. My servant and another seaman, both of whom had been with me over two years came aft to look for me and to help me. I sent them forward and told them to pass the word for each man to look out for himself. For a moment or two I was quite alone; the smoke cut me off from those further forward and there was absolute quiet and stillness.[85]
>
> Lieutenant Commander Arthur Marsden, HMS *Ardent*, 4th Flotilla

These few moments of peaceful contemplation were cruelly cut short as the Germans found them and once again opened fire.

> Then all of a sudden we were again lit up by searchlights, the enemy poured in four or five more salvoes at point blank range and then switched off her lights once more. This would be about 10 minutes from the time we were first hit. The *Ardent* gave a big lurch and I bethought myself of my Gieve waistcoat. I blew and blew without any result whatever and found that it had been shot through. Another lurch, which heeled the ship right over and threw me to the ship's side. I could feel that she was going, so flopped over into the sea, grabbing a lifebuoy that

was providentially at hand. The *Ardent*'s stern kept up for a few moments, then she slowly sank from view.[86]

Lieutenant Commander Arthur Marsden, HMS *Ardent*, 4th Flotilla

The bedraggled remnants of his crew found themselves adrift in the waves with very little prospect of survival in the cold night waters.

As the smoke and steam cleared off I could see many heads in the water – about 40 to 50 I should think. There was no support beyond lifebelts, lifebuoys and floating waistcoats, so I was afraid few of us could possibly survive, especially as I realised that all the destroyers had gone on and no big ship would dare stop, even if they saw us in the water. I spoke to many men and saw most of them die one by one. Not a man of them showed any fear of death and there was never a murmur, complaint or cry for help from a single soul. Their joy was, and they talked about it to the end, that they and the *Ardent* had "done their bit" as they put it. While there were still many alive, a German came close and fired a star shell over us. I could see her distinctly and was all for giving her a hail, but the men said, "No!" They agreed that they would sooner take the remote chance of being saved by an English ship rather than be a prisoner in Germany. I was nearly done in once or twice in the first hour by men hanging on to me in the last stages of exhaustion, and I was separated from my lifebuoy and was pulled right over in the water, but managed to recover myself and the buoy. None of the men appeared to have suffered at all; they just seemed to lie back and go to sleep. After a long weary while the sun got up and then I was feeling much more comfortable than two hours previously. I found a skiff's oar floating past me and put it under my arms. I began to feel drowsy and dropped off into a sort of sleep several times, only to be awakened again by waves slapping into my face. There was quite a swell but the surface of the water was smooth owing to the masses of oil floating about from our sunken ships. I woke again after what I felt to be a long time to hear a shout and could see ships a long way off. I took a sort of detached interest in them and gave an answering shout to, 'Stick it Ardents!' to someone in the water nearby whom I could not see. I watched the ships disappear again without much interest and dozed off again. Once again I awoke to find a flotilla leader – the *Marksman* – close alongside me.

I sang out for help and in reply got a welcoming and re-assuring shout, "You're all right, Sir! We're coming!" and once again relapsed into unconsciousness. [87]

Lieutenant Commander Arthur Marsden, HMS *Ardent*, 4th Flotilla

Marsden was picked up at around 06.00. There was only one other survivor from *Ardent*'s appropriately named crew.

At the same time, behind them, another stray British ship had blundered into the line of the High Seas Fleet. The *Black Prince* had been separated from the rest of the 1st Cruiser Squadron as the Grand Fleet was deploying at 18.20. Since then she had been trying to rejoin the fleet. Now, in a sense, she repeated the mistake of her sister ships *Defence* and *Warrior* as, in all ignorance, she wandered into the path of the High Seas Fleet. Engineer Room Assistant Otto Frost was aboard a German destroyer that had taken up her natural station at the head of the line.

Pitch dark night. The ships totally blacked out, there was only a small stern light, close to the sea. At this time, I was off watch and looking at our following fleet. There – what was that? A short flash from one of our ships. And then again shortly afterwards. Two salvoes followed. The ship following us had been hit in a shower of sparks. An English vessel had closed with our fleet and in a short time it was sunk. They said it was one of the *Black Prince* class. Was it perhaps an error by the British ship believing he was joining his own fleet? Possibly! [88]

Wachmachinist Otto Frost, *VI*, 5th Torpedo Boat Flotilla, High Seas Fleet

Cadet Heinz Bonatz saw the débâcle from the *Nassau*, which had been forced to reduce speed and drop out of the main battle line after the collision with the *Spitfire*.

We suddenly sighted a cruiser with four funnels, HMS *Black Prince*. It immediately came under fire from three other ships. Within a few minutes the cruiser was a glowing wreck and sank after a mighty explosion, a horrible but imposing sight. [89]

Cadet Heinz Bonatz, SMS *Nassau*, I Battle Squadron, High Seas Fleet

The *Black Prince* was in no position to defend herself and strike back against the calibre of adversaries she had brought upon herself. The *Thüringen, Ostfriesland, Friedrich der Grosse* and *Nassau* all joined in firing at this most helpless of targets. There was no room for sentiment.

> In a few seconds she was on fire, and sank with a terrible explosion four minutes after opening fire. The destruction of this vessel, which was so near that the crew could be seen rushing backwards and forwards on the burning deck while the searchlights disclosed the flight of the heavy projectiles till they fell and exploded, was a grand but terrible sight.[90]
> Admiral Reinhard Scheer, SMS *Friedrich der Grosse*, III Battle Squadron, High Seas Fleet

Seaman Herman Meenzenn had only joined the *Nassau* three weeks before the battle. He was not an experienced sailor. It was the first sea voyage of his entire life. He found this massacre a chilling sight.

> The *Black Prince* was 500 metres away from the *Nassau* on the starboard side. I was an eyewitness from the searchlight deck to the burning of the *Black Prince* which was over in a few minutes. To express my feelings about the battle is very difficult. I had a very strong feeling of duty, but the fire on the *Black Prince* left me feeling very sad and depressed.[91]
> Seaman Hermann Meenzen, SMS *Nassau*, I Battle Squadron, High Seas Fleet

The loss of the *Black Prince* was another reminder of the vulnerability of the outmoded armoured cruisers and the dreadful human cost as 857 men lost their lives in an episode of staggering futility. Strangely, it seems the German dreadnoughts were not the last to see the burning *Black Prince*. As she drifted away she passed close by the damaged, but still floating, *Spitfire*. The engine-room staff had discovered that three of their four boilers were still working and, as the severely stressed bulkheads were still holding out, they had begun slowly steaming home at a speed of around 6 knots. Suddenly they saw an unnervingly eerie apparition – a ghost ship lit up by the flames of its own cremation.

> "Look Out!" I looked up and saw a few hundred yards away on our starboard quarter, what appeared to be a battlecruiser on fire steering straight for our stern. We thought that she was steering for us with the

intention of cutting us in two; and we thought we were done for. I believe the majority of us lay down and waited for the crash. But no crash came. To our intense relief she missed our stern by a few feet, but so close was she to us that it seemed that we were actually lying under her guns, which were trained out on her starboard beam. She tore past us with a roar, rather like a motor roaring up a hill in low gear, and the very crackling and heat of the flames could be heard and felt. She was a mass of fire from foremast to mainmast, on deck and between decks. Flames were issuing out of her from every corner.[92]

Lieutenant Athelstan Bush, HMS *Spitfire*, 4th Flotilla

By 00.30 the 4th Flotilla had shot their bolt. They had conspicuously failed to launch co-ordinated mass torpedo attacks, but had undoubtedly fought courageously as valiant seamen all too literally stuck to their guns. The line of their resistance was clearly delineated, as the sky lit up for miles around with searchlights, star shells, fires and explosions. Unfortunately, in all the confusion and heavy press of events, not one of the destroyers' commanding officers had had the time or presence of mind to wireless in formal contact reports to Jellicoe. During the engagements they had held the future of the High Seas Fleet within their grasp, but in failing to launch co-ordinated attacks, or to report the presence of the German dreadnoughts, they had allowed it to slip through their fingers. For all their efforts they had achieved little of significance. But Jellicoe too is deeply culpable for their failure. His decision not to risk the Grand Fleet in a night engagement was entirely logical; but his failure over the previous two years to ensure that his destroyers and light cruisers were properly equipped and trained for such an eventuality was not.

Aboard the *Iron Duke*, Petty Officer Arthur Brister was one of those charged with receiving those wireless signals that did come through.

After 9pm when signal traffic had thinned out, Commander Phipps asked for a relief for me and was told there was no-one available. He therefore suggested that I laid down between the incoming or outgoing of signals, but there was only one place I could do that – on the leather seated wooden settee on which reposed the C-in-C's greatcoat. Finding no means of hanging up the coat or placing it elsewhere, I stretched myself out on the seat and spread the heavy garment over me.

The excitement of the last few hours began to fade and I was feeling pleasantly relaxed when the charthouse door opened, the trip-catch putting out the light. The door closed slowly, the light came on and staring down at me was the C-in-C. I froze, unable to think what to do or say for the moment. The Admiral was wearing an old tarnished cap and a faded blue raincoat, his weather worn face looked tired and strained, yet his eyes were clear and penetrating. What would he say to a Petty Officer who had the impertinence to make use of his coat?

It seemed ages before I struggled to get up and it was then that the Commander came to my rescue. "I told him to lie down, Sir. He has no relief." Admiral Jellicoe nodded, went to the chart table and began dictating signals and conversing in his usual soft-speaking voice. For a while I stayed on the seat looking at the back of the great little man who was carrying such a tremendous load of responsibility. What would the morrow bring for him and would he go down in history as the modern Nelson?[93]

Petty Officer Telegraphist Arthur Brister, HMS *Iron Duke*, 3rd Division, Fourth Battle Squadron

Brister resumed his station and commendably resisted the temptation that surged up inside him to remove a button from Jellicoe's coat as a souvenir! Yet the very reduction in wireless messages that allowed Brister his chance of a well-earned rest was symptomatic of the ubiquitous failure of Jellicoe's subordinate commanders to report their contacts with the High Seas Fleet. In sharp contrast, almost every German ship reported in to Scheer when they contacted a British ship.

Listening to the German ships belting away at full strength on their high-pitched swinging-toned Telefunken sets, I thought they were being stupid or contemptuous of our east coast direction finding stations.

Or did they deem it the better policy to interfere on W/T in the hope of preventing or delaying sighting reports from our ships getting through to the C-in-C? By the strength of their transmission the jamming was being carried out by capital ships and therefore the coastal D/F stations were being given the chance to chart them and to obtain an indication as to which way the German battle fleet was taking for home. But the D/F Stations would be working at a long distance, over 200 miles and accuracy would be considerably lowered by 'night-effect'. If only we had a ship fitted with a D/F set! Even a set of simple design would be sufficient under the present conditions. The Germans were giving us the heaven sent opportunity to keep track of them throughout the night and we were unprepared.[94]

Petty Officer Telegraphist Arthur Brister, HMS *Iron Duke*, 3rd Division, Fourth Battle Squadron

Throughout the night actions many of the men aboard the Grand Fleet dreadnoughts were fully aware that something was going on behind them.

About 11.45pm, there was a terrific burst of firing astern of us, fair going it, light cruisers and destroyers. It went on for about five minutes and must have been a pretty hot show. One ship was hit badly and lit up the sky in a great red flame. It looked as if there was a huge great orange sitting on the ship and it dies down and suddenly flares up again.[95]

Midshipman Geoff Congreve, HMS *Benbow*, 4th Division, Fourth Battle Squadron

A lit match can be seen for miles at night; so an exchange of gunfire stood out like a Brock's benefit.

I went forward to the heads. On the way back I hid for a few moments on the upper deck. Talk about Crystal Palace fireworks – it was better than that and I was getting paid about two shilling a day to see it.[96]

Leading Victualler Victor Dunton, HMS *Centurion*, 1st Division, Second Battle Squadron

Between these sporadic clashes, the inky darkness reinstated itself. There was a terrible responsibility for those in charge on the bridge as they steered their ships through the black night, fully aware of the consequences of a collision with another dreadnought. It required great concentration and skill to remain on station.

I took over as officer of the watch at 10.00pm and found we were in single line ahead, steering on a small blue light low down and keeping station by the amount of the mast of the next ahead visible in the field of the binoculars. Until 2.00am, when I went off watch, there was continual firing, flashes of searchlight, etc. astern, drawing across from the starboard to the port quarter.[97]

Lieutenant Patrick Lawder, HMS *Benbow*, 4th Division, Fourth Battle Squadron

Naturally, British optimism decreed that all the ships suffering behind them were German. This over-sanguine view led many to imagine that the British destroyers were beating off attacks by the Germans, with very little consideration given to alternative scenarios.

The night perhaps was even more weird and awe-inspiring than the day. Soon after darkness set in, suddenly, out of the quiet of the night, a terrific cannonade took place quite close; flashes were clearly seen and every now and then a tremendous explosion was heard and great flames 100 feet high shot up into the sky. This sort of thing went on all night until early dawn; intervals of short silence occurring which made the actions when they took place appear to be sudden and fierce. They were our destroyers attacking the remains of the enemy fleet that were escaping. The destroyers did not leave them alone apparently for a moment and, taking into consideration the anxiety one always feels even in peace time in a night attack, the Germans must have had a truly awful time seeing their ships blown up or injured and being attacked again and again. It was fascinating to watch in an awful sort of way.[98]

Captain Percy Grant, HMS *Marlborough*, 6th Division, First Battle Squadron

As the British light forces tried to prevent the passage of the High Seas Fleet another drama was unfolding. The German battlecruisers *Seydlitz* and *Moltke* had become separated from the main body of the High Seas Fleet and, conscious of their vulnerability, they surreptitiously began their efforts to pass through the British line and escape to safety. The *Seydlitz*, in particular, was badly damaged and her crew had a dreadful time trying to keep her seaworthy while preparing for possible battle.

Now darkness fell, and we had to make preparations for the next morning – for we were sure to meet the British again. Searchlights were repaired, night recognition signals rigged, and ammunition carried to the undamaged guns. At first, we could continue to follow the battlecruiser SMS *Moltke*, but soon we had to slow down, for water began to come over the forecastle as our bows settled. Steering was difficult, as was finding the right course, for the main gyro compartment was flooded and the after gyro unreliable. Its normal circuit had been destroyed, and the new connection short-circuited off and on. The shocks had made the magnetic compass entirely undependable. Sounding had its problems, too. The sounding machines in the casemates were scrap, while the hand-leads fouled the torn nets and then parted. Our charts were covered with blood and the spare charts were inaccessible in a flooded compartment. Under these circumstances it was not at all easy to make the correct course for the Horns Reef lightship. Moreover, all coal near the boilers had been used up, and bringing up more supplies from the more distant bunkers became increasingly difficult as a result of damage and the amount of water in the ship. Fortunately, our boilers could also burn oil, and supplies of this continued to flow, although the oil-pipes needed constant attention to prevent them from clogging.[99]

Kapitän zur See Moritz von Egidy, SMS *Seydlitz*, 1st Scouting Group,
High Seas Fleet

The *Moltke* pulled slowly away from the *Seydlitz* until they lost touch. Shortly afterwards, at 22.30, the *Moltke* sighted four large ships on the port beam. Not knowing who they were, she displayed her coloured German recognition lights and in doing so should have sealed her doom. For the indistinct blurs were the British dreadnoughts *Orion, Monarch, Conqueror* and *Thunderer* of the 2nd Division, Second Battle Squadron. The *Moltke* had been relatively lightly damaged in the earlier fighting, but as a battlecruiser she had no chance of surviving if these mighty ships had opened fire on her with their massed 13.5-inch guns. As he recognized them, Captain von Karpf had no option but to turn away silently back into the protection of darkness. The rear British ship, the *Thunderer*, clearly saw the coloured lights of the *Moltke* recognition signal, but amazingly did not open fire. Her captain was under the strange misapprehension that the *Moltke* was a destroyer and felt it was not worth opening fire on such a target and thereby giving away the position of the British dreadnoughts.

It was considered inadvisable to show up battle fleet unless obvious attack was intended.[100]

Captain James Fergusson, HMS *Thunderer*, 2nd Division, Second Battle Squadron

Jellicoe was subsequently to remark, 'I don't understand *Thunderer*'s action at all.'[101] He was not alone in regretting lost opportunity. Behind the *Thunderer* was the attached light cruiser *Boadicea*.

We were, of course, steaming without lights. At about 10.30pm, on the starboard side one of our gun's crew said he thought he could make out a ship steering in the opposite direction to ourselves. Hardly had he finished speaking when a string of three brilliant lights (Green, Red and Green) was switched on; obviously recognition lights suspended from the yardarm. It was impossible to identify the vessel, but it could not have been too far away, as we were able to recognise the crane derrick, which was a feature of the older German ships. It could not have been one of the more modern light cruisers because they were all fitted with normal pole derricks like our own ships. We waited round the gun expecting the order to fire, but no order was given and within a few minutes the coloured lights were switched off and the stranger disappeared in the gathering gloom. From her course, she would have passed astern of us at some distance. Our LTO in charge of the starboard tube was hopping mad and felt sure we could have torpedoed the German as soon as the lights came on had he received the order.[102]

Ordinary Seaman Walter Hamer, HMS *Boadicea*, (attached) Second Battle Squadron

Chances such as were offered to the *Thunderer* and the *Boadicea* do not linger for long. The *Moltke* was only in sight for about half a minute and then escaped unscathed into the night once more. She continued to engage in this desperate game of blind man's bluff for another hour. Twice more, at 22.55 and 23.20, she tried to slip through the British line and each time she encountered the impenetrable wall of the Second Battle Squadron. On both these occasions she was lucky to be able to turn away without being sighted. In the end Captain von Karpf gave up and steered well to the south, thereby using her superiority of speed to circle round the front of the Grand Fleet and make their way back to port independently.

The *Seydlitz* had an even closer escape, as she tried to feel her way through the Grand Fleet. She really was crippled, with her speed dropping down as low as 7 knots on a couple of occasions. She had not gone far when, at about 23.45, the worst fears of her crew seemed to be realized as they encountered the lagging 6th Division of the First Battle Squadron.

> In this situation, the aft-lookout reported: "Several large ships, darkened, approaching from astern." Our night glasses showed four huge ships, British, no more than 2,000 yards away. Blast! They must have seen us and would therefore open fire at any moment. Should we try to ram? But their guns were still trained fore and aft! Our ship was too heavily damaged to attack, and I gave the orders: "Hard-a-starboard, full speed ahead, engine room make as much smoke as possible – give British recognition signal." A yeoman flashed the latter "J", the leading ship promptly answered "O". That was the only light they showed for they had an excellently darkened ship. In a minute we got up so much smoke that they disappeared from view. When we reported this encounter by W/T, bright sparks flashed all over our rigging because torn wires touched the improvised aerials when the ship heeled over.[103]
>
> Kapitän zur See Moritz von Egidy, SMS *Seydlitz*, I Scouting Group, High Seas Fleet

Incredibly, none of the First Battle Squadron opened fire, although they had indeed sighted the nocturnal meanderings of the *Seydlitz*.

> Smoke was observed ahead of the *Marlborough*, which crossed from starboard to port and back again from port to starboard, and then came down to the starboard side. It appeared to be a large ship and was challenged by *Revenge*, who was answered by two letters, though they were not the correct ones. She then disappeared. *Revenge* says that the order to open fire was actually given, but was later countermanded.[104]
>
> Vice Admiral Sir Cecil Burney, HMS *Marlborough*, 6th Division, First Battle Squadron

It is unquestionable that just a couple of hits would have sent the *Seydlitz* to the bottom. The disasters that had dogged the British battlecruisers since the fleets had first engaged during the afternoon could have been avenged in a matter of moments. But once again nothing was done. A safety-first approach meant that, to the astonishment and intense relief of her crew, the *Seydlitz* was able to continue meandering past the Second Battle Squadron. The *Agincourt* also sighted her, but also forbore to open fire. And so it was that the *Seydlitz* was allowed to pass through the narrow 2-mile gap between the Battle Squadrons. Between them, they thus threw away the chance of capitalizing on all the destructive work that had been put in to reduce the *Seydlitz* to a sinking condition, all of which would be negated if she got back to harbour and was given the chance to rise again like a phoenix from the docks.

The *Seydlitz* and *Moltke* were not the only German capital ships sighted by the British dreadnoughts. During the desperate resistance of the 4th Flotilla, the *Westfalen* led the German battle line across the point of inter-section as their south-south-east-$^3/_4$-east course converged and crossed the wake of the southerly course of the main body of the Grand Fleet. The situation has been neatly summarized by Langhorne Gibson and Vice Admiral John Harper in their book *The Riddle of Jutland*, published in 1934.

> They steamed down the sides of a very long, very slender 'V', and it was one of the most curious circumstances of history that they did not come together at the 'V's point. A matter of minutes – of a quarter of an hour – of the fact that Scheer had sent his leading ships back to the rear of his line, while Jellicoe had drawn the British rear up to form upon the Grand Fleet leaders; of the fact that the British speed was 17 knots, while the German speed was 16. Tiny factors and no human plan, caused Jellicoe to arrive at the bottom of the 'V' and pass through the junction point, short minutes before the German ships arrived. The 'V' became an 'X' – the courses of the fleets crossed. [105]

It was indeed a truly close shave, for they crossed only 3 miles behind the Fifth Battle Squadron and the 6th Division of the First Battle Squadron, which were bringing up the rear of the fleet. It was the moment of maximum danger for Scheer. At the rear of the line the Fifth Battle Squadron had a clear view of dreadnoughts passing astern of them, as their distinctive silhouettes were clearly, if briefly, lit up by searchlights and nearby shell flashes.

We saw all sorts of actions going on astern of us. In one of these I well remember coming out of the gun control tower and looking aft saw what was obviously a German battleship of the *Nassau* class, easily recognisable by her boat crane, crossing our wake.[106]

Sub-Lieutenant Eric Brand, HMS *Valiant*, Fifth Battle Squadron

Despite several such sightings, the officers of the Fifth Battle Squadron lamentably failed either to engage the German dreadnoughts or inform Jellicoe as to what was happening at the rear of the fleet. Captain Craig Waller of the *Barham* made a valiant effort to defend the indefensible.

It is doubtful whether the various observations of enemy ships made by ships of our battle fleet ought to have been reported to the Commander in Chief. I was on the bridge all night with my Admiral, and we came to the conclusion that the situation was known to the C-in-C and that the attacks were according to plan. A stream of wireless reports from ships in company with the C-in-C seemed superfluous and uncalled for. The unnecessary use of wireless was severely discouraged as being likely to disclose our position to the enemy. The same reason probably influenced the *Marlborough*'s division. This may have been an error of judgement but cannot be termed 'amazing neglect'.[107]

Captain Craig Waller, HMS *Barham*, Fifth Battle Squadron

Waller's arguments were tendentious in the extreme, fatally flawed as they were by the idea that conforming to rules is always the right course of action whatever the situation. In his self-serving inability to recognize the stupidity of what was done, or rather not done, he loses credibility. By any criteria, their failure to engage was a serious mistake and can be usefully contrasted with the willingness of the German dreadnoughts to blast the *Black Prince* out of the water when she approached their line.

The key factor inhibiting the British from attacking German ships was the lack of an absolute conviction that they were hostile, not friendly. As has been observed, the Germans maintained regular wireless communication between ships, which, although relinquishing secrecy, did ensure that the High Seas Fleet was better informed as to what was happening around it. The British adopted the diametrically opposed view and instead laid great store by the maintenance of wireless silence. For them the fear of detection outweighed the value of awareness.

> Wireless signalling by ships at sea had to be stopped, because by means of directional wireless stations the positions of ships using wireless telegraphy could be determined by the enemy. As time went on, we felt that the enemy might be able to ascertain the class and in some cases even the name of the ship so signalling. This we deduced from the fact that we ourselves made progress in this direction.[108]
>
> Admiral Sir John Jellicoe, HMS *Iron Duke*, 3rd Division, Fourth Battle Squadron

Although the Grand Fleet Battle Orders issued by Jellicoe specifically called for sighting reports to be sent as a high priority, this was swamped by the three years of adherence to a rigid policy of maintaining wireless silence.

Yet the danger of regular wireless traffic was far greater than Scheer could ever have imagined. For the Admiralty knew exactly what Scheer was doing. Since nightfall, Room 40 had intercepted and successfully decoded several of Scheer's wireless messages that together made it crystal clear he was heading for Horns Reef. A number of these were summarized for Jellicoe in one single message sent at 22.41: 'German battle fleet ordered home at 9.14pm. Battlecruisers in rear. Course south-south-east-¾-east. Speed 16 knots.'[109] This report provided invaluable intelligence. When combined with the known position of the High Seas Fleet at that time, it was obvious that Scheer was ordering his fleet back by the Horns Reef route and that they would pass astern of the Grand Fleet on its southerly course. The signal was received aboard the *Iron Duke*, duly decoded and passed to Jellicoe sometime after 23.15. The key to the battle had been placed in Jellicoe's hands. If he had acted on it he could have adjusted his course to meet with Scheer off Horns Reef as the day dawned a few hours later. The results of that battle would not have been a foregone conclusion – Scheer might well have disappeared into the all-pervasive mists once more – but it would undoubtedly have been a splendid opportunity. Why did Jellicoe not use the key that had been presented to him to unlock the battle?

The main reason was that Jellicoe had developed a deep mistrust of the intelligence sent to him from the Admiralty. The fateful blunder whereby the Admiralty had informed him that the High Seas Fleet remained in harbour still rankled. But perhaps more importantly, a more recent Admiralty signal, sent at 21.58 and received by Jellicoe at 22.23, was also manifestly inaccurate. This signal claimed that the High Seas Fleet was some 8 miles to the south-west of the Grand Fleet at 21.00, when it was evidently still well to the north-west at that time. Ironically, this time the mistake did not lie with the Admiralty but with the incompetence of the German ship that had sent it. In a report transmitted to Scheer it included a grossly inaccurate estimate of the ship's position. The signal was disregarded by the Germans, who knew where they were, but when it was forwarded to Jellicoe it further undermined his wobbling faith in this kind of long-distance intelligence.

> It should be realised that implicit reliance could not be placed on intercepts. I could not assume, for instance that because the High Seas Fleet steered a course south south east ¾ east at some time between 9 and 10pm, this course would be maintained until I received information from the Admiralty to the contrary. I could not expect that any but a small proportion of Scheer's signals would be intercepted. It was only possible to get those made on 'Power'. It is easy after the event, with full knowledge from both sides, to make correct assumptions. Experience earlier in the day had shown that one might be misled if trusting too much to intercepts.[110]
>
> Admiral Sir John Jellicoe, HMS *Iron Duke*, 3rd Division, Fourth Battle Squadron

Jellicoe's negative view of the Admiralty reports was reinforced by other, more recent reports from his own ships. At around the same time as, or just after, Jellicoe received the Admiralty signal, he also received a signal sent earlier by Captain Arthur Duff aboard the *Birmingham* of the 2nd Light Cruiser Squadron, that reported sighting German battlecruisers to the north-east and following a southerly course. This signal was doubly unfortunate. What had actually been seen by the *Birmingham* were the dreadnoughts at the head of the German battle line turning to starboard to avoid the attacks of the 4th Flotilla. But this diversion only put them briefly on a southerly course. Just minutes after the sighting they reverted to a south-south-east-¾-east course, heading once again directly for Horns Reef. At 11.38 Jellicoe received a further wireless signal from Goodenough reporting the encounter with the Scouting Force: 'Have engaged enemy cruisers at 10.15 bearing west-south-west.'[111] Both these reports were timed after the intercepted German signals, which had prompted the vital communication from the Admiralty and they came from a source that had proved itself more reliable than most during the course of the battle. Not unreasonably, Jellicoe decided to back his men and he thus metaphorically cast aside the true key to success.

At first this failure, however explicable, appears to lie solely with Jellicoe. Yet on closer examination his culpability is not so clear-cut. For the Admiralty knew more than it had chosen to pass on to him. The signal it sent was largely based on a translation of Scheer's orders to his fleet issued at 21.10. Yet other evidence was also available that made it apparent that Horns Reef was his destination. At 21.06 Scheer had sent a signal, 'Commander in Chief to Airship Detachment: early morning reconnaissance at Horns Reef is urgently requested.'[112] Later it intercepted a signal sent at 22.32 ordering all destroyer flotillas to assemble by 02.00 at Horns Reef. This was not the end of the matter. A further series of German signals was intercepted and decoded as the night wore on. Many of these gave Scheer's course and position, and together they would have swept away the doubt in Jellicoe's mind.

> The lamentable part of the whole business is that had the Admiralty in
> the first place sent all the information which they had acquired when
> their 10.41 message was sent, there would have been little or no doubt
> in my mind as to the route by which Admiral Scheer intended to
> return.[113]
>
> Admiral Sir John Jellicoe, HMS *Iron Duke*, 3rd Division, Fourth Battle Squadron

This failure to make available all the evidence produced by the decoding experts of Room 40 was caused by a pervasive culture of secrecy. The civilian expert cryptographers were considered mere labourers unable to interpret the raw data that they gleaned from the German signals. Instead of being passed direct to Jellicoe, the signals went first to the Director of Operations. He was meant to sort the wheat from the chaff, but in doing so he fatally diluted and simplified the message so that the cumulative power of Scheer's signals was missed in an anodyne summary. Subsequently, the Admiralty excused this failure to forward the text of these signals by claiming that it had told Jellicoe what was happening. It could not possibly have been aware that Jellicoe no longer placed much credence in its bald statements and put far greater faith in local reports.

However, wireless signals were not the only indicators that he had to hand. In the second part of the conundrum the question arises: Why did Jellicoe not realize that the sights and sounds of battle behind him precisely delineated the course of the High Seas Fleet as it battered its way across the rear of his fleet, exactly as had been forewarned in the Admiralty signal? His scepticism of Admiralty intelligence should have been tempered by the evidence of great events occurring behind him. Yet Jellicoe could not clearly see what was happening; there was just a lot of sound and fury which might well have signified nothing. In the absence of wireless reports from the units involved identifying the presence of dreadnoughts, he felt certain that these were just clashes between the light forces of the opposing fleets.

> The evident signs of destroyer fighting in rear, at a long distance astern led me to think that our torpedo boat destroyers were in action with the enemy torpedo boat destroyers and supporting light cruisers, and I considered that the effect of such fighting would be to turn the enemy to the northward or westward, even if he had originally intended to take passage by the Horns Reef ... There was nothing to indicate that our destroyers were in action with enemy battleships.[114]
>
> Admiral Sir John Jellicoe, HMS *Iron Duke*, 3rd Division, Fourth Battle Squadron

When all things are considered, in the cold light of day, Jellicoe cannot entirely escape the blame. He certainly was not given all the information available to the Admiralty; his subordinates let him down in not providing situation reports. But he also did nothing to find out exactly what was going on behind him. He sent no signals to the destroyer flotillas enquiring who they were engaging and in what circumstances. Here perhaps Jellicoe's age counted against him. At 58 he stood on the cusp of old age. He must have been suffering to some extent from the psychological after-effects of a whole day of momentous decisions based on minimal infor-mation, under conditions of considerable discomfort, in physical danger and without any chance for real rest and recuperation. And it was not only Jellicoe who was suffering from the after-effects of a trying day. A telling

quotation attributed to Commodore William Goodenough perhaps holds
the clue to why so many otherwise competent officers failed to realize what
was going on:

> If only I had gone to my cabin, had a glass of port and quietly thought
> out what the enemy was likely to do.[115]
>
> Commodore William Goodenough, HMS *Southampton*, 2nd Light Cruiser
> Squadron

But there was no time for a relaxed contemplation of the problem. With
hindsight it is reasonably easy to work out what was happening, but for
the men who were there it was a deadly guessing game. Fatigue – the
natural concomitant of long hours of extreme concentration, tension and
suppressed fears – severely blurred their critical faculties.

> I had the first watch in the ordinary course, but became frightfully
> sleepy after the sandwiches. I hardly felt any interest in the second lot
> of firing at 11.30 and certainly made no attempt to draw any deductions
> from it. When Number One came up at midnight, I turned over to
> him and flumped down on the chart house settee (immediately below
> the bridge) to fall instantaneously into a heavy sleep. On looking back
> at it the following week it struck me what a remarkable thing that
> overbearing sleepiness was. I normally kept a standing First, so that was
> nothing to do with it. During the day I had no wearing decisions to
> make, I had received no obvious shock, nor had I done any physical
> work. There was nothing to account for it except the excitement, and
> possibly the noise of the day. I think now that this over-mastering
> mental fatigue is a factor in a prolonged sea fight that should never be
> overlooked. For the Commander-in-Chief, the Flag and Commanding
> Officers, for whom there was no escape from continuous and intense
> mental activity and responsibility for instant action, this effect may be
> expected to have been at least correspondingly powerful. It does seem to
> me that at night after a day action, the side who surprises the other may
> have from this cause alone an unexpectedly large advantage. I recall that
> round about 11pm, the Captain got a camp-stool on the bridge and sat
> down; I think sleeping with his back against the bridge screen.[116]
>
> Sub-Lieutenant Anthony de Salis, HMS *Moresby*, 13th Flotilla

By the end of the day the enervating stress of battle had been gradually displaced by the dull torpor of routine duties. As the minutes ticked by and nothing seemed to happen, it became more difficult to sustain the high level of concentration that the situation required. The dark was a natural womb where men, despite themselves, relaxed into the sag of their stretched nerves, fighting a constant battle in themselves against the dangerous opiate of sleep. Many were collecting their strength and thoughts, conjuring up all their mental reserves for the renewed battle that they felt certain would follow next morning. Some allowed themselves dreams of what might be. In such a state they were utterly confident that the 'noises off' to their rear were irrelevant to the main business that would be transacted 'come the dawn'.

> During the night, one thought of the changes that could come about after a 'Glorious First of June'. More help to our troops in France and perhaps for us more liberty, an end to the prison like existence at Scapa Flow within a floating steel fortress. It was worth fighting for, worth the risk. Maybe the navy could then be reduced in strength. All night the enemy ships had been near us to the westwards and north-westward. We did not know whether they were battleships, cruisers or both, but they were certainly doomed to be mopped up at daylight. We had them on toast! How could they possibly avoid us?[117]
>
> Petty Officer Telegraphist Arthur Brister, HMS *Iron Duke*, 3rd Division, Fourth Battle Squadron

Behind the Grand Fleet, the echoes of the gallant resistance of the 4th Flotilla were still dying away. Unfortunately, the British destroyer flotillas remained, in the main, paralysed by their responsibilities and an ignorance of the situation that faced them. The 11th Flotilla could yet have rehabilitated their fallen reputation by steering towards the battle, for they could all see the flashes of the guns and the funeral pyre left by the *Tipperary*. But they were marching to a different drum and, as Commander Hawksley intended, they merely held their station and continued to the south, saving their 'powder' for a morning confrontation. To the east of the 4th Flotilla lay the 13th Flotilla, the 9th and 10th Flotilla and the

12th Flotilla, all also intent on sticking to their southerly courses. Given the proximity of the engagements, these as yet unengaged ships could not but be aware of the repeated flare-ups of intensive action on the starboard beam, but seem to have been remarkably successful in restraining any sense of curiosity.

> Suddenly the night was split open by brilliant flashes of fire two miles on our starboard beam. We heard gunfire, several violent explosions and saw a British destroyer silhouetted in the glare of a searchlight. In the darkness, punctuated by blinding light, it was quite impossible to size up the situation and, though we had glimpses of moving ships, we could not distinguish friend from foe. We brought our guns to bear but saw no identifiable target at which to fire. In a short time the commotion subsided.[118]
>
> Sub-Lieutenant Harry Oram, HMS *Obdurate*, 13th Flotilla

Concerned with maintaining their flotilla formations, worried by the responsibility of giving away their position, terrified by the possibility of attacking their own ships; there seems to have been a collective desire to avoid a confrontation with the unknown. This was an entirely understandable perspective, but was not the attitude traditionally expected of Royal Navy officers. In this sense it is slightly disturbing to read the explicit intention of Captain James Farie, aboard the *Champion*, who led his 13th Flotilla deliberately away from the sound of gunfire.

> Heavy firing was opened on our starboard beam, apparently at some of our destroyers between the 13th Flotilla and the enemy. I hauled out to eastward as I was unable to attack with any of our own flotilla, our own forces being between me and the enemy. I then resumed course south.[119]
>
> Captain James Farie, HMS *Champion*, 13th Flotilla

His reasoning was entirely specious. Fully aware that his own forces were being attacked, he could have assisted in their desperate resistance to the German passage. As other instances demonstrated, there might have been recognition problems as the 13th Flotilla joined the fray. But such problems could have been overcome. Jellicoe had assigned the massed flotillas to the rear of the line for a purpose. Regrettably, he had not made it entirely clear what that purpose was. But Farie, in withdrawing to eastwards without incurring a single hit on his ten destroyers, missed an opportunity to launch a massed torpedo attack that could have wrought ruin on Scheer's mighty battle fleet. Ironically, such was his haste to vacate the scene, he turned to the east without signalling, while simultaneously increasing speed, and thereby lost all but two of his flotilla. Casting around, the rest of Farie's destroyers took up station behind the five destroyers that formed the 9th and 10th Flotilla under Commander Malcolm Goldsmith aboard the *Lydiard*. As the column of ships length-ened behind him, they were joined by another stray, the *Unity* from the 4th Flotilla. Goldsmith was sublimely unaware of these additions to his command and still believed he had only his original five destroyers following him. The night sky was lit by burning ships, but Goldsmith was determined to avoid what he saw as the rash mistakes made by the 4th Flotilla in attacking British ships in error.

> Fire was opened on us by a line of large ships which we took to be our own. *Champion* suddenly increased to high speed and disappeared to south. I continued south and eventually turned south west and west to get on the other side of the big ships – who still spasmodically opened fire towards us.[120]
>
> Commander Malcolm Goldsmith, HMS *Lydiard*, 9th and 10th Flotilla

For officers in the ships that followed him it must have been a frustrating experience. At 12.10 he turned his line to take up the south-westerly course that would take them right across the bows of the long line of big ships that many of them had discerned to starboard. It was at this point, as the flotillas steered directly across the front of the unrecognized German battle line, that the significance of the lengthened column became apparent. Goldsmith had judged his run across the head of the column still with only five ships in mind. In actual fact he had twelve. The result was disaster for the last two ships behind him, the *Petard* and *Turbulent*. As they crossed the line of the advancing column they were sighted by the leading ship, which of course was German, not British. The *Petard* got the treatment first.

> We sighted a dark mass about five or six points on our starboard bow, steering south-east, about 600 yards away. On looking at her closely there could be no doubt at all what she was, as at the angle we sighted

her at, we could see clearly large crane derricks silhouetted against the sky, and only German ships have these fittings. At the same moment the German battleships switched on recognition lights, consisting of two red lights over a white one. As *Petard* had fired all her torpedoes in the day attack, there was nothing we could do but get away, so we increased to full speed and altered course about a point to port to clear the enemy's stern. As soon as we had passed ahead of her, she switched her foremost group of searchlights on to us, but they just missed our stern on being switched on, though they were trained round to the right directly and then illuminated us perfectly. Immediately afterwards, we saw the flashes of the enemy's secondary armament being fired, and on the bridge we felt the ship tremble slightly, and guessed we had been hit aft. They seemed to give us another salvo, and then the second ship in the line – we could now see four – also joined in. This second salvo struck us further forward in the ship, but luckily missed the bridge and the midship guns' crew. At this moment, the foremost group of German searchlights were switched off us and trained round to port all together on to the *Turbulent*, my next astern.[121]

Lieutenant Commander Evelyn Thomson, HMS *Petard*, 13th Flotilla

The *Petard* crossed the German line just 200 yards ahead of the *Westfalen*. Behind her the unfortunate *Turbulent* was in a hopeless position. At the last moment, to avoid being rammed side-on, she turned to starboard and, as she sailed alongside the *Westfalen*, she was literally blown out of the water when her boilers exploded at 00.32. There were no survivors. The *Petard*, and probably also the *Turbulent*, had no torpedoes left after their brave attacks during the Run to the South. The conduct of the rest of Goldsmith's makeshift flotilla was spineless. Some considered the position unfavourable for attack; others felt that they could not find the German line in the smoke. Most simply did not, or affected not to, notice what was going on behind them and indeed Goldsmith only noticed the additions to his brood at 06.00. This complete lack of situational awareness was not a real excuse. The action could be clearly seen from the Fifth Battle Squadron further to the south.

Firing suddenly broke out and it was soon obvious that it was a destroyer attack on larger ships. The large ships were firing hard and a few minutes later one destroyer blew up. Then a lot of guns fired together and in the flash we saw that the large ships had cranes between the masts. I was on the bridge at this time, as this was my night station and there was a general cry of, "Hun!" The same flash illuminated the destroyers also – I could see them lying quite close to the Germans – the one that blew up was the *Turbulent* and, as I watched, the next in line, the *Petard*, was badly hit. Immediately afterwards the leading German ship put a searchlight on us – it was only on us for a few seconds, but at once he altered course right round to port, the whole line followed and were lost to sight. I don't know to this day what ships they were. We certainly thought that they were battleships, but at night-time everything is distorted in regard to size and distance and they may have been the new cruisers, which also had cranes.[122]

Sub-Lieutenant Clifford Caslon, HMS *Malaya*, Fifth Battle Squadron

To complete this disastrous tale of wholesale incompetence, Farie, in swinging round to the east, cut across the 12th Flotilla commanded by Captain Anselan Stirling, who was also forced to turn to the east to avoid the *Champion* and her two cohorts as they steamed across his path. Shortly after Stirling's ships swung round in considerable confusion, they were surprised by a strange ship breaking out of the darkness at short range.

Just before midnight I thought I observed smoke on our port bow, but after a good look through glasses none of us could make anything of it. I had a look round on the other bow and on looking to port again saw a light cruiser about two cables off coming straight at us at full speed. I at once put the helm hard-a-port and went half speed astern with the starboard engine. We just managed to get clear, which was lucky for us, as otherwise we should have gone to the bottom all right. This ship, which I think was German, came up in a cloud of smoke of her own making and was consequently difficult to make out in a second. As she passed us about 20 yards off she fired her after gun twice in the opposite direction to us (I suppose at the *Nonsuch* who was ahead of us in the line). She also switched on a searchlight but did not pick anyone up with it. We were too close to fire a torpedo at her and as she passed, she put her helm over to starboard, we being then stern on to her could not train our tubes far enough aft to get a shot.[123]

Lieutenant Commander Charles Poignand, HMS *Menace*, 12th Flotilla

The ship disappeared into the black night and the *Menace* rejoined her flotilla. The ship that the *Menace* had encountered was one of the two German ships, the *Frankfurt* and *Pillau,* which had become detached from the rest of the High Seas Fleet screen and were proceeding independently well to the port of the main column. But these were minor fish compared to the great game that was being played out further south.

Captain Farie and Commander Goldsmith had not only missed every opportunity that had been presented to them but, as the direct result of Farie's actions, the fifteen destroyers of the 12th Flotilla had also been forced away from their designated station and the scene of the action.

> Suddenly about midnight guns started astern of us, though there were actions in various directions continuously. We pushed on a little faster when bangs and crashes came our way from astern. Some enemy ships were firing salvoes of 11″ right into the flotilla from the rear. It was uncanny, and being pitch dark, I confess I hated that part of it. Several pitched abreast of us, ten yards off. Others between the *Narwhal* and me, and close round us all. Then it ceased as we got ahead.[124]
>
> Commander John Champion, HMS *Maenad*, 12th Flotilla

The references in this passage to the fact that they 'pushed on a little faster' and 'it ceased as we got ahead' succinctly convey the mental state of so many British officers when faced with the necessity of taking tough decisions to achieve a meaningful resolution of the night actions. Physically brave, they lacked both flexibility and determination. They were the weak link in Jellicoe's armour through which the High Seas Fleet had thrust almost unscathed.

Most of the barrier placed by Jellicoe across Scheer's line of retreat to Horns Reef had thus been ineffectually dispersed. The long line of dreadnoughts had succeeded in breaking right through the rear of the Grand Fleet without losing a single major ship. Two light cruisers the *Elbing* and *Rostock,* were in danger of sinking, but on the debit side five British destroyers had been sunk and a further five had been badly damaged. The resoluteness and skill demonstrated by the Germans had brought their just reward. They had achieved a miraculous escape from the position of peril to which Jellicoe's cautious manoeuvring had condemned them during the daylight exchanges. But not all of the

German ships would be returning home. The condition of the *Elbing* was deteriorating fast.

> Both engine rooms were flooded and we stopped. Guns were now free, but we knew that without engines, we would have been quickly a victim of English fire. It was very necessary to maintain port and starboard watches, but luckily no action ensued. Now a strong hawser was dragged from aft to port side over the shot-up bridge. This was a whole crew effort in complete darkness. We had to prepare a towline for the ship. And then a German torpedo boat appeared on the starboard side and came alongside – we could see in outline how deep our ship lay already.[125]
>
> Max Meier, SMS *Elbing*, II Scouting Group, High Seas Fleet

Preparations were put in hand to evacuate the ship while she was still afloat. But there was no panic or disintegration of discipline and, as Heinrich Bassenge had expected, the crew did not forget the wounded.

> The sailors came to fetch the wounded. I was supported on both sides to the middle deck and was then able to climb over from there into the S53. This was not easy as I could not use my burnt hands. The *Elbing* was very low in the water. There was lots of help to get me down the narrow ladder into the officers' wardroom. Already there were lots of wounded from the *Tipperary* and they laid me in a bunk. I gave a last look at the *Elbing* and then my eyelids were so swollen that I could not open them any more.[126]
>
> Lieutenant Heinrich Bassenge, SMS *Elbing*, II Scouting Group, High Seas Fleet

Once those unable to help themselves had been moved to safety, the rest of the crew also crammed aboard the destroyer.

> The injured were passed over and then came the call, "Muster in Divisions! Abandon ship to the torpedo boat!" We stood there on the upper deck side by side. The torpedo boat pushed off and the order came from the Bridge, "Action stations, torpedo tubes and guns!" The ship sped off at high speed into the dark night. We heard that our Commander, two other officers and one cutter crew had remained on the *Elbing*.[127]
>
> Max Meier, SMS *Elbing*, II Scouting Group, High Seas Fleet

Almost all of the *Elbing*'s crew were taken on board the *S53* in addition to nine British seamen already picked up from the *Tipperary*. Captain Madlung stayed aboard the *Elbing* with a few other key personnel to try to salvage the ship. Eventually he was forced to abandon ship and boarded a cutter. He passed through struggling survivors of *Tipperary* and lit flares to alert British destroyers to their presence. Finally this brave officer was picked up by a Dutch steamer and made his way back to Wilhelmshaven via Holland.

On other German ships the struggle to contain the damage proved fruitless. The need to maintain headway if they were ever to get home conflicted directly with the consequently increased pressure exerted by the sea on weakened and buckling bulkheads. The battlecruiser *Lützow* had been in desperate trouble even before the night began. The waves had been pouring into the forward compartments ever since two shells had penetrated her below the waterline at around 18.15.

> The ship is well down by the head, the deck at the bows is on a level
> with the water. I hear that practically the whole fore part of the ship is
> waterlogged, only one of the switch rooms there is clear of water and
> there are a number of men down there below the level of the water on
> the upper platform deck. To help them was impossible.[128]
>
> Commander Günther Paschen, SMS *Lützow*, I Scouting Group, High Seas Fleet

The crew busied themselves in damage control and in trying to exploit the minimal remaining steaming power. Maybe they would be lucky if they could only survive the night.

> The speed of the ship has been reduced to seven knots on the earnest
> representations of the first officer, but with the corresponding revolutions
> she probably only developed about five. The very low forecastle – *Lützow*
> had no upper deck forward – was now under water. More sea had got up
> from the south west and is breaking on the forecastle among the heaps of
> empty cartridge cases. We were all deadbeat, officers and men and the
> night dragged endlessly on. What of the morning?[129]
>
> Commander Günther Paschen, SMS *Lützow*, I Scouting Group, High Seas Fleet

Gradually hopes faded away as it became apparent that they had not been able to stabilize the ship. Ever more water filled the compartments below decks, internal bulkheads were one by one failing under the intolerable pressure. Inexorably, inevitably, the sea was dragging her down. The end was near.

> I always had hopes for the ship, but at midnight when the Captain called the senior officers to a conference, the Commander reported 7,500 tons of water on board and expressed his opinion that at the most we could keep afloat till 6am. The news was a dreadful blow. The noble ship; but it had to be; the bows were now two metres under water, which was pouring through the open doors of the casemates into the battery and through the torn up plating on to the middle deck. The great oil boiler rooms forward had had to be abandoned to save the men there. The draft forward was 17 metres. The Captain, who up till now had steadily steered the ship in the direction in which the fleet had last been seen, sadly gave in, to prevent the useless sacrifice of human life which would have occurred if she had not been abandoned.[130]
>
> Commander Günther Paschen, SMS *Lützow*, I Scouting Group, High Seas Fleet

Captain Harder accepted the reality of his situation and at last the order was given to abandon ship.

> Shortly after 1am came the order, "All aft!" and the four destroyers which had stayed with us were ordered alongside, aft on the starboard side. I had not recollected them and was agreeably surprised at not having to swim. As long as there was time I went round the ship with other officers and trusted ratings looking for wounded and men who were asleep. Sure enough I found one gallant fellow fast asleep on the bench in the gunnery flat. The sight in the 6″ Battery was indescribably desolate. Most of our casualties had been there. The disembarkation of the crew was carried out perfectly, first the wounded and then the rest without any trouble. As we cast off in the last boat I saw the ship in the grey light of morning; 'A' Turret under water, 'B' an island. Near the bridge the water was up to the superstructure. The stern was about two metres higher than usual. Then one of the destroyers fired a torpedo which hit amidships, whereupon the ship for a moment heeled over to starboard. It only needed a slight impact to hasten the sinking by one or two hours.[131]
>
> Commander Günther Paschen, SMS *Lützow*, I Scouting Group, High Seas Fleet

The *Lützow* finally slipped beneath the waves at about 01.45. She was one of the most modern German battlecruisers and represented an equivalent loss to the *Queen Mary*.

At roughly the same time the *Wiesbaden*, so many times sunk in the reports of optimistic British officers, finally really did succumb to her many mortal wounds. She was smashed almost to pieces, and most of her crew were already dead by the time she rolled over and sank. The few survivors took to makeshift rafts, but the unwelcoming seas sucked the life from their limbs one by one. Finally, just one remained alive of that magnificent crew, Stoker Hugo Zenne. He clung to his raft for thirty-eight hours before he was rescued by a passing Norwegian freighter. The epic last fight of the *Wiesbaden* had been a credit to the whole German Navy.

◆ ◆ ◆

By this time the High Seas Fleet had almost succeeded in passing unscathed through the British destroyers. Fortunately for the senior service, its reputation for decisive action was about to be restored. Captain Anselan Stirling, leading the 12th Flotilla aboard the *Faulknor*, was not to be deflected long from his duty by the evasive manoeuvring of Captain James Farie, which had earlier obstructed his command. At 12.15 Stirling had returned to his intended southerly course and was once again heading towards the German fleet. The vital difference was the time and place at which contact would be made. If Stirling had been left unimpeded he might have caused considerable damage in a well-co-ordinated attack launched in the thick of night across the head of the German battle line. Unfortunately, as it was, he and his flotilla neared the point of contact just as the short summer night was beginning to give way to the first signs of dawn at 01.45. It should be emphasized that although the opaque darkness was beginning to break up, visibility remained bad and there was still considerable scope for a fatal blunder by either side. As he became aware of a line of big ships ahead of him heading to the south-east, Stirling eyed up the situation. Although he could not identify them he was sure they were not British. Acting upon his convictions he ordered the 1st Division of his flotilla, led by Commander George Campbell in the *Obedient*, to attack. He also signalled to Jellicoe that he had sighted German battleships.

Enemy's battlefleet steering south-east, approximate bearing south-west. My position ten miles astern of 1st Battle Squadron.[132]

Captain Anselan Stirling, HMS *Faulknor*, 12th Flotilla

Exactly this sort of signal should have been pouring in to Jellicoe from all the destroyer flotillas throughout the night action. Had he been kept in touch with what was happening in this way, then the course of events on 1 June would have been very different. It is almost incredible to realize that Stirling was the first officer from the destroyer flotillas actually to mention that the German battleships were present. Although his positional information was inaccurate – it was more like 26 miles astern and well out on the port quarter of the First Battle Squadron – such a mistake would not have been overly important had it been just one of many such reports. In any case the key piece of information was the presence of the main body of the High Seas Fleet behind the Grand Fleet. It was all the more frustrating therefore that the signal failed to get through! Perhaps it was sent on the wrong frequency; perhaps the German tactic of jamming the signal traffic had been successful. Possibly other ships received it and failed to forward it to the *Iron Duke*, or maybe, in all the excitement, it was never actually transmitted. Whatever the reason, once again the strange mixture of fantastic opportunity and cussed bad luck that had dogged the Grand Fleet since nightfall continued to hold sway and Jellicoe was left in ignorance of what was happening behind the arras.

In accordance with Stirling's orders the 1st Division of the 12th Flotilla – the *Obedient, Mindful, Marvel* and *Onslaught* – moved off to begin their attack. Almost at once Campbell lost his prey in the misty conditions, most likely because the German line turned, although this is by no means certain. Another opportunity had slipped through British fingers. But Stirling did not let the situation rest. He ordered the 1st Division to fall in astern of him and he led the line himself. Presuming that the German line had turned away, he proceeded at full speed to the south-east so that he could get ahead of the German line and place himself in an ideal position for a torpedo attack. After a few minutes he turned 180 degrees to starboard and was rewarded with a view of the rearmost German dreadnoughts of the III Squadron, the pre-dreadnoughts of the II Squadron, the battlecruisers *Von der Tann* and *Derfflinger*, followed in turn by assorted light cruisers. When the 12th Flotilla launched their attack at 02.03, the Germans were not entirely sure whether the approaching destroyers were in fact British. The bulk of the German destroyers had spent an abortive night sweeping fruitlessly for the Grand Fleet. Many were now returning to the main body of the High Seas Fleet and there was every chance of making a dreadful mistake if proper identification was not made. As a result there was a distinct hesitation before the German battleships opened fire. Commander Barry Bingham, who had been picked up several hours earlier after the sinking of the *Nestor*, was aboard one of the German destroyers and he had distinctly mixed emotions as he sought to interpret events from his rather restricted perspective as a prisoner of war.

> I began to reflect about the immediate future. How was it all going to end? Assuming that the British sank this German torpedo boat destroyer – an eventuality one's patriotism demanded and thoroughly expected, because she was one of an old type and no kind of match for any of our destroyers – should we pull through, after a scuffle with the sentry, another bath in the North Sea, and, with the remote chance of being picked up by a British destroyer in the dark? Probably not. On the other hand, if the German destroyer came through unscathed, one would emerge from the business with a whole skin, with a certainty of a dreary spell of captivity, but with the hope of serving under the White Ensign at a future date. And so the long drawn torture of this ghastly night crept on until the first tinge of dawn found its way into the cabin.[133]
>
> Commander Barry Bingham, HMS *Nestor*, 13th Flotilla

Aboard the *Onslaught*, Able Seaman George Wainford was ready to spring into instantaneous action as the lithe British destroyers raced in to the attack.

> My job as a torpedoman was to load the torpedoes into the tubes. There was a sort of derrick with a little chain on it. You lift it up and you pushed it in, made certain that the warhead was on correctly and then the chief petty officer he'd do the actual firing. You had to get a direct bearing on the ship with a direction finder – you had to get the speed of your enemy, your own speed, the angle of the enemy, your angle – all coinciding before you fired. He did all that. There was a

pistol grip there and it used to detonate a charge, which blew the
torpedo out into the water and then the propeller started.[134]

Able Seaman George Wainford, HMS *Onslaught*, 12th Flotilla

Another torpedoman, Fred Knight, was on the after deck torpedo-tubes
aboard the *Onslaught*.

We went straight in to attack. It was fast breaking daylight. We carried
four 21″ torpedoes which were all fired – one hitting the third ship in the
line at a range of 1,000 yards. As we moved swiftly away, the German
light cruisers which had failed to spot us making the attack opened fire.[135]

Able Seaman Fred Knight, HMS *Onslaught*, 12th Flotilla

Finally the British destroyers revealed their true worth. As well as the
Onslaught, the *Faulknor*, *Obedient* and *Marvel* all fired two or four torpedoes,
totalling some twelve in all, from a range of about 2,000 yards before
swiftly turning away. They were the most modern type of destroyer, each
fitted with four torpedo-tubes arranged in double tubes on the centre line,
which meant that all four torpedoes could be fired simultaneously if the
opportunity arose. The torpedoes caused chaos in the German line, which
was forced to turn some 6 points away to starboard. Individual ships
desperately manoeuvred to evade the onrushing torpedoes that combed
the line searching for victims. One actually ran underneath the *Grosser
Kurfürst*, another self-detonated as it passed through the line and there were
numerous close shaves. In the end, despite all Stirling's efforts, only two
torpedoes struck home, but they had a devastating effect as they both hit
the pre-dreadnought *Pommern* at approximately 02.10. The magazine was
breached and she blew up in an instantly devastating explosion, killing
all 844 members of her crew. The blast could be heard miles away.

Having laid down on a wardroom settee, I was awoken at about 2.30
by a loud crash, just like that caused by a large armoured hatch being
dropped. I later heard that this was the time of a successful torpedo
attack on a German battleship.[136]

Lieutenant Patrick Lawder, HMS *Benbow*, 4th Division, Fourth Battle Squadron

Once doubts over the identity of these mystery destroyers had been erased
from their minds, the Germans reacted to the attack with their customary

efficiency. Searchlights flared out and guns opened fire all along the line. The attacking British destroyers were partially covered by a self-generated smoke-screen but the *Onslaught*, as the last in the line, gave the Germans more time to react and they hit her hard.

> We fired our torpedoes and of course other ships in the flotilla did the same and there was a terrific explosion and a German ship blew up. "Cor!" I said. "We got her!" And the moment I said that either one shell or a salvo hit our bridge. There was a terrific bang, a fire started the port side of the foc'sle where all the hammocks underneath the foc'sle deck were stowed. [137]
>
> Able Seaman George Wainford, HMS *Onslaught*, 12th Flotilla

The German shells raked across the destroyer, once again concentrating on the area of the bridge to considerable effect.

> They swept the ship with salvoes. One struck the bridge killing all the officers and ratings, setting the bridge on fire. The ship was left helpless until she could be brought steady by the after steering gear. The bridge was shot away – a tangled mass. [138]
>
> Able Seaman Fred Knight, HMS *Onslaught*, 12th Flotilla

The directing minds of the *Onslaught* were blown away in a veritable whirl-wind of shot and shell.

> Shell burst against the port side of the charthouse and forebridge igniting a box of cordite, causing a fire in the charthouse, completely wrecking the forebridge and destroying nearly all navigational instruments, At the time there were on the forebridge: the Captain, First Lieutenant, torpedo coxswain, two quartermasters and both signalmen, and the gunner on his way up the bridge ladder. I had just been sent down to tell the engine room to make black smoke, in order to screen our movements, and had only got to the bottom of the ladder from the forecastle deck to the upper deck. I went back to the bridge and, finding everything wrecked, the Captain mortally wounded and the First Lieutenant killed, I assumed command and gave orders for the after steering position to be connected, which was done very smartly. [139]
>
> Sub-Lieutenant Harry Kemmis, HMS *Onslaught*, 12th Flotilla

For Wainford, a youthful sailor, it was a bewildering situation. But the calm assumption of command by their inexperienced sub-lieutenant soon brought the situation back under control.

We could hear a lot of crying and talking and shouting on the foc'sle end so I went to go up there. Sub-Lieutenant Kemmis was there, he said, "Where are you going, Wainford?" I said, "On the foc'sle, Sir, to help!" He said, "Keep down below out of it, find something else to do!" I thought, "I wonder why he said that?" I found out later the forr'ard 4″ gun had had in a direct hit, they were all killed and injured. The commanding officer was killed, the Lieutenant was killed, the warrant officer was killed – that was the three officers. I think the coxswain at the wheel was killed and there were several more wounded. It was a bit of a shambles really. I saw one chap, it was horrible, his whole stomach was torn open, it was all hanging out and he was trying to push it back – and that's why I was told to keep out of it. Sub-Lieutenant Kemmis said, "Get down below and send a senior hand up here!"[140]

Able Seaman George Wainford, HMS *Onslaught*, 12th Flotilla

It was left to older, more experienced hands to collect the bodies.

We collected the dead and wounded. The Captain, Lieutenant Commander C R Onslow, was still alive but died a short time after. There was not much left of the others on the bridge which was put in sacks.[141]

Able Seaman Fred Knight, HMS *Onslaught*, 12th Flotilla

The valiant Onslow was taken below decks, where young Wainford witnessed his final moments and his unbearably poignant last words.

The skipper died in the crew's foc'sle, on the mess table. They laid him on there. I'll always remember his last words, he said, "Is the ship all right?" I said, "Yes, Sir, the ship's all right!" He said, "I'll have a little sleep now then ..." And that was it. I was there when he died.[142]

Able Seaman George Wainford, HMS *Onslaught*, 12th Flotilla

Led by Commander John Champion aboard the *Maenad*, the 2nd Division of the 12th Flotilla, comprising the *Narwhal*, *Nessus* and *Noble*, followed the 1st Division into the attack. Unfortunately, the *Maenad* was caught out by the 180 degree turn. Her torpedoes were trained to starboard and as she swung them round she delayed her turn. By the time she was ready her good companions had left her behind. Despite this misfortune, the *Maenad* soon made amends for her error by pressing on with a series of lone attacks on the German line.

> We dashed ahead to get ready to attack them. I got separated from the others and attacked three times about 2.15am. Just before 2.30, one of our torpedoes blew up the fourth ship of the line, 1,000 feet high, just like the *Defence*. There is no doubt about one and everything points to there having been two sunk. Anyhow, I claim one and at the very least the 12th Flotilla got one between them. Of course in these attacks we were fired at. Shots just short and just over and certainly between the funnels and the bridge. We bore charmed lives, it is a miracle and nothing less.[143]
>
> Commander John Champion, HMS *Maenad*, 12th Flotilla

There is considerable confusion over the fate of the torpedoes fired in this attack and it seems likely that the explosion claimed as proof of success was in fact the explosion of the unlucky *Pommern*. Ahead of the *Maenad*, the other ships of the 2nd Division also went into the attack. Unfortunately, they did not escape the reprisals of the now fully alerted German gunners. The *Nessus* was badly damaged as the others swung round for their attack run.

> I saw a line of enemy battleships on the port bow. They opened fire and almost at once we were hit by a 5.9″ shell which struck the base of the foremast cutting it in two, blowing the galley to bits, killing two officers and five ratings and wounding a further eight ratings. For a moment, from my post at the after 4″ gun I thought the foremost gun had fired, then I saw the foremast swaying and realised we had been hit. All communications to the bridge were cut so we had no information until wounded began to arrive aft. Luckily I had some first aid training so got them down in the wardroom and got busy with the first aid bags. I sent one of my gun crew to tell the Doctor, he returned to say he couldn't find him, it was not until I sent a Petty Officer forward that I found out the Doctor had been killed. Our two

worst cases were a young Ordinary Seaman who had a piece of shell
in his head which I was quite unqualified to remove and an Able
Seaman with one shoulder completely shattered. We did our best –
I was most ably assisted by our Coxswain when he was able to leave
the wheel – but we were badly handicapped as we dare not give
morphia at that time supplied in large bottles. Though I found the
Doctor's syringe, a search of his medical books failed to produce the
answer to the problem of how much to give. I was afraid of giving an
overdose.[144]

Sub-Lieutenant Eric Lees, HMS *Nessus*, 12th Flotilla

With dawn fast breaking, the 3rd Division of the 12th Flotilla was badly
disrupted in its attempted attack. The confusion caused by the first two
divisions returning in natural disorder from their torpedo runs was
exacerbated by the close attention of the German light cruisers at the
rear of the German line.

Suddenly we sighted some large ships on the starboard bow, but very
indistinctly. They proved to be some enemy ships and our leading
division, which was some way ahead of us, turned to starboard to attack
them and fired torpedoes. Before we had got to the turning point, they
were discovered and scattered, coming back at full speed in our direction
and in turn were being heavily shelled. By the time it was time for us to
turn, the leading boats of the line were coming back again and the boat
ahead of us and all others following had to turn the other way to avoid
collision. So none of us got a shot in.[145]

Lieutenant Commander Charles Poignand, HMS *Menace*, 12th Flotilla

Nevertheless, Stirling had succeeded in launching a deliberate and
determined attack on the German line, in contrast to the weak leadership
of the 11th, the 9th and 10th, and 13th Flotillas and the brave, but reactive
rather than proactive, responses of the 4th Flotilla. It was hence doubly
unfortunate that he was forced to attack from a less advantageous
position without the 'benefit' of night cover and that the Germans
skilfully managed to avoid most of the torpedoes that were fired. More
pertinently, Stirling too was let down by the lack of initiative shown by
many of his subordinates, who allowed themselves to be thwarted

by every mishap that occurred while manoeuvring in the presence of the enemy. No fewer than seven of Stirling's fifteen destroyers failed to fire any torpedoes.

There was just one last throw of the dice – and it came from an unexpected quarter. Further to the east Captain James Farie, in the light cruiser *Champion*, was still ploughing a lonely furrow on a south-easterly course, accompanied only by the *Obdurate* and *Moresby*. When they heard the sound of the 12th Flotilla attack they turned westwards and fell in with the *Marksman* and *Maenad*, which by then had lost touch with the bulk of the 12th Flotilla. At around 02.34, this motley collection of destroyers sighted four undoubted German battleships, clearly identified as *Deutschland* pre-dreadnought class, to the west of them at a range of around 4,000 yards.

> At 2.30am, we caught a glimpse of four large shadowy shapes looming
> against the still dark western horizon. *Champion*, thinking we had
> overtaken the rear ships of the Grand Fleet, turned away to avoid
> confusion. *Moresby*, our next astern, was not so sure, and, continuing
> on a closing course, identified four *Deutschland* class battleships.[146]
>
> Sub-Lieutenant Harry Oram, HMS *Obdurate*, 13th Flotilla

In the circumstances, Captain Farie's reaction was incomprehensible unless he truly believed this was the rear of the Grand Fleet, for he turned sharply away to the east. But to his credit, Lieutenant Commander Roger Alison of the *Moresby*, recognizing the opportunity that lay before him, turned out of line and at 02.37 fired a torpedo at the German ships. His initiative was partially rewarded as he scored a hit on the German destroyer *V4*. Her bow was blown clean off and she quickly sank, although accompanying destroyers rescued all but seventeen of her crew. But she was not the target that Alison had aimed at, nor the victim he craved. The last chance to strike at the German capital ships had been missed.

◆ ◆ ◆

The full onset of dawn at around 03.00 on 1 June was a relief for the tired watch keepers of the Grand Fleet. The stresses and strains of the night were alleviated by the chance to see what was going on around them.

Growing daylight revealed a cheerless morning of lowering clouds and the beginnings of a freshening wind. The visibility was poor, barely two miles, and our grey surroundings were reflected in the strained faces of the gun's crew as they flapped duffel coated arms to drive out the chill. Night action is an unnerving experience and although we had not been personally involved we had had ample evidence that swift and terrible events could have engulfed us at any moment. Our eyes were bloodshot with the strain of peering into the darkness and it was a relief to feel that now there would be some warning, however brief, of threatening onslaught. Twelve hours of tension had been wearing and wearying and though not dispirited we viewed the coming day with sombre sobriety.[147]

Sub-Lieutenant Harry Oram, HMS *Obdurate*, 13th Flotilla

Unknown to the British, Scheer had already escaped, and indeed by 03.30 the main body of the High Seas Fleet had reached the Horns Reef entrance to the Heligoland minefield. Jellicoe himself, in common with the bulk of his fleet, was still under the misapprehension that the High Seas Fleet was located to the west of the Grand Fleet. In the absence of concrete information as to the whereabouts of the High Seas Fleet, it had been his intention to reverse course to the north and drive back towards Horns Reef at 02.00. Unfortunately, despite their best intentions, the Grand Fleet were not all together in a compact formation.

The weather was misty and the visibility even less than on May 31st, being only some three or four miles, and I considered it desirable under these conditions, and in view of the fact that I was not in touch with either my cruisers or destroyers, to form single line, accepting the danger of submarine attack on a long line in order to be ready for the enemy's Battle Fleet, if suddenly sighted. The 6th Division of the Battle Fleet was not in sight at daylight, having dropped astern owing to the reduction in speed of the *Marlborough*.[148]

Admiral Sir John Jellicoe, HMS *Iron Duke*, 3rd Division, Fourth Battle Squadron

At 02.22 Jellicoe ordered all the various detached elements of the fleet to close up with the main body and at 02.39 he altered course to the north and formed a single battle line less the trailing 6th Division. But bereft of their screens, the dreadnoughts of the Grand Fleet were clearly not ready for action. His cruisers and destroyers had been scattered to the winds by the events of the night and Jellicoe hesitated to face the High Seas Fleet without them. The Grand Fleet was also fully aware that its movements were being observed from the skies.

At dawn the next morning, which was calm, sunny and misty, our division: *Marlborough, Revenge, Hercules* and ourselves were entirely on our own. The *Marlborough*'s torpedo damage had reduced her speed and we had lost touch with the Fleet. Admiral Sir Cecil Burney then shifted his flag to the *Revenge* by a light cruiser taking his staff with him, and the *Marlborough* returned to Rosyth. Shortly after this, still in the early daylight hours, we sighted a Zeppelin and, as besides having my turret, I was the anti-aircraft officer, I quickly manned our only anti-aircraft gun, a 12 pdr high angle gun. Its maximum range was about 8,000 or 9,000 yards. Nevertheless, we cheerfully engaged the airship which was probably eight or nine miles away, but it gave us something to do – and something to laugh at. Nothing daunted, the *Revenge* opened fire with her 15" guns at maximum elevation.[149]

Lieutenant Angus Cunninghame Graham, HMS *Agincourt*, 6th Division, First Battle Squadron

The sight of the enemy, however distant, was clearly too tempting; like their contemporaries in the infantry on the Western Front, the sight of an enemy flying machine brought out the sporting instinct of many gunnery officers. Yet such a salvo of huge 15-inch shells was very different from a quick fusillade of rifle fire over a parapet. What goes up must come down.

Just after dawn broke, when the whole horizon was clear, not a sign of an enemy anywhere, and suddenly out of the sky dropped a salvo of shell, about a mile from us. The Captain shouted, "Where are they? Where are they?" We learnt much later that it was merely the *Revenge*, who some 15 miles away, had fired at a Zeppelin![150]

Sub-Lieutenant Clifford Caslon, HMS *Malaya*, Fifth Battle Squadron

Traversing the heavens, in the clear light of dawn, the German airship was seen by most of the ships in the main body of the fleet and they too opened fire.

During the early hours of June 1st, a Zeppelin was sighted and we fired our 13.5″ guns at her. The guns were, I believe, loaded with armour piercing lyddite and were reloaded with shrapnel shells. None of this firing had any effect on the Zeppelin, which I heard was out of range in any case – our gunners were in fact 'bumping' their guns at extreme elevation to try and get an extra degree or so of elevation. However it was one way of unloading the guns.[151]

Boy 1st Class David Frost, HMS *Conqueror*, 2nd Division, Second Battle Squadron

Like holidaymakers swatting at a noisy fly, ship after ship relieved their frustration by firing at the insolent Zeppelin above them.

A Zeppelin hove in sight and evidently reported our position to the German Fleet. The 'Zepp' was about 18,000 yards away and fairly high up. *Benbow* presented him with a 13.5″ projectile and a salvo of 6″. *Royal Oak* gave him eight 15″. You should have seen him run when these little trifles came near him.'[152]

Assistant Paymaster Noel Wright, HMS *Benbow*, 4th Division, Fourth Battle Squadron

In the excitement of the moment, even the august *Iron Duke* could not resist joining in the 'fun'.

We closed up for an hour or so when a Zeppelin appeared on the port quarter the *Superb* firing 12″ at her! We almost immediately altered course to starboard presumably to mislead the 'Zepp' as to our course and the *Iron Duke* fired a few 13.5″ at her. She was a ripping sight in the growing light and seemed quite effortless and disinterested, however she shoved off immediately we fired – not because of the firing. I presume because she was a long way off (20,000) and we fired more or less blindly for effect. Now of course all hope of smashing the devils was gone and apparently they would have run into our open arms if the bloody 'Zepp' hadn't come and even then if the *Campania* had not disappeared and lost herself we should still have been able to know their whereabouts by aeroplane.[153]

Midshipman Arthur James, HMS *Royal Oak*, 3rd Division, Fourth Battle Squadron

The Zeppelin, *L11*, was one of those ordered out by Scheer to reconnoitre the approaches to Horns Reef.

The enemy opened fire on the airship from all the vessels with anti-
aircraft guns and guns of every calibre. The great turrets fired
broadsides; the rounds followed each other rapidly. The flash from the
muzzles of the guns could be seen although the ships were hidden by
the smoke. All the ships that came in view took up the firing with the
greatest energy, so that L11 was sometimes exposed to fire from 21 large
and numbers of small ships. Although the firing did not take effect, that
and the shrapnel bursting all around so shook the ship's frame that it
seemed advisable to take steps to increase the range.[154]

Commander Victor Schulze, Zeppelin *L11*

At around 03.45, there was a last spasm of action. The four destroyers
that had picked up the *Lutzow's* crew ran straight into Captain James Farie
and his ramshackle group of British destroyers, who were thus given one
last chance to redeem themselves.

We were galvanised by the sight of four German torpedo boats
emerging out of the pallid mist about one and a half miles away
steering an opposite course. The enemy was on the alert and both sides
opened fire simultaneously. I well remember the exhilaration of this
sudden action. The crew drilled with the precision of automata and the
gun grew hot as we pumped out shells in rapid succession. Over and
above the cacophony, I heard the Signalman's shrill warning, "Torpedo
on port bow!" and caught sight of a faint line disfiguring the sea. As we
heeled under helm, I ran to the bow and, fascinated by this deadly
menace, watched the bubbling track streak close ahead of our stem and
run away to limbo. *Champion* too had taken avoiding action and by the
time we had braced up to resume action the enemy had disengaged and
moved beyond our visibility.[155]

Sub-Lieutenant Harry Oram, HMS *Obdurate*, 13th Flotilla

Lieutenant de Salis was so deeply asleep that he had not woken during
the earlier torpedo attack made by the *Moresby*. Now he found his slumbers brought to a rude conclusion.

I was woken up at about 3.30am by the ringing of the general alarm
bells. I went up on the bridge to find that it was daylight and that two
small German destroyers were coming down past us on our starboard

side. We were in single line ahead with the *Champion* leading the line.
We opened fire as they passed and they replied; but ineffectually. We did
not turn and follow.[156]

Sub-Lieutenant Anthony de Salis, HMS *Moresby*, 13th Flotilla

Later, de Salis recognized the enormous difficulty of controlling the ship's
fire in such a brief encounter.

I remember thinking what a frightful effort it was to spot the fall of shot.
Our control arrangements were simple – a voicepipe to the guns – so
that the gun control officer (me) had to judge the range and allow the
rate correction in his head, subtracting it from his spotting correction
before ordering the latter. We got a clock and dumaresq later on and
I remember the opposition put up to them by conservative destroyer
officers who were, above everything for 'simplicity'. In this sentiment
I had, up till then, agreed completely – but I gradually came to see
after this that the kind of simplicity required is simplicity of operation,
not simplicity of gear. Intrinsic complication in some machine or other
doesn't matter a bit, provided the thing works, if it will only make
matters simpler for the man who has got to work it.[157]

Sub-Lieutenant Anthony de Salis, HMS *Moresby*, 13th Flotilla

Captain Farie, consistent at least in his responses to such opportunities,
did not attempt to pursue the four destroyers. His prey was more tempting
than was immediately apparent, for the destroyers were packed with an
invaluable human cargo of over 1,000 of the rescued crew of the *Lützow*.

Two torpedoes were fired at *Champion*, the first one passing under our
bows, the second just missing close astern. Enemy passed on opposite
course and when ship had been steadied after avoiding torpedoes, the
enemy had disappeared in the mist, and I resumed my same course.[158]

Captain James Farie, HMS *Champion*, 13th Flotilla

Rather than pursuit, Farie was far more intent on gathering together his
errant flock of destroyers which, despite his best efforts to keep them out
of action, had managed to spread themselves across the ocean.

The cherished hopes of the British battle fleet for a decisive confrontation with the High Seas Fleet were fast fading. Then at about 04.00 the

final blow fell. Jellicoe received a signal from the Admiralty informing him that at 02.30 the High Seas Fleet had been just 17 miles from Horns Reef. This truly marked the end of all the hopes and dreams of a real '*Der Tag*' on 1 June, for this unambiguous intelligence indicated that, by the time it was received, the Germans must already have reached the safety within the Horns Reef channel back to port. There was no chance of over-hauling them: the battle of Jutland was over.

On reaching Horns Reef, Scheer subsequently pretended that he seriously considered renewing the battle, but his own summary of the situation exposes such thoughts as a mere fantasy.

> From the main fleet itself no signs of the enemy were visible at daybreak. The weather was so thick that the full length of a squadron could not be made out. In our opinion the ships in a south-westerly direction as reported by L 11 could only just have come from the Channel to try, on hearing the news of the battle, to join up with their main fleet and advance against us. There was no occasion for us to shun an encounter with this group, but owing to the slight chance of meeting on account of visibility conditions, it would have been a mistake to have followed them. Added to this the reports received from the battle-cruisers showed that Scouting Division I would not be capable of sustaining a serious fight, besides which the leading ships of Squadron III could not have fought for any length of time, owing to the reduction in their supply of munitions by the long spell of firing. The *Frankfurt*, *Pillau* and *Regensburg* were the only fast light cruisers now available, and in such misty weather there was no depending on aerial reconnaissance. There was, therefore, no certain prospect of defeating the enemy reported in the south. An encounter and the consequences thereof had to be left to chance. I therefore abandoned the idea of further operations and ordered the return to port.[159]
>
> Admiral Reinhard Scheer, SMS *Friedrich der Grosse*, III Battle Squadron, High Seas Fleet

The only remaining chance for the British to cause significant damage to the High Seas Fleet lay with their submarines on their regular patrol off Horns Reef and with the new minefield laid by the fast minelayer *Abdiel*. Unfortunately, the operational orders of the submarines, designed to ensure the safety of the Grand Fleet from an accidental attack, hamstrung them to the point of irrelevance. The *E55*, *E26* and *D1* had been despatched from Harwich on 30 May and reached Horns Reef well in time to intercept the High Seas Fleet on the morning of 1 June. Unfortunately, they had been ordered to stay on the bottom until 2 June. Unable in the murky deep to receive any wireless signals, they consequently had no means of knowing that a battle was under way. As they dutifully remained dormant on the bottom, the German dreadnoughts passed over them and their golden chance to redress the balance of losses in the British favour evaporated. Meanwhile, the *Abdiel* reached the Horns Reef at 01.24 and swiftly laid down a line of some eighty mines in just half an hour. At 05.20, as the German dreadnoughts filed past, the *Ostfriesland*, bringing up the rear of the leading I Battle Squadron, struck a mine on her starboard side. The blast was enormous, causing severe damage but failing to penetrate the torpedo bulkhead. Once again the high quality of watertight compartmentation in German ships proved its value and she was soon able to take up station at the rear of the II Battle Squadron pre-dreadnoughts and continued to be able to make some 15 knots.

> The *Ostfriesland*, at 5.30am, struck a mine, one that evidently belonged to a hitherto unknown and recently laid enemy minefield. The damage was slight; the vessel shipped 400 tons of water, but her means of navigation did not suffer, and she was able to run into harbour under her own steam. I signalled, 'Keep on.' The last ships passed through the area without coming across further mines.[160]
>
> Admiral Reinhard Scheer, SMS *Friedrich der Grosse*, III Battle Squadron, High Seas Fleet

Once again Scheer's luck held and, for all Jellicoe's foresight, his failsafe had failed. Perversely, it even seems that the *Ostfriesland* had not in fact struck one of the newly laid mines, but a mine laid by the *Abdiel* on a previous mission almost a month earlier on 4 May.

The bulk of the High Seas Fleet steamed safely back into harbour between 13.00 and 14.45 in the afternoon of 1 June. Many of the crew were simply worn out and too tired to care what was going on around them.

On 1st June we went back to the harbour with *Von der Tann* to receive
hot coffee and food. Like many of my comrades I did not take them.
We lay down on the floor in a corner of the ship, we did not care where
and went to sleep as we had had no sleep for 48 hours.[161]

Seaman Carl Melms, SMS *Von der Tann*, I Scouting Group, High Seas Fleet

The worst injured of all of the German ships still left struggling back
to harbour was undoubtedly the *Seydlitz*. She had managed to rejoin the
High Seas Fleet at 06.00, but was soon once again lagging far behind the
fleet. Her survival was extremely important to the German Navy. It would
take no less than three years to build a battlecruiser from scratch, but only
a few months to repair her, if only she could be got safely back into
harbour. Ignoring their physical and mental exhaustion, her crew fought
desperately hard to save her. The once proud ship was in deep, deep
trouble.

At dawn, neither the Horns Reef light vessel nor any other ship was in
sight. Suddenly our stern wave rose high, a sign of shallow water. Before
my order "Full speed astern" could take effect our bows scraped over the
sea bottom, but soon the water became deeper again. A buoy gave us our
position, and at the lightship we got in touch with the rest of our fleet,
the light cruiser SMS *Pillau* being detached to pilot us to the Jade river.
Now a dogged fight to save the vessel began. The entire forecastle was
riddled like a sieve. Through rents, holes, leaky seams and rivets, water
entered one room after the other until only the forward torpedo flat
could be held. This big "swimming bladder" gave the forward part of the
ship just enough buoyancy. But she was so much down by the bows that
the sea started getting into the forward casemates. Their covers were
destroyed or bent, and the wood for shoring up leaks was somewhere
under the forecastle. We used everything we could lay our hands on, mess
tables, benches, eventually even the empty shelves from the shell-rooms to
the dismay of the head gunner. Quite a number of compartments had to
be kept clear by incessant bailing over a period of two days. Some
bulkheads had to be watched carefully and shored up again from time to
time. The whole ship's company was kept busy, and so sleep was possible
only in snatches. Late on June 1, pump steamers arrived but so also did a
stiff breeze from the north-west. We were off Heligoland then, with a list

of eight degrees and very little stability, and could proceed at no more than three or four knots whether going ahead bows first or stern first, which we did part of the time. When seas started breaking over the waist, the *Pillau* made a lee on our starboard bow, and a tug laid an oil-slick. That helped until the wind abated. We could not have stood a heavy gale. On June 2, we anchored near the Jade light vessel to wait for the tide, for we drew 47½ feet forward against 30 feet amidships under normal conditions. But we made it and arrived in the early morning of June 3 off Wilhelmshaven locks, where we were welcomed by hurrahs from the crews of the battleships anchored there.[162]

Kapitän zur See Moritz von Egidy, SMS *Seydlitz*, I Scouting Group, High Seas Fleet

During the battle, the *Seydlitz* had been hit by no fewer than twenty-one heavy shells and one torpedo, lost ninety-eight men killed and fifty-five injured, and had four main and two secondary armament guns put out of action. The British had missed their opportunity and the *Seydlitz* would return to the fray. In less than four months she was once more ready for action.

It was immediately apparent that, against all the odds, the German eagle had managed to pluck the British lion's beard with its talons and escape with its life. But more than that, as Admiral Scheer weighed the early assessments of the British losses and carefully counted his own, he realized that they had plenty of firm grounds for claiming a German victory. As the euphoria of his perceived 'triumph' banished lingering fatigue, he ordered champagne to be served on the bridge of his flagship and prepared to give his version of events to the world.

CHAPTER SEVEN

AFTER THE BATTLE

THE AFTERMATH OF any major battle is always grim. The Admiralty may not have covered itself in glory in the manner of its interpretation and dissemination of intelligence carefully gathered by Room 40; it may have been unduly cautious in the handling of the Harwich Force – but it certainly knew how to prepare for inevitable casualties. As soon as it realized that a major fleet action was imminent, the Admiralty swung into action and implemented long-standing arrangements for the reception of the wounded all along the east coast. The hospital ships were brought to full readiness while the battle was still under way.

> This evening after dinner two or three officers arrived on board with notebooks etc to find out what accommodation we had got for wounded, how many cots, how many stretchers, etc. and later on we got a signal to get full steam going, so as to sail at a moment's notice. It really looked as if there was going to be some work at last. We were very busy in the wards getting dressings etc ready.[1]
>
> Naval Nursing Sister Mary Clarke, HM Hospital Ship *Plassy*, Rosyth

Looking further ahead, macabrely, the grim task of coffin making also started. Shipwright Charles Petty was aboard the old battleship HMS *Victorious*, which had been converted into a floating workshop for the dockyard staff at Scapa Flow. It was to be a night that he would never forget:

> My memory of the Battle of Jutland is centred on a gruesome task upon which I was engaged all through the night which followed the battle. Several warships were returning to Scapa Flow damaged in the battle and with dead sailors aboard who were to be buried ashore. I forget the exact number but I believe that we made about 200 coffins that night. Fortunately, there was a good stock of yellow pine boards and other suitable items aboard the *Victorious*. The Shipwrights and joiners made

the coffins, which were passed on to the blacksmiths and fitters who made the handles. Other tradesmen and skilled labourers lined the coffins with some white material padded with oakum, and finally painted them with black paint and fitted brass name plates on the coffin lids. It was a frantic night's work, which went on until the morning, when all the coffins were assembled on the quarterdeck to await shipment to the ships which needed them – a saddening sight![2]

Shipwright Charles Petty, HMS *Victorious*, Scapa Flow

At the break of day on 1 June, the nurses of the *Plassy* were waiting in a state of tension as the lack of news through the night fuelled their natural trepidation as to the scale of the horrors they might have to face when the ships returned to harbour.

This morning we have been busy preparing. We got all our old patients shifted into one ward so as to leave the rest free. It has been a weird sort of day, waiting about the whole time and afraid to settle to anything for fear of any sudden news. This afternoon it has been raining in torrents, almost tropical, which did not tend to cheer us up. It seems almost certain that there has been a fight of some sort, but where, and how severe, no one knows.[3]

Naval Nursing Sister Mary Clarke, HM Hospital Ship *Plassy*, Rosyth

All they could do was wait until the fleet came home.

It was not only the fate of the human casualties that caused concern in the immediate aftermath of the battle. There was also the question of the severely damaged ships that had to be brought safe home to harbour. Nelson's last order at the battle of Trafalgar, sadly ignored by his grieving subordinates, was for his fleet to anchor to protect his ships and their hard-won prizes from an imminent storm. He was not there to enforce it and consequently when the storm broke next day, it was a terrible and often fruitless struggle to keep the damaged ships afloat. The battle of Jutland had failed to live up to anticipations. But, in the aftermath at least, there was a sad echo of Trafalgar in the eternal battle against the power of the waves which could rival the destructive capacity of any weapons system.

Several of the British ships had been left in a dire condition that left them acutely vulnerable as the weather gradually freshened and the waves tossed higher.

The most immediate problems were faced by the destroyers which had been damaged in the desperate close-quarter night actions. As the action moved on, the crews often found themselves dealing with severe fires, paradoxically while at the same time trying to hold back the all encroaching waves flooding through the holes torn in their sides. They were unable to make much headway, and their crews were all too aware that hundreds of miles of open seas lay between them and the sanctuary of their home ports. As the emotional backlash of the battle struck home, many men were sickened by the contrast between the romantic ideal so assiduously peddled of naval battle and the grim reality that faced them as daylight illuminated the full extent of the horrors that surrounded them.

Aboard the destroyer *Broke*, raked first by German gunfire and then in collision with the *Sparrowhawk*, men gazed around them in stunned disbelief.

> When we could see and I had time to think it dawned on me what a terrible scene had been enacted. We thought of the 'Honour' and 'Glory', which so many people in their ignorance say is attached to warfare. You should have seen the decks of HMS *Broke* at 4am, June 1st, 1916. There you would have seen an exhibition of the 'Honour' and 'Glory' in reality. Forty-eight of our crew lay dead and most of them shattered beyond recognition; another forty were wounded very badly. We were about five hours finding all of our dead chums, dragging them out of the wrecked messdeck and throwing their bodies over the side to be buried in the deep ocean. That was the 'Honour' and 'Glory' we had. It strikes you as being one gigantic murder. You wonder how men can have the audacity, for if we stopped to think what we were going to do we should never fight at all.[4]
>
> Telegraphist J. J. R. Croad, HMS *Broke*, 4th Flotilla

Whatever their disillusionment, they knew it was their duty was to get the crippled wreck back to 'Blighty'. Although under way, the *Broke* was in serious trouble and initially it seemed a fruitless task as the very elements seemed to conspire against them.

At 6.50am, the sea increased from the dead calm state which it had been in from the commencement of the action to a terrible fury and it seemed impossible for her to get back. The wounded were suffering terrible agonies, they could not be kept still owing to the roll of the ship, neither could they have their wounds dressed there only being one Sick Bay Attendant to attend all of them, name of Mr Pridmore who did splendid work although single handed. The Doctor was killed while in the sick bay. We could not steer any definite course, as the ship could not steam head to sea, had we done so the sea being so rough would have driven our bulkhead which was made of ⅜″ steel.[5]

Telegraphist J. J. R. Croad, HMS *Broke*, 4th Flotilla

The growing power of the wind and the waves thwarted their attempts to steer directly for home. Like a staggering drunk, they could not control their movements against the greater forces that pushed and pulled them in the direction nature had selected.

Our next difficulty was the weather, which came on from the south west driving us north as we could not head the seas and when we had headed her nicely for Scapa, the wind hauled round to the north west and blew hard with a heavy swell. That defeated us and we had to alter to the south with a little west in it and on this course we rolled like hell. Eventually the mast was rolled out of her, the rigging having been shot away. Well, we waddled along and eventually made the Tyne at 6pm on Saturday and damn glad to be in too.[6]

Lieutenant Irvine Glennie, HMS *Broke*, 4th Flotilla

The *Sparrowhawk* had been inadvertently rammed by the *Broke*, but the bulk of her damage had been caused moments later, when the *Contest* had sliced into her stern. Setting to with a will, the damage control parties worked flat out to shore up her internal bulkheads.

We could not steam, as the *Contest* in her collision with us had jammed our rudder hard over, and no matter how we worked the engines we could not do anything except steam round in circles at dead slow speed, stern first. The engineers tried to cut through the bolts holding the rudder to the ship, so as to drop the rudder off, but without success.[7]

Sub-Lieutenant Percy Wood, HMS *Sparrowhawk*, 4th Flotilla

It was to be a truly nerve-racking night for the *Sparrowhawk* crew. While they were locked in a vicious circle, a German destroyer appeared, threatening to complete their destruction.

> About 2am, being on deck again, I saw, together with most of the ship's company, a German destroyer come slowly up to us until, when about 100 yards off us, she stopped, and we prepared for one final scrap with her, with the one gun and one torpedo that were left in action. Most of the officers and men were grouped round the after gun. In the hope of saving the ship orders were given that the gun was not to fire until the enemy opened fire, and being determined to get some of his own back, the Captain took gunlayer, the First Lieutenant was the trainer, and I was to look after the spotting. The gunner stood by with his last torpedo. The rest of the gun's crew were completed by various seamen and those left without a job were ordered to lie down along the upper deck. We loaded and waited for the flashes of gunfire from the German destroyer. But none came, and suddenly, just in the same way as she had appeared, she started her engines again, gathered way, and disappeared into the darkness.[8]
>
> Sub-Lieutenant Percy Wood, HMS *Sparrowhawk*, 4th Flotilla

Perhaps the German destroyer decided that the *Sparrowhawk* was surely doomed and exercised the quality of mercy on her crew. But their ordeal was not over. At about 03.30, as the light was fast improving, an even more powerful German ship manifested itself in the distance.

> A large shape, which we knew was a big ship, then moved up out of the mist. We just prayed that it was one of our own. Every man on board was straining his eyes to try and make her out and some officers were using glasses as well. Our feelings, when we saw that she was one of the latest class of German light cruisers, may perhaps be imagined. Fellows went about sort of whispering that this must be the end of all things, and asked each other what it was like to be dead.[9]
>
> Sub-Lieutenant Percy Wood, HMS *Sparrowhawk*, 4th Flotilla

Once again they manned the gun and tried to prepare themselves for death.

> I had some spotting glasses and as it got light, I tried hard to see men on her upper deck, for she was only about a mile and a half away and after

a short time it had become really light. I thought she started to heel over to one side slightly. Then everyone else noticed it until there was actually no mistaking it. She settled down forward, very slowly and then quietly stood on her head and sank. We had seemed to be absolutely done, there had seemed to be no hope whatever, and then this happened – you can imagine what we felt like.[10]

Sub-Lieutenant Percy Wood, HMS *Sparrowhawk*, 4th Flotilla

The mysterious German light cruiser was almost certainly the abandoned *Elbing*, slipping alone to her final resting place.

The *Tipperary* had been hit early in the frenetic night actions fought by the 4th Flotilla, her flames acting for quite some time as a beacon blazing across the night sky. She too had been approached by various German destroyers, but, already clearly *in extremis*, was left for dead as a sheer waste of ammunition. The *Tipperary*'s coal bunkers were engulfed by an uncontrollable conflagration and the whole forward area of the ship was utterly impassable.

For about two hours the ship floated in this condition, during which time we employed ourselves getting the wounded aft on to the quarterdeck and covering them with officers' bedding from the cabins, and in putting out two small fires which commenced aft. We also collected all the confidential books, and placed those not already in steel chests into weighted ammunition boxes, ready to throw overboard in an emergency. We could not cope with the fire forward, it being impossible to get along the upper deck, as the ready supply of ammunition for the forward guns was exploding box by box at short intervals. All the boats were completely smashed, but two life saving floats which were undamaged were got into the water and kept alongside ready. We threw everything that could possibly catch fire overboard, in the hopes of stopping the fire spreading aft, and I think we got rid of far more things than was necessary, even throwing overboard the upper deck supply of ammunition and the two port torpedoes. Perhaps we did it more to keep ourselves employed and our minds from thinking of the forward magazine, than with any idea of being useful.[11]

Sub-Lieutenant Newton William-Powlett, HMS *Tipperary*, 4th Flotilla

The unstoppable fire was all-consuming. Just before 02.00 the flames won the struggle to control the ship. It became obvious the *Tipperary*, disfigured and broken, was going to sink.

> The First Lieutenant ordered, "Everyone for themselves!" and we clambered over the side into the sea. The small Carley float had already left and I have never heard of it being seen again. Those who were lucky enough to be in time, got on to the large Carley float, the remainder just jumped into the sea. By the time I got to the rails the stern of the ship was well up in the air and the propellers were out of the water, so I slid down a rope on to the port propeller and thence into the sea.[12]
>
> Sub-Lieutenant Newton William-Powlett, HMS *Tipperary*, 4th Flotilla

William-Powlett found himself in the water, with no place on the Carley float, his saturated sea boots already weighing him down. Crucially, he found that he had foolishly neglected to blow up his life-saving waistcoat.

> I started off trying to get clear of the ship as I was afraid of being sucked down by eddies, but could make no headway for some time, probably because I was trying to swim to windward, and it was not until I swam round the stern of the *Tipperary* and pointed down to leeward that I got any distance from her. I heard a commotion behind me, and looking over my shoulder saw the last of the stern just disappearing, so I swam hard for a bit. I now found myself some distance from the 30-odd other swimmers – amongst whom I noticed Peter, our first lieutenant's white haired terrier – with the Carley raft further to leeward. As I had little hope of being picked up, I swam slowly away from the others, preferring to drown by myself rather than with a crowd.[13]
>
> Sub-Lieutenant Newton William-Powlett, HMS *Tipperary*, 4th Flotilla

At some point during that miserable night a German ship passed close by, but although the men on the raft hailed her, they were ignored. By then William-Powlett's grim resolve to die alone had been eroded.

> The cold of the water had sort of numbed my brain and I now had only one idea left – to reach the raft – and I eventually reached it. It was overcrowded, but they pulled me up on to it, an engine room artificer on one side of me and a red haired marine on the other side, and I had

room to sit on the edge. The raft, supporting about 30 men, was about a foot under water – it's a hollow, copper, oval shaped affair, with lifelines and things to hang on by – and as the night drew on a swell got up and the seas washed up and down over our middles, like the waves when one first wades out bathing, only much colder. We sang various popular songs, but I suppose because I had got colder swimming about than the others who had been on the raft all the time, I could not think of the words and my music was all of one note. When at last daylight gradually appeared we made out the shape of a small ship, apparently steaming round and round in circles. We were now all in a dull, comatose condition, in which one didn't care whether one lived or died; so much so that, although the destroyer was only 100 yards from us, it was very difficult to get anyone to use the paddles and get there.[14]

Sub-Lieutenant Newton William-Powlett, HMS *Tipperary*, 4th Flotilla

The eccentrically circling destroyer they had spotted was the *Sparrowhawk*, still hampered by her smashed rudder. Desperately the exhausted men tried to raise the energy to cover the short distance to what they imagined would be salvation.

Somebody reported a submarine in sight and once more the after gun was manned at the run. Luckily the First Lieutenant with his glasses made out the supposed submarine to be a Carley life-saving raft full of men, for though they were only about half a mile away, the sea was so confused that we could only catch a glimpse of them now and again. They saw us and put up a sheet as a sail. We tried to work the engines to steam towards them, but without much success. As they managed to paddle nearer we heard them singing, "It's a long, long way to Tipperary", so we knew who they were, and incidentally jolly well agreed with them. It *was* a long way![15]

Sub-Lieutenant Percy Wood, HMS *Sparrowhawk*, 4th Flotilla

It took about ninety long minutes for the Carley float to get alongside. By that time, of the original twenty-three survivors, three were already dead, five died after being pulled up onto the *Sparrowhawk*'s quarterdeck and a further eight had lapsed into deep unconsciousness. After separately sighting a German light cruiser and a Dutch steamer, both of which ignored them, the men aboard the *Sparrowhawk* were eventually delighted to see the approach of another, fully able-bodied destroyer, the *Marksman*. Unfortunately, all attempts to take the *Sparrowhawk* in tow were frustrated by the steadily rising seas. Eventually, reports of nearby German submarines forced the *Marksman* to give up her salvage attempts. The survivors of the *Sparrowhawk* and *Tipperary* crews were embarked and the *Marksman* set about sinking the now derelict hulk by shell fire. Despite her parlous condition, it took eighteen shells before the *Sparrowhawk* finally slid beneath the waves.

The *Spitfire* had also been left with her bows gaping open to the seas when she had earlier rammed the *Nassau*. Immediately after the collision, her crew had swung into action in a desperate effort to stem the onrushing waters before it was too late.

> Mess tables, collision mats and shores were used to try and fill up the
> gaping bow, but they were all washed inboard again time after time, as
> the wind and sea were now fast rising. By dawn, June 1st, the sea had
> risen a good deal and the wind was still freshening from the south-west,
> and about 8.00am we had to turn the ship head to sea and ease down.
> All storerooms, shell rooms and lower mess decks forward being flooded,
> we began to get very anxious whether the fore boiler-room bulkhead
> would stand the strain. At dawn the Captain ordered a tot of rum to be
> served out all round and I must say that cheered up the men no end.[16]
>
> Lieutenant Athelstan Bush, HMS *Spitfire*, 4th Flotilla

The patriotic determination of the *Spitfire*'s crew to regain their home-land is illustrated by their refusal of the offer of assistance from a neutral Norwegian merchant ship. They were going to stick by the little ship that had served them so well in adversity. However, as the wind continued to rise, they began to fear that they were not going to make it home.

> The sea got up and the wind increased so considerably that we had to
> turn to north to keep the sea on our quarter. Our hopes of getting home
> fell during that night, as the weather gradually became worse and worse,
> and about 1.00am, we decided that the only thing to do was to fire
> distress signals, estimating that we were about 60 miles from the English,
> or it might be the Scottish, coast. As we were on the point of doing this,

at about 2.00am, suddenly – it seemed like a miracle – the wind died down, and the sea got smoother and smoother, until at 4.30am we turned to west-south-west and increased speed to about 10 knots. As the morning drew on we met a patrol drifter, which informed us we were 22 miles east north east of the Tyne. After making such a landfall as this, we came to the conclusion that *the* best aids to navigation are a torn piece of a chart, a bookcase batten as a ruler and the wake of the last met merchant ship as sailing directions![17]

Lieutenant Athelstan Bush, HMS *Spitfire*, 4th Flotilla

So, against all the odds, they too pulled into Tyneside in the early morning of 2 June. On board their forecastle they still carried a 20-foot-long steel armour plate as a memento of their head-on collision with the *Nassau*. The seamanship and endurance demonstrated by the officers and men of these battered destroyers, as they struggled back home in adverse weather conditions, deserves nothing but respect.

Of all the wounded large British ships, there is no doubt the armoured cruiser *Warrior* was in the worst shape. On the evening of 31 May her captain assessed the condition of his ship as she staggered away covered by the eccentric circling of the *Warspite* from the scene of the massacre of Rear Admiral Robert Arbuthnot's 1st Cruiser Squadron.

We had been hit at least 15 times by heavy projectiles – 11″ or 12″ – and about six times by smaller shells. Fires were raging so badly aft that it was impossible to get access to the engine room; the whole main deck was full of flame, smoke and gas from enemy shells; the upper deck was torn to pieces and every boat was damaged beyond repair. The masts still stood and so did the funnels, although the rigging had been shot away and there were many holes in both masts and funnels. But the most serious damage was that caused by an 11″ or 12″ projectile which struck us on the waterline on the port side, passed through the after reserve coal bunker, crossed the upper part of the port engine room and burst as it went through the middle line bulkhead, leaving most of its gas in the port engine room, while several large fragments of it were deflected downwards and tore a

large hole in the double bottom at the after end of the starboard
engine room.[18]

Captain Vincent Molteno, HMS *Warrior*, 1st Cruiser Squadron

Inevitably, in these circumstances, casualties were severe. There were nearly
100 killed and wounded sailors scattered all around the ship. The seriously
wounded were in desperate need of attention. The medical and surgical
teams faced the challenge before them with a cool determination.

As soon as the action ceased, medical and stretcher parties busied
themselves looking for and collecting the wounded from isolated parts of
the ship. The sick bay was left almost intact and so cases were moved
there and the adjoining part of the messdeck was cleared for the
reception of the wounded. The wounded were collected and were
temporarily made comfortable, dressings being quickly applied and
tourniquets seen to, which had been put on previously. As most of the
wounded were suffering from severe shock, one tried to combat this. The
wet clothes were taken off and they were put into dry bed gear and
wrapped up, given warm drinks and morphia. Fortunately one galley fire
was uninjured after the action. Everyone worked with a will and by about
8.30 the wounded were fairly comfortable and we could have a look
round and decide what to do. During this time several cases succumbed
to their injuries. In all we had 80 or so killed or died of wounds soon
after the action. Having sorted out the wounded as far as possible, it was
obvious that something more must be done. The wounds were very
ragged as caused by pieces of metal. Compound fractures were common
and limbs had been torn off. Of the survivors the majority had wounds
of lower extremities. Several had limbs smashed to pulp and had
embedded pieces of clothing and metal which needed removal. We
commandeered the bathroom near the sick bay for a theatre and
prepared it as quickly and as best we could. We had plenty of instruments
and water, but our stores were not too abundant, as the ship had been
badly knocked about and, in spite of our precautions in scattering the
stowage of gear, we were still short handed. The only antiseptic we had
was carbolic acid and a little perchloride. We had enough cyanide gauze
and wool however. The lighting of the theatre was the main disadvantage
and obstacle. We had only candle lamps available and these give very

little illumination for critical operations. But, one has to make what one has, do. We boiled our instruments and set to work. No gloves were served out. These would have been invaluable as in a short time one's hands became fearfully sore owing to the antiseptic solutions. The Fleet Surgeon operated, assisted by myself, and Dr Macdonald gave the anaesthetic. We commenced at 9.30 and went on until about 5 next morning when one had to cease owing to the fearful tossing the ship received in the heavy seas. All sorts of wounds were dealt with and several amputations were done – plain circular, no flaps. Needless to say several men were beyond all hope of recovery and others had died whilst waiting their turn – plainly from shock.[19]

Surgeon Lieutenant Charles Leake, HMS *Warrior*, 1st Cruiser Squadron

As the men of the *Warrior* tentatively tried to make their way back home, they had the good fortune to fall in with the seaplane carrier *Engadine*, which had been ordered to return home independently.

At 18.40 hours another cruiser was sighted, steaming towards us on our starboard bow. Steam and smoke were pouring from her, and flames were seen coming from the stern ports. We made her out to be British and when near enough we signalled, "Can we be of any assistance?" and received the reply, "Stand by me." Her name was *Warrior* and she informed us that both engine rooms were full of steam and she couldn't stop. We turned and came up on her port quarter. She had a bad list and had been holed on the water line. Her W/T had gone and she was on fire aft. She began blowing off steam and signalled that they were trying to shut off steam. When eventually this was done, she signalled, "Stand by to tow me," and we lowered our motorboat and, after a long toilsome business with tow ropes, the first of which parted, we got a steel hawser aboard, and took her in tow at 20.40 hours, but experienced great difficulty in getting her on the move.[20]

Signaller H. Y. Ganderton, HMS *Engadine*, Battlecruiser Fleet

The *Warrior* was a large ship of some 505 feet in length and 73 feet in the beam. She dwarfed the *Engadine* and the strain on the towing cable between the two ships was almost incalculable.

I'll never forget the first pull of the wire. Keep in mind that *Engadine* displaced about 1,400 tons and the *Warrior* was 14,900 – with the water in her she was probably 19,000. So the very first time all that happened was a colossal shower of sparks and she stopped dead. [21]

Flight Lieutenant Graham Donald, Royal Naval Air Service, HMS *Engadine*, Battlecruiser Fleet

At last, by dint of sheer perseverance, they overcame the forces of inertia and got the dead weight of the *Warrior* slowly moving forward towards home. The battle had long since moved on and passed far out of sight, but the two ships could make less than 10 knots and would have been at the mercy of any stray German submarines or warships that might happen upon them. Most of the crew of the *Warrior* were too busy to care.

In the darkness of the messdeck I saw a torchlight, a surgeon was searching a pile of dead bodies, looking for life – about 30 bodies of a stoker fire party. All of them had been killed by a heavy calibre shell. Down below decks, tired seamen struggled with the hand pumps to keep the ship afloat. Holes were plugged and bulkheads shored up, but the struggle all night was in vain, as the water in the ship was rising and it was a question of how long *Warrior* could stay afloat.[22]

Signalman Reuben Poole, HMS *Warrior*, 1st Cruiser Squadron

From the deck of the struggling *Engadine*, they looked back on the *Warrior* and wondered whether she would be able to survive.

It was a terrific strain on our small ship, as we struggled on against a rising sea, and she shook and trembled as the revolution indicator was pushed up from 12 to 19 knots. All through the night we struggled on, making only 8.2 knots through the water. Unfortunately the weather began to get worse and the sea became rough. Fire could still be seen coming from *Warrior*'s stern ports and even loose papers were blown out with the draught of the fire, as the ship slowly heaved to the swell. Steel hawsers were at breaking strain, stern plates and bollards nearly wrenched and torn from their seating by the tugging of the heavy cruiser astern, as she rose and sank on the heaving waves, threatening every moment to engulf her altogether. Her gallant crew, weary and battle worn, worked hard at the pumps all night long to keep her afloat.[23]

Signaller H. Y. Ganderton, HMS *Engadine*, Battlecruiser Fleet

By morning it had become apparent that the *Warrior* was doomed as the sea slowly gained the upper hand. In a domino effect, as a bulkhead gave way, neighbouring compartments inexorably filled with water, the pressure grew on the next bulkhead and so the situation got steadily worse, as the ship gradually surrendered what little buoyancy she had retained.

> My duties during the dark hours were keeping a look out and also taking my turn at hand pumping, endeavouring to keep this great ship afloat, but it was all in vain. By daylight our decks were well awash and it was too dangerous for the *Engadine* to continue towing us.[24]
>
> Signalman William Robertson, HMS *Warrior*, 1st Cruiser Squadron

Regretfully bowing to the inevitable, the *Warrior*'s crew began to finalize the preparations necessary to abandon ship. First, the wounded had to be brought up on deck.

> They carried me to the middle mess deck and while I was lying there the padre came and asked me for my home address and if I had any mates aboard from my hometown. While I was there the ship was sinking and they carried me from the mess deck up to the bows of the ship. The crew kept on working the pumps to keep her afloat.[25]
>
> Stoker 1st Class David Williams, HMS *Warrior*, 1st Cruiser Squadron

It was an eerie scene, as the stricken giant gradually lost sea way and wallowed ever lower in the waves.

> In the morning a white drifting mist, not thick enough to be called a fog, blotted out the distance and gave an air of unreality to the scene. It was cold too, with the icy cold of the North Sea. I shivered as I stood in an exposed position on the bridge and pressed closer to the protecting canvas screen as I looked at the grey waste of tumbling waters around, and watched the labouring of the heavy cruiser astern. It had been a night of tension, and reaction from the excitement of yesterday's battle had brought that nightmare feeling of impotence, when something seems to numb your power of action and you remain rooted to the spot.[26]
>
> Signaller H. Y. Ganderton, HMS *Engadine*, Battlecruiser Fleet

The dead weight of the cruiser meant that, overnight, they had only been able to make 70 miles. Such minimal progress meant that they had not yet cleared the danger zone and were vulnerable to any German sub-marine or destroyer attack. The literal point of no return had come: it was obvious that they would now never get the *Warrior* back to port.

> I was on the bridge during the early morning watch and at about 7am,
> I heard the Engineer Commander report to Captain Molteno that the
> after main bulkhead had burst and that the ship would soon sink. This
> was confirmed by the Ship's Commander. On the Captain's orders, I
> personally made a signal to the *Engadine*, by semaphore hand flags, from
> the portside of the bridge, "Come alongside, am sinking."[27]
> Signalman Reuben Poole, HMS *Warrior*, 1st Cruiser Squadron

Given the disproportionate size of the ships, this simple instruction was a good deal easier said than done.

> Already heavy seas were sweeping across the decks amidships, and it
> was plain that it was a question of moments only when she would make
> the final plunge. There were 700 men onboard, of whom many were
> wounded, and what had to be done must be done quickly. But would it
> be quick enough? Boats were out of the question, and in any case it was
> unlikely that any of the *Warrior*'s boats were undamaged.[28]
> Signaller H. Y. Ganderton, HMS *Engadine*, Battlecruiser Fleet

The waves were getting very rough and the only method of disem-barkation that offered anything like the requisite speed was for the *Engadine* to risk damage to herself by coming right alongside the waterlogged *Warrior*. Fortunately, the seaplane carrier had been a cross-Channel steamer in her peacetime years, before she had been converted to play her part in the war. One relic of this former incarnation was the thick rubbing strake that still surrounded her to facilitate going alongside jetties. This was to prove a vital buffer between the two ships.

> Tow ropes and hawsers were hurriedly cast off, and we steamed round
> in a circle to bring us astern and on her port quarter. The first attempt
> to go alongside failed owing to the heavy seas now running and we
> began to have the terrible fear that we should be too late. A second
> attempt was made. Our Captain, seemingly unperturbed, with supreme
> skill and judgement, gauged it exactly; and although at one moment

high on the crest of a huge wave it seemed that we must crash down right upon her decks now already awash, yet we managed to run right alongside, and grappled on with steel hawsers and stout hemp ropes. Men were ordered to stand by with axes to cut them through should the *Warrior* founder before they could be cast off. The two ships were grinding together horribly. With a crash part of the stout 'rubbing chock' which ran nearly the whole length of the ship near the water line and served as a fender, was splintered by some projecting piece of armour on the other ship's side. At any moment the thin plating itself might be stove in by the pounding blows that shook the whole vessel to her very keel.[29]

Signaller H. Y. Ganderton, HMS *Engadine*, Battlecruiser Fleet

Speed was of the essence. All personnel had to transfer immediately from the *Warrior* to the *Engadine*. Anyone unaccounted for and left aboard would be doomed to a lonely death on an abandoned hulk.

With vicious bumping the two ships were made fast. Captain Molteno had given the orders, "Close all watertight doors, batten down all hatches, prepare to abandon ship." As my work was finished on the bridge I was sent down to join the crew for "Abandon Ship!" I nipped down the hatchway to the messdeck for a few personal items and in the light from the hatchway I saw a worn out sailor, oblivious to the danger, fast asleep in the hammock netting. I gave him a good shaking, saying, "Come on mate, abandon ship, she'll be sinking any minute now!" I hope that seaman heeded my warning. If not, he would be battened down. The souvenirs I brought down from the bridge were one White Ensign, one Union Jack, my pair of hand semaphore flags and binoculars. From the canteen I salvaged one large carton of Players cigarettes and one large carton of Fry's Cream bars. Yeoman Parsons asked me to try to save his sewing machine as he had to stay on the bridge with the Captain – I ignored his request![30]

Signalman Reuben Poole, HMS *Warrior*, 1st Cruiser Squadron

As quickly as possible the crew gathered on the deck. Everyone was aware that at any moment the *Warrior* might sink, but their discipline held in what were severely trying circumstances.

It wasn't a very easy job so everybody had to lend a hand making odd wires fast to try and hold her tight to the *Warrior*'s side; put down fenders as best we could. It's not the sort of thing an aircraft carrier or a warship is really equipped for doing at sea as a rule. But the really nasty moment was just as we were getting ready, the *Warrior* gave a nasty sort of shudder – it just looked as if she was going to sink. It was unmistakeable. Apart from pulling us with her, just for a moment there was a slight look on all these chaps' faces – and keep in mind they'd had an awful hammering, the scuppers were running with blood and casualties. There might have been a panic. The Captain just signalled the bugler. He blew the still – just a toot of the still – every man Jack stood to attention and then they carried on in a very orderly manner.[31]

Flight Lieutenant Graham Donald, Royal Naval Air Service, HMS *Engadine*, Battlecruiser Fleet

Steadied by this act of command, the men of the *Warrior* faced their extreme danger with calm equanimity.

Warrior's crew were fallen in by divisions on her deck, in perfect order, awaiting further command. Because of the large number of men to be taken off it was decided to get all the able-bodied over first and send them below, thus leaving the deck free for handling the wounded. Then, at the word of command, the able-bodied – though very weary and battle-grimed – leapt over the short space to find an uncertain foothold upon our decks helped by our own men.[32]

Signaller H. Y. Ganderton, HMS *Engadine*, Battlecruiser Fleet

Vaulting the void that separated the ships, each man was aware that a slip or misjudgement would mean almost certain death.

The operation 'abandon ship' was carried out as smoothly and calmly as a Sunday morning divisional muster. When my turn came to abandon ship my goods and relics were thrown onto the deck of our rescue ship. Then as the ship rose with the waves, I grabbed at the *Engadine*'s taffrails and rolled inboard. What a relief! I felt as though I could go below and sleep for a week.[33]

Signalman Reuben Poole, HMS *Warrior*, 1st Cruiser Squadron

As the men leaped, rolled or stumbled across the gap between the two ships, they were met by helping hands from the *Engadine* crew.

> Our officers and men lined *Engadine*'s side and grabbed each man as he came across. The two ships were working heavily, the noise of rending steel was terrific and only orders shouted in one's ear could be heard. Davits were sheared off from their supports, *Engadine* was holed in several places, though not badly, and the fenders, mostly bundles of hazelwood sticks wired together, quickly went to pieces.[34]
>
> Flight Lieutenant Frederick Rutland, Royal Naval Air Service, HMS *Engadine*, Battlecruiser Fleet

Then it was the turn of the wounded. Because of the frenetic urgency of the situation, stretchers were simultaneously passed across from one ship to another along the entire side of the *Engadine*.

> As the ships lurched towards each other the stretchers containing the wounded were quickly and tenderly handed across the gulf to willing hands. The sea down below, like some savage beast imprisoned in a cage, madly leapt at them with foaming jaws. One poor fellow was being passed across, when the ship gave a sudden lurch, and for a moment those who were handling the stretcher on which he lay lost their hold on it, and with a cry of pity and despair from the helpless onlookers, he slipped from the stretcher and fell down into the seething waters below. Instantly several men sprang forward and would have gone over the side after their messmate had not the captain of the *Warrior* ordered them back. "It is madness to go down there!" he cried. Indeed the terrible sound of rending timber and buckling plates proclaimed all too loudly that no human being could hope to escape being crushed to death in those relentless steel jaws.[35]
>
> Signaller H. Y. Ganderton, HMS *Engadine*, Battlecruiser Fleet

More prosaically, Lieutenant Rutland looked over the side and coolly came to the same conclusion.

> The last stretcher was being passed when the wounded man slipped out of it and fell into the sea between the two ships. At that time two officers and the captain of the *Warrior* were crossing to the *Engadine*, near where

I was standing. Several officers and men jumped on the netting or bulwarks as though to go down after him, but the captain shouted that no one was to go over the side. It was in fact impossible, for the poor fellow had fallen through the gap between *Engadine*'s rubbing-strake and *Warrior* as the two ships drew apart, before taking another charge at each other. He had fetched up on a bundle of hazelwood sticks, the remains of a fender, and for the moment these supported him. But it seemed that it would be only a matter of seconds before he fell through them. So I decided that nothing could be done and went on helping the wounded, of whom there were nearly a hundred to be placed in shelter.[36]

Flight Lieutenant Frederick Rutland, Royal Naval Air Service, HMS *Engadine*, Battlecruiser Fleet

But something drew Rutland's attention back to the scene. Once again he assessed the situation and made what, to him, was a rational analysis of the risks involved in attempting a rescue.

Then I saw a group of men looking over the side, near where the wounded man had gone over board; I ran forward and saw that, though still between the ships, he had drifted far enough ahead to be rescued without any real risk. So I grabbed a rope with a bowline in it, with which two men had been trying to lasso him, told them and others to hang on to the end, went down the rope, swam to the man, brought him to the rope, put myself into the bowline, and, holding him in my arms, ordered those on deck to heave away. There was one tricky moment when we were nearly up to the deck and I saw the steel hawser from *Warrior*'s bows cutting across my rope. Had the hawser parted at the wrong moment it could have cut us both in two. Had it merely carried away our rope, it would have meant another swim. Because I have always had the habit of talking to myself in moments like this, many people heard me say to the unconscious man, "Sorry, me lad, I'm afraid we've got another dip coming." But old Hancock, the captain of the *Engadine* in peacetime and now serving in her as Lieutenant R.N.R., saw what was happening and rang the engines ahead, thus taking the strain off the hawser. Two minutes later we were aboard, the hawser had parted and the ships swung clear, with *Warrior* sinking fast. After all, the poor fellow died of his wounds. He had been very seriously wounded and it was apparently known that he had only a short time to live. As for myself, I had never been in danger, except from the steel hawser, for I had weighed up the situation in a second before going over the side and reckoned that, so long as the rubbing-strake held, I could save myself from being crushed and swim clear if I had to.[37]

Flight Lieutenant Frederick Rutland, Royal Naval Air Service, HMS *Engadine*, Battlecruiser Fleet

As is often the case with deeds of heroism, Rutland played down the extent of the risks he had taken in going to the man's rescue. To the witnesses, his actions appeared quite different. They were plainly flabbergasted by the raw courage.

Then I saw what was surely as brave a deed as any in that great battle. Lieutenant Rutland quickly seized hold of a rope, tied a bowline round his body and, telling the men to hang on to the other end, made his way forward a little towards the bows, swung himself over the bulwarks and quickly lowered himself down between the two ships. The men begged that they might go, but he forbade them to risk their lives. A confused scene of tossing water is my only impression of that moment, as he edged his way aft. I scarcely dared look down from my lofty vantage point at the end of the bridge. Now a man dangling in space, now lost to sight in a roaring cascade; a sickening thud that made the heart stand still as the ships struck – and still that persevering and gallant figure fighting on. A gasp of dismay as the rope slackened, but only for a moment. Now he had hold of the wounded man. Feverishly the men began to haul away at the rope and willing hands were stretched out to receive the poor crushed burden from the grasp of his brave rescuer. No, he did not live, poor fellow. He expired as he lay on the deck – his back broken, it was said – but he was just able to whisper, "Thank you!" before he died to the man who had risked his own life so fearlessly to save him. That was perhaps as great a reward as the Albert Medal which he afterwards received.[38]

Signaller H. Y. Ganderton, HMS *Engadine*, Battlecruiser Fleet

In all over 700 men were rescued from the stricken ship. The last to leave, as tradition dictated, was Captain Molteno.

Finally the Commander reported all hands were on board the *Engadine*, and he and I then jumped on board and the *Engadine* went astern to clear the sinking ship. As we left the old *Warrior* we gave her three hearty cheers. Every big sea washed over her decks and water poured down through the huge rents in the upper deck on to the main deck.[39]

Captain Vincent Molteno, HMS *Warrior*, 1st Cruiser Squadron

It had been a very close-run thing. The bereft crew looked back at the *Warrior* for the last time as she slipped out of sight with just a faint echo of a Viking prince sailing off to Valhalla.

Grappling irons and ropes were cast off at 08.25 and gathering speed we left the doomed ship – a truly forlorn spectacle. Derelict, battered and battle scarred, forsaken at the last, heaving in a queer dying convulsive sort of manner – and yet, with the white ensign proudly flying at the masthead, her battle ensign. *Warrior's* crew gave their old ship a cheer, and there were tears in her Captain's eyes. That was the last glimpse of the old *Warrior* we had before she was lost sight of in the mist, and vanished for ever beneath the waves of the cold grey North Sea.[40]

Signaller H. Y. Ganderton, HMS *Engadine*, Battlecruiser Fleet

When they got back into port, Captain Molteno tried to sum up the strange feelings of pride and sorrow stirred within him by the loss of his ship in an order he issued to his surviving ship's company.

I am proud to have been in command of such a fine body of men. You behaved magnificently and I have just applied to the Admiralty to keep you all together and to again put me in command of you 'Warriors'. I am proud of you and have asked for leave for you all to go home and see your friends and you can 'cock a chest', for you will get ten days, but if any of you have got to fill casualties, I hope you will keep up the traditions of the *Warrior* and go with a cheer. Your courage was magnificent, not one had any thought for himself, but everyone tried his best to save his ship and render aid to the wounded and dying. I would not have believed it possible for a ship to get into such 'hell' and come out again with so many survivors. We had 60 brave men killed, 28 seriously injured and 15 slightly wounded –

and I will see that the *Warrior*'s wounded will be well looked after. Now men, I hope you will all enjoy yourselves at home and I know that your people will be jolly well proud of you, and well they may be.[41]

Captain Vincent Molteno, HMS *Warrior*, 1st Cruiser Squadron

The main military value of the obsolescent *Warrior* undoubtedly lay in her large crew as the loss of the ship herself did not materially affect the strength of the Grand Fleet. Once rescued they could return to their home ports and then be sent out to serve their country on new ships. Manpower was short and trained seamen were in scarce supply. However, the super-dreadnought *Warspite* was an entirely different matter. The loss of such a ship would still have been a calamity even if every member of the crew were saved. After being ordered back home the injured *Warspite* made for harbour with all possible speed. But Rosyth was a long way, she had no escort, no accompanying ship to take off the crew *in extremis* and most of her lifeboats had been holed.

> When the ship got out of the range of enemy guns, the order was passed by telephone to us that turrets crews could stand easy but remain in the vicinities of the turrets. Which meant you could come out on top and walk around the top of the turret. When I got out I was amazed at what I saw. Part of the bridge was alight, a store of lifebelts under the bridge were in flames; I could see there was a fire raging in the 6″ Battery where the cordite was alight; the upper deck was riddled with shell; the funnels were holed; every boat in the ship had a hole in it and the ship looked really bad.[42]
>
> J. J. Hazelwood, HMS *Warspite*, Fifth Battle Squadron

Surgeon Ellis found a moment to pop out on deck to see what was happening. He too was stunned by the change in the ship's appearance. But his equanimity and confidence gradually revived.

> We were moving through the water slowly, heading back towards Rosyth. There was no other ship in sight, or noise of firing, anywhere. There was still a dull red glow from the sun, left in the sky, low down, but it was very hazy and impossible to see any distance. The sea was still

calm, but there was just enough breeze to make its surface tumbly. As regards the ship, it is difficult to say what one's feelings were on looking at her. Only a few hours before she had been one of the cleanest and smartest looking ships in the fleet, her decks spotlessly white and her light grey paint, freshly put on only recently, gleaming everywhere in the sunshine. Now her decks were filthy, littered with debris and in places torn up by shells, one of the quarterdeck ladders had been blown away, her funnels had ragged holes in them, the small iron ladder on 'X' Turret had been bent, twisted and broken away from its lower supports, whilst the side of the turret was covered with marks from glancing hits. Her general appearance was in about as absolute a contrast to what it had been before as well could be. A ragged and dirty White Ensign still flew from her ensign staff – which had been struck once and broken, so that it was now much shorter and at the main masthead there was flying the Union Jack. The damage fortunately, was, on the whole, more spectacular than real. She was afloat and barring bad weather, perfectly seaworthy. Our steaming powers were unimpaired and as soon as the damaged interior parts of the ship had been shored up and made secure, there seemed to be no reason why we should not proceed on our way back to port in perfect security.[43]

Surgeon Gordon Ellis, HMS *Warspite*, Fifth Battle Squadron

For the indefatigable Commander Humphrey Walwyn, 1 June was proving another busy day. His duties were truly legion: checking for damage; supervising the shoring up of bulkheads, the plugging of holes below or near the water-line, the pumping out of tons of water; making sure that existing repairs were still holding firm. With some trepidation he tackled the job of collecting the dead from below decks.

Went aft and tried to square up hole by port casemate lobby. Got half a dozen men to get the dead out of the flat below. I was afraid of myself that I should get 'cold feet' at seeing dead men, but one was so hardened that I didn't care a rap. They were badly knocked about but absolutely 'dry' and not bleeding at all. The thing that struck me was that they were not nearly so frightening as I thought they would be somehow.[44]

Commander Humphrey Walwyn, HMS *Warspite*, Fifth Battle Squadron

Walwyn's work was given added impetus by the knowledge that the *Warspite* was by no means out of the woods. The Germans knew that any British 'lame ducks' would be heading back to their bases and Scheer had therefore ordered his screen of U-boats still lurking outside Scapa Flow and the Firth of Forth to try to intercept any crippled ships returning to port.

About 7.00am the Captain sent for me and said he was certain we should be attacked by submarines and to do all I could to get everything as ready as possible. Got upper deck 6″ crews closed up and went on getting rafts etc. built. Had a strong party plugging holes up in cabins and quarterdeck aft, and used up all the blankets and bedding from the after cabins. The Captain's cabin was about a foot deep in water. I did not even then know that the capstan engine flat had been holed below the waterline and got the five ton pump underway trying to pump it out. They plugged away all the fore-noon but made no impression; this was natural as they were pumping the North Sea out and back to itself again, my fault entirely, but these things look foolish afterwards.[45]

Commander Humphrey Walwyn, HMS *Warspite*, Fifth Battle Squadron

Unless she suffered further damage, there was never any real chance of the *Warspite* sinking, as long as her engines kept going. But to her crew who had grown accustomed to her 'moods' she did not feel 'normal' beneath their feet.

During the night the breeze, from the north west still, had freshened and there was enough sea to give the ship a certain amount of motion. It was not rough, but with the ship in her present condition any sea at all was not desirable. One could feel she was sluggish, owing to her flooded compartments – or imagined it at all events – and any sea was bound to put the strength of her structure to a severe test.[46]

Surgeon Gordon Ellis, HMS *Warspite*, Fifth Battle Squadron

Extra look-outs were stationed all round the ship; tired eyes straining for any sign of a periscope or torpedo track. The 6-inch batteries were closed up and kept ready for immediate action. The main turret crews and any other spare personnel were told off into damage control parties. Other parties were ordered to bring up as many mess tables and stools as possible from the mess decks. These were then lashed together to make impromptu rafts stacked up on the quarterdeck in case of the unthinkable.

The risk of torpedo attack was made dramatically apparent as the *Warspite* ran into a concentration of submarines off the east coast of Scotland. Once again the she proved a lucky ship.

> A German submarine fired two torpedoes at us. She had misjudged
> our speed and zig-zag and had come up to attack right astern, so she
> only had our stern to aim at. She made a very good shot, the two
> torpedoes running up, one on each side of our quarterdeck. I stood
> on the quarterdeck and watched the one on the starboard side.
> It began to turn in towards the ship and looked as if it was going to
> hit, but at the last moment it reached the end of its run and sank.
> I breathed again.[47]
>
> Assistant Clerk Gilbert Bickmore, HMS *Warspite*, Fifth Battle Squadron

Down below, Ellis was busy writing up his case notes ready for transferring the wounded to hospital on arrival in port when he became aware that all was not well.

> Williamson suddenly pushed aside the curtain and informed us that a
> torpedo had just passed along the ship's side, only about some 10 feet
> off. This was a new complication and had the effect of making me feel
> I wanted to go up on deck at once – for what reason I don't know – but
> the PMO went on writing with his usual imperturbability so that for
> sheer shame I felt bound to stay also. However the job was nearly
> finished and I did not waste any time then in going up onto the
> forecastle deck, where I found a number of other officers assembled. It
> had come from astern, and, as we watched, the periscope and top of the
> conning tower of the submarine from which it had been despatched,
> emerged above the surface about half a mile distant on the port quarter.
> The gun's crew of the port 6″ on the forecastle deck immediately fired in
> its direction and the shell pitched sufficiently close for the spray to hide
> all sight of it. It probably wasn't hit, but at any rate when the spray
> subsided it was no longer visible.[48]
>
> Surgeon Gordon Ellis, HMS *Warspite*, Fifth Battle Squadron

Luckily, it was not a co-ordinated attack, for the next U-boat was also in the wrong position to have much chance of securing a hit and too close for its own comfort.

> Very shortly afterwards another one was sighted almost directly ahead. It was so close that it was impossible to bring a gun to bear, the depression being too great, but the Captain endeavoured to ram him and missed by only a matter of feet. He dived in such a hurry that his tail came up out of the water, so I imagine that his equanimity must have been quite as much, if not more so, disturbed as ours over the incident. Only a few minutes after this a third submarine appeared on the port side, about 400 yards off. He just came up and went down again, the top of his conning tower alone being caught sight of, before we had a chance to fire, and was evidently unaware until he saw us that he had misjudged his position so much. He no doubt hoped to find himself some little way ahead, on a convenient bearing for firing a torpedo.[49]
>
> Surgeon Gordon Ellis, HMS *Warspite*, Fifth Battle Squadron

If the *Warspite* not been plagued by problems that forced the steering to be conducted from the engine-room, many felt that the second U-boat could have been successfully rammed. No one knew how many more German submarines might be lurking close by and the need for a destroyer escort was becoming paramount.

> We had made urgent signals for a destroyer escort to be sent and one could only hope that they would speedily turn up. About an hour later, just after lunch, they did, six of them, and one felt comparatively safe again then. I know that I welcomed their appearance as much as anyone anyway. The chances of us seeing the Forth Bridge again had, up till then, been a question of some doubt in my mind. They weren't destroyers as a matter of fact; one was, of an old type, the remainder were torpedo boats, and at our rate of speed they had their work cut out to keep in station with us.[50]
>
> Surgeon Gordon Ellis, HMS *Warspite*, Fifth Battle Squadron

It is a credit to the essential toughness of the *Warspite* that, after all she had been through, she was still capable of making some 21 knots. Truly they were super-dreadnoughts! Eventually, on the afternoon of 1 June, they entered the Firth of Forth and her ordeal was brought to an end.

> We passed under the Forth Bridge at about 3.00pm – still on fire, with our funnels belching smoke from their many perforations. We were greeted by loud cheers from the men at work on the bridge as we passed under it.[51]

Assistant Clerk Gilbert Bickmore, HMS *Warspite*, Fifth Battle Squadron

For the nurses aboard the *Plassy*, the tension was broken when the *Warspite* arrived. Now they knew they would have work to do.

> We were all up on deck after dinner watching and waiting, when we saw through the mist and rain, two destroyers come under the Forth Bridge and following them very slowly, but still in a stately manner, the first battle scarred heroine, HMS *Warspite*.[52]

Naval Nursing Sister Mary Clarke, HM Hospital Ship *Plassy*, Rosyth

The other significant ship at risk from her injuries was the *Marlborough*. Despite the torpedo strike, she had been able to stay in line, maintaining a speed of around 17 knots, which, as has been noted, acted as a brake to the overall progress of the 6th Division, First Battle Squadron. At around 01.00 it became apparent that two of the boiler bulkheads of the forward engine-rooms were beginning to give way under the pressure of water. They were rapidly shored up and speed further reduced to around 12 knots. Under these deteriorating circumstances, Vice Admiral Sir Cecil Burney transferred his flag to the *Revenge* at 03.00. The *Marlborough* was then ordered back to port accompanied by the destroyer *Fearless*. Shortly after they commenced their journey back, it was realized that the dreadnought was in far more serious danger than had been originally thought.

> Several of the ship's compartments, including a boiler room, had been flooded as a result of the torpedo hit, but for the first few hours the pumps kept the water in check. Then at about dawn, one of the pumps became choked and the water level in the flooded compartments began to rise. Soon there was a grave risk that the bulkhead of the engine room would give way and if that large space became flooded the ship

might well founder. Brave men in diving helmets worked to clear the pump inlet, but the Captain decided that it would only be prudent to get everyone up on deck. The pipe, "Hands to abandon ship stations", brought us all doubling to our stations abreast the boat or raft to which we were allocated. My station was on the quarterdeck and most of us fell in just as we were, one or two had the sense to snatch up a greatcoat. At first one of the party for our boat, a warrant officer, was absent, but about five minutes later he came running aft. He was dressed in his best uniform, was carrying a suitcase and had a bowler hat under his arm. He was loudly cheered. Fortunately, after about half an hour the pumps were cleared, we were fallen out and returned to our action stations.[53]

Midshipman Angus Nicholl, HMS *Marlborough*, 6th Division, First Battle Squadron

At 11.00 Admiral Sir John Jellicoe was given permission to order out some of the destroyers from Tyrwhitt's Harwich Force to rendezvous with the *Marlborough* and chaperone her for the last few miles. Thanks to the earlier Admiralty intransigence in refusing to release them, this was to be the only use made of that magnificent fighting force. Safely under escort, the *Marlborough* finally reached the Humber on the morning of 2 June.

◆ ◆ ◆

The morning of 1 June brought a cold empty misery to the main body of the Grand Fleet. Ever since the signal from the Admiralty at 04.00, they knew that there was no longer any doubt that the High Seas Fleet had made good its escape. This depression was increased by news of the loss of the *Indefatigable* and the *Queen Mary*, which Jellicoe had not hitherto been aware of. For a few hours they sailed in a thoroughly desultory fashion around the 'battleground', metaphorically trailing their coats and looking for German stragglers. As they passed through the debris the crews looked about them for any survivors. There were desperately few to be found, but Able Seaman Albert Cave sighted something through his range-finder and reported as such to Captain Albert Scott of the *Dublin*.

"There's something moving in the water – it looks like a figure waving!" He altered course toward him and I said, "It looks like a German!" He

with a real good telescope could still only make out a blur. "He's got
fair hair and a moustache." The ship eventually got near and a touch,
"Astern" to engine room, stopped. The Captain said, "Well we'll hear
what he's got to say." To everyone's surprise he shouted, "Thank God!"
He had one arm on a tea box. We dropped a Jacob's ladder over the
side for him to climb up, but he was so exhausted and nearly dead. All
we could do was to send a man down with a heaving line, put a bowline
around him through a snatch block, then willing hands hauled him up
and inboard.[54]

Able Seaman William Cave, HMS *Dublin*, 2nd Light Cruiser Squadron

The rescued man, Stoker George Parkyn, one of the crew of the *Tipperary*,
had been extremely lucky. Throughout the morning there were a few such
fortunate rescues.

Early on the morning of 1st June we sighted what we thought was a
periscope but which turned out to be a Carley Float with seven survivors
of HMS *Fortune* on board. With great difficulty we hauled these men
aboard and found that some were in bad shape through shrapnel
wounds. We did our best to give them what comfort we could also
supplying them with some fresh clothes.[55]

Ordinary Seaman A. Coventry, HMS *Moresby*, 13th Flotilla

Survivors of the destroyer night actions were found by a number of ships.
Another raft full of survivors was picked up by the *Maenad*.

I came across a raft full of men of the *Fortune*, and picked up 11 of
them, but not without excitement, because just as I dropped a boat,
a submarine was sighted close to. I dashed off, and left the boat, and
returned to pick it up when it was quite ready in every way. Even then a
torpedo was fired at us, but it was a bad shot. The submarine had been
messing about, and had been hailed by the men, but of course used
them as a bait. One died after we got him on board, but the others were
landed at Queensferry.[56]

Commander John Champion, HMS *Maenad*, 12th Flotilla

Overall the vista that lay before them as they cruised around the area of
the battle was grim.

During the afternoon we passed over the scene of the action. The sea was strewn with wreckage for miles and we steamed for half an hour through large numbers of dead bodies, mostly German, floating in a mass of blood, oil, dead fish, sea-gulls, cartridge cases, etc.[57]

Midshipman Gordon Eady, HMS *New Zealand*, 2nd Battlecruiser Squadron

The tangle of destruction strangely mirrored the trail of devastation left by conflict on land.

We steamed over the scene of the action. We passed masses of floating wreckage: spars, ditty boxes, fragments of lifeboats and many bodies. After steaming about this gruesome locality – the scene of many triumphs and losses – for many hours, we shaped course for home.[58]

Able Seaman John Myers, HMS *Monarch*, 2nd Division, Second Battle Squadron

Shortly after 11.00, the Grand Fleet turned to the north-west and made directly for Scapa Flow. The battle of Jutland was over.

For some of the smaller ships, sailing back independently, returning home was rather easier said than done. The destroyer *Obdurate* was confronted by a series of problems. Although the ship had not been badly damaged, fundamentally the crew had absolutely no idea where they were! Dead reckoning was useless after the twists and turns of the battle and the sun refused to shine on them.

Homeward bound on our own we were faced with a problem of navigation. Having virtually no record of our courses and speeds during the battle it was idle to try and calculate our position and there was no gainsaying the fact that we were lost. The wind had freshened and scurrying clouds masked the sun from observation. The Captain pondered the chart and mumbling, "My guess is as good as anybody's!" drew a large circle and prodding it with his finger said, "The rocks are a long way off – steer west and let me know if it gets thick!" With this parting injunction he left the bridge for the first time for 24 hours.[59]

Sub-Lieutenant Harry Oram, HMS *Obdurate*, 13th Flotilla

More by luck than judgement the *Obdurate* made it home. But not before she was racked by one last cruel twist of fate that accentuated the tragedy of the battle.

When we had ceased fire earlier that day a nose fused lyddite shell was in the gun and, as it was a somewhat cumbrous matter to eject such a projectile, he decided that the easiest way of emptying the gun was to fire it. Having warned the Captain, I piped the gun's crew to muster and a few minutes later Petty Officer Tait, the gunlayer, hailed from the foc'sle and was told the object of the exercise. He had an able seamen with him and between them they laid and trained the gun out on the bow and, without waiting for the remainder of the gun's crew, he reported that he was ready. The First Lieutenant, satisfied that the range was clear, gave the order to, "Fire!" and together we leant over the bridge rail as the gunlayer closed up to his position at the left of the gun. As he pulled the trigger there was an explosion and, to our horror, we saw the gun burst just abaft the trunnion. The severed rear part of the gun was blown back by the force of the explosion and the breech block flying in our direction hit, and all but penetrated, the protective mattress surrounding the bridge. We hurried to the foc'sle to find the gunlayer dead and the Able Seaman lacerated and unconscious. The gun accident shocked the whole company. It was cruelly paradoxical that after battle without casualty, we should suffer loss by misadventure and the cause of the accident gave rise to much argument. There seemed to be no reason why a perfectly normal gun, which only a few hours earlier had functioned in an exemplary manner, should suddenly erupt.[60]

Sub-Lieutenant Harry Oram, HMS *Obdurate*, 13th Flotilla

Later investigation by the ordnance experts found a flaw in the barrel. When coupled with the cooling of the gun with the shell still inside it, this had caused the barrel to grip the driving band of the shell with more than usual intensity. When the gun was fired, the path of least resistance for the explosion had been the flaw in the barrel, ripping apart the gun and stealing away the life of yet another man.

The bigger ships were less troubled by the fluctuations of wind and tide. They had retained a clearer idea of their navigational position. But for those that had suffered damage and casualties in the battle there followed a grim combination of damage control, the collection of corpses and the care of the wounded. Parties of men were set to repair the damage caused by the ferocious blast of the huge guns. Many were simply tidying things up, getting them back into some kind of order, the first steps of the long process that would eventually return the ships to pristine condition.

> We were employed in cleaning up the battery. The whole place was a shambles, with twisted iron and steel everywhere, even after the debris was cleared up and it was not put right until the ship was refitted. The nose of the shell which dealt all this fearful destruction was found embedded in a tin of biscuits in the canteen. It is now mounted on a wooden base and kept on board as a relic.[61]
>
> Sub-Lieutenant Clifford Caslon, HMS *Malaya*, Fifth Battle Squadron

Officers read the roll-calls, gaps were identified and they attempted to find out what had happened to their men.

> In the afternoon we set course for Scapa and the men were fallen in and we mustered by the roll call. I read the muster for the forecastle division, to which I was attached – it was a grim business, and I was glad when it was done.[62]
>
> Sub-Lieutenant Clifford Caslon, HMS *Malaya*, Fifth Battle Squadron

Every man who failed to answer had to be accounted for. It was a time of painful discoveries: across the fleet the realization dawned that the hand of fate had passed across their future, before moving on to choose other victims. Boy 1st Class Henry Hawkins had spent the battle in 'A' Turret of the *Barham* and had seen little of the battle. When at last he emerged, the state of the ship gave him a profound shock.

> I was horrified to come on deck and see our fore-messdeck gone, sick bay patients and staff wiped out, as the sick bay received a direct hit. I thought to myself, "I must be lucky!" Because nine of us boys who had not been vaccinated during the last five years were attended to on the 30th May. On the morning of the 31st, eight went sick and were detained in the sick bay. I put up with my sore arm and remained alive.[63]
>
> Boy 1st Class Henry Hawkins, HMS *Barham*, Fifth Battle Squadron

In the chaos that reigned aboard many ships, there were many surprises lurking for the unwary.

During the morning of 1st June I went down to the messdeck to my mess. A body was lying on the mess table, I was told he was dead. I laid on the stool and fell asleep. When I woke up the body moved. He sat up and spoke to me – I wonder if my face turned white! It was Leading Signaller Last who had been wounded and unconscious and covered with newspapers. I am pleased to say he recovered.[64]

Ordinary Signalman Charles Rudall, HMS *Chester*, attached 3rd Battlecruiser Squadron

Many men were understandably shaky after their experiences. Their nerves had been stretched and there was an inevitable reaction. The veneer of glory had been stripped from the face of battle and few knew how to react.

When we were allowed to get out of the turret in the evening, the Midshipman of the turret, was longing to say something to me quietly. Then he said, "Mr Macey, I thought I was a brave person before this action and I hope now I shall never see a German again, dead or alive." I dare not answer him, for I felt very much the same.[65]

Boatswain William Macey, HMS *Tiger*, 1st Battlecruiser Squadron

Slowly, some kind of routine re-emerged aboard the ships. Normal human needs were reasserted after the unnatural privations of the battle.

We fell out from action stations at 6pm about 27 hours after we had sounded off the day before. It was a quaint sight to see us in the gunroom, black and begrimed partaking of our first meal for over 24 hours. It was only dry bread and tea but served to appease our hunger *pro tem*. I then had a refreshing wash, brushed up and spent the evening salving my belongings from the flooded gunroom.[66]

Midshipman Gordon Eady, HMS *New Zealand*, 2nd Battlecruiser Squadron

The men exchanged their tales. Over the space of a few hours they had looked death in the face, they had seen the horrors of war and they had survived. Such an experience inevitably changed them, not necessarily for the better.

I arranged to be served with a meal in the wardroom galley. As I ate, I was regaled by the cook, a true Cockney, with an account of how, the previous day, he had found his mate lying dead with the top of his head neatly sliced off, "Just as you might slice off the top of a boiled egg, Sir!" Which I myself had observed. But by that time I had become so inured to death and wounds and blood that I was able to listen unmoved, continuing with my meal the while.[67]

Sub-Lieutenant Windham Hornby, HMS *Chester*, attached 3rd Battlecruiser Squadron

The wounded had by this time been collected together and were placed under treatment. On the hardest hit ships the sick bays quickly became pitiful places of horror where pain and suffering mingled with stoicism.

My first place of call was the medical distribution space. I had heard that my friend, Teddie Brown, had been wounded. I found the place forrard to the right of 'B' Turret barbette, and overflowing on to the starboard stokers' mess deck. Brown was doing fairly well, so I moved among my wounded shipmates. What a scene it was! It was very much like that painting of the *Victory*'s cockpit, ill lit, with mutilated bodies lying everywhere. The few cots were full, all hammock places occupied. The remainder were lying on mess tables and on the hard steel lino-covered decks, pitiful wrecks of this terrible action. I stopped by the hammock of a seaman acquaintance of mine, lit a cigarette and put it between his lips. He had lost both arms, but seemed remarkably cheerful.[68]

Able Seaman Victor Hayward, HMS *Tiger*, 1st Battlecruiser Squadron

The precise effects of traumatic shock on the workings of the human mind remain a mystery, but it is certain that not everyone was able to accept their fate with the same degree of sanguine equanimity. Private John Harris had escaped from the flames sweeping through the starboard 6-inch battery aboard the *Malaya*, but he had still been badly burnt.

That night was indescribable. A long line of wounded and dying, stretcher bearers kept busy as men passed-out. Next night the officers gave up their beds for the wounded. The boy on my right kept saying, "I wish I was dead!" Someone said, "What's the matter with the kid?" So I asked the boy and he replied, "My eyes are gone." Many of our charge loaders were blinded by ignited cordite charges.[69]

Private John Harris, Royal Marine Light Infantry, HMS *Malaya*, Fifth Battle Squadron

The *Malaya*'s surgeons carried on with a complete and utter dedication. Transcending their normal physical limitations, by sheer strength of will they worked continuously until they finally dropped.

> He and I were at it from the time we began, all that day, the following night, the following day, till the next night about 2am when I fell down. I had been feeling great pain in my legs, through standing in one place so long. Our helpers worked in watches of four hours. I discovered that my legs and ankles were swollen like a case of severe dropsy. Fortunately it was at my last case that I collapsed, so we were able to get a rest. I had asked the wine caterer, who was one of our best helpers, to leave a double whisky behind the flowerpot in the wardroom. I could not walk and had to go the length of the ship on my hands and knees – and a jolly difficult thing it is to climb up and down ladders on your hands and knees! I got to the wardroom, collected the whisky, sank into a chair and lighted a cigarette. The next thing I remember was getting shaken up by some attendant to go to some case. The whisky was un-drunk, the cigarette had burnt to my fingers. I had gone dead asleep.[70]
>
> Surgeon Lieutenant Duncan Lorimer, HMS *Malaya*, Fifth Battle Squadron

The men appreciated the superhuman efforts of their medical teams.

> Our three doctors were wonderful. The terrible state of the wounded men made their task a very heavy one, and they were kept operating and bandaging for over 24 hours without ceasing. At the end of this time they were so overcome with sheer fatigue, that the last cases were bandaged with the doctors lying down beside the patient, for they could stand no longer.[71]
>
> Sub-Lieutenant Clifford Caslon, HMS *Malaya*, Fifth Battle Squadron

Many of the dead remained where they had fallen, dismembered and charred at their posts. With their names and personalities still fresh in mind, the task of collecting and identifying the corpses was one that required a strong stomach. As part of his duties, the Reverend Bradley went down the port side of the *Tiger*, where he found bodies still strewn around the 6-inch magazine.

The sight was terrible. There was a considerable amount of water. There in all of this, mixed up with rubbish and debris were bodies or bits of bodies. One had no head as far as I could see, nor legs, the left arm was gone and the right lay near with its hand hanging off. It was a mere trunk – quite naked – for the blast tore the clothes off. You could feel the little pieces of limbs under your feet as you walked ankle deep in water. It was quite dark save for the torch we had. Later on I got together a stretcher party to try and get the pieces away, but when they saw what they had to tackle they slunk away, and I must confess I was not sorry.[72]

Reverend Thomas Bradley, HMS *Tiger*, 1st Battlecruiser Squadron

The effect of the shells that had exploded in what were, in effect, crowded rooms was to create a charnel-house. Friends and shipmates, fellow human beings, had been rendered down to their constituent parts and splattered around with no vestige of human dignity.

Well, we have had our day, what we have been looking forward to and I can't say that I particularly want to see another sight like it. The poor devils that were lying about killed. Some had their heads blown off, some with no arms and legs. The pieces of shell that were found all had picric acid on them, so all the men that were wounded were poisoned, and that caused more deaths. I went down the distribution station where the first shell came in and picked up a large piece of – well it looked like gristle and it smelt awful – so I put it out of sight.[73]

Petty Officer Edward Phillips, HMS *Barham*, Fifth Battle Squadron

Amidst the squalor, one corpse was treated with special reverence aboard HMS *Lion*. The courageous action of Major Francis Harvey of the Royal Marines in flooding the magazine below 'Q' Turret had already been made known to the crew. They sought, in their own small way, to mark their gratitude.

Three of us went into the turret, we knew who had saved us with his dying breath. We found a charred piece of humanity near where the voice pipe was. We stood still, dazed, knowing that to him we owed our lives. It seemed at the same time that we had better get something special to put these poor remains in. We went down to the nearest officer's cabin that was intact and we found some linen. We took it up with us and we wrapped him in that. We took him down to the after deck and told the officer in charge there.[74]

Stoker Donald Maclachlan, HMS *Lion*, 1st Battlecruiser Squadron

As they crossed the North Sea, heading back to Rosyth, Vice Admiral Sir David Beatty signalled to his Battlecruiser Fleet that all preparations should be made for a traditional burial at sea for the majority of the corpses. The method employed was gruesomely practical.

After (as far as possible) identification, the bodies were placed in hammocks weighted with exercise projectiles ready for burial at sea. The main provider of hammocks was the boys' hammock netting raided for this purpose and so I lost my first pair of hammocks plus blankets including one just sent from home.[75]

Boy Telegraphist Arthur Lewis, HMS *Lion*, 1st Battlecruiser Squadron

The macabre nature of this age-old naval ritual gave some of the younger members of the crew a shock. There was an inescapable air of finality about the process which had been missing from the adrenalin-soaked battle.

The biggest fright at my age was to see the bodies, the canvas bags being made and the old-fashioned cannon balls being used for the burial at sea.[76]

Boy 1st Class Henry Hawkins, HMS *Barham*, Fifth Battle Squadron

The padres came together for ecumenical services to give their men a Christian send-off, however the savage indecencies of war had abused their mangled corpses.

The bodies were got together and sewn up in sackcloth – leaving their sea boots sticking out. They were then placed on the starboard superstructure. They had some difficulty in piecing together those who had been smashed up – in one or two cases the sacking with the body inside was not more than 2ft 6″ long. Word came through later that they would be buried at 6.30. A row of mess tables were placed with one end over the starboard side of the quarterdeck and the bodies were laid two on each mess table. A six inch shell was placed under their heels and tied onto their sea boots to ensure the bodies remaining at the bottom. We all collected round and the Church of England padre first of all said the burial service, then I said mine and then we both said the words of committal together.[77]

Reverend Thomas Bradley, HMS *Tiger*, 1st Battlecruiser Squadron

Surgeon Lieutenant Duncan Lorimer had come up on deck for the funerals. Like many witnesses, despite everything he had already seen he was deeply affected by the overwhelming sadness of the moment.

The ship had slowed down and there was a burial going on of the poor unrecognisable scraps of humanity from the explosion. I had been asked previously to try and identify Young and Cotton, but it was impossible. It was a gloomy scene, the grey sky, the grey sea, the stitched up hammocks, the padre with his gown blowing in the breeze. The 'Last Post' was sounded by the Marine buglers and our shipmates plunged into the sullen waters.[78]

Surgeon Lieutenant Duncan Lorimer, HMS *Malaya*, Fifth Battle Squadron

On the ships that had been hardest hit, the burial services could not be concluded quickly. The sheer number of corpses to be disposed of was intimidating and it was a long-drawn-out affair.

All the ships moved slowly. Our chaplain had been killed in the action, so Admiral Beatty took over the service. But when he started his feelings overcame him and he handed the book to Flag Captain Chatfield. Here was a scene from the brush of a great artist – the great flagship with her flag at half mast in honour of the ceremony and the marks of heavy action all over her, the smoke stained officers and men swaying to the roll of the ship and all the time the funeral party committing the remains of their late comrades to the deep. During the latter part of the ceremony we sang the hymn, 'Abide with me'. Surely never did the noble words of that beautiful hymn have a deeper significance or were ever sung to such a setting.[79]

Stoker Donald Maclachlan, HMS *Lion*, 1st Battlecruiser Squadron

The mechanics of the actual committal to the sea were brutally simple.

Two gratings were used, manned by two ratings each, one at the head
the other at the foot. Two corpses are committed to the deep at once,
one body is placed on each grating covered with a Union Jack and then
borne to the stern-most part of the upper deck, then together the two
gratings are tilted and the bodies slide off the grating and into the deep.
And so the process is continued until all the bodies had found a watery
grave. The sailors' anthem (Eternal Father Strong to Save) having been
sung with many a sad heart, the ceremony closes.[80]

Petty Officer Edwin Downing, HMS *Lion*, 1st Battlecruiser Squadron

And so the corpses dropped down into the sea.

Many did not sink immediately, but kind of floated in a horizontal
position for a time until the weights took effect, when they gradually
righted themselves to an upright position with about half of the canvas
showing above the surface before finally disappearing beneath the waves.
It was an eerie scene as though they wanted to take one last look at their
old ships before they went under.[81]

Signalman John Handley, HMS *Barham*, Fifth Battle Squadron

◆ ◆ ◆

The *Warspite* was the first ship to return to Rosyth. Word of the confrontation between the fleets had spread through the British ports and it was
inevitable that everybody in harbour and ashore was desperate for news
of the battle. As the *Warspite* docked, Assistant Clerk Bickmore was given
a task that tested his remaining stamina to the utmost.

Captain Phillpotts sent for me as we slowly steamed up to Rosyth and
gave me a note addressed to the Captain of the *Queen Elizabeth* and
told me that, as we entered the dock I was to jump ashore and take it
on board the *Queen Elizabeth*, which I did. I was taken straight down to
the Captain's cabin and delivered the note and was given a glass of
champagne while I answered questions. When I left the Captain, the
Commander was waiting for me and took me to the wardroom where
to the accompaniment of whisky, the wardroom's officers had their
turn; and then the Gun Room got hold of me, this time with beer, so
I imagine the story improved in each mess. When I went back on

board my own ship I had about as much liquid ballast as I
could carry![82]

Assistant Clerk Gilbert Bickmore, HMS *Warspite*, Fifth Battle Squadron

The super-dreadnought *Queen Elizabeth* had been confined in dry dock
and as a result had missed the battle. She was swiftly moved out of dock
to make way for her injured sister ship. Her officers and crew proved most
solicitous in looking after their opposite numbers from the *Warspite*.

The *Queen Elizabeth*'s were exceedingly kind in offering sleeping
accommodation to those of us whose cabins were unusable. Middleton
put me up in one of their cabins and I went to bed that night
surrounded by every conceivable luxury, even to a large box of his own
chocolates which Middleton brought up and put alongside my bunk for
me to help myself to in case I couldn't sleep. I did though, although I
felt so wide awake until I got between the sheets that Middleton had to
force me to go and turn in even though I was his guest![83]

Surgeon Gordon Ellis, HMS *Warspite*, Fifth Battle Squadron

Sailors have always formed attachments to their old ships. But the eccentric
nature of the *Warspite*'s double circle under the collective nose of the High
Seas Fleet, the effectiveness of her armour which shielded her crew and the
sheer military power that she exuded, gave the *Warspite* an added cachet that
from that day was to distinguish her for the rest of a long naval career.

Next morning I went and had a look all round the ship as she lay in
dock and it may have been emotional, but I felt I just loved her. And I
think now there is no other ship in the world like her. *Warspite* – may her
name always be honoured.[84]

Surgeon Gordon Ellis, HMS *Warspite*, Fifth Battle Squadron

At about 08.30 the next morning, 2 June, the survivors of the
Battlecruiser Fleet sailed into the Firth of Forth. Public knowledge of the
battle was spreading fast and the welcome for Beatty's gallant ships was
heartfelt.

It was evident that the news of our doings had gone before us as the
bridge and forts were crowded with soldiers who gave us cheer upon
cheer as we passed. All Admiral Hood's family were on the veranda of

his house waving to the ships as they came in. The first gloomy Admiralty communiqué was not issued until that evening, so they were still in ignorance of the *Invincible*'s fate. Nearly all the battlecruisers had scars to show, mainly on the funnels and upper works, or great dents in the armoured plating. All our bridge screens were hanging in tatters, our funnels and paintwork were scorched and blistered, and the former were dented from the blast from our own guns. Most of our boats were smashed and a huge gaping hole showed where 'X' Turret had been hit. Most of the badly damaged ships went straight into dock and the Forth looked strangely empty. Close to us were the buoys round which the *Queen Mary* and *Indefatigable* had swung for so long. The latter was our 'chummy' ship and each of us wrote to the parents of one of her 'snotties', just a letter of sympathy, which was the least we could do.[85]

Midshipman Gordon Eady, HMS *New Zealand*, 2nd Battlecruiser Squadron

As they sailed past under the bridge, the hospital ship *Plassy* moved out to meet them ready to receive the wounded. The nurses aboard, who had been waiting for nearly two days to take aboard the casualties, were now to go into 'action' themselves.

We received orders early to proceed at once down to the Forth Bridge and prepare to take in patients as the ships came in. There has been a tremendous battle and I am afraid we have lost a good many ships, including some say the *Queen Mary*, but I do hope that is not true. As we got to anchor, the ships began to come in, the *Lion*, the *Tiger*, the *Princess Royal*, the *Southampton*, the *Birmingham*, the *Birkenhead*, the *Inconstant*, etc. etc. etc., besides destroyers, steamed past us and our crew gave them cheer on cheer. They did not look much the worse except for a few ominous looking holes, but inside some of them had been infernos but a few hours before. Crowded on the decks in most varied rig, were survivors from the poor lost ships. The men all looked cheery even at that hour and one could hardly believe all that they must have gone through.[86]

Naval Nursing Sister Mary Clarke, HM Hospital Ship *Plassy*, Rosyth

It was not long before the grim evidence of the misery of battle was carried across to the waiting nurses. They too were brought face to face with the nature of modern warfare.

Drifters by the dozen, six or seven deep on the port and starboard sides waiting to unload their sad burdens. Poor men, they almost all had their faces and hands tied up. We started about 11 and by 12.30 had taken in over 100 and they said the worst ones, at least 90 cot cases, were still to come. We got them all into bed as quickly as possible, no easy job sometimes, and fed them with beef tea and the bad ones with brandy, and left them to settle down a bit before we attempted their dressings. We rushed up and snatched a little lunch as we could, then the bad cases began to come in, poor things it was pitiful to see some of them, with legs off, or arms off and some fearfully burnt, face, arms, legs and body. We even had destroyers up, alongside discharging patients directly on board. A tremendous thunderstorm came on in the afternoon, which didn't assist matters as everything got wringing wet. By about 3.30 they were all inboard with the exception of a few isolated cases.[87]

Naval Nursing Sister Mary Clarke, HM Hospital Ship *Plassy*, Rosyth

At Rosyth the atmosphere of heightened emotion resulted in some understandably harrowing scenes as some casualties were brought out of the ships and disgorged directly ashore.

During the battle there was little time for thought and feelings. Later when we were safely housed in the dry dock, there was a poignant scene as crowds of dockyard workers gathered on the dockside to watch the dead and wounded being carried over the gangways. The ship's male voice choir, led by their conductor, a Welsh stoker, sang 'Comrades in Arms' while this was being done. Many strong men broke down and wept. After the dead had all been carried ashore it was now the turn of the wounded. I was standing beside the Reverend Walter Carey at this time and a stretcher was being carried past with a body completely swathed in bandages with only holes for mouth, nose and eyes. As the stretcher passed we heard a voice saying, "God bless *Warspite*" and recognised it as that of Father Poland who was badly burned trying to save men in the 6″ Battery deck when the cordite ammunition was set on fire. Carey broke down and wept like a child.[88]

Engine Room Artificer 1st Class Thomas Collins, *HMS Warspite*, Fifth Battle Squadron

Private John Harris, after enduring the awful conditions in the *Malaya* sick bay, was finally landed at the docks. But by this time he had become quite delirious.

> After landing at base we were taken by hospital train to Queensferry.
> Ladies on the train handed out cigarettes. I kept shouting, "Pass up
> lyddite, pass up shrapnel!" A lady put a spoonful of jelly in my mouth
> to shut it. One chap said, "Do you know who that lady was?" I said,
> "Haven't the slightest!" He said, "That was Lady Jellicoe!"[89]
>
> Private John Harris, Royal Marine Light Infantry, HMS *Malaya*, Fifth Battle Squadron

Those who had not been wounded may have been able to cheer and celebrate their survival, but underneath many were suffering from the symptoms of suppressed shock. Though they were outwardly in control, this was often revealed in the most trivial of ways.

> The wardroom still being unfit to use as a mess, the Captain had invited
> us to dine in his fore-cabin, he himself taking the head of the table.
> The wardroom cook prepared the repast and he 'led off' with tomato
> soup, of a particularly sanguinary hue. Or so some of us thought. The
> Captain took up a spoonful. Then regarding us steadily, he observed,
> "No, Gentlemen, I think not!" And we passed to the next course.[90]
>
> Sub-Lieutenant Windham Hornby, HMS *Chester*, attached to 3rd Battlecruiser
> Squadron

The naval nurses aboard the *Plassy* were rushed off their feet. From a standing start they had been catapulted into the full range of battle wounds. As they tried to deal with the worst cases, the burns victims posed the most problems.

> We were able to set to work to see what we had got. I had the most in
> my ward with 46 acute cases besides the supervision of 'B' which was
> full up too. We started about 5.00 to do the dressings ... Some of the
> poor things hadn't been touched since Wednesday night when the first
> fight took place and had only the first picric dressings on their burns.
> It must have been agonies taking the dressings off, but very few of them
> made a moan, I never saw such bravery in my life. The smell of burns is
> awful, one gets almost nauseated sometimes. The poor things have

nearly all to be fed as nearly all have both hands tied up and masks on their faces, and their poor eyes are so bad in most cases, it takes a long time.[91]

Naval Nursing Sister Mary Clarke, HM Hospital Ship *Plassy*, Rosyth

The men had been through the most awful physical and mental trauma. It was not surprising that some lost their reason under the pressure. One man went mad and jumped overboard.

A terrible thing happened in my ward last night, one of my gas poisoning boys who has been very bad, suddenly went off his head and while the night duty man's back was turned went into the lavatory and jumped through the scuttle. He was seen swimming along towards one of the cruisers and we signalled over to them to lower a boat. He must have been stronger than we thought as he had gone about 200 yards and caught hold of their cable. They took him on board, wrapped him in blankets and gave him brandy, then sent him back to us. He does not seem much the worse but I'm afraid the shock will be very bad for him.[92]

Naval Nursing Sister Mary Clarke, HM Hospital Ship *Plassy*, Rosyth

Three hours after the Battlecruiser Fleet, at 11.30 on 2 June, the main body of the Grand Fleet arrived back at Scapa Flow. Their casualties had been minimal and their reception in the isolated anchorage was an understated affair in contrast to the dramatic scenes unfolding at Rosyth.

When we cast off, the depot ship had their large gramophone on deck playing, "We don't want to lose you, but we think you ought to go!" Three days later, when we came alongside again to repair action damage and evacuate wounded, the gramophone was again in evidence playing, "We're glad to see you back dear lady!"[93]

Sub-Lieutenant Eric Lees, HMS *Nessus*, 12th Flotilla

One ship that those ashore imagined would have suffered heavily was the *Duke of Edinburgh* – the sole surviving ship of the 1st Cruiser Squadron. Both the *Defence* and the *Black Prince* had gone down with all hands and the *Warrior* had suffered grievously.

By the time we arrived in the Flow it was common knowledge that three out of the four ships of our Squadron had gone down. It was to be

expected, therefore, that the *Duke of Edinburgh* had certainly shared in the
casualties, details of which we were asked to report by signal. The reply
was, "One case of Rubella." This was a mild form of fever contracted
by a musician in the transmitting station. Compared with our consorts
we certainly got off very lightly.[94]

Lieutenant Leslie Hollis, HMS *Duke of Edinburgh*, 1st Cruiser Squadron

Guilt is a common emotion in the aftermath of battle. Men feel that
they should have shared the fate of their comrades. Able Seaman Arthur
Ford was particularly vulnerable to such feelings. He had missed the battle,
as he had been sent on a gunnery course just five days before it. When he
heard that his erstwhile ship, the *Black Prince*, had gone down with all hands
he was mortified. Suddenly Ford was alone, bereft and struggling with
violently conflicting feelings which veered from a strange guilt to sheer relief.

My first thoughts were that I'd dodged the column and I ought to have
gone with them. I did. I don't know why but I did. I thought, "Why
should I escape when all the others went west?" That's the feeling I
had for some time. "What a horrible end I've missed..." Imagine the
different crews at their gun stations, I would know a lot of the men and
what guns they were on. They were so exposed, the six inch guns were
on deck with no shelter of any description, totally in the open. The guns
had been brought up from the lower deck to the upper deck because
they couldn't fire them in rough weather in that type of ship. Can you
imagine being half a mile away from the German High Seas Fleet with
their 12″ guns. It would just blow them clean out of the water a
broadside. Oh, it must have been a shocking, nobody able to do a thing,
I doubt if they fired a shot hardly. But of course these things when
you're young these thoughts don't last too long.[95]

Able Seaman Arthur Ford, HMS *Black Prince*, 1st Cruiser Squadron

On some of the worst hit ships, the stench of battle was not easily
washed away and provided a lingering reminder of lost shipmates. In these
cases it would be some time before their crews could forget Jutland.

By this time an awful smell had penetrated all over the ship and we had
to get busy with buckets of disinfectant and carbolic soap. Human flesh
had got into all sorts of nooks, such as voice pipes, telephones,

ventilating shafts and behind bulkheads. I remember helping to clear the
port flour store of that glutinous mass of water and flour; it was like
trying to clear out a huge pastry-mixing bowl, and we humans were the
currants![96]

Able Seaman Victor Hayward, HMS *Tiger*, 1st Battlecruiser Squadron

Yet despite all the horrors and the lengthy casualty lists it is a simple
fact that, for most of the British sailors of the Grand Fleet, life soon
returned to normal.

The ambulance came down and took the dead and dying away and the
wounded. Somebody made some tea – as usual! A mate of mine said,
"Here let's climb up on the quayside". And we had an old football
aboard and we were up there kicking this football about! We'd been so
trained to accept anything that was going to happen that it was not
exactly routine, but it had happened and that was it![97]

Able Seaman George Wainford, HMS *Onslaught*, 12th Flotilla

Their morale would survive the shock of battle. The question was: How
would the world and history come to view the battle they had fought?

CHAPTER EIGHT

WHO WON?

HAVING A SHORTER distance to travel, the Germans naturally got back into port first. This gave them an immense advantage in the war of words that was to follow over the results of what they called the battle of Skaggerak. From their perspective they had won a great victory. Scheer initially claimed to have sunk three battlecruisers, one super-dreadnought (mistakenly claiming the *Warspite*), two armoured cruisers, two light cruisers and thirteen destroyers. At this point the Germans only cautiously admitted to the loss of the *Pommern* and the *Wiesbaden*, though allowing that the *Frauenlob* and some destroyers had not yet returned. They concealed the loss of the *Lützow*, the *Elbing* and *Rostock*. As one, the German nation boiled over with exultation and patriotic jubilation. Banner headlines screamed news of the 'victory', first from every German street corner but then quickly spreading until the rest of the world was convinced that the Royal Navy had been defeated. All the august machinery of state was deployed to reinforce the national celebrations that ensued now that the long shadow of British naval supremacy seemed to have been dispelled.

> The first honour paid to the Fleet was a visit from His Majesty the Emperor on June 5, who, on board the flagship, *Friedrich der Grosse*, made a hearty speech of welcome to divisions drawn from the crews of all the ships, thanking them in the name of the Fatherland for their gallant deeds. In the afternoon the Emperor visited all the hospitals where the wounded lay, as well as the hospital ship *Sierra Ventana*, where lay Rear-Admiral Behncke, leader of Squadron III, who was wounded in the battle, and who was able to give the Emperor a detailed account of his impressions while at the head of the battleships. Several of the German princes also visited the Fleet, bringing greetings from their homes to the crews and expressing pride in the Fleet and the conduct of the men.

The Grand Dukes of Mecklenburg-Schwerin and of Oldenburg came directly after the battle and were followed very soon after by the Kings of Saxony and Bavaria.[1]

Admiral Reinhard Scheer, SMS *Friedrich der Grosse*, III Battle Squadron, High Seas Fleet

Honours and awards were showered on the fleet on an unparalleled scale. This display of triumphalism was in no way feigned. The High Seas Fleet had indeed sunk more ships than they had lost; they had conducted themselves with courageous determination throughout the battle and their ships had more than vindicated the faith of their designers in their ability to withstand almost anything that the British could throw at them.

From the other side of the North Sea the perception of what soon became known to the British as the battle of Jutland was markedly different. Popular expectations, founded on centuries of naval supremacy, had always been absurdly high. Nothing but the complete destruction of the German fleet would have been acceptable to the British public. Questions of strategy and Imperial security did not enter the public mind. They simply expected the Germans to be soundly thrashed. In the harsh light of this view what actually happened at Jutland fell far short of expectations. Even for the professionals there was no sense of triumph or victory. For Jellicoe, Beatty, the Admiralty and the men of the Royal Navy, the battle of Jutland was a distinct disappointment. Even before the Grand Fleet had actually returned to harbour, the first rumours of defeat had begun to circulate, causing deep concern in that section of the Admiralty tasked with releasing briefings and controlling the inflated public perceptions.

Our first news that there had been a battle was the German wireless message that announced to the world that 'a portion' of their High Seas Fleet had met our Grand Fleet in full force and had defeated it. Presently we got various single 'intercepts' between Sir David Beatty and the Commander in Chief of the Grand Fleet referring to losses of various ships. The damaged ships began to come into east coast ports with many hospital cases on board. Of course, wild rumours were flying about all over the country, since officers and men were wiring to their friends saying that they were all right. There was normally no censorship

of inland messages, but on this occasion messages of the nature
indicated were held up for inquiry before being sent on. It was at once
decided, however, that the number – about 6,000 – being so enormous,
it was out of the question to hold them up. In addition a great many
people in the neighbourhood of Edinburgh had learnt that a battle had
been fought at sea.[2]

Sir Douglas Brownrigg, Naval Censor, Admiralty

As the officers and men went ashore they had to cope with a strange
mixture of fact and rumour. Some found their families in mourning after
inaccurate reports had condemned their ships in error to oblivion.

As soon as I was able to go ashore after the battle I made haste to advise
my mother of my safety. Poor mother, this was less than three weeks
after the death of my brother. I was therefore horrified later to find that
my Queensferry friends had written to her sending their condolences on
my demise! When the Fleet was returning it was confidently reported
among naval circles ashore that *Indomitable* had been blown up instead of
Invincible and they had acted on this immediately. Fortunately my wire
arrived almost simultaneously. Next day I went to visit these friends.
The maid, whom I knew well, opened the door and when she saw me
she screamed and fled. You see she had the best authority for knowing
me dead. The family came tumbling out and welcomed me back to the
land of the living with joyful acclamations.[3]

Assistant Clerk Hubert Fischer, HMS *Indomitable*, 3rd Battlecruiser Squadron

The Admiralty, conscious that the Germans had already successfully
begun to peddle their version of the battle to the international press, was
keen to issue a statement as soon as possible.

We were thus faced with the situation that it was known all over the
country that there had been a great naval battle, whilst we at the
Admiralty were, officially, in ignorance of what had actually occurred.
In these circumstances, whilst fully appreciating the preoccupations of
the Commander in Chief, it was decided to ask him for a statement for
publication.[4]

Sir Douglas Brownrigg, Naval Censor, Admiralty

After receiving Jellicoe's reply giving brief reports of losses and a few words on the imagined German losses, the Admiralty decided to go ahead in issuing an outline account.

> On that bare information it was decided that it was necessary to make
> an announcement to the Press, since it was obviously impossible to
> maintain further silence. The first communiqué was therefore issued to
> the Press at 7pm on June 2, and it has been very much criticised from
> various points of view. Its wording was not arrived at without intense
> care and thought and discussion, and those who framed it were Mr
> Balfour (the First Lord), Admiral Sir Henry Jackson (the First Sea Lord),
> and Vice Admiral Sir Henry Oliver (the Chief of Staff). It cannot be
> suggested by anybody that more *brains* could have been got together in
> any Government Department, or, for that matter, in any other building
> in London.[5]
>
> Sir Douglas Brownrigg, Naval Censor, Admiralty

Despite the careful consideration, the communiqué showed all the signs of having been written by committee and it was quite startlingly frank. It was the first real source of hard information for a country gasping, palpitating for news. But in its determination to face up to some unpalatable facts it failed to put any sort of gloss on events to explain the strategic significance of the battle for the British nation. Crucially, it failed to mention that the Grand Fleet had been left in control of the seas, or that the Germans, to put it bluntly, had fled for their lives. Both of these points, which were to the immense credit of the Grand Fleet, needed to be clearly stated to counterbalance the German claims.

> On the afternoon of Wednesday May 31, a naval engagement took
> place off the coast of Jutland. The British ships on which the brunt of
> the fighting fell were the Battlecruiser Fleet and some cruisers and light
> cruisers, supported by four fast battleships. Among these the losses were
> heavy. The German Battle Fleet, aided by low visibility avoided
> prolonged action with our main forces, and soon after these appeared
> on the scene the enemy returned to port, though not before receiving
> severe damage from our battleships. The battlecruisers *Queen Mary*,
> *Indefatigable*, *Invincible*, and the cruisers *Defence* and *Black Prince* were sunk.

The *Warrior* was disabled, and after being towed for some time had
to be abandoned by her crew. It is also known that the Destroyers
Tipperary, Turbulent, Fortune, Sparrowhawk and *Ardent* were lost, and six
others are not yet accounted for. No British battleships or light cruisers
were sunk. The enemy's losses were serious. At least one battlecruiser
was destroyed, and one severely damaged; one battleship reported sunk
by our destroyers during a night attack; two light cruisers were disabled
and probably sunk. The exact number of enemy destroyers disposed of
during the action cannot be ascertained with any certainty, but it must
have been large.[6]

Admiralty Communiqué

The statement was bald, and when interpreted by the popular press next
day the results were all too predicable. Most of the newspapers simply
took their lead from the tone of the Admiralty communiqué and passed
on to their readers the sad news that '*Der Tag*' they had yearned for had
somehow ended in a German victory. Naturally, the civilian reaction was
one of stunned and horrified disbelief. In wilder spirits this even led to
some abuse of the naval personnel for having 'let them down' in the course
of the battle.

My job in harbour was to run the second picket boat and so I took the
steward in to a pier just underneath the Forth Bridge, at the bottom of
the hill, South Queensferry. There was not a very big crowd of about
30 people and their attitude was one of, "Here, what do you think you
are doing? What do you think we pay the Navy for?" Remarks like that.
We said, "Well, we have just had a battle!" "Yes," they said, "fine battle
that was. The Germans beat you didn't they? We read about it in the
papers." Now that was really a complete surprise to us and a great
shock.[7]

Midshipman John Crawford, HMS *Valiant*, Fifth Battle Squadron

The resentment caused by such behaviour among the men who had so
recently risked their lives for the common cause was deep and long-lasting.

The Admiralty Communiqué giving the supposed losses came to
increase the gloom. Later, newspapers stated that some of our wounded
had been jeered at by workers at a dockside. To be derided by one's

own people, even though those concerned were of a low type of rat, was humiliating. It hurt one's sense of pride in the Service. It was impossible to believe that the long unconquerable reign of the British Navy was coming to an end. We consoled ourselves with the thought that another smack at the German Fleet must surely come. We had faith in our C-in-C.[8]

Petty Officer Telegraphist Arthur Brister, HMS *Iron Duke*, 3rd Division, Fourth Battle Squadron

Most of the Royal Navy was incandescent with rage over the treatment it had received at the hand of the Admiralty bureaucrats. Letters of protest poured in and somewhat belatedly the Admiralty realized that, perhaps, it had not employed entirely the right tone in its statement.

I have heard from many men and women all over the world that this communiqué came as a frightful staggerer, especially to friends of this country in neutral states where German propaganda was going strong, and no doubt our exiled compatriots suffered mentally very acutely. None the less I still think, at this distance of time, that the only proper course was pursued and the only possible version given to the public from the facts as they were known at the Admiralty.[9]

Sir Douglas Brownrigg, Naval Censor, Admiralty

Bolstered by further reports from Jellicoe, the Admiralty tried to correct its defeatist tone in a second communiqué issued on 3 June which sought to boost German losses, followed by a third statement on 4 June, which grossly exaggerated them. The subsequent German confession on 7 June that they had concealed the loss of the battlecruiser *Lützow* and light cruiser *Rostock* in their first statements also helped to undermine the initial fears of outright German victory. Gradually, as it was realized that the British blockade endured unchallenged, the overall international perception of the battle slowly mutated to that of a qualified British success. When Jellicoe's Despatch on the Battle of Jutland was published on 6 July, few doubts remained in Britain that a victory had been achieved. But the helter-skelter of events that characterized the Great War had already moved on the glare of public attention. On 1 July the British and French armies launched the battle of the Somme with a military disaster on an unprecedented scale. Soon all other issues faded into near insignificance as the burgeoning casualty lists rolled from the newspaper presses. Jutland soon became 'yesterday's news'.

The overwhelming feeling of those in the Battlecruiser Fleet and Grand Fleet was of frustration at their failure to achieve the kind of success that they had expected. But they were undiminished in their confidence that they would ultimately achieve a crushing victory.

> It was an unsatisfactory show as far as results go. They were absolutely saved by the bad weather and in spite of all of Admiral Jellicoe's splendid work. All the same I am awfully glad to have been in my turret in this ship for an action after all this time of waiting. It was not of course what we expected the action to be like, not one ship against another and fought till one sinks. That will come later on...[10]
>
> Midshipman Geoff Congreve, HMS *Benbow*, 4th Division, Fourth Battle Squadron

If the Germans still fancied their chances in open battle, the men of the Royal Navy were more than willing to oblige them. Next time it would be different.

> We still have to finish the business off and they may reckon themselves able to take us on in open fight again, I can only say, "Pray God they do!" We had no luck; they had. I'm not saying so in any way to try and minimise our losses as in spite of that we defeated them. They could have engaged us again at 4.00 am Thursday but preferred to make for home.[11]
>
> Lieutenant Henry Blagrove, HMS *Tiger*, 1st Battlecruiser Squadron

Although the men of the Battlecruiser Fleet mourned their losses, such feelings were just grist to the mill to make them even more determined to 'smash the Huns'. Beatty caught the mood of many of his men soon after they returned to Rosyth.

> We have all lost friends, relatives and they have given up their lives in a most gallant manner. But these valuable lives have not been wasted and there will be a day such as we had a hundred years ago when we will account for them. Take my kindest regards to the relatives of those who died so gallantly. We have to get our ships in a good fighting condition

so that we can have the second round. We have only had 'Round One', but 'Round Two' I think they will throw in the sponge.[12]

Vice Admiral Sir David Beatty, HMS *Lion*, 1st Battlecruiser Squadron

To emphasize their continuing domination and to try to provoke a German reaction, the British light forces immediately returned to the scene of the battle.

Everyone seemed to think that the Grand Fleet had been beaten. To prove that this was not so, may I say that after the refuelling we left at daybreak the next day in company with our remaining Harwich destroyers. We swept the battle area all around Horns Reef and the Jutland Bank up to the approaches to the German minefield. We saw many signs of the action, wreckage and sunken hulls of ships. But no sign of any ship of the German Navy. [13]

Able Seaman Albert Hickson, HMS *Laurel*, 9/10th Flotillas

The Grand Fleet was ready for action again by 21.45 on 2 June. At that point Jellicoe could deploy no fewer than twenty-four intact dreadnoughts and battlecruisers ready for immediate action. This stood in sharp contrast to the mere ten available to Scheer. The British ships receiving dockyard repairs rejoined the fleet by the end of July. The damaged ships of the High Seas Fleet trickled back and Scheer was able to consider renewed action by mid August. The battlecruisers *Seydlitz* and *Derfflinger* took much longer to repair and were not released until towards the end of the year. Time imbued the cacophony of German triumphalism with a hollow ring.

Any superficial analysis of ships lost and of casualties sustained shows that the Germans did indeed have a case for celebrating a victory (see Appendices A and B).[14] In all, the British lost three battlecruisers, three armoured cruisers and eight destroyers. The Germans lost one battle-cruiser, one pre-dreadnought, four light cruisers and five destroyers. Although it can be argued that the *Invincible* and *Indefatigable* were past their prime, this is probably an unsustainable qualification. Their sister ships continued to serve in the Grand Fleet until the end of the war. In contrast, the armoured cruisers were completely obsolescent and if anything Jutland had exposed the folly of packing hundreds of trained young men into a ship that could neither fight nor flee. The Germans could point to the equal obsolescence of the *Pommern*. In the battle some 6,094 British sailors lost their lives as opposed to 2,551 Germans. The telegrams notifying families of casualties spread their misery across much of Britain to a much wider extent than is often realized. The casualty figures can be compared to the 5,774 British soldiers killed directly by enemy action (as opposed to the 16,168 succumbing later from wounds and disease) during the *whole* of the Boer War. Most of the British casualties had been caused by the explosive detonation of the three battlecruisers; had the German battlecruisers displayed an equivalent volatility then the overall picture would have been very different. Yet one of the problems with the analysis of Jutland is that experts will not consider what actually happened, but constantly imagine what might, or should, have been. The British battlecruisers *were* severely flawed, but they had been sent into battle and the Germans had made the most of their weakness.

Whatever specious claims can be constructed from an analysis of losses or casualties it remains a fact that *the British won the battle of Jutland*. In the end the material successes of the High Seas Fleet fade into complete insignificance in comparison to the crushing strategic success that the Royal Navy secured for the British Empire. The great question of the naval war had been answered. Although the High Seas Fleet did re-emerge, it would never again seriously threaten the command of the seas possessed by the Grand Fleet. The sole intention of the Germans at Jutland had been to isolate a small portion of the British fleet and, by destroying it, to allow a subsequent fleet action between relatively equal forces to follow quickly. They almost succeeded, but in the end failed. The British losses were painful, but quickly replaced. Ultimately, the British margin of superiority was not affected in the slightest by the battle. There is no room for sentiment in war, the most brutal of sciences. The mere fact that the Germans fought bravely against the odds does not materially change the result. It would only have done so if the morale of the Grand Fleet had been destroyed in the process. This was demonstrably not the case. Although proud of their achievements at Jutland, the more thoughtful German naval officers clearly acknowledged the legitimacy of the British strategic victory.

> The English fleet, by remaining a 'fleet in being', by its mere continued
> existence, had so far fully fulfilled its allotted task. The Battle of
> Skagerrak did not relax the pressure exerted by the English fleet as a
> 'fleet in being' for one minute.[15]
>
> Commander Georg von Hase, SMS *Derfflinger*, I Scouting Group, High Seas Fleet

Scheer understood this only too well. It had never been his intention to
confront the full strength of the Grand Fleet, and having inadvertently done
so, he was determined to avoid it happening again. The High Seas Fleet
did emerge once more. On 19 August Scheer led it out to try again his original pre-Jutland plan, intending to bombard Sunderland and lure the Grand
Fleet into another submarine trap. Once again the British were forewarned
by Room 40. But, in the event, through a combination of Jellicoe's legiti-
mately enhanced fears of running into precisely such a trap and a myriad
of complicating factors, the confrontation never took place, Sunderland was
left undisturbed and the High Seas Fleet returned safely once more with
nothing achieved. Back in Wilhelmshaven, Scheer realized that once again
he had been nearly trapped by the entire Grand Fleet and he lost much of
his enthusiasm for further surface adventures in the North Sea.

> In view of England's plan of campaign, there was no alternative but
> to inflict direct injury upon English commerce. We could not build a
> sufficiently great number of additional large ships to compensate for the
> inevitable losses which we were bound to suffer in the long run in a
> conflict with the numerically superior English fleet ... We ought to have
> tried earlier what the result of a victory by our fleet would be. It was a
> mistake on the part of the naval leaders not to do so.[16]
>
> Admiral Reinhard Scheer, SMS *Friedrich der Grosse*, III Battle Squadron,
> High Seas Fleet

Henceforth he advocated unrestricted submarine warfare as the naval
panacea to the parlous strategic situation that entwined Germany.

> A victorious end to the war at not too distant a date can only be looked
> for by the crushing of English economic life through U-boat action
> against English commerce. Prompted by the convictions of duty, I
> earnestly advise Your Majesty to abstain from deciding on too lenient a
> form of procedure on the ground that it is opposed to military views,

and that the risk of the boats would be out of all proportion to the expected gain, for, in spite of the greatest conscientiousness on the part of the Chiefs, it would not be possible in English waters, where American interests are so prevalent, to avoid occurrences which might force us to make humiliating concessions if we do not act with the greatest severity.[17]

Admiral Reinhard Scheer, SMS *Friedrich der Grosse*, III Battle Squadron, High Seas Fleet

In October 1916 the German Naval Staff announced a resumption of unrestricted submarine warfare. Although the High Seas Fleet briefly emerged on 18 October, it returned to harbour with nothing achieved. It was to be the last time it emerged before the end of the war. The morale of the fleet, which had briefly blossomed after the perceived German victory at Jutland, soon drained away as naval personnel realized that for them '*Der Tag*' would never dawn. When the war finally staggered to a close two long, painful years later, with the German Army in steady retreat, the High Seas Fleet mutinied rather than emerge to fight a last futile battle. The ultimate triumph of the Royal Navy was reflected in the humiliating surrender of the seventy ships of the High Seas Fleet to the Grand Fleet on 21 November 1918.

◆ ◆ ◆

The achievement of a crushing strategic victory was not enough to remove the venomous sting from the post-mortems conducted after Jutland. Although the Royal Navy had been vehement in its demands for a proper recognition of its achievements at Jutland, this by no means implied that it was in any way satisfied with its performance in the battle. It too had expected a crushing victory and it was fully aware that, whatever Jutland was, it was not a British triumph.

It was apparent that the mighty dreadnoughts, but in particular the battlecruisers, had severe weaknesses that would have to be addressed as a matter of extreme urgency.

It reminds me of the knights in armour who hammered each other with maces, battleaxes and spiked balls attached by a chain to a handle. Like the knights' armour, these 'dreadnoughts' we used to think were so wonderful, had their weaknesses as their designers and constructors should have realised.[18]

Engine Room Artificer Gordon Davies, HMS *Birkenhead*, 3rd Light Cruiser Squadron

The experts laboured on numerous technical committees preparing reports to determine the lessons of the battle. As a result, armour protection against plunging fire was increased over the magazines; comprehensive anti-flash measures were introduced to reduce the possibility of flash penetration and the consequent inevitable cataclysmic explosions that had ensued at Jutland; the introduction of director firing was accelerated and widened; new spotting and gunnery control measures were rapidly devised and introduced.

The battle had revealed many structural weaknesses and defects in our warships, which entailed speedy alterations and additions. So, for the next year or so, we were engaged in fitting additional armour plating above magazines and shell-rooms, and in installing flash proof arrangements to ammunition hoists. The electricians and fitters were frantically fitting directional firing equipment. If there *had* been another major battle our ships would have been much less vulnerable – and could have given a better account of themselves![19]

Shipwright Charles Petty, HMS *Victorious*, Scapa Flow

It also became apparent that the British shells were not as efficient as they should have been. Intelligence sources revealed that the Germans had been pleasantly surprised by their lack of penetration and destructive force.

It was astonishing that the ships had remained navigable in the state they were in. This was chiefly attributable to the faulty exploding charge of the English heavy calibre shells, their explosive effect being out of all proportion to their size. A number of bits of shell picked up clearly showed that powder only had been used in the charge. Many shells of 34cm and 38cm calibres had burst into such large pieces that, when picked up, they were easily fitted together again.[20]

Admiral Reinhard Scheer, SMS *Friedrich der Grosse*, III Squadron, High Seas Fleet

Trials under more realistic battle conditions than had previously been the norm uncovered serious defects in British shell design. This however proved an excessively long-winded and difficult matter to resolve. Indeed, the new fully efficient armour-piercing shells only became available to the Grand Fleet in the spring of 1918.

Jellicoe had learned much in the course of the battle and the Grand Fleet Battle Orders were systematically reviewed and revised to ensure that the mistakes that had been made would not be repeated. Nevertheless, the dominant theme remained the formation of a single line of battle designed to pulverize the High Seas Fleet by the massed power of the great guns. However, a little more flexibility was introduced where it was clear that the prevailing visibility or other circumstances meant that the Commander-in-Chief could not command and control the whole fleet. The response to the threat posed by German destroyer attacks was also tweaked to allow unthreatened divisions of the battle line to press on and maintain contact, while only those directly menaced by torpedoes would take such evasive measures as seemed most appropriate. The role of the British destroyer flotillas was redefined in a more offensive cast, emphasizing that the best means of defence was to threaten torpedo attacks themselves on the German line as soon as an engagement had become general. The importance of maintaining contact with the main body of the German fleet throughout the twists and turns of action, but especially at night, was also emphasized.

For all the positive changes that resounded through the Grand Fleet, human nature meant that unfortunately these went hand in hand with a thoroughly negative-minded search for scapegoats. The origins of the problem lay deep within the Battlecruiser Fleet. They had considered themselves the élite of the Grand Fleet. Now their disappointment at the results of Jutland boiled over into a widespread belief that Beatty had done everything he could to successfully deliver Scheer and the High Seas Fleet on a plate to Jellicoe and the Grand Fleet. They had then, through excessive caution and downright timidity, cast aside the ripe fruits of victory. Although Beatty had initially on the surface been supportive of his Commander-in-Chief, inside he was ablaze with frustration.

I went and saw him and I had what to me was one of the most trying
periods that I can remember at any time. I was a young commander at the
time and in his cabin, he raved that the battle fleet hadn't supported him.
He was walking up and down very excited. I was alone with him there.
I know I was sweating, I didn't know what to say, because he was very
angry at the time. I think he firmly believed that he had been deserted.[21]

Commander Hubert Dannreuther, HMS *Invincible*, 3rd Battlecruiser Squadron

Beatty and his men's viewpoint might have been countered more easily
if Jellicoe had not himself been so chastened by his failure to achieve the
victory he sought. The depression that afflicted him was exacerbated by
the loss of the *Hampshire* carrying the charismatic, if increasingly redun-
dant, Field Marshal Lord Kitchener en route for a visit to Russia on 5
June. In a foul night the *Hampshire* had the misfortune to run into one of
the mines laid by a submarine minelayer as part of Scheer's trap intended
for the Grand Fleet leaving harbour. It was not Jellicoe's fault, but he
shouldered the responsibility as he did so much else. His health, never
robust since the wound he suffered in the Boxer Rebellion of 1900, was
wavering and he seemed to have lost his confidence and zest for the fray
after Jutland. The incredibly lonely burden that he had endured since the
outbreak of the war seems to have doubled overnight. He no longer
looked forward to battle; his vital intellectual vigour had been ground
down and finally eroded.

Aware of the feeling that was building up in the Battlecruiser Fleet,
Jellicoe made a well-intentioned attempt to bind his fleet together. Once
they had been restored to full fighting strength he arranged for them to
pay a fraternal visit to the Grand Fleet at Scapa Flow, where they received
a carefully orchestrated reception.

We entered the Flow at about noon on Sunday morning, in glorious
weather, hot sun, cloudless sky and not a breath of wind. To reach our
anchorage, we had to steam through the lines of the Grand Fleet. In
accordance with our usual custom the ship's companies were drawn up
on deck standing at attention. To our surprise when we were fairly in
amongst the Fleet, as if by a given signal, they all burst into a roar of
cheering. As we passed each ship we were greeted with a fresh outburst of
cheer upon cheer. We were completely taken aback and carried on

standing to attention. We could see the Captains of the battleships, caps in hand on their forebridges giving the time for the cheers. What a difference to our reception ashore by the people in Edinburgh! To our signal of thanks from Beatty, Jellicoe replied, 'We thank you for your signal. The ships at Scapa only desired to give expression to their regard and admiration of their comrades in the Battlecruiser Fleet'. During our ten days stay we were honoured with fetes, entertainments and dinners every night by ships in the Grand Fleet. It was great – Jutland was worth it.[22]

Midshipman Gordon Eady, HMS *New Zealand*, 2nd Battlecruiser Squadron

But the effect of such placatory gestures did not endure and the simmering embers of underlying discontent soon flared up again.

On 28 November 1916 the clearly exhausted Jellicoe was called ashore to take up the equally onerous duties of First Sea Lord charged with countering the German submarine campaign. His departure allowed the Grand Fleet at Scapa to demonstrate the affection and admiration in which they held their chief. One of his staff, who had served with him aboard the *Iron Duke* since August 1914, expressed his feelings about Jellicoe in passionate terms which bordered on the hyperbole.

Jellicoe left at noon and turned over to his successor (Sir David Beatty) the most efficient fighting machine the world has ever seen. No one outside the service can or ever will realise what the world owes to J.R.J. for producing it. No other man could possibly have done it. He equals, if not excels, Nelson professionally, and has not the latter's weaknesses. He is a man whose whole heart is wrapped up in his country. It is hard to appreciate what his feeling must have been in giving up the Command of the Fleet, which for nearly two and a half years, he has been preparing for the great day on which he had hoped to have led it to complete victory. I know the thought of that day never left his mind for a moment. I was privileged to get a glimpse of his feelings, and think it was the bitterest day of his life, and yet I know he did not hesitate for a moment to take the step which he felt was for the country's good. The confidence the Fleet had in him was unbounded, and every single officer and man in the *Iron Duke* loved him, of that I am certain.[23]

Commander Matthew Best, HMS *Iron Duke*, 3rd Division, Fourth Battle Squadron

Almost inevitably, his replacement was Sir David Beatty. The Grand Fleet was not enthralled by the prospect of their new Commander-in-Chief and his reception was muted to say the least.

> Beatty was popular enough with the Battlecruiser Fleet, but the Grand Fleet had no use for him, while they just about worshipped Jellicoe whom they called 'Hellfire Jack'. Later, when Jellicoe went to the Admiralty and was succeeded by Beatty as Commander in Chief Grand Fleet, and the latter came up to take command, there was no spontaneous cheering to greet him and had not Admiral Sir Cecil Burney, Second in Command, realised what was happening and signalled an order to cheer ship, there would have been no welcome. As it was, the formal cheers were as nothing compared with the roar of cheering with which the Grand Fleet said goodbye to Jellicoe.[24]
>
> Assistant Clerk Gilbert Bickmore, HMS *Warspite*, Fifth Battle Squadron

Beatty did not long retain the *Iron Duke* as his flagship. As he was Commander-in-Chief, no one could gainsay him and in February 1917 he transferred his flag to the *Queen Elizabeth*, one of the super-dreadnoughts he had coveted for so long when he was in command of the Battlecruiser Fleet. Beatty commanded the Grand Fleet with distinction, maintaining morale under the trying years of inaction and refining the tactical doctrine inherited from Jellicoe to allow enhanced flexibility of subordinate commanders in battle conditions. But the war ended without him being offered a further chance to engage the High Seas Fleet. It was a triumph but he had not triumphed.

The lack of a further opportunity to tackle the German fleet meant that Beatty's disappointment over the battle of Jutland rankled, becoming deeper with each passing year. In the post-war period, when he was promoted to become the First Sea Lord in November 1919, he was unable to resist the temptation to misuse his position to influence materially the official accounts of the battle. His own mistakes were glossed over, the contribution of the Battlecruiser Fleet was grossly exaggerated, the role of Vice Admiral Sir Hugh Evan-Thomas and the Fifth Battle Squadron was undermined and the overall contribution of both the Grand Fleet and Jellicoe were misrepresented and traduced. The two great admirals fought again, not now side by side, but through the medium of endless nit-picking memoranda. This internecine conflict took place against a background of fully fledged attacks launched on each other by their respective friends and supporters. Jellicoe, who regained a good deal of his intellectual vigour once he had recovered from his wartime responsibilities, was able to deploy a more logical framework of arguments. He could coolly and rationally analyse the mistakes made by himself and his subordinates in the course of the battle. But Beatty never managed to overcome his intense personal disappointment and thereby to achieve a dispassionate view of the battle. Jellicoe died in November 1935. Beatty, who insisted on acting as a pallbearer despite his own poor health, followed him to the grave just months later in March 1936. Both are buried in St Paul's Cathedral. It was the nearest they would ever get to Nelson, but they had both in their different ways served their country well.

Many naval commentators have struggled to assess the relative abilities of Jellicoe and Beatty in the exercise of their commands during the battle of Jutland. Ironically, it is a sense of lingering injustice inspired by Beatty's ignoble behaviour in the post-war years which has caused many historians to take Jellicoe's side in the Jutland controversy more vehemently than might otherwise have been the case. But Beatty's post-war conduct should not affect our judgement of his competence in 1916. In theory, Beatty possessed many of the right instincts for a fighting admiral: he applauded the idea of decentralization of command and encouraged initiative in his subordinates; he did not lack the courage to take big decisions in moments of crisis and rarely did anything but close the enemy. In contrast, Jellicoe was a natural centralizer, a technocrat, with a mind like a slide rule and thought processes that travelled smoothly along the grooves of cold logic. Overwhelming all his more martial instincts was a blanket of caution. He could not – he would not – risk the Grand Fleet and the future of his country on the lottery of successfully evading a mass destroyer torpedo attack under cover of bad visibility. In the post-war years the Royal Navy rediscovered its commitment to dogged aggression as the strategic situation changed radically with the rise of the United States and Japan. As a result, the Royal Navy that fought the Second World War was clearly built on the principles that Beatty has been widely held to espouse. In a sense, therefore, Beatty could be seen as the future, while Jellicoe represented the mores of the technocrats of the Edwardian navy that had swept away the crusty cobwebs of Victoriana.

Yet the issue is surely more complex than this. Jellicoe may have been hamstrung by caution, but his country had good reason to be grateful for his cool detachment. When the crucial moment came, despite the lack of sighting reports from his subordinates, he made the perfect decision on how to deploy the Grand Fleet. He crossed the Germans' 'T' – that most desirable and difficult of naval manoeuvres – not once but twice in the ensuing engagement. He did make mistakes; it would be impossible not to in that confused battle. But endless efforts to replay the action with the restrictions to visibility and paucity of information endured by Jellicoe on the day have not uncovered any certain or safe route to a clear-cut victory at Jutland. Most radical solutions proffered to the myriad problems he faced involve a reliance on substantial leaps of faith and a large amount of luck. That was not Jellicoe's way. In the end, Jellicoe was thwarted by the poor visibility and his own tired decision to disregard the signal intelligence that he received from the Admiralty during the night.

Although Beatty performed with great gallantry at Jutland, he made a succession of mistakes. By far the most serious was his first. He had not concentrated his force, but had gone into action half-cocked, leaving the most powerful ships in the world lagging miles behind. Petty signalling disputes cannot be allowed to cloud this issue. Ultimately it was Beatty's responsibility to concentrate his forces before going into action. The men aboard the *Indefatigable* and *Queen Mary* paid the ultimate price for his failure. It is possible they would have been killed in any event, but they would surely have been joined in their watery graves by many more of the brave men serving aboard the *Lützow*, *Derfflinger*, *Seydlitz*, *Moltke* and *Von der Tann*. Beatty made other, less important mistakes throughout the battle, particularly in the confusion when the High Seas Fleet suddenly hove into sight and his failure to pass on proper intelligence of their position while Jellicoe was trying to deploy the Grand Fleet. When all is said and done, Beatty did not perform at the level that his own self-image would suggest. He did not achieve conspicuous success when he used his initiative and, despite his lip service to decentralization, whenever it came to the crunch he himself did not allow such practices in his own subordinates. His signals were as rigidly interventionist as Jellicoe's when it came to thwarting the delegation of power in the actual battle.

Jellicoe was a brilliant man saddled by a poor system of command and control in conditions of appalling visibility. As C-in-C he must bear responsibility for the failures in the command structure and night-fighting techniques endemic within the Grand Fleet. Nevertheless, his natural calmness, intelligence and clear thinking allowed him to transcend these handicaps to achieve his overriding aim safely: to retain for Britain command of the world's oceans beyond the narrow confines of the North Sea. In contrast, Beatty may have had a theoretical grasp of what was required for a complete naval victory, but he did not have either the application or the brilliance to achieve it at the moments when it mattered during the battle. The followers of the American historian Alfred Mahan in their earnest desire for a Nelsonic figure to lead the Grand Fleet to a new Trafalgar forget that he could not be found in the real world. Nelson was a unique figure in naval history and it was simply not fair to expect either Beatty or Jellicoe to match him. Perversely, as a direct result of the vigorous controversy that followed the battle, it has been the fate of Jellicoe and Beatty to be locked together in a kind of historical purgatory, endlessly analysed by naval historians. Both men deserve a better memorial to their courage and devotion to duty. It is more important to remember that in the end, together they delivered to the British people the naval victory on which ultimate success in the First World War depended.

Whatever the merits of these two commanders, the experience of the ordinary sailors in the most significant battle fought by the Royal Navy in the twentieth century must not be overlooked. Fifty years on from *Der Tag*, on 31 May 1966, some of the surviving British and German veterans met again in the North Sea. It is fitting that one of them should have the last word.

> By a coincidence the weather was almost exactly as it had been 50 years
> before, patchy mist and a flat calm sea. The two squadrons did not
> sight each other until they were within a few miles. After meeting they
> steamed on parallel courses about 30 yards apart. The ships' companies
> 'manned ship' lining the rails everyone strictly at attention. Not so the
> British and German veterans who grinned and waved like anything at
> their former antagonists. The veterans in both squadrons cast memorial
> wreaths on the sea, then each squadron cheered the other and finally
> there was an exchange of signals and mementos.[25]

Angus Nichol, HMS *Marlborough*

COMPARISON OF CASUALTIES IN SHIPS RETURNING TO PORT

SHIP TYPE	BRITISH SHIPS	KILLED	WOUNDED	TOTAL
BATTLESHIPS	Barham	26	46	72
	Colossus		9	9
	Marlborough	2	2	4
	Malaya	63	68	131
	Valiant		1	1
	Warspite	14	32	46
BATTLECRUISERS	Lion	99	51	150
	Princess Royal	22	81	103
	Tiger	24	46	70
LIGHT CRUISERS	Calliope	10	29	39
	Caroline	2		2
	Castor	13	26	39
	Chester	29	49	78
	Dublin	3	27	30
	Southampton	29	60	89
DESTROYERS	Acasta	6	1	7
	Broke	47	36	83
	Defender	1	2	3
	Moorsom		1	1
	Nessus	7	7	14
	Obdurate	1	1	2
	Onslaught	5	3	8
	Onslow	2	3	5
	Petard	9	6	15
	Porpoise	2	2	4
	Spitfire	6	20	26
TOTAL CASUALTIES SURVIVING SHIPS		422	609	1031

APPENDIX A

SHIP TYPE	GERMAN SHIPS	KILLED	WOUNDED	TOTAL
BATTLESHIPS	*Grosser Kurfürst*	15	10	25
	Kaiser		1	1
	König	45	27	72
	Markgraf	11	13	24
	Oldenburg	8	14	22
	Ostfriesland	1	10	11
	Nassau	11	16	27
	Prinzregent Luitpold		11	11
	Rheinland	10	20	30
	Schlesien	1		1
	Schleswig-Holstein	3	9	12
	Westfalen	2	8	10
BATTLECRUISERS	*Derfflinger*	157	26	183
	Moltke	17	23	40
	Seydlitz	98	55	153
	Von der Tann	11	35	46
LIGHT CRUISERS	*Frankfurt*	3	18	21
	Hamburg	14	25	39
	München	8	20	28
	Pillau	4	19	23
	Stettin	8	28	36
DESTROYERS	*B98*	2	11	13
	G40	1	2	3
	G41		5	5
	G86	1	7	8
	G87	1	5	6
	S32	3	1	4
	S36		4	4
	S51		3	3
	S52	1	1	2
TOTAL CASUALTIES SURVIVING SHIPS		436	427	863

COMPARISON OF CASUALTIES IN SHIPS SUNK

SHIP TYPE		BRITISH SHIPS KILLED	WOUNDED	POW	TOTAL
BATTLECRUISER	*Indefatigable*	1017		2	1019
	Invincible	1026	1		1027
	Queen Mary	1266	6	2	1274
PRE-DREADNOUGHT					
ARMOURED CRUISERS	*Black Prince*	857			857
	Defence	903			903
	Warrior	71	36		107
LIGHT CRUISERS					
DESTROYERS	*Ardent*	78	1		79
	Fortune	67	2		69
	Nestor	6	8	80	94
	Nomad	8	4	72	84
	Shark	86	3		89
	Sparrowhawk	6			6
	Tipperary	185	4	8	197
	Turbulent	96		13	109
TOTAL CASUALTIES SHIPS SUNK		5672	65	177	5914
TOTAL CASUALTIES SURVIVING SHIPS		422	609		1031
TOTAL BATTLE CASUALTIES		6094	674	177	6945

APPENDIX B

SHIP TYPE	GERMAN SHIPS	KILLED	WOUNDED	TOTAL
BATTLECRUISER	*Lützow*	115	50	165
PRE-DREADNOUGHT	*Pommern*	844		844
ARMOURED CRUISERS				
LIGHT CRUISERS	*Elbing*	4	12	16
	Frauenlob	320	1	321
	Rostock	14	6	20
	Wiesbaden	589	0	589
DESTROYERS	*S35*	88		88
	V4	18	4	22
	V27		3	3
	V29	33	4	37
	V48	90		90
TOTAL CASUALTIES SHIPS SUNK		2115	80	2195
TOTAL CASUALTIES SURVIVING SHIPS		436	427	863
TOTAL BATTLE CASUALTIES		2551	507	3058

NOTES TO THE TEXT

CHAPTER I

[1] A. T. Mahan, 'Address of Captain A. T. Mahan, President of U. S. Naval War College', *Proceedings*, December 1888, pp.621–39

[2] Quoted in O. Parkes, *British Battleships* (London: Seeley Service, 1956), p.435

[3] J. Jellicoe, quoted in A. Temple Patterson, *Jellicoe: A Biography* (London: Macmillan, 1969), p.34

[4] J. Jellicoe, *The Grand Fleet, 1914–1916* (London: Cassell, 1919), p.49

[5] J. Jellicoe, Grand Fleet Battle Orders, quoted by A. J. Marder, *From Dreadnought to Scapa Flow* (London: Oxford University Press, 1966), vol. iii, 20–21

[6] Jellicoe, *Grand Fleet,* 400

[7] A. Temple Patterson, *The Jellicoe Papers* (London: Naval Records Society, 1996), vol. i, p.75

[8] Temple Patterson, *Jellicoe Papers*, i, 76

[9] Temple Patterson, *Jellicoe Papers*, i, 79

[10] R. Bellairs, quoted in A. Marder, *From Dreadnought to Scapa Flow*, (London: Oxford University Press, 1920), vol. ii, p.443

[11] R. Scheer, *German High Seas Fleet in the World War* (London: Cassell, 1920), p.176

[12] Temple Patterson, *Jellicoe Papers*, i, 252

[13] *The Beatty Papers*, (Aldershot: Naval Records Society), vol. i, 297–8

[14] Temple Patterson *Jellicoe Papers*, i, 227

CHAPTER 2

[1] B. Bingham, *Falklands, Jutland and the Bight* (London: John Murray, 1919), p.133

[2] IWM DOCS: G. E. D. Ellis, Microfilm copy of manuscript diary, 30/5/1916

[3] IWM DOCS: M. Clarke, Manuscript diary, 31/5/1916

[4] IWM DOCS: Misc. 1010, R. Church Collection: H. Hayler, Manuscript letter, 30/5/1920

[5] IWM DOCS: Misc. 1010, R. Church Collection: R. B. Fairthorne, Manuscript answer to questionnaire, ca 1970–74

[6] IWM DOCS: J. C. Croome, Typescript

[7] IWM DOCS: Misc. 1010, R. Church Collection: N. E. White, Manuscript answer to questionnaire, ca 1970–74

[8] IWM DOCS: Croome, Typescript

[9] IWM DOCS: Croome:, Typescript

[10] IWM DOCS: Misc. 1010, R. Church Collection: J. J. Moss, Manuscript answer to questionnaire, ca 1970–74

[11] IWM DOCS: Misc. 1010, R. Church Collection: N. E. White, Manuscript answer to questionnaire, ca 1970–74

[12] G. von Hase, *Kiel and Jutland* (London: Skeffington,1921), 121

[13] Scheer, *German High Seas Fleet,* 133

[14] Scheer, *German High Seas Fleet,* 141

[15] J. Jellicoe, quoted in *Battle of Jutland Official Despatches* (London: HMSO), pp.1–2

[16] IWM DOCS: Misc. 1010, R. Church Collection: A. E. Cooper, Manuscript answer to questionnaire, ca 1970–74

[17] IWM DOCS: T. M. Field Collection: E. Francis, 'Impressions of Gunner's Mate at Jutland'

[18] IWM DOCS: Misc. 1010, R. Church Collection: H. Hayler, Manuscript letter, 30/5/1920

[19] IWM SR: J. G. D. Ouvry, AC 9260, Reel 1

[20] IWM DOCS: A. E. M. Chatfield, *The Navy and Defence* (London: William Heinemann, 1942), p.139

[21] A. Temple Patterson, *Jellicoe Papers*, i, p.260

[22] Hase, *Kiel and Jutland*, 129

[23] Hase, *Kiel and Jutland*, 90

[24] Hase, *Kiel and Jutland*, 127

[25] Ranft, *Beatty Papers*, 297–8

[26] IWM DOCS: Misc. 1010, R. Church Collection: H. Bassenge, Translation of answer to questionnaire, ca 1973

[27] IWM DOCS: T. Farquhar, Typescript diary, 31/5/1916

[28] IWM DOCS: Misc. 1010, R. Church Collection: H.Bassenge, Translation of answer to questionnaire, ca 1973

[29] Admiralty, *Narrative of the Battle of Jutland* (London: HMSO, 1924), p.10

[30] IWM DOCS: T. Farquhar, Typescript diary, 31/5/1916

[31] V. E. Tarrant, *Jutland: The German Perspective* (London: Brookhampton Press, 1999), p.275

[32] IWM DOCS: Misc. 1010, R. Church Collection: H. Bassenge, Translation of answer to questionnaire, ca 1973

[33] IWM DOCS: T. Farquhar, Typescript diary, 31/5/1916

[34] PRO: ADM 116/3188, H. Evan-Thomas, Letter, 14/8/1923

[35] H. Evan-Thomas Letter to Editor of *The Times* (London: 16/2/1927)

[36] *Jutland Despatches*, 444

[37] Hase, *Kiel and Jutland*, 142

[38] IWM SR: G. Donald, AC 18, Reel 9

[39] F. Rutland, quoted in H. W. Fawcett & G. W. W. Hooper, *The Fighting at Jutland: The Personal Experiences of Forty-Five Officers and Men of the British Fleet* (London: Macmillan, 1921), p.8

[40] IWM DOCS: Misc. 1010, R. Church Collection: H. Bassenge, Translation of answer to questionnaire, ca 1973

[41] F. Rutland, quoted in Fawcett & Hooper, *Fighting at Jutland*, 8

[42] IWM DOCS: H. Y. Ganderton, 'Under the White Ensign: A Bunting Tosser's Log', p.33

[43] IWM DOCS: Misc. 1010, R. Church Collection: H. D. Owen, Typescript answer to questionnaire, ca 1970–74

[44] M. von Egidy, *Jutland: A German View* (London: Purnell Partworks, History of the First World War), vol.4, no.3, p.1417

[45] Hase, *Kiel and Jutland*, 142

[46] IWM DOCS: G. M. Eady, Typescript, 'The Battle of Jutland by Snottie', p.10

[47] IWM SR: J. G. D. Ouvry, AC 9260, Reel 1

[48] IWM DOCS: C. Caslon Collection, 'Recollections of the Battle of Jutland', pp.1–2

[49] IWM DOCS: Misc. 1010, R. Church Collection: H. O. Hill, Manuscript answer to questionnaire, ca 1970–74

[50] IWM DOCS: E. E. Sharpe, Manuscript letter, 6/6/1916

[51] IWM DOCS: T. M. Field Collection: E. Francis, 'Impressions of Gunner's Mate at Jutland'

[52] IWM DOCS: Misc. 1010, R. Church Collection: F. J. Arnold, Manuscript answer to questionnaire, ca 1970–74

[53] IWM DOCS: E. M. Phillpotts Collection: H. Walwyn, Typescript memoir, 'HMS Warspite', pp.1–2

[54] IWM DOCS: G. E. D. Ellis, Microfilm copy of manuscript diary, 31/5/1916

[55] IWM DOCS: R. H. C. F. Frampton, 'An Eyewitness Account of the Battle of Jutland on 31 May, 1916

[56] IWM DOCS: Misc. 1010, R. Church Collection: G. M. Eady, Typescript answer to questionnaire, ca 1970–74

[57] IWM DOCS: Misc. 1010, R. Church Collection: H. Hayler, Manuscript letter, 30/5/1920

[58] IWM DOCS: G. M. Eady, Typescript; 'The Battle of Jutland by Snottie', p.10 and short extracts from R. Church Collection: G. M. Eady, Typescript answer to questionnaire, ca 1970–74

[59] IWM SR: J. J. Hazelwood, AC 4125, Reel 1

[60] IWM DOCS: D. Lorimer Collection: E. Brind, Typescript, p.123

[61] IWM DOCS: D. Lorimer Collection: E. Brind, Typescript, p.123

[62] Egidy, *Jutland*, 4, 1417

[63] A. Scheibe, 'The Jutland Battle', *Journal of the Royal United Service Institution*, vol. lxii, p.31

CHAPTER 3

[1] Hase, *Kiel and Jutland*, 143

[2] IWM DOCS: R. C. O. Hill, Typescript, 'Personal Experience of the Action on Wednesday, May 31st 1916'

[3] IWM DOCS: Chatfield, *Navy and Defence*, 140–41

[4] G. Paschen, 'SMS *Lützow* at Jutland', *Journal of the Royal United Service Institution*, vol. lxxii, p.33

[5] Hase, *Kiel and Jutland*, 145

[6] Chatfield, *Navy and Defence*, 140–41

[7] IWM DOCS: A. B. Combe, Typescript, 'Account of the Action on May 31st 1916'

[8] IWM DOCS: V. Hayward, Manuscript, 'HMS *Tiger*'

[9] IWM DOCS: Misc. 1010, R. Church Collection: R. C. Hogg, Manuscript answer to questionnaire, ca 1970–74

[10] IWM DOCS: T. M. Field Collection: E. Francis: 'Impressions of Gunner's Mate at Jutland', pp.4 and 7

[11] IWM DOCS: T. M. Field Collection: E. Francis: 'Impressions of Gunner's Mate at Jutland'

[12] IWM DOCS: Misc 1010, R. Church Collection: G. M. Eady, Manuscript answer to questionnaire, ca 1970–74

[13] IWM DOCS: G. M. Eady: Typescript, 'The Battle of Jutland by Snottie', p.22

[14] Hase, *Kiel and Jutland*, 146–7

[15] Hase, *Kiel and Jutland*, 147–8

[16] IWM DOCS: H. B. Pelly Collection: W. N. Lapage, Gunnery Commander's Report, 6/6/1916

[17] H. P. K. Oram, *Ready for Sea* (London: Seeley Service, 1994), pp.152–3

[18] Hase, *Kiel and Jutland*, 149

[19] Oram, *Ready for Sea*, 152–3

[20] IWM DOCS: T. F. Bradley, Manuscript Diary, 31/5/1916

[21] IWM DOCS: T. F. Bradley, Manuscript Diary, 31/5/1916

[22] Egidy, *Jutland*, 4, 1417

[23] Egidy, *Jutland*, 4, 1417

[24] IWM DOCS: Misc 1010, R. Church Collection: J. Herford, Typescript answer to questionnaire, ca 1970–74

[25] Hase, *Kiel and Jutland*, 150–51

[26] W. S. Chalmers, *The Life and Letters of David Beatty Admiral of the Fleet* (London: Hodder & Stoughton, 1951), p.231

[27] IWM DOCS: A. B. Combe, Typescript, "Account of the Action on May 31st 1916'

[28] G. Paschen, 'SMS *Lützow* at Jutland', lxxii, 33

[29] A. Mackenzie-Grieve, 'Battle of Jutland, May 31st 1916', *Cinque Ports Gazette*, 12/1934, p.60

[30] H. Willons, quoted in Naval Records, *The Beatty Papers*, i, 354

[31] Chatfield, *Navy and Defence*, 142–3

[32] Paschen, 'SMS *Lützow* at Jutland', lxxii, 34

[33] IWM DOCS: E. M. Phillpotts Collection: H. Walwyn, Typescript memoir, 'HMS Warspite', pp.2–3

[34] IWM DOCS: E. M. Phillpotts Collection: H. Walwyn, Typescript memoir, 'HMS Warspite', p.3

[35] IWM DOCS: Misc. 1010, R. Church Collection: H. Bassenge, Translation of answer to questionnaire, ca 1973

[36] IWM SR: AC 4096, Reel 1 C. Falmer

[37] IWM DOCS: C. Caslon Collection, 'Recollections of the Battle of Jutland', pp.3–4

[38] IWM DOCS: E. C. Cordeaux: Manuscript letter, ca 6/1916

[39] IWM SR: AC 4096, Reel 1 C. Falmer

[40] IWM SR: AC 4096, Reel 1 C. Falmer

[41] IWM DOCS: Misc. 1010, R. Church Collection: H. Bassenge, Translation of answer to questionnaire, ca 1973

[42] Chatfield, *Navy and Defence*, 141

[43] Peter Liddle Collection, Brotherton Library, Leeds University: E. S. Brand, Typescript memoirs

[44] IWM DOCS: Misc. 1010, R. Church Collection: C. Melms, Translation of answer to questionnaire, ca 1973

[45] Scheibe, 'Jutland Battle', lxii, 33

[46] Scheibe, 'Jutland Battle', lxii, 33–4

[47] IWM DOCS: E. M. Phillpotts Collection: H. Walwyn, Typescript memoir, 'HMS Warspite', pp.3–4

[48] IWM DOCS: R. H. C. F. Frampton, 'An Eyewitness Account of the Battle of Jutland on 31 May, 1916'

[49] IWM DOCS: E. M. Phillpotts Collection: H. Walwyn, Typescript memoir, 'HMS Warspite', p.4

[50] Chatfield, *Navy and Defence*, 143–4

[51] IWM DOCS: Misc. 1010, R. Church Collection: D. Maclachlan, Manuscript answer to questionnaire, ca 1970–74

[52] IWM DOCS: N. G. Garnons-Williams, Typescript

[53] IWM DOCS: Misc. 1010, R. Church Collection: A. R. Lewis, Manuscript answer to questionnaire, ca 1970–74

[54] IWM DOCS: T. M. Field Collection: E. Francis, 'Impressions of Gunner's Mate at Jutland'

[55] Peter Liddle Collection, Brotherton Library, Leeds University: J. L. Storey, Typescript memoir within H. H. McWilliam Collection

[56] IWM DOCS: T. M. Field Collection: E. Francis, 'Impressions of Gunner's Mate at Jutland'

[57] IWM DOCS: T. M. Field Collection: E. Francis, 'Impressions of Gunner's Mate at Jutland'

[58] IWM DOCS: T. M. Field Collection: E. Francis, 'Impressions of Gunner's Mate at Jutland'

[59] IWM DOCS: Misc. 1010, R. Church Collection: P. R. Dearden, Letter, 5/6/1916

[60] IWM DOCS: J. Lloyd Owen, Copy of account given to R. K. Dickson: manuscript

[61] IWM DOCS: T. M. Field Collection: E. Francis, 'Impressions of Gunner's Mate at Jutland'

[62] IWM DOCS: T. M. Field Collection: E. Francis, 'Impressions of Gunner's Mate at Jutland'

[63] V. Hayward, *HMS Tiger at Bay* (London: William Kimber, 1977), p.108

[64] IWM DOCS: T. M. Field Collection: E. Francis, 'Impressions of Gunner's Mate at Jutland'

[65] IWM DOCS: J. Lloyd Owen, Copy of account given to R. K. Dickson: manuscript

[66] Peter Liddle Collection, Brotherton Library, Leeds University: J. L. Storey, Typescript memoir within H. H. McWilliam Collection

[67] IWM DOCS: Misc. 1010, R. Church Collection: P. R. Dearden, Letter, 5/6/1916

[68] IWM DOCS: Misc. 1010, R. Church Collection: S. King-Hall, Typescript manuscript

[69] IWM DOCS: T. M. Field Collection: E. Francis, 'Impressions of Gunner's Mate at Jutland'

[70] Peter Liddle Collection, Brotherton Library, Leeds University: J. L. Storey, Typescript

memoir within H. H. McWilliam Collection

[71] IWM DOCS: Misc. 1010, R. Church Collection: P. R. Dearden, Letter, 5/6/1916

[72] IWM DOCS: Misc. 1010, R. Church Collection: A. T. Hickson, Manuscript answer to questionnaire, ca 1970–74

[73] IWM DOCS: Misc. 1010, R. Church Collection: P. R. Dearden, Letter, 5/6/1916

[74] Hase, *Kiel and Jutland*, 160–61

[75] Egidy, *Jutland* 4, 1417

[76] IWM DOCS: H. B. Pelly, Captain's Report, 6/6/1916

[77] IWM SR: J. G. D. Ouvry, AC 9260, Reel 2

[78] IWM DOCS: G. M. Eady, Typescript, 'The Battle of Jutland by Snottie', p.16

[79] IWM DOCS: C. Buist, Typescript manuscript

[80] Chatfield, *Navy and Defence*, 143

[81] IWM DOCS: Misc. 1010, R. Church Collection: A. R. Lewis, Manuscript answer to questionnaire, ca 1970–74

[82] IWM DOCS: Misc. 1010, R. Church Collection: A. S. Tempest, Typescript answer to questionnaire, ca 1970–74

[83] H. Willons, quoted in Naval Records, *The Beatty Papers*, i, 354

[84] IWM DOCS: Misc. 1010, R. Church Collection: A. R. Lewis, Manuscript answer to questionnaire, ca 1970–74

[85] IWM DOCS: G. M. Eady, Typescript, 'The Battle of Jutland by Snottie', p.16

[86] IWM DOCS: Misc. 1010, R. Church Collection: G. M. Eady, Typescript answer to questionnaire, ca 1970–74

[87] Hase, *Kiel and Jutland*, 86

[88] IWM DOCS: N. G. Garnons-Williams, Typescript

[89] IWM DOCS: Misc. 1010, R. Church Collection: A. S. Tempest, Typescript answer to questionnaire, ca 1970–74

[90] IWM DOCS: T. F. Bradley, Manuscript Diary, 31/5/1916

[91] B. Bingham, *Falklands, Jutland and the Bight* (London: John Murray, 1919), pp.138–9

[92] IWM DOCS: Misc. 1010, R. Church Collection: H. D. Owen, Typescript answer to questionnaire, ca 1970–74

[93] Oram, *Ready for Sea*, 155–6

[94] Oram, *Ready for Sea*, 155–6

[95] IWM DOCS: Misc. 1010, R. Church Collection: H. D. Owen, Typescript answer to questionnaire, ca 1970–74

[96] IWM DOCS: Misc. 1010, R. Church Collection: H. D. Owen, Typescript answer to questionnaire, ca 1970–74

[97] IWM DOCS: Misc. 1010, R. Church Collection: H. D. Owen, Typescript answer to questionnaire, ca 1970–74

[98] IWM DOCS: Misc. 1010, R. Church Collection: H. D. Owen, Typescript answer to questionnaire, ca 1970–74

[99] PRO: ADM 137/4808, P. Whitfield, Typescript letter, 8/6/1916

[100] E. C. O. Thomson, quoted by Fawcett & Hooper, *The Fighting at Jutland: The Personal Experiences of Forty-Five Officers and Men of the British Fleet*, 30

[101] Bingham, *Falklands, Jutland and the Bight*, 141–2

[102] IWM DOCS: Misc. 1010, R. Church Collection: H. D. Owen, Typescript answer to questionnaire, ca 1970–74

[103] IWM DOCS: Misc. 1010, R. Church Collection: H. D. Owen, Typescript answer to questionnaire, ca 1970–74

[104] IWM SR: Baynham Collection: G. Betsworth, AC 9004, Reel 1 & 2

[105] Bingham, *Falklands, Jutland and the Bight*, 141–2

[106] Bingham, *Falklands, Jutland and the Bight*, 142–3

[107] PRO: ADM 137/4808, P. Whitfield, Typescript letter, 8/6/1916

[108] E. C. O. Thomson, quoted by Fawcett & Hooper, *The Fighting at Jutland: The Personal Experiences of Forty-Five Officers and Men of the British Fleet*, 30

[109] Egidy, *Jutland*, 4, 1417–20

[110] E. C. O. Thomson, quoted by Fawcett & Hooper, *The Fighting at Jutland: The Personal Experiences of Forty-Five Officers and Men of the British Fleet*, 30

[111] Scheer, *Germany's High Seas Fleet*, 146–7

[112] IWM DOCS: Misc. 1010, R. Church Collection: G. F. Spargo, Manuscript answer to questionnaire, ca 1970–74

[113] W. Goodenough, *A Rough Record* (London: Hutchinson, 1943), p.95

[114] Chatfield, *Navy and Defence*, 144

[115] Admiralty, *Narrative of the Battle of Jutland* (London: HMSO, 1924), p.22

[116] IWM DOCS: C. Buist, Typescript memoir

[117] Goodenough, *Rough Record*, 95

[118] *Jutland Despatches*, 453

[119] Mackenzie-Grieve, 'Battle of Jutland', 12/1934, 60–61

[120] Scheer, *German High Seas Fleet*, 147

[121] A. Gordon, *Rules of the Game* (London: John Murray, 2000), pp.127–8

[122] IWM DOCS: E. M. Phillpotts Collection: H. Walwyn, Typescript memoir, 'HMS Warspite', pp.4–5

[123] IWM DOCS: D. Lorimer Collection: E. Brind, Typescript, p.124

[124] IWM DOCS: D. Lorimer Collection: E. Brind, Typescript, p.125

[125] IWM DOCS: D. Lorimer Collection: E. Brind, Typescript, p.126

[126] IWM DOCS: C. Caslon Collection, 'Recollections of the Battle of Jutland', p.6

[127] IWM DOCS: Misc. 1010, R. Church Collection: H. D. Owen, Typescript answer to questionnaire, ca 1970–74

[128] IWM DOCS: Misc. 1010, R. Church Collection: H. D. Owen, Typescript answer to questionnaire, ca 1970–74

[129] IWM DOCS: Misc. 1010, R. Church Collection: H. D. Owen, Typescript answer to questionnaire, ca 1970–74

[130] Bingham, *Falklands, Jutland and the Bight*, 143

[131] PRO: ADM 137/4808, P. Whitfield, Typescript letter, 8/6/1916

[132] Bingham, *Falklands, Jutland and the Bight*, 144

[133] Bingham, *Falklands, Jutland and the Bight*, 144–5

[134] IWM SR: Baynham Collection: G. Betsworth, AC 9004, Reel 1 & 2

[135] Bingham, *Falklands, Jutland and the Bight*, 145–6

[136] PRO: ADM 137/4809, A. Joe, Typescript report on letters of RN officer POWs

from H. Sturgis, 31/7/1916

[137] Bingham, *Falklands, Jutland and the Bight*, 146

[138] IWM SR: Baynham Collection: G. Betsworth, AC 9004, Reel 1 & 2

[139] Bingham, *Falklands, Jutland and the Bight*, 147

[140] IWM SR: Baynham Collection: G. Betsworth, AC 9004, Reel 1 & 2

[141] IWM DOCS: Misc. 1010, R. Church Collection: P. R. Dearden, Letter, 5/6/1916

[142] IWM DOCS: T. M. Field Collection: E. Francis, 'Impressions of Gunner's Mate at Jutland', pp.8–9

[143] IWM DOCS: T. M. Field Collection: E. Francis, 'Impressions of Gunner's Mate at Jutland', p.9

[144] E. C. O. Thomson, quoted by Fawcett & Hooper, *The Fighting at Jutland: The Personal Experiences of Forty-Five Officers and Men of the British Fleet*, 30

[145] IWM DOCS: T. M. Field Collection: E. Francis, 'Impressions of Gunner's Mate at Jutland', p.9

CHAPTER 4

[1] IWM DOCS: E. M. Phillpotts Collection: H. Walwyn, Typescript memoir, 'HMS Warspite', p.5

[2] IWM DOCS: Misc. 1010, R. Church Collection: S. D. Tillard, Manuscript answer to questionnaire, ca 1970–74

[3] IWM DOCS: Misc. 1010, R. Church Collection: H. A. Dawson, Manuscript answer to questionnaire, ca 1970–74

[4] IWM DOCS: Misc. 1010, R. Church Collection: S. King-Hall, Typescript manuscript

[5] IWM DOCS: A. F. de Salis: 'Narrative of HMS Moresby'

[6] IWM DOCS: A. F. de Salis: 'Narrative of HMS Moresby'

[7] IWM DOCS: E. M. Phillpotts Collection: H. Walwyn, Typescript memoir, 'HMS Warspite', p.5

[8] IWM DOCS: Misc. 1010, R. Church Collection: D. Duthy, Typescript letter, 5/6/1916

[9] IWM DOCS: G. E. D. Ellis, Microfilm copy of manuscript diary, 31/5/1916

[10] IWM DOCS: D. Lorimer Collection: E. Brind, Typescript, p.126

[11] IWM DOCS: C. Caslon Collection, 'Recollections of the Battle of Jutland', p.7

[12] IWM DOCS: D. Lorimer Collection: E. Brind, Typescript, pp.126–7

[13] IWM DOCS: Misc. 1010, R. Church Collection: J. H. Harris, Manuscript answer to questionnaire, ca 1970–74

[14] IWM DOCS: Misc.1010, R. Church Collection: J. H. Harris, Manuscript answer to questionnaire, ca 1970–74

[15] Peter Liddle Collection, Brotherton Library, Leeds University: K. M. Lawder, Transcript of interview tape 522

[16] IWM DOCS: C. Caslon Collection, 'Recollections of the Battle of Jutland', p.8

[17] IWM DOCS: C. Caslon Collection, 'Recollections of the Battle of Jutland', p.8

[18] IWM DOCS: C. Caslon Collection, 'Recollections of the Battle of Jutland', p.8

[19] IWM DOCS: Misc. 1010, R. Church Collection: J. H. Harris, Manuscript answer to questionnaire, ca 1970–74

[20] IWM DOCS: C. Caslon Collection, 'Recollections of the Battle of Jutland', pp.9-10

[21] IWM DOCS: C. Caslon Collection, 'Recollections of the Battle of Jutland', pp.10-11

[22] Peter Liddle Collection, Brotherton Library, Leeds University: G. W. Norman, Manuscript memoir

[23] IWM DOCS: Misc. 1010, R. Church Collection: F. J. Arnold, Manuscript answer to questionnaire, ca 1970–74

[24] IWM DOCS: D. Lorimer: Typescript, pp.120–21

[25] IWM DOCS: G. H. Bickmore, Typescript, p.16

[26] IWM DOCS: E. M. Phillpotts Collection: H. Walwyn, Typescript memoir, 'HMS Warspite', p.6

[27] IWM DOCS: E. M. Phillpotts Collection: H. Walwyn, Typescript memoir, 'HMS Warspite', p.7

[28] IWM DOCS: G. E. D. Ellis, Microfilm copy of manuscript diary, 31/5/1916

[29] IWM DOCS: G. E. D. Ellis, Microfilm copy of manuscript diary, 31/5/1916

[30] IWM DOCS: E. M. Phillpotts Collection: H. Walwyn, Typescript memoir, 'HMS Warspite', p.7

[31] IWM DOCS: Misc. 1010, R. Church Collection: P. F. E. Cox, Typescript manuscript

[32] IWM DOCS: E. M. Phillpotts Collection: H. Walwyn, Typescript memoir, 'HMS Warspite', pp.8–9

[33] IWM DOCS: E. M. Phillpotts Collection: H. Walwyn, Typescript memoir, 'HMS Warspite', p.11

[34] Hase, *Kiel and Jutland*, 174

[35] Hase, *Kiel and Jutland*, 171–2

CHAPTER 5

[1] IWM DOCS: A. D. B. James, Manuscript memoir, 'Battle of Jutland'

[2] Jellicoe, *Grand Fleet*, 302–4

[3] IWM DOCS: Misc. 1010, R. Church Collection: A. J. Brister, Typescript answer to questionnaire, ca 1970–74

[4] IWM DOCS: Misc. 1010, R. Church Collection: A. J. Brister, Typescript answer to questionnaire, ca 1970–74

[5] IWM DOCS: J. C. Croome, Typescript

[6] J. S. Corbett, *Naval Operations* (London: Longmans, 1923), vol. iii, p.348

[7] A. Cunninghame Graham, *Random Naval Recollections, 1905–1951* (Gartocharn: Fameddram, 1979), p.50

[8] IWM DOCS: Misc. 1010, R. Church Collection: W. C. C. Bennett, Manuscript answer to questionnaire, ca 1970–74

[9] IWM DOCS: Misc. 1010, R. Church Collection: D. M. Frost, Typescript answer to questionnaire, ca 1970–74

[10] IWM DOCS: J. E. P. Brass, 'Recollections of a Midshipman and Junior Officer, 1914–1921', p.45

[11] Peter Liddle Collection, Brotherton Library, Leeds University: W. Robinson, Manuscript memoirs

[12] IWM DOCS: Misc. 1010, R. Church Collection: V. Jensen, Typescript answer to questionnaire, ca 1970–74

[13] IWM DOCS: Misc. 1010, R. Church Collection: J. W. Beardsley, Manuscript answer to questionnaire, ca 1970–74

[14] IWM DOCS: J. E. P. Brass, 'Recollections of a Midshipman and Junior Officer, 1914–1921', p.46

[15] IWM DOCS: J. C. Croome, Typescript

[16] IWM DOCS: Misc. 1010, R. Church Collection: H. S. Wright, Manuscript answer to questionnaire, ca 1970–74

[17] IWM DOCS: Misc. 1010, R. Church Collection: F. T. Hall, Manuscript answer to questionnaire, ca 1970–74

[18] NMM: A. Marsden, Manuscript account, 'HMS Ardent and Jutland Action', 1916

[19] Jellicoe, *Grand Fleet*, 329–30

[20] J. S. Corbett, *History of the Great War: Naval Operations* (London: Longmans Green, 1923), vol. iii, p.349

[21] IWM DOCS: J. C. Croome, Typescript

[22] Jellicoe, *Grand Fleet*, 343

[23] Paschen, 'SMS *Lützow* at Jutland', lxxii, 36

[24] IWM DOCS: Misc. 1010, R. Church Collection: C. E. Rudall, Manuscript answer to questionnaire, ca 1970–74

[25] PRO, ADM 137/301: R. N. Lawson, Admiralty Report, 2/6/1916

[26] PRO, ADM 137/301: R. N. Lawson, Admiralty Report, 13/6/1916

[27] IWM DOCS: Misc. 1010, R. Church Collection: W. M. P. Hornby, Typescript answer to questionnaire, ca 1970–74

[28] IWM DOCS: Misc. 1010, R. Church Collection: R. S. Gulliver, Manuscript answer to questionnaire, ca 1970–74

[29] IWM DOCS: Misc. 1010, R. Church Collection: W. M. P. Hornby, Typescript answer to questionnaire, ca 1970–74

[30] IWM DOCS: Misc. 1010, R. Church Collection: C. E. Rudall, Manuscript answer to questionnaire, ca 1970–74

[31] IWM DOCS: J. C. Croome, Typescript

[32] IWM DOCS: J. C. Croome, Typescript

[33] J. O. Barron, quoted by H. W. Fawcett & G. W. W. Hooper, *The Fighting at Jutland: The Personal Experiences of Sixty Officers and Men of the British Fleet* (Glasgow: Maclure, 1921), p.239

[34] PRO: ADM 116/1485, W. Griffin, Report, 8/1916

[35] IWM DOCS: Misc. 1010, R. Church Collection: W. J. Clement-Ford, Manuscript answer to questionnaire, ca 1970–74

[36] J. Knox, quoted by Fawcett & Hooper, *The Fighting at Jutland: The Personal Experiences of Sixty Officers and Men of the British Fleet*, 256

[37] J. Knox, quoted by Fawcett & Hooper, *The Fighting at Jutland: The Personal Experiences of Sixty Officers and Men of the British Fleet*, 256

[38] IWM DOCS: Misc. 1010, R. Church Collection: A. W. Gutteridge, Manuscript answer to questionnaire, ca 1970–74

[39] PRO: ADM 116/1485, J. Tovey, Report, 2/6/1916

[40] Peter Liddle Collection, Brotherton Library, Leeds University: T. D'Arcy, Typescript memoirs

[41] J. Knox, quoted by Fawcett & Hooper, *The Fighting at Jutland: The Personal Experiences of Sixty Officers and Men of the British Fleet*, 256

[42] F. Dreyer, *The Sea Heritage: A Study of Maritime Warfare* (London: Museum Press, 1955), p.145

[43] Corbett, *History of the Great War*, iii, 355

[44] IWM DOCS: Misc. 1010, R. Church Collection: E. Downing, Typescript account in answer to questionnaire, ca 1970–74

[45] Corbett, *History of the Great War*, iii, 356

[46] Jellicoe, *Grand Fleet*, 346

[47] J. Jellicoe, statement quoted in Ranft, *The Beatty Papers*, 471

[48] J. Jellicoe, statement quoted in Ranft, *The Beatty Papers*, 470

[49] IWM DOCS: James Collection: T. Norman, Typescript copy of letter, 7/6/1916

[50] IWM DOCS: Misc. 1010, R. Church Collection: P. B. Lawder, Typescript account in answer to questionnaire, ca 1970–74

[51] IWM DOCS: D. Lorimer Collection: E. Brind, Typescript, p.128

[52] Corbett, *History of the Great War*, iii, 361

[53] Jellicoe, *Grand Fleet*, 348–50

[54] Dreyer, *Sea Heritage*, 146

[55] IWM DOCS: Misc. 1010, R. Church Collection: A. J. Brister, Typescript answer to questionnaire, ca 1970–74

[56] IWM DOCS: Misc. 1010, R. Church Collection: J. T. Davies, Manuscript answer to questionnaire, ca 1970–74

[57] IWM DOCS: Chatfield, *Navy and Defence*, 145

[58] IWM DOCS: L. Hollis, Typescript memoir, p.8

[59] Gordon, *Rules of the Game*, 392

[60] Paschen, 'SMS *Lützow* at Jutland', lxxii, 36

[61] Hase, *Kiel and Jutland*, 179

[62] IWM DOCS: Misc. 1010, R. Church Collection: J. P. Champion, Manuscript copy of letter, ca 1916

[63] IWM DOCS: D. Lorimer Collection: E. Brind, Typescript, p.129

[64] IWM DOCS: Misc. 1010, R. Church Collection: P. B. Lawder, Typescript account in answer to questionnaire, ca 1970–74

[65] H. Kitching, quoted by Fawcett & Hooper, *The Fighting at Jutland: The Personal Experiences of Sixty Officers and Men of the British Fleet*, 433–44

[66] H. Kitching, quoted by Fawcett & Hooper, *The Fighting at Jutland: The Personal Experiences of Sixty Officers and Men of the British Fleet*, 434

[67] IWM DOCS: Misc. 1010, R. Church Collection: R. Poole, Manuscript answer to questionnaire, ca 1970–74

[68] IWM DOCS: Misc. 1010, R. Church Collection: D. Williams, Manuscript answer to questionnaire, ca 1970–74

[69] IWM DOCS: C. E. Leake, Typescript taken from original 1917 manuscript, 1971

[70] H. Kitching, quoted by Fawcett & Hooper, *The Fighting at Jutland: The Personal Experiences of Sixty Officers and Men of the British Fleet*, 435

[71] IWM DOCS: Misc. 1010, R. Church Collection: W. Robertson, Manuscript answer to questionnaire, ca 1970–74

[72] IWM DOCS: Misc. 1010, R. Church Collection: E. Eades, Manuscript answer to

questionnaire, ca 1970–74

73 IWM DOCS: E. M. Phillpotts Collection: H. Walwyn, Typescript memoir, 'HMS Warspite', pp.18–19

74 IWM DOCS: A. F. de Salis: 'Narrative of HMS Moresby'

75 IWM DOCS: G. H. Bickmore, Typescript, p.17

76 IWM DOCS: J. Bostock, Microfilm account, 'Battle off the Coast of Jutland', pp.15–16

77 IWM DOCS: E. M. Phillpotts Collection: H. Walwyn, Typescript memoir, 'HMS Warspite', pp.15–16

78 Peter Liddle Collection, Brotherton Library, Leeds University: W. R. Fell, Manuscript letter

79 IWM DOCS: E. M. Phillpotts Collection: H. Walwyn, Typescript memoir, 'HMS Warspite', pp.14–15

80 IWM DOCS: E. M. Phillpotts Collection: H. Walwyn, Typescript memoir, 'HMS Warspite', p.19

81 IWM DOCS: G. E. D. Ellis, Microfilm copy of manuscript diary, 31/5/1916

82 IWM DOCS: E. M. Phillpotts Collection: H. Walwyn, Typescript memoir, 'HMS Warspite', p.18

83 IWM DOCS: Misc. 1010, R. Church Collection: H. E. Webber, Manuscript answer to questionnaire, ca 1970–74

84 IWM DOCS: Misc. 1010, R. Church Collection: S. D. Blackman, Manuscript answer to questionnaire, ca 1970–74

85 IWM DOCS: Misc. 1010, R. Church Collection: H. E. Webber, Manuscript answer to questionnaire, ca 1970–74

86 IWM DOCS: Misc. 1010, R. Church Collection: H. J. W. Fischer, Typescript, ca 1970–74

87 IWM DOCS: Misc. 1010, R. Church Collection: H. J. W. Fischer, Typescript, ca 1970–74

88 Hase, *Kiel and Jutland*, 181–2

89 Hase, *Kiel and Jutland*, 182

90 Paschen, 'SMS *Lützow* at Jutland', lxxii, 36–7

91 Paschen, 'SMS *Lützow* at Jutland', lxxii, 37

92 Hase, *Kiel and Jutland*, 182–3

93 A. von Trotha, Internet Source, http://www.100megsfree2.com/jjscherr/scherr/vonscheer.htm

94 Scheer, *German High Seas Fleet*, 151

95 Scheer, *German High Seas Fleet*, 151–2

96 IWM DOCS: Misc. 1010, R. Church Collection: S. King-Hall, Typescript manuscript

97 IWM SR: J. G. D. Ouvry, AC 9260, Reel 2

98 IWM DOCS: H. R. Tate, Manuscript diary, 31/5/1916

99 IWM DOCS: Misc. 1010, R. Church Collection: J. G. Farquhar, Manuscript account in answer to questionnaire, ca 1970–74

100 IWM DOCS: P. Grant, Typescript letter, 5/6/1916

101 IWM DOCS: Misc. 1010, Church Collection: R. L. Elgwood, Manuscript letter, 6/6/1916

102 IWM DOCS: Misc. 1010, R. Church Collection: H. S. Wright, Manuscript answer to questionnaire, ca 1970–74

103 IWM DOCS: Misc. 1010, R. Church Collection: N. E. White, Manuscript answer to questionnaire, ca 1970–74

104 IWM DOCS: W. Greenway, Typescript letter, 12/6/1916

105 IWM DOCS: J. E. P. Brass, 'Recollections of a Midshipman and Junior Officer, 1914–1921', pp.46–7

106 IWM DOCS: Misc. 1010, R. Church Collection: V. Jensen, Typescript answer to questionnaire, ca 1970–74

107 IWM DOCS: Misc. 1010, R. Church Collection: H. C. F. Foot, Typescript letter, 3/6/1916

108 IWM DOCS: M. V. Hoyle, Microfilm memoir, 'The Battle of Jutland'

109 IWM DOCS: R. Goldreich, 'Jottings from a Jewish Naval Officer's Notebook', from *The Jewish Ex-Serviceman*

110 IWM DOCS: Misc. 1010, R. Church Collection: J. W. Beardsley, Manuscript answer to questionnaire, ca 1970–74

111 IWM DOCS: Misc. 1010, R. Church Collection: A. E. Cooper, Manuscript answer to questionnaire, ca 1970–74

112 IWM SOUND, AC 10722, C. P. Blunt

113 IWM DOCS: Misc. 1010, R. Church Collection: W. T. Macey, Manuscript answer to questionnaire, ca 1970–74

114 IWM DOCS: H. R. Tate, Manuscript diary, 31/5/1916

115 IWM DOCS: R. Goldreich, Manuscript diary, 31/5/1916

116 IWM DOCS: Misc. 1010, R. Church Collection: G. Congreve, Typescript letter, 4/6/1916

117 IWM DOCS: N. Wright: Typescript letter, 12/7/1916

118 Paschen, 'SMS *Lützow* at Jutland', lxxii, 37

119 IWM DOCS: J. C. Croome, Typescript

120 Hase, *Kiel and Jutland*, 183

121 IWM DOCS: Misc. 1010, R. Church Collection: H. E. Dannreuther, Letter, 2/6/1916

122 Paschen, 'SMS *Lützow* at Jutland', lxxii, 37–8

123 IWM DOCS: Misc. 1010, R. Church Collection: R. H. Bowden, Manuscript answer to questionnaire, ca 1970–74

124 IWM DOCS: Misc. 1010, R. Church Collection: B. W. Gasson, Manuscript answer to questionnaire, ca 1970–74

125 IWM DOCS: J. C. Croome, Typescript

126 IWM DOCS: Misc. 1010, R. Church Collection: H. J. W. Fischer, Typescript, ca 1970–74

127 IWM DOCS: R. M. Servaes, Manuscript letter, 5/6/1916

128 IWM DOCS: Misc. 1010, R. Church Collection: S. D. Blackman, Manuscript answer to questionnaire, ca 1970–74

129 IWM DOCS: Misc. 1010, R. Church Collection: H. J. W. Fisher, Typescript, ca 1970–74

130 Hase, *Kiel and Jutland*, 184

[131] IWM SOUND, AC 20979, H. Dannreuther (recorded by Robert Church)

[132] IWM DOCS: Misc. 1010, R. Church Collection: A. S. Tempest, Typescript answer to questionnaire, ca 1970–74

[133] IWM DOCS: J. Myers, Manuscript account, 6/1916

[134] Anon officer, quoted by Fawcett & Hooper, *The Fighting at Jutland: The Personal Experiences of Sixty Officers and Men of the British Fleet*, 249–50

[135] IWM DOCS: Misc. 1010, R. Church Collection: B. W. Gasson, Manuscript answer to questionnaire, ca 1970–74

[136] IWM SR: J. G. D. Ouvry, AC 9260, Reel 2

[137] IWM DOCS: James Collection: T. Norman, Typescript copy of letter, 7/6/1916

[138] IWM DOCS: R. Sinclair: Manuscript letter, 27/6/1916

[139] IWM DOCS: J. C. Croome, Typescript

[140] Jellicoe, *Grand Fleet*, 354

[141] Scheer, *Germany's High Seas Fleet*, 153

[142] Scheer, *Germany's High Seas Fleet*, 153

[143] Paschen, 'SMS *Lützow* at Jutland', lxxii, 38

[144] Hase, *Kiel and Jutland*, 190

[145] IWM DOCS: J. E. P. Brass, 'Recollections of a Midshipman and Junior Officer, 1914–1921', p.47

[146] PRO: ADM 116/1485, W. Griffin, Report, 8/1916

[147] C. Hope, quoted in Corbett, *History of the Great War*. iii, 354

[148] IWM DOCS: J. O. G. Howell, Manuscript letter, 23/2/1917

[149] Jellicoe, *Grand Fleet*, 356

[150] IWM DOCS: A. D. Nichol, Typescript account, 'The Battle of Jutland'

[151] IWM SR: Tape Recording of G. Fox, AC 751, Reel 7

[152] IWM DOCS: C. Caslon Collection, 'Recollections of the Battle of Jutland', p.13

[153] IWM DOCS: P. Grant, Typescript letter, 5/6/1916

[154] IWM DOCS: Misc. 1010, R. Church Collection: T. C. Clark, Manuscript answer to questionnaire, ca 1970–74

[155] Scheer, *Germany's High Seas Fleet*, 155–6

[156] Admiralty, *Narrative of the Battle of Jutland* (London: HMSO, 1924), p.52

[157] IWM DOCS: Misc. 1010, R. Church Collection: H. S. Wright, Manuscript answer to questionnaire, ca 1970–74

[158] IWM DOCS: Misc. 1010, R. Church Collection: R. McLean, Manuscript answer to questionnaire, ca 1970–74

[159] IWM DOCS: A. D. B. James, Manuscript memoir, 'Battle of Jutland'

[160] IWM DOCS: Misc. 1010, R. Church Collection: J. W. Beardsley, Manuscript answer to questionnaire, ca 1970–74

[161] IWM DOCS: Misc. 1010, R. Church Collection: H. C. F. Foot, Typescript letter, 3/6/1916

[162] PRO: ADM 137/4809, A. Blessman, Typescript letter, 16/6/1916

[163] V. Tarrant, *Jutland: The German Perspective* (London: Arms & Armour, 1995)

[164] Tarrant, *Jutland*

[165] PRO: ADM 186/55: CB1548 German Navy Tactical Orders: Tactical Order No. 16, On the Tactical Employment of the II Battle Squadron 10/5/1916

166 IWM DOCS: Misc. 1010, R. Church Collection: B. von Gymnich, Translation of answer to questionnaire, ca 1973

167 Hase, *Kiel and Jutland*, 197–9

168 Hase, *Kiel and Jutland*, 199–200

169 IWM DOCS: Misc. 1010, R. Church Collection: H. C. F. Foot, Typescript letter, 3/6/1916

170 IWM DOCS: Misc. 1010, R. Church Collection: D. Joel, Manuscript answer to questionnaire, ca 1970–74

171 IWM DOCS: Misc. 1010, R. Church Collection: H. C. F. Foot, Typescript letter, 3/6/1916

172 Egidy, *Jutland*, 4, 1420

173 Egidy, *Jutland*, 4, 1420

174 IWM DOCS: Misc. 1010, R. Church Collection: C. Melms, Translation of answer to questionnaire, ca 1973

175 Paschen, 'SMS *Lützow* at Jutland', lxxii, 38

176 IWM DOCS: Misc. 1010, R. Church Collection: A. J. Brister, Typescript answer to questionnaire, ca 1970–74

177 IWM DOCS: Misc. 1010, R. Church Collection: G. Congreve, Typescript letter, 4/6/1916

178 IWM DOCS: C. Caslon Collection, 'Recollections of the Battle of Jutland', pp.10–11

179 Peter Liddle Collection, Brotherton Library, Leeds University: G. W. Norman, Manuscript memoir

180 IWM DOCS: C. Caslon Collection, 'Recollections of the Battle of Jutland', pp.10–11

181 IWM DOCS: Misc. 1010, R. Church Collection: A. J. Brister, Typescript answer to questionnaire, ca 1970–74

182 Jellicoe, *Grand Fleet*, 361

183 Jellicoe, *Grand Fleet*, 361

184 J. Jellicoe, 'Errors made in the Jutland Battle', quoted in Dreyer, *Sea Heritage*, 167

185 IWM DOCS: Misc. 1010, R. Church Collection: H. S. Phipp, Manuscript answer to questionnaire, ca 1970–74

186 IWM DOCS: W. Greenway, Typescript letter, 12/6/1916

187 INTERNET SOURCE: W. F. Fielder account at http://www.attrill.freeserve.co.uk/jutlandbattle.htm

188 IWM DOCS: Misc. 1010, R. Church Collection: A. P. Smith, Typescript letter sent in answer to questionnaire, ca 1970–74

189 INTERNET SOURCE: W. F. Fielder account at http://www.attrill.freeserve.co.uk/jutlandbattle.htm

190 IWM SR: G. Wainford, AC 9953

191 IWM SR: G. Wainford, AC 9953

192 Jellicoe, *Grand Fleet*, 364–5

193 IWM DOCS: Misc. 1010, R. Church Collection: H. Bassenge, Translation of answer to questionnaire, ca 1973

194 IWM DOCS: Misc. 1010, R. Church Collection: F. Motzler, Translation of answer

to questionnaire, ca 1973

[195] Admiralty, *Narrative of the Battle of Jutland* (London: HMSO, 1924), p.60

[196] IWM DOCS: R. M. Servaes, Manuscript letter, 5/6/1916

[197] IWM DOCS: A. T. Nickless: Typescript memoir, 'The Battle of Jutland'

[198] IWM DOCS: Misc. 1010, R. Church Collection: J. W. Algar, Manuscript answer to questionnaire, ca 1970–74

[199] IWM DOCS: Misc. 1010, R. Church Collection: J. W. Algar, Manuscript answer to questionnaire, ca 1970–74

[200] IWM DOCS: A. T. Nickless: Typescript memoir, 'The Battle of Jutland'

[201] IWM DOCS: Misc. 1010, R. Church Collection: J. W. Algar, Manuscript answer to questionnaire, ca 1970–74

[202] IWM DOCS: H. Horniman, Microfilm memoir, ca 1953

[203] Hase, *Kiel and Jutland*, 214

[204] Hase, *Kiel and Jutland*, 215

[205] IWM SR: J. G. D. Ouvry, AC 9260, Reel 2

[206] Oram, *Ready for Sea*, 167–8

[207] INTERNET SOURCE: W. F. Fielder account at http://www.attrill.freeserve.co.uk/jutlandbattle.htm

[208] T. Jerram, quoted in Corbett, *History of the Great War*, iii, 388

[209] T. Jerram, quoted in Tarrant, *Jutland*, p.179

[210] Tarrant, *Jutland*, p.179

[211] INTERNET SOURCE: W. F. Fielder account at http://www.attrill.freeserve.co.uk/jutlandbattle.htm

[212] J. Hawksley, quoted in H. H. Frost, *The Battle of Jutland* (London: United States Naval Institute, 1936), p.408

[213] IWM DOCS: J. E. P. Brass, 'Recollections of a Midshipman and Junior Officer, 1914–1921', p.48

CHAPTER 6

[1] Jellicoe, *Grand Fleet*, 372–3

[2] Jellicoe, *Grand Fleet*, 373

[3] Frost, *Battle of Jutland*, 411

[4] Jellicoe, *Grand Fleet*, 374

[5] Jellicoe, *Grand Fleet*, 374

[6] D. Beatty, quoted in Corbett, *History of the Great War*, iii, 389–90

[7] Scheer, *German High Seas Fleet*, 159

[8] Hase, *Kiel and Jutland*, 206

[9] Hase, *Kiel and Jutland*, 216–17

[10] A. von Trotha, Internet Source, http://www.100megsfree2.com/jjscherr/scherr/vonscheer.htm

[11] IWM DOCS: Misc 1010, R. Church Collection: J. C. Boldero, Typescript answer to questionnaire, ca 1970–74

[12] IWM DOCS: G. M. Eady: Typescript, 'The Battle of Jutland by Snottie', pp.24–5

[13] IWM DOCS: G. M. Eady: Typescript, 'The Battle of Jutland by Snottie', p.29

[14] IWM DOCS: T. F. Bradley, Manuscript diary, 31/5/1916

[15] IWM DOCS: A. B. Combe, Typescript, "Account of the Action on May 31st 1916'

[16] IWM DOCS: Misc. 1010, R. Church Collection: A. S. Tempest, Typescript answer to questionnaire, ca 1970–74

[17] H. Willons, quoted in Naval Records, *The Beatty Papers*, 5–6

[18] IWM DOCS: Misc. 1010, R. Church Collection: W. C. C. Bennett, Manuscript answer to questionnaire, ca 1970–74

[19] Marder, *From Dreadnought to Scapa Flow*, 135

[20] IWM DOCS: Misc. 1010, R. Church Collection: O. Frost, Translation of manuscript, ca 1973

[21] IWM DOCS: Misc. 1010, R. Church Collection: S. King-Hall, Typescript manuscript

[22] IWM DOCS: Misc. 1010, R. Church Collection: H. Bassenge, Translation of answer to questionnaire, ca 1973

[23] Anon officer, quoted by Fawcett & Hooper, *The Fighting at Jutland: The Personal Experiences of Sixty Officers and Men of the British Fleet*, 374

[24] PRO: ADM 116/1485, J. Hawksley, Report, 3/6/1916

[25] IWM DOCS: R Church Collection: H. Burroughs, Typescript manuscript

[26] S. King-Hall, *A Naval Lieutenant, 1914–1918* (London: Methuen, 1919), pp.148–9

[27] King-Hall, *A Naval Lieutenant*, 148–9

[28] IWM DOCS: R Church Collection: H. Burroughs, Typescript manuscript

[29] King-Hall, *A Naval Lieutenant*, 150

[30] Fawcett & Hooper, *Fighting at Jutland*, 160

[31] PRO: ADM 137/4808, Stolzmann, Translation of interview in *Norddeutsche Allgemeine Zeitung*, 25/6/1916

[32] PRO: ADM 137/4808, M. Müller, Translation of interview in *Norddeutsche Allgemeine Zeitung*, 25/6/1916

[33] PRO: ADM 137/4808, M. Müller, Translation of interview in *Norddeutsche Allgemeine Zeitung*, 25/6/1916

[34] IWM DOCS: R. Church Collection: H. Burroughs, Typescript manuscript

[35] IWM DOCS: Misc. 1010, R. Church Collection: A. Stewart, Manuscript answer to questionnaire, ca 1970–74

[36] IWM DOCS: Misc. 1010, R. Church Collection: A. D. Gash, Manuscript answer to questionnaire, ca 1970–74

[37] IWM DOCS: Misc. 1010, R. Church Collection: G. F. Spargo, Manuscript answer to questionnaire, ca 1970–74

[38] IWM DOCS: Misc. 1010, R. Church Collection: A. C. Scott, Manuscript letter, 18/6/1916

[39] IWM DOCS: Misc 1010, R. Church Collection: G. F. Spargo, Manuscript answer to questionnaire, ca 1970–74

[40] IWM DOCS: Misc. 1010, R. Church Collection: A. C. Scott, Manuscript letter, 18/6/1916

[41] IWM DOCS: R Church Collection: S. King-Hall, Typescript manuscript

[42] S. King-Hall, *A Naval Lieutenant*, 154

[43] IWM DOCS: Misc. 1010, R. Church Collection: A. Stewart, Manuscript answer to questionnaire, ca 1970–74

[44] IWM DOCS: R. Church Collection: S. King-Hall, Typescript manuscript

[45] IWM DOCS: Misc. 1010, R. Church Collection: C. V. Marsden, Typescript answer to questionnaire, ca 1970–74

[46] IWM DOCS: Misc. 1010, R. Church Collection: A. Stewart, Manuscript answer to questionnaire, ca 1970–74

[47] IWM DOCS: Misc. 1010, R. Church Collection: H. Bessenge, Translation of answer to questionnaire, ca 1973

[48] IWM DOCS: Misc. 1010, R. Church Collection: H. Bessenge, Translation of answer to questionnaire, ca 1973

[49] IWM DOCS: H. W. Breece, Manuscript account

[50] IWM DOCS: Misc. 1010, R. Church Collection: M. H. Cox, Manuscript answer to questionnaire, ca 1970–74

[51] IWM DOCS: Misc. 1010, R. Church Collection: M. H. Cox, Manuscript answer to questionnaire, ca 1970–74

[52] N. J. W. William-Powlett, quoted by Fawcett & Hooper, *The Fighting at Jutland: The Personal Experiences of Forty-Five Officers and Men of the British Fleet*, 190

[53] A. P. Bush, quoted by Fawcett & Hooper, *The Fighting at Jutland: The Personal Experiences of Forty-Five Officers and Men of the British Fleet*, 178

[54] IWM DOCS: Misc. 1010, R. Church Collection: M. H. Cox, Manuscript answer to questionnaire, ca 1970–74

[55] IWM DOCS: Milford Haven Collection: I. Glennie, Microfilm letter, ca 6/1916

[56] Anon officer, quoted by Fawcett & Hooper, *The Fighting at Jutland: The Personal Experiences of Forty-Five Officers and Men of the British Fleet*, 172–3

[57] IWM DOCS: Misc. 1010, R. Church Collection: M. Meier, Translation of answer to questionnaire, ca 1973

[58] IWM DOCS: Misc. 1010, R. Church Collection: H. Bassenge, Translation of answer to questionnaire, ca 1973

[59] A. P. Bush, quoted by Fawcett & Hooper, *The Fighting at Jutland: The Personal Experiences of Forty-Five Officers and Men of the British Fleet*, 178–9

[60] A. P. Bush, quoted by Fawcett & Hooper, *The Fighting at Jutland: The Personal Experiences of Forty-Five Officers and Men of the British Fleet*, 179

[61] A. P. Bush, quoted by Fawcett & Hooper, *The Fighting at Jutland: The Personal Experiences of Forty-Five Officers and Men of the British Fleet*, 179

[62] IWM DOCS: Misc. 1010, R. Church Collection: H. Bonatz, Translation of answer to questionnaire, ca 1973

[63] IWM DOCS: J. J. R. Croad, Manuscript account

[64] PRO: ADM 116/1485, W. Allen, Report, 3/6/1916

[65] IWM DOCS: Milford Haven Collection: I. Glennie, Microfilm letter, ca 6/1916

[66] IWM DOCS: J. J. R. Croad, Manuscript account

[67] IWM DOCS: Milford Haven Collection: I. Glennie, Microfilm letter, ca 6/1916

[68] IWM DOCS: J. J. R. Croad, Manuscript account

[69] P. Wood, quoted by Fawcett & Hooper, *The Fighting at Jutland: The Personal Experiences of Forty-Five Officers and Men of the British Fleet*, 184

[70] IWM DOCS: Milford Haven Collection: I. Glennie, Microfilm letter, ca 6/1916

[71] Anon Officer, quoted by Fawcett & Hooper, *The Fighting at Jutland: The Personal*

Experiences of Forty-Five Officers and Men of the British Fleet, 174

[72] P. Wood, quoted by Fawcett & Hooper, *The Fighting at Jutland: The Personal Experiences of Forty-Five Officers and Men of the British Fleet*, 185

[73] IWM DOCS: Misc. 1010, R. Church Collection: J. J. R. Croad, Manuscript answer to questionnaire, ca 1970–74

[74] IWM DOCS: Milford Haven Collection: I. Glennie, Microfilm letter, ca 6/1916

[75] IWM DOCS: Milford Haven Collection: I. Glennie, Microfilm letter, ca 6/1916

[76] IWM DOCS: J. J. R. Croad, Manuscript account

[77] IWM DOCS: H. W. Breece, Manuscript account

[78] NMM: A. Marsden, Manuscript account, 'HMS Ardent and Jutland Action', 1916

[79] IWM DOCS: Misc. 1010, R. Church Collection: T. W. Clifford, Manuscript answer to questionnaire, ca 1970–74

[80] F. O. Busch, quoted in T. Dorling, *Endless Story* (London: Hodder & Stoughton, 1932), p.207

[81] IWM DOCS: Misc. 1010, R. Church Collection: T. W. Clifford, Manuscript answer to questionnaire, ca 1970–74

[82] NMM: A. Marsden, Manuscript account, 'HMS Ardent and Jutland Action', 1916

[83] IWM DOCS: H. W. Breece Collection: G. A. Coles, Typescript report, 2/6/1916

[84] NMM: A. Marsden, Manuscript account, 'HMS Ardent and Jutland Action', 1916.

[85] NMM: A. Marsden, Manuscript account, 'HMS Ardent and Jutland Action', 1916.

[86] NMM: A. Marsden, Manuscript account, 'HMS Ardent and Jutland Action', 1916.

[87] NMM: A. Marsden, Manuscript account, 'HMS Ardent and Jutland Action', 1916.

[88] IWM DOCS: Misc. 1010, R. Church Collection: O. Frost, Translation of manuscript, ca 1973

[89] IWM DOCS: Misc. 1010, R. Church Collection: H. Bonatz, Translation of answer to questionnaire, ca 1973

[90] Scheer, *Germany's High Seas Fleet*, 161–2

[91] IWM DOCS: Misc. 1010, R. Church Collection: H. Meenzen, Translation of answer to questionnaire, ca 1973

[92] A. P. Bush, quoted by Fawcett & Hooper, *The Fighting at Jutland: The Personal Experiences of Forty-Five Officers and Men of the British Fleet*, 181

[93] IWM DOCS: Misc. 1010, R. Church Collection: A. J. Brister, Typescript answer to questionnaire, ca 1970–74

[94] IWM DOCS: Misc. 1010, R. Church Collection: A. J. Brister, Typescript answer to questionnaire, ca 1970–74

[95] IWM DOCS: Misc. 1010, R. Church Collection: G. Congreve, Typescript letter, 4/6/1916

[96] IWM DOCS: Misc. 1010, R. Church Collection: V. Dunton, Manuscript answer to questionnaire, ca 1970–74

[97] IWM DOCS: Misc 1010, R. Church Collection: P. B. Lawder, Typescript account in answer to questionnaire, ca 1970-74

[98] IWM DOCS: P. Grant, Typescript letter, 5/6/1916

[99] Egidy, *Jutland*, 4, 1420

[100] J. A. Fergusson, quoted in Marder, *From the Dreadnought to Scapa Flow*, vol. iii, p.158

[101] Jellicoe, quoted in Marder, *From the Dreadnought to Scapa Flow*, 158

[102] IWM DOCS: Misc. 1010, R. Church Collection: W. W. Hamer, Manuscript answer to questionnaire, ca 1970–74

[103] Egidy, *Jutland*, 4, 1420

[104] C. Burney, quoted in Frost, *Battle of Jutland*, 467

[105] L. Gibson & J. E. T. Harper, *The Riddle of Jutland: An Authentic History* (London: Cassell, 1934), pp.219–20

[106] Peter Liddle Collection, Brotherton Library Leeds University: E. S. Brand, Typescript memoirs

[107] C. Waller, The Fifth Battle Squadron at Jutland, *Royal United Services Journal*, 11/1935

[108] Jellicoe, *The Grand Fleet*, 57

[109] Admiralty, *Narrative of the Battle of Jutland*, 72

[110] PRO: ADM 116/3188, J. Jellicoe, 'Observations on the Narrative of the Battle of Jutland', pp.41–2

[111] J. S. Corbett, *Naval Operations*, vol. iii (London: Longmans, 1923), p.403

[112] Marder, *From Dreadnought to Scapa Flow*, 150

[113] J. Jellicoe, quoted in Marder, *From Dreadnought to Scapa Flow*, 150

[114] J. Jellicoe, quoted in Admiralty, *Narrative of the Battle of Jutland* (HMSO, London, 1924), pp.112–13

[115] Gordon, *Rules of the Game*, 478

[116] IWM DOCS: A. F. de Salis, 'Narrative of HMS Moresby'

[117] IWM DOCS: Misc. 1010, R. Church Collection: A. J. Brister, Typescript answer to questionnaire, ca 1970–74

[118] Oram, *Ready for Sea*, 170

[119] PRO: ADM 116/1485, J. Farie, Report, 3/6/1916

[120] PRO: ADM 116/1485, M. L. Goldsmith, Report, 3/6/1916

[121] E. C. O. Thomson, quoted by Fawcett & Hooper, *The Fighting at Jutland: The Personal Experiences of Forty-Five Officers and Men of the British Fleet*, 200–201

[122] IWM DOCS: C. Caslon Collection, 'Recollections of the Battle of Jutland', pp.14–15

[123] IWM DOCS: C. A. Poignand, Manuscript diary, 31/5/1916–1/6/1916

[124] IWM DOCS: Misc. 1010, R. Church Collection: J. P. Champion, Manuscript copy of letter, ca 1916

[125] IWM DOCS: Misc. 1010, R. Church Collection: M. Meier, Translation of answer to questionnaire, ca 1973

[126] IWM DOCS: Misc. 1010, R. Church Collection: H. Bassenge, Translation of answer to questionnaire, ca 1973

[127] IWM DOCS: Misc. 1010, R. Church Collection: M. Meier, Translation of answer to questionnaire, ca 1973

[128] Paschen, 'SMS *Lützow* at Jutland', lxxii, 39

[129] Paschen, 'SMS *Lützow* at Jutland', lxxii, 39

[130] Paschen, 'SMS *Lützow* at Jutland', lxxii, 40

[131] Paschen, 'SMS *Lützow* at Jutland', lxxii, 40

[132] Admiralty, *Narrative of the Battle of Jutland*, 84

[133] Bingham, *Falklands, Jutland and the Bight*, 149–50

[134] IWM SR: G. Wainford, AC 9953

[135] IWM DOCS: Misc. 1010, R. Church Collection: F. Knight, Manuscript answer to questionnaire, ca 1970–74

[136] IWM DOCS: Misc. 1010, R. Church Collection: P. B. Lawder, Typescript account in answer to questionnaire, ca 1970–74

[137] IWM SR: G. Wainford, AC 9953

[138] IWM DOCS: Misc. 1010, R. Church Collection: F. Knight, Manuscript answer to questionnaire, ca 1970–74

[139] H. W. A. Kemmis, quoted in Dorling, *Endless Story*, p.215

[140] IWM SR: G. Wainford, AC 9953

[141] IWM DOCS: Misc. 1010, R. Church Collection: F. Knight, Manuscript answer to questionnaire, ca 1970–74

[142] IWM SR: G. Wainford, AC 9953

[143] IWM DOCS: Misc. 1010, R. Church Collection: J. P. Champion, Manuscript copy of letter, ca 1916

[144] IWM DOCS: Misc. 1010, R. Church Collection: E. V. Lees, Manuscript answer to questionnaire, ca 1970–74

[145] IWM DOCS: C. A. Poignand, Manuscript diary, 31/5/1916–1/6/1916

[146] Oram, *Ready for Sea*, 171

[147] Oram, *Ready for Sea*, 172

[148] Jellicoe, *Grand Fleet*, 384

[149] Cunninghame Graham, *Random Naval Recollections*, 54

[150] IWM DOCS: C. Caslon Collection, 'Recollections of the Battle of Jutland', pp.15–16

[151] IWM DOCS: Misc. 1010, R. Church Collection: D. M. Frost, Typescript answer to questionnaire, ca 1970–74

[152] IWM DOCS: N. Wright, Typescript letter, 12/7/1916

[153] IWM DOCS: A. D. B. James, Manuscript memoir, 'Battle of Jutland'

[154] V. Schulze, quoted in Scheer, *Germany's High Seas Fleet*, 165

[155] Oram, *Ready for Sea*, 172

[156] IWM DOCS: A. F. de Salis, 'Narrative of HMS Moresby'

[157] IWM DOCS: A. F. de Salis: 'Narrative of HMS Moresby'

[158] PRO: ADM 116/1485, J. Farie, Report, 3/6/1916

[159] Scheer, *Germany's High Seas Fleet*, 165–6

[160] Scheer, *Germany's High Seas Fleet*, 166

[161] IWM DOCS: Misc. 1010, R. Church Collection: C. Melms, Translation of answer to questionnaire, ca 1973

[162] Egidy, *Jutland*, 4, 1420

CHAPTER 7

[1] IWM DOCS: M. Clarke, Manuscript diary, 31/5/1916

[2] IWM DOCS: Misc. 1010, R. Church Collection: C. H. Petty, Manuscript account in answer to questionnaire, ca 1970–74

[3] IWM DOCS: M. Clarke, Manuscript diary, 1/6/1916

[4] IWM DOCS: Misc. 1010, R. Church Collection: J. J. R. Choad, Manuscript answer

to questionnaire, ca 1970–74

[5] IWM DOCS: Misc. 1010, R. Church Collection: J. J. R. Choad, Manuscript answer to questionnaire, ca 1970–74

[6] IWM DOCS: Milford Haven Collection: I. Glennie, Microfilm letter, ca 6/1916

[7] P. Wood, quoted by Fawcett & Hooper, *The Fighting at Jutland: The Personal Experiences of Forty-Five Officers and Men of the British Fleet*, 186

[8] P. Wood, quoted by Fawcett & Hooper, *The Fighting at Jutland: The Personal Experiences of Forty-Five Officers and Men of the British Fleet*, 186

[9] P. Wood, quoted by Fawcett & Hooper, *The Fighting at Jutland: The Personal Experiences of Forty-Five Officers and Men of the British Fleet*, 186

[10] P. Wood, quoted by Fawcett & Hooper, *The Fighting at Jutland: The Personal Experiences of Forty-Five Officers and Men of the British Fleet*, 187

[11] N. J. W. William-Powlett, quoted by Fawcett & Hooper, *The Fighting at Jutland: The Personal Experiences of Forty-Five Officers and Men of the British Fleet*, 190–91

[12] N. J. W. William-Powlett, quoted by Fawcett & Hooper, *The Fighting at Jutland: The Personal Experiences of Forty-Five Officers and Men of the British Fleet*, 191

[13] N. J. W. William-Powlett, quoted by Fawcett & Hooper, *The Fighting at Jutland: The Personal Experiences of Forty-Five Officers and Men of the British Fleet*, 192

[14] N. J. W. William-Powlett, quoted by Fawcett & Hooper, *The Fighting at Jutland: The Personal Experiences of Forty-Five Officers and Men of the British Fleet*, 192

[15] P. Wood, quoted by Fawcett & Hooper, *The Fighting at Jutland: The Personal Experiences of Forty-Five Officers and Men of the British Fleet*, 187

[16] A. P. Bush, quoted by Fawcett & Hooper, *The Fighting at Jutland: The Personal Experiences of Forty-Five Officers and Men of the British Fleet*, 181

[17] A. P. Bush, quoted by Fawcett & Hooper, *The Fighting at Jutland: The Personal Experiences of Forty-Five Officers and Men of the British Fleet*, 182

[18] V. B. Molteno, quoted by Fawcett & Hooper, *The Fighting at Jutland: The Personal Experiences of Sixty Officers and Men of the British Fleet*, 162

[19] IWM DOCS: C. E. Leake, Typescript taken from original 1917 manuscript, 1971

[20] IWM DOCS: H. Y. Ganderton, 'Under the White Ensign: A Bunting Tosser's Log', pp.34–5

[21] IWM SR: G. Donald, AC 18

[22] IWM DOCS: Misc. 1010, R. Church Collection: R. Poole, Manuscript & typescript answer to questionnaire, ca 1970–74

[23] IWM DOCS: H. Y. Ganderton, 'Under the White Ensign: A Bunting Tosser's Log', p.35

[24] IWM DOCS: Misc. 1010, R. Church Collection: W. Robertson, Manuscript answer to questionnaire, ca 1970–74

[25] IWM DOCS: Misc. 1010, R. Church Collection: D. Williams, Manuscript answer to questionnaire, ca 1970–74

[26] IWM DOCS: H. Y. Ganderton, 'Under the White Ensign: A Bunting Tosser's Log', pp.35–6

[27] IWM DOCS: Misc. 1010, R. Church Collection: R. Poole, Manuscript & typescript answer to questionnaire, ca 1970–74

[28] IWM DOCS: H. Y. Ganderton, 'Under the White Ensign: A Bunting Tosser's Log', p.36

[29] IWM DOCS: H. Y. Ganderton, 'Under the White Ensign: A Bunting Tosser's Log', p.36

[30] IWM DOCS: Misc. 1010, R. Church Collection: R. Poole, Manuscript & typescript answer to questionnaire, ca 1970–74

[31] IWM SR: G. Donald, AC 18

[32] IWM DOCS: H. Y. Ganderton, 'Under the White Ensign: A Bunting Tosser's Log', pp.36–7

[33] IWM DOCS: Misc. 1010, R. Church Collection: R. Poole, Manuscript & typescript answer to questionnaire, ca 1970–74

[34] F. J. Rutland, quoted in D. Young, *Rutland of Jutland* (Cassell: London, 1963), pp.6–7

[35] IWM DOCS: H. Y. Ganderton, 'Under the White Ensign: A Bunting Tosser's Log', p.37

[36] F. J. Rutland, quoted in Young, *Rutland of Jutland*, 7

[37] F. J. Rutland, quoted in Young, *Rutland of Jutland*, 7–8

[38] IWM DOCS: H. Y. Ganderton, 'Under the White Ensign: A Bunting Tosser's Log', p.37

[39] V. B. Molteno, quoted by Fawcett & Hooper, *The Fighting at Jutland: The Personal Experiences of Sixty Officers and Men of the British Fleet*, 166

[40] IWM DOCS: H. Y. Ganderton, 'Under the White Ensign: A Bunting Tosser's Log', pp.37–8

[41] IWM DOCS: R. James Collection: V. B. Molteno, Typescript order, ca 2/6/1916

[42] IWM SR: J. J. Hazelwood, AC 4125

[43] IWM DOCS: G. E. D. Ellis, Microfilm copy of manuscript diary, 31/5/1916

[44] IWM DOCS: E. M. Phillpotts Collection: H. Walwyn, Typescript memoir, 'HMS Warspite', p.19

[45] IWM DOCS: E. M. Phillpotts Collection: H. Walwyn, Typescript memoir, 'HMS Warspite', pp.24–5

[46] IWM DOCS: G. E. D. Ellis, Microfilm copy of manuscript diary, 1/6/1916

[47] IWM DOCS: G. H. Bickmore, Typescript, p.17

[48] IWM DOCS: G. E. D. Ellis, Microfilm copy of manuscript diary, 1/6/1916

[49] IWM DOCS: G. E. D. Ellis, Microfilm copy of manuscript diary, 1/6/1916

[50] IWM DOCS: G. E. D. Ellis, Microfilm copy of manuscript diary, 1/6/1916

[51] IWM DOCS: G. H. Bickmore, Typescript, p.18

[52] IWM DOCS: M. Clarke, Manuscript diary, 1/6/1916

[53] IWM DOCS: A. D. Nicholl, Typescript account, 'The Battle of Jutland'

[54] Peter Liddle Collection, Brotherton Library, Leeds University: W. G. Cave, Typescript memoir

[55] IWM DOCS: Misc. 1010, R. Church Collection: A. Coventry, Manuscript answer to questionnaire, ca 1970–74

[56] IWM DOCS: Misc. 1010, R. Church Collection: J. P. Champion, Manuscript copy of letter, ca 1916

[57] IWM DOCS: G. M. Eady: Typescript: 'The Battle of Jutland by Snottie', p.27

[58] IWM DOCS: J. Myers, Manuscript account, 6/1916

[59] Oram, *Ready for Sea*, 174

[60] Oram, *Ready for Sea*, 174–5

[61] IWM DOCS: C. Caslon Collection, 'Recollections of the Battle of Jutland', pp.16–17

[62] IWM DOCS: C. Caslon Collection, 'Recollections of the Battle of Jutland', p.16

[63] IWM DOCS: Misc. 1010, R. Church Collection: H. R. Hawkins, Manuscript answer to questionnaire, ca 1970–74

[64] IWM DOCS: Misc. 1010, R. Church Collection: C. E. Rudall, Manuscript answer to questionnaire, ca 1970–74

[65] IWM DOCS: Misc 1010, R. Church Collection: W. Macey, Typescript answer to questionnaire, ca 1970–74

[66] IWM DOCS: G. M. Eady, Typescript: 'The Battle of Jutland by Snottie', pp.28–9

[67] IWM DOCS: Misc. 1010, R. Church Collection: W. M. P. Hornby, Typescript answer to questionnaire, ca 1970–74

[68] V. Hayward, *HMS Tiger at Bay* (London: William Kimber, 1977), pp.142–3

[69] IWM DOCS: Misc. 1010, R. Church Collection: J. H. Harris, Manuscript answer to questionnaire, ca 1970–74

[70] IWM DOCS: D. Lorimer, Typescript, p.120–21

[71] IWM DOCS: C. Caslon Collection, 'Recollections of the Battle of Jutland', p.17

[72] IWM DOCS: T. F. Bradley, Manuscript diary, 31/5/1916

[73] IWM DOCS: Misc. 1010, R. Church Collection: E. Phillips, Typescript answer to questionnaire, ca 1970–74

[74] IWM SOUND, D. Maclachlan, AC 768

[75] IWM DOCS: Misc. 1010, R. Church Collection: A. R. Lewis, Manuscript answer to questionnaire, ca 1970–74

[76] IWM DOCS: Misc. 1010, R. Church Collection: H. R. Hawkins, Manuscript answer to questionnaire, ca 1970–74

[77] IWM DOCS: T. F. Bradley, Manuscript Diary, 31/5/1916

[78] IWM DOCS: D. Lorimer, Typescript, p.122

[79] IWM DOCS: Misc. 1010, R. Church Collection: D. Maclachlan, Manuscript answer to questionnaire, ca 1970–74

[80] IWM DOCS: Misc. 1010, R. Church Collection: E. Downing, Typescript account in answer to questionnaire, ca 1970–74

[81] IWM DOCS: Misc. 1010, R. Church Collection: J. Handley, Manuscript answer to questionnaire, ca 1970–74

[82] IWM DOCS: G. H. Bickmore, Typescript, p.18

[83] IWM DOCS: G. E. D. Ellis, Microfilm copy of manuscript diary, 1/6/1916

[84] IWM DOCS: G. E. D. Ellis, Microfilm copy of manuscript diary, 1/6/1916

[85] IWM DOCS: G. M. Eady, Typescript, 'The Battle of Jutland by Snottie', pp.29–30

[86] IWM DOCS: M. Clarke, Manuscript diary, 2/6/1916

[87] IWM DOCS: M. Clarke, Manuscript diary, 2/6/1916

[88] IWM DOCS: Misc. 1010, R. Church Collection: T. R. Collins, Manuscript answer to questionnaire, ca 1970–74

[89] IWM DOCS: Misc. 1010, R. Church Collection: J. H. Harris, Manuscript answer to questionnaire, ca 1970–74

[90] IWM DOCS: Misc. 1010, R. Church Collection: W. M. P. Hornby, Typescript answer to questionnaire, ca 1970–74

[91] IWM DOCS: M. Clarke, Manuscript diary, 2/6/1916 & 3/6/1916

[92] IWM DOCS: M. Clarke, Manuscript diary, 5/6/1916

[93] IWM DOCS: Misc. 1010, R. Church Collection: E. V. Lees, Manuscript answer to questionnaire, ca 1970–74

[94] IWM DOCS: L. Hollis, Typescript memoir, p.9

[95] IWM SR: A. Ford, AC 719

[96] Hayward, *HMS Tiger*, 146–7

[97] IWM SR: G. Wainwright, AC 9953

CHAPTER 8

[1] Scheer, *Germany's High Seas Fleet*, 175–6

[2] D. Brownrigg, *Indiscretions of the Naval Censor* (London: Cassell, 1920), pp.48–9

[3] IWM DOCS: Misc. 1010, R. Church Collection: H. J. W. Fischer, Typescript, ca 1970–74

[4] Brownrigg, *Indiscretions of the Naval Censor*, p.49

[5] Brownrigg, *Indiscretions of the Naval Censor*, 49–50

[6] Brownrigg, *Indiscretions of the Naval Censor*, 50–51

[7] Peter Liddle Collection, Brotherton Library, Leeds University, J. Crawford, Typescript of Tape 503

[8] IWM DOCS: Misc. 1010, R. Church Collection: A. J. Brister, Typescript answer to questionnaire, ca 1970–74

[9] Brownrigg, *Indiscretions of the Naval Censor*, 51

[10] IWM DOCS: Misc. 1010, R. Church Collection: G. Congreve, Typescript letter, 4/6/1916

[11] IWM DOCS: H. E. C. Blagrove, Manuscript letter, 3/6/1916

[12] IWM DOCS: Misc. 1010, R. Church Collection: J. Jessamine, Typescript speech from D. Beatty included in answer to questionnaire, ca 1970–74

[13] IWM DOCS: Misc. 1010, R. Church Collection: A. T. Hickson, Manuscript answer to questionnaire, ca 1970–74

[14] All details taken from J. Campbell, *Jutland: An Analysis of the Fighting* (London: Conway Maritime Press, 1998), pp.337–41

[15] Hase, *Kiel and Jutland*, 229

[16] Scheer, *Germany's High Seas Fleet*, 360

[17] Scheer, Germany's *High Seas Fleet*, 169

[18] IWM DOCS: Misc. 1010, R. Church Collection: G. Davies, Typescript answer to questionnaire, ca 1970–74

[19] IWM DOCS: Misc. 1010, R. Church Collection: C. H. Petty, Manuscript account in answer to questionnaire, ca 1970–74

[20] Scheer, *Germany's High Seas Fleet*, 174

[21] IWM SOUND, H. Dannreuther, AC 20979 (recorded by Robert Church)

[22] IWM DOCS: G. M. Eady, Typescript, 'The Battle of Jutland by Snottie', p.27

[23] Peter Liddle Collection, Brotherton Library, Leeds University: M. R. Best, manuscript diary, 28/11/1916

[24] IWM DOCS: G. H. Bickmore, Typescript, p.19

[25] IWM DOCS: A. D. Nicholl, Typescript account, 'The Battle of Jutland'

INDEX

The index is arranged alphabetically, with subheadings shown chronologically where appropriate.

action, preparation for 170–171
Admiralty *see also* Royal Navy
  communiqués on battle 419–422
  response to Jellicoe's letter on tactics
    33
  Room 40 (intelligence) 35, 36, 41,
    46, 57, 58, 59, 339, 341, 371, 426
airship, Zeppelin *L11*: 363–365
Alexander-Sinclair, Commodore
    Edwyn 61
Algar, Boy Telegraphist James 274–275
Alison, Lieutenant Commander Roger
    V. 152, 153, 361
Allen, Commander Walter 316–317,
    319
anti-flash precautions 38, 117
Arbuthnot, Rear Admiral Sir Robert
    198, 199–200, 201
Armstrong, Stoker 139
Arndt, Stuckmeister 255
Arnold, Wireless Telegraphist
    Frederick 72, 159

Bailey, Commander 80
Barron, Lieutenant Commander John
    185
Bassenge, Lieutenant Heinrich 60–61,
    62, 66, 94, 96–97, 270, 298,
    308–309, 313, 350
battlecruiser concept 17–18
Beardsley, Private John, RMLI 172,
    223, 251

Beatty, David (later Vice Admiral Sir
    David) 24–25, 34, 36, 408
  at battle of Dogger Bank 36–37
  on *Queen Elizabeth* class battleships 43
  disposition of force 60
  responds to news of first shots fired
    62–63
  sights German ships 68
  adjusts dispositions 78
  orders ships to open fire 81
  orders change of course 86, 88
  orders 13th Flotilla to attack 100
  on loss of HMS *Queen Mary*
    113–114
  reacts to arrival of German High
    Seas Fleet 130–131
  orders Vice Admiral Evan-Thomas
    to alter course 135–136
  orders turn to north-west 151
  approaches Grand Fleet 177
  turns 360 degrees to starboard
    244–245
  suggests cutting off enemy fleet 271
  receives signal on fleet adopting
    southerly course 285–286
  reflections on battle 423–424
  frustration with Jellicoe 429–430
  appointed Commander-in-Chief
    431, 432–433
  death 433
  assessment 433–435
Beatty (née Tree), Ethel 25
Behncke, Rear Admiral Paul 238, 417
Bellairs, Lieutenant Commander
    Roger 33–34, 263
Bennett, Boy 1st Class Seaman
    William 170, 295

Bentinck, Commander 80

Best, Commander Matthew 431

Bethell (HMS *Nestor*) 46, 141, 142

Betson (HMS *Warspite*) 207–208

Betsworth, Petty Officer George 125, 142, 143, 144

Bickmore, Assistant Clerk Gilbert 161, 207–208, 395, 397, 409–410, 432

Bingham, Commander Barry, VC 46, 119, 124, 125, 126, 140, 141–142, 143–144, 145, 355

Bishop, Lieutenant 223

Blackman, Stoker Sidney 212, 232

Blagrove, Lieutenant Henry 423

Blessman, Obermatrose (Leading Seaman) Albert 252

Bloomfield, Lieutenant 181, 182

Blunt, Boy Seaman Charles 224

Bode, Lieutenant Commander 229–230

Bödicker, Konteradmiral Friedrich 94, 184

Boldero, Midshipman John 290

Boltenstern, Commander von 254

Bonatz, Cadet Heinz 315–316, 328

Borkum 22

Bostock, Midshipman John 207–208

Bowden, Leading Seaman Reginald 230

Boxer Rebellion 20, 25

Boyle, Captain Algernon 137, 156, 269

Bradley, Reverend Thomas 87–88, 118, 292, 405–406, 407–408

Brand, Sub-Lieutenant Eric 98, 338

Brass, Midshipman John 171, 172, 221, 241, 281

Breese, Surgeon Lieutenant Henry 309, 321

Bright, Able Seaman 262

Brind, Lieutenant Patrick 76–77, 134, 136, 137, 154–156, 194, 201

Brister, Petty Officer Telegraphist Arthur 167–169, 197, 261, 263, 330–332, 344, 421–422

British Expeditionary Force (BEF) 26, 44

Brown, Teddie 404

Brownrigg, Sir Douglas 418–420, 422

Buist, Sub-Lieutenant Colin 113, 131

burials at sea 407–409

Burney, Vice Admiral Sir Cecil 190, 191, 269, 336, 363, 397, 432

Burrough, Lieutenant Harold 300, 301, 304

Busch, Searchlight Control Officer Fritz Otto 323

Bush, Lieutenant Athelstan 311, 314–315, 330, 379–380

Callaghan, Admiral Sir George 18–19, 21, 23, 24, 29

Campbell, Commander George 353, 354

Carey, Reverend Walter 412

Carey, Surgeon Lieutenant 307

Caslon, Sub-Lieutenant Clifford 71, 94–95, 137, 246, 261–262, 347–348, 363, 402, 405

  on shelling of HMS *Malaya* 155, 157–158, 159

Cassin, Signalman 188

Cave, Able Seaman Albert 398–399

Chalmers, Lieutenant William 90

Champion, Commander John 201, 349, 358, 359, 399

Chatfield, Flag Captain Alfred 57, 80, 81, 92, 97, 100–101, 113, 130, 199, 408

China, Boxer Rebellion in 20, 25

Churchill, Winston 19, 21, 22, 25

Clark, Bugler Thomas, RMLI 246

Clarke, Naval Nursing Sister Mary 47, 371, 372, 397, 411, 412, 413–414

Clement Ford, Able Seaman W. J. 186

Clifford, Leading Seaman Thomas 323–324

Coles, Lieutenant Commander Gordon 324

Colley, Captain 172, 223

Collins, Engine Room Artificer 1st Class Thomas 412

Combe, Midshipman Anthony B. 81, 90, 292

commerce raiding 39–40

communications, Royal Navy 168–169

Condon, Mr (HMS *Moorsom*) 138

Congreve, Midshipman Geoff 225, 261, 332, 423

convoys 39–40

Cooper, Boy 1st Class A. E. 55–56, 223

Corbett, Sir Julian 13–14, 26, 283

Cordeaux, Sub-Lieutenant Edward 95

cordite charges 116, 224 *see also* shells, Royal Navy

Cornwell, Jack, VC 183

Coronel, battle of 29

Coventry, Ordinary Seaman 399

Cox, Leading Torpedoman Maurice 309, 310, 311

Cox, Able Seaman Gunner Percival 163

Crabbe, Commander Lewis 186

Crawford, Midshipman John 421

Croad, Telegraphist J. J. R. 316, 317, 318, 320, 321, 373–374

Cromarty Firth 34, 36

Crooke, Captain Ralph 279

Croome, Midshipman John C. 48, 49–50, 169, 173, 176, 183–184, 226, 228, 231, 237

Cross, Gunnery Instructor 20

Culme-Seymour, Admiral Sir Michael 20

Cunninghame Graham, Lieutenant Angus 170, 363

D'Arcy, Probationary Surgeon Lieutenant Thomas 188–189

Dannreuther, Gunnery Commander Hubert 229, 233, 235, 430

Davies, Engine Room Artificer Gordon 427–428

Davies, Boy 1st Class John 198

Dawson, Boy 1st Class Harold 149–150

de Salis, Sub-Lieutenant Anthony 152–153, 207, 343, 365–366

Dearden, Midshipman Peregrine 105, 108, 110, 111, 145

destroyers 28, 121–122

Dinn, Leading Signaller George 182–183

Dogger Bank, battle of 36–39

Donald, Flight Lieutenant Graham, RNAS 65–66, 382–383, 387

Downing, Petty Officer Edwin 190–191, 409

Dreyer, Captain Frederic 73, 190, 196–197

Duff, Captain Arthur 340

Dunton, Leading Victualler Victor 332

Duthy, Lieutenant Desmond 154

Eades, Able Seaman Ewart 205

Eady, Midshipman Gordon 70, 74, 75, 83, 112–113, 115–116, 290–292, 400, 403
    on return to Scotland 410–411, 430–431

Egidy, Kapitän zur See Moritz von 68, 77, 88–89, 112, 127–128, 258–259, 333–334, 336, 369–370

Elgwood, Sub-Lieutenant Reginald
    219
Elliott, Able Seaman 96
Ellis, Surgeon Gordon 47, 73, 154,
    162, 210–211, 392–393, 394, 395,
    396, 410
English Channel 22–23
Epworth, Mr (HMS *Petard*) 123
Evan-Thomas, Vice Admiral Sir Hugh
    94, 123, 133, 136, 151, 169–170,
    206, 208, 269, 432
  confusion with signals 63, 64
Ewart, Lieutenant 56, 71–72, 104,
    105

Fairthorne, Midshipman Richard
    47–48
Falklands, battle of the 29
Falmer, Signaller C. 94, 95–96
Farie, Captain James 100, 119,
    345–346, 348, 349, 353, 361, 365,
    366
Farquhar, Midshipman John 218
Farquhar, Engine Room Rating T. 61,
    62
Fell, Midshipman William 209–210
Ferdinand, Archduke Franz 18
Fergusson, Captain James 334–335
Fielder, Carpenter Frederick 267, 268,
    279–280
Fischer, Assistant Clerk Hubert 213,
    231–232, 233, 419
Fisher, Sir John 16, 17, 18, 21
Folkestone raid 45
Foot, Assistant Paymaster Harold 222,
    251, 257
Ford, Able Seaman Arthur 415
Forth Bridge 47–48, 397
Fox, George 245
Frampton, Midshipman Roger 73,
    99–100

Francis, Petty Officer Ernest 56,
    71–72, 82–83, 103, 105, 106–107,
    108–109, 145–147
Freeman (HMS *Nestor*) 142–143
Frost, Boy 1st Class David 170, 364
Frost, Wachtmachinist (Engineer Room
    Assistant) Otto 296, 328

Ganderton, Signaller H. Y. 67, 382, 383,
    384, 385–386, 387, 388, 390, 391
Garnons-Williams, Midshipman Nevill
    102, 117–118
Gash, Boy Telegraphist Arthur 304
Gasson, Royal Marine Gunner Bryan
    230–231, 235
Gautier, Lieutenant Commander 252
German Army invasion plans 26
German Navy
  Battle Squadrons
    I 52, 277, 287–288, 313
    II 52–53, 277, 288, 298, 300
    III 52, 137, 148, 154, 253, 277,
    288, 367
  cipher books obtained by Russians
    34, 35
  East Asiatic Squadron 26, 29
  expansion of 14, 15, 17
  Flotillas
    II 119, 124, 185, 260
    III 251, 260, 268
    IV 260, 261
    V 260, 272
    VI 260
    VII 260
    IX 119, 123–124, 185, 260, 261
  High Seas Fleet 26, 27, 35, 40, 41,
    58, 140, 148, 353, 425
  sets sail 52
  arrives at battle 128–130, 132
  retires 239–241
  steams back into harbour 368–369

re-emerges once more 426, 427
Scouting Division, I 129, 367
Scouting Force, 1st 35, 36–37
Scouting Groups
  I 20, 58, 60, 147, 150, 233, 254
  II 54, 58, 179, 288
  IV 54, 58, 276, 288, 300
Germany, Imperial, emergence of 14
Glennie, Lieutenant Irvine 312, 317,
  318, 319, 320, 321, 374
Goehle, Korvetten Kapitän 261
Goldreich, Midshipman Robert 222,
  225
Goldsmith, Commander Malcolm
  346, 347
Goodenough, Commodore William
  133, 176, 191, 249, 300, 301, 308,
  340–341, 343
sights enemy 130, 131, 132
Grant, Captain Percy 218, 246, 333
Green, Jimmy 96, 245
Greenway, Warrant Officer Walter
  220, 266
Grenfell (HMS *Warspite*) 93
Griffin, Torpedo Coxswain William
  185, 241
Griffiths (HMS *Warspite*) 211
Gulliver, Officers' Steward 1st Class
  Reginald 181–182
gun turrets, battlecruiser 73 *see also*
  guns, turret
gunnery, advances in 16, 18
gunnery firing systems, 'director' 21,
  73–74
gunnery problems, Royal Navy 37,
  38–39
gunnery transmitting stations 73,
  74–75, 213 *see also* range-finders
guns, turret 73, 173 *see also* shells,
  Royal Navy
  comparison 79

firing 221–222
loading 75–76, 82–83
Gutteridge, Signalman A. W. 188
Gymnich, Lieutenant Beissel von 253

Hall, Electrical Artificer Frank 174
Hamer, Ordinary Seaman Walter 335
Hamilton, L. H. K. 125
Hancock, Captain, RNR 389
Handley, Signalman John 409
Hanel, Leading Seaman 229, 233
Harder, Captain 352
Harris, Private John, RMLI 156–157,
  158, 404, 413
Hartlepool bombardment 34, 35, 36
Hartog, Captain Paul 240, 254
Harvey, Major Francis, VC 92, 406
Hase, Commander Georg von 78–79,
  86, 89–90, 103, 117, 164, 165,
  214, 215, 233
before battle 52, 58–59, 65, 70
opens fire 81, 83–84
on sinking of HMS *Queen Mary* 111
on cordite charges 116
on sinking of HMS *Defence* 200
shelled by HMS *Invincible* 229
on shelling of SMS *Derfflinger* 240,
  254–256, 276–277
night action 288, 289
after battle 426
Hauser, Lieutenant Commander 200
Hawkins, Boy 1st Class Henry 402,
  407
Hawksley, Commander James 272,
  280, 299, 344
Hayler, Seaman Torpedoman Harry
  47, 56, 74–75
Hayward, Able Seaman Victor 82,
  106, 404, 415–416
Hayward-Booth, Sub-Lieutenant 150
Hazelwood, J. J. 75–76, 392

Heligoland Bight 27–28, 284, 285
Herford, Able Seaman James 89
Hickson, Able Seaman Albert 110, 424
Hill, Lieutenant Henry 71
Hill, Midshipman Rupert 79
Hipper, Admiral Franz von 35, 36, 37,
    45, 60, 64–65, 128
  sights British battlecruisers 68
  orders battlecruisers to open fire 80
  orders change of course 88
  alters course 126
  executes 16 point turn 150
  turns north-north-west 153
  joins High Seas Fleet 186–187
  shifts his flag to *G39*: 240
  resumes command of I Scouting
    Group 288, 289
Hodgson, Lieutenant Commander
    John 122, 124, 138, 139, 140
Hogg, Boy 1st Class Richard 82
Hollis, Lieutenant Leslie, RM 199,
    414–415
Hollman, Korvettenkän 252
Hood, Rear Admiral Sir Horace 169,
    183, 184, 212, 229
Hope, Able Seaman Charles
    241–242
Hopkins, Lieutenant Commander
    Sydney 319
Hornby, Sub-Lieutenant Windham
    181, 182, 404, 413
Horniman, Paymaster Henry 276
Horns Reef 284, 285, 286, 287, 290,
    339, 341, 362, 367, 368
hospital ship (German Navy) *Sierra
    Ventana* 417
hospital ship (Royal Navy) *Plassy* 47,
    371, 372, 397, 411, 412, 413–414
Howell, Able Seaman John 241,
    242–243
Hoyle, Midshipman Michael 222

Hutchinson, Commander Reginald
    322

Ingenohl, Admiral Friedrich von 27,
    34, 35, 36, 39
intelligence, naval 34, 35 *see also*
    Admiralty, Room 40

Jackson, Captain Thomas 57, 58
James, Midshipman Arthur 166,
    250–251, 364
Jellicoe, John (later Sir John) 19,
    20–22, 28–29, 331
  description by Lieutenant
    Commander Bellairs 33–34
  during Boxer Rebellion 20
  ordered north to Scapa Flow 23–24
  Grand Fleet Battle Orders 29, 30
  letter on tactics to Admiralty 30
    October 1914: 31–33
  response to German East Coast raids
    41–42, 43
  plans for May and early June 1916: 45
  scepticism re Harwich Force joining
    fleet 53
  intentions on setting sail 53–54, 55
  responds to news of first shots fired
    62
  assessment of the naval war in 1916:
    166–167
  concerned with absence of reports
    169–170
  receives news of High Seas Fleet
    being sighted 175
  signals action is imminent 176
  and position of High Seas Fleet
    176–177
  awaits news of High Seas Fleet
    189–190
  receives news of German Grand
    Fleet 191–192, 194

and Grand Fleet tactics 192–193
signals battle orders 194–198
on action with SMS *König* 237–238
orders turn south 'by divisions'
· 243–244
orders 4th Light Cruiser Squadron
into the attack ⁄263–264
sightings of German turn away not
reported to him 269
orders Grand Fleet onto south-westerly course 270
controls the course of the battle
280–281
determines to avoid night action and
decides on southerly course
282–285
stops wireless signalling and receives
messages on German fleet's course
339–342
alters course to north and forms
single battle line 362–363
receives signal confirming enemy
had reached safety at Horns Reef
367
visits HMS *Calliope* after battle 275
depression following battle 430
appointed First Sea Lord 431
death 433
assessment 433–435
Jensen, Signalman Victor 171, 221
Jerram, Vice Admiral Sir Martyn 250,
271, 279
Joe, Surgeon Probationer A. 142–143
Joel, Flag Lieutenant David 257–258
Jutland, battle of
commences 62
contact and the run to the south 69
'Action Stations' sounded 70–72, 77
the end of the run to the south 101
German High Seas Fleet arrives
128–130, 132

the turn and run to the north 135
the arrival of the Grand Fleet 178
Jellicoe deploys 195
Scheer's battle turn away 227
Scheer's second battle turn away
247
night approaches 273
Scheer escapes 287
veterans meet in 1966: 435

Karpf, Captain von 334, 335
Kattegat channel 45
Kemble, Lieutenant 118
Kemmis, Sub-Lieutenant Harry 357,
358
Kiel Canal 17, 26
King-Hall, Lieutenant Stephen 108,
150, 217, 297, 300–302, 306–307
Kitchener, General Sir Herbert (later
Field Marshal Lord) 24, 430
Kitching, Engineer Commander
Henry 202, 203, 204–205
Knight, Able Seaman Fred 356, 357,
358
Knox, Lieutenant John 187, 188, 189

Lahs, Kapitänleutnant 184
Lane, Able Seaman 106
Lapage, Lieutenant Commander
Walter 85
Last, Leading Signaller 403
Lawder, Assistant Paymaster Keith 157
Lawder, Lieutenant Patrick 193–194,
202, 332–333, 356
Lawson, Captain Robert 179–181
Le Mesurier, Commodore Charles
272–273
Leake, Surgeon Lieutenant Charles
204, 381–382
Lees, Sub-Lieutenant Eric 359–360,
414

Lewis, Boy Telegraphist Arthur 102, 113, 115, 407
Lloyd Owen, Midshipman John 105, 107, 111
Loftus Jones, Commander, VC 185–186, 241–242, 243
Long, Able Seaman 103, 106
Longhurst, Lieutenant Commander 80, 81, 292
Lorimer, Surgeon Lieutenant Duncan 159–161, 405, 408
losses, German Navy 417, 422, 424, 425
losses, Royal Navy 420–421, 424, 425
Lowestoft bombardment 41, 44

Macey, Boatswain William 224, 403
Madlung, Captain 351
Mahan, Alfred T., USN 11–12, 14, 435
Manners, Lieutenant Commander Erol 170
maritime power 11–14
Marsden, Lieutenant Commander Arthur 174, 322, 324, 325–328
Marsden, Sub-Lieutenant Charles 307
Mauve, Rear Admiral 53, 278
May, Sir William 21
McCulloch, Lieutenant 159
Macdonald, Surgeon 204, 382
McGilp, Assistant Paymaster 145
Mackenzie-Grieve, Commander Alan 91, 132
Maclachlan, Stoker Donald 102, 406–407, 408
McLean, Midshipman Robert 250
Meenzenn, Seaman Hermann 329
Meier, Max 313, 350
Mellish (HMS Southampton) 306
Melms, Seaman Carl 98, 259, 369

Michelsen, Commodore 248
Middleton (HMS Queen Elizabeth) 410
minefields 45, 54
Molteno, Captain Vincent 381, 385, 386, 390–392
Moore, Sub-Lieutenant 188, 189
Moss, Able Seaman Torpedoman Joseph 50
Motzler, Signalman Franz 270
Müller, Machinist Max 303
Myers, Able Seaman John 234, 400

Napier, Rear Admiral Trevelyan 275–276
naval blockades 13–14, 22–23
naval forces, total 53
naval supremacy 11–14
Navy Act, 1900 (Germany) 14–15
Nelson, Horatio 12, 14, 25, 372, 435
Nicholl, Midshipman Angus 245, 397–398, 435
Nickless, Albert 274, 275
night action preparations 294–296
Nile campaign 24
Norman, Midshipman Gerald 159, 262
Norman, Lieutenant Thomas 193, 236
North Sea 51

Odensholm 35
Oliver, Rear Admiral Henry 58
Onslow, Lieutenant Commander C. R. 358
Oram, Sub-Lieutenant Harry 85, 86, 120–121, 278, 345, 361, 362, 365, 400, 401
Ouvry, Midshipman John 57, 70, 112, 217–218, 235, 277–278
Owen, Sub-Lieutenant Hilary 68, 119–120, 121, 122–123, 124–125, 138–140

Pakenham, Rear Admiral William 78, 291–292

Palmer, Able Seaman 321

Parkyn, Stoker George 399

Parsons, Yeoman 386

Paschen, Commander Günther 80, 91, 92–93, 177–178, 200, 226, 229–230, 240, 351, 352

  on shelling of SMS *Lützow* 214–215, 260

Patterson, Sub-Lieutenant 323

Pelly, Captain Henry 112

Percy, Sub-Lieutenant 145

Peters, Arthur 130

Petty, Shipwright Charles 371–372, 428

Phillips, Petty Officer Edward 406

Phillpotts, Captain Edward 210, 211, 409

Phipp, Gunner Horace, RMLI 265

Phipps, Commander 169, 197, 330

Plater, Stoker Frederick 162

Pohl, Admiral Hugo von 39, 40

Poignand, Lieutenant Commander Charles 348, 360

Pollen, Arthur 73

Pollen ('Poland'), Father 210, 211, 412

Poole, Signalman Reuben 203, 383, 385, 386, 387

Pridmore, Sick Bay Attendant 374

Pring (HMS *Warspite*) 209

range-finders 73, 74, 75, 79–80, 84–85 *see also* gunnery transmitting stations

Rawles, Petty Officer Gunners Mate 205

Riddle of Jutland, The 337

Riddles, Len 171

'Risk Fleet Theory' 15

Roberts, Engineer Officer Norman 125

Robertson, Signalman William 205, 384

Robinson, Ordinary Seaman William 171

Rosyth 36, 42, 44, 46–47

Roy, Chief Yeoman of Signals 182

Royal Navy *see also* Admiralty; hospital ship *Plassy*; ships, Royal Navy; submarines, Royal Navy

  Atlantic Fleet 25

  Battle Squadrons

    First 50, 196, 294

    Second 35, 50, 57

    Third 42

    Fourth 50

    Fifth *see* Royal Navy, Fifth Battle Squadron

  Battlecruiser Fleet (previously 1st Battlecruiser Squadron) 25, 38, 44, 46, 47, 48, 55, 147, 217, 410

    assessment of battle 429, 430–431

  Battlecruiser Fleet Orders 64

  Battlecruiser Squadrons

    1st (later Battlecruiser Fleet) 24, 27, 34, 35, 36–37, 48, 60, 63, 193

    2nd 48, 60, 63, 78

    3rd 44, 50, 166, 169, 179, 212, 213

  Channel Fleet 23

  comparison between 1805 and 1916: 167

  conflict within 15–16

  Cruiser Squadron, 1st 36, 50, 166, 198, 199, 414

  Cruiser Squadron, 2nd 50, 166

  Destroyer Flotillas

    1st 48

    4th 50, 166, 185, 294, 297, 309, 314, 316, 322, 330

9th 78, 294, 344–345, 346

10th 294, 344–345, 346

11th 50, 166, 272, 294, 297–299, 300, 344

12th 50, 166, 268, 294, 344–345, 348, 349, 354, 355, 358, 360

13th 48, 68, 78, 100, 118–119, 294, 344–345

Fifth Battle Squadron 93, 94, 97, 136, 151, 153, 164, 269

before battle 42, 43, 46, 47, 48

meets enemy 60, 63, 65

turns north 133–134, 136–137, 148

re-engages enemy 206

night action 294, 337–338

Grand Fleet 24, 26, 27, 28, 29, 34, 38, 424, 430–431

exercises 30, 33

prepares to leave Scapa Flow 48

heads towards battle 166

deploys into battle line 217–219

opens fire 221–222

after battle 398–400

returns to Scapa Flow 414

Grand Fleet Battle Orders 29, 30, 429

Harwich Force 23, 27, 28, 41, 53, 371, 398

Light Cruiser Squadrons

1st 48, 60

2nd 48, 60, 129, 131, 133, 150, 249, 294, 300

3rd 48, 60, 275–276

4th 50, 166, 263, 264, 272, 294

supremacy 11, 12

Rudall, Ordinary Signalman Charles 179, 182–183, 403

Rushton, Commander 308

Russian co-operation 34

Rutland, Flight Lieutenant Frederick, RNAS 66, 67, 388–390

Scapa Flow 22, 23, 28, 38, 42, 48–52, 413, 430

Scarborough bombardment 34, 35, 36

Scheer, Admiral Reinhard 40–41, 44, 52–53, 128–129, 133, 148, 368, 370

plans for May and early June 1916: 45, 46

intentions on setting sail 54

wireless call sign 57–58

orders turn to north-north-west 151

orders turn to north-west 154

meets Grand Fleet 216–217

orders battle turn to starboard 238–239

orders second battle turn to the east 246–249

orders battlecruisers to engage enemy 252–253

decides on escape route 286–288

on attack on HMS *Black Prince* 329

reaches safety of Horns Reef 367

on visits by the Kaiser and others 417–418

reflections on battle and future plans 426–427

on British shells 428

Scheibe, Commander Albert 77, 99

Schillig Roads 52

Schlieffen, Chief of Staff von 26

Schofield, Surgeon Commander 307

Schultz, Korvetten Kapitän Max 260

Schulze, Commander Victor 365

Scott, Captain Albert 305, 306, 398–399

seaplanes, Royal Naval Air Service 65–67

Servaes, Sub-Lieutenant Reginald 232, 272

Seymour, Vice Admiral Sir Edward 20

Seymour Flag Lieutenant Ralph 80,
    81, 101, 136
Sharpe, Able Seaman Edward 71
Sheerness 42
shells, Royal Navy 428–429 *see also*
    cordite charges; guns, turret
ships, German Navy *see also* hospital
    ship *Sierra Ventana*; submarines,
    German Navy
  Bismarck 189
  Blücher 18, 36–37, 39
  Breslau 26
  Derfflinger 78–79, 86, 117, 164, 214,
    225, 230, 233
    before battle 36, 52, 58, 59, 65, 70
    opens fire 80–81, 83–84
    shelled 89–90, 165, 215, 240,
      254–256, 276–277
    shells HMS *Queen Mary* 111
    shells HMS *Defence* 200
    shelled by HMS *Benbow* 225
    shelled by HMS *Invincible* 229
    night action 288–289, 354
    after battle 424
  Deutschland 52
  Elbing 94, 179, 298, 299, 300, 310
    before battle 60–61, 62, 64, 66
    shelled 308–309
    rammed by SMS *Posen* 313
    sinking 349–351, 375–376
  Frankfurt 93, 179, 297–298, 349, 367
  Frauenlob 300, 302–303, 304
  Friedrich der Grosse 52, 129, 206, 216,
    289, 329, 417
  G37: 185
  G41: 260–261
  G88: 252
  G104: 185
  Goeben 26
  Grosser Kurfürst 52, 153, 253–254,
    356

Hamburg 299, 300, 310
Hannover 52
Helgoland 52, 206
Hessen 52
Kaiser 52, 273
Kaiserin 52, 206
König 52, 206, 237–238, 240, 270
Kronprinz Wilhelm 52
Lützow 80, 81, 91, 92–93, 200,
    214–215, 240, 270, 272, 296
  before battle 52, 68
  shelled 153, 164, 177–178, 260
  battle damage 214–215
  shells HMS *Invincible* 236–237
  sinking 351–353
Magdeburg 34–35
Markgraf 52, 153, 238, 253, 273
Moltke 36, 52, 81, 86–87, 98, 288,
    333, 334, 335
München 276, 300
Nassau 52, 206, 310, 314–316, 328,
    329
Oldenburg 52, 206, 323, 325
Ostfriesland 52, 206, 329, 368
Pillau 179, 184, 297–298, 349, 367,
    369, 370
Pommern 52, 278, 356, 359
Posen 52, 252, 313
Prinzregent Luitpold 52, 273
Regensburg 119, 124–125, 367
Rheinland 52, 322
Rostock 300, 310, 322, 349
S35: 185, 262–263
S50: 184–185
S52: 185
S53: 350, 351
Schlesien 52, 278
Schleswig-Holstein 52, 278
Seydlitz 77, 81, 258–259, 336–337
  before battle 36, 37–38, 45–46, 52,
    68

shelled 88–89, 127–128, 134, 153,
164, 276
battle damage 333–334
after battle 369–370, 424
Stettin 300
Stuttgart 300, 310
Thuringen 52, 206, 329
V1: 296, 328
V4: 361
V28: 185
V29: 123, 124, 262
V45: 185
V48: 241, 243, 245, 252, 268
V69: 184–185
V71: 252
V73: 252
Von der Tann 52, 81, 86, 95, 98, 99,
150–151, 259
night action 288, 354, 369
Westfalen 52, 239, 287–288, 309,
310, 316–317, 321, 337, 347
Wiesbaden 179, 184, 187, 199–200,
213, 224–225, 248, 251, 353
ships, merchant
Arabic 40
Lusitania 40
N. J. Fjord 60, 61
Sussex 44
ships, Royal Navy *see also* hospital ship
Plassy; submarines, Royal Navy
Abdiel 285, 367, 368
Aboukir 27–28
Acasta 179, 185, 186, 187
Achates 309, 322
Agincourt 50, 170, 265, 336, 363
Ajax 50
Albemarle 21
Alexandria 24
Ambuscade 309, 321, 322, 324–325
Ardent 174, 309, 322, 324–328
Audacious 28

Australia 48
Badger 234–235
Barfleur 25
Barham 97–98, 99–100, 148–149,
151, 164, 338, 402, 406
before battle 44, 48, 63, 64, 67, 73
Bellerophon 50
Benbow 50, 193–194, 218, 225, 226,
261, 332–333, 356, 364, 423
Birmingham 132, 305, 340
Black Prince 177, 328–329, 415
Boadicea 335
Britannia 19, 24
Broke 309, 311–312, 313, 316–321,
373–374
Calliope 272, 273–275
Campania 51–52, 364
Camperdown 19
Canada 50
Canterbury 179
Caroline 267–268, 279–280
Castor 279, 280, 298–299
Centurion 20, 50, 260, 332
Champion 68, 345, 346, 348, 361, 366
Chester 179–183, 403, 404, 413
Christopher 179
Collingwood 50, 171, 221, 224
Colossus 50–51, 193, 219–220, 222,
251–252, 257–258, 265
Comus 170, 272, 295
Conqueror 50, 56, 223, 334, 364
Constance 272
Contest 309, 311, 320, 321, 374
Cressy 27–28, 173, 174
Defence 198, 199, 200–202
Drake 21
Dreadnought 16–17, 21
Dublin 129–130, 300, 304–306,
398–399
Duke of Edinburgh 198, 205–206,
414–415

Engadine 45, 48, 52, 65, 66, 67, 152, 382–383, 384–391

Erin 50, 250

Excellent 19

Falmouth 177

Faulknor 353, 354, 356

Fearless 397

Fortune 297, 309, 322, 323, 324

Galatea 54, 61–62, 64, 167

Garland 297, 309, 310, 311, 313, 322

Hampshire 430

Hercules 21, 50, 172, 223, 265, 363

Hogue 27–28, 173–174

Indefatigable 48, 73, 81, 86, 94, 95–97, 113, 398

Indomitable 169, 173, 176, 179, 183–184, 212–213, 214, 231–232, 233

  before battle 36, 48, 49–50

  shelled 226, 228

  sinking 237

Inflexible 50, 185, 214, 232, 236, 290

Invincible 17–18, 36, 50, 182, 183, 185, 212, 214, 228–232, 233–236

Iron Duke 167–169, 177, 190, 192, 196–197, 265, 330–331, 339, 432

  before battle 33, 48, 50

  shells SMS *König* 237–238

  shells Zeppelin 364

King George V 50, 173–174, 219, 224, 243, 249–250

Laurel 110–111, 424

Lion 73, 130, 134, 179, 190–191, 193, 199, 244, 406–407

  before battle 25, 36, 37, 46, 48, 63, 64, 67

  engages enemy 79, 80, 81

  shelled 90, 91–92, 97, 102–103

  battle damage 114–115, 117–118

  night action 292, 293–294, 295

  burials at sea 408–409

Lydiard 346

Maenad 349, 358–359, 361, 399

Magic 299

Malaya 94–95, 98, 154–161, 164, 194, 261–262, 402, 404–405, 408

  before battle 44, 48, 71, 72, 73, 76–77

  shells SMS *Seydlitz* 134

  shelled and battle damage 137, 148–149, 151, 154–161

  night action 347–348

Marksman 361, 379

Marlborough 50, 190, 193, 206, 245–246, 265, 294, 362, 363, 397–398

Marne 299

Marvel 354, 356

Menace 348–349, 360

Mindful 354

Monarch 50, 222, 260, 334, 400

Moorsom 68, 119–120, 121, 122–123, 124–125, 138–140

Moresby 152–153, 324, 343, 361, 365–366, 399

Morris 85, 119

Narborough 119

Narwhal 358

Neptune 50, 252

Nerissa 119

Nessus 358, 359–360, 414

Nestor 119, 120, 124, 125–126, 128, 140, 141–144

New Zealand 81, 82, 83, 86, 400, 403, 411

  before battle 36, 48, 68, 70, 73, 74, 75

  shelled 112, 115–116

  night action 290–292

  returns to Scapa Flow 430–431

Nicator 119, 124, 126, 138

Noble 358

Nomad 119, 123, 124, 126, 140–141

Nottingham 119, 305

Obdurate 85, 86, 119, 120–121, 278, 345, 361, 362, 365, 400–401

Obedient 353, 354, 356

Onslaught 268, 354, 355–356, 357–358

Onslow 152, 187–189

Ophelia 179, 186

Orion 50, 172, 221, 241, 250, 260, 281, 334

Pelican 119

Petard 119, 123, 126, 127, 128, 146, 346–347, 348

Phaeton 61, 62

Porpoise 309, 322

Princess Royal 36, 48, 68, 73, 81, 89, 92, 117, 276

Queen 25

Queen Elizabeth 44, 48, 409, 410, 432

Queen Elizabeth class 42–43

Queen Mary 81, 82–83, 85, 88
  before battle 48, 56, 71–72, 73
  shelled and sinks 103–108, 109, 111, 112–113

Ramillies 20

Revenge 50, 265, 336, 363

Royal Oak 50, 218, 224, 250–251, 364

Royalist 171, 279

St Vincent 50

Sans Pareil 19

Shark 179, 185, 186, 241–243

Southampton 130, 131, 150, 249, 297, 300–302, 303–304, 305, 306–308

Sparrowhawk 309, 311, 313, 318–320, 374–376, 378–379

Spitfire 309, 311, 314–315, 316, 329–330, 379–380

Superb 50, 364

Temeraire 50

Termagent 119

Thunderer 50, 222, 225, 265, 334–335

Tiger 82, 85, 86–88, 112, 118, 152–153, 235, 277–278, 292
  before battle 36, 37, 48, 57, 63, 64, 70, 71, 73, 81
  after battle 403, 404, 405–406, 407–408, 415–416

Tipperary 309–312, 314, 376–377

Turbulent 119, 126, 346, 347

Unity 309, 346

Valiant 44, 48, 71, 73, 97–98, 148–150, 151, 154, 164, 338

Vanguard 50, 220, 266

Victoria 19

Victorious 371–372, 428

Warrior 198, 199, 202–205, 206, 380–392

Warspite 93, 98, 99, 100, 148–149, 151, 153, 409, 410, 412
  before battle 44, 47–48, 72–73, 74–76
  shelled 154, 161–164, 206–211
  battle damage 380
  returns to Rosyth 392–397

Sibbald, Dr 20

Signal Book 15

Sinclair, Captain Robert, RMLI 236

Skagerrak 45, 46

Smith, Officers' Steward 2nd Class Albion 267

Smith, Midshipman T., RNR 241, 242

Some Principles of Maritime Strategy (1911) 13

Somme, battle of the 422–423

Souther (HMS *Malaya*) 157

Spargo, Telegraphist G. F. 129–130, 305–306

Spickerell (Commander Bailey's Secretary) 80

Stanley, Captain The Hon. Victor 250
Stares, Petty Officer 105
Stewart, Stoker Andrew 304, 307, 308
Stickland, Navigating Officer 306
Stirling, Captain Anselan 348,
    353–354, 360–361
Stolzmann, Midshipman 302, 303
Storey, Midshipman Jocelyn 103–104,
    107, 109, 110–111
Stosch, Lieutenant Commander von
    229
Strutt, Commander The Hon. Arthur
    80
submarine, emergence of 22
submarines, German Navy 27–28, 39,
    40, 44, 45, 46, 54, 394, 395–396,
    427
  U9: 27
  U32: 54
  U66: 54
submarines, Royal Navy
  D1: 368
  E26: 368
  E55: 368
Sunderland, planned bombardment
    45–46

tactics, Royal Navy 30–33
  Grand Fleet 192–193
Tait, Petty Officer 401
Tate, Midshipman Hugh 218, 224
Tempest, Leading Signalman Alec
    114, 118, 234, 293
Thomson, Lieutenant Commander
    Evelyn. C.O. 123, 126, 128, 146,
    346–347
Tillard, Lieutenant Commander
    Stephen 149
Tillstone (HMS *Malaya*) 95
Tirpitz, Admiral Alfred von 14, 15
torpedo attacks 264–266

Tovey, Lieutenant Commander
    John/Jack 187, 188, 189
Trafalgar, battle of 167, 372
Tree, Ethel 25
Trelawny, Lieutenant Commander
    Clarence 314, 315
Trewin, Assistant Paymaster George
    66, 67
Trotha, Chief of Staff Adolf von 216,
    289
'Two Power Standard' 15
Tryon, Admiral Sir George 19–20
Tyrwhitt, Commodore Reginald 53,
    175–176

U-boats *see* submarines, German Navy

Wainford, Able Seaman George 268,
    355–356, 357, 358, 416
Waller, Captain Craig 338
Walwyn, Commander Humphrey 93,
    99, 100, 134, 149, 153, 163–164
  before the battle 72, 73
  shelled 161–162, 206–207, 208,
    209, 210, 211
  after the battle 393–394
Webber, Ordinary Signaller Harold
    212
Wheeler, Engineer Lieutenant
    Commander 138
Whitby bombardment 35, 36
White, Electrical Artificer Nelson 50,
    219–220
Whitfield, Lieutenant Commander
    Paul 123, 126, 140–141
Wilhelm II, Kaiser 14, 417
Wilhelmshaven 26
William-Powlett, Sub–Lieutenant
    Newton 310–311, 376, 377–378
Williams, Stoker 1st Class David
    203–204, 384

Williamson (HMS *Warspite*) 395
Willons, Private H., RMLI 91, 114, 293–294
'Windy Corner' 212
Wintour, Captain Charles 309–310
wireless stations, directional-finding 35
Wood, Sub-Lieutenant Percy 318, 320, 374, 376, 378
Wood, Sergeant 'Timber' 156
Woods, Commander A. R. W. 197
world power, balance of 14
wounded, treating 87–88, 160–161, 210–211, 381–382, 405

Wright, Engine Room Artificer 4th Class Harold 173–174, 219, 249–250
Wright, Assistant Paymaster Noel 226, 364

Yarmouth bombardments 34, 41
Yeo, Petty Officer 207–208

Zenne, Stoker Hugo 353
Zeppelin *L11* airship 363–365